The Journey

*Appalachia to Paradise
to Purgatory*

The Journey

*Appalachia to Paradise
to Purgatory*

Colonel Vaughan Witten, PhD

CITIOFBOOKS, INC.
3736 Eubank NE Suite A1
Albuquerque, NM 87111-3579
www.citiofbooks.com
Hotline: 1 (877) 389-2759
Fax: 1 (505) 930-7244

Ordering Information:
Quantity sales. Special discounts are available on quantity purchases by corporations, associations, and others. For details, contact the publisher at the address above.

Printed in the United States of America.

ISBN-13:	Softcover	978-1-959682-47-9
	eBook	978-1-959682-48-6
	Hardcover	978-1-959682-62-2

Library of Congress Control Number: 2022922238

Dedicated
To

My wife Mildred, Scott, Brian, my parents, Alphonso and Arlene Witten, the immediate and extended Witten and Walker family, Mildred's (Williams) family, my Air Force comrades, my Shaw colleagues and friends I have made around the U.S. and the world as I passed through on the journey. I equally dedicate this book to the good people of Kanawha Valley and West Virginia in general for their honesty, pride, work ethic, compassion and overall integrity. Finally, to the demanding, but gentle and concerned faculty and staff of Washington High School in London for their efforts and love in preparing me for the big world outside of West Virginia. All mentioned have contributed to my confidence, education and overall world view.

More specifically-sisters and brother

Audrey- 2nd born- My sweet, innocent, loving, loyal, saintly sister. You did so much for everyone and asked for nothing in return. I will see you in heaven and Mom and Dad.

Sandra- 3rd born- Extremely intelligent and wise. Understood the world system. I love you for your grace, goodwill and understanding. I will see you in heaven also.

Janita- 4th born- Extremely intelligent, hard working, ambitious, loyal, faithful. I love you very much. I will see you in heaven.

Emma- 5th born- Ambitious, hardworking, smart, good mother, loving sister. I love you. See you in heaven.

James- 6th born- Wonderful man, hardworking, loyal, faithful, reliable. Was wild once upon a time, but I love you very much. See you in heaven with all the family.

And finally to my family in Martinsville, Va., all my mom's sisters, brothers, cousins, and all for being such a good family-Elmer, Bernice, Lizzy, Gracie and Jean. Howard, Ruth and Willie have already gone to God along with Arlene, my Mother. On Mildred's side, Ethel and Cille. Sister, Pie-Lindsay, and Henry have already passed as has her Mom and Dad.

Acknowledgements

I acknowledge with gratitude the support, editing and typing of Mrs. Kimberly Tidwell of Four Oaks, N.C. who is the secretary of the large Social Sciences Department at Shaw University. Her ability to manage her staggering Shaw workload and help my cause on nights and weekends was amazing and I cannot thank her and Mrs. Mildred Hooker, typist, enough, for their work.

I also wish to thank Mrs. Megan Spruill, the Social Sciences' secretary prior to Mrs. Tidwell, for her typing and support. This whole effort spanned ten years and many other secretaries helped me also, but to a lesser degree.

I am grateful for the friendship and support of my colleagues at Shaw University and also for the friendship of my *VFW Post 6018*, Fayetteville, N.C. *Knotty Head* members and their "can do" spirit. Also, to the U.S. Air Force for my training, world travel and sense of pride in my country.

Finally, I acknowledge my wonderful family and the contributions of Mrs. Louise Henderson and Washington High School, London, West Virginia for my primary education and positive world view.

CONTENTS

FOREWORD
WILD, WONDERFUL, WEST VIRGINIA

This journey from the friendly, exciting mountains and valleys of pristine West Virginia in the 1940s and 1950s to the military life and eye opening world view of the U.S. Air Force was exceedingly joyful. This West Virginia in which 30 counties in 1863 split off from Virginia over the issue of slavery which it opposed, and became a state in its own right; originally proposed to be named Kanawha, then Western Virginia and ultimately, West Virginia. This West Virginia with its hardy, honest, industrious people that was Jim Crow on the surface, but tolerant and integrated in its heart, was the fertile soul the Witten family and many other Blacks labored, loved and lived in pursuit of happiness and attainable success and fortune. Looking back on my youth in Kanawha County, roaming the hills and valleys barefoot, swimming in the mighty Kanawha River and exploring the coal field activities; I realize that I was truly blessed to be in a virtual paradise of physical environment and familial love. Though technically poor by economic standards, and purportedly racially oppressed, I didn't realize or perceive either of those conditions and enjoyed a healthy, free, open, exciting and wonderful childhood attributed mostly to my Mom and Dad because I didn't know I was supposed to be second class and because I didn't know I was not more poor than the typical West Virginian, I escaped the social-psychological scars and baggage that usually accompanies such a background. From such an environment as this, I left home at age 17 with my high school diploma and unlimited confidence in myself to succeed and make my mark on the world. This was the second phase of my journey that began with my enlistment in the U.S. Air Force during the Korean War in 1952.

The continuation of 27 years of globetrotting Air Force duty and the 50 years of marriage to Mildred was paradise, unrealized until it was over. My retirement from the Air Force in 1979 and the loss of my wife in 2007 spanned the years of essential purgatory where I was introduced to the real pain and suffering of life in America and the epiphany of the gradual decline of morals, values, respect and helplessness in observing our slide on the slippery slope of gradual cultural decline. This slide was mitigated by the love and support of my wife Mildred, my sons Scott and Brian and my many friends at Shaw University and different venues in my daily life, including Uncle Elmer and his wife Aunt Bernice, Aunt Gracie, my siblings James, Audrey, Sandra, Janita, Emma and my wonderful parents Arlene and Alphonso Witten until their deaths in 2000 and 1991 respectively. I realize at this writing in my 73rd year, that I have been specially blessed by God and appreciate Him even more because I have not been a faithful churchgoer, but I have been a faithful believer in Jesus and the afterlife of heaven. I feel fortunate for being born and raised in the United States of America and hope and pray that it can survive the terrorist attacks and immorality of its people in the future.

I do, however, have some regrets that I could not prolong the life of my wife, mother and father. Though I showed them love, I wish I had told them more often. I wish I had learned to play a musical instrument and one or two foreign languages. I wish I had fought Andrew Richmond on the school bus when he slapped my sister Sandra, but he and his thuggish brothers were too much for me to prevail at the time, but I regret not fighting them all anyway. I regret not encouraging Scott enough to finish his degree work, and inspiring Brian to wear his Army uniform when he would come home on leave. It was as if he was ashamed of being in the Army.

For a lifetime, these aren't too bad because I have long acknowledged my imperfection, but on the whole, I am satisfied that I lived an honorable and good life, and also know that I need Gods' grace to enter heaven and believe that he will allow me in.

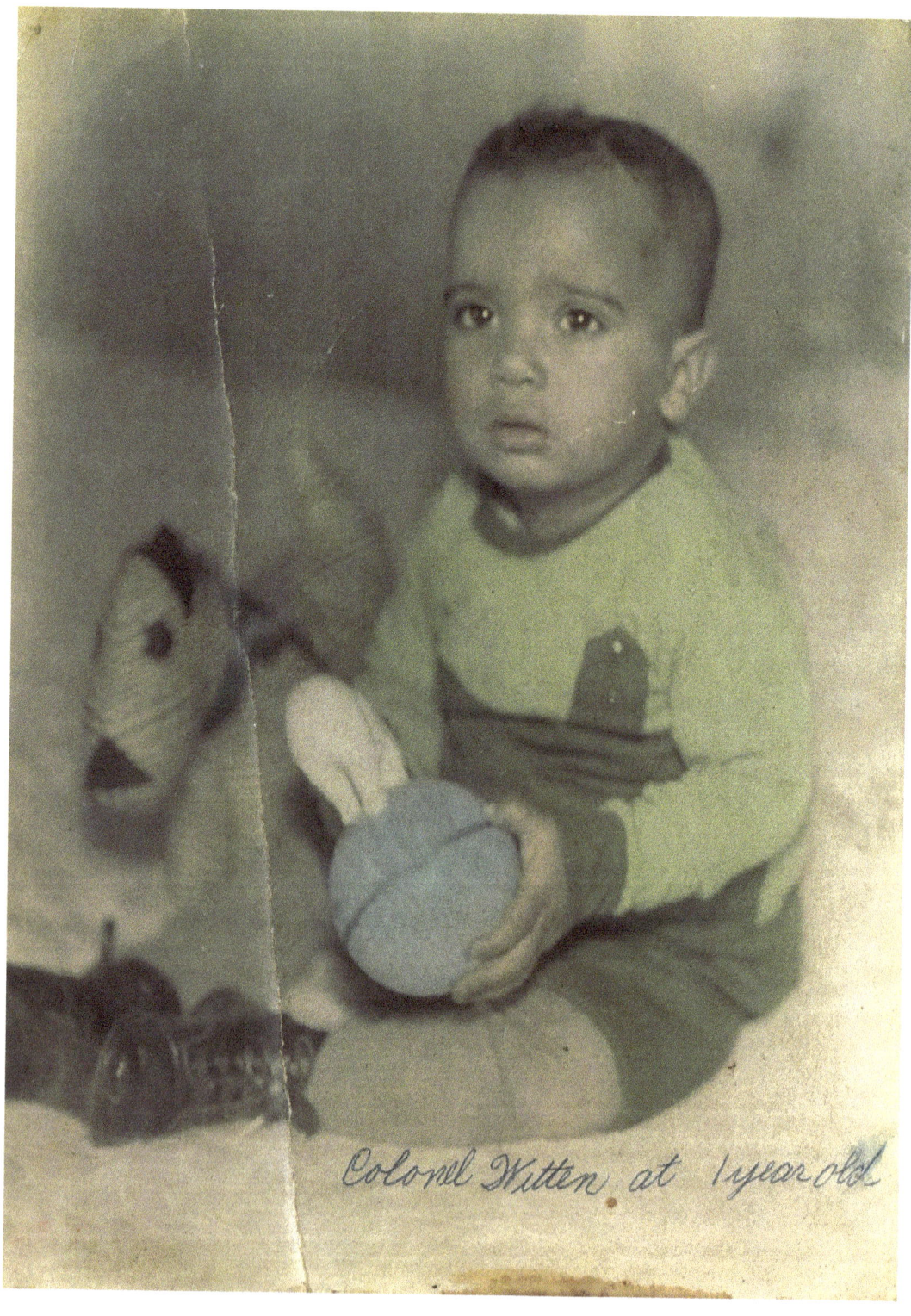

Colonel Witten at 1 year old

July 6, 1929   Sunset: January

MILDRED

MALCOMB   MURPHY

9

VFW

HOME

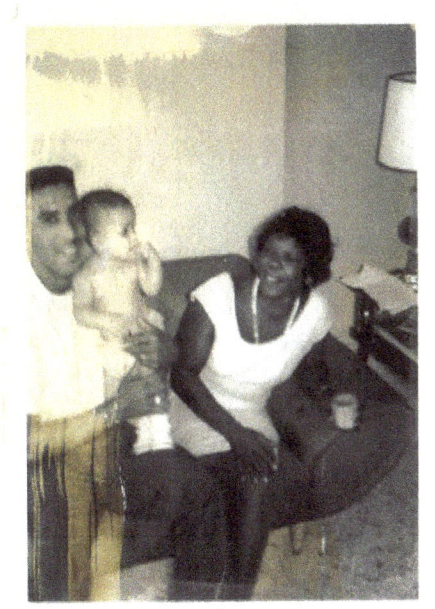

ME- MILDRED 1956

HOME 2009

HOME

HOME

ALFONSO WITTEN WARD, WVA
DADDY - YOUNG MAN

DAD

Dad
&
Mom

Scott

Brian

14

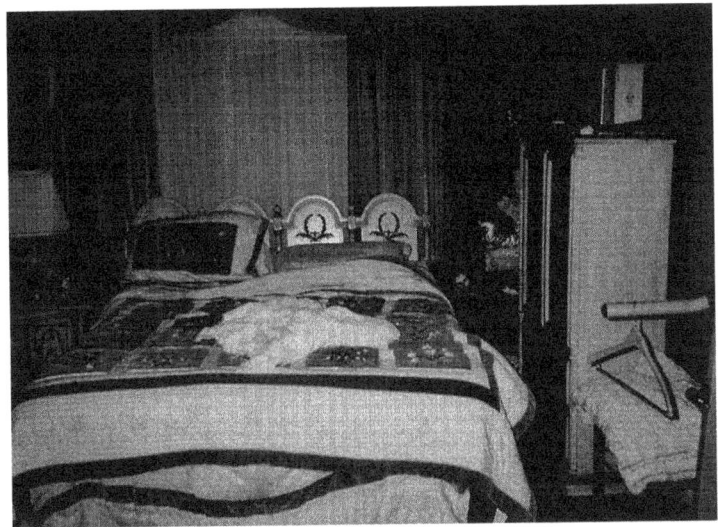

Home

Home

The Early Years in West Virginia
Colonel Vaughan Witten

I was born on 18 February 1935 in Anawalt, West Virginia to a 23-year-old warrior prince of a father and an 18-year-old saintly queen of a mother. My dad was total energy with the pride, courage and strength of a Hannibal. He was just fearless and would fight at the drop of a hat. Yet he could be kind and generous, while on the hand a strict disciplinarian and tireless uncomplaining worker. After a year or so working on railroad maintenance, he worked in the cruel, dangerous coalmines for 40 years until he had to retire with heart trouble and black lung disease from breathing in the coal dust over the years. The mines were primitive in the 1940's and the coal operators just as greedy and callous then as now. In addition to cave ins and explosions, the men had to work in four foot high shafts that required one to work on their knees for 8 to 16 hours per day. Hand loading was the method of extraction. The long wall extraction machines didn't come until later. Though it was tough hard work, the hand loaders made the most money with the use of their shovel, loading coal onto the low built tiny rail cars that brought the coal out of the mine on rails to a collection point called a tipple, that graded the coal by size and dumped it into high rail cars that transported it to the Kanawha River about 15 miles away and onto barges for transportation down the Ohio and sometimes Mississippi Rivers.

My father, Alphonso Witten, married Arlene Walker of Martinsville, Va., in 1934, and it was a good marriage except in the early years when he was so wild and reckless that he hit my mother a couple times, but she forgave him and had the grace and wisdom to see a great man underneath all that rage at times. We lived in a coal company house and shopped at the company store, which gave credit, but overcharged. I remember sometimes my dad would work several double shifts making good money and yet would not draw a dime because it all went to pay bills at the company store. The company owned everything. The rent was free in the small shotgun houses and the officials were kind and friendly. But the mining camp was like a reservation even with its own script money that was only good on the coal camp. To get real green back money you could trade $1.00 into $1.15 script if you were going to buy things on the camp. Things were relatively cheap with gas at 10 cents a gallon, movie 10 cents, pop and candy 5 cents and so on. But in the company store, things were higher priced. There was a lot of money trading, but it was legal.

I remember I took a 100 customer paper route when I was about twelve so I could give my mom a free paper everyday and she could avoid the 65 cents paper bill. This was a first class paper, the Charleston Gazette, that was about 25 miles away, but it was close enough that the papers would still be warm when the distribution truck dumped them off every morning at about 6:00a.m. I would ride my bike the two miles to the filling station drop point and then fold the papers, stuff them into my bike saddle bags and basket and be on my way to complete my

5 miles delivery up the mountain to the last customer near the mine and still get back home for some hot oatmeal and catch the school bus. I did this for about three years until I graduated from Washington High School at age 15.

My favorite toy or play weapon was the 500 shot Daisy BB gun-rifle. I was very accurate with it and shot many small birds out of the sky or from their perch. We could make toys out of about anything along with some imagination. A milk can can become a football and a small rock wrapped in layers of electrical tape became a baseball. Competition and a strong desire to win in any game revealed the skills of the poorest boys and put us far ahead of more affluent youngsters later in our adolescence. I realized later that I was very determined and motivated to prevail as a result of compensation for my small size. My smartness came natural as best I can discern. My dad was extremely smart and gifted in the mechanical or maintenance area and my mom knew how to make bricks without straw-so to speak. Through raising and feeding six kids on the little pay left my dad after the company store got it's share, my mom had plenty food, especially pinto beans, corn bread and butter milk along with the typical breakfast of oatmeal, cream of wheat and buttered toast. I took it all for granted then. Also, one usually raised a hog in the back yard, feeding it slop from the kitchen; and several chickens. I used to wring the chicken necks off and watch them flop around awhile, then soak them in hot water and take the feathers off. My dad would shoot the hog in the head and then place it onto an A-frame device for butchering. We would grind our own sausage on a small hand grinder. Also, we had a garden that was full of pole green beans, onions, tomatoes and peppers along with a few rows of corn. During World War II, these were called "victory gardens".

Neither of my parents smoked, but dad chewed tobacco, as did most miners. I remember one popular brand was Redman. You could by tobacco in a pouch already sliced up or in a solid bar that had to be bitten off to get a good chew. I was fortunate that I never had a desire for the stuff, nor were any of my black friends, but the white boys tended to go for it as they grew up.

To till the garden each year required a lot of work with a pitchfork. It was only about 100 by 50 feet of land, but I thought it was huge. At the very end of the yard past the garden, was our outhouse toilet. We didn't have running water until my mid-teens when dad drilled a well and installed an electric pump. He drilled the hole to find water by beating the pipe into the ground with his bare hands using a sledgehammer for about a week. Until we got our own water, we used a community hand pump located on a cement slab. It often required priming before any water came out, but the water was cold and good. I enjoyed going to the pump daily to get two buckets full to bring home. We bathed in a large washtub and never thought that we were deprived or impoverished. We accepted things as they were and were happy without feeling sorry for ourselves. This was the way it was and negative thought had no place in our daily routine. In fact,

17

with daddy being a favorite of the mine boss, I thought we were better off than most. Some years dad could afford to pay Tom Sherman to plow our yard with his horse. He was a nice man, but we were a little afraid of him, but yet, we would still overturn his toilet on Halloween.

There were all kinds of ways to make extra money if you didn't mind work. In addition to my newspaper jobs, I would also help unload 50 pound bags of rock dust from the rail cars that brought it in to reduce sparks in the mines and prevent explosions. I would also collect chunks of coal from the coal railroad that would fall off the cars on the way to the river. I would pile it up at home for use in our cooking stove and sell the rest to the older people in the neighborhood for a small sum. I tried everything I could to relieve the economic load off my parents. I would also cut small limbs off trees to sell as bean poles for 2 cents and tomato sticks for 1 cent. I sold Vick Salve, vegetable seeds and Easter cards house to house. I even sold minnows from the creek to fisherman for bait for a penny each. We didn't have the luxury of organized entertainment per se. We made our own toys, listened to the radio for stories like *The Shadow* which was scary, but exciting. We didn't even have telephones and television was not heard of, much less being an actual reality capable of being acquired. As I said before, we were happy, poor and appreciated even the smallest of things. I do want to mention the greasy pig contest we enjoyed at the county fair. The officials would cover a pig heavily with axel grease, then turn it loose in an enclosed circle in which everyone could try to catch. It was real funny because when someone caught the pig, it was so slippery they couldn't hold it. Eventually when someone did catch it, they could take it home for food or a pet. They also had a 15 foot greasy pole covered with axel grease in which we tried to climb and get a $10 bill at the top. Now, $10 in the 1940's was like $100 in 2008. Of course, the first 50 or so climbers didn't have a chance. They only ended up cleaning the excess grease off the pole. As more and more people tried, the pole became less slippery and finally someone reached the top. Everybody just had so much fun watching and laughing at those trying to climb the pole as well as catch the greasy pig. Finally worthy of note, a Black circus from New Orleans called *Silas Green* would come to town once a year and we would have so much fun with the rides and animals yes, Barnum and Bailey circus came around also, but nothing was as much fun as *Silas Green*.

Along with my exciting and enjoyable youth came a lot of family deaths and sadness, mostly on dad's side. His dad and mom both died when I was about 8 or 9 years old and then the most tragic of all, his two baby sisters, Helen and Rita about 12 and 13 both drowned in a mining water storage pool. They became stuck in the thick mud bottom and couldn't escape. Everyone was devastated. I particularly remember how swollen their bodies were at the funeral. It seemed like we were always going to a funeral. It was about a four-hour drive from Ward to Dad's home in Anawalt, and I dreaded that trip. Dad had so much death in his family that many things reminded him of it. One winter when I made snow structure like a fort for snow ball fighting, he made me tear it down because he thought it looked like a casket. Of course I tore it down.

Dad was somewhat superstitious about death. He believed that if a bird got in your house and flew around, that someone would die. We had a bird get in our house one day, but no one died that I recall. There were few deaths among mom's family in Martinsville. I attribute that to genes and a much slower and less dangerous life style in South Western Virginia. Agriculture and furniture manufacturing were the major industries. My Grandpa Walker, who was my favorite, worked in the furniture factories and he was very relaxed, easy going and loving. Grandma Pearl was the iron hand of the family and she ran a tight ship. Martin Walker died just as I was leaving for England and the Azores in 1960. I remember seeing his pay stub one day where he made 10 cents per hour. But you could get a loaf of bread for a penny and grandma had a cow for milk and butter. I liked to churn the milk to see the butter rise to the top.

It was fun going to Martinsville, but I was always apprehensive going to Anawalt under any conditions. The house was built high up on the side of a mountain above the highway that entered the town. It was very scary, looking like something from a haunted house movie. The steps up to the three-story building were long and steep. Grandfather was also scary. He didn't talk much, at least not to me and he had long gray hair and would sit on the top floor porch looking out over the town. The story was that he was real tough in his day and the meanest man in McDowell County. Even the sheriff was afraid of him, so the story goes. He looked Indian and I understand had some Spanish and other blood. It must be so, because his kids were named Alphonso, my Dad; Adrian, Carthetine, Orlando, Pedco and Clayton. Grandma Witten was sweet, short fat and black. I liked her, but don't remember much about our relationship. After their deaths, the old house was abandoned to ruin. I don't think anyone in today's world would live there, but in Grandpa's day it was probably the best house in Anawalt, which by the way is where I was born one year and one month after Mom and Dad married in Bassett, Virginia. My parents left there when I was 2 or 3 and went to the Ward coal-mining town where he first worked on the railroad repairing tracks before going into the mines to work. He continued to work in different mines after one would run out of coal and then to another. When a mine ran out of coal, it was call a "blow out". He did this until he was about 60 years old and also became a Baptist minister when he was about 30. He was a good preacher, but would not take money from the church. All of his churches were small over the years, from about 20 to 50 members. He was very faithful as was my mom, never missing a Sunday. I didn't go every Sunday and felt a little guilty about that. I would rather stay home and play. Dad called me his prodigal son. In fact, when I was up in the mountain playing and missing supper, Dad would whistle for me. I knew his whistle and would run home as fast as I could. My sister Audrey is the only one of the children who could whistle. I tried, but never could do it.

My high school days were very enjoyable and satisfying except for the discrimination expressed by our coach of all the sports, a Mr. Marion Meadows. He was a black man from Montgomery, W.Va, about 10 miles from the school located in London. For some reason he gave preferential treatment as to who played on the teams to the boys and girls who rode on the Montgomery bus. We had only about 300 students in the school. About two hundred rode on five or six buses from various coal camps and about 100 lived in or near London and walked to school. On the few days I missed our Ward bus, I would walk and/or hitch hike to school and still get there on time. About Mr. Meadow's prejudiced attitude, especially against the Ward kids, I think he felt the Montgomery kids, who were from the city, were better than coal miner's kids. But we Ward kids continued to try out and some eventually made his teams, even football. It's ironic that even though he called himself using the "best" players, we never beat anybody, especially football. We did a little better in basketball because for a short period, we had 3 or 4 tall kids from a single family in Montgomery who were actually good. As for myself I was very little, 5'4, 110 pounds, so I was known for my fearlessness, courage, strong spirit and toughness, but not big enough. However, after 3 years on the practice squad and not playing a game, he did let me play in my senior year--though I was still very small playing against other teams of virtual men at 6 feet or better, 180 lbs. to 220 lbs. It was found out that some of the other team players worked in the coal mines at night. There was no law at that time limiting the age of players... that came later. Anyway, after about five games in 1951, I broke my leg in our game against Dubois and there went my football career. It also threw me back in my academics by a few hundreds of a point and costing my slam-dunk for valedictorian. I lost out to Sylvia Ferguson and was salutatorian, for the senior class. Up to that time, I was known as the smallest, but smartest boy in the school. Our science teacher, Mr. Roscoe Carter, used to take me from my 9th grade class in the Junior High School on the first floor of our building, up to the physics and chemistry classes in the upstairs high school to show them up, when they couldn't answer his questions. I felt good about his confidence in me, but I didn't like showing them up for they would get mad and blame me for the embarrassment. Also while in high school, I fought this boy named Clyde Kelley every morning before school for one year. I know it sounds stupid and unbelievable, but we just didn't like each other and would wrestle in the dirt every morning. When I got into my first class, my clothes were always dirty from fighting and playing tin can football in the school yard before the first bell. I guess I was about 12 years old. Later, Clyde and I became best friends.

About football, I was the best tackler on our team regardless of size, in basketball, I was the best shooter, but in both cases, too small to make varsity until the 1951-football season. I never did make the basketball team, but I did make the baseball team because size was not a factor. I could hit, field and throw better than 90% of the other boys. Plus, I had a secret weapon. I could play catcher, a position most guys were afraid to play. I learned to play this position in sand lot games, and when Mr. Meadows found out, it was the first time he showed any interest in me. I made the baseball team.

Our graduating class in 1952 was only about 20 students, but it was an exhilarating experience. I was smart enough for college, and W.Va. State was only about 50 miles away. But the 5 or 6 hundred dollars tuition was just too much to ask of my hard working parents, so I was determined to work odd jobs until I was old enough to get a real job and pay my own way. As it turned out, my real job became the U.S. Air Force, during the Korean War in which I enlisted at age 17 with my parents' permission.

But during the time between graduation and the Air Force, I lived an undisciplined unsupervised life in which, I had no true focus. I cut grass, washed dishes, bussed tables, cut up chickens in in a local chicken slaughter house, caddied golf, set bowling pins and other things I probably have forgotten.

One episode stands out in all this. I had a job as a table boy cleaning tables and removing dishes at a high-class restaurant in Charleston. All the waitresses were white and friendly. On my first night I took the tip money as I cleaned the tables and put it in a box. I thought the tips were for me. So, about half way through the shift, one of the waitresses asked me if I had seen any tips on the tables. I said "Yes, I have it all boxed for I thought it was mine". She laughed and said "No, the money is for the waitresses". I said that I was sorry and quickly gave them the money. I thought I would be fired for stealing, but they realized I was just a dumb kid that didn't know any better. In fact, they had more respect for me for being honest and thoughtful. After that, they would each give me 10% of their nightly tips. I felt good about that.

So after two years of bumping around like this I was eligible to work in the good paying coalmines, with my parent's permission and signature. My mom however, said no way would she allow me in there to be hurt or killed. So, I then thought of the military for I always fore saw myself as a soldier patriot and not ashamed to risk myself for glory. We West Virginian's are the most decorated military people in the U.S. on a per capita basis. West Virginians for some reason are not afraid of anything, sometimes at their own peril. I think I got my warrior spirit from, my dad who was fearless, smart and the courage of a lion. I adored him, except for his harsh discipline, but I now appreciate him even for that.

One quick anecdote about Dad before I finish this section. You see, as hard a worker and good provider as he was, he had one heck of a sense of humor. So he had this pet alligator, small and young, but still an alligator. I don't know where he got it and never found out. He would carry it around in the front seat of his car and would stop to pick up hitch hikers and then laugh when they jumped in the front seat about scared to death. They would immediately jump out and run when seeing the alligator. Dad was a legend in the hills around Ward hollow with that alligator and was the subject of many funny stories when the family and friends got together.

About the discipline, I can't not report it. It was very mean. Dad would beat me with a bank belt, electric cable, anything he could get his hands on when he got mad and would just go on and on. I would be hollering and running, but he kept at it. The worst was when he plaited the peach tree limbs. It was like a whip, raising whelps on the skin. He did this up to my Senior year in high school. At this time I feared and hated him, but forgave him later in that, that was all he knew from his father. I also hated that peach tree and thought about cutting it down. ☺

Ms. Henderson, Early School Years and High School Senior Year

Ms. Louise Henderson was my elementary school teacher. She was such a wonderful, understanding and excellent teacher that it is difficult to adequately describe her. She had such patience and love for her students while teaching 4 or 5 different grades in a small one room wooden building on the middle of a field near a rocky creek bed about a half mile from the company store and another quarter mile from a large brick elementary school for white children. There were only about 20 of us Black coal miner kids in the school, but Ms. Henderson made sure we knew about all the basic Sciences, English, Math and Core Education courses. As I look back she must have been about 30 years old, very beautiful with coal black hair that stayed that way until she died at age 95.

I just loved to go to school and I loved Ms. Henderson. She was so kind and forgiving. She was generous with praise and made you feel like you were the smartest, most important kid in the world. I know I got a lot of my confidence from her as well as my parents.

In the winter time, we huddled around a pot belly stove to keep warm. I moved through the grades pretty fast because Ms. Henderson skipped me two grades because I was advanced beyond my grade level according to her. I don't remember my exact age, but I was very young when I left to go to junior high under a good teacher, Mrs. Zampere Moore, in Houston, West Virginia, not far from London. Ms. Moore, however, was mean and everybody was scared of her. I didn't like her much, but I did like the sweet persimmons we could pick off one of the nearby trees. The school burned down about a year after I arrived and all 30 or 50 students there had to go to London early to finish the 8th grade and continue on into junior high.

While at the Ward school, I couldn't wait to get outside to play at recess. I would always be so happy if I saw my mom walking down the railroad tracks past the school on the way home about a mile away, carrying groceries from the company store. She would always have a snack for me if we saw each other. She was just like an angel walking out of heaven. I really liked the Ritz cheese crackers she would sometimes buy. Also during recess, we boys would wrestle and throw rocks at each other in our war games. There were plenty of smooth flat rocks in the dry creek bed. We were all lucky that we didn't hit or hurt each other. We would also catch bull frogs and take them home. There we would cut off their legs and fry the legs in corn meal. When heated, the legs would jump out of the pan if it wasn't covered. The bull frog legs were very good as well as fried green tomatoes. But once back inside the school, it was right into the books and academic discussions. Ms. Henderson taught us like we were high school students and we knew things then that college graduates today don't know about physics, geography, science and astronomy. When I got to high school, it was very easy.

Washington High School - Senior Year

Returning from Martinsville in 1950 for my senior year at Washington High was super exciting. I was glad to see all of my old friends and teachers and eager to learn more about the world of academics, especially, science and civics. Mr. Bernard Brown, our history teacher, was my favorite teacher, and I was real glad to see him, plus, he was our band director. I played the snare drum in the band. We had the West Point type band uniforms of black trimmed in orange, our school colors, and we were quite impressive, especially for a relatively poor black high school of about three hundred students and no football field. We had a practice field only behind the school with no seats, lights, goal post or any such things. We played our home football games at West Virginia Tech College in Montgomery on top of the mountain behind the college. The field was so sloped from sideline to sideline that you could hardly see people on the other side at the ground level. But at least it had goal posts, bleachers and stripes every ten yards. This is the field where my leg was broken in October of 1950.

Sometimes during my senior year or perhaps immediately after in June 1951, I was able to come up with the $15.00 to spend a week at West Virginia Boys State, a park and institution designed to teach young boys about State Government in which each would be elected or appointed to an office and then perform the duties for a week. It was located about 80 miles from home in a mountainous region with a steep river gorge at a place called Hawks Nest. It was an honor and privilege to be able to go there, but the $15.00 cost was huge at that time. I couldn't get it from dad because he had bought me my drum and a graduation suit that year, so I wrote my Uncle Carthentine Witten in Anawalt, who was a school teacher in Gary, West Virginia. He promptly sent me the money. I have always cherished him for such a magnificent gift and regret that I never paid him back before he died. The $15.00 would equal to about $100.00 today.

Boys State was fun. I ran for Governor and lost. The fellow who did win then appointed me Highway Commissioner. I was just too young and small to influence the others to vote for me. I was 15 and most of the other 100 or so boys were 18 to 20. They pulled a lot of pranks and tricks on me because of my youth. One was to loosen the top of the salt shaker at breakfast so all the salt would spill on my food. I learned a lot of tricks and about deviant behavior at that camp. One night in the open by barracks we slept on cots, we had a pillow fight and the Administrators made us all get dressed and run around the building for an hour at 1:00 in the morning.

The week at Boys State was a wonderful experience. Though I was small and young for my level of academic achievement, I was very good at sports, especially at pitching horse shoes. I had learned to pitch horse shoes with the coal miners at home who used the game as a past time. A pit was located near our house in Ward hollow during the six month coal strikes of 1949, which was all the miners had to do for recreation. Gradually, I became better at pitching than they were and I competed regularly with the champion throwers, which were Pickle Mayfield, Doodle Booker and my dad. The miners would also gamble at cards for recreation.

So, when I found out that Boys State had a horse shoe tournament, I immediately registered to compete. Though there were some good pitchers in the camp, I won the tournament and received more recognition for that than anything else I had done during the week the week passed all too quickly, and eventually I was hitch hiking my way back home with a lifetime of memories. A state police trooper picked me up hitch hiking and drove me all the way home to Ward. He was really nice. During my adolescence, I and my two close friends, Bobby Preston and Leroy Franklin essentially lived a Daniel Boone type of life in the mountains. We would build log cabins to stay out at night, swim in the rivers in the region without fear of drowning, hop on and ride the swift coal train from the mines daily, pick blueberries in snake infested bushes, make bow and arrows to fight each other with, make sling shots to hurl small stones to kill birds, climb the tall oil and gas derrick towers and play like batman, play football with tin cans and even make our own toys from discarded metal or appliances. Speaking of football, one day we were playing with a real football when the ball rolled away to where my dad was walking. He picked it up and drop kicked it about 50 yards. I was totally surprised; I didn't even know he could play football. His stock went up with me after that performance. Imagine having a dad who could do all that he could do, and play football too. We also shot marbles and boasted about who could win the most. I traded comic books weekly by the dozen; Superman, Captain America, Wonder Woman and Flash were favorites. I practically learned to read with comic books. As far as Leroy and Bobby were concerned, they didn't really like me nor me them. You see, they were somehow related biologically in a convoluted ways and always competed to beat me at everything. I was as determined to beat them in everything as well, such as football, basketball, horseshoes, bow and arrows, snow sledding or even gathering walnuts. There was a walnut tree orchid near the top of one mountain and thousands of walnuts would be on the ground. We used to gather them in bags and bring them off the mountain to eat. But the actual nut was in a green hull that had to be removed. In doing so, the hull had a brown stain that covered and penetrated your hand skin. Once finished hulling, your hands would be walnut stained for weeks. We would put the raw nuts on top of the house to dry out in the sun. After about a month, you could take them down and crack and eat them. Our competition also included rooting for major league baseball teams. Bobby and Leroy liked the Detroit Tigers and knew everything about their players and I liked the New York Yankees and knew about them. We would get our daily stats from the newspaper and radio. There was no TV in those days or even knowledge that such an invention existed or would ever exist. So we argued daily about which team was the best. Though outnumbered by them, I had the advantage because the Yankees won most of the time. In addition to them, I had to compete with a 5 year older boy who was more like a man than we were. He was a friendly, good guy, and was good at sports. He was Jesse Woodson, nicknamed "Rat". He was also related to Bobby, so in essence it was me against the three of them, psychologically, if not physically. Jesse was so good that he was allowed to play varsity basketball at Washington High under Mr. Meadows. Now that was some feat for Mr. Meadows didn't like the Ward kids as I mentioned earlier.

There is a major episode in this story that I have yet to reveal and it was scary. One day as Bobby, Leroy and I were playing Indians, shooting arrows at each other in a hillside creek bed, I saw my Dad running from this crazy man Joe Pen, who was chasing him with a hatchet trying to kill him. I couldn't believe my eyes. This Joe Pen was an ex convict having been in the Moundsville, West Virginia State Prison for murder. He had been released and everyone knew he was dangerous, but my Dad must have said something to set him off. My Dad would not hold his tongue and wasn't afraid of anything. Anyway, as I saw Dad run across the dry creek bed, I shot my arrow at Joe Pen, but I missed, but he had to duck. Meanwhile, Dad picked up a big rock, turned around and threw it at Joe Pen, hitting him in the head and causing him to drop the hatchet. I screamed as Daddy picked up the hatchet and yelled for him to kill Joe Pen. But Dad didn't kill him; he turned the hatchet sideways and beat him down to the ground, drawing lots of blood from Pen's head. I'm not clear about what happened after that, except Joe Pen had his head wrapped in bandages for about a month and he didn't mess with my Dad after that. Also, the coal company officials ejected Mr. Pen off the camp and he had to find a job and house somewhere else. You see, once you quit or lost your job on the camp, you had to move out into t he world so to speak. Under some circumstances they would let you stay, but you would have to pay rent. I was very proud of my Dad in defeating that crazy bully and I am glad now that he didn't kill him.

During this time, there were five children, myself, Audrey, Janita and James; Emma, the baby in the family wouldn't be born until 1955, and this was 1949-51. Anyway, one day I came home from school and my mom had a new baby girl. I didn't know where it came from; I didn't even notice that my mom was pregnant. This was Janita, and by the way, one could not even say pregnant in those days. It was a bad word, and even when someone was pregnant, we called it "knocked up".

My brother James was tougher than I was as it turned out. He played integrated sports after 1955, after Brown vs. Board, and made all star everything, especially in football. But he was wild and took chances I would never take. After I went into the Air Force, I learned the he had taken my dad's pick-up truck, which my dad treasured and kept washed and shined; and drove it down to Cedar Grove without a license or even knowing how to drive. I don't know how James survived that. If I had done that, I would be lucky to be alive to write this story. Speaking of cars, in the 1980's and 1990's, there was one extraordinary episode I had with a 1981 American Motors Concorde 6 cylinder station wagon, formerly known as a Nash Motors product. This was a very simple, but reliable car for the most part. I drove it for about ten years mainly the 150 mile round trip from Fayetteville to Raleigh for work every day. The almost unbelievable part was I put over 600,000 miles on it. Yes, I know it sounds like an exaggeration, but it's true. I didn't report it to the car company since the way odometers turned over at 100,000 miles in those days, you couldn't prove it, and I didn't think they would believe me. Anyway, I carried extra oil, a water pump, fan belts and spark plugs and points in the back. If it broke down on the road, I had my tools and could change a water pump, plugs, points or belt on the side of the road in an hour or so. I hated to get rid of it, but it finally just wore out. I drove it to the junk yard with a heavy heart.

Also, I forgot about Washington High School principle Mr. Leonard Barnett, who called everybody "Mackey" he was a good guy, but tried to act tough to keep us in line. A very good principle. He looked almost white, but we knew he was Black, and he didn't try to "pass" nor did any other of our white skinned teachers. They were all tough. We had a Mrs. Morgan who would slap you in the face if she caught you cheating. I didn't cheat, but I was extra careful in her class. Other teachers I liked very much were Mr. White, who taught the Industrial Skills and Printing Press, and also was the Boy Scout Master, Br. Bolden, Assistant Football coach and Biology, Mrs. Jarret, Librarian, Mrs. Seay, Music teacher, of course, Mr. Brown, History and Band Master. Can't remember the rest, but since it's been 58 years, I'm sure you understand. But they were all good and gave us tough love, except for Mr. Meadows who I did not like and had no respect for.

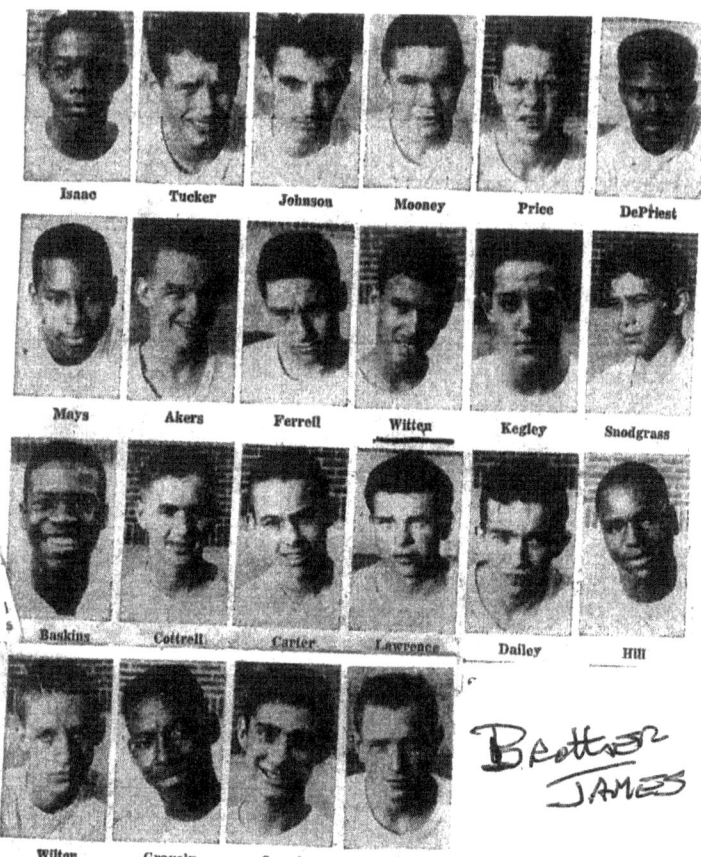

Isaac   Tucker   Johnson   Mooney   Price   DePriest

Mays   Akers   Ferrell   Witten   Kegley   Snodgrass

Baskins   Cottrell   Carter   Lawrence   Dailey   Hill

Wilton   Gravely   Sword   Landers

Brother James

1959-60?

Dailey, Witten Lead UKV Team

Charleston Gazette

Pat Dailey of Pratt and James Witten of Cedar Grove were named captains of the offensive and defensive units of the Upper Kanawha Valley Junior High Conference football team.

Dailey, the conference's leading scorer, captains the 11-player offensive unit. Witten, a tough lineman for conference champion Cedar Grove, heads the 11-player defensive team.

The Upper Kanawha Valley team was picked by the eight league coaches at a meeting held last Wednesday.

The biggest player on the team is DuPont's 118-pound Donald Isaac.

Offensive Unit

Pos.	Player	School	Gr.	Wgt.
E—	Rick Carter	C.G.	9th	133
E—	Tom Hill	Marmet	9th	160
T—	Roger Mays	Leewood	9th	150
T—	Leonard Baskins	DuPont	9th	137
G—	Tommy Tucker	Chelyan	7th	165
G—	Bill Kegley	DuPont	9th	150
C—	Bill Wilton	Midway	9th	150
B—	Pat Dailey	Pratt	9th	150
B—	Bob Gravely	Grant	9th	132
B—	Mike Akers	C.G.	9th	138
B—	Fred Landers	C.G.	9th	134

Defensive Unit

Pos.	Player	School	Gr.	Wgt.
L—	Ron Cottrell	Pratt	9th	140
L—	George Johnson	Chelyan	9th	135
L—	Mac DePriest	Grant	9th	145
L—	Bob Lawrence	Marmet	9th	150
L—	Elbert Price	Pratt	8th	140
L—	Jim Witten	C.G.	9th	122
B—	Clarence Mooney	Midway	9th	125
B—	John Ferrell	Leewood	9th	123
B—	Don Isaac	DuPont	7th	118
B—	Paul Sword	DuPont	8th	120
B—	Joel Snodgrass	Marmet	9th	120

Honorable Mention

Gene Walker and James Ward of Chelyan; Jack Ervin and Roger Powers of

I want to acknowledge all of my senior class members and others as best I can remember.

Seniors

Leroy Brockman
Charles Day
*Louise Mitchell
*Silvia Ferguson
*Lowella Holmes
Manard Ford
Doug Crider
Louie Crider
Bishop Woods
Harold Neal

Doug Plumer
Mildred Grooms
Catherine White
**Peaches-Nueline Brown
***Larry White
****Ramona Vinson
Benny Sharp
Willie Hendricks
Ean Pearls

*Very Smart
**Mr. Brown's daughter
***Mr. White's sons
****I had a crush on her-but I was too young and inexperienced for her.

Other Students

James Calloway
*Hamp Brockman
*Kenneth Brockman
Helen Harris
Lucy Harris
Larence Brownerman
*Kenny Boy Jones
Audrey Witten
Bobo Murray
Leroy Franklin
Billy Dabbs
Mary Ida Ely
Gwin Tootso Robinson

*Oswald Robinson
Bobby Robinson
*Jesse Woodson
Anita Woodson
Carol Jean Richmond
Charles "Tackhead" Ely
Gertrude Grooms
Sandra Witten
Darlene Hughes
Bobby Preston
Bobby Wilson
Alvin Sangum Robinson
Nehimah Ford

Donny Hudson
Tommy Hudson
*James Woodson
*Raney Lee
*John Ford
Betty Richmond
Arthur Richmond
Madeline Ely
Ernestine Brown
James Majors
Beatrice Taylor
Anita Woodson
*Henry Wallace

*Sports Heroes

28

The Washington High Alumni Association is looking for money to renovate the old Grant Elementary School and turn it into a community center.

Washington High Alumni Association proposes renovation of school for community center

By Jim Balow
STAFF WRITER

They called it Washington High School, not in honor of the country's father but for another famous Washington — Booker T. — who once lived down the road in Malden.

In 1925, after years of intense wrangling, black people in the Upper Kanawha Valley convinced the Kanawha school board to open a high school in London. From Cannelton to Monarch, Montgomery to Chesapeake and the far reaches of Paint Creek and Cabin Creek, black schoolchildren rode the buses to Washington High School.

The solid brick schoolhouse welcomed students until 1956, when integration reached this area. Thence the board of education renamed the school Grant Junior High and, later, Grant Elementary.

The school finally closed last June after 51 years of continuous service. Since then, Vandals have taken over, smashing out most of the windows, ripping down bulletin boards and tearing out lockers.

As soon as the school board announced the possible sale of the school last summer, a group of concerned graduates of the old black high school decided to try to save the building. Led by two retired schoolteachers, the

need somewhere to go for recreation."

Anderson, named Kanawha County Teacher of the Year a year before her retirement in 1985, is president of the nonprofit group. Her sister, Doris Payne, serves as secretary. Other officers are Karolyn Murray of Smithers, the vice president, and Helen Blackstock, treasurer.

Members of the steering committee include Robert Calloway Jr., Nora Jones, Bernice Goolsby and Sam Calloway.

Both Anderson, who graduated from Washington High in 1936, and Payne (class of '47) used to work at the school. Anderson served as secretary from 1947 to 1949 and taught there from 1951 to '56. Payne also worked as secretary as well as girls basketball coach for two years after graduating from West Virginia State College in 1951.

"I saw in the paper it was going up for sale and I thought, why don't we try to get the school for the community," said Payne.

The school board, while sympathetic to the idea, cannot sell the school to the alumni group

directly without going through public sale. An appraiser estimated the school property, including Grant Community Park behind the school, is worth about $45,000. He figured the park which lies in the flood plain, is worth $5,000. The school building is worthless, he determined, but the land on which it sits could be sold for $40,000 if the school were removed. With the school standing, the property is worth $20,000 according to the appraiser.

In December the school board agreed to sell the park land to the Kanawha County Parks and Recreation Commission for $2,500.

Washington High Alumni Association
P. O. BOX 536
MONTGOMERY W.VA. 25136

LOUISE ANDERSON
PRES.

KAROLYN K. MURRAY
VICE PRES.

DORIS PAYNE
SECT.

HELEN BLACKSTOCK
TREASURER

TO; WASHINGTON HIGH ALUMNUS, FORMER STUDENTS AND FACULTY
FROM: Alumni Executive Committee
DATE: June 24, 1987

GREETINGS! We know that you will be interested in becoming actively involved in a project to memoralize Washington High School. We have been formally organized and incorporated by the state of West Virginia to do just that--using the Washington High building to establish a community center.

Those of us who live in the area of the school have taken this monumental task upon ourselves. A few of us are actively involved and numbers are increasing every day. You can help by becoming involved in whatever way is feasible for you. The Board of Education gave us the building to use for this purpose. It was vacant for a year and has been vandalized, so we have to make repairs before we can establish the Center.

We are asking for Alumni contributions of any amount. Monthly pledges may be made. Your name will be inscribed on a plaque to be located in the front corridor if you contribute $100. This may be paid in four payments of $25 each, if necessary. If you would like a room named in memory or in honor of some person, it can be done with a $500 donation. Rooms are limited, of course. We feel that most alumni will want to help, and we have committed the Alumni Association to an annual contribution until the Center pays for itself. We have faith that there are enough loyal, "die-hard" Washingtonians to support our committment.

We are applying for federal, state, and private grants for renovation monies. Local businesses, civic and social organizations, churches, and community people are being asked to contribute. Fund-raising projects are also planned to help make the Center self-supporting.

Please let us hear from you immediately. We need your ideas; we need your financial help; we need your MANPOWER if you live nearby. We have set the second Saturday in each month at noon for meetings of the Association. If you are able, plan to attend some of our meetings. If you live far from the area, drop in to see us when you are visiting. We plan to open an office in the building before the renovation is completed so you can drop in and see what we are doing.

The Class of '47 has challenged other classes to beat their total contributions. Many of them have already contributed. Their initial total will be announced soon. We hope other Classes will accept the Challenge. Let us hear from you soon.

Enclosures

One other thing about Washington High, other than the greatest school in West Virginia and the best students and faculty ever, including our Assistant Principal, Mrs. Anderson, I believe, and our janitor, who I can't remember his name (sorry); is the fact that no one ever spoke to or told us about our Black history or the background of the Black schools we were associated with or played sports against. The schools were:

Byrd Prillerman High	Dubois High
*Stratton High	Conerly High
*Garnet High	Simmons High
*Douglas High	

There may be more, but I forget.

*West Virginia Black school powerhouses. They were in large cities with lots of students. We only had 200 students in the whole school with 20 in our graduating class.

About these named schools, we talked about them all the time, but had no idea or clue-at least I didn't-about who they were named after or why, or what these men had done in history to deserve a school name. Of course, I learned about them later. We didn't even discuss Booker T. Washington, our name sake. We were of course in a segregated school system and age, so I guess the White government and school administrators saw no reason to educate us about us. But that was only a minor deficiency as I look back, the main thing was that I received a current day equivalent college education even with the outdated (4 years average) books, because 2+2=4 in 1951, the same as it did in 1947 or 1636, (Harvard).

I did however, look up the historical background of those schools and I present them here:

Byrd Prillerman High School was named for a former slave, Byrd Prillerman, who became a famous educator and government official in West Virginia.

Byrd Prillerman and Family

BYRD PRILLERMAN

Byrd Prillerman

Having been born a slave in 1859, Byrd Prillerman and his family, after the surrender of General Lee in 1865, immediately rented a farm in Virginia on which they lived for two years. In 1868, they came to West Virginia on foot and resided in Sissonville. 1872 entered school in Charleston and taught and supervised education in West Virginia for 40 years. He secured proper legislation with Reverend G.H. Payne, D.D to create the West Virginia colored institute in 1891, eventually becoming West Virginia State University. Later became President, retiring and becoming Superintendent of Work under the West Virginia Sunday School Association. A friend and colleagues of Dr. Booker T. Washington, Dr. Prillerman became a dynamic force in the education of West Virginia Blacks.

Dubois High School was named for William Edward Burghart Dubois, 1868-1963, an American Civil Rights Activist, Pan-Africanist, Sociologist, historian, author, and editor. A contemporary of Booker T. Washington, he carried on a dialogue with the educator about segregation, political disfranchisement, and ways to improve African American life.

W. E. B. Du Bois

From Wikipedia, the free encyclopedia

William Edward Burghardt Du Bois
(pronounced /duːˈbɔɪs/ doo-BOYSS[1]) (February 23, 1868 – August 27, 1963) was an American civil rights activist, Pan-Africanist, sociologist, historian, author, and editor. At the age of 95, in 1963, he became a naturalized citizen of Ghana.[2]

Historian David Levering Lewis wrote, "In the course of his long, turbulent career, W. E. B. Du Bois attempted virtually every possible solution to the problem of twentieth-century racism— scholarship, propaganda, integration, national self-determination, human rights, cultural and economic separatism, politics, international communism, expatriation, third world solidarity."[3]

W. E. B. Du Bois

W. E. B. Du Bois, in 1918

Born	February 23, 1868 Great Barrington, Massachusetts, USA
Died	August 27, 1963 (aged 95) Accra, Ghana
Occupation	Academic, Scholar, Activist, Journalist, Sociologist
Alma mater	Harvard University
Spouse(s)	Nina Gomer Du Bois, Shirley Graham Du Bois

Du Bois was the most prominent intellectual leader and political activist on behalf of African Americans in the first half of the twentieth century. A contemporary of Booker T. Washington, he carried on a dialogue with the educator about segregation, political disfranchisement, and ways to improve African American life. He was labeled "The Father of Pan-Africanism." **Civil rights activism**

Stratton High School - opened in 1921 in Bekley, West Virginia and was named after Reverend Daniel Stratton, a former slave who became a preacher and built Baptist meeting houses throughout Southern West Virginia. By 1925, it had become a full, four year high school. Following Brown vs. Board Supreme Court Integration decision, Stratton was converted to a Junior High School in 1967, and it is now Stratton Elementary School.

History of Stratton High School

History of Stratton High School, Beckley, West Virginia

Photo from 1970 Stratton Jr. High yearbook

History of Stratton High School, 1907-1967

By MAE REID

Stratton High School, like many other great institutions, had a very humble beginning. For in 1907, it sp the Rock Quarry Elementary School located at Mabscott.

The Rock Quarry School, which had 19 pupils, served the children of the ten families then in the Beckle first teacher was Miss Mary Booze. In 1912, the school was moved to a building on Fayette Street when Hotel now stands. This building served as a tinshop. Odd Fellow Hall and the school. The teachers were and Miss Hattie Dehaven. In 1916, E. L. Morton, a man with great foresight and courage, became the pr

In 1919, through the planning of Mr. Morton and the efforts of the parents, there was established at Faye Beaver Avenue the first Negro school in Raleigh County to offer high school subjects. The building had and was named after the Reverend Daniel Stratton, a highly respected citizen.

At Stratton, all elementary subjects and those of the first year of high school were taught. There were in school department two teachers. They were E. L. Morton and Miss Louise Morton, who later became M Jeffries.

Garnet High School- was named for American Abolitionist, clergy man Henry Highland Garnet, 1815-1882. Born a Maryland slave, he escaped in 1824 and was educated at the Oneida Institute, Whitesboro, N.Y. He was an eloquent speaker, but his radicalism, calling slaves to rise and slay their masters, caused his influence to decline. He was opposed and superseded in leadership by the more moderate, Frederick Douglass. Garnet served as Presbyterian Pastor in Troy, N.Y., in New York City and in Washington, D.C. In 1881 he was appointed minister to Liberia, but died tow months after his arrival there.

Henry Highland Garnet

1815-1882

Early history and education

Garnet was born a slave near New Market in Kent County, Maryland, to George and Henrietta. His grandfather was an African warrior prince, captured in combat, which might have been the source of Garnet's fiery spirit. Receiving permission to attend a funeral, he and his family instead escaped to free-state Pennsylvania in 1824. He spent two years at sea, as a cabin boy, cook, and steward, traveling to Cuba. When he returned, he discovered that his family had split up due to threats of slave catchers. When Garnet was ten years old, the family reunited and moved to New York City, where from 1826 through 1833, Garnet attended the African Free School, and the Phoenix High School for Colored Youth. While in school, Garnet began his career in abolitionism. With fellow schoolmates, he established the Garrison Literary and Benevolent Association. It garnered mass support among whites, but the club ultimately had to move due to racist feelings. Two years later, in 1835, he started to attend the Noyes Academy in Canaan, New Hampshire, where he met his wife, Julia Williams. Together, they had three children, only one of whom one survived to adulthood. Due to his abolitionist activities, Henry Garnet was ultimately driven away from the Noyes Academy by an angry segregationist mob. He went on to further his education at the Oneida Theological Institute in Whitesboro, which had newly opened its doors to all races. Here, he was acclaimed for his wit, brilliance, and rhetorical skills. After graduation in 1839, the following year, he injured his knee playing sports. It never recovered and his leg was amputated in 1840.

<u>Simmons High School</u> was named after Roscoe Conklin Simmons, a Black journalist, orator and politician. Born in 1881, he was the greatest Black orator of his day. He wrote for the *Chicago Defender*, the nation's largest Black newspaper and was later a columnist for the *Chicago Tribune*. He forged links with Black and White leaders and often helped White Republicans rally Black voters for support. He was a fixer they summoned when in need of political help by the community. He was one of several boyfriends of Black movie star "Gone With The Wind" movie star, Hattie McDaniel-Mammy. In this role she received an <u>Oscar</u> for <u>Best Supporting Actress</u>.

Simmons High School, Montgomery, WV

ROSCOE CONKLING SIMMONS AND THE SIGNIFICANCE OF AFRICAN AMERICAN ORATORY*

ANDREW KAYE

University of Newcastle

ABSTRACT. *The black journalist and politician, Roscoe Simmons, was best known for his ability as an orator. Simmons's lecturing activities reveal the networks underlying a black public sphere upon which ambitious black leaders relied to publicize their political agendas. Those networks expanded in the first half of the twentieth century as blacks exploited the press, radio, and other technologies, and as blacks migrated in numbers from the Southern states. Meetings of African Americans served several functions: as opportunities to debate the race's prospects; to voice political concerns; and as sources of entertainment. Simmons incorporated all these principles in his platform performances, as he worked to secure valuable connections with organizations ranging from churches and fraternal bodies to Republican clubs and urban machines. Beginning with his family connection to Booker T. Washington, Simmons cultivated friendships with influential blacks and whites over a period of fifty years. His conservative ideology, however, did not suit all tastes.*

Washington High School was named for Booker Taliaferro Washington, 1856-1915, an African American educator, orator, author and a dominant leader of the nation's African American community. Among his many achievements was the founding of Tuskegee Institute in Alabama, now Tuskegee University.

Booker T. Washington

Born	April 5, 1856
	Hale's Ford, Virginia, U.S.
Died	November 14, 1915 (aged 59)
	Tuskegee, Alabama, U.S.
Occupation	Educator, Author, and African American Civil Rights Leader

Booker Taliaferro Washington (April 5, 1856 – November 14, 1915) was an African American educator, orator, author and a dominant leader of the nation's African-American community from the 1890s to his death. Born into slavery "near a crossroads post-office called Hale's Ford" in Franklin County, Virginia [1] and freed by the Civil War in 1865, he became the first leader of the new Tuskegee Institute in Alabama, then a normal teachers' college for blacks. Washington firmly believed in the Hampton system of industrial education: teaching trades like brick-making alongside book learning. Tuskegee was to become his area of operations and he literally helped build it from the ground up[2].

As a young man, he invented the surname Washington when all the other school children were giving their full names[3].

Douglas High School was named for Frederick Douglass- born Frederick Augustus Washington Bailey, 1818-1895, an American Abolitionist, women's suffragist, editor, orator, author, statesman and reformer.

Frederick Douglass

Frederick Douglass, c.1879.

Frederick Douglass as a young man

Born	c. 1818 Talbot County, Maryland, United States
Died	February 20, 1895 (aged 77) Washington, D.C., United States
Occupation	Abolitionist, author, editor, diplomat
Spouse(s)	Anna Murray (c.1839) Helen Pitts (1884)
Children	Charles Remond Douglass Rosetta Douglass Lewis Henry Douglass Frederick Douglass Jr. Annie Douglass (died at 10)
Parents	Harriet Bailey and perhaps Aaron Anthony

Signature

Frederick Douglass

Frederick Douglass (born **Frederick Augustus Washington Bailey,** (born circa 1818 – February 20, 1895) was an American abolitionist, women's suffragist, editor, orator, author, statesman and reformer. Called "The Sage of Anacostia" and "The Lion of Anacostia", Douglass is one of the most prominent figures in African American and United States history.

He was a firm believer in the equality of all people, whether black, female, Native American, or recent immigrant. He was fond of saying, "I would unite with anybody to do right and with nobody to do wrong."

<u>Conley High School</u> of Mount Hope, West Virginia was named for an African American reverend H.W. Conley, minister and teacher at Talladega College in Alabama in the 1880's. His influence in the African American community supported the freed Blacks and enhanced their efforts to obtain an education.

W. H. Conely

Conley High School 1963 State Basketball Champions

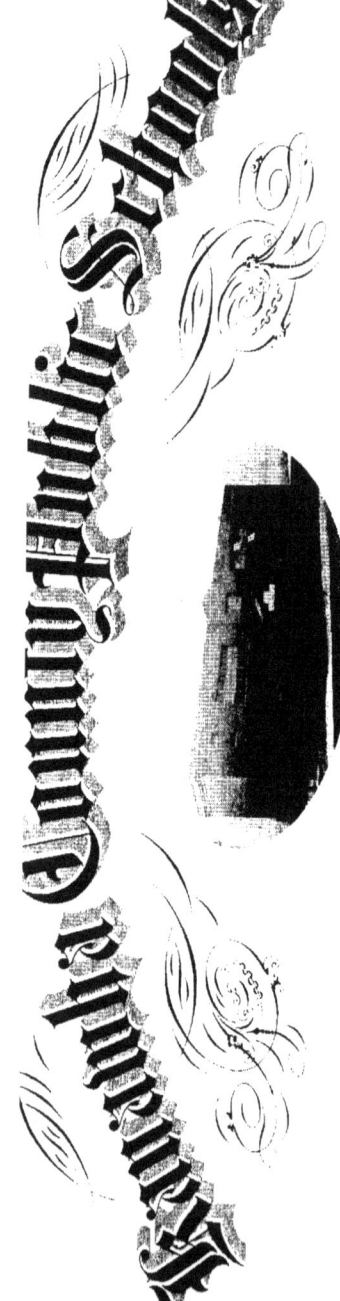

Kanawha County Public Schools

Washington High School

This Certifies That

Colonel Von Witten

Having completed the course of study prescribed by the Board of Education is hereby declared a graduate of the WASHINGTON HIGH SCHOOL and is entitled to this

DIPLOMA

Given by order of the Board of Education, in and for the County of Kanawha, Charleston, West Virginia, this 29th day of May A.D. 1951

Charles R. McCann
President Board of Education

Washington High School

W

Athletic Association

This is to certify that *Colonel Witten* has earned the Varsity W in *Football* for the year 19 *50*, meeting the provisions of Washington High School of London, West Virginia.

_____
Athletic Director

_____
Athletic Chairman

_____
Principal

_____
Student President

39 - A

HISTORY OF WASHINGTON HIGH SCHOOL (1925-1956)

Education for Blacks in West Virginia in the early 1920's ended with completion of the eighth grade because there were no secondary schools for them. A few of them from all over the state paid tuition to attend a secondary school in Institute with no reimbursement from the state. Many of those attending stayed in dormitories. This meant that most Black youth did not receive a high school education.

It became financially burdensome for those sending their children to high school. Parents became concerned and efforts were initiated to have the Board of Education provide schools for Black students. In 1923 parents of the Upper Kanawha County area banded together with B.A. Brown and his father, William, of London among the leaders, to influence the Kanawha County Board of Education to build a school for Black children. Other residents of London who played prominent roles were George Gray, Daniel Cyrus, and Julius Blaney, Sr.

Leaders in the struggle from Cedar Grove included George Lee, Dr. James Hopkins, William Beamer, Thomas Martin, Sr., James Hughes, Mr. Jones, Mattie Dingess, and Mr. Fitz. People from all sections of the valley participated in this effort.

Two sites were considered for the school – Cedar Grove and London. Attempts to locate a site in Cedar Grove met with a resounding show of racism from the white population who made it very clear that they did not want a "colored school" in their community. Blacks used their homes as collateral to raise the funds to purchase land there but were blocked in every effort by determined white citizens. No one would sell them land for the school. Fortunately, there were several Black property owners in London, and they provided land on which the school was built.

The decision to locate the school in London marked the end of many agonizing hours of strong disagreement between Black leaders of London and Cedar Grove. They put their differences aside and worked for the common good. The school which was scheduled to open in September 1925 was not ready. Therefore, school was held in the old Norris house on the hill in London until December 1925 when the students finally moved into the new building. Simmons High of Montgomery, a school in Fayette County, had been open for a short time and many Kanawha County students had been attending there. They left Simmons to attend Washington High and that was the beginning of a long time rivalry that ended with the integration of schools in 1956.

Leonard Barnett was named the first principal. He also served as a teacher. Bernard Brown and Roberta Yancey joined him as the first teachers of Washington High School. Mr. Barnett and Mr. Brown served in their capacities for the life of the school. Thirty-five students were enrolled for the first year. Andrew Calloway, Thelma Calloway and Mrs. Blackburn were added to the faculty. The school enrollment increased steadily from 35 to 184 by 1929. Albert White had also been added to the staff. The enrollment continued to increase as did the faculty. Marion Meadows, Roscoe Carter, Beatrice Morgan, Lillian Crichlow, Carrie Brown, Anna E. Gardner, and Helen McGhee were added to the faculty.

Andrew Calloway coached winning teams in the early years, course offerings were varied, and extra curricular activities were organized. Mr. Barnett sought assistance of parents and patrons to enlarge the school building so that our needs would be met. The Parent Association requested that this action be taken by the Board of Education and in 1939 this renovation was undertaken.

There was a complete renovation of the building which included new classrooms, a gymnasium and shower rooms. School was held in the First Baptist Church of London during the renovation. Crowded conditions existed, but students and teachers managed to survive. Mrs. Blackburn, Mrs. Yancey and the Calloways had resigned for other positions. Mr. Calloway was named Assistant Superintendent to serve Black schools in the county. Mr. Carter and Mr. Meadows became coaches.

The turnover of teachers was very slight. After moving in the new building, Washington High continued to flourish. Active Parent Teacher Associations and the Band Boosters were led by Mrs. Kinney, Edwina Majors, Nannie Payne and Bernice Goolsby. Helen McGhee died in the late forties, and Alma Holland became a member of the faculty. Virginia Jarrett had been hired as librarian prior to this.

The cafeteria was opened and Willa Blaney, Leona Young and Ethel Day served the school for over ten years. William Brown, Sr., who served as a disciplinarian and as a custodian, was succeeded by Lee Latham.

Athletics was a main part of the school life. Football teams and basketball teams - male and female - represented the school well. Mrs. Morgan served as coach of the girls' basketball team and coached several championship teams.

As faculty members relocated others took their places. Richard Hobson, Gladys Austin, Florence Hobson, Daisy Alston, William Robinson, Edward Bolden, Louise Anderson, Cecile McCormick, Mildred Seay, Jim Morris, Charles Q. Adams, John Turnbull and Cass Carter were members of the faculty. The band was organized by B. A. Brown who for many years gave many students a sound background in instrumental music. Charles Adams directed the band when he was hired as music teacher.

Virginia Jarrett was the first secretary employed by the Board of Education to serve Washington High School. Following her were Cecile McCormick, Ann Evans, Louise Anderson, Doris Payne, Arvonia Coleman and Garnett Pearis. Mrs. Pearis was responsible for saving those records that were saved when the school was closed as a result of integration in 1956. Other records were destroyed, unfortunately, and much of the school history was lost when segregation ended and the building was renovated to serve as a junior high school.

From the first graduating class of one – David Scott to the last with 27 graduates, many have passed through the portals of Washington High School. All can reflect on the "good ole days, those days of gladness, 'neath the Orange and the Black."

The Alma Mater
"The Orange and The Black"

Although Garnet has always favored
The violet's dark blue,
And the gentle sons of Simmons
To the gold and purple true,
We will own the lilies slender
Nor honor shall they lack,
While the Tigers stand defender
Of the Orange and the Black

Through the four long years of high school
Midst the scenes we love so well,
As the mystic charms of knowledge
We vainly seek to spell,
Or we win athletic victories
On the football field or track,
Still we fight for dear old Washington
And the Orange and the Black

When the cares of life o'er take us,
Mingled fast our locks with gray
Should our dearest hopes betray us,
False fortune fall away.
Still we banish care and sadness
As we turn our memories back,
And recall those days of gladness
'Neath the Orange and the Black

Best Wishes to all Alumni from the 2010 Reunion Committee!!

Patricia A. Wilson (Chairman), Evelyn Baskin, Helen Blackstock, Gwen Bullard, Juanita Day, Woodrow Foster, Mary German, Isabel Godfrey, Mildred Grooms, Ruth Jones, Janice Murray, Janie Nichols, Carol Saunders, John Saunders, Kenneth Thompson, and Jesse Woodson

Booker T. Washington High School
(1925–1956)

Continuing the Legacy of the Orange and the Black

North Carolina State University

On the recommendation of the Faculty and by virtue of the authority vested in them, the Trustees of the University have conferred on

Colonel Vaughan Witten

the degree of

Doctor of Philosophy

In testimony whereof, the seal of the University and the signatures of its officers are hereunto affixed this ninth day of August, nineteen eighty-nine.

Chairman of the Board of Governors

President of the University of North Carolina

Chairman of the Board of Trustees

Chancellor

Dean, Graduate School

44

THE UNITED STATES OF AMERICA

TO ALL WHO SHALL SEE THESE PRESENTS, GREETING:

THIS IS TO CERTIFY THAT

THE PRESIDENT OF THE UNITED STATES OF AMERICA
AUTHORIZED BY EXECUTIVE ORDER, AUGUST 24, 1962
HAS AWARDED

THE BRONZE STAR MEDAL

TO

SENIOR MASTER SERGEANT COLONEL V. WITTEN

FOR

MERITORIOUS SERVICE

25 January 1971 to 9 August 1971

GIVEN UNDER MY HAND IN THE CITY OF WASHINGTON

THIS   16th   DAY OF   August   19 71

SECRETARY OF THE AIR FORCE

GENERAL, USAF
COMMANDER, SEVENTH AIR FORCE

Biography

UNITED STATES AIR FORCE

82 Flying Training Wing
Office of Information
Williams AFB, AZ 85224

AV: 474-6611
Area Code: 602/988-2611

CHIEF MASTER SERGEANT COLONEL V. WITTEN

Colonel Vaughan Witten, SSAN   , AFSC 42399 is the Senior Enlisted
Advisor, 82nd Flying Training Wing. His duties as Senior Enlisted Advisor
are to assist the commander in keeping informed on matters affecting the
welfare and morale of the enlisted corps, specifically reporting significant problems with recommendations. In providing the commander with a
direct line of communication with enlisted personnel, Chief Witten is responsible for maintaining a high profile and strong liasion with the Airmen
and NCO's of the wing. Chief Witten was born in Anawalt, West Virginia,
but now calls Fayetteville, North Carolina, his home. He received his
Bachelors Degree in Sociology in 1973 at North Carolina State University
and has completed requirements for his Masters Degree in Psychology from
the University of Northern Colorado. Chief Witten enlisted in the Air
Force in May 1952 and went through Basic Training at Sampson Air Force
Base, New York. In August 1952, he entered Aircraft Maintenance School
at Sheppard Air Force Base, Texas and eventually completed advanced specialist school at Chanute AFB, Ill, as a Propeller Technician.

Chief Witten served as shop chief in the propeller career field at Grenier
AFB, NH; McGuire AFB, NJ; Lajes AB, Azores; Mildenhall AB, England; and
Cam Ranh Bay AB, Vietnam. Moving up in rank to a Master Sergeant by this
time, Chief Witten held numerous jobs as flight line chief, branch chief
and maintenance superintendent at Tachikawa AB, Japan; Langley AFB, VA;
Athen Airport, Greece; Pope AFB, NC; Tan Son Nhut AB, Vietnam; and Udorn
RTAFB, Thailand.

Chief Witten was assigned to Williams AFB, AZ in October 1974 and served
as Branch Chief, Aerospace Systems Branch 82 FMS; Maintenance Superintendent for the Deputy Commander for Maintenance, and was assigned to his
current position in April 1977. His military decorations include the
Bronze Star, Air Force Commendation Medal with two oak Leaf Clusters,
Army and Air Force Good Conduct Medals, the Vietnam Service Medal and the
Vietnam Campaign Medal.

Chief Witten, 42, his wife Mildred of Boston, Massachusetts, and their
two chidren - Scott 11, and Brian 10 reside at Williams AFB, AZ.

Colony and Dominion of Virginia

The **Colony of Virginia** was the English colony in North America that existed briefly during the 16th century, and then continuously from 1607 until the American Revolution. The colony then became the Commonwealth of Virginia in 1776, one of the original thirteen states of the United States.

Named for Queen Elizabeth I, who never married, the Virginia Colony was nicknamed "The Old Dominion" by King Charles II for its perceived loyalty to the English monarchy during the English Civil War.

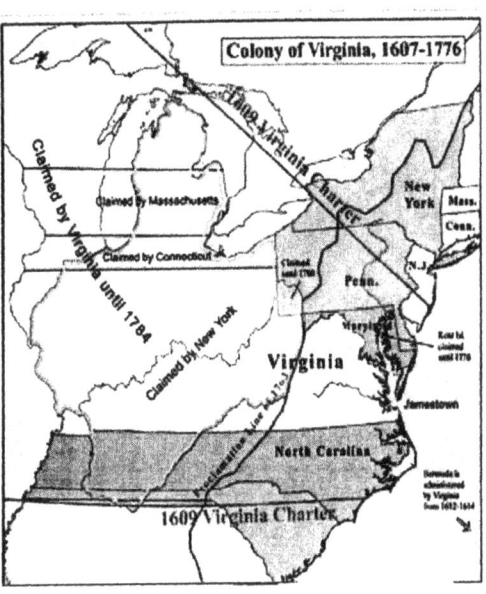

Colony of Virginia, 1607-1776

West Virginia is mostly forested land, accented by the Appalachian Mountains along its entire eastern border with Virginia.

Its most significant range (the Allegheny Mountains), extends from the southern part of the state on into Pennsylvania, Maryland and Virginia.

The highest peaks are in the central and south, running near 4,000 ft. The highest point is Spruce Knob at 4,861 ft.

Hot water mineral springs are found throughout the rolling hills of this state, with White Sulfur Springs the most famous.

Significant rivers include the Big Sandy, Ohio, and Potomac, and the Guyandotte, Great Kanawha, Little Kanawha, Monongahela and Shenandoah.

For an accurate look at the topography of West Virginia, view this map.

▶ **Landforms of America** here

▶ **Landforms of North America** here

▶ **Rivers of North America** here

▶ **West Virginia State Parks** here

Timeline of History

(1641) The first European settlers arrive

(1732) Shepherdstown becomes the first permanent settlement

(1753) European settlers journey to the area in great numbers

(1763) French loses continent and French and Indian War begins to end

(1776) Residents petition the Continental Congress for separate statehood

(1782) The Battle of Fort Henry (in Wheeling) is called the "Last Battle of the Revolutionary War"

(1836) First railroad arrives in Harpers Ferry

John Brown

(1859) Abolitionist John Brown stages raids on federal arsenal at Harpers Ferry

(1861) West Virginia refuses to secede from the Union, and separates from Virginia

(1863) West Virginia becomes the 35th U.S. State

(1885) Capital moved to Charleston

The **Kanawha River** (pronounced *kuh-NAW-uh* or *kuh-NAW*
and earlier,*kuh-NOIE*) is a tributary of the Ohio River,
approximately 97 mi (156 km) long, in the U.S. state
of West Virginia. The largest inland waterway in West
Virginia, it has formed a significant industrial region
of the state since the middle of the 19th century.

It is formed at the town of Gauley Bridge in
northwestern Fayette County, approximately 35 mi (56
km) SE of Charleston, by the confluence of the New
and Gauley rivers. It flows generally northwest, in a
winding course on the unglaciated Allegheny Plateau,
through Fayette, Kanawha, Putnam and Mason
Counties, past the cities of Charleston and St. Albans
and numerous smaller communities. It joins the Ohio
at Point Pleasant.

The river valley contains significant deposits of coal
and natural gas. In colonial times, the wildly
fluctuating level of the river prevented its use for
transportation. The removal of boulders and snags on
the lower river in the 1840s allowed navigation,
extended after the construction of locks and dams
starting in 1875. The river is now navigable to
Deepwater, an unincorporated community about 20
miles upriver from Charleston. A thriving chemical
industry along its banks provides a significant part of
the economy of West Virginia.

List of cities and towns along the

- Bancroft
- Belle
- Buffalo
- Cedar Grove
- Charleston
- Chesapeake
- Dunbar
- East Bank
- Eleanor
- Gauley Bridge
- Glasgow
- Handley
- Henderson
- Jefferson
- Leon
- Marmet
- Montgomery
- Nitro
- Poca
- Point
- Pratt
- St. A
- Smitl
- Soutl
- Winf

Kanawha River

The Kanawha River at St. Albans, West Virginia

Origin	Confluence of New River and Gauley River at Gauley Bridge
Mouth	Ohio River at Point Pleasant
Basin countries	USA
Source elevation	660 ft (201 m)
Mouth elevation	540 ft (165 m)
Avg. discharge	18,964 ft³/s (537 m³/s)
Basin area	12,236 mi² (31,690 km²)

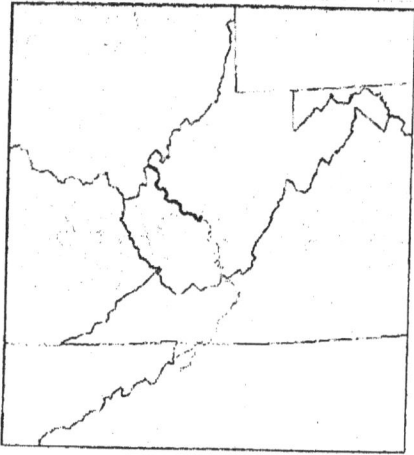

Map of the Kanawha River watershed, showing
its main tributary, the New River.

KANAWHA-COAL RIVER FIELD

Commercial mining in the field began at Cannelton in the 1850s, and the Kanawha field is currently the No. 1 producing coal field in the state. The field encompasses Boone County, the Marsh Fork district of Raleigh County, Kanawha County, Clay County, and even parts of Nicholas County. The most important seams in these areas are the medium-volatile Eagle, No. 2 Gas, Cedar Grove, Coalburg, and Winifrede. Also, Conley lumps other areas in with the Kanawha Field, but these regions actually contain the coal seams mined in the northern part of the state, and as such are the southern most extent of these coals. These areas include the region from Elmwood to Raymond City in Putnam County, and also the Elk River valley (some maps refer to this as the Coal and Coke Field). Since the coals mined in these areas are different from that mined in the southern part of the Kanawha Field, I have divded the coalfield into upper and lower portions on the map.

Modern day operations in the Kanawha-Coal River Field include Eastern Associated's Black Stallion and Lightfoot No. 2 mines, Rivers Edge Mine, Independence Coal Company's mines and their prep plant Liberty Processing, Omar Mining up the hollow from that, Goals Coal, Performance Coal Company's mines, Marfork Coal Company, Elk Run Coal Company mines and Chesss Processing plant, Pine Ridge Coal Company's Big Mountain No. 16 Mine, the Dakota/Jupiter Operation, Catenary Coal's Samples Mine, Speed Mining, Kanawha Eagle's mines, Amvest's Fola Coal, and Massey's Power Mountain/Alex Energy, to mention just a few.

THE TOWNS:

MUDDLETY (CATHERINE COAL TIPPLE)

POWELLTON

JODIE

HAREWOOD

CANNELTON

CARBONDALE

STANDARD

BURNWELL

MILBURN

KINGSTON

LEEWOOD

RED WARRIOR

History of West Virginia Mineral Industries - Coal

In 1742, John Peter Salley took an exploratory trip across the Allegheny Mountains and reported an outcropping of coal along a tributary of the Kanawha River. He and his companions named this tributary the Coal River, and his report became the first reference to coal in what is today West Virginia.

Although coal was known to occur throughout much of West Virginia, no extensive mining took place until the mid-1800s. Until that time, there was little incentive to exploit coal as a resource because of the great abundance of wood and a lack of manufacturing industries. Small amounts of coal were used by crossroads blacksmiths or by the settler whose cabin stood near an outcrop. In 1810, the people of Wheeling began to use coal obtained from a nearby mine to heat their dwellings. In 1811, the first steamboat on the Ohio burned coal from the Ohio banks. By 1817, coal began to replace charcoal as a fuel for the numerous Kanawha River salt furnaces. By 1836, the western Virginia coal fields had received so much attention that Virginia's foremost geologist, Professor William B. Rogers, was sent to visit the mines and analyze the coal in eight counties. The total coal production in 1840 for the State was about 300,000 tons, of which 200,000 tons was used in the Kanawha salt furnaces and most of the remainder was consumed by factories and homes in Wheeling. Between 1840 and 1860 many coal companies were organized, and corporations were created under the laws of Virginia for the purpose of encouraging financial investments from foreign countries.

With the outbreak of the Civil War, the Kanawha Valley mines were closed. Confederate troops set up camps in the valley, and many of the locks and dams along the river were destroyed, thus preventing shipping. Farther north, the Elkins and Fairmont fields remained active, providing coal for the Union via the Baltimore and Ohio Railroad. The coal was used for railroad engines and for heating in the east.

Following the Civil War, an awakening of interest in the State's mineral resources brought a new era of development and growth for the coal industry. The industry spread to new localities, and by 1880 there were extensive operations in Mineral, Monongalia, Marion, Fayette, Harrison, Ohio, Putnam, and Mason counties. Of the numerous coal fields which grew up in West Virginia, a few are of particular interest. One of the larger fields is the Fairmont Field, developed around the rich Pittsburgh seam. The first marketed Pittsburgh coal in western Virginia was produced around 1852 from a mine  near the present city of Fairmont. Production and marketing success of the field increased, and in 1901 the Fairmont Coal Company was formed, later to become the Consolidation Coal Company.

50

West Virginia's southern coal fields were not opened until about 1870, though they were known to exist much earlier. One of the major southern coal fields was the Flat Top-Pocahontas Field, located primarily in Mercer and McDowell counties. The Flat Top Field first shipped coal in 1883 and grew quickly from that time. Operations were consolidated into large companies, and Pocahontas Fuel Company, organized in 1907, soon dominated the other companies in McDowell County.

Many of the coal fields, such as the Kanawha, New River, Winding Gulf, Logan, and Greenbrier, owed their success to the Chesapeake and Ohio Railway. As the railway expanded its lines, coal became more available for marketing and the coal fields prospered. The Logan Field, lying in Logan and Wyoming counties, did not develop until 1904, when the railway finally reached the fields. Soon Logan became the largest coal-producing county in the State, dominated by the Island Creek Coal Company.

As the coal industry grew, mining methods and laws changed rapidly. In the earliest days, local 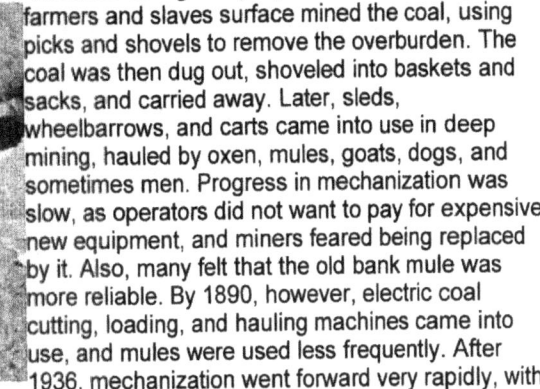 farmers and slaves surface mined the coal, using picks and shovels to remove the overburden. The coal was then dug out, shoveled into baskets and sacks, and carried away. Later, sleds, wheelbarrows, and carts came into use in deep mining, hauled by oxen, mules, goats, dogs, and sometimes men. Progress in mechanization was slow, as operators did not want to pay for expensive new equipment, and miners feared being replaced by it. Also, many felt that the old bank mule was more reliable. By 1890, however, electric coal cutting, loading, and hauling machines came into use, and mules were used less frequently. After 1936, mechanization went forward very rapidly, with shuttle cars, long trains, conveyor belts, and all kinds of large mining machinery coming into common use. Large-scale surface mining did not start until 1914, but with the development of huge shovels and draglines, the overburden can now be removed more easily and in recent years this method has become a major method of mining coal in West Virginia. Two peaks occurred in West Virginia's coal production: in 1927 production reached 146,088,121 tons and in 1947 it peaked at 173,653,816 tons.

A coal company provided not only a job but a unique way of life for West Virginia miners and their families. Since most of the mines were located too far from established towns, the coal companies built their own towns and provided inexpensive homes, a company store, a church, and often recreation facilities for the miners and their families. Because of the need for daily supplies from the company store, a simplified method of bookkeeping was established, using coal scrip. The earliest coal scrip (tokens) dates back to about 1883. Miners could get advanced credit on their earned wages (in scrip) to pay for daily necessities at the company store. This use of coal company scrip eliminated the need for the coal company to keep a large amount of U. S. currency on hand. Each mine had its own scrip symbols on the tokens, and these tokens could only be used at the local company store.

As early as the 1850s, immigrants from Wales, England, and Scotland were brought over to work in the coal mines. As the coal industry grew, most of the mining was supported by out-of-state capital and thus was run by out-of-state superintendents. These men brought in cheap

Anawalt

Tipple

COAL MINING IN WEST VIRGINIA

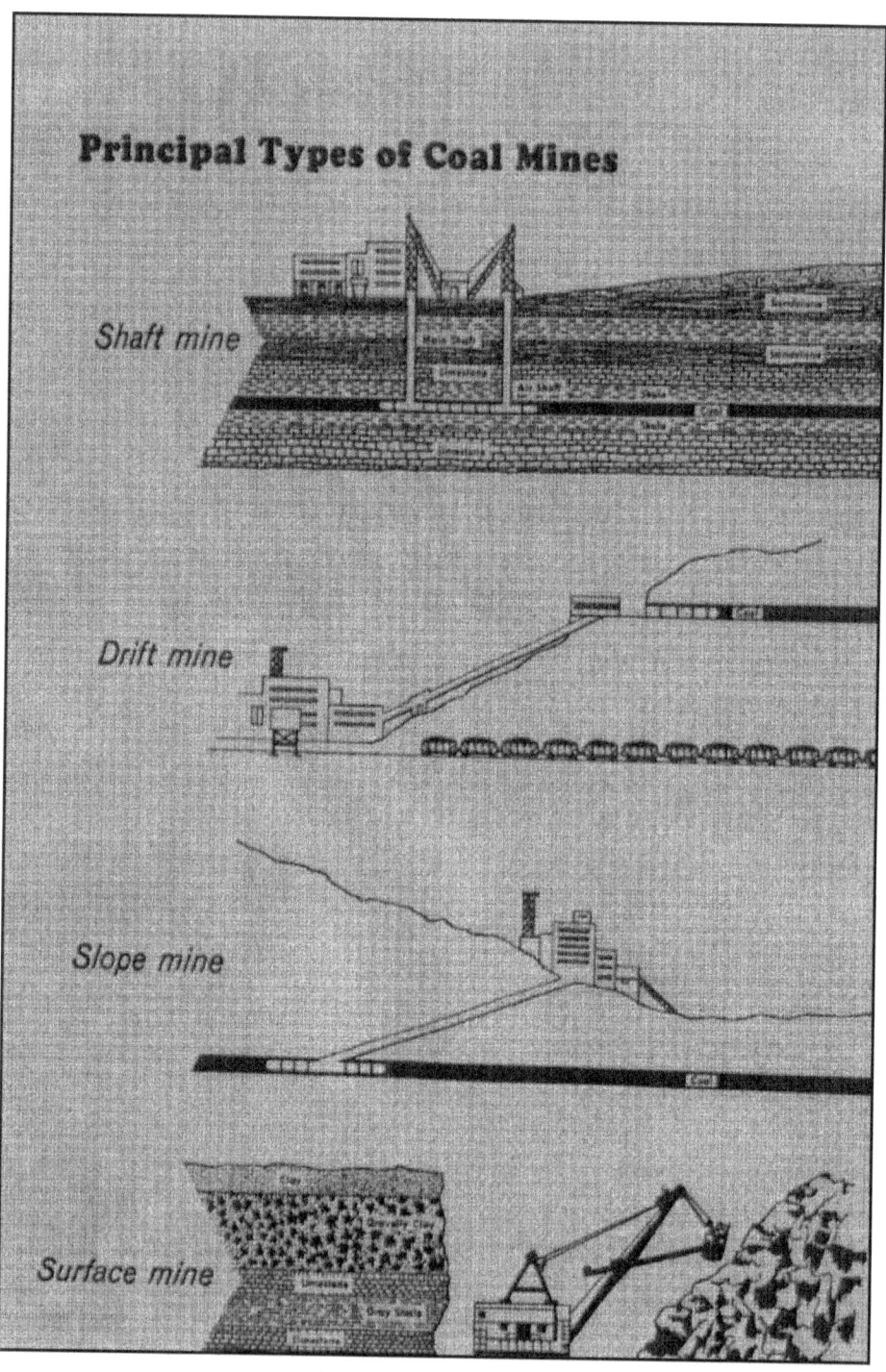

New River From Hawks Nest, West Virginia

(Coal Mining) Company Stores

In the West Virginia Coal Fields, you would almost always find a Company Store located near each coal mine. The Company Stores were stores owned and operated by the coal mining companies. Typically, during the early years that the Company Store was the *only* store in the coal mining town, as the town itself was quite literally owned by the coal company.

Click on an image: to view a larger version of the image or to select the image for an electronic post card.

Buery Company Store, Buery, West Virginia (WV). Buery was one of many coal mining towns once located in the New River Gorge. Circa 1908.

New River Company - Skelton Company Store, Skelton, near Beckley, West Virginia (WV) - circa 1960's.

Former New River Company Company Store - Mount Hope, West Virginia (WV) - July 2000.

Collins Colliery Company Store, near Glen Jean, West Virginia (WV) - circa 1908. The Collins store was a virtual duplicate of the Whipple store.

Macdonald Colliery Company, Macdonald Company Store, near Mount Hope, West Virginia (WV) - circa 1908.

Sugar Creek Company Store, Mount Hope, West Virginia (WV) - circa 1930's.

Coal Miners Life

The life of a Coal Miner in the 1880's to 1940's was very difficult, hard, impoverished, devoid of many civil rights and downright tough. But, they worked hard for nearly slave wages at times, hand loaded tons of coal a day, worked on their knees for sometimes 16 hours a day in the low 4 foot ceiling mines, with only a small lunch bucket with two sandwiches, water bottle and maybe a piece of cake to sustain them. You couldn't go out to McDonalds for lunch being two miles under a mountain. All the while, breathing in the black coal dust that would lead to Black Lung Disease or cancer twenty years later, that is, if they survived the explosions, fires and collapsed tunnels that occurred frequently. They were and are the most hardy, tough, honest and honorable people on earth. And my dad was a lion among them. He endured it all, never missed a shift except he was burned on the foot in one fire and missed about a week out of 30 years under those mountains. It is easy to be an eagle among crows, but my dad was an eagle among eagles and hawks.

Even worse than the mines themselves were the greedy coal mine owners and operators who had their own police to enforce their law, who kept wages low, disregarded safety, fought and killed to keep the unions out and overcharged everything at the company store by at least 100% and paid the miners in their own company script money of about 75% on a real U.S. dollar. You **could** spend regular American money at the store, small movie, post office and gas station, but most people only had script so they could not leave the camp to go to stores off the coal reservation. I had a paper route and handled both script and U.S. money but would trade my script for U.S. at 1.15 to 1 dollar U.S. and give to my mother. Yes, you could work off the camp as a child, but if the miner quit to work off the camp or was fired the whole family was evicted immediately for the company owned everything. The little houses were free with no heat to speak of except a pot belly stove, air condition, running water or toilets, only an outhouse, but it was better than living outdoors and most everyone adapted such that we didn't even know or think about the bad conditions. The men would often go on strike to protest the conditions and would be out of work for months without pay. The company store would issue credit for food and such but when the strike was over the families would be so far in the hole, it would take years to get out. You could buy anything at the company store, even a car. They would order it for you, but you needed the money. A new car was about $1,000. My dad worked many pay periods, 16 hour shifts and not draw a dime and my mom would always have the strength to support him, keep food on the table and love us with the confidence and power of the rich. Yes, my dad owed his soul to the company store - but we finally broke out, so to speak after about 20 years on the camp, bought a small house in the outer world and continued to work the mines - you could do that if you could afford it.

The other bad thing about the strikes were the <u>scabs</u> or replacement non-union workers who would work for less and take the regular workers jobs. They were hated by the miners and sometimes killed. There was violence at times like the 1920 Matewan Massacre and the Blair Mountain Insurrection when 15,000 miners fought the U.S. Army about the unfair and harsh treatment of the owners. They eventually surrendered but made many gains towards obtaining justice and equality. Much of the time from 1920-1960 they were led by their United Mine Worker President, John L. Lewis, who was revered and almost worshipped by the miners. He was tough and hated by some but the miners respected him for his zeal in supporting their efforts. He even challenged the President of the United States during World War II, calling a strike that had to be squashed by the Taft-Hartley Act, requiring them to go back to work. Of course now in 2010 things are better - indoor plumbing, air conditioning, etc. People are treated with respect and so on. Pay is at $200 a day vs. $5 then, in the 1920's. Scrip and the company store are gone.

The main thing about West Virginia Coal Miners and their families is that they are friendly, very proud, extremely patriotic to the United States, and ethical. Nothing stops them. They live in relative great danger every day and almost ignore it. You never want to call them a liar, thief, coward, or scab. If you do, get ready to fight. This is true of miners in Kentucky, Virginia, Pennsylvania, and Alabama also. I am just more familiar with West Virginians.

I experienced most all of these things except Matewan and Blair Mountain. This culture though poor and harsh provided me the ethics, courage, industriousness, creativity, and boldness along with my mom and dad's intelligence to move out into the world beyond Kanawha Valley and make my mark. For the love of my parents and the good people of West Virginia I will always be grateful.

Home
Site Map
Coal Miner's Son

Picture Galleries
A Coal Camp
Inside A Coal Mine

Coal Mining Facts
Mining Disasters
United Mine Workers
Coal Miner's Poetry
Coal Miner's Stamp
The Coal Miner

Links
Contact
Guest Book

A Coal Miner's Son In His Own Words

I am the son of a Kentucky coal miner, I was raised in a coal c
OWN words I want to document this life on the web site, so the
interested can read about that experience. First of all I would s
other segments of our society that have experienced hardship
just one of them.

In a coal camp, the company owned all the properties, the hou
everything associated with the camp. Miners who worked ther
for wages and the pay they received was not enough to provic
for their families. The houses were mostly four rooms without
plumbing, there were no streets, just dirt lanes filled with coal a
"warm morning" stoves that were used to heat the home. Som
had a single fireplace for heat in the cold winters.

A general store owned by the company, allowed the miners to trade for necessities. The min
company monies called script which could only be redeemed, at the company store. Tennes
had it right with the song lyrics "I owe my soul to the company store".

I went to a school that was built on the side of the mountain. I had to walk three, maybe four
there. Our basketball court was rock and dirt. some of my class mates wore torn and ragge
were not clean. Segregation was part of the poverty-ridden society back then. The African Ar
sorry to say, were worse off than the white people. A camp was provided for them separate 1
whites, and I would wonder why it had to be this way. Discrimination was prevalent and this '
me; and as a child I knew it was wrong.

Miners didn't have the luxury of full week's pay at all times. The pinto beans became the mair
miner's and their families, I truly believe the pinto bean kept some families from starvation.Co
twentieth century was very dangerous, not to mention the hard work. A lot of the mining was
safety for the coal miner was not an issue. I can remember miners getting killed quite frequer
would cave in and crush them. Coal operators would neglect safety for the better profits. Blac
prevalent and most of the miners contracted this disease. Coal mining is dirty filthy job I saw.
come home every day covered with coal dust. I made a vow that I would never go to a coal r

Organized labor came into being, thanks to the United Mine Workers and John L. Lewis. This
and mine conditions for the miner.Prior to the union, life was not easy. Folks had to "make d
opinion made stronger and better people. This life did me no harm it made me a better perso
appreciates what I have today, I am sure others who have experienced this life can give testa
made this web site for those who have experienced this life and can appreciate what it mean
miner's son or daughter.

The Company Store

Star Junction: The Company Store, circa 1900

Just about every coal patch had a Company Store, so-called because the coal company owned it. See below to learn how the coal companies took the miners' pay right back from them by forcing them to shop at the Company Store. This photograph was made in about 1900 by the Webmaster's grandfather, George A. Baughman. If you remember the Company Store from a later era (it was open through the 1950's) you remember it looking much different than it does here. At the time of this photo the front of the store faced northward toward what is now the doctor's office; the railroad tracks (now Rt. 51) would have been to the left in this photo and the original Rt. 51 and the churches to the right. When the store was enlarged the original facade was walled over and a new facade was built facing westward toward Church St.

COAL MINE SCRIP

By
John Freddie Wilson

2006

As the industrial revolution gained momentum in America during the late 1800's and early 1900's, there came a growing demand for coal to feed the hungry furnaces of industry and the mining of coal began in many states. Since most of these mines were established in remote, rugged areas far from stores and banks it was difficult to keep enough currency on hand to pay its miners. Capitalizing on the opportunity to make additional profits while filling the need to supply the miners and their families with household staples, mine owners established the company store and created the monetary system called "scrip."

The first scrip was made of paper and came in chits or booklets of different denominations and could only be used in the company store of the mine that issued the scrip. By the early 1900's token manufacturing companies began minting scrip in brass, copper, aluminum, zinc, nichol, and nichol plate, plus bi-metal pieces made of brass outer ring and lead or aluminum centers. Each company had its own version of coins, some with punched initials of the town or mine it was used in, while others were solid with pictorials or inserts. Most were round but some were scalloped or odd shaped in design. Produced in denominations from 1 cent through $5, all were different sizes much like coins of today. During World War II when metal was in short supply, fiber scrip was made in red, green, brown, white, and black colors. Other early scrip was made of celluloid, plastic and hard rubber.

The Childs Company of Chicago, Illinois was the 1st to apply for a patent of its token design or system in 1899. The Ingle Company received a sin   )19.
Ot
So   Sons

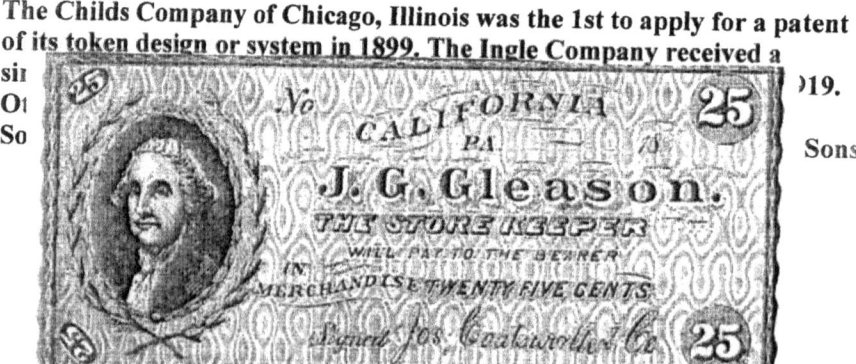

of Philadelphia, Pennsylvania and Murdock Stamp and Specialty Company. The Ingle Company later became Ingle Schierloh Company of Dayton, Ohio. In 1920 Wiley Osborne purchased Murdock Stamp and Specialty Co. and in 1924 the Insurance Credit System and changed their name to the Osborne Register Company with the trade mark "ORCO". After Ingle Schierloh Co. ceased operations, ORCO eventually became the "King" of the scrip token business.

Since about 75% of all the tokens used were in the coal fields of West Virginia, Virginia and Eastern Kentucky who called them "Scrip", that was the term adopted to describe these tokens and which we use today. Scrip was not the only name these tokens were known by however, some coal fields and other states had other colorful names such as: "Flickers", "Clackers", "Checks", "P'Lolly", "Lightweights", "Bingles", "Stickers", "Chink-tin" and "Dugaloos". But no matter the name used for these tokens, the object was the same; help the coal operators keep the wages paid to the miners in the company by forcing them to spend at the company store.

Some companies paid their miners exclusively in scrip each payday, thereby eliminating the need to keep currency on hand. Others used scrip as a credit medium that miners could use between paydays for needed supplies from the company store. A miner could request credit by scrip against work performed or work that would be performed. This scrip amount would be charged against the miners payroll account and deducted from his next pay day. Some companies would allow miners to trade scrip for cash but usually not for the full face value of the scrip. Some would pay as little as 50 cents on the dollar while others would pay as high as 80 to 85 cents per dollar. A few paid 100% but they were rare.

Being paid in scrip was like trying to work off a loan whose interest rate was so high that he was forever in debt. There was no competition in the coal fields and the company stores inflated their prices far above normal rates. By the time rent for the company house a miner lived in, any medical services he needed, utilities, and even a mandatory funeral fund were deducted along with what he had borrowed between pay days, there often was nothing left to collect on pay day.

In later years some states passed laws requiring companies to pay in U.S. currency each month. Coal companies side-stepped this law by paying in scrip for weekly or bi-weekly pay days and then cash at the end of each month. This in effect left the miner where he was before the law was enacted. Finally, in the 1950's many states outlawed the use of scrip entirely and it soon disappeared from use altogether. Scrip is now remembered mostly by those who once were paid with it and by those who

collect it as a hobby and a fascinating reminder of years gone by.

63A

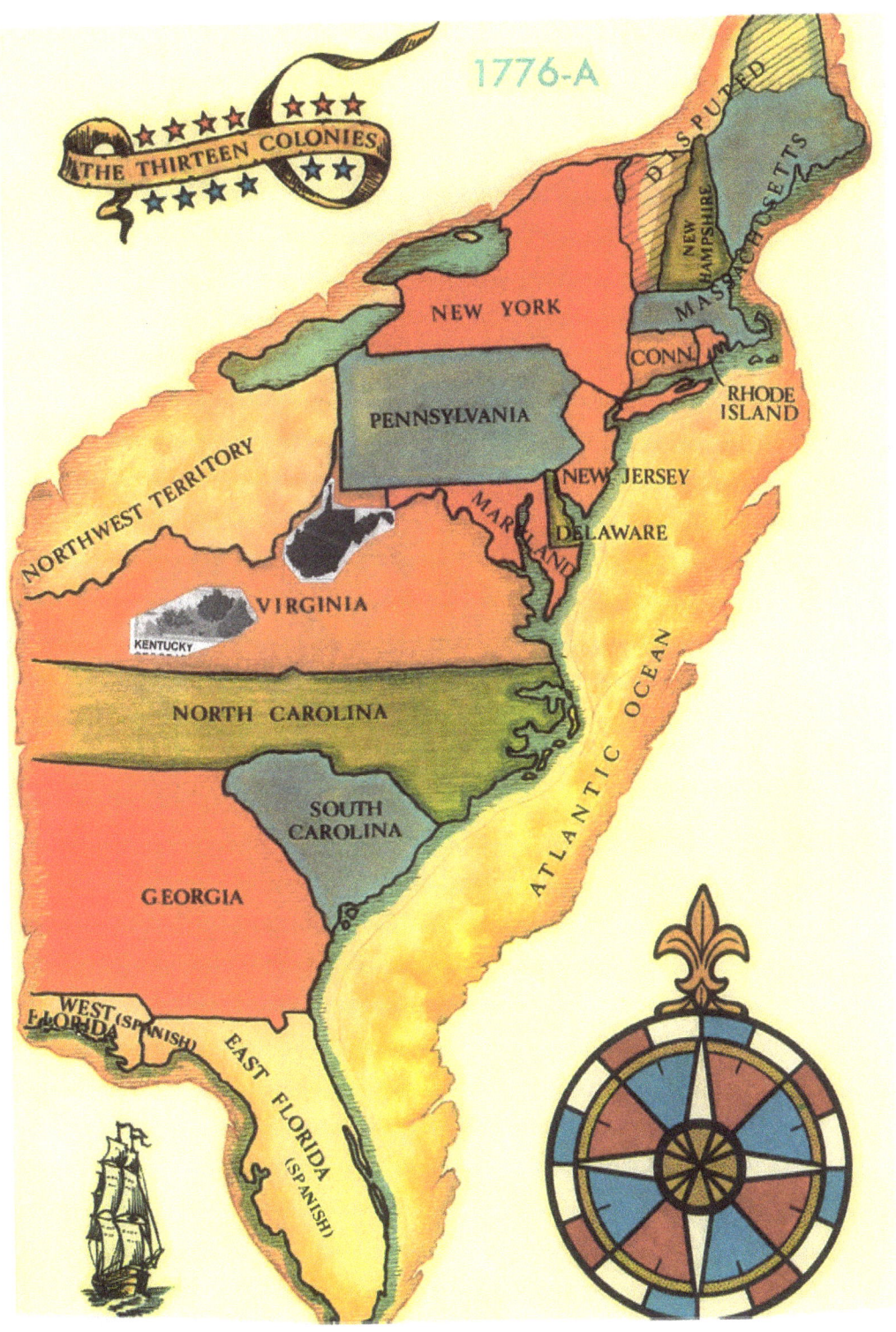

Medieval West Virginia

Page Three

The coal operators' system usually kept the miners in debt to the company store, so they could never get ahead and there was no where else to work. "There was an old saying around the coal mines in the Depression days. Somebody'd say, "How you doing?" . . . And he'd say, "Well, alright, I guess. I can't afford to die, because I owe my soul to the company store." I wrote the song Sixteen Tons around that saying," quotes Merle Travis.

> You load sixteen tons . . . what do you get?
> Another day older and deeper in debt
> Saint Peter don't you call me 'cause I can't go
> I owe my soul to the company store - by: Merle Travis (Davis).

Another song, "Coal Minin' Man," was written by Jim Mills after being inspired by watching a PBS documentary on Eastern Kentucky Coal Mines and has recently been recorded by Ricky Skaggs:

COAL MININ' MAN

> *Daylight or dark in rain or shine*
> *It don't matter down in the mines*
> *Where the tunnel is deep Lord the air gets thin*
> *That's the way of life for the minin' man*
>
> *His lungs are weak, his back is gone*
> *His sixty years are plainly shown*
> *Lived half his life down in the ground*
> *A cold steel hammer rings a mournful sound*
>
> *I'll tell you son he said to me*
> *There's just two things I pray to see*
> *That's the day my Savior Calls me Home*
> *And to see my son stop minin' coal*
>
> *Oh Daddy dear I'll tell you true*
> *There's nothing else for me to do*
> *But to make my livin' underneath this land*
> *And live and die a coal minin' man"* (Davis).

One reason that West Virginia miners wanted to be unionized was to force the companies to maintain safety rules in the mines. West Virginia had many deadly work-related accidents and had a higher death rate than other states. The largest accident was on December 6, 1907 in Marion County, which took the lives of 361 men and boys. "One historian has suggested that during World War I, a U.S. soldier had a better statistical chance of surviving in battle than did a West Virginian working in the coal mines" (West Virginia Cultural Organization).

Scenes like this were common. This photo was taken of women and children waiting to find out whether their husbands and fathers were alive or dead. This was after a mine disaster at Eccles, Raleigh County, West Virginia, on April 28, 1914, where 180 men lost their lives (Stover, Eccles). Macie Mae McMillian lost her husband, John Smith in this accident. She remarried to Edgar Clay and he died March 8, 1926 in another disaster in this same mine (Golden, Family).

People have been mining since the eighteenth century, and the lot of coal miners has only recently improved. Miners have lived with dangers the rest of us cannot even imagine: slag falls, explosions, fires, gases, cave-ins or being crippled for life either from broken bones or the 'black-lung' disease that coal miners still get from breathing in coal dust. The mines were hot and damp, and coal dust was in the air they breathed and could become explosive. There was also danger from methane gas in those mines. Water dripped from the ceilings, and the men and boys stood ankle deep in shafts and other places. Some of the coal seams, the areas in which the miners had to work, were only 20 to 28 inches which meant the miners had to lie in the water and mud on their sides while working. "I can't imagine how they managed to crawl to bring their load out. My step-father has told me that he often worked on his knees and then had to crawl in the mud and water to get to another area to work", says Gracie Stover (qtd. in Stover).

Howard Lee, attorney general for West Virginia, states, "To keep the miners' union out of the fields…the operators employed six principal methods of defense and attack: (a) injunctions; (b) martial law; (c) suzerainty over county government; (d) elaborate espionage and spy systems; (e) coercion and intimidation of workers by the use of mine guards; and (f) blacklisting all miners who favored the union……the miners asserted that they sought only to maintain their legal right to join their trade union; to regain their lost constitutional guaranties of free speech and peaceable assembly; to abolish the inhuman practices of espionage and blacklisting; to outlaw "cribbing"; to force the installation of scales to weigh the coal mined by them, as provided by law; to enforce their statutory rights to employ their own check-weigh men; to trade where they chose; to compel greater safety precautions; to dispense with all company-paid mine guards; and to enforce the "check-off," whereby the operators deduct union dues from workers' wages and pay them directly to the union" (qtd. in Lee 12).

Their only weapon was the "strike." To be successful in this, they needed to keep the company from bringing in "scabs," non-union workers brought in by the company to take their place.

John L. Lewis

From Wikipedia, the free encyclopedia

John Llewellyn Lewis (February 12, 1880 – June 11, 1969) was an American leader of organized labor who served as president of the United Mine Workers of America from 1920 to 1960. He was a major player in the history of coal mining. He was the driving force behind the founding of the Congress of Industrial Organizations, which established the United Steel Workers of America and helped organize millions of other industrial workers in the 1930s. After resigning as head of the CIO in 1941, he took the Mine Workers out of the CIO in 1942, then back into the American Federation of Labor (AFL) in 1944.

John L. Lewis

Born	February 12, 1880
	Cleveland, Iowa, U.S.
Died	June 11, 1969 (aged 89)
	Alexandria, Virginia, U.S.
Nationality	American
Occupation	Miner; Labor leader
Known for	President, United Mine Workers of America

Contents

- 1 Rise to Power
- 2 The 1950s
- 3 Retirement and Final Years
- 4 References in popular culture
- 5 Notes
- 6 References
- 7 External links

Rise to Power

Lewis was born in Cleveland, Iowa, the son of Thomas H. Lewis and Ann Watkins Lewis, both of whom had immigrated from Wales. Cleveland was a company town built around a coal mine one mile east of Lucas.[1] Lewis began working in the Big Hill Mine at Lucas as a teenager. He began working around the countryside as a "ten day miner" in the western United States. He moved to Panama, Illinois, and then to Springfield, Illinois, in 1910 with other members of his family. He joined the United Mine Workers and was eventually elected to the position of branch secretary. In 1911, Lewis began organizing for the AFL full time. After serving as statistician and then as vice-president for the UMWA, Lewis became that union's acting president in 1919. On November 1 of that year, he called the first major coal union strike, as 400,000 miners walked off their jobs. President Wilson obtained an injunction, which Lewis obeyed, telling the rank and file, "We cannot fight the Government.". In 1920 he was elected president of the UMWA. Lewis quickly asserted himself as a dominant figure in what was then the largest and most influential trade union in the country.

Lewis was considered by some a despotic leader of the Mine Workers: he expelled his political rivals within the UMWA, such as John Brophy, Alexander Howat and Adolph Germer. Communists in District 26 (Nova Scotia), including Canadian labor legend J.B. McLachlan, were banned from running

67

for the union executive after a strike in 1923. McLachlan described him as "a traitor to the working class". Lewis nonetheless commanded great loyalty from many of his followers, even those he had exiled in the past.

A powerful speaker and strategist, Lewis used the nation's dependence on coal to increase the wages and improve the safety of miners, even during several severe recessions. He masterminded a five-month strike, ensuring that the increase in wages gained during World War I would not be lost. Lewis challenged Samuel Gompers, who had led the AFL for nearly forty years, for the Presidency of the AFL in 1921. William Green, one of his subordinates within the Mine Workers at the time, nominated him; William Hutcheson, the President of the Carpenters, supported him. Gompers won. Three years later, on Gompers' death, Green succeeded him as AFL President.

John L. Lewis (right, President of the United Mine Workers (UMW), confers with Thomas Kennedy (left), Secretary-Treasurer of the UMW, and Pery Tetlow (center), president of UMW District 17, at the War Labor Board conference of January 15, 1943, discussing the anthracite coal miners' strike.

In 1924, Lewis a Republican[2], framed a plan for a three year contract between the UMWA and the coal operators, providing for a pay rate of $7.50 per day. President Coolidge and then-Secretary of Commerce Herbert Hoover were impressed with the plan and Lewis was actually offered the post of Secretary of Labor in Coolidge's cabinet. Lewis declined, a move he later regretted. Without government support, the contract talks failed and coal operators hired non-union miners. The UMWA treasury was drained, but Lewis was able to maintain the union and his position within it. He was successful in winning the 1925 anthracite miners' strike by his oratorical skills.

Historian C.L. Sulzberger later described the technique in a 1938 book called *Sit Down with John L. Lewis*, calling it the "Crust of Bread" speech. Operators who opposed a contract were often shamed into agreement by Lewis's accusations. A typical Lewis speech to operators would go, "Gentlemen, I speak to you for the miners' families... The little children are gathered around a bare table without anything to eat. They are not asking for a $100,000 yacht like yours, Mr._____..." (here, he would gesture with his cigar toward an operator), "...or for a Rolls Royce limousine like yours, Mr. _____..." (staring at another operator). They are asking only for a slim crust of bread.". With the full support of the AFL and the UMWA, Franklin D. Roosevelt was nominated and elected President in 1932, and Lewis benefited from the New Deal programs that followed. Thanks to the Wagner Act of 1935, labor union membership grew rapidly, especially in the UMWA. Lewis and the UMW were major backers of Roosevelt's reelection in 1936, and were firmly committed to the New Deal.

Lewis sent his best organizers into heavy industry in 1935-37, to organize the auto workers, the glass workers, the rubber workers and others. He supported the illegal sit-down strike (but did not use that tactic in the mines). When the AFL balked at organizing unskilled workers, Lewis withdrew his unions and formed a new organization, the CIO. By 1937-40 the CIO was spending as much time fighting the AFL as organizing, with the result that union political power was divided against itself. During the late-1930s struggle over the AFL's refusal to organize mass production workers, Green became the target of some of Lewis' most stinging attacks while Hutcheson was the recipient of a famous punch from Lewis that came to symbolize the dispute between the conservative AFL and the rebellious CIO.

West Virginia's Mine Wars

Compiled by the West Virginia State Archives

On March 12, 1883, the first carload of coal was transported from Pocahontas in Tazewell County, Virginia, on the Norfolk and Western Railway. This new railroad opened a gateway to the untapped coalfields of southwestern West Virginia, precipitating a dramatic population increase. Virtually overnight, new towns were created as the region was transformed from an agricultural to industrial economy. With the lure of good wages and inexpensive housing, thousands of European immigrants rushed into southern West Virginia. In addition, a large number of African Americans migrated from the southern states. The McDowell County black population alone increased from 0.1 percent in 1880 to 30.7 percent in 1910.

Most of these new West Virginians soon became part of an economic system controlled by the coal industry. Miners worked in company mines with company tools and equipment, which they were required to lease. The rent for company housing and cost of items from the company store were deducted from their pay. The stores themselves charged over-inflated prices, since there was no alternative for purchasing goods. To ensure that miners spent their wages at the store, coal companies developed their own monetary system. Miners were paid by scrip, in the form of tokens, currency, or credit, which could be used only at the company store. Therefore, even when wages were increased, coal companies simply increased prices at the company store to balance what they lost in pay.

Miners were also denied their proper pay through a system known as cribbing. Workers were paid based on tons of coal mined. Each car brought from the mines supposedly held a specific amount of coal, such as 2,000 pounds. However, cars were altered to hold more coal than the specified amount, so miners would be paid for 2,000 pounds when they actually had brought in 2,500. In addition, workers were docked pay for slate and rock mixed in with the coal. Since docking was a judgment on the part of the checkweighman, miners were frequently cheated.

In addition to the poor economic conditions, safety in the mines was of great concern. West Virginia fell far behind other major coal-producing states in regulating mining conditions. Between 1890 and 1912, West Virginia had a higher mine death rate than any other state. West Virginia was the site of numerous deadly coal mining accidents, including the nation's worst coal disaster. On December 6, 1907, an explosion at a mine owned by the Fairmont Coal Company in Monongah, Marion County, killed 361. One historian has suggested that during World War I, a U.S. soldier had a better statistical chance of surviving in battle than did a West Virginian working in the coal mines.

In response to poor conditions and low wages in the late 1800s, workers in most industries developed unions. Strikes generally focused on a specific problem, lasted short periods of time, and were confined to small areas. During the 1870s and 1880s, there were several attempts to combine local coal mining unions into a national organization. After several unsuccessful efforts, the United Mine Workers of America (UMWA) was formed in Columbus, Ohio, in 1890. In its first ten years, the UMWA successfully organized miners in Pennsylvania, Ohio, Indiana, and Illinois. Attempts to organize West Virginia failed in 1892, 1894, 1895, and 1897.

In 1902, the UMWA finally achieved some recognition in the Kanawha-New River Coalfield, its first success in West Virginia. Following the union successes, coal operators had formed the Kanawha County Coal Operators Association in 1903, the first such organization in the state. It hired private detectives from the Baldwin-Felts Detective Agency in Bluefield as mine guards to harass union organizers. Due to these threats, the UMWA discouraged organizers from working in southern West Virginia.

By 1912, the union had lost control of much of the Kanawha- New River Coalfield. That year, UMWA miners on Paint Creek in Kanawha County demanded wages equal to those of other area mines. The operators rejected the wage increase and miners walked off the job on April 18, beginning one of the most violent strikes in the nation's history. Miners along nearby Cabin Creek, having previously lost their union, joined the Paint Creek strikers and demanded:

- the right to organize
- recognition of their constitutional rights to free speech and assembly
- an end to blacklisting union organizers
- alternatives to company stores
- an end to the practice of using mine guards
- prohibition of cribbing
- installation of scales at all mines for accurately weighing coal
- unions be allowed to hire their own checkweighmen to make sure the companies' checkweighmen were not cheating the miners.

When the strike began, operators brought in mine guards from the Baldwin-Felts Detective Agency to evict miners and their families from company houses. The evicted miners set up tent colonies and lived in other makeshift housing. The mine guards' primary responsibility was to break the strike by making the lives of the miners as uncomfortable as possible.

As the intimidation by mine guards increased, national labor leaders, including Mary Harris "Mother" Jones, began arriving on the scene. Jones, a native of Ireland, was already a major force in the American labor movement before first coming to West Virginia during the 1897 strikes. Although she reported the year of her birth as 1830, recent research indicates she was probably born in 1845. As a leader of the UMWA's efforts to organize the state, Jones became known for her fiery (and often obscene) verbal attacks on coal operators and politicians.

Not only did the UMWA send speechmakers, it also contributed large amounts of weapons and ammunition. On September 2, Governor William E. Glasscock imposed martial law, dispatching 1,200 state militia to disarm both the miners and mine guards. Over the course of the strike, Glasscock sent in troops on three different occasions.

Both sides committed violent acts, the most notorious of which occurred on the night of February 7, 1913. An armored train, nicknamed the "Bull Moose Special," led by coal operator Quin Morton and Kanawha County Sheriff Bonner Hill, rolled through a miners' tent colony at Holly Grove on Paint Creek. Mine guards opened fire from the train, killing striker Cesco Estep. After the incident, Morton supposedly wanted to "go back and give them another round." Hill and others talked him out of it. In retaliation, miners attacked a mine guard encampment at Mucklow, present Gallagher. In a battle which lasted several hours, at least sixteen people died, mostly mine guards.

On February 13, Mother Jones was placed under house arrest at Pratt for inciting to riot. Despite the fact she was at least sixty-eight years old and suffering from pneumonia, Governor Glasscock refused to release her. On March 4, Henry D. Hatfield was sworn in as governor. Hatfield, a physician, personally examined Jones, but kept her under house arrest for over two months. During this same period, he released over thirty other individuals who had been arrested under martial law.

On April 14, Hatfield issued a series of terms for settlement of the strike, including a nine-hour work day (already in effect elsewhere in the state), the right to shop in stores other than those owned by the company, the right to elect union checkweighmen, and the elimination of discrimination against union miners. On April 25, he ordered striking miners to accept his terms or face deportation from the state. Paint Creek miners accepted the contract while those on Cabin Creek remained on strike. The settlement failed to answer the two primary grievances: the right to organize and the removal of mine guards. After additional violence on Cabin Creek, that strike was settled toward the end of July. The only gain was the removal of Baldwin- Felts detectives as mine guards from both Paint and Cabin creeks.

70

The Paint Creek-Cabin Creek strike produced a number of labor leaders who would play prominent roles in the years to come. Corrupt UMWA leaders were ousted and a group of young rank- and-file miners were elected. In November 1916, Frank Keeney was chosen president of UMWA District 17, and Fred Mooney was chosen secretary-treasurer.

Following the Paint Creek-Cabin Creek strike, the coalfields were relatively peaceful for nearly six years. U.S. entry into World War I in 1917 sparked a boom in the coal industry, increasing wages. However, the end of the war resulted in a national recession. Coal operators laid off miners and attempted to reduce wages to pre-war levels. In response to the 1912-13 strike, coal operators' associations in southern West Virginia had strengthened their system for combating labor. By 1919, the largest non-unionized coal region in the eastern United States consisted of Logan and Mingo counties. The UMWA targeted southwestern West Virginia as its top priority. The Logan Coal Operators Association paid Logan County Sheriff Don Chafin to keep union organizers out of the area. Chafin and his deputies harassed, beat, and arrested those suspected of participating in labor meetings. He hired a small army of additional deputies, paid directly by the association.

In late summer 1919, rumors reached Charleston of atrocities on the part of Chafin's men. On September 4, armed miners began gathering at Marmet for a march on Logan County. By the 5th, their numbers had grown to 5,000. Governor John J. Cornwell and Frank Keeney dissuaded most of the miners from marching in exchange for a governmental investigation into the alleged abuses. Approximately 1,500 of the 5,000 men marched to Danville, Boone County, before turning back. Cornwell appointed a commission whose findings did not support the union.

A few months later, operators lowered wages in the southern coalfields. To compound problems, the U.S. Coal Commission granted a wage increase to union miners, which excluded those in southwestern West Virginia. Non-union miners in Mingo County went on strike in the spring of 1920 and called for assistance from the District 17 office in Charleston. On May 6, Fred Mooney and Bill Blizzard, one of the leaders of the 1912-13 strike, spoke to around 3,000 miners at Matewan. Over the next two weeks, about half that number joined the UMWA. On May 19, twelve Baldwin-Felts detectives arrived in Matewan. Families of miners who had joined the union were evicted from their company-owned houses. The town's chief of police, Sid Hatfield, encouraged Matewan residents to arm themselves. Gunfire erupted when Albert and Lee Felts attempted to arrest Hatfield. At the end of the battle, seven detectives and four townspeople lay dead, including Mayor C. C. Testerman. Shortly thereafter, Hatfield married Testerman's widow, Jessie, prompting speculation that Hatfield himself had shot the mayor.

On July 1, UMWA miners went on strike in the region. By this time, over 90 percent of Mingo County's miners had joined the union. Over the next thirteen months, a virtual war existed in the county. Non-union mines were dynamited miners' tent colonies were attacked, and there were numerous deaths on both sides of the cause. During this period, governors Cornwell and Ephraim F. Morgan declared martial law on three occasions.

In late summer 1921, a series of events destroyed the UMWA's tenuous hold in southern West Virginia. On August 1, Sid Hatfield, who had been acquitted of his actions in the "Matewan Massacre," was to stand trial for a shooting at the Mohawk coal camp in McDowell County. As he and a fellow defendant, Ed Chambers, walked up the steps of the McDowell County Courthouse in Welch, shots rang out. Hatfield and Chambers were murdered by Baldwin-Felts detectives.

As a result of the Matewan Massacre, Hatfield had become a hero to many of the miners. On August 7, a crowd varyingly estimated from 700 to 5,000 gathered on the capitol grounds in Charleston to protest the killing. Among others, UMWA's leaders Frank Keeney and Bill Blizzard urged the miners to fight. Over the next two weeks, Keeney travelled around the state, calling for a march on Logan. On August 20, miners began assembling at Marmet. Mother Jones, sensing the inevitable failure of the mission, tried to discourage the miners. At one point, she held up a telegram, supposedly from President Warren G. Harding, in which he offered to end the mine guard system and help the miners if they did not march. Keeney told the miners he had checked with the White House and the telegram was a fake. To this day, it is uncertain who was lying.

On August 24, the march began as approximately 5,000 men crossed Lens Creek Mountain. The miners wore red bandanas, which earned them the nickname, "red necks." In Logan County, Don Chafin mobilized an army of deputies, mine guards, store clerks, and state police. Meanwhile, after a request by Governor

Morgan for federal troops, President Harding dispatched World War I hero Henry Bandholtz to Charleston to survey the situation. On the 26th, Bandholtz and the governor met with Keeney and Mooney and explained that if the march continued, the miners and UMWA leaders could be charged with treason. That afternoon, Keeney met a majority of the miners at a ballfield in Madison and instructed them to turn back. As a result, some of the miners ended their march. However, two factors led many to continue. First, special trains promised by Keeney to transport the miners back to Kanawha County were late in arriving. Second, the state police raided a group of miners at Sharples on the night of the 27th, killing two. In response, many miners began marching toward Sharples, just across the Logan County line.

The town of Logan was protected by a natural barrier, Blair Mountain, located south of Sharples. Chafin's forces, now under the command of Colonel William Eubank of the National Guard, took positions on the crest of Blair Mountain as the miners assembled in the town of Blair, near the bottom of the mountain. On the 28th, the marchers took their first prisoners, four Logan County deputies and the son of another deputy. On the evening of the 30th, Baptist minister James E. Wilburn organized a small armed company to support the miners. On the 31st, Wilburn's men shot and killed three of Chafin's deputies, including John Gore, the father of one of the men captured previously. During the skirmish, a deputy killed one of Wilburn's followers, Eli Kemp. Over the next three days, there was intense fighting as Eubank's troops brought in planes to drop bombs.

On September 1, President Harding finally sent federal troops from Fort Thomas, Kentucky. War hero Billy Mitchell led an air squadron from Langley Field near Washington, D.C. The squadron set up headquarters in a vacant field in the present Kanawha City section of Charleston. Several planes did not make it, crashing in such distant places as Nicholas County, Raleigh County, and southwestern Virginia, and military air power played no important part in the battle. On the 3rd, the first federal troops arrived at Jeffrey, Sharples, Blair, and Logan. Confronted with the possibility of fighting against U.S. troops, most of the miners surrendered. Some of the miners on Blair Mountain continued fighting until the 4th, at which time virtually all surrendered or returned to their homes. During the fighting, at least twelve miners and four men from Chafin's army were killed.

Those who surrendered were placed on trains and sent home. However, those perceived as leaders were to be held accountable for the actions of all the miners. Special grand juries handed down 1,217 indictments, including 325 for murder and 24 for treason against the state. The only treason conviction was against Walter Allen, who skipped bail and was never captured. The most prominent treason trial was that of Bill Blizzard, considered by authorities to be the "general" of the miners' army. In a change of venue, Blizzard's trial was held in the Jefferson County Courthouse in Charles Town, the same building in which John Brown had been convicted of treason in 1859. After several trials in different locations, all charges against Blizzard were dropped. Keeney and Mooney were also acquitted of murder charges. James E. Wilburn and his son were convicted of murdering the Logan County deputies. Both were pardoned by Governor Howard Gore after serving only three years of their eleven-year sentences.

The defeat of the miners at Blair Mountain temporarily ended the UMWA's organizing efforts in the southern coalfields. By 1924, UMWA membership in the state had dropped by about one-half of its total in 1921. Both Keeney and Mooney were forced out of the union, while Blizzard remained a strong force in District 17 until being ousted in the 1950s. In 1933, the National Industrial Recovery Act protected the rights of unions and allowed for the rapid organization of the southern coalfields.

Blair Mountain stands as a powerful symbol for workers to this day. The miners who participated vowed never to discuss the details of the march to protect themselves from the authorities. For many years, the story of the march was communicated by word of mouth as an inspiration to union activists. It serves as a vivid reminder of the deadly violence so often associated with labor-management disputes. The mine wars also demonstrate the inability of the state and federal governments to defuse the situations short of armed intervention.

Paint and Cabin Creek Murders

Francis F. Estep

Francis F. Estep and Cleve Woodrum were both shot and killed by Baldwin-Felts mine guards during the 1912-13 strike on Paint and Cabin Creeks. Both were given a bronze tablet with the seal of the United Mine Workers of America for their graves. The inscription reads,"Dedicated to the memory of _____ for distinguished service and self-sacrifice in the cause of labor and advancement of the United Mine Workers of America. Each inscription is the same except for the name.

Francis F. Estep was born at Hudnall(Kanawha Co, WV) on October 15, 1882, and used the nickname of Cesco. He married Maud Gallian, born in KY in 1890. Cesco could barely support his family, even though he worked ten hours a day and six days a week. He decided to go with the union while he was working at Acme on Cabin Creek. He then had to move out of the company house, his home and and settled in a small frame house in Holly Grove.

On May 7, 1912 the first group of Baldwin-Felts mine guards arrived at Paint Creek, and the first of June, the coal operators declared that the strikers would be evicted in five days. The Baldwin-Felts mine guards began carrying out those orders. Hundreds of miners and their families ended up living in tents in the Paint Creek area. This caused a lot of hatred and hard feelings on the part of the miners since the mine guards were ruthless in ensuring that everyone was evicted.

Martial Law was in effect twice in this area, but did not settle anything as the problems continued to escalate. On the morning of Febuary 7, 1913 there was another shootout between guards and miners at Holly Grove. Rumors began circulating that guards were going to wipe out the miners in the tents and the attack would come from the "Bull Moose Special". The "Bull Moose Special" was an armored built by the coal operators to transport scabs and mine guards.

That same night, about 10:30 P.M. Cesco Estep, his family, and other men that were visiting in his home heard the train and machine gun fire. The men ran out the door and before Cesco could get back inside, he was cut down by the hail of bullets. Over a hundred bullets pierced the side of the house, but only Cesco was killed. He was shot in the face. Maud Estep, in shock grabbed her husband's gun and emptied it at the disappearing train.

Maud Estep had to be taken to the hospital the next day and was unable to attend her husband's funeral. Guards fired into the people gathered for Cesco's funeral. He is buried at the Holly Grove Cemetery on Paint Creek.

Maud Estep never returned to their home, and eventually remarried. There was no Social Security, union benefits and no welfare to help in those times.

Battle of Matewan

From Wikipedia, the free encyclopedia

The **Battle of Matewan** (also known as the **Matewan Massacre**) was a shootout in the town of Matewan, West Virginia in Mingo County on May 19, 1920 between local miners and the Baldwin-Felts Detective Agency.

The Battle of Matewan took place on May 19, 1920 in the small coal town of Matewan, West Virginia when a contingent of the Baldwin-Felts Detective Agency arrived on the no. 29 morning train in order to evict families that had been living at the Stone Mountain Coal Camp just on the outskirts of town. The detectives carried out several evictions before they ate dinner at the Urias Hotel and, upon finishing, they walked to the train depot to catch the five o'clock train back to Bluefield, West Virginia. This is when Matewan Chief of Police Sid Hatfield decided that enough was enough, and intervened on behalf of the evicted families. Hatfield, a native of the Tug River Valley, was an adamant supporter of the miners' futile attempts to organize the UMWA in the saturated southern coalfields of West Virginia. While the detectives made their way to the train depot, the were intercepted by Hatfield, who claimed to have arrest warrants from the Mingo County sheriff. Detective Albert Felts then produced his own warrant for Sid Hatfield's arrest. Upon inspection Matewan mayor Cabell Testerman claimed it was fraudulent. Unbeknownst to the detectives, they had been surrounded by armed miners, who watched intently from the windows, doorways, and roofs of the businesses that lined Mate Street. Stories vary as to who actually fired the first shot; only unconfirmed rumors exist. Thus, on the porch of the Chambers Hardware Store, began the clash that became known as the Matewan Massacre, or The Battle of Matewan. The ensuing gun battle left seven detectives and four townspeople dead, including Felts and Testerman. This tragedy, along with events such as the Ludlow Massacre in Colorado six years earlier, marked an important turning point in the battle for miners' rights.

Battle of Matewan

Date	May 19, 1920
Location	Matewan, West Virginia, United States
Result	A setback of Miners' rights until early 1930's when the Government finally recognized American labor unions that eventually lead to the passing of the National Industrial Recovery Act (NIRA) of 1933

Belligerents

The People of Matewan	Baldwin-Felts Detective Agency

Commanders

Sid Hatfield Mayor Cabell Testerman†	Albert Felts†

Strength

Deputy Fred Burgraff and a group of local miners and residents	13 Baldwin-Felts Detectives

Casualties and losses

3 killed; 2 Miners and Mayor Cabell Testerman	7 killed; including 2 Baldwin-Felts Detectives brothers Albert and Lee Felts

The Town of Matewan

Matewan, founded in 1895, was an small independent town with only a few elected officials. The mayor at the time was Cabell Testerman, and the chief of police was Sid Hatfield. Both refused to succumb to the company's plans, and sided with the miners. In turn, the Stone Mountain Coal Corporation hired their own enforcers, the Baldwin-Felts Detective Agency, dubbed the "Baldwin Thugs" by the coal miners. The Baldwin-Felts Detectives had earned a reputation for their brutality. The coal operators hired them to evict the miners and their families from the company owned houses.[4] As a result, hundreds of miner families spent that spring in tents.

The Battle of Matewan

On the day of the fight, a group of the Baldwin-Felts enforcers arrived to evict families living at the mountain coal camp, just outside of Matewan. The sheriff and his deputy, Fred Burgraff, sensed trouble and met the Baldwin-Felts detectives at the train station. News of the evictions soon spread around the town. When Sid Hatfield approached Mr. Felts, Mr. Felts served a warrant on Sid Hatfield, which had been issued by Squire R. M. Stafford, a Justice of the Peace of Magnolia District, Mingo County, West Virginia, for the arrest of Sid Hatfield, Bas Ball, Tony Webb and others, which warrant was directed to Albert C. Felts for execution. The warrant turned out to be fraudulent. Burgraff's son reports that the detectives had sub-machine guns with them in their suitcases. Sid Hatfield, Fred Burgraff, and Mayor Cabell Testerman met with the detectives on the porch of the Chambers Hardware Store. It is still unknown whether it was Hatfield or the leading detective, Albert Felts, that shot Mayor Testerman first, though what followed was Sid Hatfield shooting Albert Felts. There are rumors that Sid shot mayor Testerman because he had feelings for his wife, but they were never confirmed, although he did remarry her after mayor Testerman's death. After the detective and mayor fell wounded, Sid kept firing, but Felts escaped. He took shelter in the Matewan Post Office, and Hatfield eventually found him there and shot him. When the shooting finally stopped, the townspeople came out, many wounded. There were casualties on both sides, including seven Baldwin-Felts Detectives, including brothers Albert and Lee Felts. One more detective had been wounded. Two miners were killed, Bob Mullins, who had just been fired for joining the union, and Tot Tinsley, an unarmed bystander. The wounded mayor was dying, and four other bystanders had been wounded.

History

At the time, the United Mine Workers of America had just elected John L. Lewis as their president. During this period, miners worked long hours in unsafe and dismal working conditions, while being paid low wages. Adding to the dilemma was the use of company scrip by the Stone Mountain Coal Company, because the scrip could only be used for those goods the company sold through their company stores, thus the miners did not have actual money that could be used elsewhere. A few months before the battle at Matewan, union miners in other parts of the country went on strike, receiving a full 27 percent pay increase for their efforts. Lewis recognized that the area was ripe for change, and planned to organize the coal fields of southern Appalachia. The union sent its top organizers, including the infamous Mary Harris "Mother" Jones.[1] Roughly 3000 men signed the union's roster in the Spring of 1920. They signed their union cards at the community church, something that they knew could cost them their jobs,

Aftermath

s their homes. The coal companies controlled many aspects of the miners' lives. [2]

Coal Corporation fought back with mass firings, harassment, and evictions. [3] Governor Cornwell ordered the state police force to take control of Matewan. Hatfield and his men cooperated, and stacked their arms inside the hardware store. The miners, cocky with the success of getting the thugs out of Matewan, improved their efforts to organize. On July 1 the miners' union went on another strike, and wide spread violence erupted. Railroad cars were blown up, and strikers were beaten and left to die by the side of the road. Tom Felts, the last remaining Felts brother, planned on avenging his brothers' deaths by sending undercover operatives to collect evidence to convict Sid Hatfield and his men. When the charges against Hatfield, and 22 other people, for the murder of Albert Felts were dismissed, Baldwin-Felts detectives assassinated Hatfield and his deputy Ed Chambers on August 1, 1921, on the steps of the McDowell County Courthouse located in Welch, West Virginia.[5]. Of those defendants whose charges were not dismissed, all were acquitted. Less than a month later, miners from the state gathered in Charleston. They were even more determined to organize the southern coal fields, and began the march to Logan county. Thousands of miners joined them along the way, culminating in what was to become known as the Battle of Blair Mountain.

Anawalt, West Virginia

From Wikipedia, the free encyclopedia

Anawalt is a town in McDowell County, West Virginia, United States. The population was 272 at the 2000 census. Anawalt was incorporated in 1949. It is named in honor of Colonel Anawalt, who was then manager of Union Supply Company, a subsidiary of the United States Steel Company. Coal mining remains the town's chief industry. Anawalt is the closest town for the unincorporated communities of Jenkinjones, O'Tool, Conklintown, Pageton, Leckie, and Little Creek.

Anawalt, West Virginia	
— Town —	
Location of Anawalt, West Virginia	
Coordinates: 37°20′9″N 81°26′14″W	
Country	United States
State	West Virginia
County	McDowell
Area	
- Total	0.7 sq mi (1.7 km^2)
- Land	0.7 sq mi (1.7 km^2)
- Water	0.0 sq mi (0.0 km^2)
Elevation	1,680 ft (512 m)
Population (2000)	
- Total	272
- Density	418.4/sq mi (161.5/km^2)
Time zone	Eastern (EST) (UTC-5)
- Summer (DST)	EDT (UTC-4)
ZIP code	24808
Area code(s)	304
FIPS code	54-01780[1]
GNIS feature ID	1534931[2]

Contents

- 1 Geography
- 2 Demographics
- 3 References
- 4 External links

Geography

Anawalt is located at 37°20′9″N 81°26′14″W (37.335800, -81.437233)[3].

According to the United States Census Bureau, the town has a total area of 0.6 square miles (1.6 km^2), all land.

Demographics

As of the census[1] of 2000, there were 272 people, 114 households, and 77 families residing in the town. The population density was 418.4 inhabitants per square mile (161.5 /km^2). There were 148 housing units at an average density of 227.7 per square mile (87.9 /km^2). The racial makeup of the town was 90.44% White, 9.19% African American, and 0.37% from two or more races.

There were 114 households out of which 25.4% had children under the age of 18 living with them, 50.0% were married couples living together, 12.3% had a female householder with no husband present,

W. Va Gamblers - Kanawha County

The Poker Game

MARTINSVILLE, VIRGINIA

During my high school days at Washington High, I forgot about the one year, eleventh grade, which I missed there because I completed that year in Martinsville, Virginia living with my maternal grandparents. A stern grandmother, Pearl, and a tender loving grandfather, Martin, called Papa. I had previously visited Martinsville many times when Mom and Dad went to visit her family. My dad would load us up in a T-model Ford, Graham or some good running car, and we would navigate those crooked roads and tall mountains. There were no four lanes or interstate highways. We were lucky to have paved roads. We would also take Grandma Pearl a rumble seat load of coal for her pot belly and cooking stove. All they had there for heat and cooking was wood and coal produced more heat. Every time we went, my parents would take food, whisky, coal and gifts. One time we had a flat tire and dad had to unload all the coal. fix the flat, and reload it. I was so proud of him. My dad was rich in their minds and he was correspondingly generous. He just liked to give things. He got more enjoyment from it than the receiver. When Arlene and Phons as he was called came to town, it was like Christmas. The clan for miles would suddenly appear for the party.

I enjoyed Martinsville so much that I asked mom in 1949 if I could spend a school year there. She agreed and grandma said okay; and so I went and had a glorious experience. The eleventh grade in Virginia was the final grade at that time so though I did my year there successfully at Albert Harris High, I chose not to graduate because I wanted to return to West Virginia to graduate in the twelfth grade; and I did.

While in Martinsville, I worked every spare hour when I was not in school. I caddied at the white golf course, carrying two bags at a time to make more money. Also, I cut grass with a non-powered push mover in the rich white section of town, set pins at the local bowling alley, of course two lanes at a time and washed dishes at the Eagle Restaurant downtown across from the Post Office. We had a steam dishwasher and when you opened it up, the dishes were so hot they burned your hands.

I worked because I always wanted to be independent to buy my own clothes and things. A pair of Thom McCann shoes was $8 dollars and socks $.15. I had a high school friend in West Virginia who went into the coal mines immediately after graduation who paid $1 for socks at the high-class Frankenberger clothing store in Charleston, and we thought he was crazy. This was James Woodson, one of our high school coach, Mr. Meadow's pets, and got to play everything. He was good however, but very conceited. Anyway, unfortunately, he died after a few years in the mines, of what, I'm not sure. Some say he had a heart attack. He was only about 19 or 20 years old.

But back to Martinsville... Even though I thought I was doing well by buying my own clothes, I found out the hard way that I should have been buying food also for the house at 1111 Roundabout Road. I had about 6 aunts and uncles living there with my grandparents. All very young, in high school or just out of the US Army from the end of WW II. I just took food for granted and didn't think I was a burden or should contribute in this way. I was, I thought, with my family similar to West Virginia, but I was wrong. One day, I proudly brought home a pair of new shoes and pants that together cost about $12 dollars and grandma really chastised me for wasting my money and not buying food. I was shocked and disappointed. I then started buying food for myself, but I didn't feel the same about being there after that.

One tragic thing did happen in the town before I left for home in West Virginia. Seven young black boys, one of whom I knew, Booker T. Milner, were accused of raping a young white girl. They denied it and were all convicted anyway and given the death sentence. Martinsville became a hot bed of controversy and anger during this time, especially among the black community. This was the Martinsville Seven case known across the country. I remember they appealed to the Virginia governor at the time, a Mr. Battle, but he turned them down and they were all electrocuted in 1952 or 1953. It was a local and national tragedy.

During my last summer as I recall in 1951, before returning to the mountains, I visited for three months, my Aunt Willie, Uncle Wilber and their four teenage boys, Billy, Jimmy, Frank and Johnny, in Reidsville, NC, where they lived on a share cropping tobacco farm. Of course, at the time I didn't know anything about share cropping. I thought they owned the farm. They tended about 50 or so acres of tobacco and had lots of chickens for food, some pigs, two cows and a mule for plowing. I tried to ride the mule, but he made my back side sore. My cousins were very lazy and slow. Though I was visiting, I had to take the cows out every morning into the field and tie them to a tree for grazing. I would also have to milk them before we departed. And yes, sometimes, the cow did kick over the milk bucket, but it was fun to milk them, which took a certain skill. After returning from the field every morning, all wet from the dew, I would bring in water from the well in the backyard. One day as I was winding the heavy bucket to the top, I slipped and released the handle which unwound and hit me in the head, knocking me out for a few seconds. Aunt Willie conserved everything and our meals were mainly squirrels and rabbits shot by Uncle Wilber while hunting. She would not let me wear my shoes except for church, which I didn't mind too much, for I went barefooted in West Virginia most of the time. Most kids went barefoot in those days. I would cut my feet often on hidden glass in the creek behind our house. And nails, I had several nails stuck 2 or 3 inches into the bottom of my feet. The pain was terrible, but we would put iodine on it and keep on going. I never did get lock jaw, which many people did get from nails in the foot.

But there were times I did need my shoes, especially when suckering and worming the tobacco plants in the fields. She would offer the five of us a quarter now and then for the one that could worm or sucker a long, long row of tobacco the fastest. I always won and my cousins didn't like that. Going barefoot so much, I eventually stubbed my toe and it became an infected stone bruise that was excruciatingly painful they didn't know what to do about it and a doctor was out of the question. I suffered with the throbbing pain for about a week until my Grandpapa and his kids came to assist in harvesting tobacco. I was real glad to see him and he knew immediately what to do. He just took out his pocket knife and cut the toe, releasing all that stuff that was inside hurting me.

I was greatly relieved and healed quickly. For the next few days, we pulled the tobacco, tied it to sticks and placed them high into a curing barn for treatment before selling. In the heated curing barn, the green tobacco turned brown and brittle. It was t hen taken down and hauled to the nearby market for sale. Uncle Wilber would give the land owner most of the money and keep a little for himself. This was a grand adventure for me, for I would never have experienced this part of life without this opportunity. It was fun and exciting.

Not long after this, I returned to West Virginia for my senior year in high school. I was glad to see my family, the mountains and my friends.

However, there is one other episode I must relate before I return to West Virginia. That is the activity of some white skinned blacks that "passed" for white to receive the better white social treatment than they would had they declared their true blackness. They were considered traitors by the regular black people. I mention this because my mom, all her siblings, mother and father and extended family were white in their skin, hair and overall appearance and behavior. But to their credit, they never "passed". They would not even consider it. They were proud to be what they were, Negros, and would never betray the black race, even though they could have benefited. Now they were often perceived as white by the real whites and sometimes given preferential treatment, but they didn't seek it or even know it most times. My Granddad was so much white in his appearance and manner that he seemed to me like he was or could be a great plantation owner controlling hundreds of people. He was laid back, confident and had an endearing manner, but firm. One time he took his two grown sons into a supposed "whites only" store by mistake and his sons were light skinned, but not enough to be mistaken as white, were told they couldn't come in. My Granddad asked why and was told he couldn't bring niggers into that store. The store owner was surprised when told that Elmer and Howard were his, Granddad's sons. Granddad was angry and immediately left the store.

In regards to being mistaken for another race, I my self have been mistaken as Spanish, Arab, Filipino, Greek and other in my travel to many nations in the world. I had occasion in Saigon and Bangkok to argue with women there when I told them I was Black, they would say, "Oh no, not Black" and I would tell them "Yes I am and happy to be so". They didn't understand and would sometime say no one wants to be Black. That's the kind of propaganda the White GIs spread about us Negros. In the 2nd World War, Germany and France, the women thought the Black GIs had tails because of the lies told by the White GIs. But they found out different at bedtime.

Martinsville, Virginia

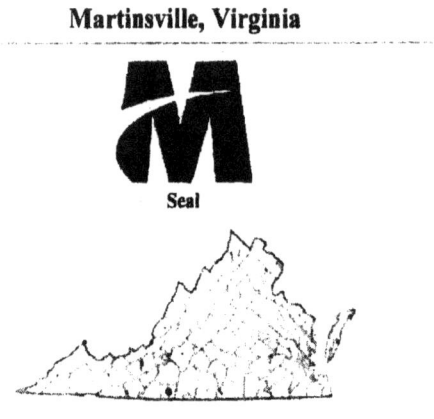

Seal

History

Martinsville was founded by American Revolutionary War General Joseph Martin (general), born in Albemarle County, whose plantation "Scuffle Hill" was located on the banks of the Smith River near the present-day southern city limits. General Martin and revolutionary patriot Patrick Henry, who lived briefly in Henry County and for whom the county is named, were good friends.

The city's main industry for a century was furniture construction, and today Virginia furniture makers still reside in the region. Shortly after World War II, DuPont built a chemical manufacturing plant. The booming chemical industry led to Martinsville declaring itself an independent city in 1928, while still retaining its status as county seat.

DuPont later built a large manufacturing plant for producing nylon, a vital war material, which made the city a target for strategic bombing during the Cold War. This nylon production jump-started the growth of the textiles industry in the area. For several years Martinsville was known as the "Sweatshirt Capital of the World." In the early 1990s, changing global economic conditions and new trade treaties made Martinsville textiles and furniture manufacturing economically unsustainable. Many firms closed shop and laid off thousands of workers. Currently, the city is repositioning itself long-term as a center for technology development and manufacturing. Due to the local government's inability to fund certain services, in the near future the city of Martinsville may decide to legally convert into the town of Martinsville.

The Martinsville Seven

Martinsville historic marker

On January 8, 1949, a group of seven young men sexually assaulted a 32-year-old woman in the city of Martinsville, Virginia. When the details of the offense were reported in the local newspaper, residents of the town were shocked that such a thing could happen in their community. The crime ......d a lot of people. The suspects had been drinking all that day and later testimony indicated that at least four of the men were intoxicated during the event. The victim, who was married to a local store manager, suffered severe physical and psychological injuries. She was hospitalized and kept in seclusion until court proceedings began during April of 1949. All seven attackers were black. The victim was white. Despite the inflammatory racial aspects of the case, the judicial atmosphere was calm and deliberate. Too deliberate, some said. "The defense attorneys stood idly by while the prosecution, the judge and the all-white jury, with unbelievable speed-up, railroaded the seven," said one newspaper account of the trials (*Daily Worker*, June 1, 1949).

The case received ample national attention, though it is not well remembered today. That's because the guilt of the defendants was never in question. They confessed upon arrest and several of the men admitted to the assault at their trials. Though civil rights groups tried to help, public support for the defendants was tempered by the fact that they were guilty beyond any reasonable doubt. After a series of six trials, which took place over a period of eleven days, the defendants were convicted of rape in the first degree. One trial required just six hours from jury selection to verdict. Pursuant to Virginia statutes, all seven men received a death sentence. There has never been a case like it in the history of American criminal justice.

The Martinsville Seven

U.S. AIRFORCE AND BASIC TRAINING

After working nickel and dime jobs in West Virginia, while waiting to turn 17 so I could get a real job in the mines or something, I asked my parents permission to go into the mines or the Air Force. They thought the Air Force was safer and so they signed for me to join the Air Force in 1952--the 3rd year of the Korean War. The Air Force was glad to have me, and I was glad also. The Army had integrated in 1947 and the Air Force became a separate service at that time. The Air Force was considered elite and smarter than the Army and to be honest, I believe it to be true with the Air Force's emphasis on education, high tech airplanes and such. Given the differences in the military branches, I always respected the other services for their mission, duty and dedication for protecting America.

I arrived by train at Sampson AFB in New York in late May 1952, I was located upstate New York near the Finger Lakes. Even in May, it was cold at night. In our barracks the cigarette butt can water would freeze at night. I didn't smoke or drink at the time and didn't until I was 21 and tried to be a "real" man. Anyway, the little 2 stripe Air Force Corporal named Elliot who was our drill Sergeant gave us all Hell during the next two months. He was the meanest little dude I had ever met, but he was fair and I liked him after the training was over. I was in flight number 1687 in the E Block area, and I actually loved the excitement and activities of Basic Training. We learned about the Government, basic drills, marching, firing weapons and general military knowledge. When Basic was completed we were all, except for a few screw ups promoted to Airman third class one stripe. I treasure that one stripe today as much as my PhD.

After Basic was over, we were assigned to go to advanced schooling at other bases depending on our aptitude scores. I had high scores in almost every field, so I was given top choices. I wanted to join the war in Korea as soon as possible, so I volunteered to go to gunnery school in Colorado and become a Tail Gunner on a B-26. I got my first choice, but then my orders were red lined, that means cancelled, for some reason and then I got another set of orders to got to Aircraft maintenance school in Wichita Falls, Texas for six months. This was a jewel of an assignment in that I liked airplanes and it was prestigious, especially for a 17 year old Black boy from West Virginia, fixing and maintaining complex airplanes that they only allowed White boys to do at the time. Yes, there was prejudice and discrimination the, but it was mild in the Air Force and it didn't hinder me much in my 27 year career as I attained the highest enlisted rank of E-9 Chief Master Sergeant by the age of 37 with 20 years of service.

Several of my fellow Airmen flew from New York to Texas in August and it was fun except for the small C-47 airplanes bouncing around in the turbulent weather enroute. When I stepped off the plane at Sheppard Air Force Base, it was so hot that it took my breath away I was very happy to be there and looked forward to this next phase of my journey.

B-29 SHEPP.RD A.FB. TX

GOONYBIRD YG-125

WASHINGTON → 750 ← SOTT

WE THREE 1952 TEXAS

GRENIER, ICELAND, GREENLAND AND MCGUIRE

My first flight aboard our wing of C-54s stationed at Grenier AFB, Manchester, NH occurred after I had been assigned to Grenier for about six months in 1953. Having a high IQ and knowledge about airplanes, coupled with my mechanical skills learned from my father before entering the Air Force in 1952 at the age of 17, I was made to order for an Air Force career. When I finished basic training at Sampson AFB, New York in August 1952, I received my first choice of going to Gunnery school in Denver, Co. However, my orders were red lined for some administrative reason and I was eventually assigned to receive training for my second choice which was Aircraft Maintenance. I trained for six months at Sheppard AFB, Texas for specialized training on propellers. I know that they may seem simple, but you almost have to be an engineer to understand, assemble, install and troubleshoot them. From Chanute, Illinois I later went to Grenier as an 18-year baby with old man's knowledge about airplanes. I was 18 and looked 15. In fact, some of my comrades took some convincing that I was even in the Air Force.

New Hampshire is like a wonderland, green forest, beautiful lakes, mountains, friendly people, clean and a vacation land for many. And I got to enjoy all this for free. We were only an hour by car from Boston; in those days the traffic was light to none. The only people on base with a car were the officers and a few high ranking NCOs. Everybody else walked, hitchhiked or caught a bus. I just loved the place especially since I was something of a celebrity being so young. Blacks and Whites gave me huge respect for my achievements and fighting – can do – spirit. But they played a lot of tricks on me in the beginning. Coming from the back woods of West Virginia, I was gung ho and very proud, but also very naïve. I had intuitive almost a priori knowledge of mechanics and repairing things, even if I had not seen them before. Anyway, my Sergeant boss told me to go around the base to get him a bucket of steam. So he gave me an empty bucket and away I went. Every place I went to said they had just run out of steam and sent me to another Unit. After half a day, I gave up and reported to the Sergeant that there was no steam on base. He and his fellow Airmen just burst out in laughter at me for being so dumb, but I got over it. Not immediately though. They pulled another stunt on me and then I finally "woke up". This time I was told to bring back a bucket of stripped paint. Again like a little dunce I went all around base and returned with an empty bucket. They laughed again, but stopped playing tricks on me after that. They treated me like a king a few months later when I saved the whole squadron from being grounded. That story is next. By the way, I learned that the old troops played pranks on all new troops when they first arrived.

It seems that I always came upon crisis situations in the Air Force that gave me a chance to shine, even though I had nothing to do with the opportunity.

One day, our Maintenance Chief approached me at coffee break and said that all of our planes were grounded because of suspected cracks in the Engine – Propeller Shafts. We had ten C-54s that flew the cargo run to Labrador, Germany, Scotland, Greenland, and New Foundland on a regular basis. Our Commander was worried that with all his planes grounded, our higher headquarters at Westover AFB, MA would be alarmed, and our Commander – Colonel was very concerned. I told him not to worry, that with the loan of some unskilled muscle, I could pull all 40 propellers that day, lay them on the ramp, inspect for cracks and get them all back on and run operational checks by the end of the day. Everyone laughed and said "Surely you jest, that would be impossible, for you're the only one who knows how to do this". So I replied that, "I could do it, just give me a chance".

So with nothing to lose, I began removing the four propellers from each airplane very carefully. Propellers that pull the airplane through the air are complex and dangerous. Yet I had all 40 off and on the ground in about three hours. I then mixed the chemicals to apply to the engine shafts to check for cracks. After checking them all and rolling the heavy maintenance stands from engine to engine, I determined that none were cracked. Now everyone was happy, but I had the prodigious task of installing all those propellers, ensuring they were safe and then starting and running all ten airplanes to make sure nothing leaked and then sign all the required documents that stated the planes were air worthy and mission capable. Can you imagine this kind of responsibility on an 18-year old two striper that didn't even shave yet? But I did it before dark. Needless to say, my stock was very high with everyone in the squadron. I was promoted to Buck Sergeant the next week over all those in front of me with more time in the service and grade. My Commander told me that I was likely the youngest three-stripe Buck Sergeant in the Air Force. I was very proud and I really enjoyed getting the $60 pay raise with the promotion.

After achieving the near impossible, the Commander allowed me several privileges. One was, he allowed me to tag along and fly with the Air Crew when I wanted to, no matter where the plane was going. So as soon as I could, I was riding in the cargo bay on my way to Germany. But after leaving Goose Bay Labrador for Frankfort, Germany, our plane flew into icy weather that coated the wings and made the plane too heavy to stay in the air. So the Aircraft Commander diverted our flight to Iceland for refueling and to wait out the bad weather. When we got there, it was snowing, but not really cold, given the country name of Iceland. I found out later that the founders of Iceland deliberately misnamed it to scare off other immigrants from coming and enjoying the mild climate, hot volcanic warmed springs, green forest and beauty. It is said that Greenland was named in the reverse because no one would come if they knew it was a gigantic block of ice.

Anyway, the crew and I went into the Keflavic Airport to clear customs and prepare to get some chow and a good night sleep in the military quarters. As I entered the airport, I was shocked to see a beautiful, but milk white woman, it was unbelievable. I could not imagine anyone being that white. She was pleasant though and assisted getting us on our way. By the way, the U.S. government had an agreement with Iceland that no black troops could be stationed there. I guess they wanted to keep their women milk white. It was okay, I guess, for a black to drop in for a night escaping danger; but I suppose you couldn't stay long. We were out of there the next day and in Germany by night fall.

After spending a couple days in Rhein-Main AFB, and Frankfort with my friend Leo Scott, the flight attendant, we departed and landed in Scotland for an overnight. We stayed in a fancy hotel, but no heat. The people in Europe used heavy quilts on beds at night for warmth. But the stay was enjoyable; I remember in the hotel bar that night that a Scottish woman wanted to touch my hair to see how it was. She hadn't seen many blacks before, I said "sure go ahead", it might have had a racist content, but I chose to see it as pure curiosity and no harm done. After leaving Scotland, we flew in to Lajes, Azores for fuel and then had an uneventful flight to Westover where we unloaded our cargo and then a half hour flight back to Grenier. I was very happy with this experience and later was delighted to get a $26 check for travel per diem to compensate for my missed meals. I wanted to do this again soon.

After this, I visited Boston and Concord, NH several times. I went to see the ship, Old Iron Sides, anchored in Charleston Harbor, Bunker Hill Monument, Harvard and MIT. When we drove into Boston, we passed MIT every time. Scott had purchased a raggedy Chrysler about ten years old worth $150, but it did run good. He couldn't afford insurance so we parked it in the woods off base. The states did not require insurance those days, so it was legal to have it on the road - but not on base.

One night coming back from Boston with our gang of Scott, Bam from LA, Marks from St. Louis, Dee Dee from New York and Hart from Baltimore, the police pulled me over, near Cambridge, with guns drawn. Everyone was asleep, but me the driver. The 3 or 4 cops asked us about a bank robbery and we of course had no clue what they were talking about. All of a sudden their radio crackled that other police had caught the robber and they abruptly left us without an apology or anything. Actually, I didn't care about an apology; they being all white were going to shoot us, maybe.

Before leaving New Hampshire, I did have the experience of fighting a forest fire in the White Mountains. My whole outfit of the 83rd Transport Squadron was ordered to spend about two weeks in the mountains fighting the fire. We lived I small pup tents and ate field rations. This was for me for it reminded me of West Virginia. Also while at Grenier, I tried my hand at boxing. I joined the boxing team as a light weight. After some training hitting the bags, I entered the local Golden Gloves tournament along with Scott, and Zatic Simpson, a heavyweight. We all lost. I fought a tough Marine and we blooded each other. I lost by decision. I didn't know three minutes were so long. I could hardly breathe in the second round and the water they pour on your head sooo ice cold. It would temporarily wake the dead.

After two years in New Hampshire, I met my future wife, Mildred Williams, in Boston. She came up to Grenier to visit a couple of times and I went to Boston after, and we would later be married in Salem, New Hampshire in 1956 where the Clerk of Court, being so used to marrying white people, put white for race by both our names on the marriage license. Mildred and I were and still are far from white.

In early 1956, my C-54 unit disbanded and most of the maintenance crews were reassigned to McGuire AFB, NJ near Wrightstown, New Egypt and Fort Dix. The principal airplane there was a larger, faster and more powerful C-118 for carrying mainly passengers to and from military bases in Europe. It was a little more difficult to work on than the C-54s, but I made the transition. After being in New Jersey for a few months, Mildred and I got married in New Hampshire and I went apartment hunting in Trenton before she came down. I found a nice apartment in West Trenton for $65 for a one bedroom. That $65 was a lot and would make a new car payment in 1956. I started my college career in Trenton, going to Trenton State for a year and also did a year of Law School at Lasalle Law School in Philadelphia. By corresponding correspondent courses was the equivalent of on-line courses today. I completed Landlord, Tenant, Bailment's, and Torts, before I left McGuire.

I was promoted to Staff Sergeant at McGuire just before my first four year enlistment expired, which put me in the category of a "fast burner", but it would be an eternity before I was promoted again. The next nine years, mostly at McGuire would be my most troubling experience with discrimination and racism. I found out that although New Jersey is in the north, the people there are more prejudiced and racist than most southern states and the base had more than its share of Rednecks, if not outright Klan. We had one fat, primitive Chief Master Sergeant who was so Neanderthalish that he openly spit his tobacco juice into trash cans. I found that many of the Senior NCOs such as this person were World War II illiterates that transferred from the Army into the Air Force when it became a separate branch in 1947. It would be another 20 years before most of these dinosaurs would retire or otherwise attrite out of the Air Force. I was an exceptional black to get as far as I had so fast and with a luckily skilled, respected job. Most of my black friends were relegated to menial jobs such as cooks, truck drivers, refuelers, grass and lawn maintenance, sports and ditch diggers. Yes, there was a legitimate job just for people to play sports if they were good enough, but they never got promoted.

In late 1956, there was an insurrection type political disruption in Hungary and the communist government allowed so may of the rebels to evacuate to the

United States. So where did they come to? You guessed it, McGuire AFB by the dozens of flights called "Operation Safe Haven". We were extremely busy handling all the refugees coming in and fixing the broken airplanes that landed.

The following year, I and many of my airmen comrades, were given orders to go to Thule, Greenland for 90 days. We all departed for Thule on several C-124 transport aircraft. Now a C-124 was a scary looking airplane from the stand point that it was not supposed to fly. It was just too big. You might think of it as a three-story warehouse with wings. I always was in awe every time I saw one take off. As it lumbered down the runway, you just knew that I would not lift off, yet it always did. The engineers who designed this behemoth should receive a medal. It was so big that it would carry two Greyhound buses and other cargo plus people. I had not flown on it before and was apprehensive that it could get us to the top of the world. It was overpowered with four huge engines, but painfully slow. It took so long to get anywhere that once on the ground, the aircrew would get an automatic 15 hour crew rest. For most aircraft, the crew would only get 3 hours rest while the plane was refueled and inspected for defects and repaired.

This trip to Thule was no different. We landed at Goose Bay, and Sondestrom, Greenland before navigating past the Glacier Mountains of Greenland before arriving at Thule. Greenland is Denmark territory and was and still is a vital communications, logistic and missile base for the United States. On Thule we had the first line of early warning devices to detect any Soviet Union Ballistic missiles launched at the U.S. over the North Pole. So it was very high priority for the Defense Department. My job on the mission was to support Air Force aircraft providing food, fuel and other logistics to Thule and Ice Island until the icebreaker could get into port and bring supplies in July, August.

Even in May, it was very cold, about 50 degrees below zero and the sun stayed up 24 hours a day. One could quickly get confused with the time as to whether it was day or night. I didn't see darkness until I returned to New Jersey. The winds and snow were sometimes off the chart and could be deadly. There were ropes running from almost all buildings connecting each other in case of a sudden wind storm blowing snow that blinded everything. These storms were called phases. If one got caught outside in one and didn't find a rope to lead to a shelter; they could and did die from the cold only a few feet from a building. The barracks were made of concrete and strongly anchored to the ground with their length side pointed to the north to decrease the chance of being blown away. The toilets were of the hand pump type. To flush them, you had to pump very hard to get the waste to go away. The only problems were that the pump would often back fire and spew the material back up into your face if you were looking directly over the commode. We learned fast how to avoid this situation. Also, the waste carrying pipes leaked outside and formed large brown ice sickles. These were humorously called Thule popsicles.

Being so isolated, it was amazing how many facilities were there to pass time and relax. There was a great library, bowling alley, movie, Base Exchange and typical things you would find on a state side base. The one thing I hated was the constant fog that kept out supply and mail planes for days at a time. I love getting letters from Mildred.

The most amazing aspects of Thule is the huge ice cap just a few miles away and the Ice Island T-3 Research Station that is located on an Iceberg about 300 miles away in the Artic Ocean north of Canada. This base has dozens of Scientists there working on who knows what, and the island literally floats back and forth with the currents of the Artic and it has an ice runway that can take a C-124 until it begins to melt in June or July. So we flew daily sorties to this island, but the main problem was finding it everyday. For you see, it moves a mile or so each day and we had to find it and then land that mountain of an airplane onto an ice runway without skidding or crashing. There is no question that the USAF has the best pilots in the world and the navigators aren't bad either. Once on the ground or should I say ice, we would off load food, fuel oil, medicine and many unknown items to sustain the people there for another year. Once the runway started to melt with holes we could no longer land and it would be about 9 months before the supply planes returned next year.

Finally, in July or August, the ice breaker arrived and several ships following her docked and began unloading heavy equipment tractors, building materials and other logistics. That was our cue to get out of dodge, and we were all ready to leave the "land of the midnight sun". When I arrived back at McGuire, I was thrilled to see green trees and grass.

After nine years at McGuire, interrupted by a tour in England and the Azores, I finally made Technical Sergeant; of course this was after filing a complaint with the Inspector General about racial discrimination. You see, I was constantly training younger inexperienced white boys, but they would get the promotion that I deserved. In 1966, I got the promotion and right after that I received orders for Vietnam. I don't know if they wanted to get rid of me or not, but I welcomed the opportunity to move out into the real Air Force of Fighter and Bomber planes and especially I wanted to go to a war zone.

And so I did, arriving in Saigon in March 1966, for a relatively uneventful year at Cam Ranh Bay except for the 30 day TDY in the Philippines.

But before going to Saigon, I must report that Mildred and I lived in the upstairs apartment of Mr. and Mrs. Baker for two years in Trenton when we first got married. Mrs. Baker was an angel of a woman and her husband, Theopolus was a good guy also, but he tried to be tough. They had three great kids that we almost grew up with, Carol, Junior and Maudine, the youngest. Maudine eventually had a son who graduated from West Point. Mildred and I were only in our early twenties ourselves, 21 and 26 respectfully. I the younger. We moved around the corner to 10 Jarvis Place in West Trenton into a larger apartment in

1958 and had a long pleasant friendship with out next door neighbors, Doris and Jimmy Rogers. Jimmy worked in the passenger railroad from Trenton to New York everyday. A real good guy, but could not improve his golf game, after years of trying ☺. Their children, Theresa, Jimmy Jr. and I forgot the other, but they honored me by naming their last child after me, Little Colonel. I could hardly believe the honor. Also, I must mention my good friends, Everett and Luvenia Bell from Georgia and Greenfield from a Trenton suburb. Everett and Greenfield worked in the prop shop at McGuire for years.

History

The United States Air Force became a separate military service on September 18, 1947, with the implementation of the National Security Act of 1947.[6] The Act created the United States Department of Defense, which was composed of three branches, the Army, Navy and a newly-created Air Force.[7] Prior to 1947, the responsibility for military aviation was divided between the Army (for land-based operations) and the Navy, for sea-based operations from aircraft carrier and amphibious aircraft. The Army created the first antecedent of the Air Force in 1907, which through a succession of changes of organization, titles, and missions advanced toward eventual separation 40 years later. The predecessor organizations of today's U.S. Air Force are:

- **Aeronautical Division, U.S. Signal Corps** (August 1, 1907 to July 18, 1914)
- **Aviation Section, U.S. Signal Corps** (July 18, 1914 to May 20, 1918)
- **Division of Military Aeronautics** (May 20, 1918 to May 24, 1918)
- **U.S. Army Air Service** (May 24, 1918 to July 2, 1926)
- **U.S. Army Air Corps** (July 2, 1926 to June 20, 1941) and
- **U.S. Army Air Forces** (June 20, 1941 to September 17, 1947)

The United States Air Force has been involved in

- World War I
- World War II
- The Cold War
- The Korean War
- The Vietnam War
- Operation Eagle Claw
- The United States invasion of Panama
- Operation Eldorado Canyon
- The Gulf War
- The Kosovo War
- Operation Enduring Freedom
- Operation Iraqi

United States Air Force

U.S. AIR FORCE

The official logo of the United States Air Force

Active	1947 -
Country	United States
Branch	Air Force
Role	"To fly and fight in Air, Space, and Cyberspace"
Size	351,800 active personnel 6,217 aircraft 1900 ICBMs
Part of	Department of Defense
Headquarters	The Pentagon
Motto	*Un Ab Alto* (unofficial)
March	The Air Force Song
Battles/wars	Korean War Vietnam War Operation Desert Storm Operation Deliberate Force Operation Desert Fox Operation Allied Force

Commanders

Commander-In-Chief	President George W. Bush
Civilian leadership	Michael Wynne *(Secretary of the Air Force)*
Military leadership	General T. Michael Moseley *(Chief of Staff of the Air Force)*

Insignia

Air Force flag	
Roundel	

Aircraft flown

Attack	F-15E, F-117, A-10, AC-130
Bomber	B-52H, B-1B, B-2
Electronic warfare	E-3, E-8, E-4, E-9, EC-130
Fighter	F-22, F-15C, F-16
Reconnaissance	U-2, RC-135, Q-4, Q-1
Trainer	T-6, T-37, T-38, T-1, TG-10
Transport	C-17, C-5, C-130, C-135, VC-

93

Honorable Discharge

DEPARTMENT OF THE AIR FORCE · UNITED STATES OF AMERICA ·

from the Armed Forces of the United States of America

This is to certify that

COLONEL V. WITTEN, Chief Master Sergeant, Regular Air Force

was Honorably Discharged from the

United States Air Force

on the 30th *day of* December 1977 *This certificate is awarded as a testimonial of Honest and Faithful Service*

JAMES K. HOPE, III, Lt Col, USAF
Williams Air Force Base, Arizona

DD FORM 256 AF PREVIOUS EDITIONS OF THIS FORM MAY BE USED.
1 NOV 51

THIS IS AN IMPORTANT RECORD — SAFEGUARD iT!

95

USAF 1953 Grenier AFB, NH

C-54 "Skymaster"

GREMLIN

OF GRENIER AIR FORCE BASE   Home of 1610th Air Transport Group ATLD-MAT

Vol. 4 No. 10 Monday November 30, 1953

Five Airmen Volunteer for Base Boxing Team for January Tourney

Five Grenier pugilists have expressed an interest in the January Northeast Area AF Boxing tournament. They will enter as a team representing the base.

The entries are: A/2c Fred Naugle, 1610 ABS; A/3c Leo Scott, M&S; A/3c Zatic Simpson, M&S; A/2c Charles Volkert, Heavy Equipment; and A/2c Colonel Whitten, M&S.

Last year, Simpson and Scott were both entered in the New England Golden Gloves tourney but were defeated.

Phil Wagman, the Golden Gloves Tournament Director in Manchester, has informed Athletic Director Tom Moore that the GG Tournament will be held on the last Saturday in January and the first two Saturday's in February.

M&S BOXERS - The 1610th M&S Sq will represent Grenier in the January Northeast Area AF Boxing Tournament. Pictured below are four members of the base team; all from the M&S Sqdn. Left to right: A/3c Zatic Simpson; A/3c Leo Scott; A/3c Willie Walker and A/2c Colonel Whitten. A/2c John Smith, Team coach, said that the team will participate in the Golden Gloves Tournament in Manchester on the last Saturday in January and the first two Saturday's in February.

Five Miler Didn't Make Race

The airplane carrying Grenier's lone entry in Boston's five mile foot race Tuesday developed engine trouble half way to Bean town and was still out when the starting time arrived.

The runner, A/2c Colonel Whitten of 1610th M&S Squadron, called S/Sgt Joe Easley at the base gymnasium for instructions. "Race started?" Joe asked. "Yes", the Colonel said. " Well, you can either run like hell and catch up with them", Joe advised, "or run back to work!"

Bowling League Stalled

Four teams have submitted letters to the Base Gym requesting official entry in the base bowling league.

S/Sgt Joe Easley, Base Gym, said that he would like to have at least 16 teams in the league. Tentative schedules have been drawn and soon as the teams are entered they will be placed on the schedule.

Bloody Noses And Over-Eating Fell Grenier Golden Glovers

Two Grenier airmen from the 1610th M&S Squadron were eliminated from the finals of the 1954 New Hampshire Golden Gloves tournament Feb 13th, at the Manchester State Armory.

In the second bout of the evening in the 135-pound class, A/2c Colonel Whitten lost a decision to Archie Auger of Tilton, New Hampshire. Both Whitten and Auger drew blood in the first round and their noses were streaming for the rest of the fight.

The first of the two heavyweight bouts which closed the evenings program matched A/3c Zatic Simpson, 1953 New Hampshire champion with Albert Brewster, of Dartmouth College.

Brewster upset the champion as he gained a TKO victory in the beginning of the third round when Simpson indicated to the referee that he had had enough. S/Sgt William Nelson, M&S, Simpson's manager, said that a heavy supper apparently was the cause of his fighter's sluggishness and inablitiy to withstand punishment.

83 ATS Crew Wins Praise For Tough Emergency Maintenance

Grenier AFB, N. H. -- In a classic example of how to keep 'em flying, S/Sgt Roscoe M. Collins and three airmen of the 83rd Air Transport Squadron pulled a remarkably quick engine change and licked a baffling maintenance problem on their C-54 aircraft at Sondrestrom AFB in Greenland.

The plane, 5503, lost an engine while approaching Sondrestrom on a scheduled trip. Sgt. Collins, crew chief on 5503, was dispatched from Grenier with A/1c Melvin G. Higden, A/1c Ronald P. Konieczny, and A/3c Paul A. Lynch to change the engine.

Immediatley after landing in Greenland, the airmen went to work. A sizzling nine hours later, the new engine was in and 5503 was ground checked and ready for a test hop -- a performance which had operations and maintenance personnel back at Grenier whistling with amazement.

At this point, the aircraft developed a flat strut. The 83rd airmen dug up the necessary parts only to find that the base didn't have the wrench needed to remove the inside

See 83rd Maintenance Page 4

very IMPORTANT *people*

As a safety precaution, engine mechanics use a rail-guarded platform when working high off the ground on a MATS airplane.

By M/Sgt. Frank W. Penniman

WHO ARE THE VIP's of the Military Air Transport Service? Pilots and aircraft observers may well head the list, but there are others who share the top spot — airmen and WAF who keep the planes flying in the biggest airline system in the world. From flight engineers who operate the airplane control panels to weather observers who track every cloud for miles around, from radio operators aboard planes and in ground stations to engine mechanics who keep the planes in flying shape — it's teamwork in MATS that counts the most.

Because MATS has many facets — communications, flying, weather, rescue, and photography — it is not difficult for the new airman and WAF to be placed in a field where their schooling and training are fully utilized. And what's more, there's room for individual advancement in the technical and administrative fields to which airmen and WAF are assigned.

In the flying phase of MATS, young servicefolk today

are making great strides in such jobs as load masters, flight traffic specialists (similar to airline hostesses), aerial engineers, and radio operators. Also, the specialized mechanics who work on the various parts of airplanes — from props to tails — are aided by the latest technical equipment.

Among the other popular fields in the MATS system of flight support is weather. Today, the airman and WAF work with the newest electronic gadgets in determining future climatic conditions so that MATS pilots may fly in greater safety. From data secured by the electronic and other scientific equipment, weather observers make their charts. These are the safety charts of the skyways that have helped MATS, and other flying units, to skirt thunderheads and to dodge tornadoes.

Without communications, flying activity would be severely curtailed. So pilots and navigators look to the control tower operators, landing control technicians, communications center specialists, radio technicians, and air

Flight engineer making an engine and instrument panel check before his "Superfort" takes off on a weather mission.

100

velocity, and other relative data which are radioed back to weather stations. The stations then warn all those in the path of the raging wind.

Another type of B-29 is flown by men of the Air Rescue Service. This plane carries a large lifeboat slung beneath its cigar-like belly. Upon reaching the scene of a sea disaster, the launch is dropped by parachute to the survivors. Each boat is equipped with provisions to sustain life until a seaplane or ship arrives.

The SA-16 "Albatross" amphibian is one of the most versatile aircraft in service today. Extensively used by ARS, this plane has been instrumental in the successful completion of many search and rescue missions.

Few men have distinguished themselves as much as the helicopter crews of the Air Rescue Service. Able to rise and descend vertically, H-5 and H-19 'copters have played a vital role in answering the call of distress. During the Korean conflict, almost a thousand servicemen were rescued from behind enemy lines by helicopter. Transferred to transport planes, many of these men were flown to hospitals in the United States within 60 hours.

Every day, MATS' planes operate between Air Force installations in 37 countries scattered throughout the world. In the past five years, they have flown almost four billion passenger miles. In view of this feat and the many other functions and accomplishments, it is small wonder the serviceman smiles with a tinge of pride when he refers to the Military Air Transport Service as "our airline."   END

The heavy doors of a "Globemaster II" easily open to let a partially dismantled H-19 'copter be loaded for flight.

Special mobile ladders are used by maintenance men to reach the C-124's towering tail section.

101

At Hickam Air Force Base in Hawaii, combat troops stand
in formation in front of their MATS C-97 "Stratocruiser."

An H-5 helicopter hovers over an SA-16 "Albatross" in the
Far East. Both planes are used by the Air Rescue Service.

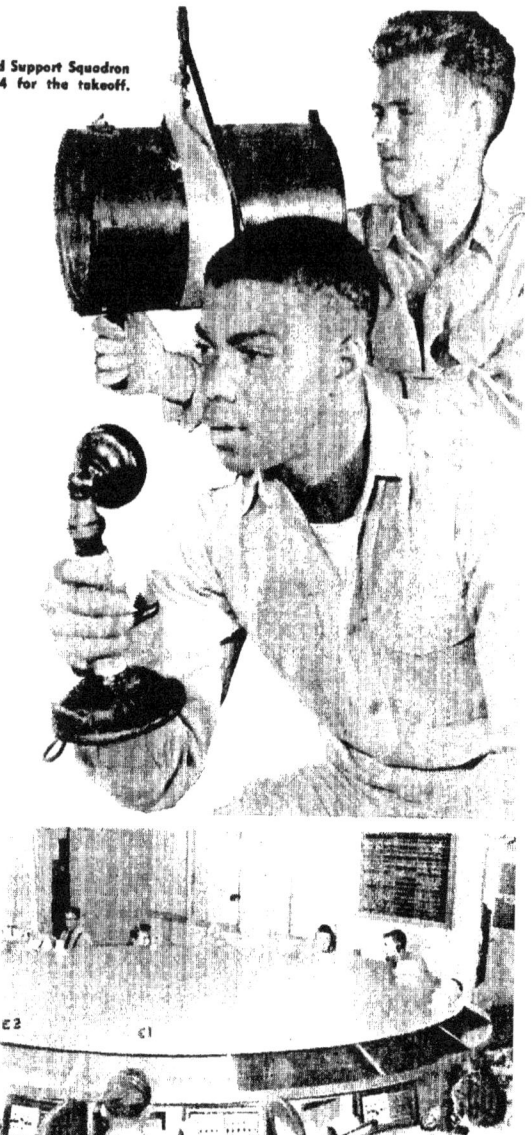

Two control tower operators of the 1502d Support Squadron on Kwajalein Atoll clear a MATS C-54 for the takeoff.

TALKING *(Continued)*

within about 40 miles of his destination, a voice over the plane's radio telephone starts guiding him in for a landing. The voice tells the pilot what course to take into the base and gives him detailed instructions every few minutes, mile after mile, until he sets his plane down safely on the runway. Such safe landings, even under the most adverse weather conditions, are commonplace with MATS' planes because of the magical qualities of Ground Controlled Approach.

Briefly, GCA is a high-precision ground radar system that enables aircraft to make a safe approach to a narrow airstrip under conditions approaching zero in visibility. Here is how it works:

A radar system scans the sky in a 360-degree arc, spotting all planes approaching as far as 30 miles from the field. GCA operators, closeted in a curtained trailer alongside the airstrip, radio the pilot continuous and accurate information on his position obtained by sensitive radar equipment. Radar plotters make calculations on their screens and relay the data to the pilot, giving the necessary flight corrections which enable him to keep the plane on the proper course.

In the last crucial minutes before the plane touches down, the GCA operator literally talks the pilot in safely. He keeps up a running conversation with the pilot, checking the plane's altitude, rate of descent, the correct headings to align the plane with the runway, and the plane's glidepath in relation to the landing. Guided by the operator's voice, the pilot obeys all instructions. He knows that the GCA man is acting as an eye in the sky for him, leading him in on an invisible beam to a safe landing.

Airways and Air Communications Service does this vital GCA job not only for MATS' planes but for other planes of the United States Air Force as well. What's more, it does this on a 24-hour-a-day basis all along the global communications chain. This marvel of electronic ingenuity makes it possible for MATS' planes to fly under all weather conditions anywhere in the world.

But important as GCA is, it is far from being the only string on AACS' bow. It also operates point-to-point and ground-to-air radio stations; airbase control towers; electronic aids to navigation — such as radio ranges, direction finders, homing beacons, marker beacons, instrument landing systems, and Loran (a long-range navigational system) — and land-line telephone facilities and teletype stations. In other words, it performs the thousands of duties necessary for the working of a mammoth communications system.

Currently, AACS is running 19 different kinds of service for the Air Force which require the efforts of some 26,000 military personnel. It operates 2,063 facilities spread over 252 strategic sites around the northern hemisphere. Nearly 70 percent of all AACS personnel are serving outside the United States in stations ranging from Alaska to Panama, from Greenland to Trinidad, and from Germany to Korea and across the Pacific.

AACS was organized primarily to lessen the risk of military flying by providing an integrated airways system under a single jurisdiction that answers directly to the top level of the Air Force command. How well it has succeeded is a matter of proud record. This incomparably valuable service has all but eliminated many of flying's greatest hazards. And the end of its development is nowhere

Interphone operators work at rotating table which provides for smooth flow of messages at the Carswell AFB, Tex., flight service center.

Iceland

Iceland, officially the **Republic of Iceland** (Icelandic: *Ísland* or *Lýðveldið Ísland*; IPA: ['lɪðvɛltɪð 'islant]) is a country of northwestern Europe, comprising the island of Iceland and its outlying islets in the North Atlantic Ocean between Greenland, Norway, Ireland, UK and the Faroe Islands.[1] As of December 2006, it had a population of 307,261. Its capital and largest city is Reykjavík.

Iceland has a history of habitation since about the year 874 when, according to *Landnámabók*, the Norwegian chieftain Ingólfur Arnarson became the first permanent Norwegian settler on the island. Others had visited the island earlier and stayed over winter. Over the next centuries, people of Nordic and Gaelic origin settled in Iceland. Until the twentieth century, the Icelandic population relied on fisheries and agriculture, and was from 1262 to 1944 a part of the Norwegian and later the Danish monarchies.

Today, Iceland is a highly developed country, the world's fifth and second in terms of gross domestic product (GDP) per capita and human development respectively. Iceland is a member of the UN, NATO, EEA, and OECD.

Lýðveldið Ísland
Republic of Iceland

| Flag | Coat of arms |

Motto: none

Anthem: *Lofsöngur*

Location of Iceland (orange)

on the European continent (white)

Capital (and largest city)	Reykjavík 64°08′N 21°56′W (http://tools.wikimedia.de/~magnus/geo/geohack.php?params=64_08_N_21_56_W_type:country(103,000))
Official languages	Icelandic (*de facto*)
Government	Constitutional republic
- President	Ólafur Ragnar Grímsson
- Prime Minister	Geir H. Haarde
Independence	from Denmark
- Home rule	1 February 1904
- Sovereignty	1 December 1918
- Republic	17 June 1944

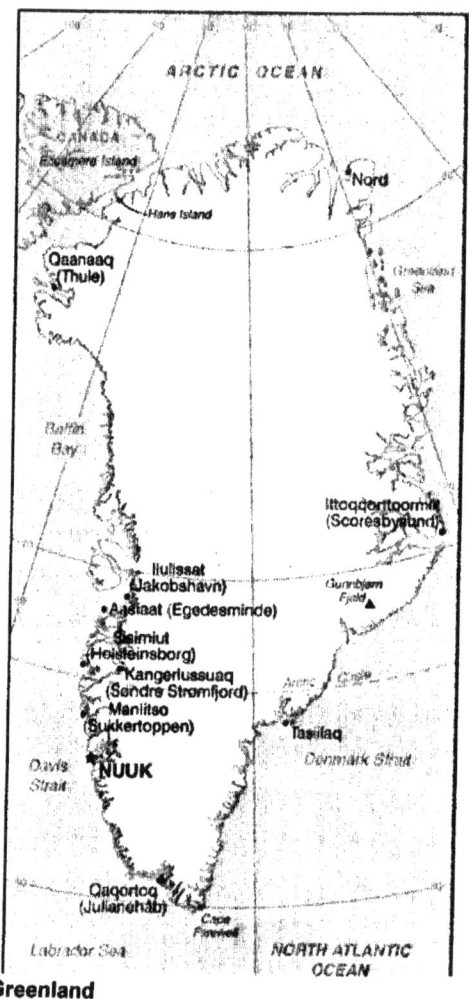

Greenland

Background:

Greenland, the world's largest island, is about 81% ice-capped. Vikings reached the island in the 10th century from Iceland; Danish colonization began in the

18th century, and Greenland was made an integral part of Denmark in 1953. It joined the European Community (now the EU) with Denmark in 1973, but withdrew in 1985 over a dispute centered on stringent fishing quotas. Greenland was granted self-government in 1979 by the Danish parliament; the law went in effect the following year. Denmark continues to exercise control of Greenland's foreign affairs in consultation with Greenland's Home Rule Government.

History

WEATHER BUREAU ARCTIC METEOROLOGICAL SERVICE

The Weather Bureau has been authorized by the Congress to establish a network of stations in the high latitudes of the Western Hemisphere in cooperation with other interested countries, for the purposes of taking surface and upper-air observations and making such other meteorological studies of Arctic weather conditions as may be practicable. During ,the past 3 months, with the assistance of the War and Navy Departments and the Civil Aeronautics Administration, hundreds of tons of cargo-quarters, furnishings, special clothing; food, medicine, instruments, tools, and other materials and supplies vital to the success of the project, have been procured and assembled at Boston for shipment north-ward. Personnel-administrators, forecasters, observers, doctors, radio-men, mechanics, and cooks-have been selected and all other detailscompleted. As the initial phase of this meteorological network, a complete surface and upper-air observation station will be established at Thule, Greenland, during the current summer. The personnel and supplies are now being transported to that place in Navy cargo ships which left Boston July 18, 1946. After construction of buildings, installation of meteorological instruments and radio facilities, and other preliminary work have been completed about the middle of September, the meteorological program will be started. Initially, it will consist of a 6-hourly surface observation, pilot-balloon observations at 0400 and 1000Z, and a rawinsonde observation, at 1500Z daily. If circumstances permit, a second daily rawinsonde and 3-hourly surface observation will be added at a later date at which time, pilot-balloon observations ,will be made at 1000 and 2200Z daily, and rawinsondes at 0300 and 1500Z. Other special observations will be undertaken as may be practicable. Mail and critical supplies will be flown into and out of Thule by War Department aircraft, For administration and coordination; of the project, a unit designated as the Arctic Meteorological Service section has been organized in the Central Office of the Weather Bureau under Mr. D. M. Little, Assistant Chief,

Thule Airbase in 1989

106

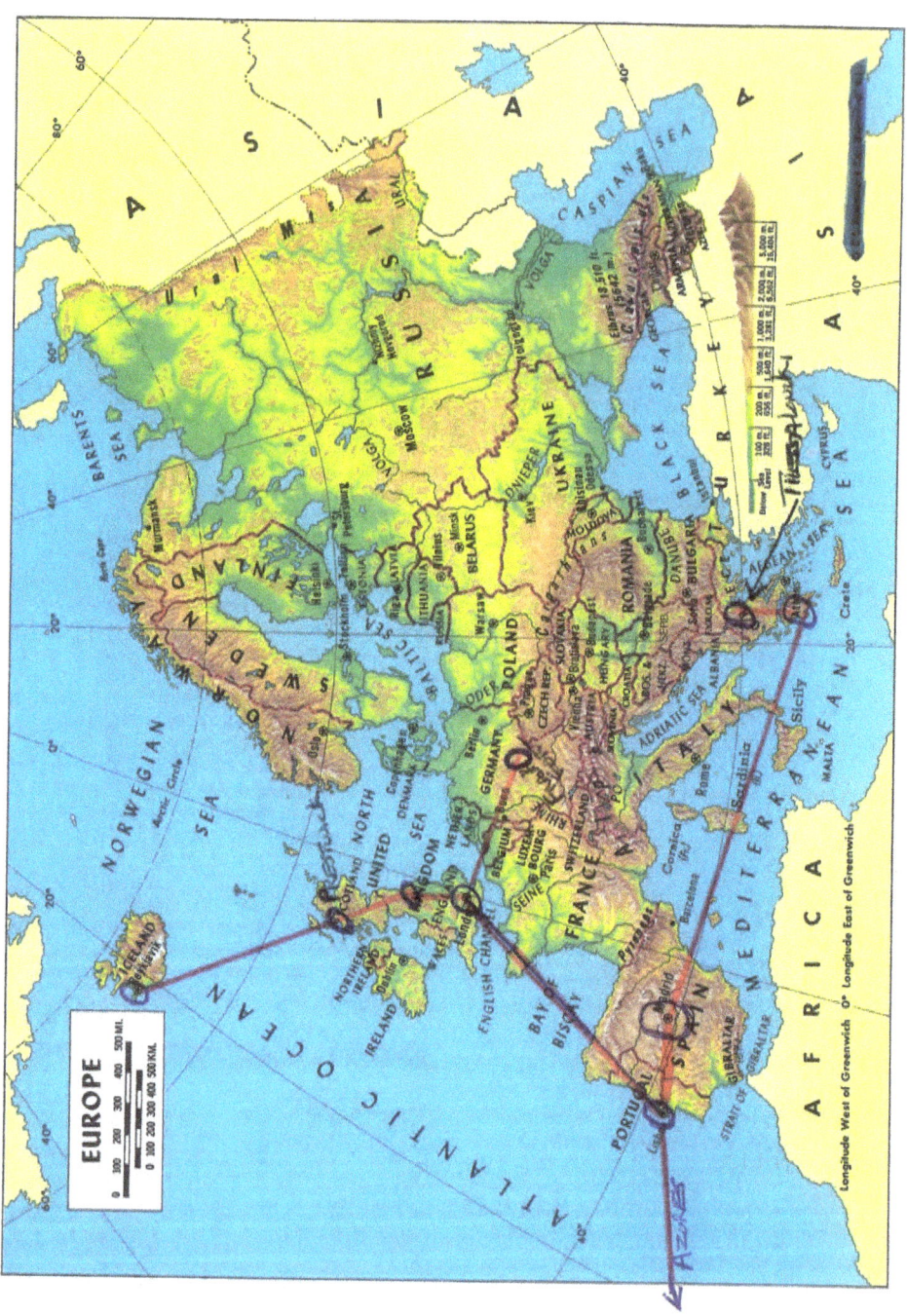

107

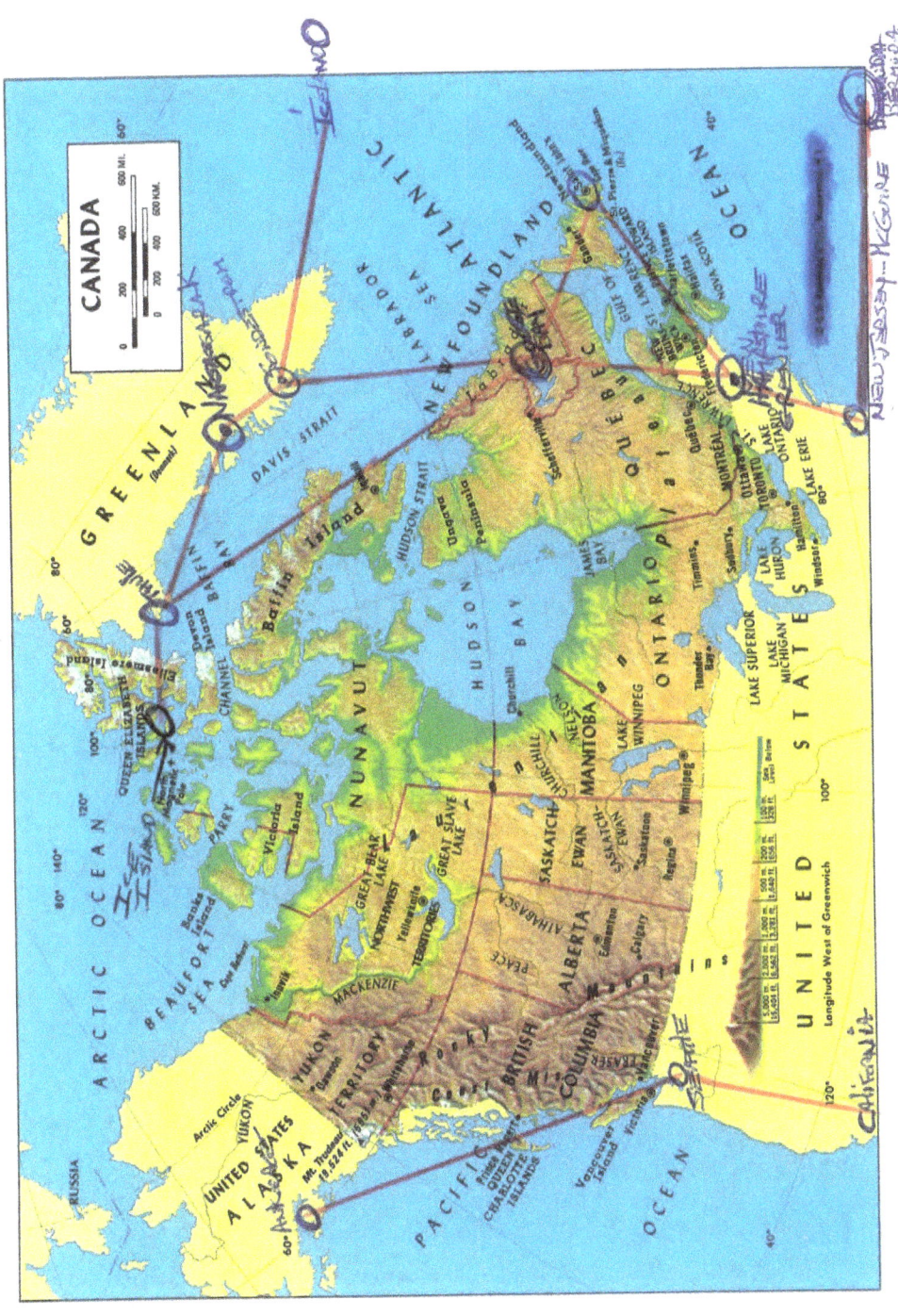

UNITED KINGDOM

HAVING COMPLETED EIGHT YEARS IN THE Air Force – mostly in New Hampshire and McGuire AFB, New Jersey, with some temporary duty in Greenland and Iceland, I was assigned to the United Kingdom in 1959, where I spent about a year in Mildenhill, Manchester, London and several small towns. I primarily maintained WB – 50 weather reconnissavee aircraft – those were similar to the B-29 bombers used to drop the atomic bomb on Hiroshima and Nagasaki. I found the English to be incredibly friendly and good people. The weather was typically rainy and cloudy – and I liked it because it reminded me of my home in West Virginia. Having attained the rank of Staff Sergeant at the tender age of 21, I was somewhat of an anomaly in charge of much older troops, but I always maintained their respect.

It was great fun visiting London and the English countryside. The roads were very narrow and curvy – with people parking anywhere alongside the road creating an environment for accidents. In the cities, motorist actually used their parking lights when they parked at night due to the heavy fog and typically poor visibility. Probably the most fun was riding the narrow gauge railroad passenger cars to Manchester, Liverpool, and other places. If you caught the Milk Run or slow train that stopped at every station, it would take all day to get anywhere. But, if you were on an express, you got there rather briskly. Liverpool was very active with the Beatles in these days just before they came to the United States.

Outside the base at Mildenhill, near the train station in Shippy Hill was a pub called the Bird in the Hand. This was where the locals and many Airmen hung out drinking the heavy English beer called Stout, and throwing darts. The standing launch point for the darts had been used so often over many years that a hole was worn in the floor at that point. And of course the talk was about soccer and betting. As I recall, there was little or no television available in those days of 1959 and 1960.

I had arrived in England with the intention of bringing my wife, Mildred, later once I was able to obtain family housing; but the list was long and by the time I got near the top, I received orders to go to Lajes AB, Azores, a Portuguese island territory in the Atlantic Ocean about one third the distance from Europe to the United States. Our WB-50 aircraft which flew daily weather missions from England to the North Pole and the South Atlantic were to be put in mothballs and the Squadron deactivated. This was a surprise and disappointing because I would now have to start all over again on a housing list in the Azores. So after clearing the base, having my last taste of the splendid fish and chips and uniquely good English tea, I departed London Heathrow on KLM airlines, Super Constellation for Lisbon, Portugal and then to the tiny refueling island of Santa Maria where I was then stranded for a week due to a hurricane that grounded all flights until it blew past the Azores Archipelago.

United Kingdom

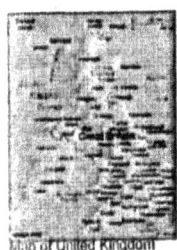

Map of United Kingdom

United Kingdom of Great Britain and Northern Ireland

Sovereign: Queen Elizabeth II (1952)

Prime Minister: Gordon Brown (2007)

Current government officials

Land area: 93,278 sq mi (241,590 sq km); **total area:** 94,526 sq mi (244,820 sq km)

Population (2007 est.): 60,776,238 (growth rate: 0.3%); birth rate: 10.7/1000; infant mortality rate: 5.0/1000; life expectancy: 78.7; density per sq mi: 652

Capital and largest city (2003 est.): London, 7,615,000 (metro. area), 7,429,200 (city proper)

Other large cities: Glasgow, 1,099,400; Birmingham, 971,800; Liverpool, 461,900; Edinburgh, 460,000; Leeds, 417,000; Bristol, 406,500; Manchester, 390,700; Bradford, 288,400

Monetary unit: Pound sterling (£)

Languages: English, Welsh, Scots Gaelic

Geography

The United Kingdom, consisting of Great Britain (England, Wales, and Scotland) and Northern Ireland, is twice the size of New York State. England, in the southeast part of the British Isles, is separated from Scotland on the north by the granite Cheviot Hills; from them the Pennine chain of uplands extends south through the center of England, reaching its highest point in the Lake District in the northwest. To the west along the border of Wales—a land of steep hills and valleys—are the Cambrian Mountains, while the Cotswolds, a range of hills in Gloucestershire, extend into the surrounding shires.

Important rivers flowing into the North Sea are the Thames, Humber, Tees, and Tyne. In the west are the Severn and Wye, which empty into the Bristol Channel and are navigable, as are the Mersey and Ribble.

Government

The United Kingdom is a constitutional monarchy and parliamentary democracy, with a queen and a parliament that has two houses: the House of Lords, with 574 life peers, 92 hereditary peers, and 26 bishops; and the House of Commons, which has 651 popularly elected members. Supreme legislative power is vested in parliament, which sits for five years unless dissolved sooner. The House of Lords was stripped of most of its power in 1911, and now its main function is to revise legislation. In Nov. 1999 hundreds of hereditary peers were expelled in an effort to make the body more democratic. The executive power of the Crown is exercised by the cabinet, headed by the prime minister.

England has existed as a unified entity since the 10th century; the union between England and Wales, begun in 1284 with the Statute of Rhuddlan, was not formalized until 1536 with an Act of Union; in another Act of Union in 1707, England and Scotland agreed to

110

Ethnicity/race: English 83.6%, Scottish 8.6%, Welsh 4.9%; Northern Irish 2.9%, black 2%, Indian 1.8%, Pakistani 1.3%, mixed 1.2%, other 1.6% (2001)

Religions: Christian (Anglican, Roman Catholic, Presbyterian, Methodist) 71.6%, Muslim 2.7%, Hindu 1%, other 1.6%, unspecified or none 23.1% (2001)

Literacy rate: 99% (2003 est.)

Economic summary: GDP/PPP (2007 est.): $2.137 trillion; per capita $35,100. **Real growth rate:** 3.1%. **Inflation:** 2.3%. **Unemployment:** 5.4%. **Arable land:** 23%. **Agriculture:** cereals, oilseed, potatoes, vegetables; cattle, sheep, poultry; fish. **Labor force:** 30.07 million; agriculture 1.5%, industry 19.1%, services 79.5% (2004). **Industries:** machine tools, electric power equipment, automation equipment, railroad equipment, shipbuilding, aircraft, motor vehicles and parts, electronics and communications equipment, metals, chemicals, coal, petroleum, paper and paper products, food processing, textiles, clothing, other consumer goods. **Natural resources:** coal, petroleum, natural gas, tin, limestone, iron ore, salt, clay, chalk, gypsum, lead, silica, arable land. **Exports:** $468.8 illion f.o.b. (2006 est.): manufactured goods, fuels, chemicals; food, beverages, tobacco. **Imports:** $603 billion f.o.b. (2006 est.): manufactured goods, machinery, fuels; foodstuffs. **Major trading partners:** U.S., Germany, France, Ireland, Netherlands, Belgium, Spain, Italy, China (2004).

Communications: Telephones: main lines in use: 32.943 million (2005); mobile cellular: 61.1 million (2004).

permanently join as Great Britain; the legislative union of Great Britain and Ireland was implemented in 1801, with the adoption of the name the United Kingdom of Great Britain and Ireland; the Anglo-Irish treaty of 1921 formalized a partition of Ireland; six northern Irish counties remained part of the United Kingdom as Northern Ireland and the current name of the country, the United Kingdom of Great Britain and Northern Ireland, was adopted in 1927.

History

Stonehenge and other examples of prehistoric culture are all that remain of the earliest inhabitants of Britain. Celtic peoples followed. Roman invasions of the 1st century B.C. brought Britain into contact with continental Europe. When the Roman legions withdrew in the 5th century A.D., Britain fell easy prey to the invading hordes of Angles, Saxons, and Jutes from Scandinavia and the Low Countries. The invasions had little effect on the Celtic peoples of Wales and Scotland. Seven large Anglo-Saxon kingdoms were established, and the original Britons were forced into Wales and Scotland. It was not until the 10th century that the country finally became united under the kings of Wessex. Following the death of Edward the Confessor (1066), a dispute about the succession arose, and William, Duke of Normandy, invaded England, defeating the Saxon king, Harold II, at the Battle of Hastings (1066). The Norman conquest introduced Norman French law and feudalism.

The reign of Henry II (1154–1189), first of the Plantagenets, saw an increasing centralization of royal power at the expense of the nobles, but in 1215 King John (1199–1216) was forced to sign the Magna Carta, which awarded the people, especially the nobles, certain basic rights. Edward I (1272–1307) continued the conquest of Ireland, reduced Wales to subjection, and made some gains in Scotland. In 1314, however, English forces led by Edward II were ousted from Scotland after the Battle of Bannockburn. The late 13th and early 14th centuries saw the development of a separate House of Commons with tax-raising powers. Edward III's claim to the throne of France led to the Hundred Years' War (1338–1453) and the loss of almost all the large English territory in France. In England, the great poverty and discontent caused by the war were intensified by the Black Death, a plague that reduced the population by about one-third. The Wars of the Roses (1455–1485), a struggle for the throne between the House of York and the House of Lancaster, ended in the victory of Henry Tudor (Henry VII) at Bosworth Field (1485).

During the reign of Henry VIII (1509–1547), the church in England asserted its independence from the Roman Catholic Church. Under Edward VI and Mary, the two extremes of religious

Bureau of European and Eurasian Affairs
July 2008

People

History

Government

Political Conditions

Economy

Defense

Foreign Relations

U.S. Relations

Travel/Business

Background Notes A-Z

Background Note: United Kingdom

PROFILE

OFFICIAL NAME:
United Kingdom of Great Britain and Northern Ireland

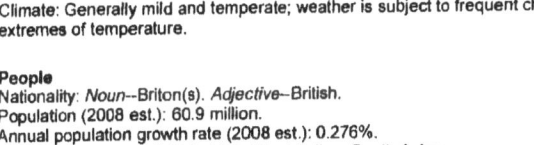

Spring flowers in front of St. Stephen's tower, containing Big Ben, London, United Kingdom, March 7, 2002. [© AP Images]

Geography
Area: 243,000 sq. km. (93,000 sq. mi.); slightly smaller than Oregon.
Cities: *Capital*–London (metropolitan pop. about 7.2 million). *Other cities*–Birmingham, Glasgow, Leeds, Sheffield, Liverpool, Bradford, Manchester, Edinburgh, Bristol, Belfast.
Terrain: 30% arable, 50% meadow and pasture, 12% waste or urban, 7% forested, 1% inland water.
Land use: 25% arable, 46% meadows and pastures, 10% forests and woodland, 19% other.
Climate: Generally mild and temperate; weather is subject to frequent changes but to few extremes of temperature.

People
Nationality: *Noun*--Briton(s). *Adjective*–British.
Population (2008 est.): 60.9 million.
Annual population growth rate (2008 est.): 0.276%.
Major ethnic groups: British, Irish, West Indian, South Asian.
Major religions: Church of England (Anglican), Roman Catholic, Church of Scotland (Presbyterian), Muslim.
Major languages: English, Welsh, Irish Gaelic, Scottish Gaelic.
Education: *Years compulsory*--12. *Attendance*–nearly 100%. *Literacy*–99%.
Health: *Infant mortality rate* (2008 est.)–4.93/1,000. *Life expectancy* (2008 est.)--males 76.37 years; females 81.46 years; total 78.85 years.
Work force (2008, 29.59 million): *Services*–80.4%; *industry*–18.2%; *agriculture*–1.4%.

Government
Type: Constitutional monarchy.
Constitution: Unwritten; partly statutes, partly common law and practice.
Branches: *Executive*–monarch (head of state), prime minister (head of government), cabinet. *Legislative*–bicameral Parliament: House of Commons, House of Lords; Scottish Parliament, Welsh Assembly, and Northern Ireland Assembly. *Judicial*–magistrates' courts, county courts, high courts, appellate courts, House of Lords.
Subdivisions: Scotland, Wales, Northern Ireland (municipalities, counties, and parliamentary constituencies).
Political parties: Great Britain--Conservative, Labour, Liberal Democrats; also, in Scotland–Scottish National Party. Wales–Plaid Cymru (Party of Wales). Northern Ireland--Ulster Unionist Party, Social Democratic and Labour Party, Democratic Unionist Party, Sinn Fein,

Alliance Party, and other smaller parties.

Suffrage: British subjects and citizens of other Commonwealth countries and the Irish Republic resident in the U.K., at 18.

Economy

GDP (at current market prices, 2007 est.): $2.15 trillion.

Annual growth rate (2007 est.): 2.9%.

Per capita GDP (2007 est.): $35,300.

Natural resources: Coal, oil, natural gas, tin, limestone, iron ore, salt, clay, chalk, gypsum, lead, silica.

Agriculture (1.1% of GDP): *Products*—cereals, oilseed, potatoes, vegetables, cattle, sheep, poultry, fish.

Industry: *Types*—steel, heavy engineering and metal manufacturing, textiles, motor vehicles and aircraft, construction (5.2% of GDP), electronics, chemicals.

Trade (2007 est.): *Exports of goods and services*—$415.6 billion: manufactured goods, fuels, chemicals; food, beverages, tobacco. *Major markets*—U.S., European Union. *Imports of goods and services*—$595.6 billion: manufactured goods, machinery, fuels, foodstuffs. *Major suppliers*—U.S., European Union, China.

PEOPLE

The United Kingdom's population in 2004 surpassed 60 million—the third-largest in the European Union. Its overall population density is one of the highest in the world. Almost one-third of the population lives in England's prosperous and fertile southeast and is predominantly urban and suburban—with about 7.2 million in the capital of London, which remains the largest city in Europe. The United Kingdom's high literacy rate (99%) is attributable to universal public education introduced for the primary level in 1870 and secondary level in 1900. Education is mandatory from ages 5 through 16. About one-fifth of British students go on to post-secondary education. The Church of England and the Church of Scotland are the official churches in their respective parts of the country, but most religions found in the world are represented in the United Kingdom.

A group of islands close to continental Europe, the British Isles have been subject to many invasions and migrations, especially from Scandinavia and the continent, including Roman occupation for several centuries. Contemporary Britons are descended mainly from the varied ethnic stocks that settled there before the 11th century. The pre-Celtic, Celtic, Roman, Anglo-Saxon, and Norse influences were blended in Britain under the Normans, Scandinavian Vikings who had lived in Northern France. Although Celtic languages persist in Wales, Scotland, and Northern Ireland, the predominant language is English, which is primarily a blend of Anglo-Saxon and Norman French.

RAF Lakenheath

From Wikipedia, the free encyclopedia

RAF Lakenheath (IATA: **LKZ**, ICAO: **EGUL**) is a Royal Air Force airfield located near Lakenheath in Suffolk, England. Although technically an RAF station, it primarily hosts United States Air Force units and personnel. The host wing is the **48th Fighter Wing** (48 FW), also known as the Liberty Wing, assigned to United States Air Forces in Europe (USAFE).

Contents

48th Fighter Wing

The 48th Fighter Wing at RAF Lakenheath is also designated the Air Force's **Statue of Liberty Wing,** and is the only USAF wing with both a numerical designation and an official name. Since its activation at Chaumont-Semoutiers Air Base, France on 10 July 1952 the Liberty Wing has been one of the premier fighter wings of the United States Air Forces in Europe, spending its over 50-year existence as part of USAFE. The 48 FW has nearly 5,700 active-duty military members, 2,000 British and U.S. civilians, and includes a geographically separated unit (GSU) at nearby RAF Feltwell.

Tactical squadrons of the 48th Operations Group are:

- 492d Fighter Squadron (F-15E)
- 493d Fighter Squadron (F-15C/D)
- 494th Fighter Squadron (F-15E)

Royal Air Force Station Lakenheath

Part of United States Air Forces in Europe (USAFE)
Located near Lakenheath, Suffolk, England

F-15E Strike Eagles of the 48th Fighter, Statue of Liberty Wing

Type	Air Force Base
Built	1941
In use	1941-1944,1947-Present
Current owner	Ministry of Defence (United Kingdom)
Controlled by	Royal Air Force United States Air Force
Garrison	Royal Air Force (1941-1948) Strategic Air Command (1951-1959) United States Air Forces In Europe (1948-1951, 1959-Present)
Battles/wars	European Theatre of World War II (RAF)

115

Home   News   Photos   Art   Library   Units   Questions   Join

Royal Air Force Mildenhall

The U.S. Air Force activated the 100th Air Refueling Wing, host wing at RAF Mildenhall, England, Feb. 1, 1992. Since its reactivation, the 100th ARW has served as the lone air refueling wing for U.S. Air Forces in Europe. The diverse mission of **aerial refueling, special operations, air mobility, reconnaissance** and **intelligence** makes RAF Mildenhall a unique U.S. Air Force base. This public site is the number one source for news about the people and mission at RAF Mildenhall. Its content is viewable from any computer worldwide.

RAF Mildenhall News

RAF Mildenhall runners participate in cross country regionals
Servicemembers and their families from all over Europe compete in a 5K run during the "United ...ates Air Force Europe Cross Country Regional's Oct. 18, 2008 in Brandon, England. The 100th Services Squadron held the event to promote fitness and camaraderie and gave qualifying runners the opportunity to participate in the finals held in Poland. (U.S. Air Force photo by Staff Sgt. Jerry Fleshman)

Against the odds: A story of courage, determination and two tiny babies
RAF MILDENHALL, England — They shouldn't be here yet. They were supposed to be a New Year's present for their parents.

Up in arms - security forces armorers keep weapons functioning, secure
Senior Airman Johnnie Waste, a 100th Security Forces Squadron armorer, clears an M4 assault rifle before storing it at the armory at RAF Mildenhall, England, Oct. ... .08. All military members who own firearms are ...uired to keep them stored at the armory. Additionally they issue and deploy government weapons to military members whose job requires them, also performing routine inspections and basic maintenance. (U.S. Air Force photo by Staff Sgt. Jerry Fleshman)

Five minutes with former Creed singer Scott Stapp
RAF MILDENHALL, England — Scott Stapp, the voice of the band Creed, performed a concert on RAF Mildenhall Oct. 16 as part of an ongoing Armed Forces and Navy Entertainment tour.

Red Ribbon Week events announced
RAF MILDENHALL, England — National Red Ribbon Observance on RAF Mildenhall and RAF Lakenheath is Oct. 23 to 29. Red Ribbon Week is dedicated to raising awareness of drug use, abuse and addiction.

Driving/Fuel Permit becomes mandatory Nov. 1
RAF MILDENHALL, England — As of Nov. 1, RAF Mildenhall drivers must have the new Driving/Fuel

Hot topic

Video

More Videos...

Commander's Access Online

Click it or ticket

Seatbelts are mandatory on RAF Mildenhall. Violators will be ticketed and could lose their driving privileges.

CLICK IT OR TICKET

Latest Videos

THE AZORES

Leaving England for the Portuguese Azores was greeted with some apprehension for I would now have to start all over with housing, learn a new organization, maintain many new airplanes that I had no experience on and acclimate to a new base culture. But on the other hand, I was excited and welcomed the new adventure, for this was why I joined the Air Force in 1952, to see the world – all of it if I could.

After leaving Heathrow and spending a day in beautiful Lisbon, I landed in Santa Maria, Azores aboard the KLM Airliner headed for Rio de Janeiro. I arrived just ahead of an impending hurricane bearing down on the island, and the airliner was just able to refuel and get out before the airport closed down.

Now Santa Maria is just a little speck of an island that was valuable mostly as a refueling stop for civilian and military aircraft. It had a relatively long runway, a small airport, a small hotel and treated everyone like a king, including me, a relatively speaking nobody Staff Sergeant in the U.S. Air Force. I would remain here for a week waiting for the hurricane to pass and it was one of the most pleasant and exciting periods of my life.

First off, I hit it good with the Portuguese in general and the hotel staff in particular for they were very kind and somewhat extraordinarily interested in me. The Air Force was paying the bill, so I was given every amenity and fantastic service. The only bad thing about the hotel was that it had no snack bar to get a cheeseburger or hotdog. Every meal was formal, two and three course service with a formal waiter, and I got so tired of that; but at least the food was good, lots of fish.

But the almost unbelievable part of this episode was the annual island basketball tournament. This tournament had been held annually for years and was the yearly social event. There were only four teams on the island and the hotel had never won the tournament. After a couple days, the hotel manager asked me if I could play for his team. I, of course, said yes because I loved the game and was pretty good, but too short to make any top notch American team including my high school of Washington High in London, West Virginia. Of course then, I was only 15 years old, even as a senior, but now I was 25 years old and much taller, but still only 5 foot 10 inches. However, I matched up well with my Portuguese opponents who played tough, foul-prone European style basketball which was almost as rough as football. But in this case, they didn't know that I was as tough as or tougher than they were, coming out of those mountains and coal fields of West Virginia. On top of my strong will and lack of fear, I could shoot long outside shots and make them, which the Portuguese in general could not. So, after getting knocked down several times inside close to the basket, I moved outside and rained down long two pointer and they couldn't stop me. I was so happy and proud to beat them. Our hotel team won two games and the tournament. What happened next is almost unbelievable even now 45 years later. I became an instant hero.

They carried me around on their shoulders and the spectators cheered and screamed like I was a Roman Conqueror. For the remainder of my stay there, I couldn't pay for anything. They showed me the entire island and celebrated until I left on the tiny almost pigmy small airplane for the Lajes Field in Teceria after the hurricane passed.

I knew about airplanes and when I saw it I was very reluctant to fly in it, even for a short hop to Lajes. As it turned out, I had good reason to doubt the plane's integrity, for we bounced around the sky like a rubber ball before we landed at Lajes where I kissed the ground. After getting settled into the base, I reported for duty in the Base Shop Hanger for repair of propellers and any aircraft that had propeller trouble.

After trouble shooting and repairing almost every airplane in the Air Force inventory, including mostly C-124, C-118, C-97 aircraft, plus many civilian types over several months, I finally got a chance to go off base and visit the towns and people. The Portuguese people were very friendly, poor and scared. They were scared of their dictator Salazar in Lisbon who ran a Stalin type iron control over the people with secret police, prisons and the like. Everyone was afraid that their neighbor or friend was a spy or collaborator and so no one trusted anyone. It was strange being in such and environment, yet the people were relatively happy and relaxed except about the police and government official who regularly carried submachine guns on their shoulder as they patrolled the towns and countryside.

The Portuguese were quite literal in their interpretation of English. If you told one to go somewhere in a car and not stop until they got there, they would run stop signs, stop lights, accidents or any other regular need to stop. They were also quite frugal. If you killed a chicken by accident, you would have to pay for the chicken and all they eggs it might lay in the future. The same for a cow, it would be the cow and the estimated future milk over the years.

Teceria is the largest of the seven island chain with San Miguel being a vacation island for them and of course Santa Maria was the small refueling island. Pria was the town just outside the town of Lajes AB and the large city of Angra de Herisimo was located across the island about ten miles away. I did a lot of sightseeing and visiting the restaurants, churches, bars, fishing piers and about everything else that could be seen there. I really liked the place, but wanted to get back to the states to my wife. It was the year 1960, the election year of President John F. Kennedy and I missed all of that. I regret not taking Portuguese and Spanish classes or learning to scuba dive while there, but I did try out for a lifeguard part-time job at the Officer's Club, but failed the test.

About the clubs, non-commissioned and commission officer, there were grand and cheap. The military allowed slot machine gambling at overseas bases at the time and the clubs were chest deep in money. They could just about provide all services free to the members. I remember some Airmen and many dependents playing the machines all day and lose their entire paycheck the Base Exchange was one of the best and the movie theater was first class.

But the wind, the wind constantly, blew hard and walking up and down the hills on base especially against the wind tired your legs out. Sometimes, the rain would come down and the wind would blow it back up before it hit the ground. It also rained constantly, my shoes in the barracks would grow mold in a week if I didn't change them out frequently. One day while working on a huge C-133 transport, a heavy rain came straight down the parking ramp and hit the side of the plane where I was working. This day I was lucky. I just walked to the other side of the wing where it was dry and waited out the rain.

There were a few Navy and Army personnel assigned to Lajes, but most people never met them because they were almost secret. The Navy folks were stationed across the runway from the airbase and conducted their quasi secret operation of hunting and killing Russian submarines in the Atlantic Ocean in the area. The Army was even scarcer, because they only had about seven soldiers in a transportation detachment on the beach that oversaw the off loading of ships by the Portuguese nationals. They had their own little mess hall, barracks, dayroom and other facilities. It was almost perfect duty, with only two or three ships docking per month. I spent one weekend there with a friend I met on base and wished I could have stayed there for the whole year I spent in Lajes.

The most exciting episode I experienced at this location was the time a huge intercontinental ballistic missile carrying C-133 aircraft landed and broke down with a missile in its belly. Being a key player in the cold war, this aircraft was monitored and controlled by the Pentagon.

After one day of intense troubleshooting by me and DOD civilian, it was determined that a feather – normal propeller switch had burned out deep under the cockpit that would not allow number 3 engine to operate. It was estimated that given the location of the malfunction that a special team from Kelly AFB, Texas would have to be the plane out of commission for about two weeks. I had so much confidence in myself that I told our maintenance officer Major Goodikuntz that I could wiggle down through the maze of cables and wires and replace the switch in a couple of hours. He believed me and put the Kelly people on hold. I did find and replaced the switch as promised, and the Major, the base and the Pentagon were very pleased, as was I . The plane took off with its missile and I received a $25 war bond and recognition as maintenance man of the month for my efforts. Needless to say that Major Goodikuntz and I had mutual respect and good will for each other for the rest of my tour. I returned to McGuire AFB and Trenton, NJ in 1961 via Bermuda and stayed there for five years until my first tour in Cam Ranh Bay, Vietnam in March 1966.

Azores

From Wikipedia, the free encyclopedia

The **Azores** (Portuguese: *Açores* pronounced [ɐ'soɾiʃ] or [ɐ'soɾʃ]) is a Portuguese archipelago in the Atlantic Ocean, about 1,500 km (950 mi) from Lisbon and about 3,900 km (2,400 mi) from the east coast of North America. The two westernmost Azorean islands (Flores and Corvo) actually lie on the North American plate and are only 1,925 km (1,200 mi) from St. John's in the Canadian province of Newfoundland and Labrador. The Azores' most significant industries are tourism, cattle raising for milk and meat, and fishing.

The nine major Azorean islands and the eight small Formigas extend for more than 600 km (373 mi) and lie in a northwest-southeast direction. The vast extent of the islands defines an immense exclusive economic zone of 1.1 million km². The westernmost point of this area is 3,380 km (2,100 mi) from the North American continent. All of the islands have volcanic origins, although Santa Maria also has some reef contribution. The mountain of Pico on Pico Island, at 2,351 m (7,713 ft) in altitude, is the highest in all of Portugal. The Azores are actually the tops of some of the tallest mountains on the planet, as measured from their base at the bottom of the ocean. The archipelago forms the **Autonomous Region of Azores**, one of the two autonomous regions of Portugal.

ACORES

A modern map of the islands.

Because these once

uninhabited, remote islands were settled sporadically over a span of two centuries, their culture, dialect, cuisine and traditions vary considerably from island to island. Farming and fishing are key industries that support the Azorean economy.

Azores Autonomous Region *Região Autónoma dos Açores*	
Flag	Coat of arms

Motto: *"Antes morrer livres que em paz sujeitos"*(Portuguese)
("Rather die free than live subjugated") (English)

Anthem: *A Portuguesa* (national)
Hino dos Açores (local)

Capital	Ponta Delgada[1] Angra do Heroísmo[2] Horta[3]
Largest city	Ponta Delgada
Official languages	Portuguese
Ethnic groups	Portuguese
Government	Autonomous region
- President	Carlos César
Establishment	
- Settled	1439
- 2001 census	241,763
- Autonomy	1976
- Density	104/km² (n/a)
	266/sq mi
Area	
Currency	Euro (km²) (EUR)
	911 sq mi
Time zone	UTC-1
Population	

Geography

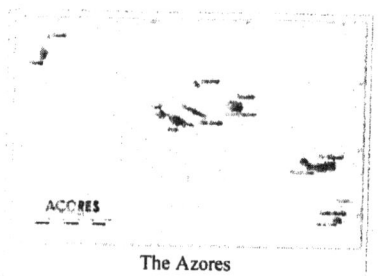

The Azores

Horta Faial.

The archipelago is spread out in the area of the parallel that passes between through Lisbon (39° 43' / 39° 55' N) and 37° N, giving it a tepid oceanic subtropical climate, with mild annual oscillation. The average annual rainfall increases from east to west and ranges from 700 to 1600 annual millimetres (27.6–63 in) on average, reaching 6,300 millimetres (250 in) in Mount Pico (the highest Portuguese mountain at 2,351 m/7,713 ft). The Azores High, an area of high atmospheric pressure, is named after the islands. The Formigas (the Portuguese word for "ants") islands (also known as Dollabarat Reefs) have rich maritime fauna, including exotic species such as the black coral and manta rays, sharks, and sea turtles. The archipelago lies in the Palearctic ecozone, forming a unique biome that includes the macaronesian subtropical laurissilva, with many endemic species of plants.

Island	Area	
São Miguel Island	759 km^2	293 sq mi
Pico Island	446 km^2	172 sq mi
Terceira Island	403 km^2	156 sq mi
São Jorge Island	246 km^2	95 sq mi
Faial Island	173 km^2	67 sq mi
Flores Island	143 km^2	55 sq mi
Santa Maria Island	97 km^2	37 sq mi
Graciosa Island	62 km^2	24 sq mi
Corvo Island	17 km^2	7 sq mi

The nine islands have a total area of 2,346 km^2 (906 sq mi). Their individual areas vary between São Miguel's 759 km^2 (293 sq mi) and Corvo's 17 km^2 (7 sq mi). Three islands (São Miguel, Pico and Terceira) are bigger in size than Malta (composed of three different islands), São Miguel Island alone being twice as big.

The nine islands are divided into three groups:

- The Eastern Group (*Grupo Oriental*) of São Miguel, Santa Maria and Formigas Islets
- The Central Group (*Grupo Central*) of Terceira, Graciosa, São Jorge, Pico and Faial
- The Western Group (*Grupo Ocidental*) of Flores and Corvo.

Geology

The islands are located atop an active triple junction between three large tectonic plates: the North American Plate, the Eurasian Plate and the African Plate. Volcanism associated with the formation of the islands arises from the fact that the Azores Triple Junction involves rifting, a process whereby the crust is spreading along three ridge legs radiating out from the triple junction.

Demographics

On 31 December 2002, the Azores' population was 238,767 at a density of 106 inhabitants per square kilometer (274.5/sq mi).

Island	Population (2002)	(% of total)	Main city/town	Municipalities
São Miguel Island	130,154	54.50	Ponta Delgada	6
Terceira Island	54,996	23.00	Angra do Heroísmo	2
Faial Island	14,934	6.25	Horta	1
Pico Island	14,579	6.11	Madalena	3
São Jorge Island	9,522	3.99	Velas	2
Santa Maria Island	5,490	2.30	Vila do Porto	1
Graciosa Island	4,708	1.97	Santa Cruz da Graciosa	1
Flores Island	3,949	1.65	Santa Cruz das Flores	2
Corvo Island	435	0.18	Vila do Corvo	1
Total	238,767		Total	19

Population

The vast majority of the inhabitants of the Azores are Portuguese, descendants of 15th century immigrants from Algarve (Southern Portugal) and from the Minho (Northern Portugal), with a minor Dutch admixture (particularly from Flanders).

Since the 17th century, many of them have emigrated, mainly to Brazil, the US and Canada.[3]

Traditional festivals from May through September Holy Ghost Festivals, or Espírito Santo Festivals, are very important to the Azorean people. The festivals are rooted in medieval traditions and typically held

Panoramic view near Sao Mateus, Terceira, June 2004

The Azores are divided into nineteen municipalities (*concelhos*); each municipality is further divided into parishes (*freguesias*). The Azores have a total of 156 parishes.

Boeing B-50 Superfortress

B-50 Superfortresses from Strategic Air Command deployed to Andersen Air Force Base, Guam, for 90-

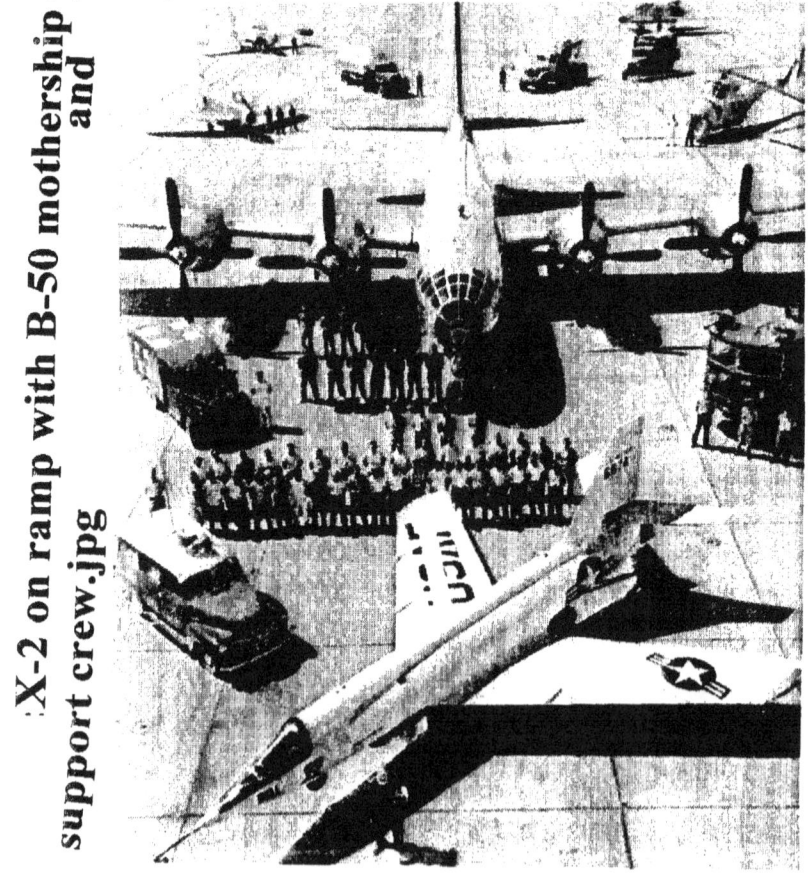

X-2 on ramp with B-50 mothership and support crew.jpg

Boeing B-52 Stratofortress

posted by Jiri Wagner

C-133 Cargomaster

Douglas C-124C *Globemaster* (Courtesy US Air Force Museum)

124

C-130 Hercules

The C-130 Hercules primarily performs the intratheater portion of the airlift mission. The aircraft is capable of operating from rough, dirt strips and is the prime transport for paradropping troops and equipment into hostile areas. Basic and specialized versions perform a diversity of roles, including airlift support, DEW Line and Arctic ice resupply, aeromedical missions, aerial spray missions, fire-fighting duties for the US Forest Service, and natural disaster relief missions. In recent years, they have been used to bring humanitarian relief to many countries, including Haiti, Bosnia, Somalia, and Rwanda.

Four decades have elapsed since the Air Force issued its original design specification, yet the remarkable C-130 remains in production. The turbo-prop, high-wing, versatile "Herc" has accumulated over 20 million flight hours. It is the preferred transport aircraft for many US Government services and over 60 foreign countries. The basic airframe has been modified to hundreds of different configurations to meet an ever-changing environment and mission requirement. The C-130 Hercules has unsurpassed versatility, performance, and mission effectiveness. Early C-130A, B, and D versions are now retired.

125

AC-130 Spectre/Spooky

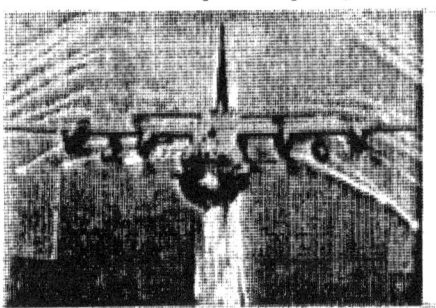

AC-130H Spectre gunship jettisons flares in 2007

C-130J Super Hercules

Views of the KC-130 operating from the Forrestal

KC-130 taking off from the Forrestal

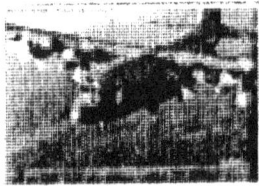

AC-130U Spooky

Gunners loading 40 mm cannon (background) and 105 mm howitzer (foreground)

RAF Hercules C.4 (C-130J-30) Kemble Airfield, Gloucestershire, England June 2004

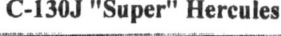

C-130J "Super" Hercules

A C-130J from the Air National Guard's 146th Airlift Wing at Channel Island ANG Base, California flies along the coast of Santa Cruz Island near California.

126

Model: C130 Hercules

GREMLIN

No. 9 Monday November 16, 1953

OF GRENIER AIR FORCE BASE

Home of 1610th Air Transport Group ATLD-MATS

FIRST 44TH CREW – The 44th ATS's first scheduled flight since going operational Nov. 1 was A-143 to Torbay, Nfld with Lt. Colonel Robert A. Wray, Jr., squadron Commander, as aircraft commander. Standing, at left, Capt. Jorgen Augustinburg, pilot; Col. Wray; and S/Sgt Earl Willis, radio operator instructor. In front, A/1c Albert Johnson, radio operator; T/Sgt Alfred Zeoli, engineer instructor; and A/1c William Hanson, engineer.

Greniers' 44th ATS Went Into Full Operation On Nov. 1 With Recent Arrival of Seven C-54s

There's a new member of the MATS team in full operation at Grenier.

The 44th Air Transport Squadron, Commanded by Lt. Colonel Robert A. Wray, Jr., became operational Nov. 1 with its first scheduled flight A-143 to Torbay, Nfld.

The 44th came into being April 20 this year at Grenier when Major Donald H. Kohl, present operations officer, and three airmen set up for business. Personnel began arriving from ATLD and other MATS bases during the early summer while both the present Commander and the first C-54-D aircraft arrived in July.

Paint brushes and hammers temporarily replaced wrenches and typewriters in the embryo 44th in July and August as rehabilitation of its buildings began. "We're working on the premise that efficiency of operation depends on a solid foundation," Col. Wray said.

It was smooth planning by the 44th to get their offices, shops and quarters in class A shape because when delivery began on their aircraft they literally "had their hands full."

There's plenty of MATS experience in the 44th's leadership. Col. Wray was commander of the Bermuda based 35th ATS and the 1610th Air Base Sq before taking the 44th reins. Major Kohl has more than 5,000 of his total of 7,000 hours flying time on MATS C-54s.

Under the supervision of experienced MATS NCOs the 44th's personnel from line mechanic to orderly room clerk are getting the right MATS training to deliver the goods as a full member of the MATS family.

The 44th's first trip to Argentia was flown Nov. 1 with Col. Wray as aircraft commander and Capt. Jorgen Augustinburg as pilot. The crew consisted of A/1c Albert A. Johnson, engineer, and A/1c Wildie Derrow as radio operator. T/Sgt Alfred Zeoli and S/Sgt Earl Willis were engineer and radio operator instructors, respectively. A/1c William Hanson was engineer on the return trip.

See 44TH ATS On Page 3

O'Seas Assignments In December

Grenier will get 25 to 30 overseas assignments in December M/Sgt Donald Dostie, 1610th ATG Personnel Sergeant Major, said today.

"We'll also lose a large number to the new units setting up at Dover AFB, Del., he said. "However, we're expecting nearly 50 replacements in December from overseas duty and tech school graduates", he pointed out.

Airmen desiring early release and meet all qualifications can still apply 'til Dec. 31

cial Hours Set For Turkey Eighteen Dish Feast 26th

renier's chefs are billing next Thursday Thanksgiving Day feast as the "dinner year". Their menu, topped by roast y, includes 18 delectable items.

nursday's special hours, M/Sgt Still Y. , Mess Supervisor said, will be 2 to 5 k for dinner and 7 until 9 o'clock for 'ast.

ersonnel planning to bring their family Consolidated Dining Hall or the Of- Club for Thanksgiving Dinner must heir reservations by 5 o'clock this Sgt Bailey said. Officers may call 9. while enlisted personnel can make eservations at Ext 477 or 563.

he charge will be one dollar plus a 20¢ e charge for officers, separated ra- enlisted personnel and civilians. Child- der twelve will be charged 50¢ plus a ervice charge. Enlisted personnel on te rations, but who are on duty Thurs- ill be charged the ususal 40¢.

ere's the menu for Thanksgiving Din- Thursday Nov. 26, 1953:

BX Toyland Opened Last Week

Grenier's Toyland opened on the second floor of the Base Exchange last week. Lt. Bennett Hardy, BX Officer, said the $9,000 assortment represents hundreds of items that were selected according to a formula devised to provide something for children of all ages at practically any price range.

The toyland hours will be the same as the BX sales store and will be open in the evenings in late December.

Dressing - Giblet Gravy - Cranberry Sauce - Mashed Potatoes - Buttered Peas - Corn O'- Brien - Waldorf Salad - Parker House Rolls - Butter - Pumpkin Pie with Whipped Cream - Fruit Cake - Assorted Candy - Mixed Nuts

VIETNAM I AND THE PHILLLIPINES

In March 1966, I was ordered to an assignment at Cam Ranh Bay, Vietnam. The flight there seemed to take forever, even in a 600 mile per hour jet aircraft. The leg from Hickam, Hawaii to Guam was the longest, about eight hours as I recall, then a short hop to the Philippines and then on to Saigon, where I stayed about a week before hitching a ride on a C-123 transport up country to Cam Ranh. Saigon was impossibly crowded with so much noise and cars and bicycles and about anything else that would move with a lawn mower engine for power. The people were friendly and the city was bustling so that one would not think that a war was going on. But, it was, of course, the North Vietnamese Army and the Viet Cong Guerrillas who were ever more bold and active, attacking many cities and American bases. I was part of a major troop build up that would eventually total over 500,000 with 58,000 being eventually killed. But before leaving Saigon, I ran into an old friend, Jesse "Doc" Payne from my Grenier experience. He was a little older than me and a really nice guy. A Staff Sergeant when I was a two striper. We met at the Tan Son hut NCO Club by accident and he was on his way back to America. How I envied him. Anyway, he introduced me to the drink called a Black Russian. We had a good time and I caught a C-123 up country the next morning to Cam Ranh Bay.

My job being in Aircraft Maintenance was to fix shot up airplanes and any other airplanes that had routine and sundry malfunctions. Airplanes are very fickle and fragile in some ways. The smallest unit or component can fail and ground the airplane. Some in flight failures can lead to fire and eventually crashes that may kill all on board from one to several hundred. Maintenance is a very precise, strict and diligent operation. The fear of making a mistake is a constant companion because the pilot and crew take your word and signed document that the aircraft is airworthy, and therefore, trust you. It is an awesome responsibility that always reminds you to be perfect in your job. On top of this, you never know which of the planes you fix will be the one you fly on to go somewhere. So one is also thinking about ones own safety in the air. I am proud to say that no plane ever crashed due to any failure or mistake on my part.

Cam Ranh Bay Air Base was a major logistics and transportation base, but it also had a fighter-bomber wing of F-4s that launched daily missions all over into Indo-China, especially North Vietnam. The sand was ubiquitous, everywhere sand, and walking in it constantly hurt your legs because you would sink into it and have to pull out at every step. But it was a relatively safe base located on the Cam Ranh peninsula on the South China Sea about two hundred miles north of Saigon. The base was constantly busy with war planes taking off and landing in addition to all kinds of transport and civilian planes bringing in supplies. I remember once we had to stop bombing for a couple of days because we ran out of bomb fins to attach to our bombs. It gave us a little break, but we got those fins delivered in a hurry. Another episode I remember was very silly and reflected some of the stupidity demonstrated in the war. In 1966, President Johnson and Defense Secretary McNamara visited the base flight line for a few hours for a morale booster pep talk. We had to empty all of the tattered old sandbags in our gun positions and check points and fill shiny new sandbags for the President to see. What a waste. Many of us saw first hand how ridiculous politics can be.

There were many fun moments though. We could go swimming in the sea when the security level was low enough. However, you had to fight jelly fish that were everywhere with their painful stings. Once I hitchhiked about 10 miles down the peninsula to the Navy area to go out into the bay to a seaplane tender to get some ice-cream. The Navy always had good food. The Army also had tons of frozen chicken, steak and beer on South Beach. They couldn't get liquor and we Air Force couldn't get food except for c-rations and regular meals. So we would make a weekly trip and trade dozens of bottles of cheap gin and vodka for dozens of cases of chicken and steak. Each of our twelve men tent-hooches had a cut in half 50 gallon oil drum for cooking outside, so there was generally a barbeque every week.

The most eventful episode I experienced was a 30-day TDY trip to Mactan Island in the Philippines to perform routine Aircraft maintenance. Mactan is a small island across the Vesaya Strait from Cebu, a much larger island. Mactan is where Ferdinand Magellan was killed on his 1519-1522 voyage around the world. The village of Lapu Lapu was the location and they were very proud of Magellan's defeat, exhibiting many paintings and sporting Magellan's name on almost everything. Even the expensive hotel in Cebu City was named Magellan.

I did enjoy the south sea paradise, but had some grief from a cracker white supervisor who tried to throw his rank around and order me to do work that I wasn't supposed to do. I was a technical sergeant at the time and he was a Master Sergeant. But I got through it okay. I liked to ride the ferry from Mactan to Cebu, but it was so old and crowded, I expected it to sink some day. When you missed it, you could hire a small canoe taxi called a Banka for the three-mile journey.

After returning from the Philippines, the remainder of the tour was mundane with the daily cold showers from a raised airplane gas tank, the long walk to the flight line and the exciting work on airplanes on the ramp. Everything about the Air Force was fun to me. I would have done my time without pay if I didn't need to support my family.

During my tour of Cam Ranh, the major achievement was probably helping to build a new base on West Cam Ranh Air Base with concrete runways and ramps, infrastructure housing, etc. I actually didn't build it; it was constructed by civilian contractor RMK, who built most all civilian works contracted by the government. The Air Force construction engineers or Red Horse assigned to Cam Ranh did most of the military construction under enemy fire when necessary.

My day finally arrive to leave for home a Freedom Bird-Pan Am jetliner in March 1967. I was reassigned to the Tactical Air Command base at Langley Air Force Base, Virginia in Hampton, Virginia. I would spend the next four years at Langley until I returned to Vietnam in Saigon.

Cam Ranh Bay AB

Cam Ranh Bay AB — view from the east.

Location of Cam Ranh Bay in southern Vietnam

Refueling

F-4 Phantom II

©Jerry Stephan 2002

F-4E from 347th TFW dropping 500 lb (230 kg) Mark 82 bombs

Role	Fighter-bomber
National origin	United States
Manufacturer	McDonnell Aircraft/ McDonnell Douglas
First flight	27 May 1958
Introduction	30 December 1960
Status	744 active in non-US service, and as drones, as of 2001
Primary users	United States Air Force United States Navy United States Marine Corps
Produced	1958–1981
Number built	5,195
Unit cost	US$2.4 million when new (F-4E)

F-4M Phantom in flight

USAF F-4E

USAF F-4E Phantom and F-5 Tiger

German F-4F

Philippines"

From Wikipedia, the free encyclopedia

Republic of the Philippines **Republika ng Pilipinas**	
Flag	
Motto: "Maka-Diyos, Maka-Tao, Makakalikasan, at Makabansa" English: "For God, People, Nature, and Country" [1]	
Anthem: "Lupang Hinirang" (English: "Chosen Land")	

Capital	Manila 14°35′N 121°0′E (http://stable.toolserver.org/geohack/geohack.php?pagename=Philippines&par
Largest city	Quezon City
Official languages	Filipino, and English
Recognised regional languages	Tagalog, Bikol, Cebuano, Ilocano, Hiligaynon, Kapampangan, Pangasinan, and Waray-W
National language	Filipino
Ethnic groups	Aeta · Ati · Bajau · Bicolano · Ibanag · Igorot · Ilocano · Ivatan · Kapampangan · Lumad · Pangasinan· Sambal · Tagalog · Visayans · Chinese · European · Spanish · Mestizo · Chab.
Demonym	Filipino, Pinoy, Philippine
Government	Unitary presidential constitutional republic
- President - Self-government	Gloria Macapagal-Arroyo March 24, 1934
- Vice President - Independence recognized	Noli De Castro July 4, 1946
Independence - Current constitution - Established	from Spain February 2, 1987 from United States 1565
Area	

The **Philippines** (Filipino: Pilipinas, officially known as the **Republic of the Philippines**, Filipino: Republika ng Pilipinas), is an Island country located in Southeast Asia with Manila as its capital city. The Philippines comprises 7,107 islands in the western Pacific Ocean, sharing maritime borders with Indonesia, Malaysia, Palau, the Republic of China (Taiwan), and Vietnam. The Philippines is the world's 12th most populous country with a population of 90 million people.[4][6] Its national economy is the 46th largest in the world with an estimated 2008 gross domestic product (GDP) of over US$154.073 billion.[6] There are more than 11 million overseas Filipinos worldwide, about 11% of the total population of the Philippines. It is a multi-ethnic country. Ecologically, The Philippines is considered to be among 17 of the most megadiverse countries in the world.[8]

Prior to the arrival of Europeans in 1521,[9] the Philippines was already settled by Austronesian (Malayo Polynesian) peoples. The Philippines became a Spanish colony in the 16th century, and a territory of the United States at the beginning of the 20th century. In 1896, rebellion led the Philippine Revolution that won independence from Spain. American occupation of the Philippines during the Spanish-American War led to the outbreak of the Philippine-American War. A Commonwealth government was established in 1935, which allowed self-governance. The country gained its independence from the United States on July 4, 1946 after World War II. Martial law was declared in 1972 which led to the insurgencies of the New People's Army and the Moro National Liberation Front. Liberal parties then led People Power Revolution of 1986, which would bring the country back to democracy.[3]

The Philippines is one of only two predominantly Roman Catholic countries in Asia-Pacific, the other being East Timor. Pre-Hispanic indigenous rituals still exist; and there are also followers of Islam.[10] Spanish was an official language of the Philippines until 1973. Since then, the two official languages are Filipino, and English.[3]

The name Philippines was derived from King Philip II of Spain in the 16th century. The Spanish explorer Ruy López de Villalobos used the name Las Islas Filipinas (The Philippine Islands) in honor of the then Crown Prince during his expedition to the Philippines, originally referring to the islands of Leyte and Samar. Despite the presence of other names, the name Filipinas (Philippines) was eventually adopted as the name of the entire archipelago

The Chocolate Hills in Bohol

Mayon Volcano, the most active volcano in the Philippines.

The Philippines constitutes an archipelago of 7,107 islands with a total land area of approximately 300,000 square kilometers (116,000 sq mi). It generally lies

The limestone islands of El Nido, Palawan

between 116° 40' and 126° 34' E. longitude, and 4° 40' and 21° 10' N. latitude, and borders the Philippine Sea on the east, the South China Sea on the west, and the Celebes Sea on the south. The island of Borneo lies a few hundred kilometers southwest and Taiwan directly north. The Moluccas and Sulawesi are to the south/southwest, and Palau is to the east beyond the Philippine Sea.[2]

Cebu

(toolserver.org/geohack/geohack.php?pagename=Cebu&params=10_25_35_N_123_47_53_E_region:PH_type:isle)

Cebu is one of the provinces of the Philippines. It lies to the east of Negros Island; to the west of Leyte and to the southeast is Bohol province. It is flanked on both sides by the straits of Bohol (between Cebu and Bohol) and Tañon (between Cebu and Negros). Cebu is located between 9°25'N and 11°15'N latitude and between 123°13'E and 124°5'E longitude in the center of the archipelago.

Cebu Island is a long narrow island stretching 225 km (140 mi) from north to south, surrounded by 167 neighboring smaller islands, that includes Mactan Island, Bantayan, Malapascua, Olango and the Camotes Islands. Of the hundreds of small islands some are uninhabited which make them the targets of adventure-seeking tourists.

Cebu is known for its narrow coastlines, limestone plateaus, and coastal plains, all characteristics of a typical tropical island. Cebu also has predominant rolling hills and rugged mountain ranges traversing the northern and southern lengths of the island. Cebu's steep mountains reach over 1,000 meters. Flat tracts of land can be found in the city of Bogo and in the towns of San Remigio, Medellin, and Daanbantayan at the northern tip of the province.

Its capital is **Cebu City**, the oldest city in the country, which forms part of the **Cebu Metropolitan Area** together with 6 neighboring cities Carcar City, Danao City, Lapu-Lapu City, Mandaue City, Naga City, Bogo, and Talisay City and 6 other municipalities. Cebu is served by Mactan-Cebu International Airport in Mactan Island, thirty minutes drive from downtown Cebu City.

Cebu is one of the most developed provinces in the country and the main center of commerce, trade, education and industry in the central and southern parts of the archipelago. It has five-star hotels, casinos, white sand beaches, world-class golf courses, convention centers, and shopping malls.

Province of Cebu

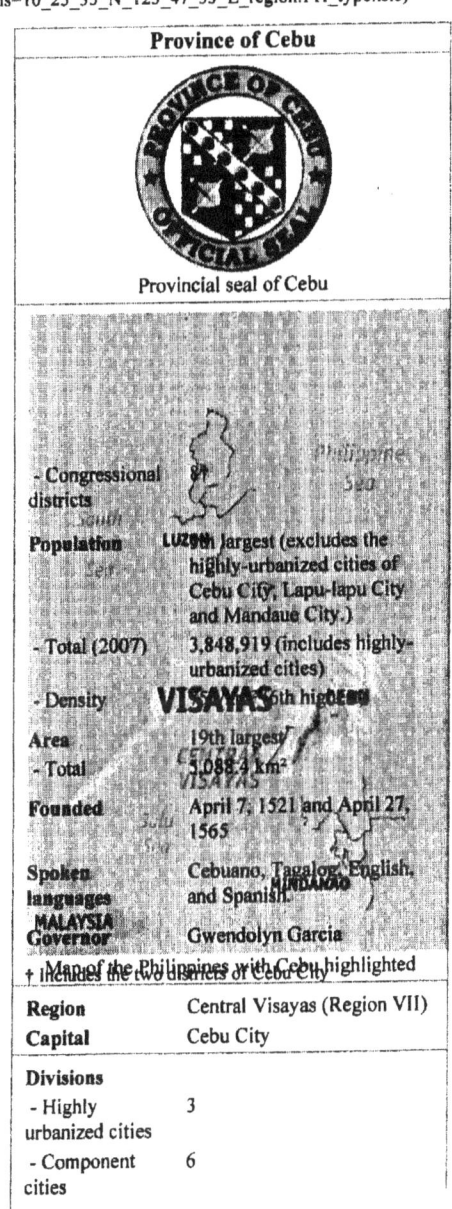

Provincial seal of Cebu

- Congressional districts	8
Population	10th largest (excludes the highly-urbanized cities of Cebu City, Lapu-lapu City and Mandaue City.)
- Total (2007)	3,848,919 (includes highly-urbanized cities)
- Density	6th highest
Area	19th largest
- Total	5,088.4 km²
Founded	April 7, 1521 and April 27, 1565
Spoken languages	Cebuano, Tagalog, English, and Spanish.
Governor	Gwendolyn Garcia

† Map of the Philippines with Cebu highlighted

Region	Central Visayas (Region VII)
Capital	Cebu City
Divisions	
- Highly urbanized cities	3
- Component cities	6

History

Before the arrival of the Spaniards, Cebu then known as Zubu (or *Sugbo*) was a trading post, with trade routes to Borneo, Indonesia, China and Arabia.

The Magellan Expedition

Losing favor for his plan of reaching the Spice Islands by sailing westward from King Manuel I of Portugal, Portuguese maritime explorer Ferdinand Magellan offered his services to the Holy Roman Emperor, Charles V of Spain. On September 20, 1519, Magellan led a flotilla of five ships with a crew of 250 out of the Spanish port of San Lucar de Barrameda enroute to the Spice Islands via the Americas and Pacific Ocean.

They reached the Philippine Archipelago on March 16, 1521. Rajah Kolambu of Mazzaua in Mindanao told them to head for Cebu, where they could trade and have provisions.

One of Magellan's ships circumnavigated the globe, finishing 16 months after the explorer's death.

Pigafetta's ilustrations of Cebuanos during the expedition.

Arriving in Cebu City, Magellan, with Enrique of Malacca as translator, befriended Rajah Humabon of Cebu and persuaded the Raja of allegiance to Emperor Charles V of Spain. Later Raja Humabon and his wife were baptized as King Carlos and Queen Juana. The Santo Niño was presented to Cebu's Queen as a symbol of peace between the Spaniards and the Cebuanos. On April 14, Magellan erected a large wooden cross on the shores of Cebu. Afterwards, some 800 native Cebuanos were baptized.

Hoping to make the new Christian King Carlos (Humabon) supreme in the region, Magellan be-friended Humabon and alliances developed between the two people. Magellan soon heard of a tribal ruler named, Rajah Lapu-Lapu, in nearby Mactan Island. It was thought that Rajah Humabon and Lapu-Lapu have been fighting for control of the flourishing trade in the area.

On April 27, the historic Battle of Mactan occurred where Magellan

was killed and his men were driven off the island by the natives of Mactan. According to historian and chronicler, Antonio Pigafetta, Magellan's body was never recovered despite efforts to trade for it with spice and jewels.

Magellan's second-in-command, Juan Sebastián Elcano took his place and sailed the remainder of the fleet back to Spain, circumnavigating the world.

The Spanish conquest and colonial period

Survivors of the Magellan Expedition brought tales of a savage island in the Orient with them when they returned to Spain. Consequently, several follow-up expeditions were sent but all ended in failure.

Forty-four years after Magellan first set foot in Cebu, in 1565, conquistador Miguel López de Legazpi and his 500 armed soldiers together with several Augustinian and Franciscan friars arrived and declared that the Spanish crown succeeded in colonizing the islands. López de Legazpi and his men then marched through Zugbo and bombarded the palisades of chieftain Rajah Tupas and destroyed the village. He and his men, later rebuilt it and called it *Villa del Santissimo Nombre de Jesús* (Village of the Most Holy Name of Jesus). Thus, in 1569, it became the first Spanish settlement established by the Spanish Cortés in the Philippines.

On August 14, 1571, Cebu (*Villa del Santissimo Nombre de Jesús*) became a Diocese. Legazpi departed for Manila in 1571, and employed garrisons, a governor and half of his soldiers in Cebu.

In 1860, Cebu opened its ports to foreign trade (Mojares xiv). The first printing house ("Imprenta de Escondrillas y Cia") was established in 1873. In 1880, Colegio de la Inmaculada Concepcion was established. The first periodical ("El Boletin de Cebu") started publishing in 1886.

> *See also: Manila galleon*

On June 12, 1898 marked the end of the Spanish era and the onset of the American regime. In 1901, Cebu became a municipality and on February 24, 1937 became a chartered city.

World War II

Cebu, being the most densely populated island in the country, served as a vital Japanese base during the Japanese occupation in World War II which began with the landing of the Japanese Imperial Army in April 1942. Almost three years later in March 1945, the Filipino and American forces landed and reoccupied the city.

Cebuano guerrillas led by an American, James Cushing, is credited for the capture of the Koga Papers which is said to have changed the American plans to retake the Philippines from the Japanese in 1944, by helping United States & the Philippine Commonwealth troops entered in Cebu in 1945.

137

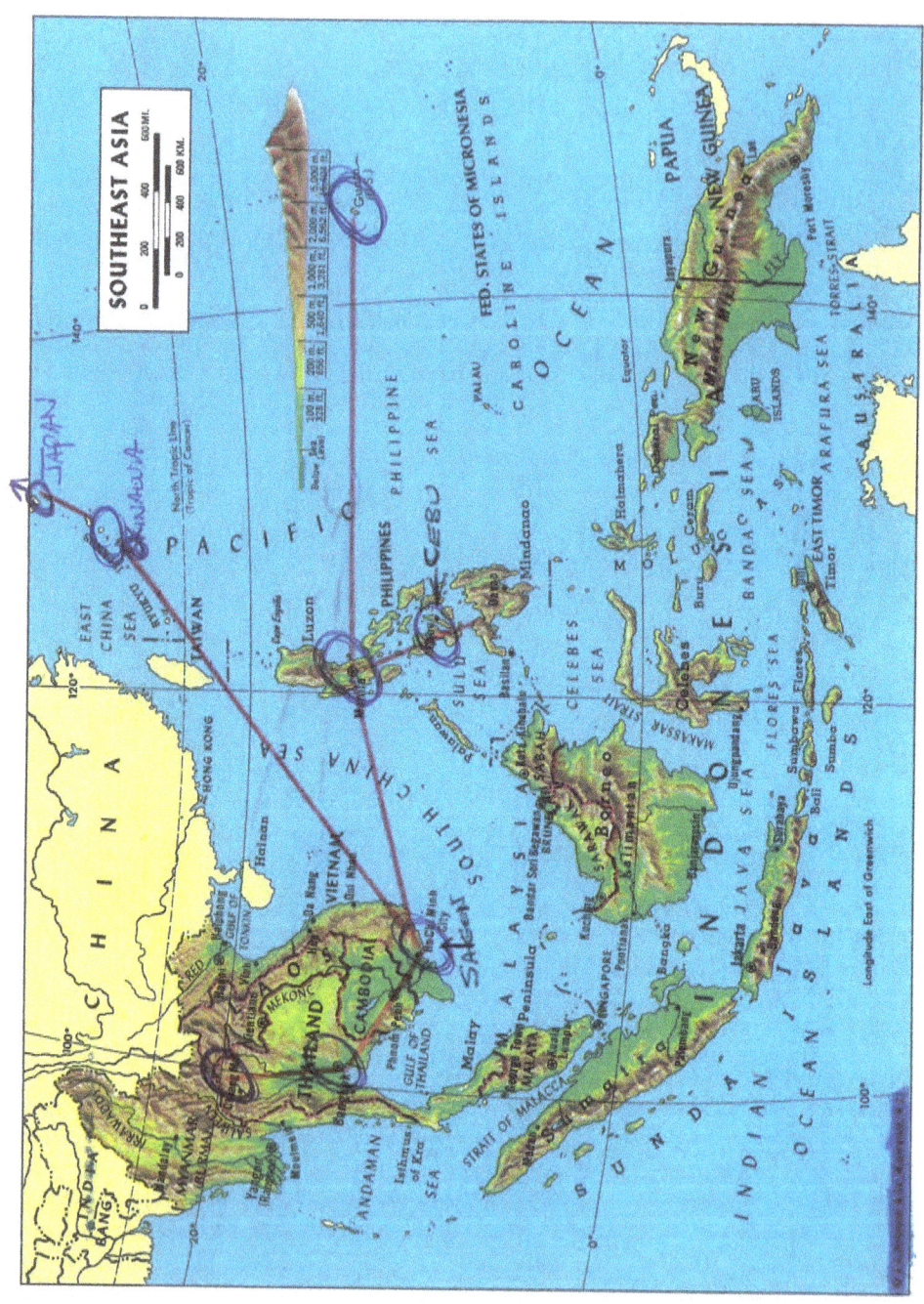

139

VIETNAM

50 REGISTER
5 P
20 CENTES
US

PHILIPPINES

1 PESO
5 CENTS
US

THAILAND

10 BAHT
50 CENTS US

SOUTH
VIET
NAM

20 P - PIASTRE
SVN
10 CENTS US

THE PUEBLO, TET, VIETNAM 1 ½ AND LANGELY

Langley Air Force Base was a great assignment and not very far from my parent's home in Ward, West Virginia, which Mildred and I visited often. We operated three squadrons of C-130 Turbo Prop Aircraft for normal duties and one squadron of C-130 Blackbirds for secret missions.

After an uneventful four months at Langley, I received orders for a 30-day temporary duty assignment for a NATO operation in Greece, called "Sunshine Express". After refueling in the Azores and Madrid, Spain, our squadron of eighteen, C-130 arrived in Athens, Greece for deployment. It was September and very hot. We were quartered at a resort hotel on Vula Beach on the Agean Sea about five miles from downtown Athens. I was awed by the Greek Architecture and historical buildings and temples. The Acropolis on a hill in downtown with the partially destroyed temple and outdoor theaters was very beautiful and almost sacred. Thousands of people paid to come there and visit on a daily basis, and I got to see it free, compliments of Uncle Sam. It was against the law to pick up and take even a small stone or pebble for a souvenir. I was surprised by the Greek countryside, with no trees anywhere, even on the mountains. I was told that the trees had long ago been stripped for wood to heat and build ships in the ancient days.

After a few leisure days on the beach, we saddled up and flew up to Thessalonika to deliver Spanish troops on a NATO exercise. Our planes parked on the ramp at the International Airport and we camped out in the mountains in tents at a Greek base already occupied by British Army troops. The British really know how to live outdoors. Their tents were fixed up like small apartments and they were so casual about everything. I visited the churches in Thessalonika, saw the Roman Hadrian Wall, and saw many communist troops visiting from nearby Macedonia for the World Trade Fair going on at the time. All in all, this was very exciting. One night, we had to change an engine on one of our planes and we were able to move about in the airport in our fatigue work uniforms with no problem. Everywhere we went people were friendly and happy to be with Americans.

The thirty days went fast and we were out of there and back to Langley after a stop in the Azores where our plane broke down, but with all the mechanics on board, it didn't take long to get the plane airworthy. After returning to Langley and being promoted to Master Sergeant, our squadron was ordered to Tackikaw, Japan to support a possible war with North Korea after they took our Navy ship "Peublo" on the high seas.

The North Koreans challenged the unarmed Pueblo with several gun ships and threatened to sink her. The Pueblo Captain Bucher ordered his men to destroy as much classified equipment and information as possible and surrendered the ship to North Korea to preserve the lives of his crew of sixty-eight. The ship was towed to Wonsan Harbor and Bucher and the crew were imprisoned. Needless to say, the White House and Pentagon moved to a war footing and sent everything, but the kitchen sinks to Japan for a possible massive strike on North Korea unless she returned our men and the ship.

Being in TAC or Tactical Air Command, my unit was automatically called upon to support this possible war situation. It was said of TAC, "that if the world sneezes, TAC will be there to wipe its nose". So our entire wing of C-130s went to North Carolina and loaded up and flew the 4th TAC Fighter Wings troops and equipment to Tackikawa Air Force Base in Japan outside Tokyo.

After arriving in Japan and quartered in Yomato, Japanese Auxiliary Base, we set up to deliver equipment to South Korea in case of war with the North. After a month or so of diplomatic activity, the North Koreans released our men, but kept the ship. However, in the meantime, the North Vietnamese had decided to sharply increase their attacks on South Vietnamese cities in what was called the New Year TET offensive. The war heated up tremendously which required more men and equipment from America. Since my unit was already half way to Vietnam and no longer needed in Japan, we were sent to South Vietnam to support our response to TET. We were all disappointed because most of our troops wanted to go back home, especially me, for I had just left Vietnam about ten months earlier.

So there I was, right back in the hot rainy monsoon weather in Vietnam. This time, it was Nha Trang near Cam Ranh Bay, but we regularly flew back to Tackikawa, which wasn't too bad. Being aVeteran of Vietnam, I helped our administrators in the orderly room manage their activities so far from Langley. I remember our First Sergeant who was a good guy, but afraid to fly, especially in Vietnam, wanted to get down there to qualify for combat pay and tax exemption. I convinced him it was okay, and after he went back to Japan in one piece, I was one of his favorite people.

On a mission from Cam Ranh Bay to Tachikawa, Japan, the C-130 was flying on tangled with a terrible typhoon late one night in June 1968. Winds were so powerful that our aircraft was buffeted and shaken like a rag doll. I was really scared for I thought that we would crash into the Pacific and never be heard from again. Somehow that Cadillac of an airplane together with its very skilled pilot survived some system failures and got us to Japan in one piece. I was 33 years old and it was the first time I had knowingly faced death and it disturbed me. After that, I stopped volunteering for dangerous missions and cut my flying down to a minimum.

After returning to Langley via Alaska, I was promoted to Senior Master Sergeant and eventually ordered back to Vietnam, Tan Sahn Knut AB, Saigon in 1970. On this next trip to Vietnam, I would have much better living conditions and ironically earn the Bronze Star Medal for participation in the LAOS Lamson 719 Invasion of LAOS by the South Vietnamese Army.

142

USS PUEBLO (AGER-2)

Official Navy Photograph
Provided by Steve Woelk

The USS PUEBLO was a U. S. Navy vessel sent on an intelligence mission off the coast of North Korea. On January 23, 1968, the USS PUEBLO was attacked by North Korean naval vessels and MiG jets. One man was killed and several were wounded. The Eighty-two surviving crew members were captured and held prisoner for 11 months.

143

USS *Pueblo* (AGER-2, originally AKL-44), 1967-____

USS *Pueblo*, an 850-ton environmental research ship, was built at Kewaunee, Wisconsin, in 1944 as the the U.S. Army cargo ship *FP-344*. She was transferred to the Navy in April 1966 and renamed *Pueblo*. Initially designated a light cargo ship (AKL-44), she soon began conversion to a research ship and was redesignated AGER-2 shortly before commissioning in May 1967. Following training operations off the U.S. west coast, in November 1967 *Pueblo* departed for the Far East to undertake electronic intelligence collection and other duties.

On 23 January 1968, while off Wonsan, North Korea, *Pueblo* was attacked by local forces and seized. One crewmember was killed in the assault and the other eighty-two men on board were taken prisoner. The North Koreans contended that the ship had violated their territorial waters, a claim vigorously denied by the United States. After eleven months in captivity, often under inhumane conditions, *Pueblo*'s crew were repatriated on 23 December 1968. The ship was retained by North Korea, though she is still the property of the U.S. Navy. She was exhibited at Wonsan and Hungham for three decades and is now a museum at Pyongyang, the North Korean capital city.

144

Tokyo

Tokyo (東京 *Tōkyō?*), officially **Tokyo Metropolis** (東京都 *Tōkyō-to?*),[1] is one of the 47 prefectures of Japan and located on the eastern side of the main island Honshū. The twenty-three special wards of Tokyo, each governed as a city, cover the area that was once the city of Tokyo in the eastern part of the prefecture, and total over 8 million people. The population of the prefecture exceeds 12 million.

Tokyo is the seat of the Japanese government and the Imperial Palace, and the home of the Japanese Imperial Family.

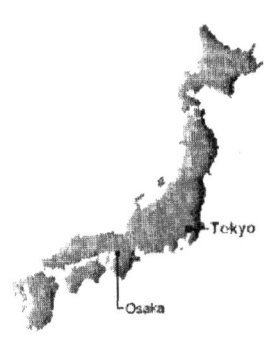

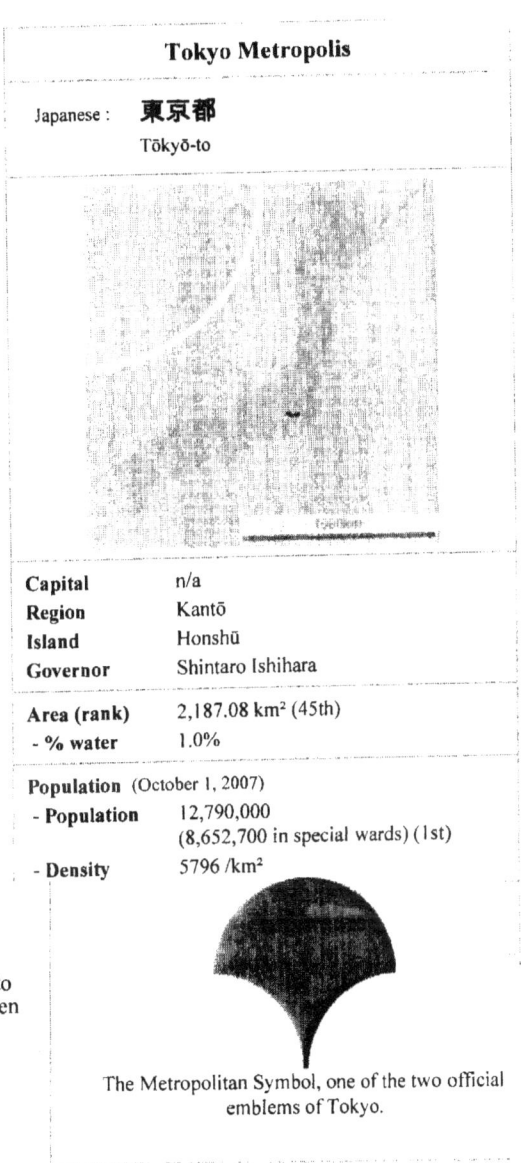

Tokyo Metropolis	
Japanese :	**東京都** Tōkyō-to
Capital	n/a
Region	Kantō
Island	Honshū
Governor	Shintaro Ishihara
Area (rank)	2,187.08 km² (45th)
- % water	1.0%
Population (October 1, 2007)	
- Population	12,790,000 (8,652,700 in special wards) (1st)
- Density	5796 /km²

The Metropolitan Symbol, one of the two official emblems of Tokyo.

Tokyo was originally known as Edo, meaning estuary.[2] Its name was changed to Tokyo (*Tōkyō: tō* (east) + *kyō* (capital)) when it became the imperial capital in 1868.[2] During the early Meiji period, the city was also called "Tōkei", an alternative pronunciation for the same Chinese characters representing "Tokyo". Some surviving official English documents use the spelling "Tokei".[3] This pronunciation is now obsolete.[4]

Panoramic view of Tokyo Imperial Palace as seen from Marunouchi.

Sakura in Tokyo Imperial Palace.

Rainbow Bridge and Tokyo Tower

Tokyo is Japan's capital and the country's largest city.

Tokyo is also one of Japan's 47 prefectures, but is called a metropolis (
than a prefecture (ken). The metropolis of Tokyo consists of 23 city war
cities, 5 towns and 8 villages, including the Izu and Ogasawara Islands
small Pacific Islands in the south of Japan's main island Honshu.

The 23 city wards (ku) are the center of Tokyo and make up about one
metropolis' area, while housing roughly eight of Tokyo's approximately
million residents.

Prior to 1868, Tokyo was known as Edo. A small castle town in the 16t
Edo became Japan's political center in 1603 when Tokugawa Ieyasu e
his feudal government there. A few decades later, Edo had grown into
world's most populous cities.

VIET NAM HELMET + MEDALS

AF MESS DRESS UNIFORM

WORLD TRAVEL

VIETNAM AUTHOR - TENT
CAM RAN BAY 1966

1966 AUTHOR RVN
TENT - M - ILE

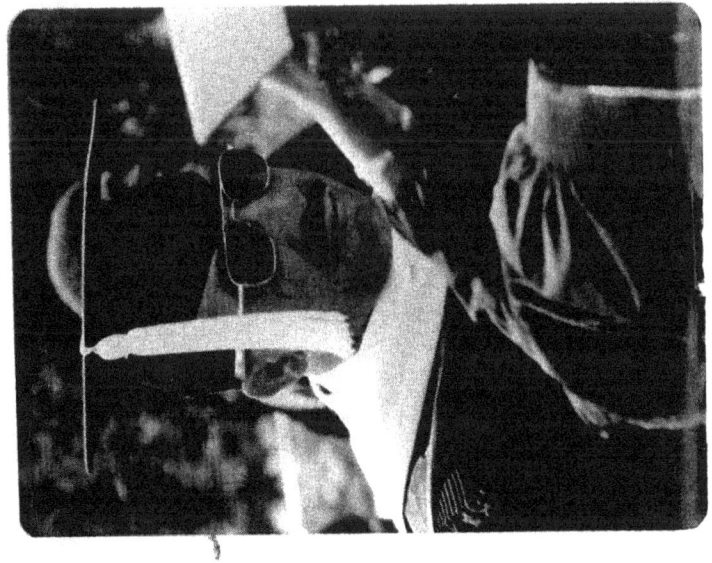

SHAW GRADUATION
1970's

VIETNAM II

In August 1970, I was reassigned to my second full Vietnam tour at Tan Son Nhut AB outside Saigon. The base was combined with the Saigon International Airport and was headquarters for the Vietnamese Air Force and 7th Air Force U.S. Operations. The long 13,000 Mile flight to Saigon was very boring and tiring as usual, with stops in San Francisco, Honolulu, Guam, Manila and finally Tan San Nhut. This was my third trip to Southeast Asia in four years with one more to Thailand in 1973. The living conditions at Tan Son Nhut were much more like normal living than in the sand dunes and jungles in the country of Vietnam. I had running water and regular toilets in a barracks near the NCO Club and the access to the commissary in Cholon, the Chinese section of Saigon, to buy regular food, which could be cooked in the small kitchen in the barracks. Because of my high rank of Senior Master Sergeant, I lucked up and got assigned to this billet. I was however, the only Black among all the 25 or so troops living there. This was no real problem, but I could detect some subtle racism from some of the White Boys. They were obviously racist towards the Vietnamese Police in their white shirts and hats trying to direct traffic in the mess. These police were affectionately called White Mice.

Though chaotic and dangerous, going to downtown Saigon was fun with so much to see. The docks, clubs, sports, topless women in the bars, music and constant movement were exciting. The kids were very curious and clever. They would mark up your boots with chalk while you walked and then offer you a shoe shine for 50 Piaster, about 5 cents. Anytime you drove a military vehicle to Cholon or other places that required parking, you had to hire them to watch your vehicle. If you didn't, then your tires would be missing when you came back. Another popular place to visit was the Soul Alley, a small neighborhood off Plantation Road in West Saigon. This was the only place that one could get corn bread, pinto beans and soul food in general. It was essentially isolated to most people and almost occupied by soldiers who were AWOL or otherwise running from the police. If you were respectful, they would not harm another regular G.I. but you had to do the "dap" when they approached you. The "dap" was touching your fist against the other guy's fist in a sort of ritual handshake. I would do the dap, get me some corn bread and beans and get out of there as soon as possible.

The black market was rampant on the dock on the Saigon River. Incoming supplies were stolen as soon as they were off loaded from the ships. You couldn't buy some clothing items on base because of shortage, but you could buy almost everything except a tank on the docks.

I had to be careful whom I went downtown with. The "VC", Viet Cong, would randomly kill white soldiers and those close by if you were with them. They seemed to avoid killing Blacks, if possible. The claymore mines they used did not discriminate. If you were close to a detonation on the sidewalk, well that was just your bad day. The Vietnamese were basically good and friendly people. If they liked you, the called you "number one" and if not, you were "number ten". If they thought you were silly or crazy, you were "dinky dow". When it was time to go, then the term was "DD mow" or just "DD out of here". The GIs, of course, picked up and used a lot of this slang among themselves.

Back at the base, I had it made for the first six months of my year tour. I really had no job worthy of the name. The Air Force had sent too many people over there in some skills and you had no job to do except doing something out of your field. I had the flunky job at first, chasing expensive and hard to obtain Aircraft parts, to keeping them in the maintenance repair system. I didn't like it, but I wasn't going to fight the guy holding my position and I got paid the same anyway.

As fate would have it, I accidentally met Colonel Green on base that I knew at Langley AFB. He knew my abilities and skills. Once he found out I had this cushy job in the Reconnaissance Wing and there was a dire need for my skills in the 834th, C-130 outfit across the runway at Tan Son Nhut, I immediately got orders to report to a combat outfit actually engaged in warfare activities.

I welcomed the chance to be a part of the real war and the 834th Commander was glad to receive me. This outfit flew in country sorties delivering to men food, mail and about anything you could get on a C-130, everyday. In fact, the C-130s were affectionately called Trash Haulers since at the end of the day, lots of trash and debris was on the floor after handling supplies, Vietnamese soldiers, their families, chickens, pigs and donkeys to every little dirt strip or Special Forces camp in the South of Vietnam.

Once in the 834th, I earned my pay. I was constantly repairing propeller systems, changing engines, flying in country delivering troops and other things. One of my favorite missions was going into Ben Cat and picking up the last of Thailand's Troops and taking them to Bangkok as Thailand pulled out of the war in 1971. It was on this mission and one week later when we provided Air Lift in the Lamson 719 Laos invasion that I won the Bronze Star. The troops we ferried into battle were so young and inexperienced that I knew they would lose the fight against the North Vietnamese that they would face. And I was right. The Army of Republic Vietnam ("ARVN") South was routed by the North in the Laos battle. It was so bad that we had to dispatch B-52s out of Guam to bomb and destroy the weapons and supplies that the ARVN soldiers left on the battlefield. This was to deny them to the North. Many of the young South Vietnamese men had bought their way out of the Army leaving the poor to do the fighting and defending.

After Bangkok and Laos, my time was about up and I would soon be assigned to Pope AFB, Fayetteville, NC. It was of course another C-130 base and I liked that.

Viet Cong. Wikimedia Commons (Public Domain)

Related pictures

Viet Cong

The Columbia Encyclopedia, Sixth Edition | Date: 2008

Viet Cong , officially Viet Nam Cong San [Vietnamese Communists], People's Liberation Armed Forces in South Vietnam. The term was originally applied by Diem's regime to Communist troops (about 10,000) left in hideouts in South Vietnam after the Geneva Conference of 1954, following the French Indochina War (1946-54). Most Communist troops, according to the agreements, had withdrawn to North Vietnam. Supported and later directed by North Vietnam, the Viet Cong first tried subversive tactics to overthrow the South Vietnamese regime, then resorted to open warfare (see Vietnam War). They were subsequently reinforced by huge numbers of North Vietnamese troops infiltrating south, and aided in the reunification of Vietnam following the collapse of South Vietnam in 1975.

Author not available, VIET CONG., The Columbia Encyclopedia, Sixth Edition 2008

VC TUNNEL COMPLEX

During the Vietnam war, the Viet Cong built up highly complex tunnel systems over large parts of South Vietnam. Whole companies of Viet Cong were able to survive and fight for long periods of time within these systems.

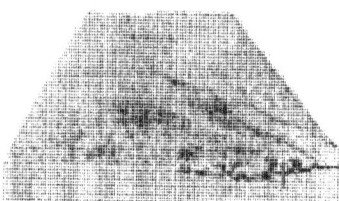

Bunkers as shown here were often linked by tunnels to

1. escape holes
2. underground food and supplies storage
3. medical area
4. kitchens
5. rest areas
6. HQ centres

⬇The image above, left, gives an overall view of a tunnel system. Below are 2 overlapping enlargements to show detail. Images from the book NAM; The Vietnam Experience 1965/75 by Hamlyn ISBN 0 600 563 111

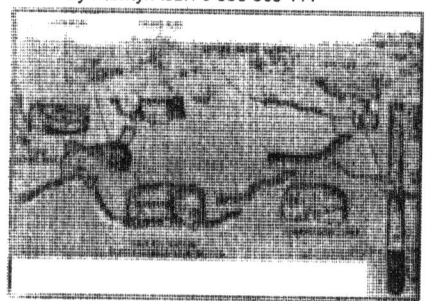

1st Battalion, Royal Australian Regiment, left South Vietnam, having completed almost a full year of combat duty. In leaving, the "diggers" could point with pride to a creditable performance during their stay, highlighted by participation in no fewer than nineteen major operations. Of particular note was an operation conducted in January 1966 which resulted in one of the biggest intelligence coups of the war up to that time. During a sweep of the so-called Iron Triangle, an area near Saigo heavily fortified and controlled by the Viet Cong, the Australian unit discovered a vast complex of tunnels, dug 60 feet deep in some places which turned out to be a Viet Cong headquarters. In addition to capturing five new Chinese Communist anti-aircraft guns, the Australians discovered 6,000 documents, many revealing names and locations of Viet Cong agents.

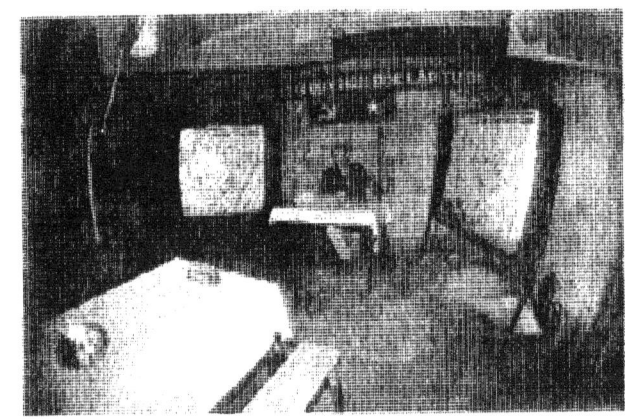

VC tunnels

Re-creation of underground conference room from which Tet offensive was planned

The tunnel system, built over 25 years starting in the 1940s, let the Viet Minh and, later, the Viet Cong, control a huge rural area. It was an underground city with living areas, kitchens, storage, weapons factories, field hospitals, command centres. In places, it was several stories deep and housed up to 10,000 people who virtually lived underground for years.... getting married, giving birth, going to school. They only came out at night to furtively tend their crops.

The ground here is hard clay, which made this whole thing possible. But even so, the planning and construction was incredible. People dug all this with hand tools, filling reed baskets and dumping the dirt into bomb craters. They installed large vents so they could hear approaching helicopters, smaller vents for air and baffled vents to dissipate cooking smoke. There were also hidden trap doors and gruesomely effective bamboo-stake booby traps.

Of course, the U.S. military knew about the tunnels. The tunnels not only allowed guerrilla communication, they allowed surprise attacks, even within the perimeters of U.S. military bases. The U.S. retaliated with bombs, eventually turning the region into what writers Tom Mangold and John Penycate called "the most bombed, shelled, gassed, defoliated and generally devastated area in the history of warfare."

Opening to a bunker system, found by Australian soldiers on Operation Coburg.

153

Tan Son Nhut Air Base

Ton Son Nhut Air Base - June 1968

Tan Son Nhut Air Base (1955-1975) was a Republic of Vietnam Air Force Force (VNAF) facility. It is located near the city of Saigon in southern Vietnam. The United States used it as a major base during the Vietnam War (1959-1975), stationing Army, Air Force, Navy, and Marine units there. The APO for Tan Son Nhut Air Base was APO San Francisco, 96307

Tan Son Nhat International Airport, (IATA: **SGN**, ICAO: **VVTS**) has been a major Vietnamese civil airport since the 1920s.

Early history

Tan Son Nhut Airport was built by the French in the 1920s when the French Colonial government of Indochina constructed a small unpaved airport, known as Tan Son Nhut Airfield in the village of Tan Son Nhut to serve as Saigon's commercial airport. Flights to and from France, as well as within Southeast Asia were available prior to World War II. During World War II, the Imperial Japanese Army used Tan Son Nhut as a transport base. When Japan surrendered in August 1945 the French Air Force flew a contingent of 150 troops into Tan Son Nhut.

After World War II, Tan Son Nhut served domestic as well as international flights from Saigon. In 1952, the French Air Force moved the 312th Special Mission Squadron to TSN from Nha Trang Air Base, consisting of French Douglas C-47 Skytrains and Beechcraft Model 18s for carrying cargo and military passengers to support French forces.

Lockheed C-130A-45-LM Hercules Serial 57-460 of the South Vietnamese Air Force. The aircraft served with the VNAF from October 1972 to April 1975. During the fall of Saigon, it was flown from Tan Son Nhut Air Base to Singapore, carrying about 350 Vietnamese.

Returned to USAF service in August 1975, it was assigned to the 16th Special Operations Squadron (SOS) at Korat Royal Thai Air Force Base, Thailand, then used by the United States Air Force Air National Guard for many years before being retired in 1989.

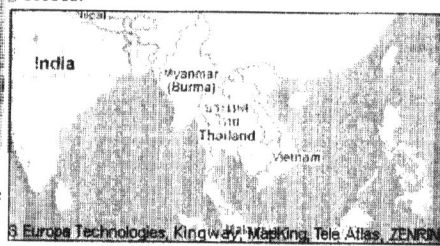

Image results for thailand - Report images

NVA troops overrunning the base area of the 429th Transport Squadron at Tan Son Nhut air base - 30 April 1975

Thailand

VNAF C-47s of the 413th Transportation Squadron on the very crowded flightline at Tan Son Nhut.

C-119Gs of the VNAF 819th Transport Squadron - Tan Son Nhut Air Base

VC tunnels

Re-creation of
underground conference
room from which Tet
offensive was planned

The tunnel system, built over 25 years starting in the 1940s, let the Viet Minh and, later, the Viet Cong, control a huge rural area. It was an underground city with living areas, kitchens, storage, weapons factories, field hospitals, command centres. In places, it was several stories deep and housed up to 10,000 people who virtually lived underground for years.... getting married, giving birth, going to school. They only came out at night to furtively tend their crops.

The ground here is hard clay, which made this whole thing possible. But even so, the planning and construction was incredible. People dug all this with hand tools, filling reed baskets and dumping the dirt into bomb craters. They installed large vents so they could hear approaching helicopters, smaller vents for air and baffled vents to dissipate cooking smoke. There were also hidden trap doors and gruesomely effective bamboo-stake booby traps.

Of course, the U.S. military knew about the tunnels. The tunnels not only allowed guerrilla communication, they allowed surprise attacks, even within the perimeters of U.S. military bases. The U.S. retaliated with bombs, eventually turning the region into what writers Tom Mangold and John Penycate called "the most bombed, shelled, gassed, defoliated and generally devastated area in the history of warfare."

Opening to a bunker system, found by Australian soldiers on Operation Coburg.

Tan Son Nhut Air Base

Ton Son Nhut Air Base - June 1968

Tan Son Nhut Air Base (1955-1975) was a Republic of Vietnam Air Force Force (VNAF) facility. It is located near the city of Saigon in southern Vietnam. The United States used it as a major base during the Vietnam War (1959-1975), stationing Army, Air Force, Navy, and Marine units there. The APO for Tan Son Nhut Air Base was APO San Francisco, 96307

Tan Son Nhat International Airport, (IATA: **SGN**, ICAO: **VVTS**) has been a major Vietnamese civil airport since the 1920s.

Early history

Tan Son Nhut Airport was built by the French in the 1920s when the French Colonial government of Indochina constructed a small unpaved airport, known as Tan Son Nhut Airfield in the village of Tan Son Nhut to serve as Saigon's commercial airport. Flights to and from France, as well as within Southeast Asia were available prior to World War II. During World War II, the Imperial Japanese Army used Tan Son Nhut as a transport base. When Japan surrendered in August 1945 the French Air Force flew a contingent of 150 troops into Tan Son Nhut.

After World War II, Tan Son Nhut served domestic as well as international flights from Saigon. In 1952, the French Air Force moved the 312th Special Mission Squadron to TSN from Nha Trang Air Base, consisting of French Douglas C-47 Skytrains and Beechcraft Model 18s for carrying cargo and military passengers to support French forces.

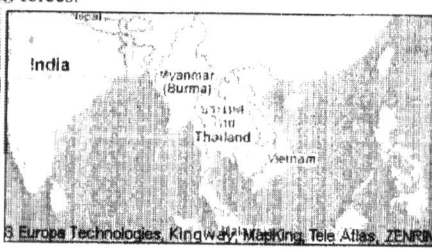

Thailand

Lockheed C-130A-45-LM Hercules Serial 57-460 of the South Vietnamese Air Force. The aircraft served with the VNAF from October 1972 to April 1975. During the fall of Saigon, it was flown from Tan Son Nhut Air Base to Singapore, carrying about 350 Vietnamese.

Returned to USAF service in August 1975, it was assigned to the 16th Special Operations Squadron (SOS) at Korat Royal Thai Air Force Base, Thailand, then used by the United States Air Force Air National Guard for many years before being retired in 1989.

Image results for **thailand** - Report images

NVA troops overrunning the base area of the 429th Transport Squadron at Tan Son Nhut air base - 30 April 1975

VNAF C-47s of the 413th Transportation Squadron on the very crowded flightline at Tan Son Nhut.

C-119Gs of the VNAF 819th Transport Squadron - Tan Son Nhut Air Base

Saigon

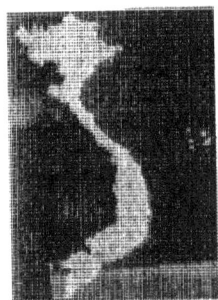

Like many cities in Vietnam, Saigon did not escape the wrath of war. Since the beginning, Saigon has had quite a traumatic history. There are many citations to birth of Saigon and the origin of its name. In the 15th century, this area were swamps, marshes and thick forests. By the early 17th century, a small township formed. According to one theory, Saigon or Sai Con has its root in a Khmer wor Prei Kor (Kapok Tree Forest).

The name Saigon was used officially in 1698, when Lord Nguyen Phuc Chu sen Mr. Nguyen Huu Canh to this region to create various districts and to form a government for this southern outpost. Because of its strategic location for trade a commerce as well as military importance, Saigon continued to grow and became bonafide city. By 1772, Mr. Nguyen Cuu Dam began to fill many of the canals t

Ho Chi Minh City
Thành phố Hồ Chí Minh
Formerly Saigon (Vietnamese: Sài Gòn)

Saigon Skyline

Ho Chi Minh City Hall

Tan Son Nhut Air Base

460th Tactical
Reconnaissance Wing
1966-1971

315th Air Commando
Wing, Troop Carrier
1966-1967

377th Air Base Wing
1966-1973

United States Pacific
Air Forces
1961-1973

Military Assistance
Advisory Group -
Vietnam
1961-1962

2d Air Division
1962-1966

7th Air Force
1966-1973

a production-model B-50 with a regular
crew made the first nonstop flight around the world.
By Bruce D. Callander

156

173d Airborne Yearbook, 3rd Year, Pictorial History

Paratroopers

Indochina

From Wikipedia, the free encyclopedia

Indochina, or the **Indochinese Peninsula**, is a region in Southeast Asia. It lies roughly east of India, south of China. The name has its origins in the French, *Indochine*, and was adopted when French colonizers in Vietnam began expanding their territory to bordering countries.

Historically, the countries of Mainland Southeast Asia were culturally influenced by China and India, but to varying degrees. Indochina refers to an area inhabited by different Mongoloid races having significant Indian cultural influences. Some Southeast Asian cultures, such as that of Laos and Thailand are heavily influenced by Indian culture as well as by Cambodian culture. Cambodia exhibits little Indian cultural influence, exhibiting many strong Chinese cultural influences, found in Cambodian cuisine and Cambodian clothing. Together with Java, these influences have been present since the era of the Khmer Empire.

Myanmar appears to be equally influenced by Indian and Chinese cultures.

Others, such as Vietnam, are more heavily influenced by Chinese culture, with only minor cultural influences from India, largely via the Champa civilization that Vietnam conquered during its southward expansion.

Malaysia and Singapore were at first strongly influenced by Indian culture followed by Islamic influences. Later, Chinese culture becomes a major influence following large numbers of Chinese immigration and settlement.

Indochina 1886

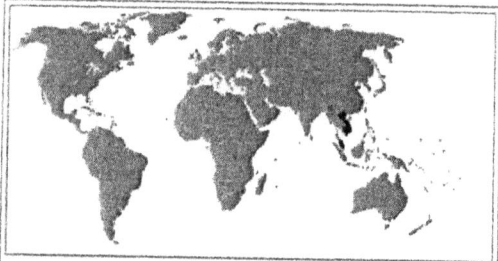

Dark green: always included, Light green: usually included, Red: sometimes included

Today, most of these countries also show pronounced Western cultural influences which began during colonialism of western countries in Southeast Asia.

In a strict sense, Indochina comprises the territory of the former French Indochina:

- Cambodia
- Laos
- Vietnam

158

However, in a wider sense, the cultural region is better described as **Mainland Southeast Asia** in which sense it also includes:

- Peninsular Malaysia (the southern end of the Malay peninsula excluding the Malay islands)
- Myanmar (formerly Burma--part of British India until 1937)
- Singapore (also considered part of Maritime Southeast Asia if the Johor-Singapore Causeway is not taken into account)
- Thailand (formerly Siam)

Note that the term *Sino-Indian* is used to describe things relating to India and China. (e.g. *Sino-Indian relations*).

See also

- ASEAN
- East Indies
- French Indochina
- Malay Peninsula
- Maritime Southeast Asia
- Indochina War
- Indochina Time UTC+7
- Serindia

External links

- History of the mountain people of southern Indochina up to 1945 (Bernard Bourotte, i.e. Jacques Méry, U.S. Agency for International Development, 195? (http://pdf.usaid.gov/pdf_docs/PNADG750.pdf)

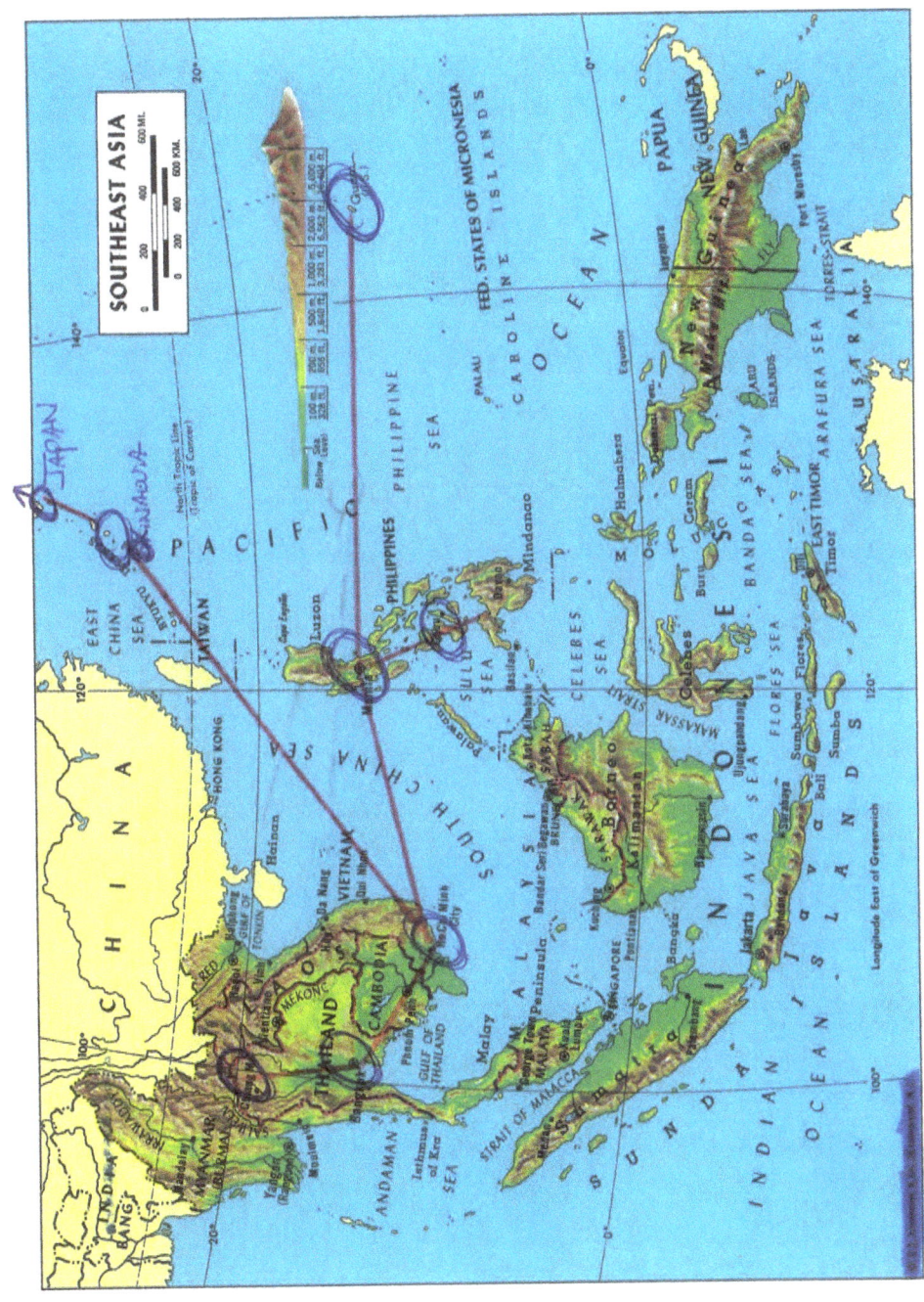

POPE AFB AND FAYETTEVILLE

Arriving at Pope in August 1971, Mildred and I set about buying a house that we intended to live in after retirement which I knew would be coming around in a few years – actually 1979.

The house we selected was a medium-sized three bedroom, partially constructed unit in the Oakdale subdivision of Fayetteville. We lived in an apartment with our two sons, Scott and Brian for about a month while it was being completed. It was good in a way that the house was still under construction for this allowed us to make some building changes in the decision before completion. We eventually added about 800 square feet of renovations and additions in the next thirty years, providing an equivalent separate apartment type kitchen, bath, bedroom for Scott, who at the time was on end-stage kidney dialysis for five years. During the time of the new construction, Scott received a new kidney in a transplant operation at Duke University Hospital in Durham, North Carolina, March 2004.

Fayetteville is a military town anchored by Fort Bragg, approximately 50,000 soldiers and Pope Air Force Base, 7,000 airmen, plus about 20,000 dependents. Both bases are essentially logistic independent, but many soldiers, airmen and families live off base in Fayetteville, Spring Lake, Southern Pines, Pinehurst, Lumberton, Sanford and dozens of small towns. The climate is hot in the summer, with great spring and fall temperatures and mild winters. Interstate I-95 runs through the area and the Cape Fear River and several lakes provide for good fishing. There is light manufacturing, lots of tobacco farms, soy beans, corn and sweet potatoes raised in the regions with the largest hog processing meat plant in the world, Smithfield in the town of Tar Hill.

My tour at Pope was a relatively short one, of two years, but after getting settled in, I transferred all of my college credits from The College of William and Mary, Trenton State and Christopher Newport College into North Carolina State University, taking a curriculum in Sociology. I graduated with a Bachelors degree in May 1973 just before I was reassigned back to Southeast Asia. I was also promoted to E-9 Chief Master Sergeant, the military's highest enlisted rank, while at Pope.

I was initially assigned to maintain C-130s on the flight line and overhaul the giant four bladed turbo propellers that pulled the plane through the air. The C-130 was the workhorse of the Air Force's tactical airlift capability and me being an expert and supervisor on this system; I was in high demand, especially in the Vietnam-Thailand-Laos war zone.

After about a year on the flight line, I was reassigned on base to the Aerospace Ground Equipment Branch to provide leadership, but most immediately to diffuse a racially charged work environment. AGE Equipment is very important in the Air Force, for it is the equipment used to facilitate work on

163

airplanes on the ground. The low and high tech equipment varies from electrical power carts, hydraulic lifts, bomb carrier-loaders, night lighting units, air pressure machines and a plethora of assorted gadgets, gizmos and accessories. Without AGE, the Air Force doesn't fly – no matter how expensive or sophisticated the aircraft.

Well, at the Chief level, my specialty code presumed and required me to know these systems and hydraulics as well as my primary job as an Aircraft Maintenance Superintendent. It was okay, because I knew in theory how it all worked and came together. Besides, as the Chief, I didn't actually have to know every detail of AGE, but primarily to ensure that the ones that did know it, did their jobs, promptly and accurately. At first, my new troops were a little apprehensive of me, partly, because I came from Aircraft; not one of their own and because I was Black and a Chief. The Air Force didn't have many Black Chiefs, especially young ones who hadn't even reached the twenty-year mark to qualify for retirement. In addition, I was a no nonsense hard nose military type that didn't accept excuses for failure.

Though most of the sixty or so men in the unit were White, there were about a dozen Blacks that were into the 70s civil rights movements and were reaching their "Blackness", in many ways irritating and threatening to whites. What they were doing wasn't really serious or a threat to unit effectiveness, but they were not understood by the White supervisor and White airmen and thus, were somewhat demonized mainly out of fear and ignorance. This is where I came in. I was supposed to deal with the unrest and personal conflict. And I did.

There were two main problems. First and most difficult was the attitude and demeanor of the White E-7 Master Sergeant Supervisor. He was only a couple clicks from the Klan. He was basically an ignorant, abrasive, overt racist. The other problem easier to deal with was the Blacks brandishing the red, green and yellow headbands and other paraphernalia that symbolized the black freedom civil right movement, which irritated the White airmen.

I had a one on one meeting with the supervisor and encouraged him to tone down his anti-Black behavior and I met with all the men in a general meeting to clear the air and put everything on the table. There was some resistance because some of the most outspoken ones didn't trust me and thought I would destroy their culture and comfort level. I told them I would be fair, but firm in my management style, but they should just watch what I do and not what I say. In a few months, the situation eased and we had a normal running operation. I also told the Black guys to cool it with the Black power rhetoric and the green, red and yellow power symbols, and they did, in the interest of harmony.

Other than this episode, the tour at Pope was essentially unremarkable. The pace was slow and simple except for the one situation in which the base was subject to a no-notice Air Force Inspector General visit where the inspecting team tried to find every big or small deficiency in the operation. The team had a fanatical General who was possessed with failing a base and successfully failed the Pope Wing, which resulted in the Commander being relieved and shipped out to Korea. It was blatantly unfair. Take for instance, one of our high-priced, high tech electrical MD-3 Power Units was failed because one of the four tires air pressure was one pound too low. That one pound had no relevance to mission capability and should not have been a factor in the decision of combat worthiness. Anyway, the General and his team treated the whole base this way and saw a bogeyman under every rock. I said I would never forget his name, but I did. He was definitely forgettable.

Mildred and I had our most enjoyable experiences off base getting our boys into a good kindergarten and first grade school. Mildred and the kids stayed in Fayetteville while I did my tour in Thailand and we then moved to Williams AFB, Arizona outside Phoenix in 1974, upon my return.

UNITED STATES OF AMERICA

BETSY ROSS 1st STARS & STRIPES

KNOTTY HEADS ANONYMOUS

MEMBER OF THE YEAR AWARD
2008-2009

TO

Vaughan Witten, Ph.D.
President

PROCLAMATION

Whereas, Vaughan Witten has conducted himself in a manner befitting a gentleman in his activities as a Knotty Head Member;

Whereas, Vaughan Witten has continually contributed his time and energy to the principles, ethics and missions of the Knotty Head Anonymous;

Whereas, Vaughan Witten has demonstrated distinguished leadership in executing the goals and objectives of Knotty Head Anonymous, such as, directing the repairing and painting of the ballroom of VFW Post 6018, installing mesh wires on the post windows and other valuable projects;

Whereas, Vaughan Witten has served as a model of excellence in his attitude and behavior, expressing good will to his colleagues in the VFW and community at large;

Now, Therefore, be it resolved, that **Vaughan Witten** is recognized and praised as the 2008-2009 Knotty Head Anonymous' Member of the Year with all the rights, privileges, and benefits appertaining; and to receive the Award of Knotty Head Anonymous' Member of the Year 2008-2009.

By my hand this day
25 July 2009

JAMES P. ALLEN
Vice President

Fayetteville, North Carolina

Fayetteville is a city located in Cumberland County, North Carolina. As of the 2000 census, the city had a total population of 121,015. It is the county seat of Cumberland County [GR6], and is best known as the home of Fort Bragg, a U.S. Army post located northwest of the city.

As of 2006 the city of Fayetteville has a population over 174,000 and ranks as the sixth largest municipality in North Carolina. Fayetteville is located near the Sandhills in the western part of the Coastal Plain region, on the Cape Fear River. With a population of 341,363, the Fayetteville metropolitan area is the largest in southeastern North Carolina, and the fourth largest in the state.

or suburban areas of the Fayetteville metro include Hope Mills, Spring Lake, and Raeford. Fayetteville is expected to annex portions of Fort Bragg as soon as 2007. This would push the city's population well over 200,000.

Fayetteville, North Carolina

City seal

City nickname: "All-American City" "City of Dogwoods"

Location in the U.S. state of North Carolina

County	Cumberland
Area	
- Total	93.55 mi²
Population	
- Total (2005)	174,000
- Density	911.5/mi²
- Metropolitan	341,363 (2006 est.)
Time zone	Eastern: UTC−5
Mayor	Anthony G. Chavonne
City Manager	Dale E. Iman
City website (http://www.cityoffayetteville.org/)	

167

Famous People from Fayetteville

- Chris Armstrong - ex-Arena Football League player
- Chip Beck - Professional PGA Golfer
- Bunkie Blackburn - NASCAR driver
- Christopher Daniels - Professional wrestler for Total Nonstop Action Wrestling
- Brad Edwards - Former Washington Redskins Player, and Super Bowl winner
- Henry Evans - Free black Methodist preacher who established Methodism in the Cape Fear River valley of North Carolina.
- Raymond Floyd - Professional PGA Golfer
- Frank P. Graham - President of the University of North Carolina and United States Senator
- Moonlight Graham - New York Giants outfielder for two innings on May 25, 1905; represented in the novel Shoeless Joe and the movie Field of Dreams
- Joe Horn - National Football League wide receiver
- Edward M Joyner Jr. - Canadian Football League Offensive Line for the Ottawa Rough Riders. Grey Cup winners 1968 and 1969
- Michael Joiner - standout basketball player for Florida State Seminoles
- Jimmy Raye - former NFL wide receiver
- Hiram Rhodes Revels - first African American member of Congress
- Robert Strange - United States Senator

Henry Evans (circa 1760-1810) built the first Methodist church in Fayetteville in 1793 and is known as the "Father of Methodism" for blacks and whites in the area.

The Confederate arsenal in Fayetteville was destroyed in March 1865 by Union Gen. William Sherman during the Civil War.

The Civil War Era

In March 1865, Gen. William T. Sherman and his 60,000-man army moved into Fayetteville. The Confederate arsenal was totally destroyed. Sherman's troops also destroyed foundries and cotton factories and the offices of *The Fayetteville Observer*. Not far from Fayetteville, Confederate and Union troops engaged in the last cavalry battle of the Civil War, the Battle of Monroe's Crossroads.

Cross Creek Linear Park

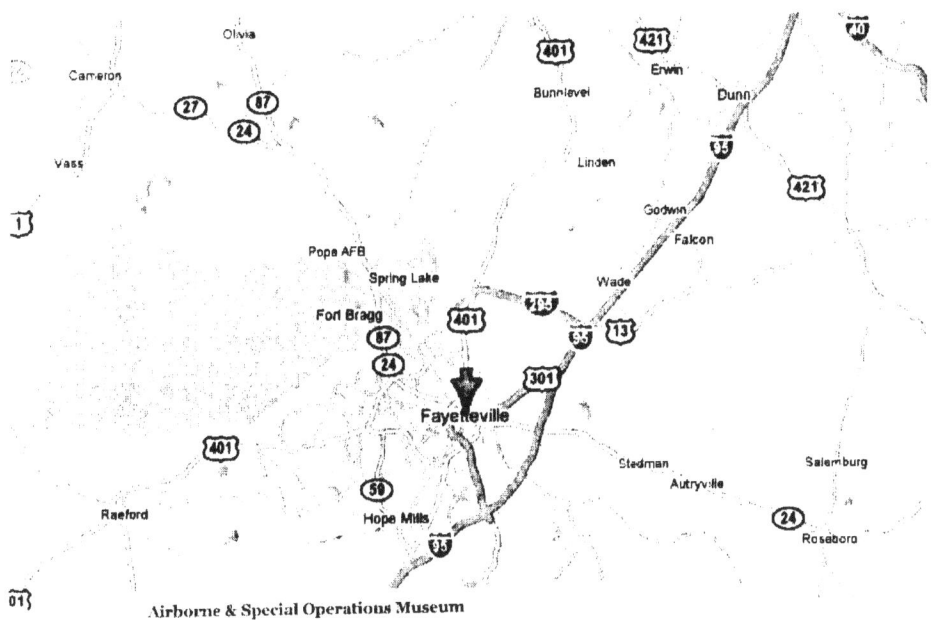

Airborne & Special Operations Museum

The Airborne & Special Operations Museum is run jointly by the non-profit Museu
civic and government leaders, and the Department of the Army. Opened August 20
teamwork that Fayetteville and Fort Bragg have developed over the past eighty yea
intersection with Hay Street, the museum is an anchor for downtown revitalization
community's belief in the importance and viability of this historic part of the city.

A part of the U.S. Army Museum System, the museum tells the story of Army airbo
1940 origin and movement to the Fayetteville area in March of 1942, through the p
dollar museum houses many rare and impressive artifacts, including a C-47 "Skytr
complete with a paratrooper in the door. A fully restored CG-4A glider, one of only
display, along with two helicopters, a Sheridan tank, and a complete collection of u
the sixty-year history of this exciting segment of the armed forces.

DAD + MOM - BACK   Colonel + Milored - Front

HOME - WVA

Milored
+
Scott
Fayetteville

1984
Olds

BRIAN   Colonel + Jaulita

BRIAN - SCOTT
ALLADIN HOTEL - LAS VEGAS
1979

CILLEY & ETHEL - FAYETTEVILLE

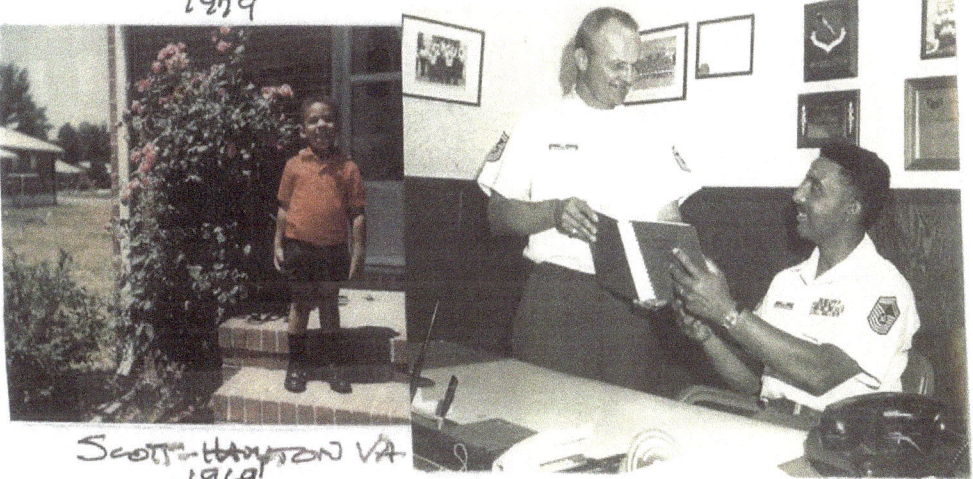

SCOTT - HAMPTON VA
1969

MS JIM NOTE - CMS WITTEN
SENIOR ENLISTED ADV.
WILLIAMS AFB AZ
1978

MILDRED - FAR LEFT
ME IN RED
AT AUNT LIZZIE'S
MARTINSVILLE - FIGSBORO, VA
1973

171

BUDDIES IN ENGLAND

Mildred - EARLY MARRIAGE

BUDDIES Mildred hill

EMMA PUTT - BABY JUYA

SOFTBALL THAILAND
UDORN

SEA-VIEW LAKES
AZORES - PORTUGAL

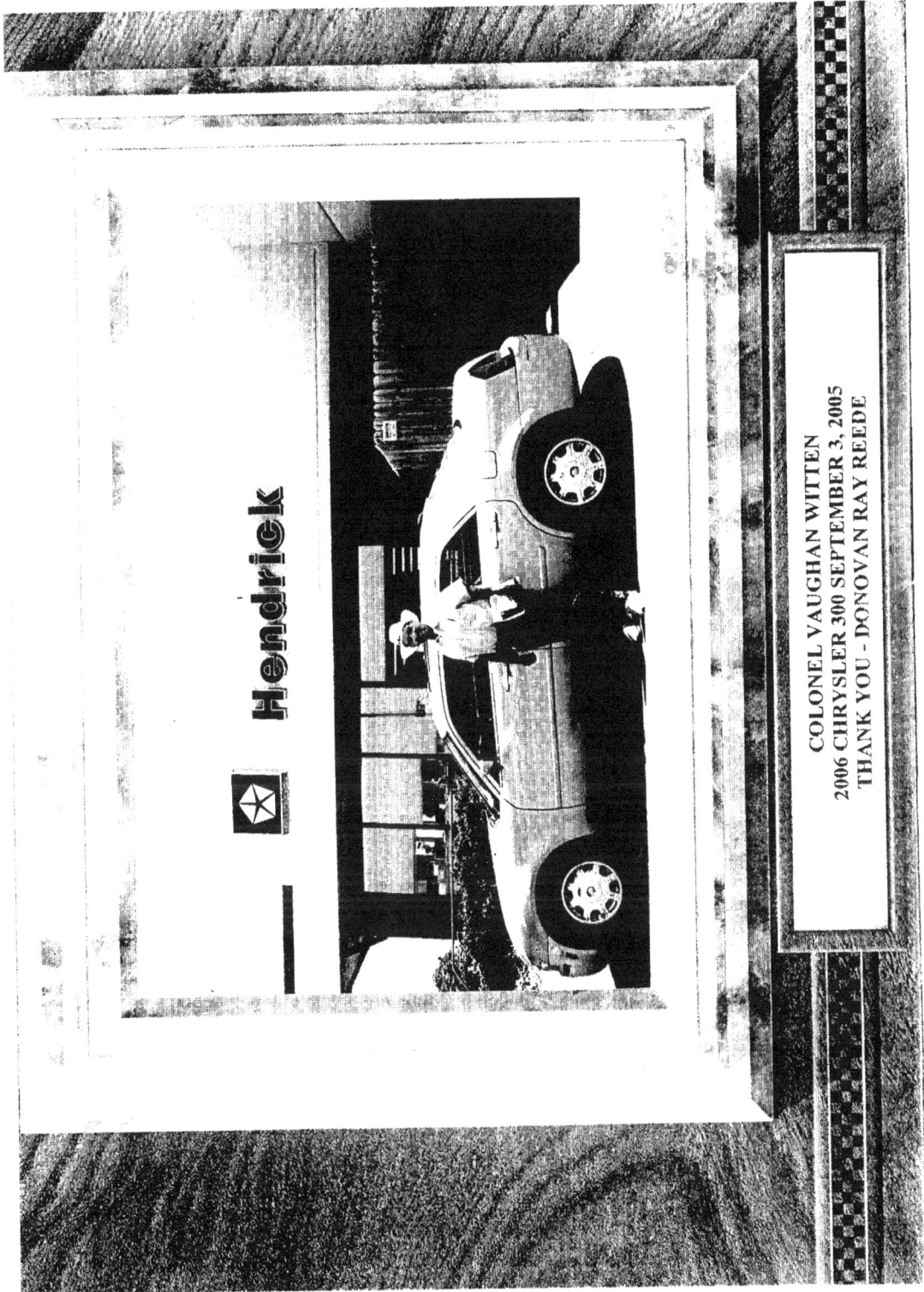

COLONEL VAUGHAN WITTEN
2006 CHRYSLER 300 SEPTEMBER 3, 2005
THANK YOU - DONOVAN RAY REEDE

VFW Post 6018

Knotty Head
Conex

Tuskeegee Airmen
1943

THAILAND AND WILLY

In August 1973, I departed Pope AFB, North Carolina for my final overseas assignment in Udorn, Thailand. I had already been to Thailand on my 1971 Saigon assignment and transported the final Thai army contingent to Bangkok as Thailand pulled out of the Vietnam War. I remember getting some of the best ham sandwiches in Southeast Asia, from a "momason" on one of the small food shacks on a Bangkok airport taxi way. Her reputation for her ham sandwiches was well known throughout Vietnam. I forgot her name, but I'm sure my friend and a fellow Air Force colleague, James A.P. Davis of Hampton, Virginia does. He and his wife, Helen, as well as my wife, Mildred, could always remember every detail of an activity.

In any regard, I did make the long boring flight to Bangkok and then up country to Udorn Thani. Udorn was a Thai-American Airbase in Northern Thailand used primarily for launching recon and bomber missions against the North Vietnamese. My purpose or mission was to support the effort in the area of maintaining weapons and bomb loading equipment as well as all the generic aerospace ground equipment on base. It was quite a heavy responsibility and I had about two hundred troops under my supervision. The base was beautiful and well managed. We had Thai women to clean the dorm rooms, wash our clothes and general housekeeping for the coast of a pittance. They were friendly and loyal to America. The Thai countryside and local towns were breathtaking in their beauty and could easily be characterized as exotic. I liked it here, but still missed Mildred, Scott and Brian.

I went to some of the "must see" things in the country and was especially impressed by the White Temple Buddha Complex in Bangkok. It was beautiful beyond description. There were hundreds of young Buddhist monks there in those orange wrap around uniforms and 58 Buddha statues lined around an internal mall, all in a different pose or position. It was awesome to see.

After spending one year at Udorn supporting the bombing of North Vietnam and Cambodia primarily, I returned to the United States to be assigned to a base in Arizona. I tried to get assigned to the east coast, but was eventually stationed to Williams AFB, outside Chandler, Arizona about 30 miles from Phoenix.

At first, I hated this assignment to "Willy" as it was affectionately called. It was hot, hot, all the time and located in the wilderness near the Superstitious Mountains. Plus, it was far from North Carolina and I would have to move my family into this oven. Willy was an Air Training command undergraduate pilot training base, and was in itself a pleasant assignment with good people.

After flying to Fayetteville in December 1974, Mildred, the boys and I drove to Arizona in January 1975. I had already obtained base housing and arranged for our furniture to be delivered by our arrival date. We also arranged to

175

have our pet dog, Huey, flown into Phoenix where we picked him up at Sky Harbor. Huey was almost human in his behavior and understanding. We loved him very much and he gave us much joy.

We stopped on the way to visit many parks and monuments including the Meteor Crater and the Petrified Forest. We went up to the Grand Canyon and Mexico later. After moving in to our small three bedroom house on base, we were very happy. Scott and Brian had their own room and Mildred and I were like celebrities since I was a high-ranking noncommissioned officer and the base gave us huge respect, especially since I was a black, college graduate, bronze star holder and Vietnam Veteran. Scott and Brian were enrolled in the elementary school on base. I believe in the 4th and 3rd grades, respectively. They did well in their studies and excelled in their school activities, including both playing baseball in the Babe Ruth League and Brian, being an outstanding basketball player and hero in winning the Arizona Military Baseball Championship by hitting a home run in the 9th inning to beat the Marine team for El Toro.

One of the greatest thrills Mildred and I had in Arizona was the activities of Scott and Brian in the Cub Scouts and the week encampment they had in remote campgrounds as part of their training.

After driving several hours into a deserted moonscape, we finally arrived at Geronimo Boy Scout Camp. It was beautiful in a Boy Scout way. Wooden buildings, camp fire sited, rifle ranges, bow and arrow ranges, canoe stalls with a large lake and many other facilities. After checking the boys in, we had dinner and Mildred and I headed back to Willy. After a week, we returned for the last day of camp and observed the boys finish up their training. They did well in rifle and bow shooting, but sometimes had a problem keeping the two man canoe straight as they rowed across the lake. They had great fun, as did Mildred and I. With this training and certification, they were promoted to the highest Cub Scout rank of Weblo, having already obtained Bear and Wolf rank. They were later inducted into an elaborately arranged ceremony for membership in the Arrow of Light. They were now the ultimate Cub Scouts and ready for admission into the Boy Scouts. Theirs was an honor and experience that few Boy Scouts have attained.

Another memorable experience with the boys was our trip to Globe, Arizona and the Apache Indian Reservation. We drove through the desert for about three hours and Brian fell asleep on the way. Upon arrival we saw the dilapidated, grimy almost primitive living conditions of the Indians and even I was surprised. When Brian awoke, he looked around and said "is this it?" He was expecting the Hollywood Indian and cowboy version of a reservation. He was really funny in his disappointment. What few Indians we did see were lethargic or drunk, hanging around the Trading Post which had overpriced goods and meat that had turned brown from old age. They did have a small hospital, a small jail with Indian Police; also a Post Office. But, in the Post Office, the supervisor was White.

The trip to the Apache Reservation was quite educational for all of us. I learned that the Indians received a check each month and could leave the reservation anytime they wanted to, to go to town and work or whatever. They then could come back when they wanted to and, of course, keep getting their check. Reservations are like mini sovereign territories under treaty with the United States.

After a year on base working for the Chief of Aircraft Maintenance in a basically nothing job, I was selected by the new Wing Commander, Col. Larry Cooper to became the next Wing Senior Enlisted Advisor which made me the Chief of all the other 30 Chiefs on base and the 6,000 enlisted troops. It was a very high honor, especially since I was the first Black to hold this high position and be involved in a high level of administrative decisions. This, of course, elevated Mildred's position of influence with the big wigs. She was appointed to the head of the Commissary Advisory Committee. This made a lot of the Black wives jealous, but that was their problem.

As part of my duties, I was the Commissioner of Little League Baseball and Softball for the base with about 17 leagues and 600 children from T-Ball to teen baseball. It was quite a job dealing with the umpires and parents. The players were no problem. I was also on the Queen Creek school board that included the Willy elementary school.

My mom and dad came to visit us one summer and were amazed that we had a lemon and grapefruit tree in our backyard. They were all over the base. You could just grab a grapefruit from a tree or the sidewalk if you wanted it and take it to work.

Mildred, the boys and I went to the Grand Canyon one winter in the snow above Flagstaff. We visited many of the Arizona landmarks and went to Nogales, Mexico a couple of times. We really enjoyed Arizona. Eventually, my time to retire came around and we moved to North Carolina after stopping off for a couple of day in Las Vegas. I forgot that we also visited my sister, Sandra in Los Angeles and went to Disneyland and Universal Studios. We were there when "Jaws" was the big hit and we had a scary – but fun – encounter with him while on tour.

As I said before Mildred was a force of nature. One of a kind and I was lucky to be married to her. Not perfect, but in the 99th percentile. She was loving, dependable, smart and brave. I admired her courage and her cooking. She could cook so good that I should weigh 300 pounds instead of 200. We argued early in our marriage about money because we were both trying to manage our little poverty wages at the time. Finally, I said to her "Just let me make the money and manage the money. You can spend it and stay home with the kids and manage the house." She agreed and we did that for 50 years. She liked to plant flowers and work with plants and loved beautiful things, furniture and such. But she wasn't at all that crazy about buying expensive clothes though she had plenty and a gazillion pairs of shoes, but I guess all women have tons of shoes. I always bought her a new car for safety and comfort and I would drive the old one to work. It paid off in the long run for me for when her new car got old in 6 or so years it was still in good shape. So, I would buy her another good new car and take her old car for myself which was still practically new.

She was very loyal and faithful to me and I did everything I could for her, but I just couldn't keep her alive. I know she lived 77 years, but I thought she would live forever. She had a massive heart attack at the dinner table while cooking. It happened right in front of me. Thank goodness I had just arrived home about 15 minutes before. I called out to her, slapped her gently with no response, got on the phone to 911 and told them to hurry while answering all their questions. The fire truck pulled up before I hung up. They were just around the corner. They and EMS rushed her to Cape Fear Hospital only two miles away but they could not save her. I followed EMS in my car and waited for the news from the doctor. He came out and told me she had died and they tried everything that they could. I haven't been the same since. She is buried in a cemetery about a half mile from our house and near the road. I drive by and see the headstone which has my name on it also, and blow my horn to let her know I'm thinking of her.

She was born and raised in Hephzibah, Georgia near Augusta and has a wonderful family, Ethel, Cille, Sister, Henry and a real comical brother called Pie. Pie, Sister and Henry have passed on and Ethel and Cille now live in Worcester, Massachusetts where Mildred and I spent a lot of time during our early years, including Boston and New Hampshire. I haven't visited Worcester since her death but intend to do so this Thanksgiving 2009.

Mildred loved to read the paper. She would read it religiously every day, front to back. She was probably the most and best reader in Cumberland County. If the paperboy had not delivered the paper by 6:00 am when I went to work, I would go to the nearby gas station buy one and leave it on the front step. She had a problem getting up and down the hill of our front yard.

She loved animals even more, watching all the TV animal shows and always having a pet. We had a dog of one kind or the other for 50 years. They led a good life, food, travel, and medical. Better than many people. My favorite was Huey. He lived to be about 13 or 91 in people years. He traveled to Arizona by Airplane and was almost human. The last ones we got – the only time we ever had more than one at a time were Murphy, an Llasa opso and Malcolm, a Shih Tzu. Murphy is outgoing and stubborn and will bite if irritated. Malcolm, at 13 pounds is sweet, obedient and always hungry for a snack of baloney or ham. They are up in age now about 10 years – dog, losing their eyesight and becoming senile or some type of personality change. Murphy is just strange now and won't obey any command or request until he wants to do it. Malcolm acts as if he is afraid of everything now and hides out in any nook or cranny he can find. I have to look all over the house each day to find him. However, if he hears the refrigerator door open, he will come running because he knows food is there and he won't miss that. In fact that's the way I often get him out of his hideout. He will eat his snack, run outside to pee, come back, and hideout again. They keep me going and guessing, but I love them and know that they can't help being what God has made them to be.

C-130 Hercules - Military Aircraft

C-130 Hercules - Military Aircraft

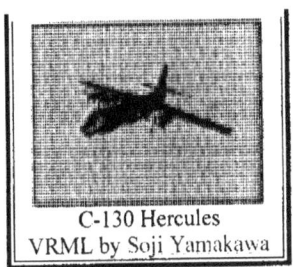

C-130 Hercules
VRML by Soji Yamakawa

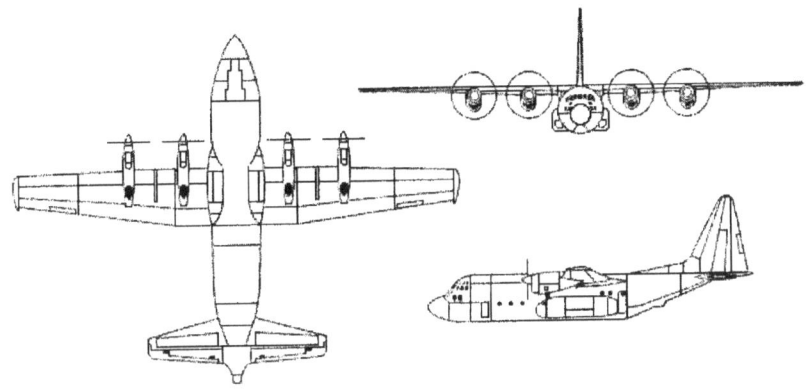

Williams Air Force Base

From Wikipedia, the free encyclopedia

Williams Air Force Base

Part of Air Training Command (ATC)
Located in Mesa, Arizona

Williams AFB, 8 May 1997

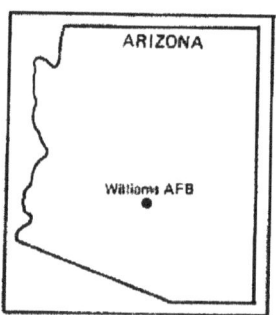

Location of Williams AFB

Type	Air Force Base
Coordinates	33°18′29.00″N 111°39′35.81″W (http://stable.toolserver.org/geohack/geohack.php? pagename=Williams_Air_Force_Base&params=33_18_29.00_N_111_39_35.81_W_type:airpc
Built	1941
In use	1941-1993
Controlled by	United States Air Force

MILITARY

Williams AFB

Units

-

Official Homepage

- Williams Gateway Airport

Williams Air Force Base (Williams AFB) is in Mesa, Maricopa County, Arizona, approximately 30 miles southeast of Phoenix and just east of Chandler. Williams AFB, constructed in 1941, operated primarily as a flight training school from 1942 until the base closed on September 30, 1993.

The former Williams Air Force Base played a strategic role in America's aviation history. Over a span of 52 years, more than 26,500 men and women earned their wings at Williams. Gearing up for the combat pilot demands of World War II, the Army Air Corps broke ground in Southeast Mesa, Ariz. for its Advanced Flying School on July 16, 1941. In February 1942, the growing military base's name was changed to Williams Field to honor Charles Linton Williams, an Arizona-born pilot. The facility was redesignated as Williams Air Force Base (WAFB) in January 1948. WAFB was the U.S. Air Force's foremost pilot training facility, graduating more student pilots and instructors than any other base in the country and supplying 25 percent of the Air Force's pilots annually. WAFB provided training for a variety of fighter and bomber aircraft including the AT-9, AT-17, P-38, AT-6, B-17, B-24, P-51, P-47, F-86, F-100, T-33, T-37 and T-38.

WAFB was closed in 1993 and created a loss of more than 3,800 jobs and $300 million in annual economic activity. The state and communities began work immediately to redevelop the base after the announcement of closure in 1991. Upon closing, Williams AFB was transferred to the Air Force Base Conversion Agency (AFBCA). AFBCA assumed responsibilities for the restoration and reuse of the base and worked with the Restoration Advisory Board and Williams redevelopment partnership to maximize reuse. On February 17, 1995, the Air Force signed the Record of Decision (ROD) for the Disposal and Reuse of Williams AFB. The decision in this ROD is to dispose of the aviation-related portion of Williams AFB in a manner that will enable the development of a regional airport with the capacity for expanding commercial and industrial development.

The Department of Defense is retaining 10.74 acres for the U.S. Army Reserves, and 8 acres of the U.S. Air Force for continued military use. DOD recommended changing the 1991 BRAC vote to move the base's Armstrong Laboratory Aircrew Training Research Facility to Orlando, Fla. The Defense Base Closure and Realignment Commission agreed, and the lab will remain at Williams.

Garrison	Air Training Command
Occupants	82d Training Wing (1973-1993)

Williams Air Force Base is a former United States Air Force (USAF) base, located in Mesa, and about 30 miles southeast of Phoenix, Arizona.

It was active as a training base for both the United States Army Air Forces, as well as the USAF from 1941 until its closure in 1993. Williams was the leading pilot training facility of the USAF, supplying 25% of all pilots.

Contents

- 1 Current status
- 2 History
    - 2.1 Base Operating Units
    - 2.2 Major Commands Assigned
    - 2.3 Operational history
- 3 See also
- 4 References
- 5 External links

Current status

Since its closure most of the base has since been annexed as part of Mesa, Arizona. Some property was retained by the US government while other portions were conveyed and converted into the civilian Williams Gateway Airport which was later renamed Phoenix-Mesa Gateway Airport and an educational campus anchored by Arizona State University Polytechnic Campus and Chandler-Gilbert Community College.

History

The base was named in honor of Arizona native 1st Lt Charles Linton Williams (1898-1927). Lieutenant Williams died on 6 Jul 1927 when his Boeing PW-9A pursuit aircraft crashed near Fort DeRussy, Hawaii. The airfield was designated as Williams Air Force Base (WAFB) in January 1948.

Previous names of the base were:

- Mesa Military Airport, Higley, Arizona, 19 Jun 1941
- Higley Field, Oct 1941
- Williams Field, 24 Feb 1942.

Base Operating Units

- 89th Base HQ and Air Base Sq (advance detachment), 16 Oct 1941 - 4 Dec 1941
- 89th Base HQ and Air Base Sq, 4 Dec 1941 - 1 May 1944
- 3010th AAF Base Unit, 1 May 1944 - 26 Sep 1947
- 3010th AF Base Unit, 26 Sep 1947 - 26 Aug 1948

Williams Air Force Base -

- 3525th Air Base Gp, 26 Aug 1948 - 1 Jul 1958
- 4530th Air Base Gp, 1 Jul 1958 - 1 Oct 1960
- 3525th Air Base Gp, 1 Oct 1960 - 1 Feb 1973
- 82d Air Base Gp, 1 Feb 1973 - 30 Jun 1993

Major Commands Assigned

- Air Corps Flying Training Comd, 23 Jan 1942
- AAF Flying Training Comd, 15 Mar 1942
- AAF Training Comd, 31 Jul 1943
- Tactical Air Command 1 July 1958 - 1 October 1960
- Air Training Command 1 Jul 1946 - 1 July 1958, 1 October 1960 - Jun 1993

Operational history

The United States Army Air Forces broke ground for its Advance Flying School there on July 16, 1941. During the fifty-two years it was operational, the base graduated more pilots and instructors than any other base in the country and supplied twenty-five percent of the Air Force's pilots annually.

Construction of the base started on 16 July 1941 and the initial construction was completed in December, making the base oprational, although the airfield was not ready for 4-engined aircraft until late 1943. During World War II, Williams Field was under the command of the 89th Army Air Force Base Unit, AAF West Coast Training Center. The training mission of the base 4-engined aircraft transtitonal training predominated during 1944-1945, but was changed to fighter pilot training in early 1945.

During the 1950s, a fighter gunnery school was added in 1954, however the base's mission returned exclusively to undergraduate pilot training in 1961.

The primary training aircraft used during the 1970s, 1980s, and 1990s were the Cessna T-37 "Tweet" and the Northrop T-38 Talon. Both trainers were two-seat, dual-engine jet aircraft.

The undergraduate flight training program lasted just less than one full year and involved classroom, simulator, and aircraft training activities. Graduates were selected to remain as instructors, after an intensive training course, or went on to train in their primary weapon system aircraft.

Students proceeded from the academic phase of classroom and simulator instruction around the six-week point of the program. The first flight was largely a 'demo' flight in the T-37 aircraft with the instructor orienting the student to the aircraft, the local training area, and some basic flight maneuvers.

The approximately 4,127 acre base was closed 30 September 1993 as a result of BRAC 1991. The host unit, the 82d Flying Training Wing and its squadrons (96, 97, 98, and 99th FTS) were inactivated.

Williams AFB, Az

ME-NCO of the year 1976

ARIZONA

Thailand

From Wikipedia, the free encyclopedia

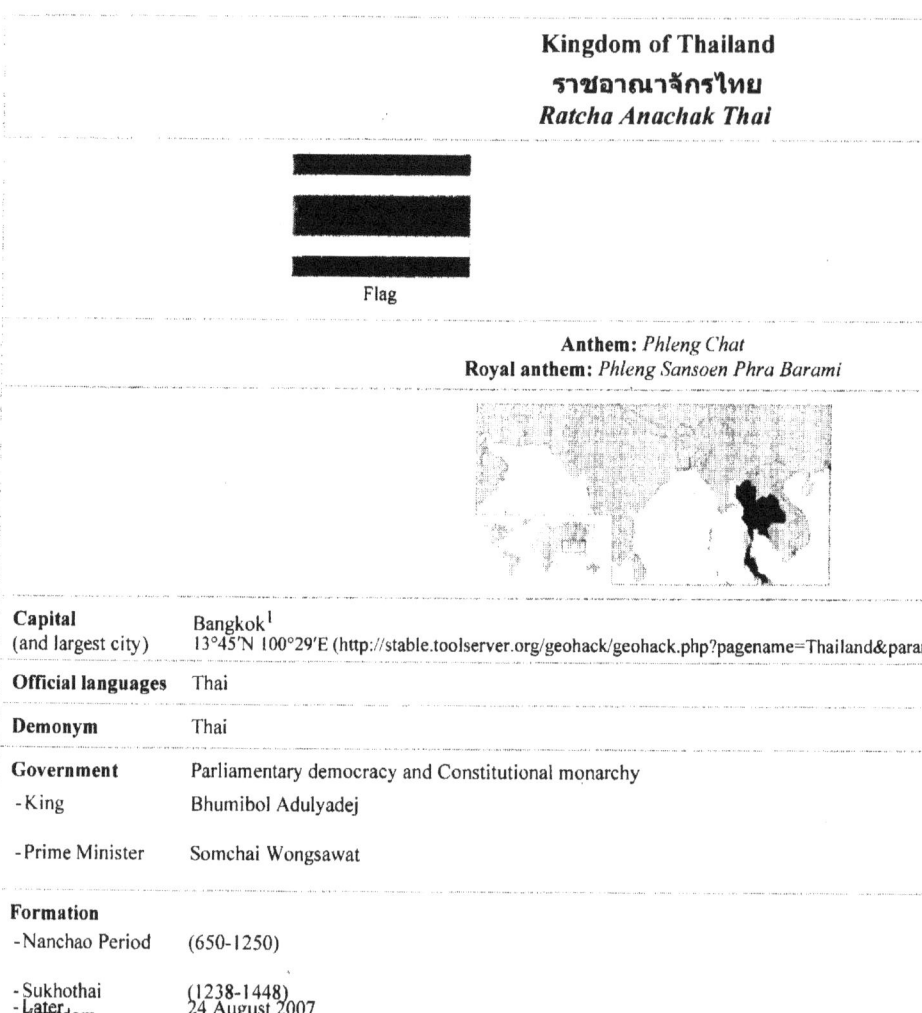

Kingdom of Thailand
ราชอาณาจักรไทย
Ratcha Anachak Thai

Flag

Anthem: *Phleng Chat*
Royal anthem: *Phleng Sansoen Phra Barami*

Capital (and largest city)	Bangkok[1] 13°45′N 100°29′E (http://stable.toolserver.org/geohack/geohack.php?pagename=Thailand&parar
Official languages	Thai
Demonym	Thai
Government	Parliamentary democracy and Constitutional monarchy
- King	Bhumibol Adulyadej
- Prime Minister	Somchai Wongsawat
Formation	
- Nanchao Period	(650-1250)
- Sukhothai	(1238-1448)
- Later kingdom	24 August 2007

The **Kingdom of Thailand** (IPA: /ˈtaɪlænd/, Thai: ราชอาณาจักรไทย   Ratcha Anajak Thai ,
IPA: [râːtɕʰa-ʔaːnaːtɕɑ̀k-tʰɑj]) is an independent country which lies in the heart of Southeast Asia. The country is bordered to the north by Laos and Burma, to the east by Laos and Cambodia, to the south by the Gulf of Thailand and Malaysia, and to the west by the Andaman Sea and Burma. By the maritime boundary, the country is bordered to the southeast by Vietnam in the Gulf of Thailand, to the southwest by Indonesia and India in the Andaman Sea.

The capital and largest city of Thailand is Bangkok. It is also the country's centre of political,

Thailand -

commercial, industrial and cultural activities. Bangkok is known in Thai as "Krung Thep Mahanakorn," or, more colloquially, "Krung Thep."

Thailand is considered to be the world's 50th largest country in terms of total area, with a surface area of approximately 513,000 km² (198,000 sq mi), and the world's 20th largest country in terms of population with approximately 63 million people. The population consists 80% of Thais, 10% of Chinese, and 3% of Malay. The rest are minorities such as Mons, Khmers, and various hill tribes. The country's official spoken and written language is Thai.

Thailand is one of the most strongly Buddhist countries in the world. The national religion is Theravada Buddhism which is practiced by more than 95% of all Thais (2002).[3] The cultures and traditions in Thailand are significantly influenced by those of India, China, Cambodia, as well as various countries in Southeast Asia. As a result, seniority plays an important role in the country's cultures. Respect for the elders is essential to Thai's spiritual practices as well as daily lifestyles. Thais are also well-known for their friendliness and hospitality, leading to the country's so called reputation as the "Land of Smiles."

Thailand is a constitutional monarchy with His Majesty King Bhumibol Adulyadej, or King Rama IX, the ninth king of the Chakri Dynasty, as the present king. The King has reigned for more than half a century, making him the longest reigning Thai monarch. His Majesty the King is recognised as the Head of State, the Head of the Armed Forces, the Upholder of the Buddhist religion, and the Upholder of all religions. Due to the government of the Monarch, Thailand is the only country in Southeast Asia that has never been colonized or taken over by a European power.

Udornthani, Thailand

Thailand

189

Along the Old West Highway headed for the San Carlos Indian Reservation

Around Town

A few sites near the town of San Carlos out to the lake and back to Globe.

Geronimo

Geronimo

See a few of the early photos of this years time at Geronimo

Camp Geronimo - Summer 2007

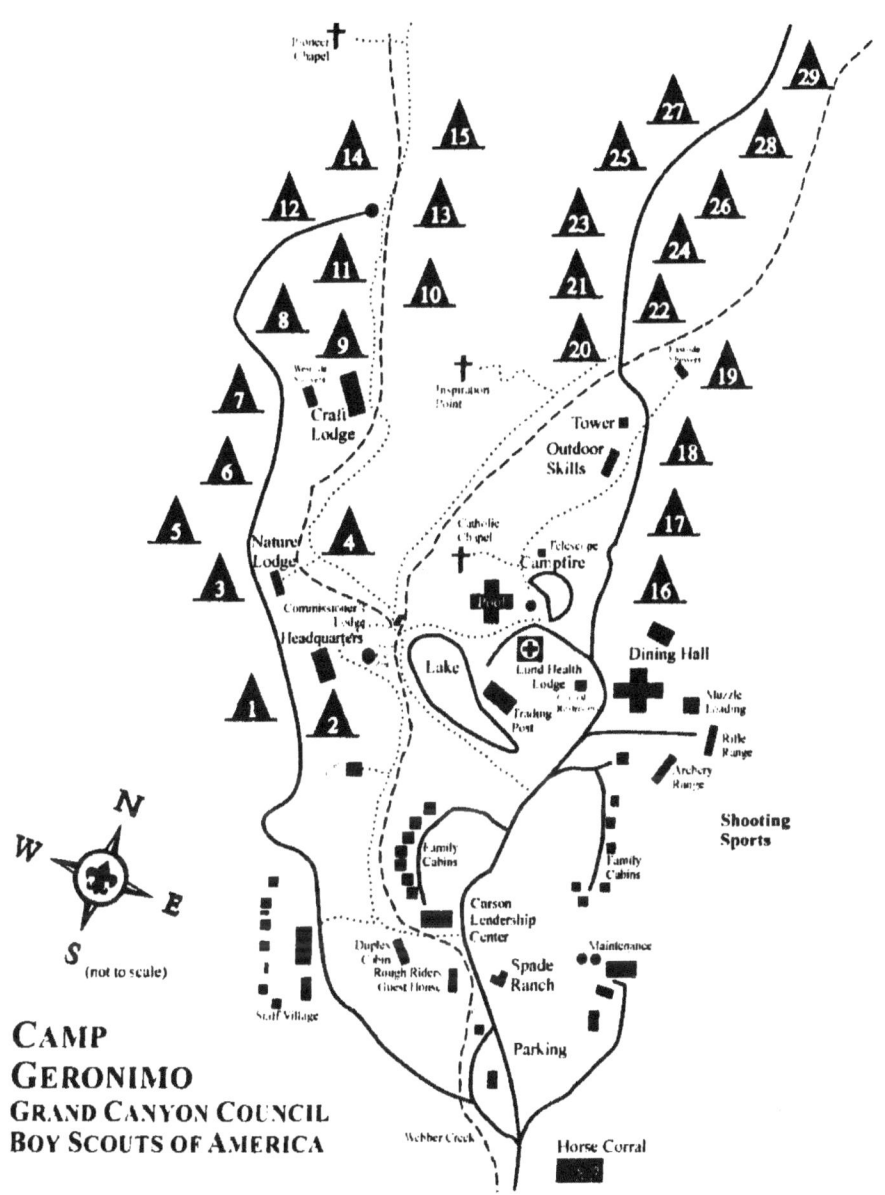

CAMP
GERONIMO
GRAND CANYON COUNCIL
BOY SCOUTS OF AMERICA

11-'Troop Formation' Thurs dinner

08-Spade Ranch house

09-Spade Ranch house 2

10-Outdoor code

Camp Geronimo 2004

CLOTHING ITEMS
- Pajamas
- Scout uniform*
- Sweater or jacket
- Poncho or rain gear
- Hat or visor
- Rugged pants (Levis)
- T-Shirts
- Underwear
- Hiking boots and proper socks
- Tennis shoes or moccasins with proper socks
- Swim suit and towel
- Old tennis shoes

CAMPING GEAR

MERIT BADGE ITEMS
- Merit badge books
- Scout handbook
- Writing items: paper, pencil or pen
- CPR pocket certificate

CAMP NECESSITIES
- Flashlight with fresh batteries
- Clothesline and pins
- Pocket knife (NOT a sheath knife) & Tot n' Chip
- Fishing gear
- Compass

LEAVE AT HOME
- Fireworks
- Radios/tape & CD/DVD players
- Sheath knives
- Weapons
- Water balloons
- Water balloon launchers
- Sling shots
- Wrist rockets
- Skateboards/rollerblades
- Bicycles
- Matches, lighters, Hot Spark kits

The Boy Scout uniform consists of the following: official Scout shirt; official Scout pants (long or short) official Scout socks worn with shorts; and a Scouting belt. Hats and neckerchiefs are optional, but must be

Camp Geronimo, AZ

Camp Geronimo is a **locale** in **Gila County, Arizona**. It has an elevation of **5,600 feet**.

Degrees Minutes Seconds:
Latitude: 342431N
Longitude: 1112234W

Decimal Degrees:
Latitude: 34.40861
Longitude: -111.37611

Military in action

Contributed and staff archived photos, clockwise, from top left, World War II, the Korean War, Grenada, Iraq, Panama and the Vietnam War. For a slide show of past Veterans Day activities in the Cape Fear region, view our "Remember This?" slide show at **fayobserver.com**.

195 - A

B-36 BOMBER?

HOOVER DAM - CAR BROKE DOWN
1 July 1979 - WORRIED
BRIAN + MILDRED + MESMLEY

World Fair
NY 1956
Dad, Mom, Emma

Jerome Ghost
Mining Town, AZ

Universal Studios

Mexico

Scott Huey

Mildred, Scott, Brian
Cub Scout Dinner
Arrow of Light

Phoenix Zoo

Montezuma Castle
Indian Homes carved in cliff

Williams AFB
Air Show

BRIAN - CACTUS

BRIAN PAINTED
DESERT AZ

Scott Mildred, AZ

Scott - near Williams AFB
AZ

THE FAYETTEVILLE OBSERVER

WEDNESDAY, DECEMBER 22, 2010

Would-be soldiers can't pass exam

**By Christine Armario
and Dorie Turner**
The Associated Press

MIAMI — Nearly one-fourth of the students who try to join the U.S. Army fail its entrance exam, painting a grim picture of an education system that produces graduates who can't answer basic math, science and reading questions, according to a new study released Tuesday.

The report by The Education Trust bolsters a growing worry among military and education leaders that the pool of young people qualified for military service will grow too small.

"Too many of our high school students are not graduating ready to begin college or a career — and many are not eligible to serve in our armed forces," U.S. Education Secretary Arne Duncan said. "I am deeply troubled by the national security burden created by America's underperforming education system."

MANY FAILING MILITARY APTITUDE TEST

Between 2004 and 2009, nearly 23 percent of 17 to 20-year-olds failed to get the minimum score needed to join the military.

Percentage of applicants who failed aptitude test

10 to 15 16 to 20 21 to 25 26 to 30 31 to 35 36 to 40

By state:

Lowest:
W.Y. 13%

Highest:
H.L. 36%

By race:

Hispanic: 29%
White: 16%

R.I.
Del.
D.C.

NOTE: Numbers
rounded to nearest percent

Sources: Education Trust, U.S. Army

AP graphic

graduates are unable to pass a test of basic skills.

"It's surprising and shocking that we are still having students who are walking across the stage who really don't deserve to be (there) and haven't earned that right," said Tim Callahan with the Professional Association of Georgia Educators, a group that represents more than 80,000 educators.

This is the first time that the U.S. Army has released this test data publicly, said Amy Wilkins of The Education Trust, a Washington, D.C.-based children's advocacy group. The study examined the scores of nearly 350,000 high school graduates, ages 17 to 20, who took the ASVAB exam between 2004 and 2009. About half of the applicants went on to join the Army.

Recruits must score at least a 31 out of 99 on the first stage of the three-hour test to get into the Army. The Marines, Air Force, Navy and Coast Guard recruits need higher scores.

Further tests determine what kind of job the recruit can do with questions on mechanical maintenance, accounting, word comprehension, mathematics and science.

The study shows wide disparities in scores among white and minority students, similar to racial gaps on other standardized tests. Nearly 40 percent of black students

and 30 percent of Hispanics don't pass, compared with 16 percent of whites. The average score for blacks is 38 and for Hispanics is 44, compared to whites' average score of 55.

Even those passing muster on the Armed Services Vocational Aptitude Battery, or ASVAB, usually aren't getting scores high enough to snag the best jobs.

"A lot of times, schools have failed to step up and challenge these young people, thinking it didn't really matter — they'll straighten up when they get into the military," said Kati Haycock, president of the Education Trust. "The military doesn't think that way."

The military exam results are also worrisome because the test is given to a limited pool of people: Pentagon data shows that 75 percent of those aged 17 to 24 don't even qualify to take the test because they are physically unfit, have a criminal record or didn't graduate high school.

Educators expressed dismay that so many high school

The effect of the low eligibility rate might not noticeable now — the Department of Defense says it meeting its recruitment goals — but that could change as the economy improves, said retired Navy Rear Admiral Jamie Barnett.

"If you can't get the people that you need, there's a potential for a decline in your readiness," said Barnett, who is part of the group Mission: Readiness, a coalition of retired military leaders working to bring awareness to the high ineligibility rates.

The report by The Education Trust found that 23 percent of recent high school graduates don't get the minimum score needed on the enlistment test to join any branch of the military. Questions are often basic, such as: "If 2 plus x equals 4, what is the value of x?"

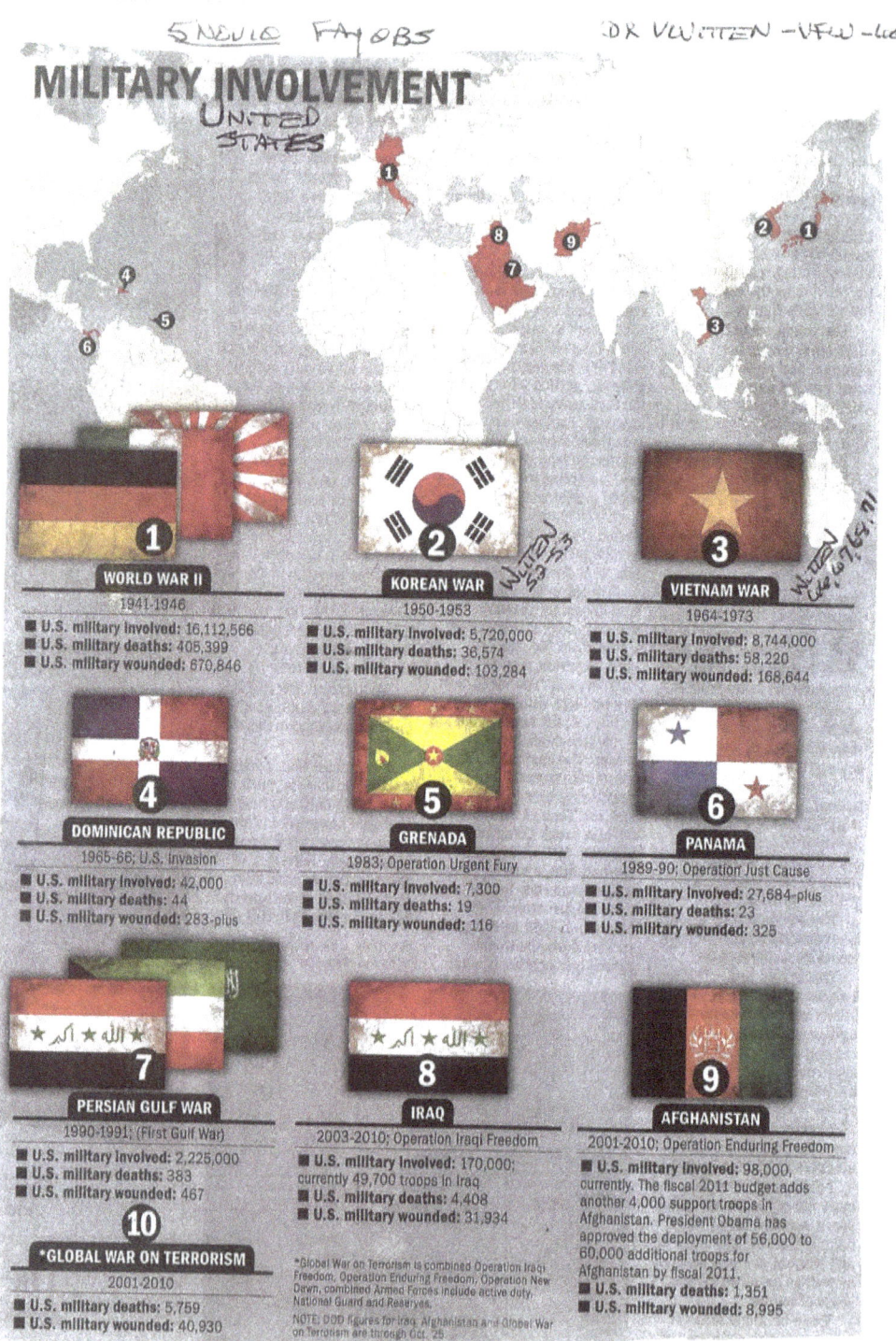

MILITARY INVOLVEMENT

1 — WORLD WAR II
1941-1946
- U.S. military involved: 16,112,566
- U.S. military deaths: 405,399
- U.S. military wounded: 670,846

2 — KOREAN WAR
1950-1953
- U.S. military involved: 5,720,000
- U.S. military deaths: 36,574
- U.S. military wounded: 103,284

3 — VIETNAM WAR
1964-1973
- U.S. military involved: 8,744,000
- U.S. military deaths: 58,220
- U.S. military wounded: 168,644

4 — DOMINICAN REPUBLIC
1965-66; U.S. Invasion
- U.S. military involved: 42,000
- U.S. military deaths: 44
- U.S. military wounded: 283-plus

5 — GRENADA
1983; Operation Urgent Fury
- U.S. military involved: 7,300
- U.S. military deaths: 19
- U.S. military wounded: 116

6 — PANAMA
1989-90; Operation Just Cause
- U.S. military involved: 27,684-plus
- U.S. military deaths: 23
- U.S. military wounded: 325

7 — PERSIAN GULF WAR
1990-1991; (First Gulf War)
- U.S. military involved: 2,225,000
- U.S. military deaths: 383
- U.S. military wounded: 467

8 — IRAQ
2003-2010; Operation Iraqi Freedom
- U.S. military involved: 170,000; currently 49,700 troops in Iraq
- U.S. military deaths: 4,408
- U.S. military wounded: 31,934

9 — AFGHANISTAN
2001-2010; Operation Enduring Freedom
- U.S. military involved: 98,000, currently. The fiscal 2011 budget adds another 4,000 support troops in Afghanistan. President Obama has approved the deployment of 56,000 to 60,000 additional troops for Afghanistan by fiscal 2011.
- U.S. military deaths: 1,351
- U.S. military wounded: 8,995

10 — *GLOBAL WAR ON TERRORISM
2001-2010
- U.S. military deaths: 5,759
- U.S. military wounded: 40,930

*Global War on Terrorism is combined Operation Iraqi Freedom, Operation Enduring Freedom, Operation New Dawn, combined Armed Forces include active duty, National Guard and Reserves.

NOTE: DOD figures for Iraq, Afghanistan and Global War on Terrorism are through Oct. 25

197

AIR FORCE RETIREMENT
AND
SHAW UNIVERSITY

Having lived a life in virtual paradise in the Air Force for 27 years, even with long separation from Mildred, on 1 July 1979, Mildred, Scott, Brian and I left Arizona for the cross country drive to North Carolina via Las Vegas. We were now retired from the Air Force after 27 years and I was a civilian. The freedom from military life though was great and felt good. The first part of the trip up to Nevada was uneventful until we reached the Hoover Dam where the car broke down. It was a good car, 1975 Pontiac that was running well, but all of a sudden as we came down a mountain to the dam, the engine began to knock and sounded like it would explode. I became very concerned about the consequences and costs if the engine needed repair or replacement. We were in the middle of nowhere and would require a tow to Las Vegas about 60 miles away, plus the cost of repair or a new engine.

I eased down the slope to the nearest parking lot on the dam and looked under the hood, checking for obvious damage. After a few minutes, Mildred and I agreed to try to drive it slowly into Las Vegas for maintenance and hope the engine wouldn't explode. Being a mechanic, I suspected that a rod bearing was loose and would break. We began the long trip into Las Vegas, driving slowly about 35 mph to minimize damage to the engine. The road at that time was only two lanes and I had traffic backed up for miles behind me and they were irritated with me, to say the least, honking horns and cursing.

Eventually, we arrived in Las Vegas and were prepared to go to our hotel, The Aladdin; but I needed gas, so I stopped, got gas and intended to take the car, still knocking to a mechanic the next day. I anticipated at least a $2,000 repair bill and a 3-day delay in Vegas waiting on the car. As I filled the tank, I saw a display of STP Engine Oil Additive by the pump and reasoned that if my engine had a blocked valve lifter, the STP might clear it. The small can of STP only cost $1.00 and I had nothing to lose, so I purchased and poured the can into the engine. Then magic happened, before I got to the hotel about two miles away, the engine quieted down and began to run normally. I could hardly believe it and was scared that it would begin knocking again, but it didn't.

Anyway, I relaxed and enjoyed two days in Vegas with Mildred and the kids. Mildred liked to gamble, so she was very happy and the kids, Scott and Brian, swam in the pool and played kid games. But I was still nervous and apprehensive, because I knew I had a 2,000 mile trip to North Carolina with a car having dubious reliability and subject to breakdown any moment. But the time came to depart and I nursed the engine for about 100 miles, afraid to open it up for fear of disaster. However, I gained confidence with each mile that the engine hummed along with no problem. Finally, somewhere in Utah, I opened it up and drove around 70 mph the rest of the way.

We stopped in St. George, Utah and had the best salmon cakes for lunch I had ever tasted. We stopped at Best Western hotels most of the way and eventually arrived in Saginaw, Michigan where we visited with my sister, Audrey, and her husband, Herman for a few days. Herman was also retired from the Air Force, a Master Sergeant KC-97 Tanker In-flight Boom Operator.

Leaving Saginaw, we drove to Raleigh, North Carolina where we stayed temporarily in a motel while we looked for an apartment or townhouse to settle in to. We had our own house in Fayetteville about 60 miles away, but it was being rented at that time. I wanted to try and establish my post Air Force career in Raleigh which at the time I thought was more sophisticated and had better job opportunities. I found out later that it was very provincial and socially backwards compared to Fayetteville, at least among Blacks. I had no idea as to what I might do for work since I had only a Masters degree in Psychology and only two years of college teaching experience. So, one day after filling out papers at the unemployment office, I took a chance and walked onto the campus of Shaw University and asked if they needed a Psychology teacher. I didn't get a direct yes or no, but they said they would call me in a day or so. As it turned out, the new President had fired most of the faculty and everyone had to reapply for their job, thus causing an administrative nightmare. After a couple of days, I received a mailgram asking me to come work. They had been calling me for two days, but my phone had a constant busy signal, so the mailed me. I was very glad to be employed because I couldn't support my family on my Air Force retirement alone.

As a new teacher, I had to start from scratch with everything, from writing my syllabi, getting my books, writing lesson plans, getting an office and learning the University culture. Everyone was friendly, but the students were lazy, didn't want to work and many resisted my authority and demands for excellence. But we got along, although I flunked over half of them my first year.

The President, Stanley Smith, was pompous, strange and dictatorial. He thought he was President of the US, Russia and Japan, instead of a small Black college. He honored no laws established by the US Department of Education and often encouraged his administrators to skirt or break a law in order to keep government funds rolling in. He was very vain and egotistical, signing all checks, especially pay checks and small $2 or $3 dollar checks for services just to let everyone know he was the boss. He wouldn't pay many University bills and Shaw's reputation was a joke in Raleigh. Of course, we never got a pay raise during his tenure, and when we went belly-up insolvent in 1986, the Trustee Board fired him.

Stanley Smith was from Trinidad-Tobago in the Caribbean islands, and had an arrogance and superior view of himself that is often attributed to people from the West Indies. He liked to party though. He would invite the faculty and staff to his University purchased house in Raleigh and provide big liquor and good food. He had a bar with enough liquor to supply a state ABC store. Overall, he was a pretty good guy, once you got to know and understand him. He was a captive of his island culture and he was what he was. However, he was a disaster as a college president and Shaw escaped his incompetence by the skin of her teeth. He was eventually fired by the Board of Trustees after we were in critical condition. For instance, one payday, the business manager told him that he didn't have enough money to cover the $600,000 payroll, and asked what he should do.

The President told him to release the checks and let the money go as far as it could. $200,000 in checks bounced that month. No one ever figured out how such a slob and incompetent person could ever be selected President of the School.

After his departure, the school struggled along to keep the doors open. Faculty and staff were not paid for three months and many were hurt financially. But the Trustee Board stepped up to the plate, mortgaging their houses to obtain grants and loans to pay employees and critical bills while searching for a new president. Dr. John Lucas of Durham was named interim President and he and Dr. George Debnam, a prominent Raleigh physician and other Board Members provided the energy, leadership and money, along with others to keep the school afloat until a new president, Dr. Talbert O'Shaw from Jamaica and Morgan State University arrived to take leadership in November 1987.

Dr. Shaw was a relatively good President compared to the others. He was fiscally responsible, tough and pompous, but effective. He was successful in bringing the school out of the despair mainly because he had brought with him and administrative genius in a Dr. Ernest Pickens, also a Morgan State graduate. They were both no-nonsense and dedicated to the University. I got along well with both of them, but one had to be careful what you said and how you said it around Talbert O'Shaw. He was a perfectionist and looked for any flaw in ones' behavior for criticism. Talbert Shaw was a brick and mortar man. He built many new buildings, renovated another and made the campus respectable to look at. Academically, it was another story. It was the usual delusion and propaganda of quality education with no quality. Ernest Pickens was the real power behind the throne, but he too had to walk gently around "Julius Caesar" Shaw or risk his head to Talbert's retribution.

Under President Shaw, the school did prosper in brick and mortar, but suffered on the humanitarian and psychological level. Enrollment increased and new majors added, but the quality of students remained as low as ever before. He and his monster academic Vice President, Ramsey, didn't care as long as students qualified for federal grant and loan money to be funneled to the University. Shaw was all about money and glory for himself. His pompous demeanor and critical tongue kept most people at length and intimidated the bearer of truth. He basically lived a delusion of grandeur that he was superior, perfect and The Boss. He was also vain in many ways including keeping his gray mustache dyed black all the time. A basic narcissist.

He did have one redeeming factor in that he believed in giving the faculty and staff a raise every year and kept the bills paid. We all respected him for that. He was like a strong patriarch, taking care of his children.

The faculty however, were quality, but the students were about 9th grade equivalent and were not pushed to attain a true college education. When a faculty member tried to demand excellence and flunked those that didn't produce, the faculty was threatened with dismissal. So, most faculty went along and passed and eventually graduated incompetent students, perpetuating a fraud with a degree. Even with such low standards, our graduation rate was only 13% in four years and 24% in five years. It was really pathetic, but who would tell the "King" that he had on no clothes?

One summer Talbert and several others HBCU Presidents visited the State of Israel and since he met the President of Israel, he came back equating his position to that of Israel, a small, but strong world power. He was given credit though, for increasing faculty pay. For the 16 years of his tenure, the faculty and staff received from 3-6% cost of living increase each year, I received 10% when I got my PhD. Under Stanley Smith, we received nothing. Another thing he did that was far reaching and positive was to bring on to the Board of Trustees, a Shaw alumnus who was a famous and wealthy lawyer in the person of Willie Gary. Mr. Gary was a force of nature and carried the University on his back almost alone for years. In addition to donating millions of dollars to the endowment and operating funds, he sponsored and essentially brought back and paid the millions for the return of football in 2002, absent since 1978, the days of Stanley Smith. Dr. Shaw didn't really want it back because of the expense, but the alumni wanted it for the prestige and glory. So with Mr. Gary's help, it happened. One thing I found out about Black people after I returned to civilian life is that they like flashy, noisy, dressy, superficial things that provide them a venue or opportunity to show off, dance, perform or otherwise get attention. Football fit this need perfectly. Today we call this *bling-bling*.

President Shaw was a stubborn, strong, imperious man, who thought he was a king. His ego was boundless and he had a terrible temper that got him into trouble with students and the press. He was very much in love with himself. Again, no one dared to tell the king that he was naked. So, the University suffered through another 16 years with an ego maniac, where a few new buildings were erected while the academic program continued to sink to ocean bottom levels. He even had the nerve to name a new dormitory after himself while he was still in office. Another thing I learned about Blacks in high office is that they have no shame, humility or compassion for the under dog and little people. They tend to be indulged in their own greatness, importance and pursuit of money and prestige for themselves. The typical faculty and staff dislike and fear them, but are trapped into economic servitude and grin and bear their burden of working for an unappreciative tyrant. It is like they, the Presidents, have read Macceavelli and believe it is better to be feared than loved. But receiving praise or "Thank you" for a good job would ever come from him. He lived large, belonging to the Raleigh elite set, world travel, expensive banquets, humongous house, jaguar and all at University expense, plus a huge salary. He was like Stanley Smith in that he had no shame and both were Islanders.

One indication of his huge ego was the jeweled bowl incident. The government of Saudi Arabia, in recognition of the Muslim Mosque on campus, which they paid for, presented the University an expensive jeweled bowl in the shape of a sailing ship. When the Emissary said the bowl was for Shaw, President Shaw interpreted that statement to mean it was meant for him. So guess what? He took the bowl home and kept it. After some months, when the newspapers found out about this unethical and perhaps, illegal behavior, they exposed the whole thing in the paper. Talbert used every excuse in the book for taking the gift for himself saying among other things that he was Shaw and thought it was a personal gift. Anyway, to diffuse this embarrassing situation, Talbert sold the bowl on auction at Southerbys of New York. He said that the bowl was appraised as a cheap version of an expensive item and fetched a low price at auction. Of course, no one believed him. He eventually donated the proceeds to the University, according to his press release.

Under Talbert Shaw, I received my PhD in Psychology at NC State in 1989 and was promoted to Vice President for Student Affairs in 1993. This promotion came out of the blue, but I believe it was because there was a vacancy of course, but mainly because I publicly defended him in a faculty-staff meeting when he had been accused of adultery and fraud. I didn't have any proof, but believed that even with his faults, he was not guilty of the things attributed to him. My response was spontaneous and I think he appreciated it for he was about to be disgraced and perhaps even fired. I was very pleased with new job and pay, but had no idea that being on his Cabinet and close to his Presidential power that it would be miserable. And it was. I suffered him for ten years, refusing to quit. In fact, I earned a Shaw Bachelors degree in 1999 for I wanted to be a Shaw Alumnus and the status that went with it when I retired. You see, people on the outside believe Shaw is honorable and great. Actually, the mission and conceptual ethos of Shaw is honorable in theory and as an institution. It's just that the Presidents and high Administrators are weak, corrupt, narcissistic, greedy and unethical, thereby dragging the school over the cliff into the financial and functional abyss. It is only the inside faculty and staff that knows Shaw is actually an educational fraud, non relevant and a glorified███ High School. It is difficult and sad for me to say this, especially having worked and served her for 30 years, but I must tell the truth about this situation. I thought I could make a difference, but I didn't. Me and others like me were ignored or intimidated by ignorance and stupidity on the level of a tsunami.

In 2003, a new President was hired, this one an American, at least, born and raised in the United States. As mentioned earlier, this was Clarence G. Newsome. However, he was a very sorry President. At first, everyone had high hopes and expectations for Dr. Newsome especially since he was a Duke University Graduate, a former Dean of the Howard University Divinity School in Washington, D.C. and was an excellent speaker, which as it later turned out was rhetoric and propaganda. He brought in his cronies from D.C., paid them twice the salaries of the old staff and hired five secretaries to do the job of the one that served the previous President. He was totally deluded into thinking he was President of the world and began to systematically overspend, live like a king and looted the University. Within three years he could not make payroll or pay bills. About a third of the staff was fired on the pretext of restructuring and the "work at will" law that was legal in North Carolina. All University property was mortgaged, pawned and the buildings were used as collateral for a $30 million loan from Bank of America. During his tenure, the University sank to levels unfathomable even beyond the Stanley Smith days. President Newsome, a preacher, was a total disaster, overspending and living higher than even Talbert Shaw, but no money to pay for it. He was a consummate liar and spin master, living a grandiose lifestyle that raped the University spiritually and economically. Newsome brought in a passel of cronies and high priced secretaries from his previous position as Dean of the Divinity School at Howard University, Washington, D.C. His primary hatchet man was Mr. Ansi Perry, along with a stupid Hilterian type, disbarred Virginia lawyer, Charles Chambliss, and a vain incompetent, Claude Flythe, as Special Assistant who was 70 and attempted to look and act like a 40 year old. They also brought in five secretaries given various titles at $50,000 per year, doing the same job that one secretary at $35,000 was previously doing. In fact, these secretaries with nothing to do had their moving expenses paid from D.C. and were making more money that the typical faculty member with a doctorate. Though Shaw was a tight fisted tyrannical ego maniac, Newsome was worse, a coward who drained the University's wealth with his corrupt unethical behavior and continuous propaganda, spinning night into day and dismal failure into excellence. He would have put Hitler's minister of propaganda Gerbels to shame. Of course this was Clarence Newsome.

The school had a penchant for hiring incompetent Administrators and some faculty who were either worthless alcoholics, and or cruel and abusive to their subordinates. The irony is that these monsters had degrees from prestigious Universities like Brown and Harvard. There was on alcoholic chairman from Harvard who married his new secretary after only one week on the job. They divorced a month later. The monster from Brown never learned to conjugate verbs from elementary school and murdered the English language during her five years there. The Academic Dean, Dr. Wilmouth Carter, was a very good

Administrator and strong leader, but she had so much riff raff and lazy subordinates that she could not deliver the kind of product that she desired. For example, her assistant, a ███████████ would come to work at 9:30am, go to coffee break, read the paper, then take a two and a half hour lunch break with his crony friends and leave early at 4:30. To add insult to injury, this wind bag became the next Dean when Dr. Carter retried. The poor University didn't have a chance to succeed and most of the students were just cannon fodder with a graduation rate of 13% in four years. Of course, the President didn't do anything about this for he was busy being important, mingling with Washington Congressman and Bureaucrats pursuing grandiose schemes to get money and grants that never materialized. The school decayed and self destructed before our very eyes.

In 1985, the faculty and staff went three months without pay, Smith was finally fired and we limped along until a White man, Mr. Spellman, with a reputation for saving drowning colleges came in and made a few simple logical decisions that breathed life into the campus. The first thing he did was double the tuition and changed the infrastructure and things improved. In 2006, Shaw was mortgaged to several large banks and the school limped along with a disgusted faculty and staff and a student body of mostly 9th graders perpetrating college students, who were essentially out of control and brought the ghetto to the heart of Shaw University.

Of course, President Clarence Newsome was above the fray, flying around the country on Shaw's American Express card and being the "Imperial" President. He apparently believed his own propaganda, boasting that we had the best students in decades and always stressed the concept of excellence in his speeches. It was a farce and a joke, but not funny to the faculty, staff and about 5% of students. He would have made Hitler proud, for his propaganda rivaled that of Heirich Himmler and Herman Gerbels.

Dr. Newsome was very insecure and suspicious of others who knew more about something than he did. He would prefer to remove established Administrators and bring in new "know nothings" that he was more comfortable with. It didn't matter that the organization suffered from many mistakes and blunders because of his decisions, it was only important that his ego was satisfied and that he had "yes" men to tell him he was wonderful and important.

That is another common characteristic I found among the three Presidents I served at Shaw. They were all Black, insecure, ego centered, narcissistic, domineering, afraid of the truth if it didn't please them and basically incompetent- with the exception of Talbert Shaw who had the luck of wisdom to have Ernest Pickens to run the University. My observation of Black college Presidents is that they abuse power, are vain, authoritarian and hide behind hatchet men in many cases who do their dirty work. They inflate their achievements and the value and effect of their institutions.

They also fail or refuse to see that only about 15% of their students are real college students, but admit pretty much anyone especially the poor Black that can qualify for U.S. Federal Financial aid, which is almost everyone. The sad thing is that about 80% of the students drop or flunk out before graduation and the U.S. tax payer foots the bill for all the wasted grant and loan money that served no tangible purpose. Of course, this make the parents happy to send their non prepared students to college because they have high hopes that the colleges will perform magic and somehow make productive citizens of their children who would otherwise end up in prison, on drugs, the streets or grave yard. I understand the parents need for hope, but it is basically false hope because the Black colleges are not prepared to meet the needs of the students and a charade and fraud is perpetrated on a perpetual basis.

If anyone blows the whistle or attempts to expose the corruption and fraud then they are called racist, not a team player and summarily fired or surreptitiously removed from the situation. Of course the White power structure knows about this fraud but they would rather pay the monetary price of supporting ineffective primarily private Black colleges than to let them die and have to put up with the millions of poorly educated Black high school student coming to their schools. So it was a quid pro quo with the top officials giving a wink and a nod to continue this situation with the cultural effect of lowering racial tensions and providing an escape valve for the 5 or 10% of serious qualified Blacks to lift themselves into the mainstream culture and have a shot at the American Dream. This was and is Shaw University. But for my advanced years I would make a run for her Presidency, knowing and acknowledging her strengths and weaknesses without the fragile ego of the past several Presidents. But alas, I know this sounds self serving and I really don't have the time or energy to turn the metaphoric Titanic in a few years. So, I will continue to do my duty and all that I can to help her survive until someone comes along with the skills and money to make her viable again and return her to the glory of the late 19th and early 20th centuries. I am happy to say that in May 2009, the Board of Trustees woke up and saw what the faculty, staff and students saw for 4 years. They fired Newsome and many of his cronies. Shaw would now have a chance to survive under new leadership. I have high hopes that that will happen.

Oops-my bad

I thought I was through with Shaw since we disposed of the incompetent, propagandist President Newsome, but neither I, nor anyone else of right mind had any clue or conception that we could get somebody worse to replace him. Now you might think I'm kidding or writing science fiction, but that is what has happened. Our Trustee Board, bless their heart, thought they were making an improvement by bringing in a temporary, one year transit president to right the ship, but what they got was a heavy handed, arrogant dictator with an agenda to fire or replace as many of us as she could in one year, reducing the budget outlay, destroy faculty and staff morale and essentially destroy the academic universities sense of purpose, freedom and individual dignity in order to save the physical and fiscal side of the university. This is or was a relatively happy campus even though the financial axe has been over our heads for years. But this new regime is unbelievable. We had no idea that out situation could get worse. We have gone from the extreme philosophical left of incompetent clowns to the extreme philosophical right of Nazi's, especially the narcissistic, Hitler type dean of the College of Arts and Sciences. A Dr. Adolph, he constantly harasses, intimidates and threatens faculty with sanctions and loss of employment for any minor infraction or omission. He either doesn't care or is oblivious to the damage he is doing and the stress he is placing on the faculty. I'm afraid that the anger may rise to the postal level. I sure hope not, but if it does, I don't want to be around at the time.

So, we continue on with a new chapter in this 144 year saga of Shaw and hope again that it will survive yet another group of bumbling, incompetent administrators who think they can either tell the big lie and delude themselves of success or use the iron fist of Nazism and punishment to achieve success. Either way is wrong and the students, faculty, staff and legacy of Shaw deserves better.

Shaw University

From Wikipedia, the free encyclopedia

Shaw University is a historically black college located in Raleigh, North Carolina. It offers several undergraduate degrees in the fine and liberal arts as well as natural science, and also degrees in allied health, business, public administration, education and computer science. Shaw Divinity School offers a Master of Divinity and Master of Religious Education. Shaw University is the oldest HBCU in the American South. A liberal arts university, Shaw is associated with the Baptist church and, as of 2004, enrolls over 2,300 students.

History

Shaw University was the first African American college in the Southern United States.[1] (http://www.shawuniversity.edu/) Started as a theology class by the Rev. Henry Martin Tupper in December 1865, the present university was called the Raleigh Institute from 1866 until 1870, when it was renamed Shaw Collegiate Institute after Elijah Shaw, the

Shaw University

Established	1865
Type	Private
President	Dr. Clarence G. Newsome
Undergraduates	2,500
Location	Raleigh, North Carolina, USA
Campus	Urban
Athletics	14 Varsity Teams
Mascot	Bear
Athletics	14 varsity teams
Website	www.shawuniversity.edu (http://www.shawuniversity.edu/)

benefactor of Shaw Hall, the college's first building. In 1875, it became Shaw University. In 1873, Estey Hall was erected for female students, making it the first such dormitory in the U.S. on a coeducational campus. The Leonard Medical School, now closed, was founded in 1885 as the first four-year medical school in the South to train black doctors and pharmacists.

The Student Nonviolent Coordinating Committee, a major force in the American Civil Rights movement, began at a conference held at Shaw in 1960.

Shaw University

Upon the recommendation of the Faculty and by the authority of the Board of Trustees, has conferred on

Colonel Vaughan Witten

the degree of

Bachelor of Arts

Liberal Studies

with all the rights, honors, and privileges thereunto appertaining.

In witness whereof, the seal of the University and the signatures of the Chairman of the Board of Trustees and the President are hereunto affixed.

Given at Raleigh, North Carolina this eighth day of May, 1999.

Chairman, Board of Trustees

President

208

North Carolina State University

On the recommendation of the Faculty and by virtue of the authority vested in them, the Trustees of the University have conferred on

Colonel Vaughan Witten

the degree of

Doctor of Philosophy

In testimony whereof, the seal of the University and the signatures of its officers are hereunto affixed this ninth day of August, nineteen eighty-nine.

Chairman of the Board of Governors

President of the University of North Carolina

Chairman of the Board of Trustees

Chancellor

Dean, Graduate School

209

SHAW Psychology OFFICE

SHAW ESTEY HALL

LEONARD HALL   TYLER HALL

RALEIGH SKYLINE

SHAW INTERNATIONAL STUDY BLDG
SOCIAL SCIENCES

[Handwritten annotation at top of page:] So much for Hope. This is an example of a good, noble man who in effect gave his life for Shaw — and an example of how he was horribly treated, and disrespected by Shaw's Administrative leadership, President. The toxic environment and jaded contempt for faculty and staff was obvious in this matter. Please Read. [signature] Colonel Walter [?] PhD 26 Oct 09

Witten, Dr. Vaughn

From:	Nelson Jr., James
Sent:	Monday, October 26, 2009 8:22 AM
To:	Faculty; Cape Directors; Wilson, P.E.; Library
Cc:	ps@williegary.com; lleb820@aol.com; ejpejj@yahoo.com; Sutton-Haywood, Dr. Marilyn; Monroe, Dr. Lee; Smith, Dr. Jeffrey A.; Lewis, Dr. Donnell; Bell, Dr. Joseph; Bryan, Linda
Subject:	Dr. Frederick Jones: An Extraordinary Life
Attachments:	Dr. Jones to Dr. Yancy.doc

One could traverse an entire lifetime and never meet a more caring man than Dr. Frederick Jones. Dr. Jones, who passed away on October 18, 2009, left a legacy of goodwill, scholarship, and concern for his fellow colleagues at Shaw University.

Faced with an ethical crisis affecting the lives of others, most of us recoil timidly in order to protect our own jobs. Without fanfare, Dr. Jones sacrificed his entire career and life so that others would not suffer. When Dr. Jones observed some detrimental personnel actions last summer, he quietly sent the attached letter to Dr. Yancy on July 13. This letter clearly delineated the concerns that would lead to his resignation a month later. Please observe that not one concern in this two-page letter indicates any personal injustice Shaw did to him. In this letter, Dr. Jones simply highlights the harm done to two fellow colleagues. Despite his personal interest to remain at Shaw, Dr. Jones informed Dr. Yancy, and many of us, that his integrity would not allow him to perform his duties if the injustices to two faculty members were not rectified.

Dr. Jones did resign from Shaw University in August without having another full-time job. Because of this, Dr. Jones toiled teaching six adjunct courses both day and night in a hectic schedule at two schools. His pay was one-third that of Shaw with no benefits. Despite this strenuous schedule for a senior citizen, Dr. Jones told his former colleagues he was relieved by his decision to leave Shaw. However, he continued to worry about his colleagues remaining at Shaw in a toxic environment. In an article to the Triangle Tribune on September 6, Dr. Jones reiterated that he was not planning to leave Shaw, but had to leave because of the ethical issues. As recently as ten days ago, Dr. Jones conveyed an eternal optimism in his new life and his hope that conditions would improve for his former colleagues.

Others will speak about Dr. Jones immense service to students, his untiring devotion to the Humanities Department, and his wise leadership in the College of Arts & Sciences. As a consequence, if someone writes about the recent history of Shaw, please include our hero and honor the contributions of Dr. Frederick Jones. Let all know that between 2003 and 2009, a noble man worked in our midst. This extraordinary man personified concern and love in a life rich with dignity. He left us an unmatched legacy of integrity that all can cherish. For these reasons, we salute Dr. Frederick Jones

July 13, 2009

Dear Dr. Yancy,

I am writing to respond to your e-mail requesting me to indicate to you the administrative issues I need to be clarified.

First of all, I have an Employment Agreement for 2009-10, dated March 31, 2009, that I signed on April 22, 2009. It states, among other things, that my appointment as Assistant Dean of the College of Arts and Sciences was being renewed for the 2009-10 academic year. I also know that Dr. Elvira Williams received and accepted a similar reappointment letter as Dean of the College of Arts and Sciences. Dr. Williams had to go on medical leave from June 30 for at least two weeks. Through her lead Administrative Assistant, she sent out a notice to the College's Department Chairs on Monday, June 29, to the effect that, in her absence, I would be the "point of contact until further notice." As of June 29, therefore, neither Dr. Williams, nor I had received any official indication that Dr. Williams had been terminated as Dean of the College. I was therefore stunned by the information that came from "Newswire" on July 2 that "Shaw University today named Dr. David Marshall the Interim Dean of the College of Arts and Sciences effective immediately." While I understand that a dean serves at the pleasure of the President of the University, I do not understand how two people could concurrently be appointed to the position of Dean for the same period of time. I know that Dr. Williams was not relieved of the position of Dean before Dr. Marshall was offered the same position. This is one of the administrative issues I need clarity on.

The second issue is in regard to faculty governance. As a department chair and assistant dean, I need to be very clear on every issue regarding faculty. The Faculty Handbook clearly states that if a faculty member is not to be rehired by the University, that faculty member should be given notice of that decision not later than December 31 for a termination that should be effective as of the following May. A faculty member in the Department of Mass Communications, which Dr. Marshall was the chair of, in the college of which I am the assistant dean, Mr. Russell Robinson, received and signed a reappointment letter for the 2009-10 academic year in April 2009. To the best of my knowledge, no provable incident that can reasonably be categorized as "cause" occurred between April and June 20, when he received a termination letter, which you signed, from the University.

The third administrative issue, which relates to the first two, concerns the appointment of Dr. David Marshall as Interim Dean. This is itself an issue for concern because of the following reasons: (a) There is an outstanding EEOC complaint from Mr. Robinson against Dr. Marshall regarding his leadership conduct; (b) Dr. Marshall resigned from Shaw University as of June 30, 2009, after one year in a position in which he supervised only two people; (c) SACS requires that an institution must demonstrate that its administrative and academic officers have the "experience, competence, and capacity to lead the institution." The Academic Positions section of Dr. Marshall's curriculum vitae shows that he had only had one full time academic position, lasting one year, before he

214

came to Shaw University. I am concerned that Dr. Marshall does not seem to have the qualification or experience to be Dean of the largest college of the university with over 70 faculty members in it. Moreover, the SACS *Principles of Accreditation* emphasizes the need for "institutions to make reasonable and responsible decisions consistent with the spirit of integrity in all matters."

In addition, I value my own integrity and would be unable to carry out my duties as Assistant Dean or Department Chair under the leadership of Dr. Marshall as Dean. It is in light of the above issues that I wrote an e-mail to your Administrative Assistant on July 9 requesting to see you.

As you know, Dr. Yancy, the President of the Faculty Senate, responding to expressions of concern by many faculty members, called an emergency faculty meeting on Wednesday, July 8. That meeting was very well attended and some recommendations were made that are on their way to your desk if they have not already reached it. So, I am not alone in my quest for an explanation of recent administrative issues at Shaw University.

I would be able to explain further if you grant me audience.

I thank you for giving me this opportunity to express my request for clarity in regard to these disturbing administrative issues, and I look forward to meeting with you.

Yours truly,

Frederick C. Jones, Ph.D.

Chair, Department of Humanities and

Assistant Dean, College of Arts & Sciences

Shaw University

SEE **HEALTH**, PAGE 6A

Fired, sued, hired by Shaw

School aware of checkered pasts

By Josh Shaffer
STAFF WRITER

RALEIGH – Shaw University, deeply indebted and aggressively seeking donors, has hired a vice president who was successfully sued for sexual harassment and a dean dismissed from the only other administrative job on his résumé.

The vice president, Lee Monroe, a Shaw alumnus, was hired this summer after his 2007 departure as president of Voorhees College in Denmark, S.C., where a jury awarded $500,000 to a professor who accused him of punishing her for rejecting repeated sexual advances. A university spokeswoman said Tuesday that Shaw officials knew about the lawsuit when they hired Monroe.

The dean of arts and sciences, David Marshall, was appointed in July after his contract was not renewed in 2006 at McNeese State University in Lake Charles, La., for issues that include his unapproved use of school foundation money, according to records from the Louisiana state university system.

Marshall's hiring — and the firing of a professor — triggered a sharp rebuke from a top faculty member. In an open letter e-mailed to colleagues last week, Faculty Senate President James Nelson said that the rescue mission has been undermined by a "moral crisis" brought on by personnel decisions, including Marshall's hiring.

"We say we wish to restore our financial base," Nelson wrote. "Our actions suggest we waste much of this base on a few individuals."

THE NEWS & OBSERVER +
WEDNESDAY, AUGUST 19, 2009

SHAW
CONTINUED FROM PAGE 1A

Marshall comes at a time of turmoil for the school. Interim President Dorothy Yancy is tasked with eliminating more than $20 million in debt and has called on supporters to revive Shaw, the oldest historically black college in the South.

Monroe is VP at Shaw University

Top officials at Shaw declined requests for comment. Board Chairman Willie Gary, a Florida lawyer, did not return repeated calls. Yancy did not answer a telephone message or respond to written questions hand-delivered to her office.

In an interview Tuesday, Shaw spokeswoman Tanya Wiley stressed the skills and hard work of both Monroe and Marshall, adding, "There's some people out there with an ax to grind."

Wiley also said Shaw officials knew of the lawsuit against Monroe but added that it "has nothing to do with his track record for raising money. It has nothing to do with his track record as a leader."

In a separate interview last week, Monroe downplayed the impact of the sexual harassment judgment on his ability to right Shaw's finances. He said he had recently statutory cap that reduced the amount a jury initially awarded her.

The suit filed in South Carolina was the second harassment action brought against Monroe as a college president. The first, in 1995, came from Marilyn Marshall, a former vice president at Paul Quinn College in Dallas, who alleged Monroe repeatedly made inappropriate remarks about her appearance, court records said. That suit was dismissed after a year because of a lack of evidence.

> 'I am appalled. It's the misuse of power. They are recycling these people that they put in there. The presidents are being recycled by their friends.'

MOREEN JOSEPH SUED LEE MONROE FOR SEXUAL HARASSMENT AT ANOTHER SCHOOL

snared a big donation despite his legal defeat.

"With those court documents in place, we got a commitment for $1 million," Monroe said. "So you go figure."

Marshall said Tuesday that Nelson's letter does not represent the feelings of Shaw's whole faculty, just that of one man. "He found something, he thought it was sexy, he sent it out," the dean said.

A loyal alumni base

Shaw supporters look to the campus as the mother of North Carolina's historically black schools. As a small institution with 2,750 students, Shaw produces graduates with fierce loyalty and appreciation for the doors it opened.

In May, President Clarence Newsome accepted a year's paid sabbatical and left his post amid criticism over poor finances and crumbling infrastructure. At the time, Gary described a debt of at least $20 million and said each Shaw board member would contribute $50,000 of his or her own money. But officials also lamented the school's graduation rate, which was hovering around 36 percent.

The South Carolina sex case was not his only problem at Voorhees.

In 2006, Denmark shut off water to the campus citing consistently late bills and partial payments, said city administrator Heyward Robinson. Monroe disputed the debt and paid with personal money.

"I remember he took out a check and wrote a check in my office," he said.

Shortly afterward, the city manager noted that Voorhees had also not paid for its share of a ladder truck needed to fight fires in multi-story buildings.

"We've had a rough go of it," Wiley said. "There's a national economic disaster going on."

Monroe, who turns 66 this month, is a Shaw graduate whose résumé includes jobs heading three historically black schools and serving as senior adviser for education to Gov. Jim Martin.

Alumni already praise Monroe's work for the troubled school, especially his reaching out to graduates through Internet seminars.

"He has been nothing but giving," said Emily Perry, president of the national alumni association. "I have nothing but good things to say about Doctor Monroe."

But Moreen Joseph, who successfully sued Monroe in South Carolina, called his hiring at Shaw an outrage and attributed it to the network of friends who hire each other for top jobs at historically black schools.

"I am appalled," Joseph said, adding she has tried unsuccessfully to get a job at Shaw. "It's the misuse of power. They are recycling these people that they put in there. The presidents are being recycled by their friends."

Joseph collected $136,000 plus attorneys' fees under a

Stint at McNeese State

Marshall came to Shaw after several short stints as professor and chairman of the McNeese State mass communications department, according to his résumé. He received his first reprimand in July 2005 after a month on the job, according to records from the grievance committee of the Board of Supervisors for the University of Louisiana system.

Marshall's appeal to the grievance committee was denied. In its decision, the committee A letter of reprimand was kept confidential.

JDMAYLO SHAW UNIVERSITY *FAYOBS*

Alumni association seeks board ouster

The Associated Press

RALEIGH — The national alumni association of Shaw University, one of the oldest historically black colleges in the South, has called for the board of trustees to step down or be dismissed because of continuing financial problems.

The News & Observer of Raleigh reported that the alumni association of Shaw University in Raleigh addressed its letter to the school board chairman Willie Gary, an alumnus and multimillionaire lawyer whose office is based in Stuart, Fla.

Shaw's board consists of educators, business people and Baptist officials in North Carolina, Florida and New York, as well as boxer Evander Holyfield and boxing promoter Don King, Shaw's website says. The school is searching for a new president and must renew its accreditation in 2012.

"We can no longer stand by and allow Shaw to appear to deteriorate due to poor judgment. ... We have serious concerns regarding conflict of interest, fiduciary responsibilities, adverse interest and commitment," says the May 14 letter from association president Emily Perry.

The letter isn't the first criticism from alumni about Shaw, a school of about 2,700 students that has debt of more than $20 million. In March, the school's Florida alumni group sent a letter to Shaw administrators saying it was "amazed" that giving among board members totaled only $41,089 since July, despite Gary's pledge that each of the roughly 40 board members would chip in $50,000.

Gary said Thursday that he doesn't plan to step down or request that anyone else do so. He said he hasn't kept up with his 1991 pledge to donate $10 million, at the rate of $250,000 a year, because of the recession.

"Whether I've given any money to Shaw in the last year or so? No, because of the economic times," Gary said. "We don't have it."

He promised to resume his donations once the economy improves.

Perry's letter, which was sent to board of trustee and alumni association members, suggests the board eliminate ineffective members to make way for the future.

"Now is the time for a new board of trustees that can effectively attend to the fiduciary responsibilities of Shaw," the letter reads.

Earlier this year, Shaw University secured a $31 million federal loan with help from U.S. Rep. Bob Etheridge.

30MAY10 FAYOBS

President destroying his own country

The man in our White House is plunging our country into a civil war, dividing the citizens in this great United States. He is determined to destroy us, from within and from without, one way or another.

On the inside, he says states cannot take it upon themselves to enforce federal law to protect their state from drugs, drug lords, weapons sales, murder, kidnapping and destruction of property caused by illegal immigrants coming into the U.S.

On the outside, he is disarming our country, thinking he is encouraging peace and favor with our enemies when the enemy does nothing except lie. He apologizes for us being a free and patriotic people.

He has spent and is spending money like a man gone wild from day one, always in a helicopter or Air Force One going somewhere to politic or have a photo op.

He is going to cause our country to collapse under a mountain of debt with programs he proposed and a stupid Congress voted into law. We fear for our children and grandchildren.

What have some of the American people voted into the White House? A man gone greedy for power and control of the greatest nation on Earth. He is unpatriotic and pretends to be a Christian. How can we take three more years of this?

Another thought; why do we waste money venturing into outer space when it is needed so desperately on Earth? Hello, American leaders, are you in space or spaced out?

Betty Lowrance
Clinton

217

ROUNDUP

8 Nov 2008

Shaw wins CIAA championship

A staff and wire report

DURHAM — Shaw broke open a close game with a dominating second half to win the CIAA championship in a 36-7 rout of Elizabeth City State on Saturday.

Quarterback Travis Robinson led Shaw (8-3) by passing for 309 yards and three touchdowns.

Shaw only led 13-7 at halftime but shut out the Vikings in the second half.

Three different receivers, Tyrone Bolden, Lenell King and James Pettway caught touchdown passes for Shaw.

Shaw had a balanced offense with 201 yards rushing, led by Raymon Williams with 96 yards and Aaron Ellison with 90.

■ San Diego 28, Davidson 24 — In Davidson, Sebastian Trujillo threw three touchdown passes and ran for the game-winning score as San Diego rallied to defeat Davidson.

The Wildcats (3-8, 2-4 Pioneer Football League) led 21-0 before Trujillo, who was 22 of 27 for 265 yards, began the comeback for the Toreros (7-2, 4-2).

■ Winston-Salem State 27, Delaware State 26 — In Dover, Del., Jarrett Dunston scored from 8 yards out with 4:19 to play to seal a comeback victory for Winston-Salem State against Delaware State.

Dunston completed 5 of 10 passes for 97 yards with two interceptions, adding 16 yards and two scores on nine carries for the Rams (3-6).

■ Appalachian State 49, Chattanooga 7 — In Chattanooga, T—

casins (1-9, 0-6) 655 yards to 227.

Appalachian State's Robert Welton scored three rushing touchdowns in the first half before taking the second half off.

He scored from 18 yards out, and followed a 76-yard run by Edwards with a 1-yard dive. Welton scored in the second quarter from 1-yard out for a 28-7 lead.

Edwards threw a 48-yard touchdown pass to T.J. Courman with 10 seconds left in the first half.

■ Elon 33, Western Carolina 14 — In Elon, Scott Riddle

quarter. Andrew Wilcox, who made a 47-yard field goal in the first, added a 34-yarder in the second to put Elon ahead 13-0.

■ Coastal Carolina 23, Gardner-Webb 18 — In Boiling Springs, Zach MacDowall threw for 292 yards and three touchdowns to lead Coastal Carolina to a win against Gardner-Webb.

The Chanticleers (5-5, 1-3 Big South Conference) won despite being outgained 439-344 by the Bulldogs (5-6, 2-2).

■ Florida A&M 45, North Carolina A&T 7 — In Greensboro, Curtis Pulley threw three touchdown passes to lead Florida A&M to a win against North Carolina A&T.

Pulley completed 14 of 28 passes for 201 yards for the Rattlers (7-3, The Rattlers (7-3, 3-3 Mid-Eastern Athletic Conference) outgained the Aggies (3-8, 1-6) 283-102, and capitalized on four turnovers en route to the victory.

No Democratic mandate

WASHINGTON — The national election Tuesday was not only historic for the election of the first African-American president in the nation's history but also for how little the avalanche of Democratic votes changed the political alignment in Congress.

The first Democratic Electoral College landslide in decades did not result in a tight race for control of Congress.

When Franklin D. Roosevelt won his second term for president in 1936, the defeated Republican candidate, Gov. Alf Landon of Kansas, won only two states, Maine and Vermont, and Democrats controlled both houses of Congress by wide margins.

But Obama's win was nothing like that. He may have opened the door to enactment of the long-deferred liberal agenda, but he neither received a broad mandate from the public nor the needed large congressional majorities.

The Democrats fell several

ROBERT NOVAK

votes short of the 60-vote filibuster-proof Senate that they were seeking and also failed to get rid of a key Senate target: Republican leader Mitch McConnell of Kentucky.

Republicans, though discouraged by the election's outcome, believe Obama will be hard-pressed not so much to enact his agenda but to keep his popular majority, which he considers centrist, as he moves to enact ultra-liberal legislation, particularly the demands of organized labor.

Robert Novak is a syndicated columnist. Readers may write to him at info@creators.com (with his name in the subject line) or Creators Syndicate, 5777 W. Century Blvd., Suite 700, Los Angeles, CA 90045.

Witten, Dr. Vaughn

From: Nelson Jr., James
Sent: Wednesday, September 30, 2009 6:08 AM
To: Faculty; Cape Directors; Wilson, P.E.; Library
Cc: ps@williegary.com; lleb820@aol.com; ejpejj@yahoo.com; Sutton-Haywood, Dr. Marilyn; Monroe, Dr. Lee
Subject: Restoring a Shaw that Cares

Many of us have expressed concerns about how Shaw treats us. No one seems to listen to or care about employees. Communications to employees are frequently laced with vitriol suggesting little need for us or our services.

Shaw's traditional mission supports humanity

Shaw was founded in December, 1865 to educate the freedmen who stood on the bottom rung of the social structure. Shaw's founders resisted the oppressors of that time who used fear, intimidation and force to keep freedmen on that bottom rung. Shaw's motto in English became "For Christ and Humanity". Throughout our history, Shaw's goal has been to meet the needs of disadvantaged groups.

Shaw currently strays from its traditional mission

Many lovers of Shaw deplore those who use our oppressor's tactics of fear, intimidation and force to achieve their objectives. Insensitive treatment of our colleagues at Shaw frequently strays from our traditional humane mission. Small groups of people usually end up denying voices to the masses by limiting their chances to redress grievances or giving them at-will contracts. *Shaw's current oppressions should be relegated to the dungeons of our past.*

We desire a Shaw of trust and fairness

Let us become committed to giving every employee a voice to be heard and treated with dignity. Let us engage in dialogue. Let's cooperate with every request as long as the basic principles of integrity and fairness are not compromised. Let's make our University fit, have healthy values, and value people. Let's do this because valuing people is our true road to prosperity. As a result, let's treat our colleagues with fairness and equality because we recognize their unique contributions and value to Shaw University. Let's create a positive work environment at Shaw by listening to employees. Let's help our University build trust by respecting staff, students and faculty. Let's encourage our leaders to listen to our voices and not perceive input as criticism deserving dismissal.

Shaw's wall of fear cracks

Some of us have responded to Shaw's challenges by honoring our past. When students started a recent petition supporting a teacher they admired, they were told they may lose their financial aid for signing it. Many signed it anyway and submitted the petition to Chairman Gary. When faculty were asked to sign a letter supporting due process, most signed it directly in front of the Vice President. When faculty members were told that the Senate President's job may be in danger, many came to Estey Hall to pray for our trustees, administrators and University. When faculty kept being reminded by their interim dean that their job was in danger for not doing what many saw as unnecessary tasks, some objected and requested a vote of no confidence in this manager. When two teachers could not abide by

9/30/2009

unethical practices at Shaw beneath their standards, they abruptly quit their jobs. Some employees have even become whistleblowers, informing outsiders of our flaws.

Our founder's vision must be carefully moved from our present dungeon and spread into the bright light of our new future. Leading to this goal, we are asking every employee of Shaw University to approve the following new initiatives:

1. Universal Mediation for all Employees

Our University needs effective employees. Becoming an effective employee is difficult when you spend enormous amounts of time nursing grudges. Small problems at Shaw become major crises because of years of neglect. We propose the establishment of a mediation group made up of students, faculty, staff, and administrators. This mediation group will give everybody a chance to be heard and respected. It will give every person an opportunity to negotiate and create a positive atmosphere of caring and goodwill before anything escalates to grievance level.

2. Universal Due Process for all Employees

Our University needs to treat employees fairly. Some issues cannot be decided amicably by mediation, so a person may sometimes face disciplinary actions, including termination. We propose that in cases where the facts are in dispute, that all employees be given the chance to appeal to a Grievance Committee where employees can be informed of charges against them, allowed a chance to be heard in his or her defense, and allowed a chance to bring witnesses in their defense.

3. Appointment Letters that Support Employee Loyalty to Shaw

Our University needs to value employees. At-will contracts were created after slavery to maintain the aristocrats' system of subjugation and control. Shaw's current practices deny staff yearly reappointment letters and insert restrictive clauses in faculty's reappointment letters that limit their rights to redress grievances.

4. Monthly Town Hall Meetings to Identify and Solve Problems

Our University needs to fix employee problems. Problems cannot be fixed if there is an unwillingness to recognize their existence. If problems continue forever, they do serious damage to our University. A monthly town hall meeting can help us identify problems and solve them before they reach destructive proportions.

Please discuss these initiatives in your area. Post them on your wall. Let's have a meeting soon to consider adoption of them. Then, let's hold hands together restoring a great University that shows respect for the views, tolerance of the beliefs, and concern for the welfare of all employees.

9/30/2009

Former assistant dean blasts Shaw's ethics

Published Wednesday, September 2, 2009 7:00 am
by Sommer Brokaw>

RALEIGH – In light of the immediate appointment of David Marshall as interim dean of the College of Arts and Sciences at Shaw University, the assistant dean retired.

Frederick Jones, who served as chair of the Department of Humanities for five years and assistant dean for two years, resigned last month under the new presidential administration of Dr. Dorothy Yancy who confirmed Marshall's appointment.

Marshall has come under fire recently for failing to disclose information that he was fired as chair of the Department of Mass Communications at McNeese State. Particularly disturbing was one of the grievances alleged mishandling of foundation money, and Shaw is still recovering from $20 million in debt. But Marshall denies the allegation.

Jones, who interviewed him for the position, said he wasn't told that Marshall had been fired; instead, he was told he left Louisiana because of Hurricane Katrina.

"I wasn't planning to leave at this time, but I brought it to the attention of the authorities that I wasn't going to serve under Dr. Marshall as dean. I wasn't comfortable with his credentials," Jones said. "Dr. Yancy wasn't going to do anything about it."

Jones detailed three major ethical issues that he listed in a letter to Yancy earlier this year.

First, Dr. Elvira Williams received and accepted a reappointment letter as dean of the College of Arts and Sciences for the 2009-10 academic year. "It's just unethical," Jones said. "You reappoint the person and then you appoint someone else to the same position, and this person that you appoint to the same position doesn't have the experience or the qualifications to be dean of the largest college of the university."

Second, the faculty handbook says written notice that an appointment is not to be renewed shall be given to full-time faculty in advance of the expiration of any appointment, no later than December 31 by certified mail. Jones wrote that Russell Robinson, a faculty member in the communications department, received and signed a reappointment letter for the new academic year in April, but he didn't receive a termination letter until June, signed by Yancy.

"This was in complete violation of the regulations, and Dr. Marshall was instrumental in that firing because I know that he had tried several times to get Mr. Robinson fired," Jones said. "One of the reasons I think he did that is because Mr. Robinson had discovered that his past was fishy, that he had not been upfront about why he left Louisiana, so he became vindictive."

Third, Jones said Marshall isn't qualified for the position based on two reasons: One, Robinson has an outstanding EEOC complaint against Marshall; and second, Marshall only had one other full-time academic position before he came to Shaw, which lasted one year.

With Shaw preparing for re-accreditation in 2012, he added that the Southern Association of Colleges and Schools require that an institution demonstrate its administrative and academic officers have the "experience, competence and capacity to lead the institution."

Marshall denies that he had any personal vendetta against Robinson. "It's ridiculous on its face to suggest that I would walk into a job without any preparation."

Witten, Dr. Vaughn

From: Nelson Jr., James
Sent: Monday, February 15, 2010 8:10 AM
To: Nelson Jr., James; Faculty; Cape Directors; Wilson, P.E.; Library
Cc: ps@williegary.com; lleb820@aol.com; ejpejj@yahoo.com; Sutton-Haywood, Dr. Marilyn; Monroe, Dr. Lee; Smith, Dr. Jeffrey A.; Lewis, Dr. Donnell; Bell, Dr. Joseph; Bryan, Linda; Yancy, Dr. Dorothy C.; dcforbes@bellsouth.net; mspaulding50@aol.com; Fillingham, Sherri; Wiley, Tanya; ateresachavis@hotmail.com; silver1282@aol.com; accurateset@verizon.net; isaachorton@remotelight.com; MFSpaulding50@aol.com; Woods, Janine

Subject: Shaw's Inequities Mirror Our Sad Past

Throughout its history, Shaw's accomplishments have been noteworthy. Shaw had successful professional schools of medicine, pharmacy, and law. Shaw was among the first to admit women students and construct a dormitory for females. Shaw's hospital and teacher education programs admirably served the needs of North Carolina's disadvantaged people. The Student Nonviolent Coordinating Committee (SNCC) was organized on Shaw's campus in April 1960. However, even before SNCC founder, Ella Baker, graduated from Shaw in 1927 as class valedictorian, she frequently challenged Shaw's policies she thought were unfair.

So, forty years ago, Shaw's leaders should have known better. These leaders were grounded in a civil rights movement that sought tolerance and opportunity for all people. They knew about Shaw's rich tradition. Yet, these leaders created a Shaw that closely paralleled the inequities we endured from our European bondage. In this issue, we discuss how Shaw's post-civil rights inequity started, its consequences, and what we can do to eliminate it now.

Shaw Creates System of Inequities

During the 1960's, President James Cheek instituted a number of progressive initiatives. Two such programs were granting half-year salaries to mostly African-American faculty willing to go back to obtain the PhD and also doubling the average salary of faculty. However, accrediting agencies, newspapers and some other influential whites often denigrated Shaw's quality. Facing financial exigencies, Shaw abandoned many costly programs benefiting the mostly African-American faculty and students. As a result, many African-American professionals started withdrawing support to Shaw.

Despite eliminating the costly program supporting the largely African-American faculty who obtained their PhD's, Shaw gained instant credibility with a low cost solution. Shaw would import low-paid PhD's largely from working class whites and foreign born nationals. Differing from their pre-civil rights counterparts, few of these newcomers had civil rights backgrounds or experience aiding blacks. In spite of these obvious deficiencies, few newcomers were integrated into Shaw's community. Even worse, Shaw retained its inbred, detached and well-connected African-American leadership.

By the late 1970's, Shaw was inhabited by a divisive mix of agendas. Many black intellectuals had become disillusioned that they were losing their beloved Shaw. Many "outsiders" were aware that they had no real role in governance but were being exploited for their PhD's to give an appearance of quality. Capitalizing on our mistrust of each other, Shaw's self-serving entrenched leadership produced a financial crisis during this past decade largely by aggravating the tensions, withdrawing services for faculty and students to dangerous levels, abandoning our infrastructure, and enriching themselves. Before anyone would stop this abuse, Shaw was in shambles with its two-tier system of inequities deep-rooted

Shaw's bottom tier struggles to survive

Shaw's bottom tier is composed of the majority of African-Americans not lucky enough to join the top tier. They share the bottom with virtually all whites and persons of foreign descent. Devoid of a grievance process to settle differences or clauses that guarantee job security, individuals in these groups frequently tussle for modest personal gains.

Most live with continual fear. Every step they take; every hour, every minute and every second they live; any wrong move they make might lead to unemployment. Any criticism they share, any disloyalty others perceive, any act of independence could lead to homelessness. There's no way of knowing when their last day at Shaw will be. There's never any way of knowing!

Shaw's top tier struggles to maintain control

Shaw's top tier is led by roughly twenty Board members and a few administrators. An elite subgroup of approximately four Board members and an administrator craft virtually all of Shaw's important decisions. Devoid of processes that ensure fairness or input, this group gives perks to members of the bottom tier based largely on loyalty and developed relationships.

Most members of our top tier also live with continual fear. They fear Shaw's closure. Their self-declared mission is to save Shaw. Every potential student that is not enrolled, any tuition that is not received, every criticism from members of the Shaw community, any distraction from raising money, every negative newspaper article could lead to closing Shaw. There's no way of knowing when Shaw will close. There's never any way of knowing!

Many of Shaw's leaders have religious or civil rights backgrounds. But from this, little benefit is garnered. These righteous backgrounds have not impeded members of this group from inflicting pain on the bottom tier. Such pains to the bottom tier are well-known and include residing in poorly maintained buildings, receiving low and disparate pay, earning no pension match to sustain them when they age, and working under at-will clauses where they are dismissed without any due process. When a few brave souls bring up those troubling contradictions, they are immediately ostracized. Moreover, leaders quickly justify why they must endure the pain. "All problems cannot be solved immediately", they say. "Besides, if Shaw closes, the bottom tier loses their jobs anyway."

Shaw improves when we stop creating fear

The common denominator uniting most of us is fear. Shaw improves when we stop creating fear. We must be courageous enough to give all members of our Shaw community far more chances to learn sharing, to challenge thoughtfully, to work safely, to grow harmoniously, and to thrive utilizing inherent abilities we all possess.

Finally, we must reduce fear because imitating inequities of past destructive European cultures is not Shaw's way. Sharing our limited resources, showing compassion to the least fortunate of us, giving love to all people, and working to ensure disadvantaged people have a brighter future all combine to make up OUR tradition at Shaw. Let's refocus our efforts towards honoring our noble tradition.

2/15/2010

Faculty and Course Evaluation Comments, Spring 2009

Instructor	Instructor/Class/Location	Please describe one specific learning activity that was particularly useful in helping you meet the student learning outcomes for this course.	What specific suggestions do you have toward making this course a better learning experience?	Please share any additional comments you may have.
Witten, Colonel	Witten, Colonel - PSY47001, Raleigh Day		none	Dr. Witten tought his class as if it was on the graduate level, because of this I'm now able to prepare for grad school with confidence.
		Doing the 8-10 page research paper was useful in helping me meet the outcome for this course because my paper was on sigmund freud and he plays a major part in psychology. I learned so much about him in ding the research paper.	none..continue teaching the same way because i've learned so much	This is a great class and you will leave out of there with so much knowledge about psychology.
		We really didn't have learning activities, he lectured more and gave you life examples to help you have a better understanding writing a bio of someone we learned about.	Nothing.	He is a very tough teacher, but only because he cares about your future. Study hard, and things will be fine
	Witten, Colonel - PSY49201, Raleigh Day	The examples Dr Witten gave during class help to better understand the material and a good way of remembering it too.	give a study guide of what is exactly on the quiz and tests	Dr Witten is a outstanding teacher. In class he doesn't just tell us what we are suppose to be learning but, he goes further to inform us with extra material that we may benefit from in the future. It is a good thing for him to want us to know the materia
		This course inhance my critical thinking skills. What i learned from this class, it really teaches you to think outside the box.		

224

Who's Who
AMONG STUDENTS IN
American Universities
& Colleges

This is to certify that

VAUGHAN C. WITTEN

has been elected to
Who's Who Among Students in
American Universities & Colleges
in recognition of outstanding merit and
accomplishment as a student at

SHAW UNIVERSITY

1998-99

Director

*Birthdays rekindle
warm feelings for those
who have touched our lives
in a special way.*

connections
from *Hallmark*

THOMAS KINKADE™
Painter of Light™

Thomas Kinkade is America's most collected living artist,
a painter-communicator whose tranquil light-infused paintings
bring hope and joy to millions each year.
Each painting he creates is a quiet messenger in the home,
affirming the basic values of family, health, faith in God,
and the luminous beauty of nature.

Inspired by A Peaceful Retreat © 2002 Thomas Kinkade.

THIS CARD IS MADE
WITH RECYCLED PAPER.
20% Recycled Fiber

Hallmark.com

U.S.A. 2.44
Canada 3.49
GAB 436 E
© HALLMARK LICENSING, INC.
HALLMARK CARDS, INC.
KANSAS CITY, MO 64141
TORONTO, CANADA M2J 1P6
MADE IN U.S.A.

0 92100 42075 8

2-18-10

Happy Birthday—

from just one of the many
you've touched
with your caring heart →
and your loving spirit. ___

Happy Birthday
to "My Hero."

Love,
Kimberly Colwell

Dr. Witten,

All I can say is "Thank you" for allowing me to type "The Journey". It was so wonderful to learn about history from someone who lived it. I love the fact that our ideas & morals are the same. I look up to you and respect you as more like a father and enjoy gleaning knowledge from you. Thank you for all you have done and for just being you. In case you were wondering, I'm always telling my family about our conversations and because I think so highly of you, David refers to you as "my hero."

Kimberly

227

DECLINE OF THE FAMILY AND CULTURE

A <u>significant</u> portion of the population began a rapid change in behavior beginning in the mid 1970's. White boys in their teen and early twenties began wearing long hair, like women, which was unthinkable before. Parents started losing control over their children, partly from neglect and partly from excessive government intervention in the family. Laws were passed to prevent child abuse, but went too far, stripping the parents of their usual authority to punish, spank and otherwise keep children in line and teach them manners, pride, fear of God, humility, and general civil behavior and principles of honesty and hard work. Children became wild and generally lazy, often challenging their parent's authority and even killing them in some cases. Parents on the other hand, lost much of their caring and responsibility for their kids, leaving them to fend for themselves after school was out each day, while they, the parents worked two jobs to make ends meet. Children with so much unsupervised time often got in trouble, broke the law, took drugs, smoked cigarettes and often wound up in prison for crimes including murder. There was a swift increase in parent killing of children, by cooking them in microwave ovens, throwing them off bridges into rivers, and many other forms of murder, just to get rid of them.

Abortion

To make the moral decline worse was the US Supreme Court decision in Roe vs. Wade, 1973, which legalized abortion. The abortion rate exploded. Teenagers would get pregnant and just have a "routine" abortion. Lives became less valuable and the law prevented the parents from having any say about their daughter's decision to abort.

But this was only the tip of the iceberg of an imploding culture that was moving away from God and towards Sodom and Gomorrah. An estimated 1 ½ million babies were aborted each year or about 45 million since 1973. Now this is the crux of the debate or argument over abortion. The liberals believe that life begins at birth and the antiabortionist conservatives believe that life begins at conception. So the abortionists don't think a person is killed at abortion. In this regard, the Supreme Court did temper its decision by ruling that unlimited abortion could only be practiced during the first and second trimester or six months into pregnancy and not during the last three months, although some violate this rule and kill their babies close to the ninth month.

Black Power, Pride and Stupidity

In 1964, the US Congress passed the Civil Rights Act to all, but primarily Blacks, the right to public accommodations such as hotels, transportation and restaurants without discrimination. The 1954 Brown vs. Board of Education, Topeka, Kansas had already declared Blacks should receive integrated equal education as/and with Whites, and the 1965 Voting Rights Act gave equal voting rights to Blacks as well as Whites. With all these legal victories, one would think that Blacks would excel and prosper, but the opposite occurred. Yes, Blacks now could go to school with Whites, though Whites resisted the integration, it was eventually implemented after 30 years of turmoil, fighting and busing. But the whole concept backfired. After 40 years, Blacks on average can't read or write even when graduating from high school. The whole education system has been dumbed down to where Whites also receive inferior education. Blacks score at least 20 pints less on standardized tests that are culture fair and have little sense of loyalty and concern for the institutions that hold the country together.

How could this happen? Well, Blacks after being held in slavery 250 years and social racism for another 150 years became almost wild and unmanagble with their freedom gained in the 1950's, 60's and 70's. They were all about "Black is Beautiful, Black Power" and so on. They were high on rhetoric, but no substance. A subculture of consumers, but with no wealth or economic or political power, like a child in a candy store with $500.00 to spend. They became a separate entity to the normal Black and White culture. They became deliberately different with outlandish clothes, wearing pants hanging off their ass, creating irreverent rap-stupid music, working two an d three $6.00 an hour jobs to survive, rob, steal and kill. The murder rate of Black on Black went off the charts and the prison population exploded with about 70% of prisoners in city, state and federal prisons being Black, but only comprising 13% of the population. They were unaware of their own impending doom of self destruction which is now occurring and having a negative effect on the normal Black and White population. The average person is afraid to be around Black men for fear of being robbed or murdered. The whole culture is now apprehensive of each other. Everyone is afraid of the other because they trust no one. Once you could hitch hike across the country. People trusted each other to give and accept a ride. Now both parties are afraid of each other and the cars just pass you by. Once we would stop to help a stranded motorist, now the cars just pass the motorist in distress as though they are invisible. Everyone is suspicious of the other one and might get robbed, carjacked or murdered.

As far as Black Pride is concerned, that is really a misnomer. The young Blacks of today, 2008, have no pride, no shame and essentially no future. They will do anything; say anything without any concern of its consequences, pain to others or anything. It is like we have produced a bunch of mindless, stupid monsters that are digging a deeper hole to destruction, but have no cognizance of knowledge of what they are doing. And the most absurd part of this whole situation is that they and their parents believe that if they go to college, the few that do, think a college education even a diluted one will save them. One thinks back to WEB Dubois in the 1920's about his comments on the talented tenth. That is about 10% of the Black race will become educated and provide leadership for the rest. Now it's about the talented 20th, or 5% will be qualified to lead and those will be women. The Black young male is an endangered, dying species with about 60% in prison, on drugs, gay or have AIDS. The young Black female of the future will have only Whites, Hispanics or other nationalities as eligible marriage partners.

There are more Black males in prison than in college. The prison population is saturated with them and they continue to commit crime(s) at a record pace. Mostly the crimes are violence, robbery, murder against other Blacks. They are typically afraid of White people in general, but have a pent up of hate just under the surface. The young men appear to be retarded, deliberately wearing their pants below their butt, while continually pulling them up, sometimes having a belt, but often not. This is supposed to emulate the Blacks in prison who are not allowed to have belts. The young women wear pins stuck in their tongues, in their nose and other places. They all just want to defy and defeat the White man and gloat and celebrate and brag at the White led government troubles, problems and defeats. They bask in other countries making the United States look bad. If they hate America so much, why do they stay here. I would gladly ship them away if I could to any where they wanted to go for free. And the Black candidate, Obama, running for President, if he wins, they will probably burn down America celebrating, them along with the stupid Whites who are deluded into believing he will save them. They know not what they do for I predict Obama will lie, sell the U.S. down the river and set the stage for an internal rebellion by true Americans that already detect his deceit, criminal and Muslim connections and liberal, Marxist policies. If he is not elected President, then the Blacks will say that the election was fixed or stolen. Things are only fair if they, we, Blacks win. I am of course Black also, that's one reason why I know and understand them so well. Yes, Blacks are the racists today, and that racist attitude feeds their ego and allows them to rationalize their lack of success, poverty, and second class status on to the Whites via the interaction of projection and displacement-always shielding themselves from the blame that is rightfully theirs. Yes, I am a Psychologist and have an added insight beyond my experience.

The Hispanic Problem-Illegal Immigration

Our country has now become a haven with a practically open door to illegal immigrants from Mexico and other Central and South American countries. We now have about 12 million illegal and some estimate at least 20 million. They are on average hard workers and dependable employees, they are usually preferred over Blacks and many lower class Whites because they do come to work on time and produce a product. The problem with them is legal, economic and political. Legal in that they are not supposed to be here and should go home, but they won't because our laws are not tough enough to round them up and ship them out. Plus they claim discrimination, but have such a good deal making 10 times the money they could get in Mexico that they use every legal and illegal trick to stay here. Economics, in that they get free schooling, medical and other services from our communities and drive some cities bankrupt, though they are illegal to start with. Go figure. It's a mystery to me also. Political in that they are constantly stirring up sympathy for their plight in the US and causing debate about what to do about them. They come here illegal and pregnant then have a legal baby on our soil who in 18 years can vote to have a Mexican president here. At the rate they are expanding we will be a Hispanic nation in 50 years and Americans will have to learn Spanish rather than English.

The National and State Governments are trying to cope with this problem by building fences along our southern border, tighter passport-visa laws, deport the criminals we have in jail and other measure. They are heavy drinkers, alcoholics, law breakers, won't buy car insurance, drive without licenses, you name it. They ignore our laws and then complain that we abuse them-even though they are illegal just by being here. Again, it boggles the mind to think that we have come to this. I must admit they are good, reliable workers and generally preferred over unreliable Blacks.

Rapid Black Decline after 1965

There was a time when although oppressed with racism and discrimination, Blacks over 40 or so and our ancestors were united, had normal pride, were independent thinkers, took care of their children, tied their shoes, kept clean houses, paid their bills and were basically good decent American citizens-and could read and write by 3rd grade. We could get out of bed, be on time and do a good days work for meager pay to support our family. But now, it's turned upside down. The young of today have little to zero respect for anyone or anything, especially Blacks. They don't even respect and honor their own mother and father. Most grow up in a single family mother home anyway. They tend to be unreliable, irresponsible, won't pay their debts, not interested in a higher education, unless they can get it easy, without hard work. In fact, the work ethic is gone and replaced with a "get over it" mentality laced with deception and lies. Hardly anyone trusts them or feels comfortable around them without fear or an impending calamity, crime, insult or other unsocial behavior. They are essentially man-children with limited true verbal and written skills outside Ebonics or Rap. Many with college degrees can't even fill out an employment application sufficiently to qualify for a job, but they think they know everything and their elders know little or nothing. Girls want to have babies at 12 and 13 years old and those babies do the same thing 13 years later, with babies having babies, mothers become great-grandmothers in their 40's and 50's. The grand parents generally raise the mother's children while the mother is working two McDonald's jobs to pay for her car and cell phone. As for a cell-mobile phone goes, everyone has one even if they are starving, they will take their last dollar to pay the phone bill because they love it sooo much. The girls in many cases are so psychologically lonely and have such low self esteem that they have their own real live baby so they can have someone e to love and someone to love them. It is so sad. It's difficult to see a young person in any activity without having the phone to their ear while driving, walking across traffic, sitting alone, eating, everywhere. They and adults are stupid enough to send text messages while driving-and causing accidents. Finally, the last nail in the coffins for Blacks is that they are now more racist than Whites. They see everything in terms of Black and White and blames "Whitey" for everything. They don't aspire to overcome their problems and take responsibility for their plight. The White man knows this and is just waiting for their destruction.

911 and War on Terror

On the morning of September 11, 2001 at about 8:30am, two large passenger jet airplanes with hundreds of innocent people on board were deliberately flown into the two World Trade Center towers in New York City. The towers burned for an hour or so and eventually collapsed killing over 3,000 people, including over 300 firefighters and police trying to put the fires out. These planes were flown by Muslim radicals in a holy jihad war against the United States from Saudi Arabia and several other Middle Eastern countries. There were 19 of t hem in all that hijacked these two planes and two more that same day, which I will discuss later. The "master mind" in this attack on America was a Saudi named Osama Bin Laden, and his disaster group called "Al-Qaeda". About the same time that morning, a third hijacked plane flew into the Pentagon in Washington, D.C., killing about 100 military and civilian personnel. The last plane which was apparently headed for White House was disrupted in its evil mission by the passengers on board who heroically counter attacked them in the airplane without weapons and fought them until the plane crashed in a field outside Shanksville, Pa. killing all aboard. It is believed this plane was destined for the White House or the US Capitol Building.

The President, George W. Bush, his administration, the military and the American people were shocked, traumatized and outraged. The perpetrators were deemed to have come primarily from previously protected training camps in Afghanistan. Once the country gained its balance, treated the causalities, found and buried the dead, the Congress declared war on these monsters and went on a war of deploying military forces into the Afghan, Pakistan, Iraq regions to retaliate and punish them for their cowardly attack. There was a strong effort to kill the Taliban and other fanatical jihadist, especially Bin Laden. We almost had him at Tora Bora Mountain, but the B-52 and other bombing attacks could not get him and he apparently escaped in to Pakistan. Since 2001, he has been on the run and we don't know where he is, seven years later. It is believed that he is hiding in caves, in the mountains of Pakistan.

The war in Afghanistan and the hunt for Osama continues and will continue until the insurgents, Taliban and Osama are killed, captured or otherwise pacified. We then lost about 5,000 US military in this war so far that is not even nearly over.

Iraq War 2003-Present-Persian Gulf War II

Subsequent to the 911 attacks, the President of Iraq, Sadam Hussien, having being a belligerent in 1991, against the US and NATO Forces, after invading Kuwait, again challenged the world with his arrogance and suspected possession of nuclear weapons. U.S. President, George W. Bush, of the first Persian Gulf War, convinced the United Nations that force was needed to bring Sadam down and rid him of weapons of destruction. So in March 2003, the U.S. invaded Iraq and defeated his forces in about three weeks. No weapons of mass destruction were found and the war appeared to be over. But there was so much religious hate and rivalry between the Sunni and Shiite branch of the Islam religion previously held in check by Saddam's iron hand, that it exploded into an insurgency and civil war that almost defeated the U.S. forces caught in the middle of their war. At this time, the U.S has essentially recovered from near defeat and has nearly brought the situation under control at the cost of over 5,000 dead, 30,000 wounded and nearly 800 billion dollars in treasurer. The political impact of this venture has been tremendous on the U.S. people about why we went into the war and when are we getting out.

The Housing Crisis and Wall Street Meltdown

In 2007, after years of shoddy mortgage practices by banks and mortgage companies that had been lending to people that actually didn't qualify for big loans they couldn't afford, the borrowers began defaulting when their low teaser loan rates increased via the variable interest increases that often doubled or tripled the house payments. These easy loans were made by what was called "sub-prime" mortgage loans to weak income borrowers. Then the bubble burst and thousands of people were put out of their homes by foreclosure, the banks that held these toxic bad loans began to fail and fall like flies. Huge investment banks like Bear Sterns, Merrill Lynch, insurance giant AIG and savings bank Washington Mutual lost billions and either went bankrupt or was bought up by other surviving institutions as their stock prices dropped to fire sale prices of 2 to 8 dollars on average. Even the humongously large quasi governmental mortgage companies Fannie Mae and Freddie Mac holding over half of mortgages in the United States, went under with stock dropping to $1.50 per share. They were taken over by the U.S. treasury and exacerbated the meltdown that forced the government to tackle a problem so serious it threatened to bring down the entire U.S. financial system with massive bank failures, millions of job losses by working citizens and loss of confidence in the capitalistic economic ethos. The Congress was in crisis or near panic mode in October 2008 to hammer out a proposed $700 billion bailout and package for the Wall Street blunders and stupid-supposed to be smart bankers. The American people were outraged as was Congress with the situation, but something had to be done. After weeks of debate, argument, shock and finger pointing, the Congress agreed to provide a three pronged approach to bailing out the situation that may or may not work out in the future.

Warning to America

We are in danger of being <u>too</u> politically correct. Mentally challenged instead of retarded, Administrative Assistant instead of secretary, physically challenged instead of handicapped, man made incident instead of terrorist. I could go on, but I think you get the drift. We want to be sweet and respectful to our enemies, radical Islamist terrorist, when they want to <u>kill</u> us and they make no apologies about that. So we have become so weak of spirit and commitment to our nation that we just give up to these punks who believe that if they kill us by jihad or blowing themselves into pieces to achieve their insane purpose, they will have 72 virgins waiting on them in their heaven. I say we send them to the virgins by <u>killing them first</u> and hope they run out of virgins. Have we lost our American pride and righteousness? It seems so, especially the liberal faction that would lead us down the path of self destruction because we became too stupid to protect ourselves from our enemies. Why do we enable and embolden a group holding a knife to our throat? The airline business will soon collapse with everyone afraid to fly, even if we fly naked. But of course with incompetent, so called leaders like Homeland Security Secretary, Janet Napolitano, saying "the system worked" when the Nigerian boy bumbled and failed to blow up a plane in Detroit, Christmas 2009, we have no chance of success.

Internally, we are just as weak in other areas. We're afraid to accept the idea of winners and losers anymore. We must be politically correct and make everybody a winner even if they don't deserve it. We give "F" grade student's a "C" just so we don't hurt their feelings. Nothing is as it seems. We can't take reality, so we just change the name of something to make it sound good, and then <u>we believe</u> it. It's a national delusion. But we go on pretending that we are what we are not. Many have nickel and dime income, yet attempt to live the rich life of big house, car, boat, cruises and jewelry, but it's all based on debt or credit cards. If the economy sneezes we go bankrupt and then complain about the system. Then Obama comes along and promises us that he will fix it and take from the rich by spreading the wealth. We then proclaim him the messiah and elect him President. This is so stupid and foolish, for we have succumbed to the Anti-Christ and will pay with regrets for generations to come. A lie cannot last and our deluded sense of self will have no basis in reality.

We must <u>stop killing</u> our babies and calling it abortion. We have killed 60 million babies since the 1973 *Roe vs. Wade* Supreme Court abortion decision. We could now have around 350 million Americans to fight the terrorist. The conservative's belief life begins at conception and the liberals believe it begins at birth, so the killing doesn't bother them.

We definitely must stop dumbing down the educational system. We give "A's" to "D" students and graduate high schoolers with an 8th grade knowledge level. They basically can't read, write, add or subtract. And Lord, please don't ask them to multiply. They can't even multiply by ten. It is so sad. Also, the cell phones and "bling-bling" should go in the trash. People will pay the cell bill with no food in the house, talk and text while driving and use it for a companion just as 13 year old girls have a baby to comfort and love them when they feel unloved and neglected by society. Its babies having babies. Yes, the Chinese, terrorists, Indians, Hispanics are laughing and waiting for out total collapse just like Ancient Rome and Egypt.

I know many will deny or rationalize my message of impending disaster, but it will be at their peril for we are only 2 or 3 generations from a third class nation status and the abyss of failure when we once had it all. When you add that five states now allow immoral homosexual marriage, what more can be said except that our routinely high crime and murder rate coupled with a 50% divorce rate? These statistics illustrate how far we have strayed from God and how close we must be to the Resurrection.

2008 PRESIDENTIAL ELECTION. BARACK OBAMA VS. JOHN MCCAIN

Black Obama and White McCain engaged in a titanic struggle for their candidacy and election to the Presidency. I use Black and White here because it is largely a Political race tainted with racism, at least among Blacks who love Obama just because he is Black and are, were mesmerized with his rhetoric like children. They almost all say we will finally get us a Black President, like he will be God or a Messiah that will save the world. More than likely he will lead us down to a defeat from terrorism and economic and economic decay that we may never recover. In any case it won't directly affect me because my time here is running short, for at 73, I don't have many years left. Actually, I will be glad to join my wife and parents in heaven.

In the meantime, John McCain a Navy Vietnam War hero and U.S. Senator as well as Obama is a Senator, is fighting an uphill battle against the 95% Black population, the liberal press which degrades him at every opportunity and the large liberal population that love Democratic Party ideals, ethics and policies. I think McCain is the better man and should win, but am skeptical because of the daunting economic, political and racial climate he has to overcome. How this plays out will be the subject for another book by another person in the future.

As an afterthought on Obama, it is imperative that I provide my insight and prediction about his presidency. First, about him. He has, over the past six months as President, conducted himself as unworthy. He doesn't act or behave as a real American. By that, I mean, he appears to hate America and does every thing to belittle our past accomplishments and our wonderful history and legacy of liberty and freedom. He goes around the world apologizing for America. Duh. We don't have to apologize to anyone for what we are, nor bow to some Middle East King as though we are inferior. He is obviously a closet Muslim, born in

Kenya or Indonesia, though he denies it. He refused to show his original birth certificate claiming Hawaii as place of birth. He only shows a certificate that authenticates the original, one that could be produced on a computer by any 8th grade students. He even declares that America is no longer a Christian nation.

He is manisfestly ashamed of America and wants to destroy her from within by replacing Capitalism with Socialism and attaining complete government control over private enterprise. He has a 60 vote veto proof Democratic Senate and a fifty vote majority in the House of Representatives. So, he can pretty much pass any legislation he wants, no matter how misguided or stupid.

Speaking of stupid, he thinks he is superior and elite above others and that the American people are stupid. His several trillion dollar stimulus plan and "porkulous" budgets have killed the stock market, bankrupted the financial system, bankrupted GM and Chrysler and generated 9.5% unemployment, yet he thinks he is smart. As Rush Limbaugh said, elections have consequences. We are suffering the consequences of electing this man-child. Our only hope is that, even if he isn't impeached by then, in 2010 we vote his party out of power and he can swing in the wind until 2012. You see, Obama had portrayed himself as a Messiah who would deliver to the American masses all the things they lacked, for free. More jobs, though we have lost 3 million since he became President, better inexpensive health care, less racism, though he has contributed to more racial tension, and on and on. He was in his mantra for hope and change, yes, but what did he deliver? So far, nothing, but pain, lies, arrogance and stupidity. But when the masses drink the koolaid like in Jonestown, Hitler, Germany or any totalitarian regime making grandiose promises, it always ends up in poverty, loss of liberty and death.

Obama is smart and stupid at the same time. He has learned the art of deceit from the master of lies and deception. That is he has read and studied 15th century Niccolo Machiavelli in his treatise of the book, The Prince. In t he book Machiavelli expounds on methods and strategies for gaining and attaining power. Tell the people anything they want to hear, promise them everything, then lie and distort the situation later when things turn sour. Create an enemy to divert their attention, invent a boogy man for them to hate, so they can love you as their savior. Seek to be loved and feared, but if you can't have both, it is better to be feared than loved, for when people stop loving you, they will turn on you.

He has applied Machiavelli to American politics similar to most dictators such as Stalin who kept a copy of The Prince by his bedside. For Obama is in effect the pre-Antichrist, with the original model coming later out of Europe according to the Bible.

Now that the "proles" or proletariats, (peasants) as George Orwelle describes them in his 1949 novel 1984, were under the total government control even of ones thoughts through the thought police and ubiqutous telescreens in every house reporting continuously to the government, these proles will see their world crumble before them and when they realize their fate, they will be speaking Chinese, Indian, Russian, Japanese, or German or maybe Brazilian. For you see, these will be your future Super Powers and we Americans will have faded into history as a defeated country and culture due to lack of industriousness, faith in ourselves and moral courage to defend ourselves against the external and internal enemy, just like the Romans.

But to their credit, some, even many of the "true believers" are waking up to the coffee; they realize that Obama is a fraud, a fake, a false prophet who will destroy us if not blocked. So again, the only hope is the 2010 ballot. If we don't stop this madness then, we deserve the subsequent consequences.

Back to Shaw and my Family

Of course there is a kernel of value and benefit of a Shaw, if one looks hard enough and works hard enough. My son Brian, after attending two White universities on basketball scholarships, attended Shaw for his final two years and received a degree in Business and a minor in Psychology. Having a need to have a total Shaw experience, I enrolled in the Liberal Studies Program in 1996 and received my Bachelors degree in 1999. I went to every class and did all the required work while serving as Vice President and was careful not receive any special treatment. I received the actual experience as a student and found out and reinforced the belief that a quality educational experience was possible. I was the only faculty member at Shaw in its history to obtain a Shaw Undergraduate degree while employed at the University and holding a PhD at the same time.

After graduating from Shaw, Brian served four years in the U.S. Army and eventually settled in California working in the pharmaceutical field. Scott dropped out of Pembroke State University in his senior year majoring in journalism and went to work as a reporter in the local Robeson county newspaper where he worked his way up to Managing Editor. I never got a clear answer as to why he never completed his degree work. He did however work his way to the top by becoming the paper's Manager Editor 20 years later. I was very proud of him, his work ethic, values and being a good son.

Mildred was home supporting all of us in our various activities. She was the true power and strength in the family. Her wisdom, patience and work ethic was phenomenal and incapable of sufficient characterization. She was a rare force of nature and I was fortunate enough to marry her. We were married 50 years for which I was blessed. Oh, we had our ups and downs, arguments typical marriage disagreements, but overall, we were happy and loved each other. Mildred died suddenly in January 2007, and it ripped the heart and spirit out of me, for which I never recovered. After her death, I just existed like a mechanical person, but I wasn't really alive. I rapidly arranged for my burial plot next to hers and updated my will and insurance in preparation to joining her soon. I felt almost guilty remaining here without her, but decided to suffer through the remaining life God gave me and complete this journey, until He says it's time.

Four months after her death, I discovered cancer in my colon. The surgeon cut it out and said it had not spread and gave me a 98% chance of it not recurring. I hope he is right. I am 73 years old and don't have many years remaining no matter if he is right or wrong. I don't have any joy in life anyway, so what is the purpose of just "living"?

This journey has been a gift from God that I had no clue as to his benevolence and love. I accepted everything without really thinking about how lucky, fortunate and blessed I was. I had a prince and princess for a father and mother, a loving queen of a wife, five wonderful siblings, a great extended family, good health, a good education, a blessed and wonderful country, a good military profession and honorable culture to develop in a good job at Shaw University notwithstanding its trials and tribulations.

A last word on Obama. He has been a total disgrace as a President. Martin Luther King had a dream and delivered a nightmare in Obama. This man is a radical liberal socialist who hates America. A half White-Black man that wants to destroy capitalism, liberty and freedom in this country. A Harvard educated stupid fool of a man. The problem is he has the votes in Congress to enforce his agenda-for now. His and the Democratic parties Waterloo will be November 2010, if we last that long. He has set the Black race back 50 years for the Whites that he mesmerized are waking up and will now say, "We have finally given Blacks what they wanted, a Black President, and what did we get-a damn ignorant fool. Never again. They can't play the guilt card anymore and we realize what a mistake we made". Amen.

The Journey – Vaughan Witten

Advice and warning for African-Americans/Blacks

(For those who this shoe fits)

Throw away the cell phones and "bling-bling". 2. Get out of bed and report on time. Read, read, read – books, newspapers, anything. 3. Take personal responsibility and stop blaming others for your inadequacies, flaws, poverty. 4. Be proud of yourself and don't depend on others for your self-worth, self-esteem and value. 5. Work hard, respect self and others. Be truthful, honest and get it done-no excuses-no complaints. Otherwise you will continue to be treated and perceived as second, third class, and the Whites, Chinese, Indians, Hispanics will disregard and destroy you as irrelevant and unworthy of a seat at the table. The old saying about Blacks: "If you want to keep a secret from them – Write It Down."

I am continuing this section in the reprint – not in the original manuscript. I am somewhat reluctant to say this, but if only one person understands or agrees, then it is worth it. So here goes. Many but not all of us Blacks enjoy our victimization status. This is primarily young Blacks who have been conditioned by the Government to be dependent on it for survival, primarily to get us to love it, support it and keep them, primarily Democrats in power. So the more food stamps we get -- even if we don't quality, section 8 housing, anything free or purportedly free, we pursue. In effect we become defacto slaves to the Government and often refuse to move from our dependent comfort zone to one of independence and freedom. Hans Selye, the famous psychologist calls this learned helplessness. Now don't get mad. I'm not characterizing all Blacks this way. But a significant number – which does not include the proud hard working people of West Virginia. Eric Fromm, another psychologist has a similar theory of Escape from Freedom. In other words, many Blacks and Whites prefer the comfort of protection and sympathy to the risk of being free and subject to the vagaries and problems of life that comes with true liberty and freedom. Yes, we have a class society of achievement, money, education and sophisticated manners. Most of us love to work for these. But freedom is not free and liberty must be a constant pursuit.

It is a pity that we –not all- have lost our Christian spirit and values we had when in physical bondage and turned Martin Luther King's philosophy on its head by now - judging people by the color of their skin instead of the content of their character. Many of us who have succumbed to the entitlement and welfare state would vote for a retarded criminal Black over a White Socrates, Lincoln, Truman and Descartes wrapped into one. Blacks and Whites of my generation will be ok, but the pampered, weak, delusional bunch that will soon control America – I can only see poverty, decay, subjugation and third world status for the future.

Finally, we have moved from responsibility, accountability and obedience to God, to worship the golden calf, to the self-destruction of covet. From need to want, earn and pay to hook me up, to get over – defraud the system with no guilt and education without study. We want as much as we can get from others for free. We violate daily, the Thou shall Not Covet commandment of the Ten from Moses and God, much less the other 603 from Moses that most don't even know about. Our childish indulgence in outrageous liberty and behavior is chipping away at our basic freedom and will undo everything we have gained since 1865. Think about it. This is primarily directed to the 40 and under crowd.

Covet – To strongly want something another person has, to long for with envy-greedy. To want to possess another's money, goods, wife, husband, house and etc.

239

My Final, Final Topic – Health and God

I thought I was finished when I took my draft of this book to the publisher last month, but the recent mine explosion earlier this month in Montcoal West Virginia, about 25 miles from Charleston and 45 miles from Ward with 29 miners killed, brought some more thoughts that I should put to paper. If you have read this far, it's not much farther to the end.

<u>**My Health**</u>

I haven't thought too much about it, but I realize that my genes, the mountain environment and God blessed me and my siblings, mom and dad with very good health. I don't remember any of us ever being sick or even injured except for my bout of diphtheria in Martinsville when I was about two years. Diphtheria is a respiratory disease caused by a bassillus that I suppose could kill you if untreated. I remember my parents and a doctor talking over me in a small house near Grandma Walker's house. It had a tin roof and I liked to hear the rain drops hit the roof. I like the sound even today. Anyway I survived that illness and the only other thing was a habitual nose bleed that occurred often until I was about 14. It would just start bleeding, especially if it was real hot. We tried all kinds of home remedies including a wad of paper under my top lip, but nothing really worked. I just went away by itself. About doctors, there were no doctors basically, you might see one in the hospital, otherwise you were on your own with home remedies – which often worked.

Of course we took shots and vaccinations that warded off disease like Small Pox but I still had the Chicken Pox, Measles, and Mumps as I remember but I wasn't really sick. All of my family escaped Polio which was the big bad disease of that day. I must say that the West Virginia Public Health Service was excellent. Nurses would come to all the schools, Black and White to give shots, check our teeth and every thing; they were also pretty.

My big health risk was the constantly cut feet from glass and nail punctures both from going barefooted as much as possible. I guess I should include catching the coal train going from the tipple to the river in Cedar Grove. I realize now that it was dangerous but in those days we thought we were immortal. Also, there were the ever present snakes but handled them okay - by avoiding or killing them. I didn't like to wear shoes, nor did the other boys. But we never got tetanus or lock jaw, as it was called. I was always small probably because I was perpetual motion. I never stopped or slowed down until night time for bed and right up again at 5-6 o'clock running again. Everything was so much fun, the schooling, playing, working; I was just happy to be alive - and still am today. I only weighed about 120 pounds when I joined the Air Force.

My mom and dad died from colon cancer at 84 and 78 respectively. I also had it at 72 but my operation caught it before it spread. Mom and dad were not that fortunate but they lived a full happy life in the Lord and with Jesus as their guide and Savior. I'll be glad to see them again along with Mildred and my friends who believed and lived the life of Jesus. Yes, I know none of us can really do enough to go to heaven but we are still saved by God's grace and the approval of Jesus.

Now About God

From the precivilized, caveman, Neanderthal to our current Homo Sapiens through the Chaldeians, Egyptians, Persians, Carthaginians, Greeks, Romans and primitive Europeans as well as the Mongoloids, Africans and American Indians, man has believed and worshipped some higher power to help him understand and survive nature. He has worshipped animals, the moon, the sun; you name it and often worshipped several Gods at once with no thought of an after life in many cases. The idea of one living all powerful, all knowing, ever present being or God is a relatively new concept or belief growing out of the Judeo-Neoplatonism philosophy and religion that worshippers yahweh.

But let me digress, you see humans have always attempted to explain natural events that like thunder, lightening, rainbows, death, illness, dreams, and the like, projecting human attributes onto nature. For example, the earth may become angry and have an earthquake. Looking at nature as though it was alive is called <u>animism</u>, and the projection of human attributes on nature is called <u>anthropomorphism</u>. Another approach was to assume that a ghost or spirit dwelt in everything including humans and these spirits were just as real as rocks, trees, animals and the moon. The word spirit in Latin means <u>breath</u>, ghost, psych, soul, and gives life to things. But when it leaves, death occurs. They believed that if something could be thought of or dreamed of it must exist.

So someone who had died and dreamed of would still exist.

In the fifth and sixth century B.C., the Greeks explanation of things was still predominantly religious in nature. The two major theologies were <u>Olympian</u> Gods who showed little concern with the problems and anxieties of ordinary humans and tended to be amoral and unconcerned with human morality. This was the religion of the rich and believed that the breath-soul survives death but had no memory of the things the body did so they were encouraged to live the enjoyable life for there was no punishment after death. The ideal life was the pursuit of glory, lordliness, rationality, and intellectual activity.

The opposing religion of the poor, peasants and uneducated slaves was <u>dionysiac-orphic</u>. Their belief was the transmigration of the soul. The soul was once pure and dwelled among the Gods. But then it sinned and was punished by being locked into a physical body which acted as a prison. The soul then longed for liberation to return to God and journeyed from human, to animal to plant, to human until it freed itself and again became divine. The orphic idea that the soul seeks to escape its contaminated earthly existence and enter a heavenly state gained popularity and became an integral part of our Judeo-Christian religion.

Moving beyond the Greek philosophers of Socrates, Plato, Aristotle and Philo I will now address the early Christian church, Jesus, Paul, Constantine, St. Augustine, St. Anselm, Erasmus, Martin Luther, and Spinoza as they teach, propose and attempt to seek the ultimate truth of who God is and how can we know him.

Philo - The Jewish Plato, 25BC-50AD, took the Biblical account of the creation as the starting point for his philosophy. From that account he learned that the human body was created from the earth but that the human soul was of God himself. God formed man from the dust and breathed life into him; the body being low and despicable and the soul a fragment of the divine. The person can then move downward or away from God or away from the experiences of the flesh and upward, towards God. For Philo, all knowledge comes from God but to receive God's wisdom the soul or mind must be purified. The soul must be purged of all influences of the flesh. Once purified, God's knowledge can enter, for man knows nothing and can know nothing but through God.

Jesus - Had no formal philosophy nor wrote anything about his mission or purpose. He taught among other things that knowledge of good and evil were revealed by God and once revealed, such knowledge should guide human conduct. He was a simple man and yet of God, was God and delivered the message that he was the truth and the life and no man could be with God but by him, Jesus. All those who formalized Jesus' teachings never met him but through the faith and teaching of Paul, the assistance of Roman Emperor Constantine, the death and sacrifice of his followers, and primarily though his resurrection, the Christian religion w as formed and perpetuated.

St. Paul AD 10-64 - was the first to claim and preach that Jesus of Nazareth was the messiah. While on the road to Damascus, Paul had a vision that Jesus was the Messiah and converted from Saul of Tarsus to Paul and Christianity was born. Paul learned that one God created the universe and has all power over everything and everyone. To this Paul added the belief that God Sacrificed his son to atone for man's sin and through Jesus could have a relationship with God. "For in Adam all die so also in Jesus all may be made live". Acceptance of Christ was the only way to redemption.

Only through Paul did Christianity survive for he so preached the word and influenced the world that Christianity could be called Paulinistry. Paul placed faith above reason and believed that only through faith in Christ could one receive salvation.

242

Emperor Constantine 272-337 AD

In 312, the Emperor Constantine was said to be the person who loosened the shackles of hate from the Christians. Having received a "sign" from God that he would win a major battle, he credited the Christians – he did win – and became more concerned with Christian affairs. In 313, he signed the EDICT of Milan making Christianity a tolerated religion of the Roman Empire. It did not make it the official Roman religion. This was accomplished later in 385 when Theodosius I made Christianity the official religion of the Roman Empire. In 325 Constantine convened the Council of Nicaea of bishops throughout the empire who after debate declared God the Father and Jesus the Son had equal status. He also had the bishops to write a general book of rules and doctrine about Christianity organizing all or most of the many books on Christianity into a Constantine Bible. It was later lost, but later in 367 after Anasius, the powerful bishop of Alexandria decreed that only Matthew, Mark, Luke, and John would be the only Gospels accepted of the 40 written and only 27 books of the scores would be included in the New Testament. Constantine was baptized a Christian on his death bed in 337.

St. Augustine - Opposed to St. Jerome, who argued that non-Christian philosophy should be condemned, St. Augustine successfully supported St. Ambrose who argued for using compatible philosophy and went on to combine Platonism with stoicism who believed in God's will being dominant. Neoplatonism emphasized the mystical aspects of Plato Philosophy which included a jealous God, individual immortality and passionate faith combined with Judaism; resulting in a powerful Christian world view. Augustine was mainly concerned with mans spirituality. God was the author of all forms (Plato) and Augustine continued that the ultimate knowledge consisted of knowing God. The human was seen as corrupt with an animal like body and a spirit part close to God. The war between the two aspects of human nature, already present in platonism philosophy, became the Christian struggle between heaven and hell –that is between God and Satan. He also believed that God speaks to man through his soul, but the individual need not listen.

St. Anselm - was basically an Augustinian but departed from him in his belief that we could know God by reason more than faith. His argument was that if we can think of something, something must be causing the thought. Truth is when we think of things, there must exist real things corresponding to those thoughts (Reification). He reasoned that we could think of a thing that is better or greater and greater and greater until the thought of a perfect being which would be God, and because we can think of him he must exist. Of course he says the same logic in reverse would prove the Devil as well as God. St. Anselm, of God, said "I long to understand in some degree thy truth, which my heart believes and loves. For I do not seek to understand so I may believe, but I believe in order to understand. For this also I believe – that unless I believe, I should not understand".

Desiderius Erasmus 1466-1536 - was opposed to strong belief in anything. He was fond in pointing out mistakes in anything done by humans. He encouraged people to take their lessons from the simple life of Jesus instead of from the pomp and circumstances of the organized church. He said war was nothing more than homicide and was disturbed by bishops becoming rich from war. He especially criticized the Pope and Catholic Church for its corruption and the idea that one could buy their way into heaven by paying a money <u>indulgence</u> to the Pope. He said the Pope had too much power and skirt chasing monks and priests were shameless tyrants. Erasmus was so critical of the Catholic Church that it is said that Erasmus laid the reformist egg and Luther hatched it.

Martin Luther 1483-1546, an Augustinian Priest and biblical scholar was even more critical of the Catholic Church. His 95 Theses or complaints against the church nailed to the church at Wittenburg began the process of splitting the church by way of Reformation and the start of Protestation including Lutheranism and Calvinism. Luther was against indulgences and believed man could have a direct relationship with God and not go through a priest. He said the church had drifted away from Jesus and the Bible. He believed married couples are as capable of doing Gods work as any nun or priest and that nuns and priest should marry if they desired. He disagreed with Erasmus and said that man has no free will and is captive either to the will of God or Satan. As far as why God allows evil to exist, Luther had no answer but to say the answer is unfathomable to humans and therefore must remain a mystery. In other words, only God knows. Augustine however attributed free will to man but agreed that salvation is granted only by God's grace and independent of any human action or endeavor. Luther denied free will but agreed that salvation is attained by God's grace alone.

Baruch Spinoza 1632-1677, A Portuguese Jew disagreed with Rene Descartes who proposed that God is a power that set the world in motion and then stepped away and is no longer involved with it, and instead believed that God not only started the world into motion but was also continually present everywhere in nature. To understand the laws of nature was to understand God. For Spinoza, God was nature, that God is present everywhere and in everything - Pantheism.

Spinoza believed that man has no free will; that everything he does is determined by God. He goes on to say that "men think themselves free as they are conscious of their volitions and desires, and never even dream, in their ignorance, of the causes which have disposed them to so, to wish and desire." According to Spinoza, it makes no sense to view God as the cause of all things <u>and</u> at the same time, to believe that humans possess a free will. Spinoza insists the best life was when one lives with a knowledge of the cause of things. The closest we can get to freedom is understanding what causes our behavior and thoughts: The freeman is one conscious of the necessities that compel him. He says the murderer is no more responsible for his or her behavior than is a river that floods a village. If both causes were understood, however, the aversive events could be controlled and prevented.

Witten 2010

After reading Plato, Aristotle, Socrates, Erasmus, Luther, Empedocles, St. Paul, St. Augustine, St. Anselm, Spinoza, and studying the psychology of Freud who says behavior is controlled by unconscious forces of sex and aggression and the behaviorist Skinner and Watson who say our behavior is controlled by environmental forces of rewards and punishers, it is very difficult to conclude who is correct about God, freewill, man's behavior or most of the complex issues involving God and man. Sigmund Freud among others suggests that there even is no God. He says instead of God creating man, man created God because man realizing his mortality and vulnerability in life needed a superior father or protector that we could look up to for some comfort or help in adapting and surviving - even before the idea of a heaven and after life. Then, according to Freud, man forgot he invented God and believed God was always here. Some theory huh! I don't believe Freud but it does make you think. Bottom line I do believe in God and He invented man. I must say, overall, I don't know anything just as Socrates said, in that the only thing we know is that we don't know anything. I leave it there. God bless you and thank you for reading this book on my life experiences, some social and cultural-political opinions and a quick view of the issues and speculations that learned men through the ages have of God.

COUNTRIES AND CITIES VISITED

Japan
Tokyo
Itazuke
Fukioka
Tachikawa
Iwakuni
Okinawa

Philippines
Manila
Cebu
Cebu City
Mactan
Lapa Lapa

Thailand
Bangkok
Udorn Thani
Korat

Vietnam
Saigon
Cholon
Nha Trang
Ben Kat
Cam Ranh Bay

Puerto Rico
Aricebo
San Juan
Ponce
Carolina
Bayamon

Labrador-Canada
Goose Bay

Greece
Athens
Hellikinon
Thessaloniki

Portugal
Lisbon
Azores
Lajes
Angra De Herisimo
Santa Maria
Pria

United Kingdom
England
London
Mildenhall
Alconbury
Liverpool
Ely
Cambridge
Lakenheith
Skulthorpe
Shippy Hill

Scotland
Prestwick

Korea
Osan

Greenland
Thule
Sondestrom
Narsasserak

Canada
New Foundland
Labrador

Iceland
Keflavik

Germany
Frankfort

Spain
Madrid

Wake Island

Guam

United States
Albuqueqe
Sante Fe
New York
Boston
Atlanta
Philadelphia
Miami
Los Angeles
Manchester, NH

Unites States (Continued)
Portland, MA
Chicago
Washington, DC
Seattle
Tucumcari
Charleston, WV
Charleston, SC
New Orleans
Phoenix
Tucson
Baltimore
Pittsburg
San Francisco
San Diego
Oklahoma City
St. Louis
Cincinnati
Memphis
Raleigh
Richmond, VA
Naples, FL
Jacksonville, FL
Fort Lauderdale
San Antonio

EPILOGUE
SUMMARY

Appalachia

1 Wonderful parents

2 Great siblings and family life

3 Beautiful, wild, West Virginia

4 Freedom, confidence, hope of successful future

5 Knowledge of high intellect

6 Fearless

7 Unscathed by racism and mild segregation

8 Wonderful teachers and educational experience

9 Very smart and class salutatorian

10 Good health

11 Good Athlete

12 Respected by friends and foes

13 Didn't know I was poor or ostensibly deprived.

14 Happy

<u>Paradise</u>

1   50 year marriage to Mildred

2   Raising two sons Scott and Brian

3   27 years experience in the Air Force

4   World travel – Free

5   Pride in defending my nation

6   Meeting people of all cultures rapid promotion and rise to top of Air Force – Enlisted rank-Commander Chief Master Sergeant E-9

7   Joy of raising and providing for my family

8   Overall good health until cancer at age 72.

9   Held in high esteem and respect by most people

10   Receiving numerous honors and awards

11   Attaining high education – 2 Bachelors degrees, 1 Masters degree and 1 PhD in Psychology.

12   Early working years at Shaw University as Assistant and Associate Professor of Psychology

13   Wonderful parents and good and frequent interaction with extended family

14   Observing positive attitudes and success of my sons.

15   Love of my wife who had unlimited belief and confidence in me.

16   Very smart and class Salutatorian

17   Good athlete

18   Respected by friends and foes

19   Didn't know I was poor or ostensibly deprived

20   Happy

<u>Purgatory</u>

1 Loss of respect and honor of youth for family and traditional morality
2 Increased use of abortion and laws making it legal
3 Demise and degradation of Black family and Black culture in general
4 Lack of respect for law and order
5 Increased crime, robbery and murder
6 Outrageous behavior and stupid activities accepted and even rewarded by many in society
7 Fear to speak the truth by threat of the politically correct mentality
8 Low achievements and aspirations of Blacks
9 Reverse racism-Blacks more racist while whites attempt to reduce racism
10 Blacks blaming Whites for all his problems while not accepting responsibility for their situation
11 Destruction and low standards of educational system – dumbing down everything to be nice.
12 Devaluation of the dollar and increased inflation.
13 Extremely high gas and food prices
14 Death of my wife
15 Death of my Mom and Dad
16 Death of most of my friends in early West Virginia life
17 Demise of Shaw University
18 Life without Mildred
19 Attacks on America by radical Muslim killers
20 Increased American debt
21 Increased drug and alcohol use by citizens
22 Lack of or decreasing trust among people
23 Uncontrolled illegal immigration of Hispanics
24 Biased Liberal press that supports stupid, outrageous, illegal, obnoxious and cultural destructive behavior and ideas
25 Increased greediness of banks and Wall Street
26 Black racism and hatred of their own country
27 Many too stupid to see Obama as the Anti-Christ who would destroy America if became or becomes President, essentially he is a half-breed elitist with ties to Muslim mentality, no love for America and a irrational liberal who will or would pull the house of America down upon itself, yet the giddy Blacks and White think he is so wonderful, but as the Chinese say, "Be careful what you wish for."
28 Unhappy

ARTICLES

&

CARTOONS

The journey begins

Barack Obama has always been about the words. And so it was Tuesday. For all the grandeur of the setting and the breathtaking and seemingly endless crowd arrayed before him, it was still about the words.

He officially began his improbable journey on a frigid day in Springfield, Ill., a little less than two years ago with words that promised he was running "not just to hold an office, but to gather with you to transform a nation."

Tuesday, he took his office, and now he will begin on the transformation. It is not guaranteed. It will not be easy. But he will, he said, make a start.

He looked very serious, almost somber, throughout his inaugural ceremony. And as he has done repeatedly in the last few weeks, he listed the barriers America faces, the mountains we have yet to climb.

"Our nation is at war, against a far-reaching network of violence and hatred," he said. "Our economy is badly weakened, a consequence of greed and irresponsibility on the part of some, but also our collective failure to make hard choices and prepare the nation for a new age."

He talked about lost homes and shuttered businesses and then talked about something even worse: "a sapping of confidence across our land — a nagging fear that America's decline is inevitable, and that the next generation must lower its sights."

But this, he said, he will not let

ROGER SIMON

happen. "On this day, we gather because we have chosen hope over fear, unity of purpose over conflict and discord."

And he called for what Americans say they are willing to provide, but have not in recent years been called upon to do: sacrifice. "We remain a young nation, but in the words of Scripture, the time has come to set aside childish things," he said.

The speech had political moments. President Obama served notice that he was ending the era of Ronald Reagan and those who cling to the idea that government must be small because it is the problem and not the solution.

"The question we ask today is not whether our government is too big or too small, but whether it works — whether it helps families find jobs at a decent wage, care they can afford, a retirement that is dignified," he said.

Obama also signaled the end of the era of George W. Bush.

"As for our common defense, we reject as false the choice between our safety and our ideals," Obama said.

Obama also addressed a political concern within his own party:

Democrats who remain fearful that he will delay his pledge to end the war in Iraq. Without mentioning a timetable, Obama said: "We will begin to responsibly leave Iraq to its people and forge a hard-earned peace in Afghanistan."

And then boldly he reached out a hand to the Muslim world, but also remonstrated extremists within it.

His reference to the historic fact that he was the nation's first African-American president was brief but poignant: "This is the meaning of our liberty and our creed — why men and women and children of every race and every faith can join in celebration across this magnificent mall, and why a man whose father less than 60 years ago might not have been served at a local restaurant can now stand before you to take a most sacred oath."

Will any of these words someday be carved in marble? That depends not on the words, but on the presidency.

Nobody remembers the words of failed administrations. Great words are made immortal by great presidents.

Barack Obama now has this burden and this opportunity. His journey and ours begins.

Roger Simon is the chief political columnist of politico.com, an award-winning journalist and a New York Times best-selling author.

Creators Syndicate

251

HOPE AND DISAPPOINTMENT

A year into the Obama presidency, many who expected big change are disillusioned by politics as usual

By Pauline Arrillaga
The Associated Press

A year ago, on an Inauguration Day like no other, Barack Obama placed his hand upon the Lincoln Bible and then assured a weary nation that, with hope and virtue, we could "brave once more the icy currents and endure what storms may come."

Across the country, in Seattle, Glen Boyd had only just entered his own economic storm. A couple of

weeks out of work as a DirecTV salesman, the Obama supporter nevertheless watched the inauguration on TV with a kind of goose-pimply, things-are-bound-to-get-better anticipation. He really felt it, that thing which the poet Alexander Pope said springs eternal.

"I felt a tremendous sense of pride. I felt like he was the right guy. I felt a sense of optimism," recalls Boyd.

Now, a year later, Boyd writes this in his blog: "We believed what the man said in all those 'yes, we can' speeches. My one question is, where are all those reassuring speeches now?"

"To say I'm disappointed by the Obama presidency thus far would be an understatement."

Forget "can," "change" and, above all, "hope." The new word echoing in the blogosphere and beyond as Obama enters Year 2.

disappointment.

The polls have shown a wide decline in Americans' approval of Obama since he first took office last Jan. 20. In fact, according to the latest Gallup Poll, he entered his second year with one of the lowest approval ratings of any president in the last half-century (50 percent of Americans approved of his job performance at the first of January, and 44 percent

See OBAMA, Page 17A

disapproved.)

John Connelly, a registered Republican who describes himself as an archconservative, feels no disappointment because he never placed any hope in Obama's presidency in the first place. "I knew what was coming even before he was elected," says the 68-year-old retired attorney who lives in Carolina Shores, N.C.

Rather, some of the truest Obama believers are among the most let-down.

Still others are more disappointed in their fellow Americans' impatience.

"You pick your issue of the day, and no one's happy because he hasn't tackled that one individual issue with fervor," says fish biologist Tracii Hickman of Walla Walla, Wash., an Obama voter.

She was so inspired by his election that she wrote in a newspaper commentary on inauguration eve last yea "I am optimistic that the massive problems facing our nation will be addressed and that we wi come out on the other sid of this huge mess a better people and country."

But others do, and they feel so strongly that they are moved to write about their disenchantment — or the Web and in letters to the editor, some in anger, others in sorrow, in language intemperate or aggrieved.

"Yes, we can?" writes Boyd. "How about no, we can't?"

... It was so exciting, so refreshing, so inspiring," Sullivan says.

And, one year later, so disheartening.

"What happened to that guy?" Sullivan asks. "Wha happened to his vision for the country and for the world? It seems to have vanished."

Sullivan is disappointed by health care, the economy, energy program But what angers him the most are two wars that, he believes, have damaged America's image abroad and jeopardized the country's safety.

"Essentially, it's the same rhetoric that Bush used, just with a higher level of intelligence," Sullivan says.

Perhaps even deeper than his discouragement with Obama is Sullivan's disillusionment with the entire political system, the sense that if Obama — with all his leadership skills, charisma and determination — cannot change it, nothing can.

"It shakes your belief that representative democracy will actually work for people at large."

252

One year out: Obama's fall

What went wrong? A year ago, he was king of the world. Now President Obama's approval rating, according to CBS, has dropped to 46 percent — and his disapproval rating is the highest ever recorded by Gallup at the beginning of an elected president's second year.

A year ago, he was leader of a liberal ascendancy that would last 40 years (James Carville). A year ago, conservatism was dead (Sam Tanenhaus). Now the race to fill Ted Kennedy's Senate seat in bluest of blue Massachusetts is surprisingly close, with a virtually unknown state senator bursting on the scene by turning the election into a mini-referendum on Obama and his agenda, most particularly health care reform.

A year ago, Obama was the most charismatic politician on earth. Today the thrill is gone, the doubts growing — even among erstwhile believers.

Liberals try to attribute Obama's political decline to matters of style. He's too cool, detached, uninvolved. He's not tough, angry or aggressive enough with

Charles Krauthammer

opponents. He's contracted out too much of his agenda to Congress.

These stylistic and tactical complaints may be true, but they miss the major point: The reason for today's vast discontent, presaged by spontaneous national Tea Party opposition, is not that Obama is too cool or compliant but that he's too left.

It's not about style; it's about substance. About which Obama has been admirably candid. This out-of-nowhere, least-known of presidents dropped the veil most dramatically in the single most important political event of 2009, his Feb. 24 first address to Congress. With remarkable political honesty and courage, Obama unveiled the most radical (in American terms) ideological agenda since the New Deal:

the fundamental restructuring of three pillars of American society — health care, education and energy.

Then began the descent — when, more amazingly still, Obama devoted himself to turning these statist visions into legislative reality. First energy, with cap-and-trade, an unprecedented federal intrusion into American industry and commerce. It got through the House, with its Democratic majority and Supreme Soviet-style rules. But it will never get out of the Senate.

Then, the keystone: a health care revolution in which the federal government will regulate in crushing detail one-sixth of the U.S. economy. By essentially abolishing medical underwriting (actuarially based risk assessment) and replacing it with government fiat, Obamacare turns the health insurance companies into utilities, their every significant move dictated by government regulators.

At first, health care reform was sustained politically by Obama's own popularity. But then gravity took hold, and Obamacare's profound unpopularity dragged him down with it.

After 29 speeches and a fortune in squandered political capital, it still will not sell.

Obama did not just act, however. He acted ideologically. To his credit, Obama didn't just come to Washington to be someone. Like Reagan, he came to Washington to do something — to introduce a powerful social democratic stream into America's deeply and historically individualist polity.

Perhaps Obama thought he'd been sent to the White House to do just that. If so, he vastly over-read his mandate. His own electoral success — twinned with handy victories and large majorities in both houses of Congress — was a referendum on his predecessor's governance and the post-Lehman financial collapse. It was not an endorsement of European-style social democracy.

Hence the resistance. Hence the fall. The system may not always work, but it does take its revenge.

Charles Krauthammer is a Washington Post columnist. Readers may write to him at letters@charleskrauthammer.com or Washington Post Writers Group, 1150 15th St. NW, Washington, D.C. 20071.

253

'Wish for Black America' given for new year

Ethnically Speaking

Larry G. Meeks

Dear Readers: Very early in this column's history, as a New Year's resolution, I wrote "My Wish for Black America." Since that time, it has been my most requested column. In celebration of the new year, I would like to continue my tradition, along with a few updates:

My wish for black America:

I wish black fathers would assume responsibility for the children they create and stop acting like some flying insect that goes from flower to flower trying to see how many blossoms it can fertilize.

I wish education, not sports, were considered the top priority for schools.

I wish the school systems would demand appropriate behavior and stop making excuses as to why blacks cannot make the grade.

I wish high-achieving black students were not labeled as acting white.

I wish America would stop patronizing non-achieving black Americans and treating them like misbehaving children.

I wish degrading music that sexualizes women, fosters racism and extols violence were eliminated.

I wish blacks would not make race the first consideration when there is a situation.

I wish blacks would realize that institutionalized racism is over and the path for success is open.

I wish minorities would stop stereotyping and saying all whites are alike.

I wish black leaders would stop trying to exploit their followers by trying to make them believe the world is against them and their only path to success is keeping them in power.

I wish blacks would realize they are being politically taken for granted and know that being loyal to one party makes them irrelevant. A minority's power is being the deciding vote.

I wish black people would realize that no one owes them anything except equal treatment under the law and that the best hand up is at the end of their own arm.

I wish white America would stop feeling guilty for the sins of their forefathers, because that guilt prevents whites from treating blacks as equals.

I wish our new president would use his race to unite the nation and speak out extolling the values that made us a great nation. I pray he will advocate those values, which make us come together, rather than allow the nation to break into separate groups.

I wish everyone, regardless of race, would love one another and work together to make this an even better country.

Finally, I wish God's blessings upon us so we may remain free and continue to have happy years.

Creators Syndicate

To find out more about Larry G. Meeks, visit the Creators Syndicate Web page at www.creators.com.

254

Obama's disturbing reactions

5 JAN.2010 Fy 885 NC

WASHINGTON — Janet Napolitano — former Arizona governor, now overmatched secretary of homeland security — will forever be remembered for having said of the attempt to bring down an airliner over Detroit: "The system worked." The attacker's concerned father had warned U.S. authorities about his son's jihadist tendencies. The would-be bomber paid cash and checked no luggage on a transoceanic flight. He was nonetheless allowed to fly, and would have killed 288 people in the air alone, save for a faulty detonator and quick actions by a few passengers.

Heck of a job, Brownie.

The reason the country is uneasy about the Obama administration's response to this attack is a distinct sense of not just incompetence but incomprehension. From the very beginning, President Obama has relentlessly tried to downplay and deny the nature of the terrorist threat we continue to face. Napolitano renames terrorism "man-caused disasters." Obama goes abroad and pledges to cleanse America of its post-9/11 counterterrorist sins. Hence, Guantanamo will close, CIA interrogators will face a special prosecutor, and Khalid Sheik

Charles Krauthammer

Mohammed will bask in a civilian trial in New York — a trifecta of political correctness and image management.

And just to make sure even the dimmest understand, Obama banishes the term "war on terror." It's over — that is, if it ever existed.

Obama may have declared the war over. Unfortunately al-Qaeda has not. This gives new meaning to the term "asymmetric warfare." And it produces linguistic — and logical — oddities that littered Obama's public pronouncements following the Christmas Day attack.

In his first statement, Obama referred to Umar Farouk Abdulmutallab as "an isolated extremist." This is the same president who, after the Ford Hood shooting, warned us "against jumping to conclusions" — code for daring to associate Nidal Hasan's mass murder with his Islamist ideology.

Yet, with Abdulmutallab, Obama jumped immediately to the conclusion, against all existing evidence, that the bomber acted alone.

More jarring still were Obama's references to the terrorist as a "suspect" who "allegedly tried to ignite an explosive device."

Obama reassured the nation that this "suspect" had been charged. Reassurance? The president should be saying: We have captured an enemy combatant — an illegal combatant under the laws of war: no uniform, direct attack on civilians — and now to prevent future attacks, he is being interrogated regarding information he may have about al-Qaeda in Yemen.

Instead, Abdulmutallab is dispatched to some Detroit-area jail and immediately lawyered up. At which point — surprise! — he stops talking.

This absurdity renders hollow Obama's declaration that "we will not rest until we find all who were involved." Once we've given Abdulmutallab the right to remain silent, we have gratuitously forfeited our right to find out from him precisely who else was involved, namely those who trained, instructed, armed and sent him.

This is all quite mad even in Obama's terms. He sends

30,000 troops to fight terror overseas, yet if any terrorists come to attack us here, they are magically transformed from enemy into defendant.

The logic is perverse. If we find Abdulmutallab in an al-Qaeda training camp in Yemen, where he is merely preparing for a terror attack, we snuff him out with a Predator — no judge, no jury, no qualms. But if we catch him in the United States in the very act of mass murder, he instantly acquires protection even from interrogation.

The president said that this incident highlights "the nature of those who threaten our homeland." But the president is constantly denying the nature of those who threaten our homeland.

Any government can through laxity let someone slip through the cracks. But a government that refuses to admit that we are at war, indeed, refuses even to name the enemy — jihadist is a word banished from the Obama lexicon — turns laxity into a governing philosophy.

Charles Krauthammer is a Washington Post columnist. Readers may write to him at letters@charleskrauthammer.con or Washington Post Writers Group, 1150 15th St. NW, Washington, D.C. 20071.

AN ANALYSIS

AP photos

Massachusetts state Sen. Scott Brown, left, a Republican, is running against Attorney General Martha Coakley, right, a Democrat in a special election to fill the U.S. Senate seat left empty by the death of Sen. Edward M. Kennedy.

Voter ire evident in Senate race

■ Losing the Massachusetts election to replace Ted Kennedy would hobble Democrats.

By Liz Sidoti
The Associated Press

WASHINGTON — The ill winds of an angry electorate are blowing against Democrats, the warning signs clear in a closer-than-expected Massachusetts Senate race that may doom President Obama's health care agenda and foreshadow the party's election prospects this fall.

Anti-incumbent, anti-establishment sentiment is rampant. Independents are leaving Obama. Republicans are energized. Democrats are subdued. None of it bodes well for the party in power.

"It's going to be a hard November for Democrats," Howard Dean, the Democratic Party chairman in the 2006 and 2008 elections when the party took control of the White House and Congress, told The Associated Press in an interview. "Our base is demoralized."

While he praised Obama as a good president, Dean said the Democrat hasn't turned out to be the "change agent" the party thought it elected, and voters who supported Democrats in back-to-back elections now are turned off. Said Dean: "They really thought the revolution was at hand but it wasn't, and now they're getting the back of the hand."

Just how much voters have soured since Obama took over a country in chaos is reflected in the president's late-game decision to rush to Massachusetts today to try to stave off a Republican upset in the race for a Senate seat held by Democrats for more than half a century.

Obama faced a no-win situation as he pondered whether to campaign with Democrat Martha Coakley. Had he decided against going, he would have enraged the base and been blamed if she lost. But a Coakley defeat following a presidential visit would be embarrassing, raising questions about Obama's popularity and political muscle.

Once heavily favored to cruise to victory, Coakley is in a tight fight with Republican Scott Brown, a little-known state senator, for the race to fill the seat left vacant when Sen. Edward M. Kennedy died.

Losing the race would cost the Democrats their 60-vote coalition in the Senate. The president has been relying on that big edge to stop Republican filibusters and pass not only his health care overhaul but also the rest of his legislative agenda heading into the first elections since he took office.

A Suffolk University poll released late Thursday showed Brown with 50 percent of the vote and Coakley with 46 percent. The survey indicated that Brown's supporters — disaffected Democrats, a large number of Republicans and a majority of independents — are far more enthusiastic than Coakley's backers.

Voters are down on Washington. They are deeply divided over the health care plan in Congress, and a majority thinks the country is on the wrong track. Nearly all remain anxious about the prolonged recession even though there are signs of recovery. Only about half approve of Obama's job performance. Excessive spending and big government irk them. They've lost faith in institutions.

Brown ushers in new mantra

WASHINGTON — There will be much harrumphing and punditry in the next few days about the meaning of Scott Brown's victory and his phenomenal campaign for Ted Kennedy's U.S. Senate seat.

How, in the final days of an election all but certain to go to the Democrats, did Brown, a mere state senator, manage to raise millions and rattle the machinery of his blue-hearted state?

Democrats who see the world through denial-colored glasses want to blame their candidate, state Attorney General Martha Coakley, for her halfhearted, tone-deaf campaign. Certainly she has earned some of that criticism.

Coakley presumed her ascendancy without bothering to work for the vote, even once saying: What am I supposed to do, shake hands in the freezing cold outside Fenway Park? That's like the pope saying: What am I supposed to do, celebrate Mass in St. Peter's Square?

While Coakley was ignoring the tsunami looming outside her window, Brown was hanging ten on a wave of dissatisfaction — standing on street corners, hand-delivering yard signs and, yes, shaking hands in the freezing cold. Coakley's remark that devout Catholics shouldn't work in emergency rooms if their pro-life consciences conflicted with the law of

Kathleen Parker

the land was insensitive.

Finally, and not least, Coakley's comment that former Boston Red Sox pitcher Curt Schilling is a Yankee fan put her squarely in the category of clueless.

Brown, by contrast, was the people's genius, a guy's guy who conveyed genuineness — the antithesis of everything Americans despise in Washington. He was a reformer promising change to a people weary of hope.

Democrats trying to paint Republicans as the "Party of No" were simply being crushed by a candidate who was saying, "Oh, yes we can, but not like this." Remorseful independents who had voted for the unifying and faux-centrist Barack Obama responded to the candidate who seemed to be in touch with their reality.

The meaning of Scott Brown should be clear to Democrats facing midterm elections in November. Not least, Republicans have learned how to use the Internet to build momentum and raise money. It can't go unmentioned that Brown also benefited from the strategic

brilliance of Mitt Romney loyalists Peter Flaherty and Eric Fehrnstrom, who guided him from relative obscurity to talk-of-the-nation.

Health care issue

Although Democrats flail against the obvious, the real message of Scott Brown's ascendancy signifies opposition to current health care reform. His surge has been a mirror image of 1994, when backlash to Hillary Clinton's attempt to overhaul health care sparked a Republican takeover of Congress.

Brown couldn't have come close to victory in a statewide race without the health care issue. He couldn't have raised so much money except for welling anger throughout the country.

As important as the Massachusetts special election was to the health care debate, it also represents a come-to-Jesus moment for the GOP. What kind of party will it be?

On the surface, Brown's success, especially among independents, suggests that the GOP tent is expanding to make room even for moderate, pro-choice candidates such as Brown. Have fiscal conservatives displaced social conservatives as the base? Or have the Palin-Huckabee Republicans made room at the inn out of expediency? Perhaps the party has embraced the philosophy of a retired state

GOP chairman, who once said to me: "A good Republican is a Republican who wins."

Then again, Coakley's social positions were politically extreme, even by Massachusetts standards. Whatever the case, it would be a mistake to fashion Brown into a party savior, say insiders close to the race. Brown is sui generis — a candidate uniquely suited to his time and place. As one GOP operative put it:

"No one should expect him to be a conservative icon, because he's not," she said. "He's a Massachusetts man of the people."

Yes, those Republicans who did everything possible to elect him proved themselves to be pragmatic. They understood that someone such as Jim DeMint of South Carolina couldn't win in Massachusetts. But ultimately, as others, including the president, can attest, no one can live up to iconic status.

What can be inferred from the Brown-Coakley race is that a new national mantra has emerged from the electorate that bodes ill for Democrats.

It's no longer hope and change, but something sturdier: Reform or die.

Kathleen Parker is a syndicated columnist. Readers may write to her at kathleenparker@washpost.com or the Washington Post Writers Group, 1150 15th St. NW, Washington, D.C. 200701.

Fall election may determine America's fate

When a baseball player has come to bat after failing to get a hit 20 times in a row, some fans say he is "due" for a hit. But statisticians say he is no more likely to get a hit in this at bat than at any other time. In other words, there is no such thing as being "due."

After the Republicans went from being the dominant party, at both the state and national levels, just a few years ago, and got clobbered at the polls by the Democrats two elections in a row, some people think the Republicans are "due" to make a comeback in this fall's elections.

Maybe it will happen. The polls show that the voting public is getting more and more fed up with the Obama administration and with both houses of Congress that are dominated by Democrats. But, when election day comes, nobody can vote for polls. It still takes a candidate to beat a candidate — and the question is whether the Republicans come up with the kinds of candidates that can win.

Political dangers

Thomas Sowell

difficult for Americans even to imagine that it could happen, much less what a horror it would be to live under hate-filled fanatics such as the current Iranian leaders. But Japan had likewise never surrendered in its entire history until it was hit with two nuclear bombs.

Unlike us, Iranian leaders — going back to the Ayatollah Khomeini — have said plainly that they are willing to see their country destroyed as the price of destroying the enemies of Islam — which, in their view of the world, includes the United States.

Perhaps serious sanctions might have been enough to stop the Iranian nuclear program a few years ago, by crippling their economy. But nobody in the West had the stomach for

Those of us who are not Republicans nevertheless have a huge stake in this fall's elections, because the current administration in Washington is not merely deficient but dangerous, both at home and abroad.

In just one year in power, the Obama administration has not merely tripled the deficit and circumvented the Constitution with their "czars" who rule by decree, but have moved to dictate the medical treatment of all Americans — which is to say, they are moving toward getting the power of life and death, to add to all the other powers they have seized.

Increasing numbers of Americans are saying that they are having trouble recognizing the country in which they were born and grew up. They will have even more trouble recognizing America if the Washington juggernaut does not lose a substantial part of its power in this year's election.

A nuclear Iran

The dangers are not only in domestic policy but even more so in the Obama administration's foreign policy. Their diddling around while fanatical leaders of a terrorist-sponsoring nation such as Iran are moving toward producing nuclear bombs can take us and the world to a point of no return.

No nation on earth will let three of its cities be annihilated by nuclear bombs without surrendering. The fact that the United States has never surrendered may make it

that.

The longer we wait, the higher the price goes — the price of either action or inaction.

Just three years ago, the people currently at the top in Washington — including President Barack Obama and Secretary of State Hillary Clinton — were ready to turn tail and run in Iraq.

It would take a leader with extraordinary courage, pride in America and dedication to the values, traditions and the people of America, to stand up to enemies who could annihilate Los Angeles, Chicago and New York with nuclear weapons.

Does this sound anything like the president who has gone around the world apologizing for this country and literally bowing to foreign leaders?

The stakes in this fall's elections go far beyond the fate of either the Republican Party or the Democratic Party. The fate of America is on the line. The Republicans need to understand that — and to understand that they are not simply "due" because of polls.

They have a job to do, and what will happen to our children and grandchildren will depend on how well they do it.

Thomas Sowell is a syndicated columnist. Readers may write to him at www.tsowell.com, at info@creators.com (with his name in the subject line) or Creators Syndicate, 5777 W. Century Blvd., Suite 700, Los Angeles, CA 90045.

258

A decade of deceit

By Tim Rutten

Looking back over the last 10 years, it's hard not to feel as W.H. Auden did one dreary September day in 1939:
"I sit in one of the dives
"On Fifty-second Street
"Uncertain and afraid
"As the clever hopes expire
"Of a low dishonest decade."

Still, if we're looking for a literary progenitor for the era now past, it would not be Auden but Herman Melville's "The Confidence-Man," for these were the years of the great con and the sweeping swindle. From Bernie Ebbers and WorldCom to Jeff Skilling and the Enron boys, to Bernie Madoff's Ponzi scheme, to the bait-and-switch that Bush and Cheney used to take the country into war, this was the decade of deception.

Family damage

No deceit was more malevolently corrosive than the fiction that this was a period of expansive prosperity in which significant numbers of our people were able to share in the American dream of financial security. All the triumphalist rhetoric emanating from Wall Street and the White House notwithstanding, this was — materially speaking — a disastrous decade for U.S. families.

For the first time since World War II, according to the departments of Commerce and Labor, an average American's net worth actually fell — by a

whopping 13 percent. By way of comparison, and to demonstrate just how anomalous such a decline is, consider that net worth grew 44 percent in the 1990s; 35 percent in the 1980s; 12 percent in the 1970s (even with the Carter administration's "stagflation"); 25 percent in the 1960s; and 26 percent in the 1950s.

The employment picture was no better. Though the U.S. population has grown by 35 million since 2000, employment has increased just 0.5 percent over the last 10 years. For the first time since the federal government began keeping such statistics, the number of private sector jobs actually declined. (In both the 1980s and 1990s, employment grew by 20 percent, and in the 1960s it climbed by 31 percent.)

Meanwhile, the private sector's flight from its pension obligations became

virtually general. Tens of millions of Americans were compelled to trust their retirements to the equity markets through 401(k) accounts. It was a bonanza for Wall Street, which raked in commissions and fees, and a disaster for working families, because the decade ended without any gains in the stock averages.

A tiny minority of insiders and the privileged, on the other hand, did very well for themselves. According to economists Emmanuel Saez of Berkeley and Thomas Piketty of the Paris School of Economics, the highest-earning 0.1 percent of Americans accounted for 8.2 percent of the country's total pretax income. That's the highest concentration of wealth since 1917.

Former Clinton administration Secretary of Labor Robert Reich recently pointed out that

all these factors combined to play a major, but largely unrecognized, role in the current financial crisis. Even though most American families had two working adults throughout the last decade, many had to borrow simply to maintain their standard of living. People maxed out their credit cards and tapped their homes' equity — something that proved catastrophic when the value of houses collapsed.

With incomes and employment stagnant, families had nowhere to turn. Not so employers.

Layoffs and overtime

While most lacked the managerial creativity to grow their businesses, they found a way to keep profits up by laying off huge numbers of people and simply working those who remained — too frightened to protest — harder. That accounts for the striking productivity gains recorded over the past several quarters. The sputtering economic recovery now under way essentially is a 21st century version of the old-fashioned speedup.

Democratic Party executives from President Obama to Mayor Antonio Villaraigosa have said that their priority for the year ahead is to create good jobs that pay decent wages. As the experience of this deceitful decade demonstrates, the need never has been more urgent.

Timothy Rutten is a columnist for the Los Angeles Times. Readers may send him e-mail at timothy.rutten@latimes.com.

Not everyone is celebrating

■ Some people are not convinced that Barack Obama will be good for the country.

By Andrew Barksdale
Staff writer

While many Americans heralded their new president Tuesday, some remained skeptical about the new administration and its policies.

After watching the inauguration on television, Hubert Owens said he remains unconvinced that Barack Obama is the right man to lead the country.

Owens

"The world is going to test him, and is he strong enough to protect this country like President Bush has?" he asked.

Owens, who is 30 and lives in Fayetteville, is a former soldier who was injured in Iraq by a roadside bomb. Today, he is an order-filler for the Wal-Mart distribution center. He voted for John McCain in November.

Owens, who is black, said he was moved by the ceremony. Black people have overcome so much, he said.

"It is good to see history being made on that note," he said.

Nationwide, Obama captured 53 percent of the vote. He also carried North Carolina and Cumberland County.

Still, 58 million people voted against Obama.

One was Alan Hendrix, who is 44 and owns a small but growing security firm in Fayetteville. He said Obama looked flat and uninspiring during his speech Tuesday.

"He is my president, and I will give him all my support," he said. "And he'll have my prayers."

Hendrix said Obama's approach to solving problems is growing the size of government. He disagrees with that philosophy.

"We have been successful in our country for over 200 years allowing capitalism to thrive and keeping government small," he said.

Ralph Reagan, chairman of the Cumberland County Republican Party, said many Obama dissenters are now hoping for the best in the new president.

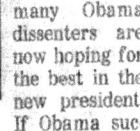

Reagan

If Obama succeeds, Americans win, too, Reagan said.

But he still worries that the country is headed in a socialist direction. Case in point, he said, is talk of bailing out several ailing industries.

"It will encourage the slothful, and it's going to prop up businesses that should fail and become efficient," he said.

Reagan spent part of Tuesday thinking about how the Grand Old Party could regain its momentum and put people back into office.

"Today is encouraging me to be even more determined that there will not be another inauguration of a Democrat," he said.

Staff writer Andrew Barksdale can be reached at barksdalea@fayobserver.com or 486-3565.

Obama fatigue sets in

By Steven Hill

President Barack Obama is approaching the first anniversary of his inauguration, and already signs of "Obama fatigue" are evident. When the president's happy or frowning visage comes on the TV, one can gauge the gut-level reactions.

My family and friends run the gamut of the political spectrum. The moderates and conservatives are both Republican and Democrat, and most of them actually voted for Obama, convinced by the candidate's soaring rhetoric and his elderly opponent John McCain's creaky appearance that the first black president in American history should be given a chance. Yet when Obama's face comes on the tube, every one of them now reacts negatively.

Some shook their heads, kind of smirking. Others were more visceral in their grimaces and body language. They voiced the usual conservative talking points about "big government takeover," but they also complained about the bailout of wealthy bank executives and auto companies while "the little guy" suffered. Some agreed that financial re-regulation was necessary, not only over the conservative punching bags of Fannie and Freddie Mac but also reinstatement of Glass-Steagall restrictions between investment and commercial banks.

January 2009

When I pointed out that the congressional Republicans seem dead set on opposing anything Obama does, most of them agreed, but they were interested in results, not excuses.

The reaction of the liberals in the family was even more surprising. Most of them were even more visceral in their disgust with Obama than the conservatives. Having been ecstatic when Obama was voted in, having felt themselves part of a historical wave that had elected what they thought was a transformative figure like Franklin Roosevelt, now they were deeply suspicious.

"I can't believe a word he says," said one. "He completely duped us. On the campaign trail, he showed us one face, and now as president another."

Similar complaints

Interestingly, they were upset over some of the same things as the conservatives,

such as the bailout of the banks, lack of strong financial re-regulation proposals, and the inability to solve the health care problem.

When I pointed out the complexity of the problems he had inherited, including a collapsing economy and a Congress beholden to special interests, they acknowledged those challenges but didn't cut Obama any slack. When I pointed out that he needs votes from 60 out of 100 Senators to get anything done — meaning that the 40 Republican senators representing only a third of the nation, joined by a single conservative Democrat or independent, can halt everything — they were impatient.

"Whatever happened to the Internet presidency, where he was going to mobilize Obama's army to pressure recalcitrant Democratic senators?" said one liberal friend. "Personally, I don't think he

really cares about the public option, or many other things he said on the campaign trail. He lets the wealthy set the agenda, all these politicians are the same."

Liberals and conservatives wanted solutions to the country's many challenges. What none of them had patience for was the gripping sense that the country is stalled.

Despite all of Obama's soaring oratory about pulling together as a nation to solve deep economic, health care and global warming crises, they all felt Obama is not delivering. Whether his inabilities are related to personal shortcomings or the defects of America's antiquated political system, they were not much interested. All they were interested in was results. And a year into his presidency, Obama was failing to produce much of those.

So, when seeing Obama on their TV screens, nearly all of them shook their heads, grimaced, snorted or chuckled, and then quickly changed the channel. I don't recall George W. Bush reaching this point in his presidency until near the end of his first term. If that's a bellwether, then Obama is in trouble.

Steven Hill is director of the Political Reform Program for the New America Foundation. His new book, "Europe's Promise: Why the European Way is the Best Hope in an Insecure Age," was published this month.

Californians pass proposal to ban same-sex marriage

By David Crary and Lisa Leff
The Associated Press

LOS ANGELES — In a heartbreaking defeat for the gay-rights movement, California voters put a stop to gay marriage, creating uncertainty about the legal status of 18,000 same-sex couples who tied the knot during a four-month window of opportunity opened by the state's highest court.

Passage of a constitutional amendment against gay marriage — in a state so often at the forefront of liberal social change — elated religious conservatives who had little else to cheer about in Tuesday's elections. Gay activists were disappointed and began looking for battlegrounds elsewhere in the back-and-forth fight to allow gays to wed.

"There's something deeply wrong with putting the rights of a minority up to a majority vote," said Evan Wolfson, a gay-rights lawyer who heads a group called Freedom to Marry. "If this were being done to almost any other minority, people would see how un-American this is."

Legal skirmishing began immediately, with gay-rights groups challenging the newly passed ban in court Wednesday and vowing to resist any effort to invalidate the same-sex marriages that took place following the state Supreme Court decision in May.

The amendment, which passed with 52 percent of the vote, overrides that court ruling by defining marriage as the union of one man and one woman. Thirty states now have adopted such measures, but the California vote marks the first time a state took away gay marriage after it had been legalized.

Gay-marriage bans also passed Tuesday in Arizona and Florida, with 57 percent and 62 percent ...

THE FAYETTEVILLE OBSERVER

minority up to a majority vote.'

Evan Wolfson,
a gay-rights lawyer

while Arkansas voters approved a measure aimed at gays that bars unmarried couples from serving as adoptive or foster parents.

Massachusetts and Connecticut are now the only states to allow same-sex marriage.

Even as the last votes were being counted in California, the American Civil Liberties Union and other opponents of the ban filed a challenge with the state Supreme Court.

The measure's passage casts a shadow of uncertainty over the marriages performed in the past four months. California State Attorney General Jerry Brown has said existing gay marriages will remain valid, but other legal experts said challenges are likely.

Proposition 8 became the focus of the most expensive social-issues campaign in U.S. history, with the rival sides raising a combined $74 million.

Exit polls revealed dramatic demographic gaps in the gay-marriage vote. While 63 percent of voters under 30 opposed the ban, 59 percent of those 65 and older supported it. There were sharp racial discrepancies as well. Even as black voters overwhelmingly backed Barack Obama — a gay-rights supporter — in the presidential race, 70 percent of them voted against gay marriage, compared with 47 percent of white voters.

OPINION

EDITORIALS · LETTERS · COLUMNS   www.fayobserver.com/opinion

Black teen murder rates rise

By Lara Jakes
The Associated Press

WASHINGTON — The number of young black men and teenagers who either killed or were killed in shootings has risen at an alarming rate since 2000, a new study shows.

The study, to be released today by criminologists at Northeastern University in Boston, comes as FBI data is showing that murders have leveled off nationwide.

Not so for black teens, the youngest of whom saw dramatic increases in shooting deaths, the Northeastern report concluded.

Last year, for example, 426 black males ages 14 to 17 were killed in gun crimes, the study shows. That marked a 40 percent increase from 2000.

Similarly, an estimated 964 in the same age group committed fatal shootings in 2007 — a 38 percent increase from seven

years earlier. The number of offenders is estimated because not all crimes are reported, said Northeastern criminologist James Alan Fox, who co-authored the study.

Seizing on President-elect Obama's incoming administration as an opportunity for more funding, Fox added: "There is an urgency for reinvestment in children and families. In essence, we need a bailout for kids at risk."

The study partly blamed Bush administration grant cuts to local police and juvenile crime prevention programs for the surge in crimes by young black men and teens. Incoming Vice President Joe Biden has promised funding to put 50,000 new police officers on the street to help bring violent crime rates back to a decade-long annual decline that began in the mid-1990s.

Nationwide, the number of murders and violent crimes over-

all dropped last year after increasing in 2005 and 2006, according to annual data compiled by the FBI. Overall, however, murders have risen by about 8 percent between 2000 and 2007.

The FBI reported 10,067 arrests in murder and non-negligent manslaughter cases in 2007. Half the people arrested — 5,078 — were black. Almost 10 percent of black people arrested for murder were under 18, the FBI data show.

The number of young white men who committed gun-related homicides also rose over the same period, the Northeastern study showed, but not as dramatically. In 2007, an estimated 384 white males age 14 to 17 shot someone to death, up from 368 in 2000.

The numbers of homicides committed by women and teenage girls — whether black or white — were relatively few, the study found.

Where's Obama's Birth Certificate?

By Alan Caruba Friday, July 31, 2009

It's the question and/or controversy that will not go away. Where was President Barack Hussein Obama born and why won't he produce a birth certificate?

Sometime ago I received an affidavit filed in the U.S. District Court, Eastern District of Pennsylvania, by Philip J. Berg, an attorney who briefly gained media attention when he asserted that President Obama is not a natural born citizen of the United States and, under the U.S. Constitution, was disqualified from running for or holding the position of President.

The problem Berg presents is that he reportedly was a supporter of Hillary Clinton's bid for the Democrat nomination and thus had a very political reason to challenge Obama's citizenship. The courts, however, appear to have been extraordinarily reluctant to address the question.

Among the Berg documents I have seen is an affidavit attesting to

a transcribed conversation between Bishop Kwele Shuhudra, Bishop of the Anabaptists Churches of North America, and Sarah Obama, the President's grandmother or aunt, who confirmed that she was present when he was born in Kenya. Could she be mistaken? There also appears to be some confusion over which hospital in Hawaii Obama was born; if he was born there. No attending physician has ever stepped forth to confirm it.

Democrat spin doctors are, of course, circling the wagons around Obama who is alleged to have spent nearly a million dollars on lawyers to keep his birth and other public records secret.

The obvious question is why.

The problem for his defenders is that no birth certificate has been made available to the public and the Hawaii Certificate of Live Birth that was briefly shown on an Obama website has raised more questions than answers about its authenticity and has been challenged as a forgery.

Obama's birth father met his mother, Stanley Ann Dunham, when they were students at the University of Hawaii. It is entirely possible that she gave birth to Obama in Hawaii though there is some question whether a ceremony occurred generating a marriage certificate. Obama senior was already married to an African wife at the time. What is known is that Obama's mother later married an Indonesian in 1965 and Obama spent his early years in Jakarta, starting in 1967.

The reason I am a "birther", i.e., someone who remains skeptical, is fairly simple. I began my career as a journalist. I was trained to be skeptical and to expect to see documentation and proof that whatever is asserted is true.

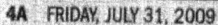

From left, Vice President Joe Biden, Harvard professor Henry Louis Gates Jr., Cambridge, Mass., police Sgt. James Crowley and President Obama talk while having beers in the Rose Garden of the White House in Washington on Thursday.

Fay BARS, NC

Colleges tighten admissions

■ Budget crunches mean caps on enrollment and cuts in classes.

By Terence Chea
The Associated Press

SAN FRANCISCO — College applicants are facing one of the toughest years ever to gain admission to the nation's public colleges and universities as schools grapple with deep budget cuts and record numbers of applications.

As cash-poor state governments slash budgets, colleges are capping or cutting enrollment despite a surge in applications from high school seniors, community college students and unemployed workers returning to school.

The increased competition means more students will be turned away, forced to attend pricier private institutions or shut out of college altogether.

Colleges that previously accepted all qualified students are becoming selective, while selective schools are becoming more so. Most community colleges have open-access policies, but demand for classes is so intense that many students can't get the courses they need.

"We're hearing a lot of panic," said Gerna Benz, a partner at California San Francisco Bay Area College Planning Specialists.

Benz is encouraging more families to consider private colleges, which may be more expensive but offer less crowded classes and the chance to graduate in four years.

Applications to private colleges are holding steady, while public universities around the country are seeing record demand as cost-conscious families look for good value, said Barmak Nassirian, associate executive director of the American Association of Collegiate Registrars and Admissions Officers.

Low-income, minority students could face the roughest road to admission because they often can't afford private colleges and don't have the re-sources or academic credentials to compete with students from wealthier families and better high schools, he said.

The caps could also threaten President Obama's goal of making the U.S. the leader in college attainment by 2020, college officials say.

"We're reducing enrollment when we should be increasing it," said Scott Lay, president of the Community College League of California. Experts say states should increase access to college during a recession so that unemployed workers can train for new jobs.

@
■ Check your e-mail in the morning for top stories.
Sign up for @lerts at **fayobserver.com**.

266

A CENTER FOR INDEPENDENT MEDIA SITE

THE WASHINGTON INDEPENDENT™

National News in Context

'Birther' Movement Dogs Republicans

Ten Members of Congress Sign on to Presidential Birth Certificate Bill

By David Weigel 7/17/09 6:00 AM

Kris Kobach campaigns in Wichita, Kans. (YouTube: WichitaLiberty)

Kris Kobach is a law professor with degrees from Harvard, Yale and Oxford, and a veteran of George W. Bush's administration who, after Sept. 11, helped craft the policy on domestic registration of foreign visitors to the United States. In May, he announced a run for Kansas secretary of state, campaigning for photo ID requirements at the voting booth. He's considered a clear front-runner for the job. But over the weekend, Kobach spoke at a Republican Party barbecue and committed a minor gaffe. According to the Lawrence Journal-World, Kobach "asked what President Obama and God had in common, with the punchline being neither has a birth certificate."

Kansas Democrats pounced. "While Kris Kobach has in the past associated himself with extremists who frequently show poor taste," said state Democratic Party Executive Director Kenny Johnston, "his latest attempt at humor has gone too far." Kobach told the Democrats to "lighten up" before walking back the comment, explaining that "until a court says otherwise, I believe Barack Obama is a natural-born citizen."

Kobach could have offered another defense. The joke was not his. One month earlier, Rush Limbaugh made the same remark on his radio show. "Barack Obama has one thing in common with God," Limbaugh said. "Know what it is? God does not have a birth certificate either." And Limbaugh may not have been writing his own material, either. At Patriot Depot, a conservative web site that sells books by Glenn Beck and signs designed for anti-tax Tea Parties, buyers can pay $10 to get two bumper stickers that read: "Obama & God Have ONLY ONE THING in Common: NO BIRTH CERTIFICATE! The Difference Is God Doesn't Think He's Obama!"According to a salesman for Patriot Depot, the company has sold "hundreds" of this and another birth certificate sticker since advertising them with the conservative opinion sites GOPUSA.com and Townhall.com.

Six months into Obama's presidency, after scores of embarrassing legal defeats, and even after tussles between the attoneys who've turned frivolous lawsuits about the president's citizenship into full-time jobs, the cottage industry of conspiracy theories about the president's birth shows no signs of disappearing. The theories have found a home in talk radio and on conservative web sites such as Free Republic and WorldNetDaily. Conspiracy theorists are increasingly sending letters to their local papers, embarrassing members of Congress at town hall meetings, and hounding Hill staffers about challenges to the president's citizenship.   ." While Posey initially said that he disbelieved conspiracy theories about the president's birth, he told the host of an Internet radio show that he'd discussed the possibility of Obama being removed from office over "the eligibility issue" with "high-ranking members of our Judiciary Committee." As of July 15, nine fellow Republican members of Congress were backing the bill. While Rep. Randy Neugebauer (R-Texas) has said that he supports the bill because he didn't know whether Obama was a citizen, other sponsors say that they weighed in to pour cold water on the conspiracy theories.

"It's a good idea," said John Donnelly, a spokesman for Rep. Dan Burton (R-Ind.), who became one of the bill's co-sponsors this month. "If candidates provided that information to the Federal Election Commission you wouldn't have all this hullaballoo. You don't want to needlessly expose presidents to crazy conspiracy theories."

www.fayobserver.com

DECEMBER 1, 2008

Study: Students lie, cheat and steal

By David Crary
The Associated Press

NEW YORK — In the past year, 30 percent of U.S. high school students have stolen from a store and 64 percent have cheated on a test, according to a new, large-scale survey suggesting that Americans are too apathetic about ethical standards.

Educators reacting to the findings questioned any suggestion that today's young people are less honest than previous generations, but several agreed that intensified pressures are prompting many students to cut corners.

"The competition is greater, the pressures on kids have increased dramatically," said Mel Riddle of the National Association of Secondary School Principals. "They have opportunities their predecessors didn't have (to cheat). The temptation is greater."

The Josephson Institute, a Los Angeles-based ethics institute, surveyed 29,760 students at 100 randomly selected high schools nationwide, both public and private. All students in the selected schools were given the survey in class; their anonymity was assured.

Michael Josephson, the institute's founder and president, said he was most dismayed by the findings about theft. The survey found that 35 percent of boys and 26 percent of girls — 30 percent overall — acknowledged stealing from a store within the past year. One-fifth

Dishonesty

From **Page 1A**

said they stole something from a friend; 23 percent said they stole something from a parent or other relative.

"What is the social cost of that — not to mention the implication for the next generation of mortgage brokers?" Josephson remarked in an interview. "In a society drenched with cynicism, young people can look at it and say 'Why shouldn't we? Everyone else does it.'"

Other findings from the survey:

■ Cheating in school is rampant and getting worse. Sixty-four percent of students cheated on a test in the past year and 38 percent did so two or more times, up from 60 percent and 35 percent in a 2006 survey.

■ Thirty-six percent said they used the Internet to plagiarize an assignment, up from 33 percent in 2004.

Despite such responses, 93 percent of the students said they were satisfied with their personal ethics and character, and 77 percent affirmed that "when it comes to doing what is right, I am better than most people I know."

'Scapegoat'

Nijmie Dzurinko, executive director of the Philadelphia Student Union, said the findings were not at all reflective of the inner-city students she works with as an advocate for better curriculum and school funding.

"A lot of people like to blame society's problems on young people, without recognizing that young people aren't making the decisions about what's happening in society," said Dzurinko, 32. "They're very easy to scapegoat."

Peter Anderson, principal of Andover High School in Andover, Mass., said he and his colleagues had detected very little cheating on tests or Internet-based plagiarism. He has, however, noticed an uptick in students sharing homework in unauthorized ways.

"This generation is leading incredibly busy lives — involved in athletics, clubs, so many with part-time jobs, and — for seniors — an incredibly demand-

ing and anxiety-producing college search," he offered as an explanation.

Riddle, who for four decades was a high school teacher and principal in northern Virginia, agreed that more pressure could lead to more cheating, yet spoke in defense of today's students.

"I would take these students over other generations," he said. "I found them to be more responsive, more rewarding to work with, more appreciative of support that adults give them.

"We have to create situations where it's easy for kids to do the right things," he added.

On Long Island, an alliance of school superintendents and college presidents recently embarked on a campaign to draw attention to academic integrity problems and to crack down on plagiarism and cheating.

Roberta Gerold, superintendent of the Middle Country School District and a leader of the campaign, said parents and school officials need to be more diligent — for example, emphasizing to students the distinctions between original and borrowed work.

DISHONEST HABITS

In a recent survey more than one in three boys and one-fourth of girls admitted to stealing from a store within the past year.

Students' ethical behavior

Admitted stealing from a store in the last year and

boys	35%
girls	26
... from a friend	20
	14

Sometimes lied to save money.

	49
	35

Had lied to a parent about something significant (public and religious private schools):

	83

Had cheated on a test:

2006	60
2008	64

Used the Internet to plagiarize an assignment

2004	33
2008	36

Source: Josephson Institute   AP graphic

Report: Grad rate dismal

■ A study says children are less likely to get a diploma than their parents were.

By Libby Quaid
The Associated Press

WASHINGTON — Your child is less likely to graduate from high school than you were, and most states are doing little to hold schools accountable, according to a study by a children's advocacy group.

More than half the states have graduation targets that don't make schools get better, the Education Trust says in a report released Thursday.

The numbers are dismal: One in four kids is dropping out of school, a rate that hasn't budged for at least five years.

"The U.S. is stagnating while other industrialized countries are surpassing us," said Anna Habash, author of the report by Education Trust, which advocates on behalf of minority and poor children. "And that is go-ing to have a dramatic impact on our ability to compete," she said.

In fact, the United States is now the only industrialized country where young people are less likely than their parents to earn a diploma, the report said, citing data compiled by the international Organization for Economic Cooperation and Development.

High schools are required to meet graduation targets every year as part of the 2002 federal No Child Left Behind law.

But those targets are set by states, not by the federal government. And most states allow schools to graduate low percentages of students by saying any progress, or even the status quo in some cases, is acceptable.

■ In North Carolina, schools must improve by 0.1 percentage point each year. At that rate, it would take nearly a century to raise the graduation rate, now 72 percent, to the state goal of 80 percent.

■ In Maryland, schools must improve their graduation rate by 0.01 percentage point each year. At that rate, it would take most of a millennium for the graduation rate among African-American students, now 71 per-cent, to reach the state goal of 90 percent.

■ In Delaware and New Mexico, schools will never have to meet a state graduation goal as long as they maintain the same graduation rate. Dela-ware's graduation rate is 76 percent; New Mexico's is 67 percent.

Why are states setting the bar so low?

Because they can, said Bob Balfanz, a researcher at Johns Hopkins University.

State and school officials are under pressure to improve test scores under No Child Left Be-hind or face penalties. But they got a break on graduation rates: Schools must meet annual goals, but the government lets each state set its own goal.

"A lot of states said, 'Well, we're under a lot of pressure; let's not make this too hard on ourselves,'" Balfanz said. "They were given a loophole, and they took it."

So in North Carolina — which has won praise for a se-ries of innovations to keep kids in school — the graduation goal has not changed. Officials are coming up with a new goal but are hoping No Child Left Behind will be rewritten to be less punitive.

"To be candid, we're waiting for NCLB to change," said June Atkinson, North Carolina's state schools superintendent. "Those numbers do not tell the story. Our mission is that 100 percent of our students will graduate from high school. Needless to say, we have a lot of work to do."

In Maryland, officials say their slower goal is more realis-tic.

"If you really want to bring about change, you have to have reachable goals that people be-lieve they can work toward," said Ronald A. Peiffer, Mary-land's deputy superintendent for academic policy.

"By not making these num-bers pie-in-the-sky, I think we have a better chance," Peiffer said.

FRIDAY
September 19, 2008

The Fayetteville Observer

The cost of racial hype

Sometimes you don't know when you are lucky. Certainly, I did not consider myself lucky when I left home at 17 and discovered the hard way that there was no great demand for a black teenage dropout with no experience and no skill.

In retrospect, however, those days of struggling to earn money to pay the rent and buy food left little time or energy for navel-gazing over things such as "identity."

All this came back to me recently when I saw a font-page story about middle-class blacks worrying about their racial identity. There, on the front page of the Wall Street Journal, was a picture of a black teenager whose mother was fixing his bow tie as he was getting dressed in a tuxedo, in preparation for a cotillion.

When I was that kid's age, I had real problems that taught me real lessons to remember when times got better, not navel-gazing problems that can distract you from reality for a lifetime.

Apparently there are middle-class blacks who spend a lot of time and energy worrying about losing their roots and losing touch with their black brothers back in the 'hood.

In one sense, it is good that there are people who think about others less fortunate than themselves. That's fine but, like most good things, it can be carried to the point where it is ridiculous and counterproductive for all concerned.

In a world where an absolute majority of black children are born and raised in fatherless homes, where most black kids never finish high school and

THOMAS SOWELL

where the murder rate among blacks is several times the national average, surely there must be more urgent priorities than preserving a lifestyle and an identity.

Tribalistic identity

During decades of researching racial and ethnic groups in countries around the world — with special attention to those who began in poverty and then rose to prosperity — I have yet to find one so preoccupied with tribalistic identity as to want to maintain solidarity with all members of their group, regardless of what they do or how they do it.

Any group that rises has to have norms, and that means repudiating those who violate those norms, if you are serious. Blind tribalism means letting the lowest common denominator determine the norms and the fate of the whole group.

There was a time when most blacks understood this common sense. But that was before the romanticizing of identity took over, beginning in the 1960s.

Back in 19th century America, the Catholic church took on the task of changing the behavior of the poverty-stricken Irish immigrants, in order to prepare them to rise in American society. As this transformation succeeded, employers' signs that said "No Irish Need Apply" began to disappear in the 20th century.

The Jewish community likewise made many efforts to change the behavior of immigrants from Eastern Europe, to enable them to better fit into American society — and to rise in that society.

The Urban League and other black uplift groups made similar efforts to prepare their fellow blacks to rise in American society. In fact, those efforts began to pay off in dramatic reductions in poverty among blacks, even before the civil rights laws of the 1960s.

The unanswered question is why an approach with a proven track record, not only in American society but in various other countries around the world, has been superseded by a philosophy of tribal identity overriding issues of behavior and performance.

Part of the problem is the "multicultural" ideology that says all cultures are equally valid.

Will time and energy spent on rap music and wearing low-riding baggy pants like guys in prison — as badges of identity — provide as good a future for young people as learning math, computers and the English language?

Romantic self-indulgence and self-deception are things that some people can afford when they reach the point where they can afford identity angst. But millions of other people will remain mired in poverty if they believe such notions.

Thomas Sowell is a syndicated columnist. Readers may write to him at www.tsowell.com, at info@creators.com (with his name in the subject line) or Creators Syndicate, 5777 W. Century Blvd., Suite 700, Los Angeles, CA 90045.

MONDAY, SEPTEMBER 15, 2008   NORTH CAROLINA'S OLDEST NEWSPAPER

The Fayetteville

ESTABLISHED 1816

Observer

Report says students not ready for college

By Justin Pope
The Associated Press

It's a tough lesson for millions of students arriving on campus: even if you have a high school diploma, you may not be ready for college.

In fact, a new study calculates, one-third of American college students have to enroll in remedial classes. The bill to colleges and taxpayers for trying to bring them up to speed on material they were supposed to learn in high school comes to between $2.3 billion and $2.9 billion annually.

"That is a very large cost, but there is an additional cost and that's the cost to the students," said former Colorado governor Roy Romer, chair of the group Strong American Schools, which is issuing the report "Diploma to Nowhere" today. "These students come out of high school really misled. They think they're prepared. They got a 3.0 and got through the curriculum they needed to get admitted, but they find what they learned wasn't adequate."

Christina Jeronimo was an "A" student in high school En-

REMEDIATION NATION

One-third of American college students have to enroll in remedial classes.

Percent of students enrolled in remedial classes, 2004

TYPE OF PUBLIC COLLEGE

Four-year   29%

Two-year   43%

Source: Strong American Schools   AP graphic

---

glish, but was placed in a remedial course when she arrived at Long Beach Community College in California. The course was valuable in some ways but frustrating and time-consuming. Now in her third year of community college, she'd hoped to transfer to UCLA by now.

Like many college students, she wishes she'd been worked a little harder in high school.

"There's a gap," said Jeronimo, who hopes to study psychology. "The demands of the high school teachers aren't as great as the demands for college."

The problem of colleges devoting huge amounts of time and money to remediation isn't

---

new, though its scale and cost has been difficult to measure. The latest report gives somewhat larger estimates than some previous studies, though it is not out of line with trends suggested in others, said Hunter Boylan, an expert at Appalachian State University, who was not connected with the report.

Analyzing federal data, the report estimates 43 percent of community college students require remediation, as do 29 percent of students at public four-year universities, with higher numbers in some places. For instance, four in five Oklahoma community college students need remedial coursework, and three in five in the California State university system need help in English, math or both.

The cost per student runs to as much as $2,000 per student in community colleges and $2,500 in four-year universities.

Boylan says colleges are learning such courses must also teach study skills to be effective.

Students often report that the hardest aspect of the transition to college is the new rhythm and structure of college-level work.

WEDNESDAY, DECEMBER 10, 2008   www.fuyobserver.com

50¢

'CORRUPTION CRIME SPREE'

Illnois Gov. Rod Blagojevich.

Feds arrest Illinois governor

■ Prosecutors say wiretaps caught the Democrat scheming to sell an appointment to the U.S. Senate.

By Mike Robinson
The Associated Press

CHICAGO — Illinois Gov. Rod Blagojevich was roused from bed and arrested Tuesday after prosecutors said he was caught on wiretaps audaciously scheming to sell Barack Obama's vacant Senate seat for cash or a plum job for himself in the new administration.

"I've got this thing and it's (expletive) golden," the 51-year-old Democrat said of his authority to appoint Obama's replacement, "and I'm just not giving it up for

See **ARREST**, Page 4A

Arrest: Blagojevich considered appointing himself to Senate

From **Page 1A**

(expletive) nothing. I'm not gonna do it."

Prosecutors did not accuse Obama himself of any wrongdoing or even knowing about the matter. The president-elect said: "I had no contact with the governor or his office, and so I was not aware of what was happening."

FBI agents arrested the governor before daybreak at his Chicago home and took him away while his family was still asleep, saying the wiretaps convinced them that Blagojevich's "political corruption crime spree" had to be stopped before it was too late.

"The Senate seat, as recently as days ago, seemed to be on the verge of being auctioned off," U.S. Attorney Patrick Fitzgerald said. "The conduct would make Lincoln roll over in his grave."

Federal investigators bugged the governor's campaign offices and tapped his home phone, capturing conversations laced with profanity and tough-guy talk from the governor. Chicago FBI chief Robert Grant said even seasoned investigators were stunned by what they heard, particularly since the governor had known for at least three years that he was under investigation for alleged hiring fraud and clearly realized agents might be listening in.

The FBI said in court papers that the governor was overheard conspiring to sell the Senate seat for campaign cash or lucrative jobs for himself or his wife, Patti, a real estate agent. He spoke of using the Senate appointment to land a job with a nonprofit foundation or a union-affiliated group, and even held out hope of getting appointed as Obama's secretary of health and human services or an ambassador.

According to court papers, the governor tried to make it known through emissaries, including union officials and fundraisers, that the seat could be had for the right price. Blagojevich allegedly had a salary in mind — $250,000 to $300,000 a year — and also spoke of collecting half-million and million-dollar political contributions.

The governor has repeatedly denied any wrongdoing. As recently as Monday, he told reporters: "I don't care whether you tape me privately or publicly. I can tell you that whatever I say is always lawful."

The governor's lawyer, Sheldon Sorosky, said he didn't know of any immediate plans for the governor to resign. Blagojevich believes he didn't do anything wrong and asks Illinois residents to have faith in him, Sorosky said.

Blagojevich was charged with two counts: conspiracy to commit fraud, which carries a maximum penalty of 20 years in prison, and solicitation to commit bribery, which is punishable by up to 10 years. He was released on his own recognizance.

Blagojevich, a former congressman, state lawmaker and prosecutor, also was charged with illegally threatening to withhold state assistance to Tribune Co., owner of the Chicago Tribune, in an attempt to strong-arm the newspaper into firing editorial writers who had criticized him.

In addition, the governor was accused of engaging in pay-to-play politics — that is, doling out jobs, contracts and appointments in return for campaign contributions.

Court papers portray Blagojevich as a greedy, vindictive pol who couldn't wait to find ways to cash in on the Senate appointment. The charges also

274

THURSDAY
January 8, 2009

www.fayobserver.com/opinion

Team Obama dabbles in drama

ROGER SIMON

For an outfit known for its lack of drama, Team Obama has become a downright thrill show. Bill Richardson! Rick Warren! Rod Blagojevich! Roland Burris! Talk about a ride through the fun house.

President-elect Barack Obama doesn't bear responsibility for all these speed bumps on the road to a better, happier, more respected America, but he certainly bears responsibility for some of them.

Obama's selection of Bill Richardson for secretary of commerce didn't seem like an awful idea. Richardson certainly has accomplished some things in his life. But Richardson clearly did not get the vetting that is supposed to go along with high office.

Jonathan Martin of Politico recently reported: "Barack Obama's transition team pressed Bill Richardson about a federal probe into 'pay to play' allegations against his office. ... But a Democratic source said Obama's questioners came away empty-handed."

Jake Tapper of ABC News recently reported that "officials on the Obama transition team feel that, before he was formally offered the job of commerce secretary, New Mexico Gov. Bill Richardson was not forthcoming with them about the federal investigation that is looking into whether the governor steered a state contract toward a major financial contributor."

See something slightly off-kilter?

How come somebody didn't say to Obama: "Before we name this guy, let's keep looking into this. After all, a late appointment is better than an embarrassing appointment."

So, blame this drama on Team Obama.

Then there is the matter of Rick Warren, the pastor of the Saddleback Church in Orange County, Calif., whom Obama has invited to give the invocation at his inauguration. Warren has done good works, including fighting global poverty and AIDS, but he also was a prominent supporter of California's Proposition 8, which outlaws gay marriage in the state.

Obama opposes gay marriage, but he also opposed Proposition 8, calling it "divisive and discriminatory."

So why did Obama give a prominent role in his inauguration to Warren? The Democrats want to reach out to evangelical voters, and Warren is considered a moderate by many. But the angry reaction of the gay community and others caught the Obama people flat-footed.

Nor was Obama's defense especially satisfying. Obama said that Warren had invited Obama to Saddleback Church to give a speech, and now Obama was inviting Warren to speak. But this isn't just any speech. It is an inaugural invocation.

So for this drama, blame Obama.

As for Rod Blagojevich and Roland Burris, neither has learned the difference between being spectacular and being a spectacle.

More on them in the future, but Obama has shown a wise amount of distance from both. Their drama cannot be laid at his feet. But, unavoidably, he is going to have to bear their burden on his shoulders.

Roger Simon is the chief political columnist of politico.com, an award-winning journalist and a New York Times best-selling author.

Creators Syndicate

LETTERS TO THE OBSERVER

OPINION

6A

FRIDAY
January 9, 2009

EDITORIALS · LETTERS · COLUMNS

www.fayobserver.com/opinion

PRINCIPLES OF LEADERSHIP
BY
ABRAHAM LINCOLN

Abraham Lincoln overcame the almost insurmountable problems of holding a nation together that was torn by civil war and divided on the issue of slavery. He was able to win the war, free the slaves and preserve the nation as a whole body under a constitution as amended; grounded on the principles of liberty, justice, freedom and the pursuit of happiness. His strong leadership in this endeavor was supported by the following leadership principles which can be applied to corporations and educational institutions today.

I. It is important that people know you come among them without fear.

II. Seek casual contact with your subordinates. It is as meaningful as a formal gathering, if not more so.

III. Remember, everyone likes a compliment.

IV. You must seek and require access to reliable and up-to-date information.

V. Give your subordinates a fair chance with equal freedom and opportunity for success.

VI. Wage only one war at a time and choose your battles.

VII. When you extinguish hope, you create desperation.

VIII. Never crush a man out, thereby making him and his friends, permanent enemies of your organization.

IX. Remember: your organization will take on the personality of its top leader.

X. Make no explanation to your enemies. What they want is a squabble and fuss; and that they can have if you explain, and they cannot have if you don't.

XI. Try not to feel insecure or threatened by your followers.

XII. Always let your subordinates know that the honor will be theirs if they succeed and the blame will be yours if they fail.

XIII. Surround yourself with people who really know their business, and avoid "yes" men.

XIV. Remember that the best leaders never stop learning.

Compiled and edited by,

Vaughan Witten, Ph.D Psychologist
Vice President for Student Affairs Shaw University and
Chief Master Sergeant USAF (RET)

277

WALL STREET

Jobless rate jump sends stocks sliding

9 JAN 09

By Madlen Read
and Stephen Bernard
The Associated Press

NEW YORK — The first full week of 2009 didn't bring Wall Street any huge shocks, but it didn't bring much for investors to be happy about, either.

A jump in unemployment sent stocks sharply lower Friday as investors feared that Americans won't soon deviate from their tightened budgets. The Dow Jones industrial average fell 143 points to end the week down nearly 5 percent, its worst week since November.

The Labor Department's much-anticipated report showed employers cut 524,000 jobs in December, a smaller decline than the loss of 550,000 jobs economists forecast. But the unemployment rate jumped to a 16-year high of 7.2 percent — more than the 7 percent economists predicted — from 6.8 percent in November.

Lost jobs were not a shock to Wall Street, but the news still stung.

Rising unemployment tends to erode consumer spending, which accounts for more than two-thirds of U.S. economic activity. For all of 2008, the economy lost 2.6 million jobs — the most since 1945. Retailers have been reporting dismal holiday sales figures, and Wall Street is concerned about how long the economy will be suffering a pullback in consumer spending.

President-elect Obama on Friday called December's jobs loss "a stark reminder of how urgently action is needed" to revive

the nation's staggering economy. Obama is planning on a stimulus package costing about $800 billion, consisting of tax cuts and other ways to try to help individuals and businesses.

But investors were worried about the prospects for the economy. Warnings from industry leaders during the week about business conditions underscored the economy's troubles.

The Dow Jones industrial average fell 143.28, or 1.64 percent, to 8,599.18. The blue chips' 4.8 percent decline for the week was the biggest point and percentage loss since the week ended Nov. 21.

Broader stock indicators also lost ground. The Standard & Poor's 500 index fell 19.38, or 2.13 percent, to 890.35, and the Nasdaq composite index fell 45.42, or 2.81 percent, to 1,571.59.

For the week, the S&P 500 slid 4.5 percent, and the Nasdaq lost 3.7 percent.

DIVIDENDS

FRIDAY DIVIDENDS DECLARED

STOCK		Period	Stk rate	of rec.	payable
Ablequctions Inc	x				
x-1 for 12 reverse split, effective 1-16					
Village SuperMkt	x			12-29	1-22
x-2 for 1 split.					
INCREASED					
Duncan Engy Prtrs	Q	.4275	1-30	2-9	
Pennichuck Corp	Q	.175	2-9	3-2	
REDUCED					
Greenbrier Cos	Q	.04	1-26	2-16	
HRPT Properties	Q	.12	1-20	1-30	
REGULAR					
Cabot Corp	Q	.18	2-27	3-13	
Compass Diversif	Q	.24	1-23	1-30	
Connecticut Water	Q	.2225	3-2	3-16	
Diamond Foods	Q	.045	1-14	1-29	
Finish Line A	Q	.03	2-27	3-16	
Golden Enterp	Q	.03125	1-16	1-28	
Hospitality Prp	Q	.77	1-21	1-21	
NiSource Inc	Q	.23	1-30	2-20	
Paychex Inc	Q	.31	2-1	2-16	
Tanger Fact Out	Q	.38	1-30	1-30	
g-payable in Canadian funds					

Hamas is to blame for civilian deaths

Jerusalem Post, on the war in Gaza:

How do Israelis feel when our artillery strikes a UN-run school building, killing dozens of people? The answer is deeply shaken, profoundly distressed, sorrowful at the catastrophic loss of life.

But we do not feel guilt. We are angry at Hamas for forcing this war on us; for habitually using Gaza's civilians as human shields; and for transforming a center where people had sought refuge into a shooting gallery and weapons depot.

To paraphrase Golda Meir, there may come a time when we will forgive the Arabs for killing our sons, "but it will be harder for us to forgive them for having forced us to kill their sons."

Images of carnage take on a momentum of their own, and it requires a certain amount of savvy to realize that, sometimes, a picture is not worth 1,000 words. Images that jumble people's thinking and distort reality are less than worthless — they're propagandistic.

Cynically thrusting pictures of dead toddlers at readers and viewers obfuscates truth, bedevils news consumers, and robotically demonizes those "who could do such a thing." What a devious way of giving succor to the uncompromising fanatics who are really to blame for the horror of it all.

A parachute drops near the MV Sirius Star on Friday at anchor as a reported $3 million ransom is paid for the hijacked ship.

10 Jan 09

Negotiator: Tanker released for $3 million

The Associated Press

MOGADISHU, Somalia — After reportedly receiving a $3 million ransom dropped by parachute, pirates said they released a captured Saudi supertanker Friday, ending a two-month drama that helped galvanize international efforts to fight piracy off Africa's coast.

U.S. Navy photos showed a parachute, carrying what they described as "an apparent payment," floating toward the tanker, which had been held with its 25-member crew since Nov. 15.

Mohamed Said, a negotiator with the pirates, said the ship was released and traveling to "safe waters" after the payment of $3 million, far less than the $25 million initially sought.

The seizure of the Sirius Star, which is the size of an aircraft carrier and filled with two million barrels of oil valued at about $100 million, capped a string of increasingly audacious attacks by Somalian pirates. It was the largest ship to have been hijacked and was taken in the Indian Ocean, more than 500 miles southeast of Mombasa, Kenya.

SHIPS HELD

More than a dozen vessels and about 300 crew are in pirate hands, according to the International Maritime Bureau piracy reporting center.

■ **Ukrainian cargo ship** MV Faina, seized in September. The pirates had asked for $20 million for the ship, its tanks and its tanks and other heavy weapons.

■ **Liberian-flagged** MV Biscaglia, seized in November, with 30 crew.

■ **Turkish tanker** Karagol, seized in November carrying 4,500 tons of chemicals and 14 Turkish personnel.

■ **Chinese** fishing vessel Tian No. 8, seized mid-November.

■ **African** Sanderling, a bulk carrier, with 21 Filipino crewmen, seized in October.

■ **Egyptian** cargo ship Blue Star with 28 crew, seized in January.

GAS PRICES

Average per-gallon cost of regular unleaded gas in Fayetteville

Source: AAA Carolinas

YESTERDAY	MONTH AGO	YEAR AGO
$1.698	$1.677	$3.088

Mayor indicted on theft charges

By Ben Nuckols
The Associated Press

BALTIMORE — From Best Buy to Saks Fifth Avenue, from Old Navy to Giorgio Armani, prosecutors allege Mayor Sheila Dixon went shopping in a big way with other people's money.

Dixon was indicted Friday on 12 counts, including perjury and theft, mostly for activity that occurred while she was City Council president.

Most of the charges against her suggest an affinity for both high-end and big-box retail.

At one point in December 2005, the indictment says, Dixon brazenly called an unnamed developer and hit him up for $500 worth of Best Buy gift cards, which she said would be donated to needy families.

Instead, five days later — and a week before Christmas — the future mayor allegedly strolled into a Best Buy in downtown Baltimore and spent 19 of the 20 gift cards, walking out with a digital camcorder and a PlayStation 2 controller, among other goods.

Similar scenarios played out several times, always around Christmas, always with gift cards that, at least in name, were supposed to be handed out to the poor, the indictment says.

"The allegation is that she stole from little children at Christmastime," said David Gray, a law professor at the University of Maryland, Baltimore. "The indictment is alleging that she was a Grinch of the worst kind."

The indictment against Dixon was the culmination of a wide-ranging investigation of city government that lasted nearly three years. It includes no allegations that she let cash or gifts influence the way she did her job. But, at the very least, it hints that the mayor, whose salary is $151,700, likes to shop but would rather not have to pay.

The charges against Dixon include four counts of perjury and two counts of theft under $500. The perjury counts relate to her failure to disclose gifts from Ronald H. Lipscomb, a developer who received tax breaks from the city.

Lipscomb, who dated Dixon briefly in late 2003 and early 2004, first bought gift cards for Dixon under the auspices of handing them out to the poor in December 2004, according to the indictment. Dixon held onto them for a year before using them during her Christmas shopping in 2005, the indictment says.

Dixon's lawyer, Arnold M. Weiner, said most of the gift cards she received went to the intended recipients and characterized the ones she kept for herself as private gifts that she was under no obligation to disclose.

10 Jan 09

Calls for resolution ignored

■ The death toll mounts as Israel and Hamas keep fighting.

**By Ibrahim Barzak
and Jason Keyser**
The Associated Press

GAZA CITY, Gaza Strip — Israeli jets and ground troops hammered at Hamas targets in the Gaza Strip and Islamic militants fired barrages of rockets at southern Israeli cities Friday, ignoring a U.N. resolution calling for an immediate cease-fire after two weeks of combat.

The Israeli prime minister's office said the U.N. action was not practical, and senior Cabinet ministers decided to press on with the offensive. Israel will stop only when it succeeds in ending rocket fire from the Hamas-ruled territory, the government said.

Hopes that Thursday night's U.N. Security Council resolution would end Gaza's worst fighting in decades were further tempered by dismissive remarks from Hamas, angry that it was not consulted during exhaustive diplomatic efforts at the world body.

Israel launched a heavy air bombardment Dec. 27 in response to intensified rocket fire that has disrupted life in southern Israel. A week later, ground troops moved in.

Seven members of the Salha family were killed by an Israeli airstrike on their house overnight, militants said. On Friday, crowds in neat rows bowed in prayer in front of their bodies, wrapped in funeral shrouds and flags.

In a hospital in Beit Lahiya, a northern Gaza town that has been particularly hard-hit, doctors treated a young girl whose left arm was torn off at the shoulder. She lay on a stretcher with a terrified expression on her face.

Smoke from Israeli military operations hangs over the Gaza City skyline Friday.

AP photo

U.N. rights commissioner calls for investigation of Gaza abuses

The Associated Press

GENEVA — The U.N. High Commissioner for Human Rights called Friday for an independent war crimes investigation in Gaza after reports that Israeli forces shelled a house full of Palestinian civilians, killing 30 people.

Navi Pillay told an emergency meeting of the U.N. Human Rights Council that the harm to Israeli civilians caused by Hamas rockets was unacceptable, but did not excuse any abuses carried out by Israeli forces in response.

In Washington, Secretary of State Condoleezza Rice said it is difficult to protect civilians in a place as densely populated as Gaza.

Pillay went further in an interview with the British Broadcasting Corp., saying an incident in Gaza City this week "appears to have all the elements of war crimes."

The U.N. Office for the Coordination of Humanitarian Affairs said Israeli troops evacuated Palestinian civilians to a house in the Zeitoun neighborhood on Jan. 4, then shelled the building 24 hours later. The U.N. agency said 110 people were in the house, according to testimony from four witnesses.

By Friday evening, more than 20 Palestinians had been reported killed during the day, pushing the death toll for the in Gaza.

The Security Council resolution called for an immediate, durable and fully respected cease-fire, leading to the full withdrawal of Israeli troops from Gaza.

While the call was tantamount to a demand on Israel and Hamas to stop fighting, it did not require that Israel's troops withdraw until there was a durable cease-fire. The resolution also urged U.N. member states to intensify efforts to provide guarantees in Gaza to sustain a lasting truce, including prevention of arms smuggling — a key Israeli concern.

In Israel's first official response to the U.N. resolution, Prime Minister Ehud Olmert's office said more Hamas rockets fired Friday "only prove that the U.N.'s decision is not practical and will not be kept in practice by the Palestinian murder organizations."

ROD BLAGOJEVICH

Lawmakers impeach Ill. governor

By Christopher Wills
The Associated Press

SPRINGFIELD, Ill. — Gov. Rod Blagojevich was impeached Friday by Illinois lawmakers furious that he turned state government into a "freak show," setting the stage for an unprecedented trial in the state Senate that could get him thrown out of office.

The 114-1 vote in the Illinois House came exactly a month after Blagojevich's arrest on charges that included trying to sell President-elect Obama's vacant Senate seat. The debate took less than 90 minutes, and not a single legislator rose in defense of the governor, who was jogging in the snow in Chicago.

Later, a defiant Blagojevich insisted again that he committed no crime and declared: "I'm going to fight every step of the way." He portrayed himself as a victim of political payback by the House for his efforts to extend health care and other relief to the ordinary people of Illinois.

"The causes of the impeachment are because I've done things to fight for families," the 52-year-old Democrat said at a news conference, where he sur-

Illinois Gov. Rod Blagojevich meets with the media Friday after the House voted to impeach him.
AP photo

rounded himself with some of the people he claimed to have helped, including a man in a wheelchair and a transplant recipient. He took no questions.

Blagojevich becomes the first U.S. governor in more than 20 years to be impeached. Arizona's Evan Mecham was impeached, convicted and removed from office in 1988 for trying to thwart an investigation into a death threat allegedly made by an aide.

No other Illinois governor has ever been impeached, despite the state's storied history of graft. Blagojevich's immediate predecessor, George Ryan,

is behind bars for corruption, and two earlier governors also went to prison.

The Senate trial is set to begin Jan. 26. While impeachment in the House required only a simple majority, or 60 votes, a two-thirds vote would be needed for conviction in the 59-member Senate.

During the House debate, lawmakers complained that Blagojevich had made a laughingstock out of the state.

"It's our duty to clean up the mess and stop the freak show that's become Illinois government," said Democratic Rep. Jack Franks.

The criminal case against the

governor included charges he tried to sell the Senate seat for campaign cash or a plum for himself or his wife and pressured people into making campaign contributions.

The impeachment case was based on the criminal charges plus other allegations — that Blagojevich expanded a health care program without authority, that he circumvented hiring laws to give jobs to political allies and that he spent millions on flu vaccine that he knew couldn't be brought into the country.

Blagojevich did not testify before the House impeachment committee and has not offered an explanation for the criminal charges.

"His silence in this grave matter is deafening," said House Majority Leader Barbara Flynn Currie, a Chicago Democrat.

The Illinois Senate is working to draft rules for the impeachment trial. The state constitution does not specify what is an impeachable offense and does not lay out a standard for conviction, other than that senators must "do justice according to law." The chief justice of the Illinois Supreme Court will preside.

281

Bush will be vindicated

CHARLES KRAUTHAMMER

WASHINGTON — Except for Richard Nixon, no president since Harry Truman leaves office more unloved than George W. Bush. Truman's rehabilitation took decades. Bush's will come sooner. Indeed, it has already begun. The chief revisionist? Barack Obama.

Vindication is being expressed not in words but in deeds — the tacit endorsement conveyed by the Obama continuity-we-can-believe-in transition. It's not just the retention of such key figures as Secretary of Defense Bob Gates or Treasury Secretary nominee Timothy Geithner, who, as president of the New York Fed, has been instrumental in guiding the Bush financial rescue over the last year. It's the continuity of policy.

It is the repeated pledge to conduct a withdrawal from Iraq that does not destabilize its new democracy and that, as Vice President-elect Joe Biden said just this week in Baghdad, adheres to the Bush-negotiated status of forces agreement that envisions a U.S. withdrawal over three years, not the 16-month timetable on which Obama campaigned.

It is the great care Obama is taking in not pre-emptively abandoning the anti-terror infrastructure that the Bush administration leaves behind. While still a candidate, Obama voted for the expanded presidential wiretapping (FISA) powers that Bush had fervently pursued. And while Obama opposes waterboarding (already banned, by the way, by Bush's CIA in 2006), he declined George Stephanopoulos' invitation (on ABC's "This Week") to outlaw all interrogation not permitted by the Army Field Manual. Explained Obama: "Dick Cheney's advice was good, which is let's make sure we know everything that's being done," i.e., before throwing out methods simply because Obama campaigned against them.

Citing as sage the advice offered by "the most dangerous vice president we've had probably in American history" (according to Joe Biden) — advice paraphrased by Obama as "we shouldn't be making judgments on the basis of incomplete information or campaign rhetoric" — is a startlingly early sign of a newly respectful consideration of the Bush-Cheney legacy.

The beauty of democratic rotations of power is that when the opposition takes office, cheap criticism and calumny will no longer do.

Which is why Obama is consciously creating a gulf between what he now dismissively calls "campaign rhetoric" and the policy choices he must now make as president. Obama will be loath to throw away the tools that have kept the homeland safe. Just as he will be loath to jeopardize the remarkable turnaround in American fortunes in Iraq.

Whatever venom the war generated is concentrated on Bush himself. By having personalized the responsibility for the awfulness of the war, Bush has done his successor a favor. Obama enters office with a strategic success on his hands — while Bush leaves the scene taking a shoe for his country.

Which is why I suspect Bush showed such equanimity during a private farewell interview at the White House a few weeks ago. He leaves behind the sinews of war, for the creation of which he has been so vilified but which will serve his successor — and his country — well over the coming years. The very continuation by Democrats of Bush's policies will be grudging, if silent, acknowledgment of how much he got right.

Charles Krauthammer is a Washington Post columnist. Readers may write to him at letters@charleskrauthammer.com or Washington Post Writers Group, 1150 15th St. NW, Washington, D.C. 20071.

Can I avoid paying my taxes?

Would it be OK if I stopped paying my taxes until Barack Obama names me to be his secretary of the treasury?

That is a deal I would like to get. That is the deal financial wizard Timothy Geithner got.

He didn't pay all of his federal taxes for years. Then, after Obama decided to name him treasury secretary, Obama's vetting team discovered Geithner's little oversight.

Not paying your taxes is considered serious for some people. But not for Geithner, a Wall Street "wonder boy" — he is 47 — who is president of the Federal Reserve Bank of New York and was instrumental in putting together the recent Wall Street bailout package.

You would think a guy such as this would know about paying taxes, but no. Mistakes were made.

Geithner failed to pay the proper self-employment taxes for 2001, 2002, 2003 and 2004, even though he was sent documents telling him he had to do so.

But in 2006, Geithner got a document he couldn't ignore. The IRS sent Geithner a notice saying he had not paid his taxes for 2003 and 2004, and Geithner paid up.

But he did not pay up for 2001 and 2002, even though he must have known that he skipped taxes for those years, too.

He didn't pay those taxes until Barack Obama decided he wanted

**ROGER
SIMON**
19 JAN 09

Geithner to head the treasury and Obama sent vetters to look into Geithner's past.

The vetters discovered Geithner's little tax error in November and told Geithner. Then Geithner paid up, with interest. The vetters also told Obama, of course.

At the end of the day, a source said, "Barack decided that he was the best person for a really important job."

OK, I get it. The economy is teetering on the brink, and we need to cut corners a little. We can't be all that scrupulous and nitpicky when the future of the nation is at stake.

So, in November, Team Obama announced that Geithner had this little problem and was paying his back taxes with interest and that it was all an honest mistake and no big deal, right?

Wrong. They decided to keep it a secret. But The Wall Street Journal discovered it and blew the whistle Tuesday.

The Senate Finance Committee has been looking into Geithner — it has to vote on his appointment — and discovered something else.

According to Gordon and Parnes: "In addition, Geithner included payments to overnight camps in calculating his dependent child care credit in 2001, 2004 and 2005. His accountant informed him in 2006 that the camps were not allowable expenses. The committee notes that Geithner did not file amended returns to fix the mistake."

The Geithner foul-up is different than the Bill Richardson foul-up. The Obama vetters were unable to get Richardson to give them all the background information they needed, but Obama went ahead and appointed Richardson to the Cabinet anyway. Then that blew up, and Richardson withdrew his name.

With Geithner, the vetters found the bad stuff — yay! — but everybody thought they could sweep it under the rug. Boo. Now Republicans are forcing a delay on the Geithner hearing until after Obama is inaugurated.

Team Obama says Geithner made "honest mistakes."

OK. I'll buy that. But as secretary of the treasury, Geithner would be in charge of the Internal Revenue Service. And we will see how easy he is on other people when they say they made "honest mistakes."

Roger Simon is the chief political columnist of politico.com, an award-winning journalist and a New York Times best-selling author.

Creators Syndicate

Lincoln's real legacy *18 JAN09*

On Tuesday, Barack Obama will stand on the steps of the U.S. Capitol and take an oath making him the nation's first president of African heritage.

The statue of Abraham Lincoln, which sits facing the Capitol in a temple two miles away, will not give two thumbs up. Neither will it weep, commune with the spirit of Martin Luther King Jr. or dance the Macarena of joy.

The point is obvious, yes, but also necessary given that when Obama was elected in November, every third political cartoonist seemed to use an image of a celebrating Lincoln to comment upon the milestone that had occurred. Lincoln, they told us, would have been overjoyed.

Actually, Lincoln likely would have been appalled. He was a 19th-century white man who famously said in 1858 that "there is a physical difference between the white and black races, which ... will forever forbid the two races living together upon terms of social and political equality."

How do you reconcile that with all those cartoons of Lincoln congratulating Obama? You don't. You simply recognize it for what it is: yet another illustration of how shallow our comprehension of history is, yet another instance where myth supersedes reality.

Not that this is anything new — or that political cartoonists are the only

LEONARD PITTS JR.

ones susceptible. Indeed, blacks once tended to regard Lincoln with an almost religious reverence. Consider another Lincoln statue, this one in a park east of the Capitol: It depicts Lincoln towering over a newly freed black man who kneels at his feet. While modern eyes might find the image unbearably paternalistic, it represented the heartfelt sentiment of the black men and women who gave it to the city in 1876 in gratitude, they said, for Lincoln freeing the slaves.

Of course, Lincoln freed no slaves. That's the myth. His Emancipation Proclamation was a military measure to demoralize and destabilize the rebellious South; it covered states he did not govern, but did not apply in slaveholding states that remained under his jurisdiction.

None of which is to deny or diminish the greatness of the 16th president. We would be a very different nation, a lesser nation, without his political genius, his dogged faith in the unsundered Union, his refusal to accept less than

Union, even when haunted by reversals and setbacks that would have broken anyone else.

No, the argument is not about Lincoln's greatness. Rather, it is about our tendency to cherish untextured myths that affirm our preferred narratives.

Abraham Lincoln did not believe in the equality of black people. He did, however — and this was no minor distinction in his era — believe in their humanity. He also abhorred slavery. But he was willing to countenance it if doing so would have vindicated his primary goal: to save the Union.

For him, nothing mattered more. Lincoln held with an indefatigable fervor to the belief that there was something unique, something necessary to preserve, in the union of American states, this government of, by, and for the people.

So, remarkable as it is that America has elected a black man its 44th president, Lincoln might find it more remarkable simply that the country has elected a 44th president at all. That was not always a certainty. He would be glad to know that, 144 years after his death, America continues to surprise itself.

The Union endures.

Leonard Pitts Jr. is a syndicated columnist. Readers may write to him at lpitts@herald.com or the Miami Herald, 1 Herald Plaza, Miami, FL 33132.

CEASE-FIRE

Israel stops offensive in Gaza

18 JAN 09

■ The country insists on keeping troops in the region, which could lead to a stalemate with Hamas.

By Matti Friedman and Ibrahim Barzak
The Associated Press

JERUSALEM — Israel implemented a unilateral cease-fire early today in its 22-day offensive that turned Gaza neighborhoods into battlegrounds and dealt a stinging blow to the Islamic militants of Hamas. But Israeli troops will stay in the Palestinian territory for now, and Hamas threatened to keep fighting until they leave.

In announcing the cease-fire late Saturday, Prime Minister Ehud Olmert said Israel had achieved its goals and more.

"Hamas was hit hard, in its military arms and in its government institutions. Its leaders are in hiding, and many of its men have been killed," Olmert said.

Israel launched the offensive Dec. 27 to stop years of rocket fire from Gaza at southern Israeli towns. But the rockets did not stop coming throughout the assault. Militants fired about 30 rockets

See CEASE-FIRE, Page 5A

Cease-fire: Pales

18 JAN

From **Page 1A**

into Israel on Saturday, eight of them around the time Olmert spoke.

More than 1,100 Palestinians have been killed in the offensive, about half of them civilians, according to Palestinian and U.N. officials. At least 13 Israelis also have been killed.

According to Olmert's statement, the cease-fire went into effect at 2 a.m. local time (7 p.m. Saturday EST). The military warned in a statement early today that attacks on soldiers or civilians "will be met with a harsh response."

If Hamas holds its fire, the military "will weigh pulling out of Gaza at a time that befits us," Olmert said. If not, Israel "will continue to act to defend our residents."

Israel's insistence on keeping troops in Gaza raises the specter of a stalemate with Hamas, which has insisted that it will not respect any cease-fire until Israel pulls out of the territory, with a population of 1.4 million.

to withdraw

stinians ask leaders to pressure Israel

09

OPINION

EDITORIALS · LETTERS · COLUMNS

www.fayobserver.com/opinion

RADIO ADDRESS

Bush reminds U.S. to remain vigilant

The Associated Press

WASHINGTON — In his final radio address as president, George W. Bush reminded the nation Saturday that it still faces a serious threat from enemies that he warned are patient and determined to strike again.

The president urged Americans not to become complacent just because the attacks of Sept. 11, 2001, are fading from memory.

"We must keep our resolve, and we must never let down our guard," he said.

At the same time, Bush said that the U.S. must not isolate itself or retreat from engagement with the rest of the world.

"Retreating behind our borders would only invite danger," he said. "In the 21st century, security and prosperity at home depend on the expansion of liberty abroad. If America does not lead the cause of freedom, that cause will not be led."

Bush and his wife are spending the weekend at Camp David, the presidential retreat in Maryland.

After the inauguration Tuesday, they will fly to Midland, Texas, to attend a welcome home rally, and then fly on to their ranch in Crawford.

OPINION

WEDNESDAY
January 21, 2009

EDITORIALS · LETTERS · COLUMNS

www.fayobserver.com/opinion

287

The Journey - Vaughan Witten

Hamas rallies celebrate 'win'

By Karin Laub
and Ibrahim Barzak
The Associated Press

GAZA CITY, Gaza Strip — Waving green Islamic flags atop the ruins of Gaza, Hamas proclaimed victory in rallies attended by thousands of supporters Tuesday, saying it survived Israel's military onslaught despite the destruction and death toll suffered by Gazans.

Hamas offered no plans, however, for rebuilding Gaza, which suffered some $2 billion in damage during three weeks of fighting. Gaza's borders with Israel and Egypt, largely sealed since the Islamic militants seized power 19 months ago, remain closed.

Israel also has claimed victory, but neither side is a clear winner.

The fighting killed some 1,300 Gazans, the vast majority civilians, and thousands of Palestinian homes were destroyed. Israel emerged from the war with 13 dead, including 10 soldiers, but halted fire before reaching its objectives. No inter-

A Hamas militant and his two children participate in a rally in Palestine Square in Gaza City on Tuesday.
AP photo

nationally backed truce deal is in place to prevent Hamas rocket fire on southern Israel or arms smuggling into Gaza.

Israel had withdrawn the bulk of its forces from Gaza by Tuesday evening. However, the temporary cease-fire remained shaky. Israel's air force struck a Gaza mortar squad after it

shelled Israel, the military said.

Hamas held more than a dozen victory rallies across Gaza, choosing bombed-out buildings as backdrops to underscore its message of defiance and its claim to have survived battle against a vastly more powerful enemy.

U.N. chief Ban Ki-moon

toured the local U.N. headquarters, inspecting damage from an Israeli shelling last week. It hit three warehouses where flour, oil and other food rations for Gaza's needy were stored.

Israel has said troops responded to fire from militants from the area, a claim the U.N. has vehemently denied.

Perhaps the best is to come

I hate to say it, but I am having a hard time believing Barack Obama. I want to give the guy a break, but he keeps saying one thing over and over. He keeps trying to sell something to us that we may not want to buy.

During his campaign, his motto was, "Yes, we can." Today, his motto is, "The worst is yet to come."

Me, I don't believe it. I have covered presidential inaugurals since Jimmy Carter's in 1977, and I have never seen so much hope, so much optimism and so much sheer joy as in Washington last week.

Even some Republicans who voted for John McCain are telling me how happy they are that Barack Obama won. It is like the nation has received a giant shot of adrenalin, that all things are possible and happy days will soon be here again.

Which is exactly what Obama is worried about. For weeks, he has been trying to talk Americans out of what he feels is their irrational exuberance. Never has an incoming president sold gloom so hard.

On Dec. 7 on "Meet the Press," Obama said, "If you look at the unemployment numbers that came out yesterday, if you think about almost 2 million jobs lost so far, if you think about the fragility of the financial system ... this is a big problem, and it's going to get worse."

ROGER SIMON

And just in case anybody missed his point, Obama said later in the same interview, "Things are going to get worse before they get better."

On Dec. 22, introducing his new economic team, Obama said: "We are facing a crisis of historic proportions. The economy is likely to get worse before it gets better. Full recovery will not happen immediately."

In his weekly radio address Jan. 10, he said, "Recovery won't happen overnight, and it's likely that things will get worse before they get better."

On his whistle-stop tour Jan. 17, he began in Philadelphia with a cheery: "Only a handful of times in our history has a generation been confronted with challenges so vast. An economy that is faltering. Two wars, one that needs to be ended responsibly, one that needs to be waged wisely. A planet that is warming from our unsustainable dependence on oil."

He followed this in Wilmington, Del., with: "Together, we know that America faces its own crossroads — a nation at war, an eco

turmoil, an American Dream that feels like it's slipping away."

And Jan. 18: "Millions of Americans' are losing their jobs and their homes; they're worried about how they'll afford college for their kids or pay the stack of bills on their kitchen table. And most of all, they are anxious and uncertain about the future — about whether this generation of Americans will be able to pass on what's best about this country to our children and their children."

Obama is smart enough to know you don't brag about your political capital. You spend it quietly with results that make a big noise in public. Until then, you prepare people for the worst, while always reminding them that we will prevail.

"There is no doubt that our road will be long, that our climb will be steep," Obama said at the Lincoln Memorial. "But never forget that the true character of our nation is revealed not during times of comfort and ease, but by the right we do when the moment is hard."

The moment is hard. But it is equally hard not to believe that hope is at hand.

Roger Simon is the chief political columnist of politico.com, an award-winning journalist and a New York Times best-selling author.

Political speeches and 'firsts'

If making speeches is one of the tests of a president of the United States, then Barack Obama passed his first test with flying colors. He has understood the varied constituencies, and the various hopes and fears he had to address. He said the kinds of things that these constituencies wanted to hear.

As a speech, it was the best inaugural address since Ronald Reagan. This is not to judge the substantive merits or demerits of what he said. Anyone who judges any political speech by its substance is likely to be disappointed.

THOMAS SOWELL

to arrest him.

It was an auspicious beginning. But presidencies are not measured by their beginnings.

Race

Inevitably, much is being made of the fact that Barack Obama is the first black president of the United States.

He is indeed the first "African American" president, unlike the millions of other black Americans whose ancestors were here longer than millions of white Americans. By the time that there was a United States of America, most black Americans had never seen Africa and neither had their grandparents.

There is no group less eligible to be called hyphenated Americans. Nevertheless, Barack Obama is one of them — symbolically, at least — and race is part of the symbolism of this moment.

Those who doubted that a black man could be elected to the highest office in the land no longer have a leg to stand on. That can be a force for good, when young blacks can no longer be told that there is no point in their trying to get ahead in this society because "the man" is going to stop them.

Now that we have the first black president of the United States, maybe we can move ahead to the time when we can forget about "the first" whatever do to what. There is too much serious work to do to spend more time on that.

Thomas Sowell is a syndicated columnist. Readers may write to him at www.tsowell.com, at info@creators.com (with his name in the subject line) or Creators Syndicate, 5777 W. Century Blvd., Suite 700, Los Angeles, CA 90045.

EDITORIALS · LETTERS · COLUMNS · www.fayobserver.com/opinion

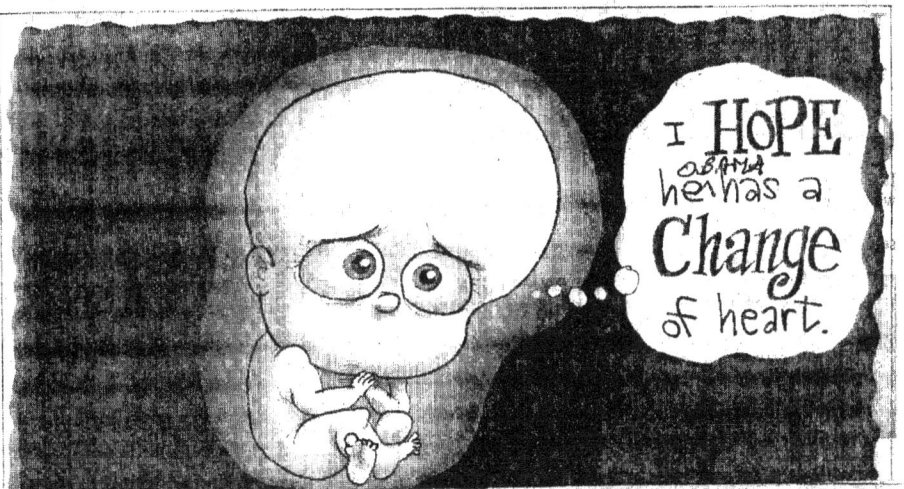

Opening speech was atypical

CHARLES KRAUTHAMMER

WASHINGTON — Fascinating speech. It was so rhetorically flat, so lacking in rhythm and cadence, one almost has to believe he did it on purpose. Best not to dazzle on Opening Day. Otherwise, they'll expect magic all the time.

The most striking characteristic of Barack Obama is not his nimble mind, engaging manner or wide-ranging intellectual curiosity. It's the absence of neediness. He's Bill Clinton, master politician, but without the hunger.

Clinton craves your adulation. Obama will take it, but he can leave it, too. He is self-contained. He gives what he must to advance his goals, his programs, his ambitions. But no more. He has no need to.

Which seems to me the only way to understand the mediocrity of his inaugural address. This is odd because Obama is so clearly capable of more. But he decisively left behind the candidate who made audiences swoon and the impressionable faint.

Candidate Obama had promised the moon. In soaring cadences, he described a world laid waste by Bush, a world that President Obama would redeem — bringing boundless hope and universal health, receding oceans and a healing planet.

Now that Obama was president, the redeemer was withholding, the tone newly sober, even dour. In a stunning exercise in lowered expectations, Obama offered not quite blood, sweat and tears, but responsibility, work, sacrifice and service.

When candidate Obama said "it's not about me, it's about you," that was sheer chicanery. But now he means it, because he really cannot part the waters.

On the issue of race, he was even more withholding, and admirably so. He understood that his very presence was enough to mark the monumentality of the moment. Words would be superfluous. This was surprising, given that the announced theme of the inaugural — "a new birth of freedom" — invited grandiose comparison to Lincoln. Yet in the inaugural address, Obama abandoned the conceit. Remarkably, he instead reached back — over Martin Luther King Jr. and Lincoln — to George

Washington. He rooted the values he cherishes most (and wants us to renew) in the Founders, in the First Republic, the slave-tainted one (as our schoolchildren are incessantly reminded) that had to await Lincoln for its cleansing.

Obama's unapologetic celebration of Washington and the founders of the original imperfect union was a declaration of his own emancipation from — or better, transcendence of — the civil rights movement. If we ever have a post-racial future, this moment will mark its beginning.

Obama did this in prose, not his usual poetry. And he buried it in an otherwise undistinguished speech marred by a foreign-policy section featuring the mushy internationalism of his still-bizarre Berlin adventure.

Perhaps that was just a bone to appease the faithful he had otherwise left hungry. We have no way of knowing. A complicated man, this new president. Opaque, contradictory and subtle. And that's just day one.

Charles Krauthammer is a Washington Post columnist. Readers may write to him at letters@charleskrauthammer.com or Washington Post Writers Group, 1150 15th St. NW, Washington, D.C. 20071.

www.fayobserver.com

JANUARY 28, 2009

FAYETTEVILLE STATE

Nursing scores worst in N.C.

■ Only 39 percent of students passed the 2008 state licensure exam, marking the second straight year of sub-par test results.

By Corey G. Johnson
Staff writer

Fayetteville State nursing graduates had the worst pass rates in the state on the 2008 licensure exam, according to final data from the state Board of Nursing.

Only 24 of 61 FSU students passed the exam on the first try, giving the university a 39 percent pass rate, according to a Dec. 31 tally of scores from the nursing board.

The results meant FSU finished last out of 60 state nursing programs whose students took the exam last year.

The final scores for the nursing program at Fayetteville Technical Community College showed an 88 percent pass rate. The pass rate at UNC-Pembroke was 80 percent.

The state average was 88 percent.

FSU's scores mark the second consecutive year of sub-par test results

See **SCORES**, Page 4A

Scores: State board will decide nursing program's future in May

From **Page 1A**

for the school's bachelor of science in nursing program. The school's pass rate was 64 percent in 2007.

Student complaints and faculty dissension have gripped the program since it began in 2005. The program has been on probation with the state Board of Nursing since 2007 for multiple violations of state rules.

The state nursing board will meet in May to decide the program's future, spokesman David Kalbacker said. Although program closings are rare, Kalbacker said the board would be taking a serious look at FSU.

FSU and University of North Carolina system officials had been closely monitoring the 2008 nursing student scores for months.

According to UNC system policy, any nursing program failing to pass at least 75 percent of its students for two consecutive years could be closed.

FSU Chancellor James Anderson was unavailable for comment Tuesday.

UNC spokeswoman Joni Worthington said UNC system officials who oversee nursing programs were out of the office, as well.

Phyllis Morgan, chairwoman of FSU's nursing department, said the scores were a disappointment.

Morgan, who has been a professor in the program since 2005, took over leadership in August. She said staff has been aggressively instituting changes to ensure improvement. The department hired two specialists this month to better track student progress and to offer additional help in developing test-

taking skills, Morgan said. The program also is revising the curriculum to better prepare students, she said.

"We're really, really focused on improving our board scores," Morgan said. "Now we have better resources and a better understanding of how to support our students so that they can be successful."

FSU's administration, faculty and staff have showered the nursing program with support and encouragement since an Observer report in November about the school's low preliminary scores on the licensure exam. Many of the nursing department's proposed curriculum changes were fast-tracked through FSU's faculty senate review process, with some faculty members sacrificing their personal time to look at nursing documents, said John Mattox, chairman of FSU's faculty senate.

Jon Young, interim FSU provost, said the gesture signaled a commitment throughout the university to the success of the nursing program.

"There is no other member of the faculty working harder than the nursing faculty," Young said in a previous interview. "Improving this program is vital to the university."

In 2007, FSU and UNC-Pembroke's nursing programs — then in their first years — had the lowest pass rates for UNC system schools, scoring 64 percent and 68 percent on the licensure exam.

UNC-Pembroke's scores improved in 2008, with 24 of 30 nursing graduates passing the licensure exam.

Staff writer Corey G. Johnson can be reached at johnsonc@fayobserver.com or 325-4848, ext. 467.

www.fayobserver.com   27 Jan 09   50¢

IMPEACHMENT TRIAL

Illinois vote ousts Blagojevich

■ The state's Senate bans the governor from holding public office in the state again.

By Christopher Wills
The Associated Press

SPRINGFIELD, Ill. — Gov. Rod Blagojevich was thrown out of office Thursday without a single lawmaker coming to his defense, brought down by a government-for-sale scandal that stretched from Chicago to Capitol Hill and turned the foul-mouthed politician into a national punchline.

Blagojevich, accused of trying to sell Barack Obama's vacant Senate seat, becomes the first U.S. governor in more than 20 years to be removed by impeachment.

After a four-day trial, the Illinois Senate voted 59-0 to convict him of abuse of power, automatically ousting the second-term Democrat. In a second, identical vote, lawmakers further

See BLAGOJEVICH, Page 4A

Illinois Gov. Rod Blagojevich was arrested last month on a variety of federal corruption charges.

Many ordinary Illinoisans were glad to see him go.

"It's very embarrassing. I think it's a shame that with our city and Illinois, everybody thinks we're all corrupt," Gene Ciepierski, 54, said after watching the trial's conclusion on a TV at Chicago's Billy Goat Tavern. "To think he would do something like that, it hurts more than anything."

Final verdict

In a solemn scene, more than 30 lawmakers rose one by one on the Senate floor to accuse Blagojevich of abusing his office and embarrassing the state. They denounced him as a hypocrite, saying he cynically tried to enrich himself and then posed as the brave protector of the poor and "wrapped himself in the constitution."

They sprinkled their remarks with historical references, including Pearl Harbor's "day of infamy" and "The whole world is watching" chant from the riots that broke out during the 1968 Democratic National Convention in Chicago. They cited Abraham Lincoln, Martin Luther King Jr. and Jesus as they called for the governor's removal.

"We have this thing called impeachment, and it's bleeping golden, and we've used it the right way," Democratic Sen. James Meeks of Chicago said during the debate, mocking Blagojevich's expletive-laden words as captured by the FBI on a wiretap.

Blagojevich did not stick around to hear the vote. He took a state plane back to Chicago.

The verdict capped a head-spinning string of developments that began with his arrest by the FBI on Dec. 9. Federal prosecutors had been investigating Blagojevich's administration for years, and some of his closest cronies already have been convicted.

OPINION

The Fayetteville Observer

2 FASG

CEOs enjoy gold parachutes

By David G. Wilson
Fayetteville

The boat is sinking, my fellow Americans, and the lifeboat list has been completed. Most of us are not on it.

Wilson

Wall Street bankers, brokers and high-buck executives did make the cut. It would seem they are rewarded for stupidity, greed and outright thievery.

Consider one John Thain, former Merrill Lynch CEO. After continuing the wrecking of the old and highly respected Wall Street brokerage (The Bull), he reached out a begging hand to equally dubious Bank of America CEO Ken Lewis.

These guys are paid to be smart and act accordingly. Apparently, being honest and forthright is not a job requirement.

So Thain takes over Merrill Lynch after his predecessor, Stan O'Neal, was ushered out the door last fall. O'Neal, you may remember, led Merrill Lynch into a disastrous third-quarter $2.3 billion loss after acknowledging a $7.9 billion bad-debt exposure.

Bankers call those bad debts non-performing assets. You and I would call them the

result of outrageous incompetence. But this situation was part of a greed-driven looting of the global economy.

O'Neal, it could be argued, did not understand about lending to those who could not pay back. Or maybe he did, but he didn't worry about it. Subprime mortgages and all of that nonsense interfered with his golf games.

A new era?

So this leads us to recently canned Merrill Lynch CEO John Thain. He was to bring a new era of discipline and control to the time-honored brokerage house.

He began by hiring the decorator for the stars, Michael S. Smith, to apply a $1.2 million redo to his office. Given the problems that prevailed in the company he was hired to run, that was not so smart.

Then he asked the CEO of floundering Bank of America for a life ring when it was apparent that Merrill was going down for the count. The bank that bought Countrywide Financial Services agreed to buy Merrill Lynch. Those of us on the outside looking in thought, "Oh, my God."

But, again no worries. Lewis and Thain held a press conference. They looked tall, tanned, rested and exuded confidence. All is not only well, they claimed, it is wonderful. Thain's words were, "This merger is a

Thain   **Lewis**

beautiful thing." Lewis promised that the combined businesses would touch two out of every three households in America.

We now know that Lewis was wrong. The combined businesses will touch every household in America because every household in America is bailing them out to the tune of tens of billions of taxpayer dollars.

Lewis, it should be noted, originally maintained that BoA did not need any TARP funds, but he took $25 billion anyway because it was out there. Only recently another $10 billion was needed by BoA to stay afloat. Holy IRS Form 1040.

Thain went on the equivalent of a "smash and grab" after his ascendancy to the top Merrill spot. He requested a $40 million to $50 million bonus for his part in the destruction of the company, realizing full well that the money would come off the backs of American taxpayers. His knuckles were publicly rapped by New York Attorney General Andrew Cuomo and Senate Majority

Leader Harry Reid, to the point that he withdrew his request. Then, he claimed he never asked for the bonus money in the first place. Would you buy a used car from this man?

Abrupt termination

Evidently Ken Lewis would not. In what may prove a futile effort to keep himself from drowning, Lewis abruptly fired Thain several weeks ago. One wonders why this one-time Wall Street whiz kid was so out of touch. Mercifully, he can relax for now at his ski house in Vail. Did I tell you that Lewis found out about Merrill's disastrous fourth-quarter losses, which have amounted to $15.3 billion, not from Thain, but from BoA's transition team? Not good, John. The boss always likes to get bad news without delay and from the guy in charge.

On a positive note, John Thain was a big John McCain supporter. He was in line for a top slot in the McCain White House, where he would have had access to trillions. Mercifully, the Arizona senator still is just that, and Thain, for now, will enjoy his parachute of gold, much of which was made with your tax dollars and mine.

David G. Wilson is a retired former president of Fasco Industries' consumer products division. He can be reached at Davedeepse@aol.com.

Greatest bank robbery ever

This is a story of the greatest bank robbery in the history of the world.

This was no carefully timed eight-minute holdup. This one happened in slow motion, and it's continuing as this column is written.

The banks are holding guns to their heads as they empty our pockets, threatening to pull the trigger and fall down dead if we don't give it up.

The first overt act of this holdup began at the end of 2007, when the five largest American securities firms paid their top people $66 billion in bonuses based on their "profits" the preceding year — profits that weren't profits at all, but huge, unimaginable losses.

In the following months, those same five firms took write-offs of more than $100 billion worth of worthless assets — the mortgage-based bundles of bad paper that were the foundations of their houses of cards.

We're talking about people who, by the end of 2007, had to know that their mortgage securities were cooked, their books were cooked and their gooses were cooked. And still they pocketed those bonus checks for billions.

Then there are the big banks, big bankers whose vaults likewise filled with worthless those same mortgage

JOE GALLOWAY

Here, the bank robbery was definitely an inside job.

Four months ago, the 10 largest banks in America had a market capitalization of $722.73 billion. This week, that figure had dropped by two-thirds, to $237.83 billion. In four short months, the bankers robbed their stockholders of $484.9 billion, even as they were robbing the American taxpayer and the Treasury of an additional $250 billion in bailout money.

Congress and the taxpayers intended the bailout money to prime the pump, but the big 10 banks just sat on our billions and did nothing as the market, day by day, wrote down their toilet paper assets for them.

They did spend some of the money to buy up smaller, better-run banks and bigger, poorly run brokerage got bigger, using themselves so dared let them fail.

And now they're back, hands out, begging the Treasury for another handout of hundreds of billions.

Since we're already in pain and in for much more of the same, how about we just let these sleazebags go belly up? Or better yet, earmark about $200 billion to buy all 10 of the biggest American bank companies, fire all their executives without severance and install new management teams composed of people who have run successful businesses.

In the movies, bank robbers always meet a bad end. John Dillinger and Bonnie and Clyde died in hails of gunfire. Willie Sutton and Alvin "Creepy" Karpis spent half their lives in prison.

What are we to do with the new generation of bank robbers? There's a harsh wind blowing through the concrete canyons of New York's financial district this winter, and I hope it's blowing ice-cold on the necks of the arrogant, incompetent, foolish bank robbers as they get in their limousines for the tedious trip home to their penthouse apartments or their suburban McMansions.

Joe Galloway is a syndicated columnist. Readers may write to him at Joe Galloway, P.O. Box 399, Bayside, TX 78340.

Soldier suicides at 30-year high mark

Report blames stress of war

By Pauline Jelinek
The Associated Press

WASHINGTON — Suicides among U.S. soldiers rose last year to the highest level in decades, the Army said Thursday.

At least 128 soldiers killed themselves in 2008. The final count is likely to be higher because 15 more suspicious deaths are being investigated and could turn out to be self-inflicted, the Army said.

A training and prevention effort will start next week.

The new suicide figure compares with 115 in 2007

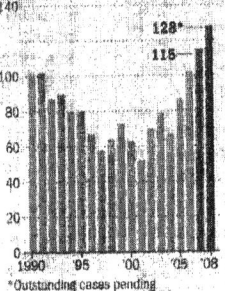

SUICIDES UP 11 PERCENT IN 2008

During 2007 and 2008, approximately 243 active duty Army soldiers committed suicide, the most during any two-year period since 1990.

Source: Department of the Army   AP

So much for hope

"A failure to act, and act now, will turn crisis into a catastrophe."
— President Obama, Feb. 4.

CHARLES KRAUTHAMMER

WASHINGTON — Catastrophe, mind you. So much for the president who in his inaugural address two weeks earlier declared "we have chosen hope over fear." Until, that is, you need fear to pass a bill.

And so much for the promise to banish the money-changers and influence peddlers from the temple. An ostentatious executive order banning lobbyists was immediately followed by the nomination of at least a dozen current or former lobbyists to high position. Followed by a Treasury secretary who allegedly couldn't understand the payroll tax provisions in his 1040. Followed by Tom Daschle, who had to fall on his sword according to the new Washington rule that no Cabinet can have more than one tax delinquent.

The Daschle affair was more serious because his offense involved more than taxes. As Michael Kinsley once observed, in Washington the real scandal isn't what's illegal, but what's legal. Not paying taxes is one thing. But what made this case intolerable was the perfectly legal dealings that amassed Daschle $5.2 million in just two years.

He'd been getting $1 million per year from a law firm. But he's not a lawyer, nor a registered lobbyist. You don't get paid this kind of money to instruct partners on the Senate markup process. You get it for picking up the phone and peddling influence.

At least Tim Geithner, the tax-challenged Treasury secretary, had been working for years as a humble international civil servant earning non-stratospheric wages. Daschle, who had made another cool million a year (plus chauffeur and Caddy) for unspecified services to a pal's private equity firm, represented everything Obama said he'd come to Washington to upend.

And yet more damaging to Obama's image than all the hypocrisies in the appointment process is his signature bill: the stimulus package. He inexplicably delegated the writing to Nancy Pelosi and the barons of the House. The product, which inevitably carries Obama's name, was not just bad, not just flawed, but a legislative abomination.

It's not just pages and pages of special-interest tax breaks, giveaways and protections, one of which would set off a ruinous Smoot-Hawley trade war. It's not just the waste, such as the $88.6 million for new construction for Milwaukee Public Schools, which, reports the Milwaukee Journal Sentinel, have shrinking enrollment, 15 vacant schools and, quite logically, no plans for new construction.

It's the essential fraud of rushing through a bill in which the normal rules (committee hearings, finding revenue to pay for the programs) are suspended on the grounds that a national emergency requires an immediate job-creating stimulus — and then throwing into it hundreds of billions that have nothing to do with stimulus, that Congress' own budget office says won't be spent until 2011 and beyond, and that are little more than the back-scratching, special-interest, lobby-driven parochialism that Obama came to Washington to abolish. He said.

The Age of Obama begins with perhaps the greatest frenzy of old-politics influence peddling ever seen in Washington. By the time the stimulus bill reached the Senate, reports The Wall Street Journal, pharmaceutical and high-tech companies were lobbying furiously for a new plan to repatriate overseas profits that would yield major tax savings. California wine growers and Florida citrus producers were fighting to change a single phrase in one provision. Substituting "planted" for "ready to market" would mean a windfall garnered from a new "bonus depreciation" incentive.

After Obama's miraculous 2008 presidential campaign, it was clear that at some point the magical mystery tour would have to end.

I thought the awakening would take six months. It took 2½ weeks.

Charles Krauthammer is a Washington Post columnist. Readers may write to him at letters@charleskrauthammer.com or Washington Post Writers Group, 1150 15th St. NW, Washington, D.C. 20071.

Nothing new in the new standard

President Barack Obama is on the right track with his plan to cap at $500,000 per year the salaries of Wall Street big-shots who get federal bailout money. But he is off by $499,999.99.

There is no reason for taxpayers to continue to reward unlimited ignorance and unbridled greed. These Wall Street firms were run into the ground by financiers who were too stupid to understand the true risks of what they were doing and too greedy to stop doing it.

And now they deserve a half-million dollars a year? Some of them deserve six to 12 in Allenwood.

But, as I said, Obama is on the right track. He said Wednesday: "We all need to take responsibility. And this includes executives at major financial firms who turned to the American people, hat in hand, when they were in trouble, even as they paid themselves their customary lavish bonuses. As I said last week, that's the height of irresponsibility. That's shameful."

You know what else is shameful? Barack Obama pressing ahead with appointment of Cabinet secretaries who he knew were tax evaders.

Those people, despite their

ROGER SIMON

qualifications, were not taking responsibility for their actions, and neither was Obama.

Tim Geithner, our new secretary of the treasury, knew he had evaded paying taxes for years, but he didn't pay up until Obama appointed him to the Cabinet.

Tom Daschle knew he owed taxes on the round-the-clock limousine and chauffeur he got from a wealthy financier for two years, but he didn't pay up until he was appointed to the Cabinet. He now admits he was "naive"?

Naive? A guy gives me a car and driver for two years, I figure he wants something. I am not saying I will give it to him, but I figure he wants it. And I don't whine afterward about being naive.

But that is not the problem. The problem is that President Obama continued to back Daschle after Daschle admitted that he had not paid his taxes.

That is not the "responsibility" that Obama

talked about Wednesday.

Now I keep seeing all these talking heads on TV telling me how nice guys like Tom Daschle have fallen victim to the "new high standards" of Washington that the Obama administration has set.

But when did paying your taxes become a new high standard? Tens of millions of Americans do it every year. And they do it even before they get named to the Obama Cabinet.

And this is part of the reason that Obama's bailout and stimulus plans are unpopular with so many Americans. To them, it is just another way to reward a special, privileged class.

Wall Street moguls who screw up get bailed out. Main Street shop owners who can't afford to meet their payrolls go under.

Ordinary people who don't pay their taxes get arrested. Big shots who don't pay their taxes get government jobs (including, in Geithner's case, being put in charge of the Internal Revenue Service).

We don't need new standards. We just need to respect the old ones.

Roger Simon is the chief political columnist of politico.com, an award-winning journalist and a New York Times best-selling author.

Creators Syndicate

Burris changes fundraising story

■ **The Illinois senator acknowledges he tried to raise money for the impeached governor.**

By John O'Connor
The Associated Press

SPRINGFIELD, Ill. — U.S. Sen. Roland Burris acknowledges attempting to raise money for ousted Gov. Rod Blagojevich — an explosive twist in his evolving story on how he landed a coveted Senate appointment from the man accused of trying to sell the seat.

Burris made the admission to reporters late Monday, after releasing an affidavit over the weekend saying he had more contact with Blagojevich advisers about the Senate seat than he had described under oath to the state House panel that recommended Blagojevich's impeachment. The Democrat also said in the affidavit, but not before the panel, that the governor's brother asked him for fundraising help.

Though Burris insists he never raised money for Blagojevich while the governor was considering whom to appoint to the seat President Obama vacated, the revelation that he had attempted to do so is likely to increase calls for Burris' resignation and an investigation into whether he committed perjury before the panel.

Illinois Democrats have sent documents related to Burris' testimony to a county prosecutor for review. In Washington, a good-government group recommended Burris' expulsion from the Senate if an ethics committee investigation shows he lied to Senate leaders.

Burris

Burris, in the middle of a previously scheduled tour of northern and central Illinois cities, would not discuss his attempts to raise funds for Blagojevich, but said he didn't do anything wrong and encouraged officials to look into the matter.

"I welcome the opportunity to go before any and all investigative bodies ... to answer any questions they have," he told reporters in Peoria, before declining to answer questions.

Burris told reporters Monday night that he had reached out to friends after Blagojevich's brother, Robert, called him before Obama's election asking him to raise $10,000 or $15,000 for the governor.

297

FRIDAY
February 27, 2009

EDITORIALS · LETTERS · COLUMNS   www.fayobserver.com/opinion

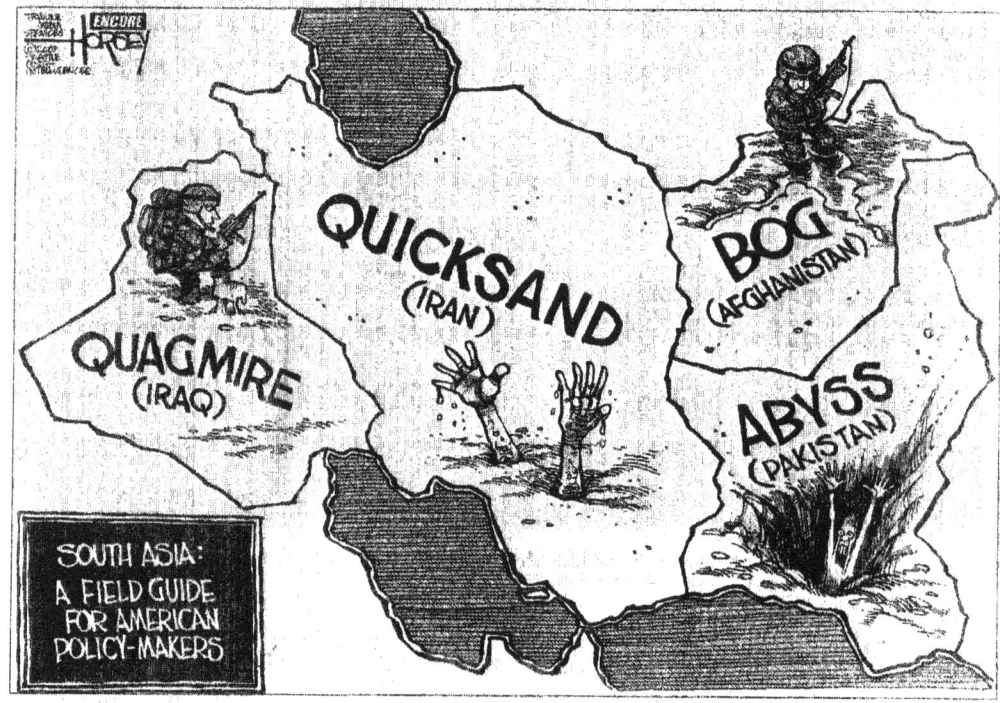

OPINION

6A

THURSDAY
March 12, 2009

EDITORIALS · LETTERS · COLUMNS

www.fayobserver.com/opinion

SATURDAY, APRIL 11, 2009

It's your country too, Mr. President

In his major foreign policy address in Prague committing the United States to a world without nuclear weapons, President Obama took note of North Korea's missile launch just hours earlier and then grandiloquently proclaimed:

Charles Krauthammer

"Rules must be binding. Violations must be punished. Words must mean something. The world must stand together to prevent the spread of these weapons. Now is the time for a strong international response."

What "strong international response" did Obama muster to North Korea's brazen defiance of a Chapter 7 U.N. resolution prohibiting such a launch?

The obligatory emergency Security Council session produced nothing. No sanctions. No resolution. Not even a statement. China and Russia professed to find no violation whatsoever.

Having thus bravely rallied the international community and summoned the U.N. — a fiction and a farce, respectively — what was Obama's further response? The very next day, his defense secretary announced drastic cuts in missile defense, including halting further deployment of Alaska-based interceptors designed precisely to shoot down North Korean ICBMs.

Rather than relying on America's technological edge in missile defenses to provide a measure of nuclear safety, Obama will instead boldly deploy the force of example. How? By committing his country to disarmament gestures — such as, he promised in Prague, ratifying the Comprehensive Nuclear Test Ban Treaty.

How does U.S. ratification of that treaty — which America has, in any case, voluntarily abided by for 17 years — cause North Korea to cease and desist, and cause Iran to turn nukes into plowshares?

I'm not against gift-giving in international relations. But it would be nice to see some reciprocity.

With varying degrees of directness or obliqueness, Obama indicted his own people for arrogance, for genocide, for torture, for Hiroshima, for Guantanamo and for insufficient respect for the Muslim world.

And what did he get for this obsessive denigration of his own country? He wanted more NATO combat troops in Afghanistan to match the surge of 17,000 Americans. He was rudely rebuffed.

He wanted more stimulus spending from Europe. He got nothing.

From Russia, he got no help on Iran. From China, he got the blocking of any action on North Korea.

And what did he get for Guantanamo? France, population 64 million, will take one prisoner. One! The Austrians said they would take none. As Interior Minister Maria Fekter explained with impeccable Germanic logic, if they're not dangerous, why not just keep them in America?

When Austria is mocking you, you're having a bad week. Yet who can blame Frau Fekter, considering the disdain Obama showed his own country while on foreign soil?

After all, it was Obama, not some envious anti-American leader, who noted that a new financial order is being created today by 20 countries, rather than by "just Roosevelt and Churchill sitting in a room with a brandy."

It is passing strange for a world leader to celebrate his own country's decline. A few more such overseas tours, and Obama will have a lot more decline to celebrate.

Charles Krauthammer is a Washington Post columnist. Readers may write to him at letters@charleskrauthammer.com or Washington Post Writers Group, 1150 15th St. NW, Washington, D.C. 20071.

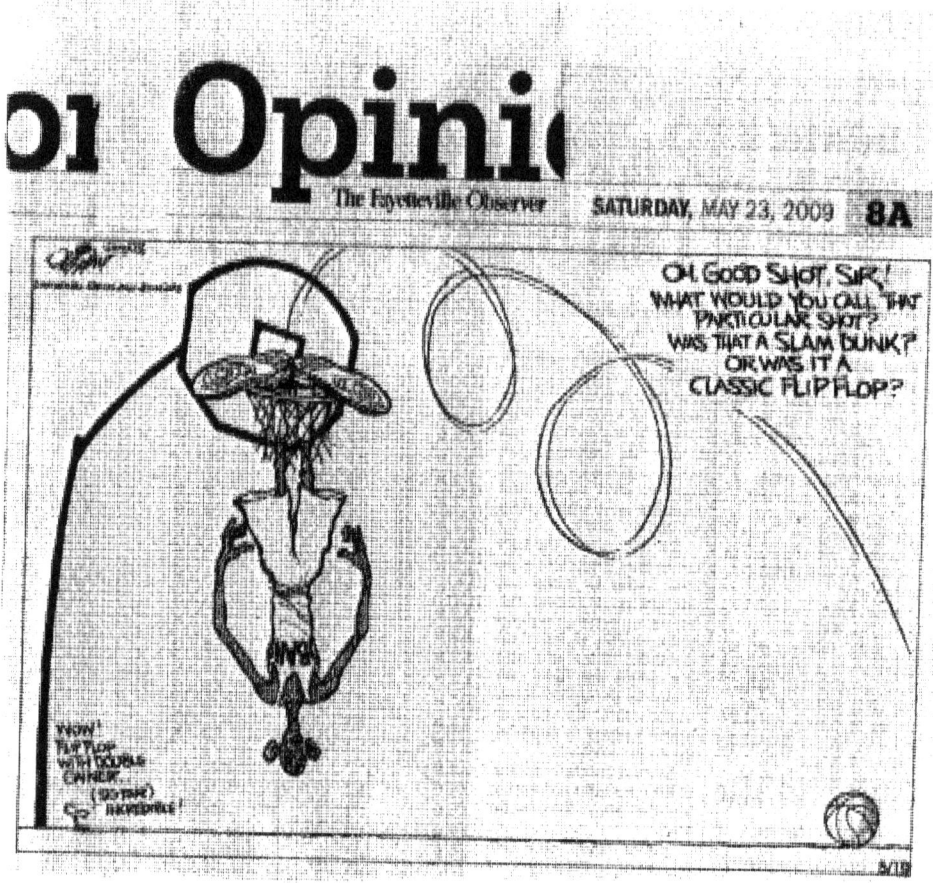

Playing the race card?

L ike a stopped clock that is accurate twice a day, Rush Limbaugh sometimes is actually funny.

After Supreme Court nominee Sonia Sotomayor tripped and broke her ankle Monday, Limbaugh said, "I hope she can find a wise Latina doctor to set that ankle, as opposed to an average white doctor, because the wise Latina doctor has much richer experience with broken ankles."

That is at least reasonably clever, Sotomayor having said in 2001, "I would hope that a wise Latina woman with the richness of her experiences would more often than not reach a better conclusion than a white male who hasn't lived that life."

Sotomayor has been making the rounds on Capitol Hill, assuring senators that what she really meant to say was that "there is only one law" and that "ultimately and completely" she would follow that law.

You can see why Democrats are nervous. Roland Burris, a political

Roger Simon

hack, muscled his way into the U.S. Senate by nakedly playing the race card, and now everybody is jumpy about any comments that seem to indicate one race should be favored over another. (Unless it is white people being favored, in which case there is rarely a controversy.)

Burris was appointed to the U.S. Senate by Illinois Gov. Rod Blagojevich, who a few weeks earlier had been led away in handcuffs for trying to sell that Senate seat.

Initially, the White House and the Democratic leadership of the Senate wanted to delay Burris' appointment until Blagojevich was impeached.

But Team Burris quickly moved into action.

"There are no African-Americans in the Senate, and I don't think that anyone, any U.S. senator who is sitting right now, would want to go on record to deny one African-American from being seated in the U.S. Senate," said Rep. Bobby Rush, a Democrat from the South Side of Chicago. "I don't think they want to go on record doing that."

Opposition to the quick seating of Burris collapsed.

Two weeks ago, however, the transcript of a secretly recorded phone call between Burris and the brother of Blagojevich was released in federal court. In the phone call, Burris offers to write a check to the Rod Blagojevich campaign and says, "I'm very much interested in, in trying to replace Obama, OK."

Some senators are now nervous and angry. They are aflame over what they see as Sonia Sotomayor's playing of the same card.

Sen. Jeff Sessions of Alabama, the ranking Republican on the Judiciary Committee, said on "Meet the Press" with David Gregory that while he would not use the word "racist" to describe Sotomayor: "I think that she is a person who believes that her background can influence her decision. That's what troubles me."

In what certainly must be her most poetic defense, Senate Majority Leader Harry Reid wrote an op-ed piece recently in The Miami Herald. He writes that several things shaped his life, just as Sotomayor's life "as a Latina" shaped hers. He says he talked to Sotomayor recently.

"I realized that I was sitting across from a person who took hardship and turned it into the anvil that shaped her character," Reid says. "She is the quintessential American story. How is this a detriment to the highest court in the land?"

A good question. And, as her nomination hearings begin July 13, one that is sure to be asked repeatedly.

Roger Simon is the chief political columnist at politics.com, an award-winning journalist and a New York Times best-selling author.

23 JUN 309

Stakes high for Obama this fall

WASHINGTON — It probably was inevitable that the elections for governor, taking place in November in New Jersey and Virginia, would be seen by many people outside those states as a referendum on Barack Obama's performance as president.

Those will be the first statewide contests since he entered the White House, and they are taking place in states he won last year. But forces of history and economics add to the presidential stakes in the outcomes.

History: In 1993, a year after the last previous Democratic president, Bill Clinton, was elected, Republicans captured the Virginia governorship with George Allen and New Jersey's with Christine Todd Whitman. Their victories set the stage for the GOP takeover of Congress in 1994 that in turn prepared the way for George Bush's presidency.

Economics: When the current Democratic governors of New Jersey and Virginia were elected in 2005, the

David Broder

unemployment rates were, respectively, 4.7 percent and 3.4 percent. This April, the latest reported month, showed the ranks of the jobless had grown to 8.4 percent in New Jersey and 6.8 percent in Virginia.

In both states, the economy has become the biggest issue for voters — and a problem for Democrats. With their party in control of both houses of the New Jersey Legislature and one house in Virginia, plus the governorships, Democrats have been wrestling with budget cuts and calls for tax relief.

Just as Obama has blamed the Bush administration for the recession he inherited, the Democrats running in these two states have invoked Bush's name and tied him to their opponents. The results

may well show how much of the responsibility for the bad economy has shifted to their shoulders — and, implicitly, to Obama's.

New Jersey is tough territory for the GOP. Whitman was the last Republican to win a statewide race, and the Democratic registration edge and Election Day margins have been increasing.

But Gov. Jon Corzine, who made a fortune on Wall Street and used it to finance successful campaigns, first for the Senate and then the governorship, has had a very rocky first term.

Republicans charge that he has failed to deliver on his key promises — to balance the budget and reduce some of the nation's highest property taxes.

The Republican challenger, Chris Christie, made his reputation as the Bush-appointed U.S. attorney, tackling public corruption and convicting more than 130 public officials.

In Virginia, Obama and term-limited Gov. Tim

Kaine, now doubling as chairman of the Democratic National Committee, were heartened by the results of last week's Democratic primary, where state Sen. R. Creigh Deeds defeated Clinton buddy Terry McAuliffe and liberal legislator Brian Moran.

A Rasmussen poll taken right after the primary showed Deeds leading Republican Robert McDonnell, 47 percent to 41 percent.

A victory by either McDonnell or Christie would likely strengthen the pragmatist camp in internal Republican debates — the people who argue that mobilizing the conservative base is not enough for victory in competitive races. And that's another reason Obama will be working to defeat them.

David Broder is a Washington Post columnist. Readers may write to him at davidbroder@washpost.com or Washington Post Writers Group, 1150 15th St. NW, Washington, D.C. 20071.

When did the Obama of change disappear?

Joe Galloway

Who stole our change? Who hijacked a popular uprising that was going to put a stop to business as usual in Washington?

What happened to Barack Obama on his way to the White House?

The Republicans have been so busy trying to paint President Obama as a socialist, as a radical, as a Marxist, as a Muslim, as the Devil, that they haven't even noticed that he has become one of them.

What a difference a year can make. A year ago Barack Obama was on the campaign trail, promising an American electorate disheartened and disgusted by eight years of George W. Bush and Dick Cheney that he was going to change everything if he was elected president.

He would be the new broom, sweeping out the dirt, collecting the trash, fixing everything that was broken and tarnished and perverted in our government, in our nation's capital, in our White House.

He swept into office on a high tide of good will and anticipation. He was going to fix Wall Street. He was going to end the war in Iraq. He was going to bring a new era of transparency to government. He was going to stimulate a faltering economy and give new hope to a shrinking, frightened middle class. He was going to close the prison at Guantanamo and end the torture policies of his predecessors. There was even a hope that we would investigate how we went wrong and who ordered it.

He came to town on a white horse, riding a staggering wave of popular approval in the polls, a golden leader in a golden moment with a golden opportunity, and then he did what? Nothing much. Nothing different.

Oh, he can still talk the talk and he does that incessantly. But he seemingly can't walk the walk.

He may still sound like a revolutionary but more and more he looks and acts like George W. Bush, albeit a George W. Bush who can speak a complete sentence in the English language.

Obama's approval ratings are beginning to unwind and begin a long downward spiral among those who had believed in the promises of change. There was a golden moment when change was possible, but it is gone now.

There was one thing Obama absolutely had to do, even before tackling an economic meltdown and the Wall Street and big bank ripoffs:

He had to reassure Americans that we all live under the rule of law, that no one by virtue of holding the highest offices in the land, or having the biggest bank account, is above the law.

It was incumbent on new President Obama to step back and let justice be done. Let the investigators do their job. Not only to let justice be done but let justice be seen to be done.

But no. He said he wanted to focus on the future, not revisit the past. He needed to get moving on stimulating a foundering economy. And he screwed that up, too, reaching out to the very pirates who had looted their stockholders, their own companies, their own country to find someone to appoint as treasury secretary, thus reassuring Wall Street that he wasn't going to turn over any apple carts.

He declared that we, as a nation and people, would no longer torture our enemies and suspected enemies; would no longer lock them up and throw away the key; would no longer violate our own laws and those of the international conventions governing warfare.

But he trooped over to the Central Intelligence Agency headquarters to reassure those who had "only followed orders" when they tortured and abused helpless prisoners that they would never face justice. Nor would those who gave those illegal orders.

He promised to release another big batch of torture photos from our concentration camps in Afghanistan and Iraq and then reneged on that promise under pressure from the national security mavens.

His promises of transparency in government weren't worth a pitcher of warm spit. He sent the new, cleaner Justice Department lawyers into court to use the same limp arguments of national security to ask judges to back off on doing their jobs.

And bit by bit the possibility of change disappeared; bit by bit the hope of a renewed and reinvigorated American democracy and way of government faded away. Those who had held a dream in their hand closed their hand and crushed the dream.

Joe Galloway is a syndicated columnist. Readers may write to him at Joe Galloway, P.O. Box 399, Bayside, TX 78340.

Republicans in the wilderness

Thomas Sowell

A Gallup poll last week showed that far more Americans describe themselves as "conservatives" than as "liberals." Yet Republicans have been clobbered by the Democrats in both the 2008 elections and the 2006 elections.

In a country with more conservatives than liberals, it is puzzling — in fact, amazing — that we have the furthest left President of the United States in history, as well as the furthest left Speaker of the House of Representatives.

Republicans, especially, need to think about what this means. If you lose when you have the high cards and still keep taking a beating, then you need to re-think how you are playing the game.

The current intramural fighting among Republicans does not necessarily mean any fundamental re-thinking of their policies or tactics. These tussles may be nothing more than a longstanding jockeying for position between the liberal and conservative wings of that party.

The stakes in all this are far higher than which element becomes dominant in which party or which party wins more elections.

A quadrupling of the national debt in just one year and accepting a nuclear-armed sponsor of international terrorism like Iran are not things from which any country is guaranteed to recover.

Just two nuclear bombs were enough to get Japan to surrender in World War II.

Perhaps people who are busy gushing over the Obama cult today might do well to stop and think about what it would mean for their granddaughters to live under sharia law.

The glib pieties in Barack Obama's televised sermonettes will not stop Iran from becoming a nuclear terrorist nation. Time is running out fast, and

we will be lucky if it doesn't happen in the first term of this president. If he gets elected to a second term — which is quite possible, despite whatever economic disasters he leads us into — our fate as a nation may be sealed.

Unfortunately, the only political party with any chance of displacing the current leadership in Washington is the Republican Party.

The "smart money" says that the way for the Republicans to win elections is to appeal to a wider range of voters, including minorities, by supporting more of the kinds of positions that Democrats use to get elected. This sounds good on the surface, which is as far as many people go, when it comes to politics.

However plausible all this may seem, it goes directly counter to what has actually happened in politics in this generation. For example, Democrats studiously avoided presenting alternatives to what the Republican-controlled Congress and the Bush administration were doing,

and just lambasted them at every turn. That is how the Democrats replaced Republicans at both ends of Pennsylvania Avenue.

Ronald Reagan won two elections in a landslide by being Ronald Reagan — and, most important of all — explaining to a broad electorate how what he advocated would be best for them and for the country. Newt Gingrich likewise led a Republican takeover of the House of Representatives by explaining how the Republican agenda would benefit a wide range of people.

Neither of them won by pretending to be Democrats. It is the mushy "moderates" — the "kinder and gentler" Bush 41, Bob Dole and John McCain — who lost disastrously, even in two cases to Democrats who were initially very little known, but who knew how to talk.

Thomas Sowell is a syndicated columnist. Readers may write to him at www.tsowell.com, at info@creators.com (with his name in the subject line) or Creators Syndicate, 5777 W. Century Blvd., Suite 700, Los Angeles, CA 90045.

Madoff gets 150 years

By Tom Hays
and Larry Neumeister
The Associated Press

NEW YORK — A federal judge rejected Bernard Madoff's plea for leniency Monday, sentencing the 71-year-old swindler to spend the rest of his life in prison for an "extraordinarily evil" fraud that took a staggering toll on thousands of victims.

U.S. District Judge Denny Chin cited the unprecedented nature of the multibillion-dollar fraud as he sentenced Madoff to the maximum of 150 years in prison, a term comparable only to those given in the past to terrorists, traitors and the most violent criminals. There is no parole in federal prison.

"Here the m······

AP photo

This courtroom sketch shows Bernard Madoff, center, seated in front of some of his victims who spoke during his sentencing Monday in Manhattan federal court in New York.

It's a privilege to be here

I am writing in response to the article "Society and Immigration," which appeared in the Information Exchange, an insert in a recent edition of The Herald.

About 15 years ago, I applied for permission to reside in the United States. After about three years of waiting, I received my Resident Alien Card, commonly known as Green Card. Two years ago, when I renewed my Green Card, I received a new card renamed to "Permanent Resident."

The writer of the article states the following: "It is degrading to use the terms 'alien' and 'illegal alien,' which describe undocumented immigrants as inhuman outsiders who come to the U.S with questionable motivations."

At no time in the 10 years that I was an "Alien" did I feel like an inhuman outsider. To the contrary, I felt privileged to be allowed to reside in the United States of America. I felt privileged because that is what it is, a privilege, not a right. I don't know where it might be written that it is a right to reside in the United States if you were born in another country. (Unless you are like my children, who were born in Canada to an

American mother, and then registered at the U.S. Embassy as American citizens.)

Many of my Canadian friends would love the privilege of being called "Resident Aliens" in the United States.

The writer also takes exception to the term "illegal immigrant," stating that 40 percent of the people living illegally in the United States entered the country legally and then overstayed their visa. To me, that's like saying it's not illegal to open a checking account with $100 and then write a check in the amount of $1,000. When someone comes to this country on a visa and then immediately hides so they can't be found, to me, that seems illegal. I also suspect that people who hide have "questionable motivations." Didn't the 9/11 terrorists enter the country legally on visas and then overstay their visa?

As an aside, to become a "Resident Alien," I had to prove that I had enough financial resources to reside in the United States. I was also not eligible for any form of social assistance, such as welfare, unemployment benefits or food stamps. In fact, I had to sign an affidavit stating that if I did apply for any social assistance, I was aware that such an act made me liable to deportation from the United States.

I have three new Canadian flags, because to fly a Canadian flag in Montreal, Canada, in many cases is asking for your home to be vandalized. These flags remain unpacked because, in my opinion, to fly a Canadian flag at my home in the United States of America diminishes my thankfulness of being given the PRIVILEGE of living in these wonderful United States of America.

Ken Fitzgerald
Gor An Farm Road, Selma

Rest in peace, U.S. media

I wish to offer an obituary for the "free press" in this country. It seems that the broadcast and print media have given up even the appearance of objectivity now that ABC has decided to present the news from the White House and air a special on the president's health care plan. ABC even announced it would air no opposing views to the president's plan.

There was a time when the American media at least paid lip service to the lack of press freedom in places like China and the Soviet Union. Those days are long passed. Our media have become no better than the Chinese state-run outlets, parroting what the "dear leader" tells them. It is no wonder that newspaper circulation is declining and network news broadcasts have dismally low ratings. The people can no longer trust that the information we receive is, in any way, unbiased. News reporters have gone from being Edward R. Murrow to Joseph Goebbels. You in the media have no one to blame but yourselves for your decline.

Thomas C. Imler

Fayetteville Observer
17 July 09

Psalm 23, revised for today

The 23rd Psalm, updated:

(1) Obama's my shepherd;

(2) He maketh me pay taxes in lean times; he leadeth me into sure devastation.

(3) He restoreth my fear; he leadeth me in the paths of socialism for his name's sake.

(4) Yea though I walk through the valley of liberal fanatics, I will fear the evil; for evil surrounds me; thy Senate and Congress discomfort me.

(5) Thou preparest a Cabinet before me who are all mine enemies: thou anointest the unions with payback, thy debt runneth over.

(6) Surely inflation and uncertainty shall follow me the rest of the days of my life: and I will dwell in the poor house forever.

Alan M. Huntre
Camero

FRIDAY, JULY 17, 2009 9A

.0020   GOLD ▼ -4.00
$935.10

Jobless woes add mortgage pressures

The Associated Press

WASHINGTON — Rising unemployment is triggering more home foreclosures, threatening the Obama administration's efforts to end the housing crisis and diminishing hopes the economy will rebound with vigor.

In past recessions, the housing industry helped get the economy back on track. Home builders ramped up production, expecting buyers to take advantage of lower prices and jump into the market. But not this time.

These days, many homeowners who got fixed-rate prime mortgages because they had good credit can't make their payments because they're out of work. That means even more foreclosures and further declines in home values.

The initial surge in foreclosures in 2007 and 2008 was tied to subprime mortgages issued during the housing boom to people with shaky credit. That crisis has ebbed and been replaced by more traditional foreclosures tied to the recession.

Unemployment stood at 9.5 percent in June and is expected to rise past 10 percent and well into next year. The last time the economy was mired in a recession with such high unemployment was 1981 and 1982.

Almost 4 percent of homeowners with a mortgage are in foreclosure, and 8 percent on top of that are at least a month behind on payments — the highest levels since the Great Depression.

Because home values have declined so dramatically, many people can't refinance.

More than 1.5 million households were threatened with losing their homes in the first six months of this year, foreclosure listing service RealtyTrac Inc. said.

According to April figures, some of the highest unemployment rates in the country are in California cities such as Merced, Modesto and Fresno that have been struck hardest by the foreclosure crisis. In those areas, home prices have been cut in half.

309

Fnyßßs 24 Jny cq

ANALYSIS

Obama makes foray into race debate

By Jesse Washington
The Associated Press

Making his first foray into a divisive racial issue, President Obama sided with Henry Louis Gates Jr. after the black scholar's arrest by a white police officer, a striking departure from Obama's "post-racial" impartiality.

Saying that the white sergeant acted "stupidly" in arresting Gates, Obama inflamed an already volatile topic. Although he backed off that comment slightly Thursday, Obama stood by his assessment that the arrest of the Harvard professor "doesn't make sense."

After years of deftly defusing racial land mines, why did Obama speak out now? Because Gates is a friend and fellow Harvard man? Because racial profiling is an issue close to the president's heart?

Or could Obama, contemplating the idea of a white cop questioning a black man in his own home, have lost his legendary cool?

"I think he was responding emotionally. It was a visceral reaction," said Mary Frances Berry, a University of Pennsylvania history professor and former chair of the U.S. Commission on Civil Rights.

"It is a milestone, in a sense" said Berry, who was watching the news conference when Obama made the original statement. "It's his first foray into putting his tippy-toe into the water, to respond directly to something about race."

sible break-in. Sgt. James Crowley arrived to find Gates inside the house and demanded to see some ID.

Gates says Crowley treated him rudely and refused to provide his badge number; Crowley says Gates yelled at him, accused him of racism and refused to calm down. Gates was charged with disorderly conduct and spent a few hours in custody. The charges were quickly dropped.

At the end of a news conference Wednesday night, Obama was asked about the arrest. After saying that he didn't know the details of what happened, the president plunged into uncharted waters.

"I think it's fair to say, number one, any of us would be pretty angry," Obama said. "Number two, that the Cambridge police acted stupidly in arresting somebody when there was already proof that they were in their own home. And number three — what I think we know separate and apart from this incident — is that there is a long history in this country of African-Americans and Latinos being stopped by law enforcement disproportionately, and that's just a fact."

In an interview with ABC on Thursday, Obama said he was surprised by the reaction to his comments. He didn't take back his words, but he did offer that he understood Crowley was an "outstanding police officer."

"My suspicion is that

words were exchanged between the police officer and Mr. Gates," he said, "and that everybody should have just settled down and cooler heads should have prevailed."

But for many black men, the history and humiliation of racial profiling makes it almost impossible to keep cool.

In his book "The Audacity of Hope," Obama said he has personally felt its sting: "Security guards tailing me as I shop in department stores, white couples who toss me their keys as I stand outside a restaurant waiting for the valet, police cars pulling me over for no apparent reason. I know what it's like to have people tell me I can't do something because of my color, and I know the bitter swill of swallowed-back anger."

So did this history lead Obama to step, however briefly, out of character — or maybe back INTO it?

"The notion of a friend, of a fellow human being, being humiliated in their home cuts to the core," answered Benjamin Todd Jealous, CEO of the NAACP, which is pushing for a federal ban on profiling.

"Racial profiling is like lightning, it's a form of humiliation that strikes randomly," he said. "It humiliates black men in front of their children, in their homes, in stores."

In 2004, Obama's star was born with his speech at the Democratic National Con-

vention calling for unity among all Americans. Since then, he had largely declined to delve into racial issues, choosing a middle ground that reflected his biracial parentage.

The journalist Ellis Cose, author of "The Rage of a Privileged Class," about anger among successful blacks, pointed out that Obama had sponsored legislation while an Illinois state senator to combat racial profiling.

"To the extent that he did drop his sort of nonracial face, so to speak, it was because this is an issue he feels personally passionate about and an issue that has clearly touched most black men in America of a certain age," Cose said. "I think he was personally outraged."

From the start, Gates' claims that he was racially profiled seemed like a case from the divided past, when truth was subjective, sympathies color-coded — and most presidents stayed neutral.

The Harvard history professor and prominent intellectual returned home from a trip to China last week and had to force open his jammed front door. A white woman who works nearby called police to report a pos-

310

Polls ca

Obama is at crucial time in pushing agenda

By Susan Page
USA TODAY

WASHINGTON -- A president's standing after his first six months in office doesn't forecast whether he'll have a successful four-year term, but it does signal how much political juice he'll have for his second six months in office.

That's the lesson of history.

Barack Obama, who completed six months in office Monday, has a 55% approval rating in the USA TODAY/Gallup Poll, putting him 10th among the dozen presidents who have served since World War II at this point in their tenures.

That's not as bad for Obama as it may sound: The six-month mark hasn't proved to be a particularly good indicator of how a president ultimately will fare.

Two-thirds of Americans approved of the jobs Jimmy Carter and George H.W. Bush were doing at six months, but both would lose their bids for re-election.

And though the younger Bush and Bill Clinton had significantly lower ratings at 180 days -- Clinton had sunk to 41% approval -- both won second terms.

Even so, a president's standing at the moment is more than a matter of vanity. It affects his ability to hold the members of his own party and persuade those on the other side to support him, at least on the occasional issue.

"Approval ratings are absolutely critical for a president achieving his agenda," says Republican pollster Whit Ayres.

For Obama, the timing of his slide in ratings is particularly unhelpful: He has intensified his push to pass health care bills in the House and Senate before Congress leaves on its August recess. He'll press his case at a news conference at 8 p.m. Wednesday.

His overall approval rating has dropped 9 percentage points since his inauguration in January, and his disapproval rate has jumped 16 points, to 41%.

USA TODAY Gallup Poll

Do you approve of the way Barack Obama is handling the economy?

- Now — 47%
- May — 55%
- March — 56%
- February — 59%

Approval for President Obama's handling of:

- The situation in Iraq — 57%
- Foreign affairs — 57%
- The situation in Afghanistan — 56%
- The economy — 47%
- Taxes — 45%
- Health care policy — 44%

The However, there is a widening disconnect between Obama's personal standing and support for the policies he advocates:

▶ By 49%-47%, those surveyed disapprove of how he is handling the economy, a turnaround from his 55%-42% approval in May. The steepest drop came from conservative and moderate Democrats.

▶ By 50%-44%, they disapprove of how he is handling health care policy.

▶ A 59% majority say his proposals call for too much government spending and 52% say they call for too much expansion of government power.

▶ Expectations of the economy's turnaround are souring a bit. In February, the average prediction for a recovery was 4.1 years; now it's 5.5 years.

▶ The administration's stimulus package isn't seen as a benefit by most whether viewed in the short term or the long term, in how it will impact the economy or individuals. Only a third think it will help their own family's finances in the long run.

Obama "might make the policies more popular by being associated with him," says historian H.W. Brands of the University of Texas-Austin. "But it's almost equally possible that it will make him less popular by linking him with those policies."

The poll of 1,006 adults, taken Friday through Sunday by land line and cellphone, has a margin of error of +/- 4 percentage points.

Obama's proposals to address the major problems facing the country call for:

- Too much government spending — 59
- The right amount of government spending — 27%
- Not enough government spending — 11%

Obama's proposals to address the major problems facing the country call for:

- Too much expansion of government power — 52%
- The right amount of government power — 35%
- Not enough expansion of government power — 10%

Presidential Approval Tracker

▪ No. 44 vs. others back to Truman? See usatoday.com.
▪ Obama's dip, 6A

Economic jitters tug at Obama in poll

Disconnect widens on likability, policies

By Susan Page
USA TODAY

WASHINGTON -- Qualms about President Obama's stewardship of the economy are growing, a USA TODAY/Gallup Poll finds, as Americans become more pessimistic about when they predict the recession will end.

At six months in office, Obama's 55% approval rating puts him 10th among the 12 post-World War II presidents at this point in their tenures. When he took office, he ranked seventh.

"His ratings have certainly come back down to Earth in a very short time period," Republican pollster Whit Ayres says.

White House adviser David Axelrod calls the "turbulence" predictable, given the nation's economic woes and Obama's ambitious agenda.

"People fundamentally like this president, and they believe he's smart and capable and strong and trying to do the right thing," Axelrod says.

The findings forecast the rough patch that probably is ahead for Obama if unemployment continues to increase, as the administration predicts.

Lower ratings could make it more difficult for him to prevail on his top legislative priority. The president met with doctors and nurses at the Children's National Medical Center on Monday as he pushed the House and Senate to pass health-care overhauls before leaving on their August recess.

Obama continues to be highly regarded personally. Two-thirds see him as a strong and decisive leader

---

From Truman to Obama

Where presidents ranked in job-approval ratings six months into their first terms:

- Harry Truman — 82%
- John Kennedy — 75%
- Lyndon Johnson — 74%
- Dwight Eisenhower — 73%
- Jimmy Carter — 67%
- Richard Nixon — 65%
- George H.W. Bush — 66%
- Ronald Reagan — 60%
- George W. Bush — 56%
- Barack Obama — 55%
- Bill Clinton — 41%
- Gerald Ford — 39%

Source: Gallup Polls since 1945 taken closest to the

Gates says time to move past arres

Associated Press

BOSTON — Black Harvard holar Henry Louis Gates Jr. ys he's ready to move on m his arrest by a white po- e officer, hoping to use the counter to improve fairness the criminal justice system d saying "in the end, this is t about me at all."

After a phone call from President Obama urging calm in the aftermath of his arrest last week, Gates said he would accept Obama's invitation to the White House for a beer with him and Cambridge po-lice Sgt. James Crowley.

In a statement posted Fri-day on The Root, a Web site Gates oversees, the scholar

Gates   **Crowley**

said he told Obama he'd be happy to meet with Crowley,

whom Gates had accused of racial profiling.

"I told the president that my principal regret was that all of the attention paid to his deeply supportive remarks during his press conference had distracted attention from his health care initiative," Gates said. "I am pleased that he, too, is eager to use my ex-

perience as a teachin ment."

It was a marked cha tone for Gates, who days following his gathered up his legal and said he was conte ing a lawsuit. He even to make a documentary arrest to tie into a larg ject about racial profi

6A SUNDAY, JULY 26, 2009

Obama talks with officer, scholar

■ The president faults his own comments in an attempt to defuse the uproar over last weekend's arrest.

The Associated Press

WASHINGTON — Trying to tamp down an uproar over race, President Obama said Friday he used an unfortunate choice of words in comment-ing on the arrest of black scholar Henry Louis Gates Jr. and could have "calibrated those words differently."

The president said he had telephoned the white police-man who arrested Gates, and he said the conversation confirmed his belief that the officer is a good man and an outstanding officer.

Obama said later that he had spoken to Gates as well.

The president caused a stir when he said at a prime-time news conference earlier this week that Cambridge, Mass., police had "acted stupidly" by arresting Gates, a Harvard scholar and friend of the pres-ident's, for disorderly conduct.

On Friday, Obama made an impromptu appearance at the daily White House brief-ing in an effort to contain the controversy. He said he con-tinued to believe that both the officer, Sgt. James Crowley, and Gates had overreacted during the incident, but fault-ed his own comments.

"This has been ratcheting up, and I obviously helped to contribute ratcheting it up," he said. "I want to make clear that in my choice of words, I think I unfortunate-ly gave an impression that I was maligning the Cam-bridge police department and Sgt. Crowley specifical-ly. And I could've calibrated those words differently."

The incident began when police went to Gates' home last week after a passer-by reported a potential break-in. It turned out Gates had tried to jimmy open his own stuck door, and there was no intruder. Gates protested the police actions and was ar-rested, although the charges have since been dropped.

Before Obama's appear-ance Friday, a multiracial group of police officers stood with Crowley in Mas-sachusetts and asked Obama and the state's governor, De-val Patrick, to apologize for comments they called insult-ing. Patrick has said Gates' arrest was "every black man's nightmare."

ANALYSIS

Race is daunting issue for Obama

By Charles Babington
The Associated Press

WASHINGTON — Presi-dent Obama's summary of the furor over a black Harvard professor's arrest was so un-derstated, and perhaps obvi-ous, that it barely rose above the cable-news driven din.

"Race is still a troubling as-pect of our society," the na-tion's first black president said Friday, as he tried to tamp down a controversy he had

Obama

helped fuel two days earlier.

Without doubt.

What's less clear, however, is whether Obama's histo-ry-making election is triggering changes in the day-to-day racial inter-actions of ordinary Ameri-cans. After all, if one of the country's most prominent black scholars can be arrested in his home after a heated ex-change with a white police of-ficer, doesn't that suggest Oba-ma's racial breakthroughs ap-

No, say a variety of people who welcomed his plunge into the controversy, even if it caused the president a little heartburn. He is uniquely po-sitioned, they say, to pour light on one troubling issue — racial profiling by police — and to nudge the nation to talk more openly about race in general, if only for a short while, as he did with a widely followed speech in March 2008.

"Obama's election gives us someone in a position of au-thority to speak personally to this experience," said James Lai, director of the Ethnic Studies program at Santa Clara University in Califor-nia. Questions of whether po-lice officers disproportionate-ly stop minorities for ques-tioning and frisking "will get a much more thorough debate now," he said.

But Obama "has to walk a very fine line" when dis-cussing race, Lai said. "He must be careful not to fall in-to the box of being the black candidate."

Surprising uproar

Even Obama was sur-prised by the intensity of the uproar over the arrest of professor Henry Louis Gates Jr. by Cambridge, Mass., of-ficers who were checking a possible burglary report, which proved unfounded. At a Wednesday news confer-ence, Obama said the offi-cers had "acted stupidly" af-ter they realized Gates was in his own home.

.0066   GOLD $939.00 ▼ -14.30

FAYOBS, NC

Index falls on consumer worries

■ Confidence is weaker than expected as job concerns hinder shoppers from spending.

By Anne D'Innocenzio
The Associated Press

NEW YORK — Americans are looking past the stock market surge and signs of a stabilizing economy and focusing on something more personal — job worries.

Consumer confidence fell this month, the Conference Board said Tuesday, presenting a big obstacle for already hammered stores as they head into the critical back-to-school shopping season.

The confidence index fell to 46.6, down from 49.3 in June and weaker than what economists were expecting. It takes a reading above 90 to signal Americans believe the economy is on solid footing.

The second straight month of declining confidence followed an upbeat report offering more evidence that the real estate market is showing signs of life. According to a widely watched index, home prices in May posted their first monthly increase since the summer of 2006.

But vanishing job security and reduced work hours continue to plague shoppers, who are relying more on their paychecks as two previous sources of money — credit cards and home equity loans — have shrunk.

Where's our post-racial president?

Many people hoped that the election of a black president of the United States would mark our entering a "post-racial" era, when we could finally put some ugly aspects of our history behind us.

Those who were shocked at President Obama's cheap shot at the Cambridge police for being "stupid" in arresting Henry Louis Gates must have been among those who let their wishes prevail over the obvious implications of Obama's 20 years of association with the Rev. Jeremiah Wright.

The racial profiling issue is a great vote-getter. And if it polarizes the society, that is a price that politicians are willing to pay.

President Obama's background as a community organizer has received far too little attention, though it should have been a high-alert warning that this was no post-racial figure.

What does a community

Thomas Sowell

organizer do? What he organizes are the resentments and paranoia within a community, directing those feelings against other communities, from whom either benefits or revenge are to be gotten, using whatever rhetoric or tactics will accomplish that purpose.

Barack Obama's present tells the same story. His appointment of an attorney general who called America "a nation of cowards" for not dialoguing about race was a foretaste of what to expect from Eric Holder.

The way Attorney General Holder has refused to prosecute young black thugs who gathered at a voting site with menacing

clubs, in blatant violation of federal laws against intimidating voters, speaks louder than any words from him or his president.

President Obama's first nominee to the Supreme Court is, like Obama himself, someone with a background of years of affiliation with an organization dedicated to promoting racial resentments and a sense of racial entitlement.

An 18th century philosopher said, "When I speak I put on a mask. When I act I am forced to take it off." Barack Obama's mask slipped for a moment last week but he quickly recovered, with the help of the media. But we should never forget what we saw.

Thomas Sowell is a syndicated columnist. Readers may write to him at www.tsowell.com, at info@creators.com (with his name in the subject line) or Creators Syndicate, 5777 W. Century Blvd., Suite 700, Los Angeles, CA 90045.

FAY OBSERVER NC 31 July 2009

Fear, seen through black eyes

Leonard Pitts

I'll tell you why Barack Obama said what he did.

When he was asked last week about the racially charged arrest of Harvard professor Henry Louis Gates, the president could have — and as a political matter, should have — given a diplomatic non-answer. Instead, he gave a forthright response he later had to apologize for: police in Cambridge, Mass., he said, acted "stupidly" in arresting Gates, a prominent black scholar, at his own home, committing no crime.

So why did Obama, usually the smartest cookie in the jar, not do the politically intelligent thing?

I think it's simple. I think he looked at Henry Louis Gates and saw his brother-in-law, his nephew, maybe himself if he were not who he is. I think he did what black men habitually do when news breaks of some brother beat down, gunned down or simply thrown down and handcuffed for no good reason: He breathed, "There, but for the grace of God ..."

Of course, Americans of many cultural stripes have put themselves in Gates' shoes in recent days. And many have found him wanting. They say he caused his own plight by being — to what degree is a matter of dispute — uncooperative with a police officer. They fault him for crying racism when it's just as likely, they say, his arrest, misguided as it was, had nothing to do with race.

The first argument misses the point. Certainly few people would dispute that Gates failed Black 101 and, for that matter, Common Sense 101 in being uncooperative to whatever degree. But it's equally obvious to some of us that a white man, whose only "crime" was complaining, would likely have enjoyed more leeway than Gates did.

The second argument is naive. One white guy I know recounts his own experience — cop barged into his home at 3 a.m., rousting him from bed, demanding I.D. — and says: "This (expletive) happens all over the place and it has nothing to do with race."

And I say: I'll see your 3 a.m. roust and raise you Tony, jacked up on a street in Harlem; Bill, with a cop's gun to his head; Bryan, pulled over for an air freshener on his rear-view mirror; James, ordered to pull down his pants and lie on the curb; Robert, threatened with injury for drinking beer in the parking lot with friends after work. And that's just among guys I know, including three preachers.

Now, broaden it to include the bridegroom shot to death on his wedding day, the African immigrant killed while reaching for his wallet, the Maryland man beaten senseless as he lay in bed, the Miami man beaten to death for speeding, the dozens of men jailed on manufactured evidence in Los Angeles and manufactured police testimony in Tulia, Texas, the man sodomized with a broomstick in New York.

And if this expletive has nothing to do with race, then where are the stories of white men sodomized with brooms or shot while reaching for wallets? Are we supposed to believe it coincidence that the men this happens to always happen to be black?

Some of us do. Some of us have the luxury of never connecting the dots, seeing instead one discrete incident over here and tsk-tsk, how terrible that is, and another discrete incident over there and tsk-tsk again. And then move on and leave it behind.

But others don't have that luxury, don't get to move on and leave it behind. Others carry it like luggage, wear the residue like sweat, into every encounter with every cop, both good and bad: not always memories of what did happen, but fear of what could. Unnecessary fear? Sometimes. There are many great cops out there. Perfectly valid fear? All too often.

Here, then, is the take-away of the Gates affair: apparently every black man knows what that fear is like, be he professor, preacher, pundit.

Or president.

Leonard Pitts Jr. is a syndicated columnist. Readers may write to him at lpitts@herald.com or the Miami Herald, 1 Herald Plaza, Miami, FL 33132.

From left, Vice President Joe Biden, Harvard professor Henry Louis Gates Jr., Cambridge, Mass., police Sgt. James Crowley and President Obama talk while having beers in the Rose Garden of the White House in Washington on Thursday.

4 Aug 09

Opinio

The Fayetteville Observer

Obama's confidence can hut us

BUDGET TROUBLES

POSTAL CUTBACKS COULD HIT LOCALLY

■ The Haymount station is among hundreds to be considered for possible shutdown or consolidation.

A staff and wire report

WASHINGTON — The neighborhood post office is facing major changes as postal officials consider closings or consolidating services at hundreds of locations across the United States, including the Haymount branch in Fayetteville.

The Haymount Post Office is one of seven in North Carolina that will be studied further. Five are in Charlotte; one is in Asheville.

Any potential closures wouldn't happen until autumn at the earliest.

Some of the offices could be closed while others could have some of their functions consolidated with other offices. For example, in some cases preparing mail for delivery may be shifted from Office A to nearby Office B, but the first office might still offer such services as selling stamps and mailing parcels and letters. In other cases, one

See **POST OFFICE**, Page 4A

After many a disappointment with someone, and especially after a disaster, we may be able to look back at numerous clues that should have warned us that the person we trusted did not deserve our trust.

When that person is the President of the United States, the potential for disaster is virtually unlimited.

Many people are rightly worried about what this administration's reckless spending will do to the economy.

He is heading this country toward disaster on many fronts, including a nuclear Iran. We cannot put that genie back in the bottle — and neither can generations yet unborn. They may yet curse us all for leaving them hostages to nuclear terror.

Conceivably, Israel can spare us that fate by taking out the Iranian nuclear facilities, instead of relying on Obama's ability to talk the Iranians out of going nuclear.

What the Israelis cannot spare us, however, are our own internal problems, of which the current flap over President Obama's injecting himself into a local police issue is just a small sign of a very big danger.

Nothing has torn more countries apart from inside like racial and ethnic polarization. Just this year, a decades-long civil war, filled with unspeakable atrocities, has finally ended in Sri Lanka. Group identity politics led to group preferences and quotas that escalated into polarization and ultimately civil war.

Group identity politics has poisoned many other countries, including Kenya, Czechoslovakia, Fiji, Guyana, Canada, Nigeria, India, and Rwanda.

Thomas Sowell

Like so many before him who have ruined countries around the world, Obama has a greatly inflated idea of his own capabilities. Often this has been accompanied by an ignorance of history.

During a recent TV interview, when President Obama was asked about the prospects of victory in Afghanistan, he replied that it would not be victory like in World War II, with "Hirohito coming down and signing a surrender to MacArthur." In reality, it was more than a year after Japanese officials surrendered on the battleship Missouri before Hirohito met General Douglas MacArthur for the first time.

This is not the first betrayal of his ignorance by Obama, nor the first overlooked by the media. Moreover, ignorance by itself is not nearly as bad as charging full steam ahead, pretending to know. Barack Obama is doing that on a lot of issues, not just history or a local police incident in Massachusetts.

These repeated demonstrations of his amateurism will not go unnoticed by this country's enemies. And it is the American people who will pay the price.

Thomas Sowell is a syndicated columnist. Readers may write to him at www.tsowell.com, at info@creators.com (with his name in the subject line) or Creators Syndicate, 5777 W. Century Blvd., Suite 700, Los Angeles, CA 90045.

316

Time to get out of Iraq 7AUG09

Defense Secretary Robert Gates has suggested that he might speed up our withdrawal from Iraq by pulling out an additional brigade combat team by year's end. Good idea! How about pulling out FIVE more brigades by then?

It is an idea whose time clearly has arrived, as evidenced by the remarkable memo from a senior U.S. military adviser in Baghdad, Col. Timothy R. Reese, that was leaked last week.

Reese, who spent his most recent tour as an adviser to the Iraqi army's Baghdad command, says in his memo that it is time for us to "declare victory and go home."

He recommends that we accelerate the pullout so that all U.S. combat troops and virtually all the rest of the Americans now serving in Iraq are gone by Aug. 2010, 15 months earlier than presently planned.

To stay longer, the colonel wrote, will do little to improve the performance of the Iraqi army but will do much to fuel a growing resentment at our presence among the Iraqi pe...

Joe Galloway

Reese wrote that the huge advisory effort that has partnered U.S. combat troops with the Iraqi security forces "isn't yielding benefits commensurate with the effort and is now generating its own opposition."

What makes Col. Reese's blunt observations and recommendations even more cogent is that he is one of the Army's thinking warriors — formerly director of the Combat Studies Institute at Fort Leavenworth and author of the official Army history of the Iraq War, "ON POINT II: Transition to the New Campaign."

The Reese memo, which the Pentagon says was written in early July and was not meant for distribution outside the U.S. command in Baghdad, notes that since the new Status of Forces Agreement between the U.S. and Iraq went int...

decided cooling of Iraqi Army relations with their American advisers, a forcible Iraqi takeover of a checkpoint in the Green Zone and Iraqi units are now less willing to do joint operations with the Americans to pursue targets the U.S. considers high value.

Reese said that all our efforts to plant the seeds of a professional military culture in the Iraqi forces have failed. "The military culture of the Baathist-Soviet model under Saddam Hussein remains entrenched and will not change."

He goes on to delineate a score of points to prove that the Iraqi army isn't very good by our standards but they are good enough to do what their political leadership demands.

At this point, the colonel declares, it is time for us to declare victory and go home before things get a whole lot worse.

We have suggested a speedup in our Iraq withdrawal several times before in this column. Doubtless we will do so many more times in the future.

another two years at such a phenomenal cost, when their hosts, the Iraqi people, don't want them there anymore?

We have other, more pressing issues to deal with at home and abroad. It is going to take time to reset our Army and rebuild and refurbish or replace hundreds of billions of dollars worth of equipment chewed up or used up in six-plus years of war in Iraq.

Our eight-year war in Afghanistan suddenly needs more attention, money and soldiers and Marines because we didn't finish the job in 2002.

The only things that can happen in Iraq with an old strategy are bad things: It's hard to declare victory and leave with your head high if the old civil war comes roaring back; if the old communal butchery and murder resumes with a vengeance; if killing American troops again becomes the favorite sport of every side in the fight.

It's high time to get while the getting's good.

Joe Galloway is a syndicated columnist. Readers may write

I'M SICK AND TIRED OF BEING UNEMPLOYED!!

AND I'M SICK OF YOU SPENDING OUR NATION INTO GENERATIONS OF DEBT!!

The American people have expressed to me their need for health care.

FRIDAY, AUGUST 7, 2009

317

17 August 2009

Where's our post-racial America?

Whatever happened to that "post-racial" America we were supposed to be living in?

Whatever happened to those warm and fuzzy feelings we got when we elected America's first black president?

Whatever happened to being so proud of ourselves for having bridged the racial divide?

Didn't last very long.

Today, America does not seem to be very post-racial or very united. Just about a year ago, we were able to laugh about things that don't seem very funny today.

In July 2008, The New Yorker ran a cover depicting Barack and Michelle Obama standing in the Oval Office with an American flag burning in the fireplace and a portrait of Osama bin Laden hanging on the wall. Obama was dressed in traditional Muslim clothing, including a turban. Michelle was sporting a huge Afro, wearing camouflage trousers with combat boots and shouldering a Kalashnikov assault rifle with a bandolier of bullets. The two were bumping fists.

The cover succeeded (at least to me) in being so absurd that it poked fun of

Roger Simon

the people who believed the Obamas were dangerous, traitorous or foreign. As David Remnick, the editor of The New Yorker, said at that time, the cover "combines a number of fantastical images about the Obamas and shows them for the obvious distortions they are."

Today, those "obvious distortions" plus new ones get serious hearings on talk radio and cable TV.

Today, "birthers" claim that Obama is not an American at all and that his election shows merely that Obama is an alien who successfully hid himself among us for years.

And Obama's comments regarding the Cambridge police department and the arrest of professor Henry Louis Gates Jr. released reactions that seem over the top even in the world of talk TV. Glenn Beck, a popular commentator for Fox News,

said: "This president, I think, has exposed himself as a guy, over and over and over again, who has a deep-seated hatred for white people or the white culture, I don't know what it is. I'm not saying that he doesn't like white people. I'm saying he has a problem. This guy is, I believe, a racist."

Largely overlooked in the understandably good feelings generated by the election of our first black president was the simple fact that white America did not vote for him.

Most white Americans voted for John McCain. While Obama won the overall vote by 53 percent to 46 percent, he lost among white voters by 55 percent to 43 percent.

When I give speeches and mention that no Democratic president since Lyndon Johnson has won the white vote, I always see some head shaking in the audience as if that could not possibly be true.

But it is. Three Democrats have become president since Lyndon Johnson — Jimmy Carter, Bill Clinton and Obama — but none of them has won a majority of white votes.

How did they become president? By picking up enough white votes along with enough minority votes to

build a winning coalition. In Obama's case, he got 43 percent of the white vote, 95 percent of the black vote, 67 percent of the Latino vote and 62 percent of the Asian vote.

During the campaign, the Obama campaign constantly said America was changing and that younger Americans had moved beyond race.

That could be true. Among white voters aged 18-29, Obama won by a margin of 54 percent to 44 percent.

It would be absurd to say that everybody who voted against Obama is a racist (and just because exit polls divide people into racial groups does not mean people cast their votes for racial reasons).

But it also may be absurd or at least prematurely optimistic, to say we are living in a post-racial America, where divides have been bridged, gaps closed and wounds healed.

We are not. We may be getting there. But there are going to be bumps in the road and mountains yet to climb.

Roger Simon is the chief political columnist of politico.com, an award-winning journalist and a New York Times best-selling author.

6 Sept 2009

Obama adviser quits

The Associated Press

WASHINGTON — The White House says President Barack Obama's adviser Van Jones is resigning amid controversy over past inflammatory statements.

Van Jones, an administration official specializing in environmentally friendly "green jobs," is linked to efforts suggesting a governmental role in the 2001 terror attacks and to derogatory comments about Republicans.

Pers

The Fayetteville Observer

Here&There

Obama's bumpy road

New York Times columnist David Brooks:

The number of Americans who trust President Obama to make the right decisions has fallen by roughly 17 percentage points. Obama's job approval is down to about 50 percent. All presidents fall from their honeymoon highs, but in the history of polling, no newly elected American president has fallen this far this fast.

Trust in government rose when Obama took office. It has fallen back to historic lows.

The public has soured on Obama's policy proposals. Voters often have only a fuzzy sense of what each individual proposal actually does, but more and more have a growing conviction that if the president is proposing it, it must involve big spending, big government and a fundamental departure from the traditional American approach.

Most Americans still admire Obama and want him to succeed. But if he doesn't proceed in a manner consistent with the spirit of the nation and the times, voters will find a way to stop him.

DAY, SEPTEMBER 6, 2009   7B

40-year sentence given for child porn

The Associated Press

WALHALLA, S.C. — A South Carolina man who state prosecutors said had the biggest collection of child pornography they had ever seen has been sentenced to 40 years in prison.

The Anderson Independent-Mail reports that 41-year-old Larry Douglas Smith pleaded guilty Friday to three counts of sexual exploitation of a minor and one count of criminal sexual conduct with a minor.

Prosecutor Chrissy Adams says Smith had 606 videos and 126,000 separate images of child porn. She says the South Carolina attorney general's office has never seen such a large collection of illegal images.

Smith's lawyer says his client could have faced more than a million years in prison if prosecutors had filed all the charges they could have.

Repeat offenders plague city's police

They steal by the dark of night. Sometimes by the light of day.

"Pulling on door handles ..." Fayetteville police Chief Tom Bergamine says about burglars who vandalize vehicles and homes in this community.

Meet Brandon McMorrough.

He is 22.

He tugs on door handles, and his criminal rap sheet says it all.

He is a thief.

He's in jail again, thanks to a Haymount resident who works as

Bill Kirby Jr.

an assistant district attorney in Hoke County, and often prosecutes criminals such as McMorrough. Mike

Hardin, 38, usually is more benign in a courtroom, but he was more animated in the wee hours of Aug. 28, when Hardin says he and his wife saw McMorrough snooping around their vehicles and a neighbor's home.

Hardin served notice to McMorrough to cease and desist,

and until police arrived, he held the man at gunpoint.

Better Hardin on the other side of the 9 mm than 75-year-old Walter

319

Afghanistan isn't worth it

7Sep09
FAYOBSER.

The debate over our creeping military mission in distant Afghanistan grows ever hotter, and before we march even deeper into trouble, perhaps it's time to dig out the old Powell Doctrine and answer the eight questions it poses.

Gen. Colin Powell, then chairman of the Joint Chiefs of Staff, said these questions all must be answered with a loud "yes" before the United States takes military action. He listed his questions in the 1990 run-up to the Persian Gulf War, drawing heavily on the Weinberger Doctrine that was laid down by former Secretary of Defense Caspar Weinberger during the debate over America's ends and means in Lebanon.

(1) Is a vital national security interest threatened?

(2) Do we have a clear, attainable objective?

(3) Have the risks and costs been fully and frankly analyzed?

(4) Have all non-violent policy means been exhausted?

(5) Is there a plausible exit strategy to avoid endless entanglement?

(6) Have all the consequences of our action been fully considered?

Joe Galloway

by the American people?

(8) Do we have broad international support?

Those questions weren't asked and answered before we invaded Afghanistan late in 2001, and by the time we invaded Iraq early in 2003, then-Defense Secretary Donald H. Rumsfeld was declaring the Powell Doctrine "outmoded" as he ran premature victory laps around a fleeting success in Afghanistan.

The Bush administration is gone, but Iraq and Afghanistan are still with us, and now a new president is overseeing a slow-motion U.S. withdrawal from Iraq and a slow-motion U.S. escalation in Afghanistan.

It can fairly be argued that not a single affirmative answer can be given to Powell's eight questions with regard to the actions now planned or under way in Afghanistan. Had those questions been asked about Iraq in early 2003, not a single affirmative answer

There was, in the beginning in Afghanistan, a vital national security interest in toppling the Taliban government and killing or capturing the Taliban's murderous guests, Osama bin Laden's al-Qaida terrorists. We toppled the Taliban, but we let al-Qaida flee over the rugged, mountainous border into Pakistan.

Even before that, we began to let Afghanistan fester, starved of U.S. manpower and money, and turned our attention to Iraq.

We no longer have a vital national security interest or a clearly attainable goal in Afghanistan.

The new U.S. military commander in Kabul, Army Gen. Stanley McChrystal, wants more U.S. troops to fight the newly resurgent Taliban guerrillas who control well over half the country, but he's been told that he shouldn't ask for them anytime soon.

With the country in recession, the budget deficit spinning into the trillions of dollars, American casualty rates in Afghanistan at record highs and public approval of the president and the war in Afghanistan falling like rocks, the White House desperately wants some breathing room.

it runs counter to an important corollary to the Powell Doctrine: If you're determined to fight a war, choose a commander whom you trust and a strategy that you back, and then give your military leaders all the resources they say they need to achieve your objective.

If you can't do that, if your objective isn't clear, if the American people and the international community aren't with you, then order a withdrawal and explain why.

For eight years, we've heard presidents and other politicians talk about setting conditions for a democratic central government in a country — really a bunch of tribes and clans — that's never had such a thing in 2,000 years and seemingly doesn't want one now.

It's time to make a decision, Mr. President, and I hope that, for our sake and yours, you make the right one. Afghanistan isn't worth the life of one more American soldier, much less the hundreds and thousands that an open-ended commitment to a war that we cannot win would cost.

Joe Galloway is a syndicated columnist. Readers may write to him at Joe Galloway, P.O. Box

Official resigns amid flap

Controversy over 9/11 remarks fells Obama's top environmental adviser

By Will Lester
The Associated Press

WASHINGTON — The White House environmental adviser under fire for inflammatory statements made before he joined the administration resigned after what he called a "vicious smear campaign against me."

Van Jones "understood that he was going to get in the way" of President Obama's agenda, White House spokesman Robert Gibbs said Sunday.

The resignation was disclosed without advance notice by the White House in a dead-of-the-night e-mail on a holiday weekend. It came as

Jones

Obama is working to regain his footing in the contentious health care debate.

Jones, who specialized in environmentally friendly "green jobs" with the White House Council on Environmental Quality, was linked to efforts suggesting a government role in the Sept. 11 attacks and to derogatory comments about Republicans.

Gibbs said Obama did not endorse Van Jones' comments but thanked him for his service.

"What Van Jones decided was that the agenda of this president was bigger than any one individual," Gibbs said on ABC's "This Week."

Recent news reports cited a derogatory comment Jones made in the past about Republicans, and separately, of Jones' name appearing on a petition connected to the events surrounding the Sept. 11, 2001, attacks. That 2004 petition had asked for congressional hearings and other investigations into whether high-level government officials had allowed the attacks to occur.

"On the eve of historic fights for health care and clean energy, opponents of

reform have mounted a vicious smear campaign against me," Jones said in his resignation statement. "They are using lies and distortions to distract and divide."

Obama's top political adviser, David Axelrod, said on NBC's "Meet the Press" that Jones "showed his commitment to the cause of creating green jobs in this country by removing himself as an issue."

Jones said in an earlier statement that he did not agree with the petition's stand on the Sept. 11 attacks and that "it certainly does not reflect my views, now or ever."

320

3 Sept 09

Surrender of the West *3 Sep 09*

Thomas Sowell

Britain's release of Abdel Baset al-Megrahi — the Libyan terrorist whose bomb blew up a plane over Lockerbie, Scotland in 1988, killing 270 people — is galling enough in itself. But it is even more profoundly troubling as a sign of a larger mood that has been growing in the Western democracies in our time.

In ways large and small, domestically and internationally, the West is surrendering on the installment plan to Islamic extremists.

The late Aleksandr Solzhenitsyn put his finger on the problem when he said: "The timid civilized world has found nothing with which to oppose the onslaught of a sudden revival of barefaced barbarity, other than concessions and smiles."

He wrote this long before Barack Obama became president of the United States. But this administration epitomizes the "concessions and smiles" approach to countries that are our implacable enemies.

Western Europe has gone down that path before us but we now seem to be trying to catch up.

Still, the release of a mass-murdering terrorist, who went home to a hero's welcome in Libya, shows that President Obama is not the only one who wants to move away from the idea of a "war on terror" — as if that will stop the terrorists' war on us.

Forgotten lessons

The ostensible reason for releasing al-Megrahi was compassion for a man terminally ill. It is ironic that this was said in Scotland, for exactly 250 years ago another Scotsman — Adam Smith — said, "Mercy to the guilty is cruelty to the innocent."

That lesson seems to have been forgotten in America, as well, where so many people seem to have been far more concerned about whether we have been nice enough to the mass-murdering terrorists in our custody than those critics have ever been about the innocent people beheaded or blown up by the terrorists themselves.

Tragically, those with this strange inversion of values include the attorney general of the United States, Eric Holder. Although President Obama has said that he does not want to revisit the past, this is only the latest example of how his administration's actions are the direct opposite of his lofty words.

It is not just a question of looking backward. The decision to second-guess CIA agents who extracted information to save American lives is even worse when you look forward.

Years from now, long after Barack Obama is gone, CIA agents dealing with hardened terrorists will have to worry about whether what they do to get information out of them to save American lives will make these agents themselves liable to prosecution that can destroy their careers and ruin their lives.

This is not simply an injustice to those who have tried to keep this country safe, it is a danger recklessly imposed on future Americans whose safety cannot always be guaranteed by sweet and gentle measures against hardened murderers.

Those who are pushing for legal action against CIA agents may talk about "upholding the law" but they are doing no such thing. Neither the Constitution of the United States nor the Geneva Conventions give rights to terrorists who operate outside the law.

There was a time when everybody understood this. German soldiers who put on American military uniforms, in order to infiltrate American lines during the Battle of the Bulge, were simply lined up against a wall and shot — and nobody wrung their hands over it. Nor did the U.S. Army try to conceal what it had done. The executions were filmed and the film has been shown on the History Channel.

So many "rights" have been conjured up out of thin air that many people seem unaware that rights and obligations derive from explicit laws, not from politically correct pieties. If you don't meet the terms of the Geneva Conventions, then the Geneva Conventions don't protect you. If you are not an American citizen, then the rights guaranteed to American citizens do not apply to you.

That should be especially obvious if you are part of an international network bent on killing Americans. But bending over backward to be nice to our enemies is one of the many self-indulgences of those who engage in moral preening.

But getting other people killed so that you can feel puffed up about yourself is profoundly immoral. So is betraying the country you took an oath to protect.

Thomas Sowell is a syndicated columnist. Readers may write to him at www.tsowell.com, at info@creators.com (with his name in the subject line) or Creators Syndicate, 5777 W. Century Blvd., Suite 700, Los Angeles, CA 90045.

Rude, but not racist

20 SEPT 09 FAYOBS NC

When Kanye West rushed onstage and grabbed the microphone away from Taylor Swift at the MTV Video Music Awards the other day, was he being a racist? Or was he just being rude?

Me, I thought he was just being rude. In any case, he apologized. And life moved on.

When Serena Williams yelled at a line judge at the U.S. Open last Saturday night, was Williams being a racist? Or was she just losing control of her temper during a hard-fought match?

Me, I thought Williams was just losing control of her temper during a hard-fought match. In any case, she apologized. And life moved on.

When Joe Wilson yelled at President Barack Obama during a joint session of Congress last Wednesday, was Wilson being a racist? Or was he just being an incredible jerk?

Me, I thought he was just being an incredible jerk. But others thought he was being a racist.

In any case, Wilson apologized. But life has not moved on.

First, the House of Representatives demanded

Roger Simon

that Wilson apologize again, and when he refused, the House passed a "resolution of disapproval" against him.

I watched the House debate figuring that at least one or two of the representatives would denounce Wilson for racism. But not a single one did.

Even President Obama, who could have used Wilson to create a "teachable moment" on race in America, did not. Instead, Obama said he "appreciated" Wilson's apology, though Obama did think the incident was an example of the "coarsening of our political dialogue."

It looked like things would move on. And then came Jimmy Carter, who seems to believe that if something is worth stating, it is worth overstating.

"I think an overwhelming portion of the intensely demonstrated animosity

toward President Barack Obama is based on the fact that he's a black man," Carter told NBC's Brian Williams.

I think it is impossible to disagree that some of the animosity directed against Obama is racist. You can't look at some of the disgusting signs that people have carried at protest marches and listen to some of the deplorable things people have said and believe otherwise.

But Carter has decided that "an overwhelming portion of the intensely demonstrated animosity" is racist.

I do remember that the extreme right wing also hated Bill Clinton, a white guy.

Also, having been in college in the late '60s, I do remember the extreme left wing hating not only some Republicans, but some Democrats, too. ("Hey, hey, LBJ, how many kids did you kill today?" was not a love song.)

So extreme feelings can be based on things other than race. And people can act rudely and not be racists.

But Jimmy Carter sees it differently when it comes to the attacks against Obama.

He could be right. But as

Jason Zengerle, a senior editor at the New Republic, wrote, if Carter "wants to help Obama, he should just shut up."

Why? Because Carter is describing an America that Obama says does not exist. Certainly there is racism in America, but Obama has always insisted that it is not as big a deal as some think. (And he was, after all, elected president. Let's not forget that as we scourge ourselves.)

Obama officially took issue with Carter through White House spokesman Robert Gibbs. "The president does not believe that the criticism comes based on the color of his skin," Gibbs said. "We understand that people have disagreements with some of the decisions that we've made."

So is it not race, but merely disagreement over decisions? Or does race still lurk? Along with rudeness. And extremism. And a coarsening of the political dialogue.

All of the above, anyone?

Roger Simon is the chief political columnist of politico.com, an award-winning journalist and a New York Times best-selling author.

Panel expands Rangel probe

By Larry Margasak
The Associated Press

WASHINGTON — The House ethics committee on Thursday expanded its investigation of Rep. Charles Rangel to include his belated financial disclosure of hundreds of thousands of dollars in previously unreported assets and income.

Rangel

and expanded several times while it pushes closer to the 2010 election year.

Republicans have forced House votes three times, the latest this week, on removing Rangel from his tax-writing position. While Democrats easily defeated each attempt, the issue has allowed Republicans to ridicule Pelosi's refrain that Democrats would drain the swamp of ethical misconduct that previously plagued Republicans.

The expansion only increases the political burden that the Ways and Means Committee chairman from Harlem places on House Speaker Nancy Pelosi, who refuses to make him step down from his post.

Pelosi and Majority Leader Steny Hoyer have said they would take no action while the ethics investigation of the New York Democrat is under way, but the inquiry has dragged on for a year

The committee said it would now investigate whether Rangel broke House rules "with respect to all financial disclosure statements and all amendments filed in calendar year 2009" as required under the Ethics In Government Act.

The law requires annual financial reports filed by all members of Congress showing ranges of assets and income.

WEDNESDAY, OCTOBER 21, 2009   12A

HIV vaccine loses luster

By David Brown
The Washington Post

WASHINGTON — The "modest" success of an HIV vaccine clinical trial in Thailand, trumpeted by researchers last month as a milestone in the AIDS pandemic, is turning out to be even more modest than originally advertised.

Full details of the study, released Tuesday at a scientific meeting in Paris, show that the vaccine provides no protection to people at the highest risk of HIV infection. In people at lower risk, the benefits may start to wane after a year. Furthermore, when the results of the three-year experiment are ana-

lyzed using alternative methods, the protective effect falls short of formal statistical significance.

Despite the new caveats, many AIDS researchers say the findings still are important.

"This is a modest effect at best, but I believe it has relevance and is a real effect that needs to be built upon," said Anthony Fauci, director of the National Institute of Allergy and Infectious Diseases, which paid for much of the $105 million study.

Some other observers, however, think the results have been oversold in a potentially damaging way.

"When this was rolled out a couple of weeks ago, it was

terribly hyped by the investigators," said Gregg Gonsalves, an AIDS activist for nearly two decades. "Some people think you have to dangle the slimmest morsels of hope in front of the general public in order to keep them interested in an AIDS vaccine. But I think that damages the credibility of the effort."

Initial results of the RV144 trial were revealed by press release and interview in late September. The presentation in Paris provided much more detail, as does a paper released simultaneously by the New England Journal of Medicine, where it will eventually be published.

The effort to make an HIV vaccine has been dogged by failure for two decades. The Thai trial, which employed a two-component vaccine and a total of six injections, was the first one to show protection. It was conducted principally by Thailand's Ministry of Public Health, the U.S. Army, and the Royal Thai Army.

The vaccine was tested in 16,402 Thai men and women. When the analysis included everyone, there was a trend suggesting that the vaccine provided protection, but the results were not statistically significant by the definition used in most medical research.

Election promises fade away

You may remember all those Obama campaign cheerleaders for change chanting, "Yes, we can!" during last year's campaign events.

This year, in the 10th month of his presidency, it doesn't really seem they can, or that he can. Nothing much has changed except the size of the federal budget deficit and the national debt, both swelling and swollen by the humongous bailout of Wall Street and the big banking corporations.

Any hope we would witness and celebrate a return to the rule of law after the departure of George W. Bush and his unindicted co-conspirators has long gone a' glimmering. President Barack Obama would rather face an uncertain future than look back at an ugly past.

Never mind this nation was founded on the concept that no man, however powerful, is above the law, not even a king.

The president-to-be promised a swift withdrawal from the Iraqi quicksand, but that hasn't come to pass, either. Instead, we witness a slow-mo pullout that will sort of end things on the Bush

Joe Galloway

administration's timetable of late 2011 for the last American combat troops to be gone, and God only knows when for the rest to leave. That's if the Iraqi parliament can pass a new election law in time for elections to be held on schedule in January.

Obama promised America's Devil's Island, the prison for terrorists and not-terrorists at Guantanamo Bay in Cuba, would be emptied and shut down by January 2010. That doesn't look very likely now, either.

There was the promise of real reform of our faltering and very expensive health care system, which doesn't cover upward of 49 million human beings. This administration would include a public option to provide competition for the insurance companies and a negotiating lever to lower

the price of pharmaceuticals.

Months were wasted as Blue Dog Democrats negotiated with Just Plain Dog Republicans on the Senate Finance Committee, supposedly trying to write a compromise health care bill that would attract some, a few, OK, just one, Republican vote to satisfy the desire for bipartisan support.

The White House sat back and let the Congress critters wheel and deal in the back room while the health care lobbyists poured more into the legislators' back pockets.

Candidate Obama, while promising to get us out of Iraq, also promised to refocus our attention on Afghanistan, the war long neglected by the Bush administration he said really mattered when it came to our national security.

When he got into office, the new president promptly threw in another 20,000 American troops the commanders said were urgently needed in Afghanistan. Now they're back lobbying for another 45,000.

Obama and his national security advisers are rethinking the whole Afghan thing, they say. Given their track record to date, can

there be any doubt they'll solomonically decide to cut the baby in half and call it a compromise?

We'll end up neither in nor out, with no hope of victory, even if some of the wise men could define what victory in Afghanistan might look like.

Those who elected Obama president hoped he would be an agent for desperately needed change in America. Turns out he's more of a politician, more a creature of Capitol Hill, than they could ever have imagined.

At a time when we need a display of raw courage and a commitment to lead America in a drive to reclaim what was right about our country and our people and restore a better vision of what we could become, instead we get compromise; we get a search for bipartisanship from those who will never deliver it; we get a bowl of mush in place of cojones.

I guess the answer really is: No, We Can't!

Joe Galloway is a syndicated columnist. Readers may write to him at Joe Galloway, P.O. Box 399, Bayside, TX 78340.

Stimulus job count inflated, data show

By Brett J. Blackledge and Matt Apuzzo
The Associated Press

WASHINGTON — A Colorado company said it created 4,231 jobs with the help of President Obama's economic recovery plan. The real number: fewer than 1,000.

A child care center in Florida said it saved 129 jobs with the help of stimulus money. Instead, it gave raises to its existing employees.

Elsewhere in the U.S., some jobs credited to the stimulus program were counted two, three, four or even more times.

The government has overstated by thousands the number of jobs it has created or saved with federal contracts under the $787 billion recovery program, according to an Associated Press review of data in the program's first progress report.

See STIMULUS, Page 4A
From Page 1A

The errors could be magnified Friday when a much larger round of reports is released. It is expected to show hundreds of thousands of jobs repairing public housing, building schools, repaving highways and keeping teachers on local payrolls.

The White House seized on an initial report from a government oversight board weeks ago that claimed federal contracts awarded to businesses under the recovery plan already had helped pay for more than 30,000 jobs. The administration said the number was evidence that the stimulus program had exceeded early expectations toward reaching the president's promise of creating or saving 3.5 million jobs by the end of next year.

But the 30,000 figure is overstated by thousands — at the very least by nearly 5,000, or one in six, based on AP's limited review of some of the contracts. Some federal agencies and recipients of the money provided incorrect job counts. The review found some counts were

more than 10 times as high as the actual number of jobs; some jobs were credited to stimulus spending when, in fact, none were produced.

The White House says it is aware there are problems. Ed DeSeve, an Obama adviser helping to oversee the stimulus program, said agencies have been working with businesses that received the money to correct mistakes. Other errors discovered by the public will be corrected, he said.

"If there's an error that was made, let's get it fixed," DeSeve said.

There's no evidence the White House sought to inflate job numbers in the report, but the administration embraced the flawed figures the moment they were released.

US AIRWAYS

Airline cutting jobs, flights

By Linda Loyd
The Philadelphia Inquirer

PHILADELPHIA — US Airways Group Inc. on Wednesday said it will cut 1,000 jobs next year, including 200 pilots, 150 flight attendants and 600 airport workers.

Many of the job cuts will be at Las Vegas, Boston and New York's LaGuardia airport.

US Airways will suspend five international destinations from Philadelphia next year — Birmingham and London Gatwick in the United Kingdom; Milan, Italy; Shannon, Ireland; and Stockholm, Sweden, which have not shown "economic resiliency or profitability" in the current economic downturn, Chairman and CEO Doug Parker said in a memo to employees.

The airline will drop its planned route to Beijing, which was postponed from 2009 to 2010. Now, the airline said it will return the route authority to the U.S. Department of Transportation "until economic conditions improve, while retaining the option to reapply for this authority in the future."

Once the changes are made, flights will be focused out of US Airways' hubs in Charlotte, Philadelphia, Phoenix and Washington's Reagan National Airport.

US Airways, in reporting a third-quarter loss of $80 million last week, said it planned to reduce international flying. The Tempe, Ariz., carrier lost $800 million in 2008 and Wednesday projected "another large loss for 2009."

US Airways will cut Las Vegas flights from 64 to 36 departures a day by February because of high fuel prices and "continued weak demand."

It will drop all flights to Wichita, Kan., and Colorado Springs, Colo.

Crew bases will be closed in Las Vegas and New York LaGuardia by Jan. 31 and in Boston by May 2. Some flight crews now based in those cities may fly out of Philadelphia in the future, an airline spokesman said.

Also Wednesday, American Airlines said it will close a maintenance base in Kansas City, Mo., and shrink other repair shops next September.

The moves will eliminate up to 700 jobs nationwide, The Associated Press reported.

THURSDAY, OCTOBER 29, 2009 **3A**

Auto lender GMAC looks for more aid

By Dan Strumpf
The Associated Press

NEW YORK — GMAC, the former lending arm of General Motors Co., is in talks with the Treasury Department for a third injection of taxpayer money.

The government mandated earlier this year that GMAC Financial Services raise an additional $11.5 billion in capital by early November after undergoing a "stress test" along with 18 other banks. While other banks deemed undercapitalized have been able to raise money from private investors, GMAC has been forced to go back to the government.

Separately, the company said Wednesday that the Federal Deposit Insurance Corp. would back a $2.9 billion debt offering.

GMAC is a crucial player in the U.S. auto industry, providing wholesale financing to many General Motors and Chrysler dealerships to pay for the vehicles on their lots. The company also operates a mortgage lending unit — Residential Capital — which has been pummeled by the housing market downturn. It also runs an insurance unit and an online banking unit called Ally Bank.

"Having a healthy GMAC is important to us," GM CEO Fritz Henderson said Wednesday, calling the lender "the source of financing" for GM and Chrysler.

A Treasury Department spokesman confirmed that the department is in talks with GMAC about a third helping of aid. The government already owns a 35 percent stake in GMAC after providing $12.5 billion to the lender. It also owns a majority stake in GM and a smaller stake in Chrysler.

Dismantling America

4 Nov 09

Just one year ago, would you have believed that an unelected government official, not even a Cabinet member confirmed by the Senate but simply one of the many "czars" appointed by the president, could arbitrarily cut the pay of executives in private businesses by 50 percent or 90 percent?

Did you think that another "czar" would be talking about restricting talk radio? That there would be plans afloat to subsidize newspapers?

Did you imagine that anyone would even be talking about having a panel of so-called "experts" deciding who could and could not get life-saving medical treatments?

How much of America would be left if the federal government continued on this path? How far the president will go depends of course on how much resistance he meets. But the direction in which he is trying to go tells us more than all his media spin.

Among the people appointed as czars by President Obama have been people who have praised enemy dictators, who have seen the public schools as places to promote sexual practices contrary to the values of most Americans.

Those who say that the

Thomas Sowell

Obama administration should have investigated those people more thoroughly before appointing them are missing the point. Why should we assume that Barack Obama didn't know what such people were like, when he had been associating with these kinds of people for decades before he reached the White House?

Nothing so epitomizes President Obama's contempt for American values and traditions like trying to ram two bills through Congress in his first year. That he succeeded only the first time says that some people are starting to wake up. Whether enough people will wake up in time to keep America from being dismantled, piece by piece, is another question — and the biggest question for this generation.

Thomas Sowell is a syndicated columnist. Readers may write to him at www.tsowell.com, at info@creators.com (with his name in the subject line) or Creators Syndicate, 5777 W. Century Blvd., Suite 700, Los Angeles, CA 90045.

Gay-marriage f...oes hold slight lead in Maine

4 Nov 09

By Glenn Adams and David Crary
The Associated Press

PORTLAND, Maine — Gay marriage appeared in danger in Maine in a closely watched referendum Tuesday that the nation's gay rights movement had hoped would yield a breakthrough victory at the ballot box.

Voters were asked to decide whether to repeal or affirm a state law that would allow gay couples to wed. The law was passed by the Legislature in May but never took effect because of a petition drive by conservatives.

With 481 of 608 precincts reporting, the pro-repeal side had 52 percent to 48 percent for gay-marriage's supporters.

A vote to uphold the law would mark the first time that the electorate in any state endorsed gay marriage. That could energize activists nationwide and blunt conservative claims that same-sex marriage is being foisted on states by judges or lawmakers over the will of the public.

However, repeal — in New England, the region of the country most supportive of gay couples — would be another heartbreaking defeat for the marriage-equality movement, following the vote against gay marriage in California a year ago.

It also would mark the first time voters had torpedoed a gay-marriage law enacted by a legislature. When Californians rejected same-sex marriage, it was in response to a court ruling, not legislation.

Maine's secretary of state, Matthew Dunlap, said turnout seemed higher than expected for an off-year election, and voter interest appeared intense. Even before Tuesday, more than 100,000 people — out of about 1 million registered voters — had voted by absentee ballot or early voting.

Five other states have legalized gay marriage — Iowa, Massachusetts, Vermont, New Hampshire and Connecticut — but all did so through legislation or court rulings, not by popular vote.

In contrast, constitutional amendments banning gay marriage have been approved in all 30 states where they have been on the ballot.

Both sides in Maine drew volunteers and contributions from out of state, but the money edge went to the campaign in defense of gay marriage, Protect Maine Equality. It raised $4 million, compared with $2.5 million for Stand for Marriage Maine.

MONDAY, NOVEMBER 2, 2009 **7A**

Prelude to drama

David Broder

WASHINGTON — The first key votes of the Obama era take place this week, not on the floor of the House or Senate, where health care legislation still languishes, but in Virginia, New Jersey and northern New York state, where President Obama's endorsements of threatened Democratic candidates will test his political clout a year after his own election.

Late polls say the odds are against R. Creigh Deeds, the Democratic state senator battling former Attorney General Bob McDonnell to hold the Virginia governorship that has been in Democratic hands for the past eight years.

Up the coast in New Jersey, Republican Chris Christie, a former U.S. attorney, has been the aggressor all year against Democratic Gov. Jon Corzine, the multimillionaire transplant from Wall Street. Corzine's vulnerability for not solving the state's chronic dependence on high property taxes could elect Christie. But New Jersey has a far more solid Democratic voter base than does Virginia.

The third contest is a special election in New York's 23rd Congressional District, crowding the Canadian border. Obama set up the race by appointing Rep. John McHugh, a moderate Republican, as his secretary of the Army.

Republican district caucuses turned to state Assemblywoman Dede Scozzafava, another moderate who fits the profile

of the district. But the man she beat for the Republican nomination, businessman Doug Hoffman, grabbed the Conservative Party nomination and became the favorite of many movement conservative leaders.

The open split on the Republican side has opened the way for Democrat Bill Owens. A win in the 23rd and a Corzine victory in New Jersey would go a long way toward salving the wounds of seeing Virginia follow its historical pattern of voting against the party occupying the White House.

Tuesday's voting is merely the curtain-raiser on a full year of Senate and statehouse races that will go a long way toward defining the landscape of Obama's political future.

The winners of these and other gubernatorial battles will have a large voice in the redistricting that will follow the 2010 census. With other major states facing Republican gubernatorial primaries and potential Democratic comebacks, there will be drama from coast to coast.

David Broder is a Washington Post columnist. Readers may write to him at davidbroder@washpost.com or Washington Post Writers Group, 1150 15th St. NW, Washington, D.C. 20071.

GOP
Republican

BIG WINS
4 Nov 09
in Virginia, New Jersey

AT A GLANCE

VIRGINIA

■ Republican Bob McDonnell easily won the state's governor's race as independent voters who last year delivered the state to President Obama shifted to the GOP, handing the party a convincing sweep of statewide offices.

NEW JERSEY

■ Moderate Republican Chris Christie ousted incumbent Gov. Jon Corzine, an unpopular Democrat for whom Obama personally campaigned. Christie became the first Republican to win a statewide contest in 12 years.

The envelope, please

2 Nov 09

WASHINGTON — Old Soviet joke: Moscow, 1953. Stalin calls in Khrushchev.

"Niki, I'm dying. Don't have much to leave you. Just three envelopes. Open them, one at a time, when you get into big trouble."

A few years later, first crisis. Khrushchev opens envelope 1: "Blame everything on me. Uncle Joe."

A few years later, a really big crisis. Opens envelope 2: "Blame everything on me. Again. Good luck, Uncle Joe."

Third crisis. Opens envelope 3: "Prepare three envelopes."

In the Barack Obama version, there are 50 or so such blame-Bush free passes before the gig is up. By my calculation, Obama has already burned through a good 49. Is there anything he hasn't blamed George W. Bush for? The economy, global warming, the credit crisis, Middle East stalemate, the deficit, anti-Americanism abroad – everything but swine flu.

This compulsion to atta his predecessor is as stale it is unseemly. Obama wa elected a year ago. He

Charles Krauthammer

became commander in chief two months later. He then solemnly announced his own "comprehensive new strategy" for Afghanistan seven months ago.

"My administration has heard from our military commanders, as well as our diplomats," the president assured us. "We've consulted with the Afghan and Pakistani governments, with our partners and our NATO allies, and with other donors and international organizations" and "with members of Congress. "

Obama is obviously unhappy with the path he

a considered readjustment of policies that have failed. In each war, quick initial low-casualty campaigns toppled enemy governments. In the subsequent occupation stage, two policy choices presented themselves: the light or heavy "footprint."

In Iraq and Afghanistan, we initially chose the light footprint. For obvious reasons: less risk and fewer losses for our troops, while reducing the intrusiveness of the occupation and thus the chances of creating an anti-foreigner backlash that would fan an insurgency.

This was the considered judgment of our commanders at the time, most especially Centcom commander (2003-2007) Gen. John Abizaid. It was a perfectly reasonable assumption, but it proved wrong. What they needed, argued Gen. David Petraeus against much Pentagon brass opposition, was population

longer for the Taliban to regroup, the failure of the light footprint did not become evident until more recently when an uneasy stalemate began to deteriorate into steady Taliban advances.

That's where we are now in Afghanistan. Obama is facing the same decision on Afghanistan that Bush faced in late 2006 in deciding to surge in Iraq.

In both places, the deterioration of the military situation was not the result of "drift," but of considered policies that seemed reasonable, cautious and culturally sensitive at the time, but ultimately turned out to be wrong. Which is evidently what Obama now thinks of the policy choice he made March 27.

He is to be commended for reconsidering. But it is time he acted like a president and decided. Afghanistan is his. He's used up his envelopes.

Price tag for health bill likely to top $1.2 trillion

By David Espo
The Associated Press

2 Nov 09

WASHINGTON — The health care bill headed for a vote in the House this week costs $1.2 trillion or more over a decade, according to numerous Democratic officials and figures contained in an analysis by congressional budget experts, far higher than the $900 billion cited by President Obama as a price tag for his reform plan.

While the Congressional Budget Office has put the cost of expanding coverage in the legislation at roughly $1 trillion, Democrats added billions more on higher spending for public health, a reinsurance program to hold

down retiree health costs, payments for preventive services and more.

Many of the additions are designed to improve benefits or ease access to coverage in government programs.

House Speaker Nancy Pelosi has referred repeatedly to the bill's net cost of $894 billion over a decade for coverage.

Asked about the higher estimate, Pelosi spokesman Brendan Daly said the measure won't "add one dime to the deficit."

Republicans put the cost of the bill at nearly $1.3 trillion.

"Our goal is to make it as difficult as possible for" Democrats to pass it, House

Republican leader John Boehner, R-Ohio, said at a news conference. "We believe it is the wrong prescription."

One day after announcing Republicans would have an alternative measure, Boehner offered few details.

He said it would omit one of the central provisions in Democratic bills — a ban on the insurance industry's practice of denying coverage on the basis of pre-existing medical conditions.

Instead, he said the Republicans would encourage creation of insurance pools for high-risk individuals and take other steps to ease their access to coverage.

Trouble ahead for Democrats?

6 NOV 09
FAYOBSER

WASHINGTON — A year after Barack Obama's election stirred broad hopes for change among American voters, persistent high unemployment and the spectacle of continued gridlock in Washington threaten Democratic dominance of the political landscape.

Tuesday's defeats in gubernatorial elections in Virginia and New Jersey not only ended a decade or more of Democratic gains in those states but signaled possible trouble ahead in the midterm elections at the national level.

At the same time, the loss of another Republican House seat in a special election — the fourth such defeat in the last two years — showed how bitter ideological conflict within the party could cripple the GOP's prospects for a comeback.

Despite White House efforts to discount the importance of the loss of the only two governorships on the off-year ballot, especially in New Jersey, where Obama had campaigned heavily for embattled Gov. Jon Corzine, the implications were clear to other Democrats.

Rep. Jim Cooper of Tennessee, a leader of the moderate-conservative "Blue Dogs," called the result "a

David Broder

wake-up call for Congress. A tidal wave could be coming."

His fellow Tennessean, Republican Sen. Lamar Alexander, said that Obama "retains his personal popularity, but his policies, and those pushed by the congressional Democrats, are scaring the daylights out of people."

Democratic pollster Peter Hart, in a memo to his clients, warned of the possible consequences of "the disappointment and disgust the American public feels toward Washington. It is as strongly negative as the period of 1979-80 and 1973-74." Both those cycles saw wholesale changes in Congress, the Democrats benefiting in the latter and the Republicans in the former.

For Obama and the Democratic congressional leadership, the off-year results arrived at a moment when their fragile internal coalitions are facing severe tests. The White House is

attempting to stage-manage a crucial vote-counting exercise in the House and Senate to determine if Democrats can risk bringing landmark health care bills to the floor. And within weeks, Obama may precipitate a similar test of support on a new policy toward Afghanistan.

Former Republican Rep. Vin Weber said he sees the Democrats in "a difficult position. A year ago, they thought they were entering a new progressive era. But within a couple months, it began to turn around, and worries about spending and big government came to the fore. In New Jersey and Virginia, we're seeing the voters return to a center-right agenda. But I think Obama and the Democratic congressional leaders are locked into that progressive agenda, and that leaves them in a risky position."

Weber conceded that "the grass-roots energy" fueling signs of a Republican comeback "can be destructive" when it is less well managed than it was in the two successful gubernatorial campaigns. In both New Jersey and Virginia, candidates with clear conservative histories and credentials, former prosecutors Chris Christie

and Bob McDonnell, focused their races on their opposition to higher taxes and their proposals for attracting jobs.

On the other hand, the GOP civil war that broke loose in New York's 23rd District special election resulted in the loss of a seat that had been Republican for more than a century.

Democrats have a larger worry: the unemployment crisis that crippled John McCain and the Republicans in 2008 is hanging on — and now is being blamed on Democrats.

Exit polls in New Jersey and Virginia showed that the more worried voters were about keeping or finding a job, the more likely they were to vote Republican.

Last week, I heard the lead economist for a major New York bank predict that unemployment next November will still linger at 9.5 percent or more.

If that is the case, this week's Democratic losses could seem minor by comparison.

David Broder is a Washington Post columnist. Readers may write to him at davidbroder@washpost.com or Washington Post Writers Group, 1150 15th St. NW, Washington, D.C. 20071.

331

TERRY SANFORD HIGH SCHOOL

Principal suspended amid grades probe

■ A spokeswoman says Diane Antolak is cooperating with an investigation into fraud allegations.

By Sarah A. Reid and Earl Vaughan Jr.
Staff writers

Diane Antolak has about 30 years of experience in education and has been principal of Terry Sanford since 2006.

The principal of Terry Sanford High School has been suspended with pay while officials investigate allegations of grade fraud, Superintendent Frank Till Jr. said.

Diane Antolak was suspended Wednesday and escorted off school grounds. Till would not discuss specifics about the allegations, but he said there was more than one. The allegations do not involve student-athletes, and the high school's sports eligibility is not affected, he said.

Till said he doesn't expect the investigation to take long.

"There should be no negative consequences for Terry

Principal

From **Page 1A**

Sanford," Till said.

Antolak said she could not comment on the suspension. She will continue to collect her $102,406 salary during the investigation.

"I trust the system. I trust Cumberland County," she said. "The process is a positive process. Sometimes, things need to be followed with procedures, and I support the procedure 100 percent."

Antolak is a veteran educator who has been principal of Terry Sanford — one of Cumberland County's highest-performing high schools — since 2006. She formerly was principal at Reid Ross Classical School.

She has about 30 years of experience in education, with 13 years spent in Cumberland County. She was largely credited with the success of Reid Ross after it opened in 1999.

Till has appointed Terry Sanford's assistant principal, Robert Guzman, to lead the school until the investigation is complete.

"I am treating this as if

Diane was sick," Till said. "He would be the senior person."

Till spent 30 minutes after school on Thursday with Terry Sanford faculty. He answered questions and informed them about the suspension, Till said.

Wanda McPhaul, a spokeswoman for the school system, said Antolak is cooperating in the investigation.

"Anytime there is a situation where a superintendent feels like an investigation should be warranted, generally an employee would be suspended with pay while that investigation is completed," McPhaul said.

Antolak is not allowed on school property until the investigation is complete, McPhaul said.

School board members reached by phone wouldn't discuss the situation. Chairman Greg West said he only knew that Antolak had been suspended.

Till will make a recommendation about Antolak's job to the school board, which will ultimately decide her fate.

Staff writer Sarah A. Reid can be reached at reids@fayobserver.com or 486-3569.
Staff writer Earl Vaughan Jr. can be reached at vaughane@fayobserver.com or 486-3519.

Report: Pool of recruits shrinking

6 Nov 09

■ Obesity or a lack of education are affecting the number of military applicants who are fit to serve.

By Henry Cuningham
Military editor

Three-fourths of young males in the United States are unfit to serve in the military due to obesity, poor health or education or criminal records, a study finds.

The report shows that North Carolina is worse than the national average in overweight youths and failure to graduate from high school on time.

However, the state traditionally ranks at the top of the nation in Army recruiting, which is probably largely due to the military presence and influence, officials said.

About 90 retired officers have come together in a project known as Mission: Readiness, Military Leaders for Kids. The group's report is "Ready, Willing, and Unable to Serve."

Retired Gen. Hugh Shelton of North Carolina is among the members. He has said technology is increasing the need for better qualified military recruits at the same time the number of qualified candidates is declining.

U.S. Secretary of Education Arne Duncan spoke Thursday in a news conference with several of the retired officials in Washington, D.C.

"A quality education is really an issue of national security," Duncan said. "If

Jobless rate at 26-year high

■ Unemployment hits 10.2 percent in October, and analysts expect it to rise further.

By Christopher S. Rugaber
The Associated Press

WASHINGTON — The unemployment rate has hit double digits for the first time since 1983 — and is likely to go higher.

The 10.2 percent jobless rate for October shows how weak the economy remains even though it is growing. The rising jobless rate could threaten the recovery if it saps consumers' confidence and makes them more cautious about spending as the holiday season approaches.

The October unemployment rate — reflecting nearly 16 million jobless people — jumped from 9.8 percent in September, the Labor Department said Friday. The job losses occurred across most industries, from manufacturing and construction to retail and financial

Economists say the unemployment rate could surpass 10.5 percent next year because employers are reluctant to hire.

President Obama called the jobs report another illustration of why much more work is needed to spur business creation and consumer spending. Noting legislation he's signing to provide additional unemployment benefits for laid-off workers, Obama said, "I will not rest until all Americans who want work can find work."

The government's monthly unemployment report is based on two surveys, one of households, one of companies' payrolls. The household survey showed that about 558,000 more people were unemployed last month than in September, raising the total to 15.7 million. The company survey, however, showed only a third as many job losses — 190,000.

The disparity can be explained by the fact that the company survey doesn't count people who are self-employed and undercounts employees of small businesses. That's why some analysts, like Diane Swonk,

chief economist at Mesirow Financial, say last month's household survey could be an ominous sign for the economy.

One struggling small business, Miller and Smith Inc., a home builder in McLean, Va., has trimmed its work force to about 97 from 350 at the height of the housing market in 2005. The company has been hurt by a slowdown in building and surging health care costs.

Miller and Smith faced a 44 percent increase in the cost of health insurance over the past year, which it managed to reduce to 23 percent.

"You can have ... one person get in a traffic accident on the weekend, and it completely blows your claim experience out of the water," Human Resources Director Selina Burke said.

Troubles for small businesses could have a disproportionate effect on the economy, because they account for about 60 percent of the nation's jobs. They tend to rely on credit cards and home equity lines to maintain their cash flow. Banks have tightened credit in many of these areas.

The 10.2 percent unemployment rate does not include people without jobs who have stopped looking for work or those who have settled for part-time jobs. If those people were counted, the unemployment rate would be 17.5 percent, the highest on records dating from 1994.

"It's not a good report," said Dan Greenhaus, chief economic strategist for New York-based investment firm Miller Tabak & Co. "What we're seeing is a validation of the idea that a jobless recovery is perfectly on track."

2010

Midterm elections bringing fear, hope

By Liz Sidoti
The Associated Press

WASHINGTON — Oh, how the tables have turned.

Nervous Democrats are on defense and emboldened Republicans sense opportunity heading into 2010 and the midterm elections. It was just three years ago that the GOP lost the House and Senate, as well as governors' races in a cross-country Democratic wave.

Now, with most states under their control and comfortable majorities in Congress, Democrats must protect far more seats than Republicans: 19 governors' mansions, 17 Senate seats and as many as 60 House districts in moderate-to-conservative regions and swing-voting areas.

At this point, Democrats must do it in a more difficult political environment than in 2006 and 2008.

President Obama clearly recognizes as much. One year after his historic victory, he pleaded for his backers to be patient and asked them to stick with him.

"The challenges might not be met in one year or one term," he said in a video message last week. "We're making progress."

Fear about the economy, and anger at incumbents are coursing through the country, while independents wary of government expansion and federal spending under the president they helped elect are shifting toward Republicans.

Democrats will be forced to explain votes and positions on the expensive economic stimulus plan, climate change legislation and, probably, the health care overhaul. Although Democrats have a popular president on their side, there are limits to Obama's clout; Democratic gubernatorial candidates in New Jersey and Virginia lost last week even though he campaigned for them.

Republicans hope to pick up seats by harnessing the sour public mood and voter wariness over Obama's policies. The GOP is re-energized but faces tension between conservatives and moderates over the party's direction, just as Democrats did between liberals and moderates when they were out of power.

The Republican Party also lacks a leader, though presidential aspirants such as Minnesota Gov. Tim Pawlenty, former Alaska Gov. Sarah Palin and former Massachusetts Gov. Mitt Romney are jockeying for position as they campaign and raise money for GOP candidates.

Most governor's seats, more than one-third of the Senate, all 435 House districts and state legislatures will be on the general election ballot.

7 Nov 2009

The 2009 'rump' rebellion

WASHINGTON — Sure, Election Day 2009 will scare moderate Democrats and make passage of Obamacare more difficult. Sure, it makes it easier for resurgent Republicans to raise money and recruit candidates for 2010. But the most important effect of Tuesday's elections is historical. It demolishes the great realignment myth of 2008.

In the aftermath of last year's Obama sweep, we heard endlessly about its fundamental, revolutionary, transformational nature. How it was ushering in an FDR-like realignment for the 21st century in which new demographics — most prominently, rising minorities and the young — would bury the GOP far into the future. One book proclaimed "The Death of Conservatism," while the more modest merely predicted the terminal decline of the Republican Party into a regional party of the Deep South or a rump party of marginalized angry white men.

This was all ridiculous from the beginning. 2008 was a historical anomaly. A uniquely charismatic candidate was running at a time of deep war weariness, with an intensely unpopular Republican president, against

Charles Krauthammer

a politically incompetent opponent, amid the greatest financial collapse since the Great Depression. And still he won by only seven points.

Exactly a year later comes the empirical validation of that skepticism. Virginia — presumed harbinger of the new realignment, having gone Democratic in '08 for the first time in 44 years — went red again. With a vengeance. Barack Obama had carried it by six points. The Republican gubernatorial candidate won by 17 — a 23-point swing. New Jersey went from plus 15 Democratic in 2008 to minus 4 in 2009. A 19-point swing.

What happened? The vaunted Obama realignment vanished. In 2009 in Virginia, the black vote was down by 20 percent; the under-30 vote by 50 percent. And as for independents, the ultimate prize of any realignment, they bolted. In Virginia and New Jersey they'd gone narrowly for Obama in '08.

This year they went Republican by a staggering 33 points in Virginia and by an equally shocking 30 points in New Jersey.

The Obama coattails of 2008 are gone. The expansion of the electorate, the excitement of the young, came in uniquely propitious Democratic circumstances and amid unparalleled enthusiasm for electing the first African-American president.

November '08 was one-shot, one-time, never to be replicated. Nor was November '09 a realignment. It was a return to the norm — and definitive confirmation that 2008 was one of the great flukes in American political history.

The irony of 2009 is that the anti-Democratic tide overshot the norm — deeply blue New Jersey, for example, elected a Republican governor for the first time in 12 years — because Democrats so thoroughly misread 2008 and the mandate they assumed it bestowed. Obama saw himself as anointed by a watershed victory to remake American life. Not letting the cup pass from his lips, he declared to Congress only five weeks after his swearing-in his "New Foundation" for America — from remaking the one-sixth

of the American economy that is health care to massive government regulation of the economic lifeblood that is energy.

Moreover, the same conventional wisdom that proclaimed the dawning of a new age last November dismissed the inevitable popular reaction to Obama's hubristic expansion of government, taxation, spending and debt as a raging rabble of resentful reactionaries, AstroTurf-phony and Fox News-deranged.

Some rump. Just last month, Gallup found that conservatives outnumber liberals by 2 to 1 (40 percent to 20 percent) and even outnumber moderates (at 36 percent). So on Tuesday, the "rump" rebelled. It's the natural reaction of a center-right country to a governing party seeking to rush through a left-wing agenda using temporary majorities created by the one-shot election of 2008. The misreading of that election is the fundamental cause of the Democratic debacle of 2009.

Charles Krauthammer is a Washington Post columnist. Readers may write to him at letters@charleskrauthammer.com or Washington Post Writers Group, 1150 15th St. NW, Washington, D.C. 20071.

Treading water sinks peace hopes

Haaretz, Tel Aviv, Israel, on Barack Obama's promise of peace in the Middle East:

A year after Barack Obama's election as president of the United States, it has become clear that, with regard to the Israeli-Arab conflict, the change he promised boils down to high-flown rhetoric and a confused policy. Instead of restarting negotiations on a final-status agreement between Israel and the Palestinians, and promoting the two-state solution with all his might, the world's greatest power is treading water in the swamp of the settlements.

Ever since the current Israeli government took office, the highest levels of the U.S. administration have been demanding that it completely halt construction in the settlements, as required by the road map peace plan. But Prime Minister Benjamin Netanyahu has refused to implement a total freeze.

Palestinian Authority President Mahmoud Abbas has made a freeze in settlement construction a precondition for resuming negotiations. In so doing, he relied on the American stance. But America's messages have been mixed.

The crisis of trust between Netanyahu and Abbas, and the huge gap between their positions, necessitates a determined and consistent American stance whose goal is to restart the negotiations and conclude them, instead of wasting time and prestige in endless discussions over empty formulas for limiting settlement construction.

The 'good war' not worth fighting

The Guardian, London, on Afghanistan:

The dimensions of the unfolding disaster in Afghanistan are becoming bigger and more daunting by the day. Once-staunch defenders of the "good war" are starting to break ranks. Kim Howells, a former Foreign Office minister with responsibility for Afghanistan and current chairman of the parliamentary intelligence and security committee, questions the central tenet of the government's case for fighting in Afghanistan: that it is the frontline of a war that would otherwise be conducted on British streets. Howells said counterterrorism would be better served by bringing the majority of servicemen home.

Afghanistan is a political failure, a fact over which the international community continue to be in denial. If they were not, neither America nor Britain would be toying with the notion that they can pressure Hamid Karzai into forming a clean government.

Barack Obama is now left clinging to one tarnished man to deliver the central plank of his fight against the Taliban and al-Qaida. And while he clings to him, any hope of re-centering aid efforts on local communities or on reforming parliament will be subverted just as the election was. Wait for the next announcement on troop levels. It will be groundhog day all over again.

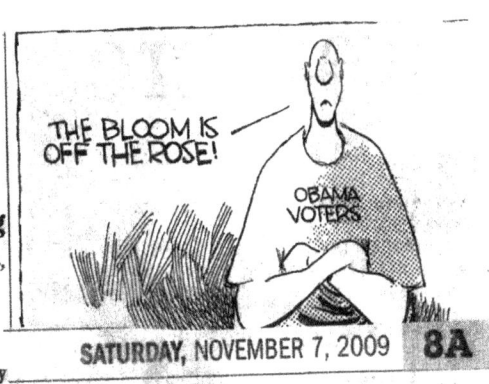

SATURDAY, NOVEMBER 7, 2009   **8A**

336

GUANTANAMO REPORT

Mistakes wipe out closure timetable

By Steven Thomma
McClatchy Newspapers

WASHINGTON — President Obama's decision to close the Guantanamo Bay, Cuba, military prison by Jan. 22 was followed by a series of mistakes and missteps by his administration that will delay the prison's closure for months, according to a report from a policy organization with close ties to the White House.

Those mistakes — which ranged from initially having too few people on board to handle the workload to misreading Congress — have put the timetable months behind schedule and will push the prison's closure well beyond the January deadline, which Obama announced with great fanfare two days after he took office.

The White House declined to comment on the report.

The administration is expected to announce within days the results of its review of legal cases against the remaining detainees at Guantanamo, a review that originally was scheduled to be finished in July. Among its conclusions, the administration is expected to say whether it will prosecute the accused mastermind of the Sept. 11, 2001, terrorist attacks.

"We hope we'll see the announcement very soon on the 9/11 case, that they're going to prosecute Khalid Sheikh Mohammed and the other conspirators in federal court," said Ken Gude, a scholar at the Center for American Progress and the author of its new report on Guantanamo. The liberal policy organization enjoys close relations with the Obama administration, which has hired several of its scholars for senior positions.

In his study, Gude said the White House made mistakes in implementing the high-profile Guantanamo policy from the very beginning.

A key problem was that the Obama administration was hours old and didn't have enough people to follow through quickly after Obama announced the closing plan. Those who were there couldn't find needed files quickly.

'Biggest mistake'

With little groundwork done to move some Guantanamo detainees to the U.S or elsewhere, the Obama administration made who Gude called its "biggest mistake" in April by asking Congress for $80 million t finance the prison closing.

"Asking Congress for money for Guantanam opened the door for conservatives on Capitol Hill, an the Obama administration was caught completely off guard when they began a gressively pushing ba against the funding," Gu said in his report.

Gude called the backla "ridiculous" because it w based on the implied argument that the country's maximum security prisons couldn't hold terrorists transferred from Guantanamo and that the closing of Guantanamo thus would endanger Americans.

Popularity not worth appearing weak

The world doesn't "like" us any better. They liked us fine before. They just need to be reminded. Ask a Frenchman if he speaks German, and if he says "no," reply "You're welcome." Remind him of the 60,757 Americans buried in France, giving their lives to restore France's freedom. The same throughout Europe: There are more than 104,000 American serviceman buried there. All we asked in return was a place to bury our dead. How many French, Dutch, Italians, Belgians or Brits are buried on U.S. soil, defending us against our enemies?

We don't ask for praise, but we don't need to apologize, which is what our president did on his recent trip overseas. And that deserves a peace prize? He has made us appear weak so, of course, they like us. Many other deserving people who have been mentioned in other letters have been passed over for this honor.

How about Obama staying home and making us feel better about ourselves?

Do we really care if the other countries like us? They want our money, they want to come to our country and not learn our language, and still accept our charity here also.

It may be that Rush Limbaugh speaks the truth you are afraid to hear. He's really quite intelligent and undeserving of name-calling.

Also the "motivational" speech given to school children? The final speech was totally different than originally planned. It was changed after many parents complained upon hearing it.

Mary Anne Lauer
Foxfire Village

USDA common sense flew the coop

The Oct. 21 article, "Farmer advocates want

Sammy Sosa, a whiter shade of male

Dear Sammy Sosa: Are you happy with yourself now? Are you more confident and self-assured? When you look in the mirror, do you like yourself better, now that you are white?

As you know, photos taken of you at an awards show earlier this month have the whole country talking. Last time we saw you, you were a brown man from the Dominican Republic, star slugger for the Chicago Cubs. Now you are white, facing the camera with a complexion strikingly reminiscent of Dracula's.

You claim you've been using a skin-softening cream and that it, combined with the bright lights under which the photos were taken, made your face look whiter than it is. Which is an extraordinarily lame excuse. Indeed, if that excuse were a horse, you'd shoot it.

While it is admirably metro-sexual of you to be so concerned with the softness of your skin, I must say: if I slathered something on my face that was supposed to render it tender and it left me looking like the Joker instead, I'd sue. You, on the other hand, are reported to be considering an endorsement deal.

"Skin softening" my fanny. "Skin bleaching" is more like it.

What's missing?

So I want to know if it's made you happy, being white, if it's given you what you felt you lacked. Me, I'd have thought you already had the brass ring by both hands: you were a handsome sports hero, had made beaucoup dollars, had the requisite gorgeous wife. What could be missing?

Whiteness, apparently.

You know how transsexuals will sometimes say they never felt at home

Leonard Pitts

in their original gender? Was that what it was like for you? Was there always a white man inside you trying to get out?

Sorry if I can't relate, Sammy, but I'm a child of the era when James Brown sang, "Say it loud! I'm black and I'm proud!" It was a seminal moment in the history of a nation, which had always taken for granted that negritude and pride were mutually exclusive. Those years found black people shrugging off the idea that they should be judged by what other people deemed beautiful. It was like a butterfly leaving a cocoon ... if butterflies wore Afros and dashikis.

We walked with a brand-new swagger in that era, Sammy, having buried the Negro — and all the attendant connotations of obsequious servitude and knowing your place — for good. From now on, we

AP file photo

Sammy Sosa says a cosmetic cream he uses to soften his skin is the reason for his lighter skin tone.

would be black. "Black is beautiful, baby," we said.

And it was possible to believe something fundamental had changed, that the Rubicon had been well and truly crossed.

Bitter pill

So you can imagine what a bitter pill the last 20 years or so have been for some of us, what a harsh lesson in the changeability of change. We spent those years watching Michael Jackson use creams and surgery to scrape Africa from his face; listening as "entertainers" made fortunes selling coonish caricatures of black life; cringing as black children decreed academic achievement synonymous with "acting white"; aching as teenage filmmaker Kiri Davis re-enacted the old "doll test" and found black children still choose white dolls as prettier or more desirable than black ones; and fuming as black people clung, stubbornly and stupidly, to the custom of referring to themselves by a certain six-letter epithet that begins with N.

But I'll bet you don't see any of that when you look in the mirror. I'll bet you don't see 400 years of internalized inferiority, little girls crying for lack of "good hair," black folks obsessively categorizing themselves by a color scheme which holds, in the words of the old saying, the lighter, the brighter, the better.

No, I'll bet you see a face you've always dreamt of seeing — white and smiling you. And I'll bet you're not embarrassed in the least. But that's all right, Sammy.

I'm embarrassed for you.

Leonard Pitts Jr. is a syndicated columnist. Readers may write to him at lpitts@herald.com or the Miami Herald, 1 Herald Plaza, Miami, FL 33132.

Cosmetics or self-image? *29Nov69*

Leonard Pitts

Please indulge me as I answer an e-mail from a guy named Dunbar.

It says in part:

"Your column on Sammy Sosa's skin cream use is off base and sends a wrong message. The issue is the man's character — not the color of his skin. Your column seemingly assumes he lightens his skin color out of shame and fails to recognize that he may simply be doing it out of vanity or his own sense of personal style. Plenty of fair-skinned people use skin-darkening creams, sun baths, tanning beds for that purpose and the only criticism leveled at them is vanity and stupidity for ignoring skin cancer warnings. The same should hold for Sammy.

"I think I know what point you are trying to make and that is a laudable one. But your delivery was clumsy and it might come across to some as 'methinks thee doth protest too much.'"

Dear Dunbar:

Thank you for writing. It's always a treat to receive such a thoughtful dissent.

Hope you don't mind my using your e-mail as a vehicle for revisiting my recent column on Sosa, the once-black former baseball star who now looks like a photo negative of himself.

I'm intrigued that you "think" you know what point I was trying to make. The fact that you have to guess, that it wasn't starkly obvious to you, suggests that what we have here is a gulf between life experiences. It brings to mind a parable to the effect that the rabbit and the bear will never agree on how threatening is the dog.

I'm going to assume — I apologize if I'm wrong — that you're not black. I say that because I've not yet encountered a single African-American reader who did not know immediately what my point was. My white readers were more likely to see me as chiding Sosa for what they regarded as a benign cosmetic choice, such as when they color their hair, inject Botox in their faces or lie under the sun to get a tan. From where they sit, it's the same when a black man lightens his skin.

I'm here to tell you: it isn't.

I'd like you to do something for me. Go to YouTube and look up a movie: "A Girl Like Me," directed by Kiri Davis.

The centerpiece of the film is a recreation of the old "doll test" conducted by a black psychologist, Dr. Kenneth Clark, in the 1940s. Clark found that black children, asked to choose between otherwise identical black and white baby dolls which one is "nice" and which one is "bad," overwhelmingly favored the white one. Davis found that nothing has changed, six decades later.

Why is that the nice doll, the unseen researcher asks a little boy. "Because she's white," he replies. Why does that one look bad, the researcher asks a girl. "Because it's black," the child says. Then the researcher asks this girl to indicate "the doll that looks like you."

She jiggles the white doll, obviously wanting to choose it. When she surrenders to reality and slides the black doll forward, it is with a deflated reluctance that sears you.

I submit that what you see in that moment is not a cosmetic preference. Rather, it is distressing evidence of how early and how profoundly the self-image of black children is maimed. We are taught from birth in a thousand ways, big and small, to hate the darkness of our very skin.

Some of us grow up to recognize and reject that brainwashing. But some of us are never able, no matter how many home runs they hit — or hit records they sell — to be at home in their God-given skin.

I understand if you can't understand. You and I discussing Sosa are like the bear and the rabbit discussing the dog. You see a cosmetic choice.

I'm afraid I see something else entirely.

Leonard Pitts Jr. is a syndicated columnist. Readers may write to him at lpitts@herald.com or the Miami Herald, 1 Herald Plaza, Miami, FL 33132.

339

Woods' weird week grows stranger

ORLANDO, Fla. — Tiger Woods strangely and suspiciously runs his car into a fire hydrant in front of his Isleworth House at 2:20 a.m. Friday and then hits a tree in his neighbor's yard. See what happens when you're in a rush to get to Best Buy for the Black Friday door-buster sale?

But, seriously, what an awful week it's been for Tiger.

He gets loudly booed at his alma mater (Stanford) during a speech at the Cal-Stanford football game (OK, so, the booing reportedly came from the Cal fans). He gets involved in a minor but mysterious car accident in front of his house and the world comes to a screeching halt for three hours when the news breaks Friday. And, worst of all, Tiger's on the cover of this week's National Enquirer, which accuses him of cheating on his wife Elin and having an affair with bombshell Rachel Uchitel.

Mike Bianchi

Here's hoping Tiger's superficial injuries from the car crash heal quickly and that the National Enquirer story turns out to be just scandalous tabloid gossip.

I don't know about you, but I've always loved Tiger because he represented all that is right about sports — on and off the course. Think about it: When's the last time you heard Tiger's name mentioned in relation to guns, drugs or sex?

How about never? The man has never embarrassed himself, his family or his sport.

Fortunately, it appears Tiger's chiseled body escaped serious physical harm in the car accident. I'm starting to wonder if his pristine reputation will remain unscathed as well.

Mike Bianchi is a columnist for the Orlando Sentinel.

GOLF

Tiger: Crash was my fault

■ The golf star refuses to talk to troopers for the third straight day.

By Fred Goodall
The Associated Press

WINDERMERE, Fla. — Tiger Woods finally gave his side of the story Sunday — on his Web site, not to police — and took the blame for an "embarrassing" car crash that gave him cuts, bruises and public scrutiny like never before.

His statement failed to clear up any questions about the middle-of-the-night accident outside his Isleworth estate in which his wife told police she used a golf club to smash the back windows of the Cadillac SUV to help him out.

"This situation is my fault, and it's obviously embarrassing to my family and me," Woods said on his Web site. "I'm human and I'm not perfect. I will certainly make sure this doesn't happen again."

Woods

The statement was posted around 2 p.m. Sunday, about an hour after Woods' attorney told the Florida Highway Patrol that for the third straight day golf's No. 1 player would be unavailable to talk to troopers.

This time, the meeting was not rescheduled.

Even so, Sgt. Kim Montes of FHP said troopers went to Woods' $2.4 million estate anyway, only for attorney Mark NeJame to turn them away. The attorney gave troopers Woods' driver's license, registration and insurance as required by law for such accidents.

Woods defends wife

Woods said the crash was a private matter, and he intended to keep it that way.

"Although I understand there is curiosity, the many false, unfounded and malicious rumors that are currently circulating about my family and me are irresponsible," he said. "The only person responsible for the accident is me. My wife, Elin, acted courageously when she saw I was hurt and in trouble. She was the first person to help me. Any other assertion is absolutely false."

Woods is scheduled to compete at his Chevron World Challenge, which starts Thursday in Thousand

See **TIGER**, Page 3C

340

Tiger

From Page 1C

Oaks, Calif., although his tournament director did not know Woods' status for the tournament — whether he would play or even attend.

Even with his first public comments on the 2:25 a.m. Friday accident, Woods left several questions.

■ Where he was going at that time of the night?

■ How did he lose control of his SUV at such a speed that the air bags didn't deploy?

■ Why were both rear windows of the Cadillac Escalade smashed?

■ If it was a careless mistake, why not speak to state troopers trying to wrap the investigation?

"We have been informed by the Florida Highway Patrol that further discussion with them is both voluntary and optional," Mark Steinberg, his agent at IMG, said in an e-mail. "Although Tiger realizes that there is a great deal of public curiosity, it has been conveyed to FHP that he simply has nothing more to add and wishes to protect the privacy of his family."

Woods' wife turned troopers away from their home in the exclusive gated community outside Orlando on Friday, the day of the accident, because she said he was sleeping. Steinberg called troopers en route to Woods' house on Saturday and postponed the meeting until Sunday.

"We're just continuing our traffic crash investigation," Montes said. "If we have somebody who we feel is pertinent to the investigation, then we will interview them."

She said the 911 caller was interviewed Saturday, and investigators might speak with other people who were at the scene as well.

The FHP released the 911 call from an unidentified neighbor on Sunday.

"I have a neighbor, he hit the tree. And we came out here just to see what was going on. I see him and he's laying down," the neighbor told dispatchers without ever identifying the victim as Woods.

Asked if the victim was unconscious, the neighbor replied, "Yes."

Part of the call were inaudible because of a bad connection. At one point, the voice of a woman is heard yelling, "What happened!"

"We're just trying to get the police here right now," the neighbor says to the woman. "We don't know what happened. We're figuring that out right now. I'm on the phone with the police right now."

According to the FHP accident report, Woods had just pulled out of his driveway when he struck a fire hydrant and then a tree. Woods said he had cuts, bruising and "right now I'm a little sore."

Montes said the Woods' car was towed for "safekeeping," and authorities have already documented where the damage is on the vehicle and the point of impact.

Tiger Woods, shown with his daughter Sam and wife Elin last week at the Stanford-California football game, is expected to discuss Friday's crash outside his home with Florida state troopers sometime today.
AP photo

341

Kill the bill and start over

30 NOV 09

The United States has the best health care in the world — but because of its inefficiencies, also the most expensive. The fundamental problem with the 2,074-page Senate health-care bill (as with its 2,014-page House counterpart) is that it wildly compounds the complexity by adding hundreds of new provisions, regulations, mandates, committees and other arbitrary bureaucratic inventions.

Worse, they are packed into a monstrous package without any regard to each other. The only thing linking these changes — such as 118 new boards, commissions and programs — is political expediency. Each must be able to garner just enough votes to pass. There is not even a pretense of a unifying vision or conceptual harmony.

The result is an overregulated, overbureaucratized system of surpassing arbitrariness and inefficiency. Throw a dart at the Senate tome:

■ You'll find mandates with financial penalties — the amounts picked out of a hat.

■ You'll find insurance companies (which live and die by their actuarial skills) told exactly what weight to give risk factors, such as

Charles Krauthammer

age. Currently insurance premiums for 20-somethings are about one-sixth the premiums for 60-somethings. The House bill says the young should pay at least one-half; the Senate bill, one-third — numbers picked out of a hat.

■ You'll find sliding scales for health-insurance subsidies — percentages picked out of a hat — that will radically raise income tax rates for middle-class recipients, among other crazy unintended consequences.

The bill is irredeemable. It should not only be defeated. It should be immolated, its ashes scattered over the Senate swimming pool.

Then do health care the right way — one reform at a time, each simple and simplifying, aimed at reducing complexity, arbitrariness and inefficiency.

First, tort reform. This is money — the low-end estimate is about half a trillion per decade — wasted

in two ways. Part is hemorrhaged into the legal system to benefit a few lawsuit winners and an army of rich malpractice lawyers such as John Edwards.

The rest is wasted within the medical system in the millions of unnecessary tests, procedures and referrals undertaken solely to fend off lawsuits — resources wasted on patients who don't need them and which could be redirected to the uninsured who really do.

Second, even more simple and simplifying, abolish the prohibition against buying health insurance across state lines.

Some states have very few health insurers. Rates are high. So why not allow interstate competition? After all, you can buy oranges across state lines. If you couldn't, oranges would be extremely expensive in Wisconsin, especially in winter.

And the answer to the resulting high Wisconsin orange prices wouldn't be the establishment of a public option — a federally run orange-growing company in Wisconsin — to introduce "competition." It would be to allow Wisconsin residents to buy Florida oranges.

Neither bill lifts the prohibition on interstate competition for health

insurance. Because this would obviate the excuse for the public option, which the left wing of the Democratic Party sees as the royal road to fully socialized medicine.

Third, tax employer-provided health insurance. This is an accrued inefficiency of 65 years, an accident of World War II wage controls. It creates a $250 billion annual loss of federal revenues.

This reform is the most difficult to enact for two reasons: The unions oppose it. And the Obama campaign savaged the idea when John McCain proposed it during last year's election.

Insuring the uninsured is a moral imperative. The problem is that the Democrats have chosen the worst possible method — a $1 trillion new entitlement of stupefying arbitrariness and inefficiency.

The better choice is targeted measures that attack the inefficiencies of the current system one by one and provide the funds to cover the uninsured without wrecking both U.S. health care and the U.S. Treasury.

Charles Krauthammer is a Washington Post columnist. Readers may write to him at letters@charleskrauthammer.com or Washington Post Writers Group, 1150 15th St. NW, Washington, D.C. 20071.

New president, same old mess

It is traditional to count our blessings this time of year, but given the general state of affairs and Washington's whole lot of talk and no action, it's hard to get into the holiday spirit.

Harder still if you are one of the many in the unemployment lines or one of the many who are cleaning out the shelves of the charity food pantries so their children don't go hungry.

The national treasury is pretty much empty and our line of credit with China is drying up. We still have plenty of paper and ink, though, and the Treasury's printing presses are running 24/7 with no sign of falling apart. The dollars they crank out are sinking like the Titanic, and gold is at $1,300 an ounce and rising fast.

Our new president is either snake-bit or vampire-bit and hasn't managed to keep even a token number of his campaign promises. But that's about to change with the Decider act on Afghanistan, when he will up the ante by an additional 34,000 U.S. troops, bringing our total investment in a losing situation to more than 100,000 by the time they all get there next year.

He did promise to do something about that 8-year-old war, and he did not promise that it would be the right something.

Joe Galloway

Health-care reform — which was supposed to be passed and signed into law by last August — isn't even halfway done yet and will likely be pushed off to next year.

Poor state of health

Our president left this badly needed fix to our broken-down health care system to the tender mercies of a Congress largely bought and paid for by the big health care and pharmaceutical and insurance corporations.

Predictably, they have neutered the bills of any real possibility of reform, turning even the thought of a public option alternative to the robber barons into an exercise in Socialism, Communism and Nazism.

Like nobody in America ever heard of Medicare or the Veterans Administration medical system — both very popular programs run by and paid for by the big bad government.

What's the point in having a Democrat in the White House and Democratic majorities in both houses of Congress if they are all going to act like Republicans?

The new president arrived on the scene in the middle of a very scary recession triggered by the unabashed greed and incompetence of a bunch of Wall Street bankers and brokers and insurers. A trillion dollars of taxpayer money was flung at them on the grounds that they were "too big to fail," and reforms were promised that would restore some semblance of order and legality to what had become a nest of pirates and looters.

Now we approach end-of-the-year bonus time on Wall Street and you can believe the bankers and brokers are already salivating as they wait for their millions in ransom money to arrive.

Nothing has been reformed. Nothing has been done to keep the thieves from doing it all over again. They feel quite secure if no one else in America does. After all, the new president put some of Wall Street's favorite handmaidens in charge of the Treasury, the Securities Exchange Commission, and our very economy itself.

Happy days are here again. Or still.

Now, let's turn back to Afghanistan. There are several good reasons that sending 34,000 more U.S. troops there is a very bad decision. The terrorist enemy they are supposedly going there to fight, al-Qaida, isn't there at all. They are really going there to fight the Taliban, who are 100 percent Afghan, on behalf of one of the most corrupt governments we have ever installed anywhere.

We have politely asked President Hamid Karzai and his kleptomaniacs to stop stealing most of the millions we've sent to help rebuild a country torn apart by four decades of war. We've asked Karzai to counsel his family to get out of the opium and heroin trade. They've all promised to do much better and no doubt they will.

So billions more of the money we can't afford will be poured down the Afghan rat hole, and hundreds more fine young American men and women will die and thousands more will be injured or wounded in pursuit of an impossible dream.

If this is the best the new president and his Congress can do, then God help us. We might just as well have kept George W. Bush and Dick Cheney for another four years. Nobody's hopes would have been dashed with those guys.

Joe Galloway is a syndicated columnist. Readers may write to him at Joe Galloway, P.O. Box 399, Bayside, TX 78340.

15 DEC 09
Fay OBSERVER

Tiger's crash makes sponsors wary

By Emily Fredrix
The Associated Press

The self-destruction of Tiger Inc. is calling into question whether companies can afford the risk of signing multimillion-dollar contracts with celebrity endorsers.

Done right, celebrity endorsers can help boost both the sale of products and their maker's image. But Woods' hasty and stunning downfall shows how quickly things can sour when a superstar athlete's life choices are exposed in a negative light by today's real-time tabloid news culture.

Woods and his advisers spent years cultivating a good-guy image to go along with his winning ways, which is how he became sports' first — and perhaps last — $1 billion earner. It's also what has made his fall even more jarring.

"The billion-dollar athlete might be a thing of the past," said Laura Ries, president of marketing consulting firm Ries & Ries. Companies "want a safe choice and it seems like there's almost no safe choice out there."

Most of Woods' $100 million in annual earnings came not from tournament winnings but from companies like Accenture that wanted to be associated with his persona. These image ads are the types that are least likely to endure. Ultimately that could mean few other sports figures will follow in Tiger Woods' footsteps.

"There has to be trust and he's just taken a grenade to any kind of traditional agreement that you'd normally have," said John Sweeney, director of sports communication at the University of North Carolina at Chapel Hill's School of Journalism and Mass Communication.

Accenture severed ties with Woods on Sunday, two days after he announced an indefinite leave from golf to work on his marriage after admitting infidelities. It said

> 'The billion-dollar athlete might be a thing of the past. Companies want a safe choice and it seems like there's almost no safe choice out there.'
>
> **Laura Ries, marketing expert**

he was "no longer the right representative" of the company's values.

That's not surprising since the global consulting firm had pinned its entire identity on the golfer and bragged that he embodied Accenture's values of perfection and integrity.

AT&T said it is also is evaluating its relationship with Woods, as is Swiss watchmaker Tag Heuer.

Procter & Gamble's Gillette brand announced over the weekend it was distancing itself from him by not airing ads featuring Woods. Nike, PepsiCo Inc.'s Gatorade and EA Sports say they are standing by him.

Other companies are likely to use the implosion of Tiger Inc. as a warning that they must closely scrutinize all off-the-field behavior of any sports star they're considering hiring and just how much benefit they're getting.

Even then, they'll likely be wary of ads that bank on a celebrity's image and instead go for that star's endorsement of a product.

"Brands continually will come back to individuals who they believe will help them sell more product," said Rick Burton, former chief marketing officer of the United States Olympic Committee and now a sports marketing professor at Syracuse University.

"The capitalism of all this is if Tiger can help somebody sell a brand in the future, they're going to use Tiger."

344

PAMALEE DRIVE AND HELEN STREET

7 JAN 10
FAYO85

MAN KILLED IN WRECK; CHASE SUSPECT SOUGHT

■ A man fleeing police in a stolen pickup causes a fatal crash and runs from the scene.

By Nancy McCleary
Staff writer

John Velandra was scheduled to teach a class Wednesday at Highland Presbyterian Church, where he was in charge of health and wellness.

Instead, his friends were mourning the loss of the personal trainer known for caring passionately about his work and clients.

Velandra was killed early Wednesday by a man who was speeding from police in a stolen pickup.

The driver has been identified as Percyful Junior Mcintyre, 24, according to WRAL-TV in Raleigh.

After the collision at Pamalee Drive and Helen Street, Mcintyre ran from the scene and hadn't been found as of Wednesday night.

The pickup was reported

See **WRECK**, Page 4A

John Velandra who was killed in Wednesday' wreck, was the fitness director at Highland Presbyterian Church.

Wreck: Personal trainer killed in crash recalled as 'caring fellow'

From Page 1A

stolen at 5:15 a.m. by a woman who lives on Ingleside Drive in LaGrange, said police Lt. Chris Davis. The woman's husband briefly followed the truck, a Ford F-150, Davis said.

The truck drove through the Cottonade and Firefox neighborhoods to Santa Fe Drive, Davis said. The driver nearly crashed at the Bragg Boulevard intersection, Davis said. At some point, one of the truck's tires went flat, but the man kept driving to Johnson Street, to Blanton Road and to Pamalee Drive.

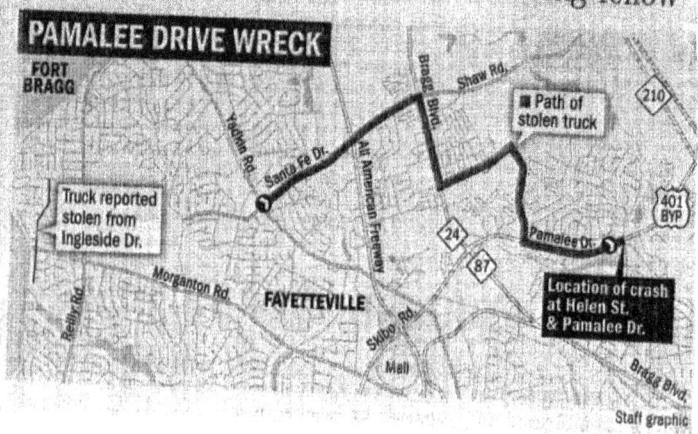

PAMALEE DRIVE WRECK

FORT BRAGG

Truck reported stolen from Ingleside Dr.

■ Path of stolen truck

Location of crash at Helen St. & Pamalee Dr.

FAYETTEVILLE

Staff graphic

WRECK—CONTINUED

Speeds reached about 70 mph during the pursuit, and the man drove through red lights and stop signs, Davis said.

Two police officers blocked Pamalee Drive and Helen Street ahead of the chase, Davis said. Their patrol cars, with the blue lights activated, were parked to stop traffic from Helen Street and Cain Road.

As the chase reached the Helen Street intersection, the pursuing officers slowed as they saw that the signal for traffic on Pamalee Drive had turned red, Davis said.

Velandra, driving a Chrysler PT Cruiser, had stopped for a red light at Helen Street, a couple of blocks from his home on Swann Street. He pulled into the intersection when the light turned green, into the path of the speeding pickup. It was not known why Velandra drove around one of the police vehicles.

Velandra, a member of Manna Church, was in charge of the health and wellness programs offered through Highland Presbyterian, said the Rev. Ernie Johnson of Highland Velandra also worked with clients at his business, Designs by Fitness & CrossFit Cape Fear.

Velandra had done personal training since 1985 and started the business in 1997, according to his Web site.

"He was a caring fellow who took his work seriously," Johnson said. "We're going to miss him. He had a preacher's heart."

For several years, Velandra was a contributing columnist on health and fitness issues for NEXT! magazine, published by the Fayetteville Publishing Co.

Davis said the police officers involved in the chase followed proper procedures, which include using two vehicles — one to pursue, and one to handle radio traffic. The officers were put on administrative duty until an internal investigation is completed, Davis said.

Staff writer Nancy McCleary can be reached at mcclearyn@fayobserver.com or 486-3568.

FRIDAY, JANUARY 8, 2010 B

Suspect in wreck surrenders

Percyful McIntyre has a record of vehicle break-in charges

By Nancy McCleary
Staff writer

The man wanted for causing a fatal traffic accident in a stolen pickup in Fayetteville turned himself in to police Thursday night.

Percyful Junior McIntyre, 24, of Yucca Court, turned himself in at the Fayetteville Police Department about 9:30 p.m., according to a news release from the department.

Police had been looking for McIntyre since Wednesday morning, after he allegedly fled the scene of the fatal crash at the intersection of Pamalee Drive, Helen Street and Cain Road. Police had been chasing the stolen pickup when it plowed into a car driven by John Velandra, 43, of Swann Street.

Police said McIntyre ran from the scene while officers tended to

McIntyre

Velandra, who was pronounced dead at Cape Fear Valley Medical Center.

Officers had used dogs to search for McIntyre but were unsuccessful.

On Thursday, before McIntyre turned himself in, his mother, Paulette McIntyre, said she had not heard from her son and she didn't know where he was.

She declined further comment.

McIntyre, who is unemployed, has had several scrapes with the law, according to court records.

He was charged in June 2006 with breaking into a motor vehicle and conspiracy, but those charges were dismissed in Cumberland District Court, according to records.

McIntyre did plead guilty to tampering with a vehicle, which is a misdemeanor.

The law defines tampering as secretly altering or breaking any parts of a vehicle or entering a vehicle with the intent to tamper with any parts.

McIntyre was ordered to pay

See WRECK, Page 4B

THE FAYETTEVILLE OBSERVER

InBrief

MARYLAND

Baltimore mayor takes plea, resigns

BALTIMORE — Mayor Sheila Dixon resigned as part of a deal with prosecutors Wednesday.

Dixon, 56, was convicted last month of misappropriating about $500 in gift cards donated to the city for needy families during her time as City Council president.

On Wednesday, she pleaded guilty to a perjury charge for failing to disclose thousands of dollars in gifts from her ex-boyfriend, a developer who received tax breaks from the city.

Dixon

Voters look for change

STATE OF THE UNION

■ President Obama's supporters see a more realistic leader who has learned from his failures.

By Adam Geller
The Associated Press

WASHINGTON — It was billed as President Obama's best, maybe even his last, chance. After a year of frustrated ambition and sinking poll numbers, he stepped before Americans to lay out plans for starting over again.

But when Dolores Earle, a retired accountant in the Chicago suburb of Brookield, Ill., settled into her recliner for Obama's State of the Union address, she heard and saw it very differently.

If Obama was going to recast his presidency, she wanted to hear a leader who'd learned some lessons from the lumps he'd taken.

A year ago, Obama "was

AP file photo

President Obama delivers his State of the Union address on Capitol Hill in Washington on Wednesday.

icans with a chance to take fresh measure of the substance and style, the accomplishments and aspirations of the nation's leader.

But when the president stepped to the podium in the House chamber last week, Earle and many other voters

— from the failure to pass health care reform to high unemployment — greatly tempered those expectations.

Scrutiny

And so instead, voters scrutinized Obama's tone

willing to fight for a more incremental version of the change he promised.

Earle was among hundreds of American who gave Obama high approval marks in an Associated Press-GfK poll conducted in early February 2009, just days after he took office. During a euphoric electoral honeymoon that now seems far more distant than a year ago, 67 percent of Americans approved of Obama's handling of the presidency, and just one in four disapproved.

A year later, a poll conducted by AP-GfK in the days leading up to the State of the Union tells a very different story. Obama's approval rating has fallen to 56 percent, and the number of those who disapprove has jumped to 42 percent.

The diminished expectations are clear in conversation with voters who were among the president's strongest sup-

MONDAY, FEBRUARY 1, 2010 **6A**

NATION

FRIDAY, JANUARY 15, 2010   3A

Fay Obs, NC

Colleges tighten admissions

■ Budget crunches mean caps on enrollment and cuts in classes.

By Terence Chea
The Associated Press

SAN FRANCISCO — College applicants are facing one of the toughest years ever to gain admission to the nation's public colleges and universities as schools grapple with deep budget cuts and record numbers of applications.

As cash-poor state governments slash budgets, colleges are capping or cutting enrollment despite a surge in applications from high school seniors, community college students and unemployed workers returning to school.

The increased competition means more students will be turned away, forced to attend pricier private institutions or shut out of college altogether.

Colleges that previously accepted all qualified students are becoming selective, while selective schools are becoming more so. Most community colleges have open-access policies, but demand for classes is so intense that many students can't get the courses they need.

"We're hearing a lot of panic," said

@

■ Check your e-mail in the morning for top stories.
Sign up for @lerts at fayobserver.com.

Gerna Benz, a partner at California San Francisco Bay Area College Planning Specialists.

Benz is encouraging more families to consider private colleges, which may be more expensive but offer less crowded classes and the chance to graduate in four years.

Applications to private colleges are holding steady, while public universities around the country are seeing record demand as cost-conscious families look for good value, said Barmak Nassirian, associate executive director of the American Association of Collegiate Registrars and Admissions Officers.

Low-income, minority students could face the roughest road to admission because they often can't afford private colleges and don't have the resources or academic credentials to compete with students from wealthier families and better high schools, he said.

The caps could also threaten President Obama's goal of making the U.S. the leader in college attainment by 2020, college officials say.

"We're reducing enrollment when we should be increasing it," said Scott Lay, president of the Community College League of California. Experts say states should increase access to college during a recession so that unemployed workers can train for new jobs.

Don't ask: Readiness comes first

WASHINGTON — Repealing "Don't ask, don't tell" may be the right thing to do, but there's only one reason to do it: military effectiveness.

Yet, repeatedly, we hear the argument that disallowing gays and lesbians to be "openly gay" in the military is a denial of their civil rights. This argument isn't only mistaken, it is misplaced. Approaching DADT as a civil rights issue is appealing and convenient, but it's really not quite that. Or rather, it isn't only that.

The military may be a microcosm of society in some ways, but it most definitely is not a democracy. Individuals don't have the usual rights that we honor in civilian society and, in fact, forfeit their freedoms when they wear the uniform.

If you want to test free speech rights, try criticizing your commanding officer.

This issue is so fraught with emotion and personal conflict that it's difficult to summon the necessary dispassion. It feels silly and patronizing to say that gays and lesbians are equal to the task of serving in the military, because it is so obvious and true.

Moreover, gays and lesbians already have served honorably and valiantly, so

Kathleen Parker

what, one might ask, is the big deal?

Then again, is that really the most relevant question? Given the nature of the military, the more pressing concern is whether changing the current policy will enhance military performance.

In combat, unit cohesion is crucial. Whether serving as "openly gay," the definition and ramifications of which remain unclear, will affect that cohesion is the great X-factor — the thing that can't be measured or fully understood in advance. The enlightened views of a few urban dwellers for whom "unit cohesion" is an abstraction are not necessarily useful to the debate.

Does the fact that society as a whole has become more accepting of gays mean that the military environment will be equally welcoming? Or will we see special training camps for guys who just can't get with the program?

I posit these questions with open heart and mind. As

a civilian without military experience, I accept my limitations in making such judgments, but would urge those contemplating a new policy to check that their motivations are moored to military rather than civilian imperatives.

There's no question that attitudes toward gays have relaxed in the 16 years since "Don't Ask, Don't Tell" was passed. A new generation of Americans has been raised to respect and accept gays and lesbians without prejudice. Views also have softened among older Americans, including Defense Secretary Robert Gates and Joint Chiefs Chairman Mike Mullen, who favor repealing DADT.

Even my Marine vet brother, who survived Khe Sanh in 1968, insisted for years that gays would have been a huge problem in Vietnam. Today he says: "Gay schmay. If he has the guts to go through the things I did, then good for him. ... No doubt we all served with gay guys and never knew it. Gays aren't stupid and they darn sure know who is friendly and who isn't. I say leave it to the troops and forget about it."

The operative words in his mellower assessment may be "never knew it," which remain central to arguments in favor of keeping DADT intact.

Among sober arguments favoring repeal of the current law is the particular idiocy of banning or removing someone who is otherwise useful to the military only because of sexual orientation. The several Arabic-speaking gays who were scrubbed when the military was sorely lacking in communications personnel in Iraq come to mind.

Equally absurd is the notion that gays cannot abide by the same rules against fraternization as heterosexuals. There's simply no evidence that gays are less able to control their libidos than are heterosexuals.

More questions remain than can be posed, much less answered, in this space, and Gates may need every minute of the 11 months he has requested to study the issue. Whatever one's personal opinion, the guiding principle should be only what is best for military effectiveness.

"Be all that you can be" was a nice recruiting slogan, but the military really is not about you. And the right to serve belongs to no one.

Kathleen Parker is a syndicated columnist. Readers may write to her at kathleenparker@washpost.com or the Washington Post Writers Group, 1150 15th St. NW, Washington, D.C. 20071.

The peasant revolt of 2010

WASHINGTON — "I am not an ideologue," protested President Obama at a gathering with Republican House members last week. Perhaps, but he does have a tenacious commitment to a set of political convictions.

Compare his 2010 State of the Union to his first address to Congress a year earlier. The consistency is remarkable. In 2009, after passing a $787 billion (now $862 billion) stimulus package, the largest spending bill in galactic history, he unveiled a manifesto for fundamentally restructuring the commanding heights of American society — health care, education and energy.

A year later, after stunning Democratic setbacks in Virginia, New Jersey and Massachusetts, Obama gave a stay-the-course State of the Union address (a) pledging not to walk away from health care reform, (b) seeking to turn college education increasingly into a federal entitlement, and (c) asking again for cap-and-trade energy legislation. Plus, of course, another stimulus package, this time renamed a "jobs bill."

This being a democracy, don't the Democrats see that clinging to this agenda will march them over a cliff?

Well, they understand it through a prism of two

Charles Krauthammer

cherished axioms: (1) The people are stupid and (2) Republicans are bad. Result? The dim, led by the malicious, vote incorrectly.

Liberal expressions of disdain for the intelligence and emotional maturity of the electorate have been, post-Massachusetts, remarkably unguarded. New York Times columnist Charles Blow chided Obama for not understanding the necessity of speaking "in the plain words of plain folks," because the people are "suspicious of complexity." Counseled Blow: "The next time he gives a speech, someone should tap him on the ankle and say, 'Mr. President, we're down here.' "

A Time magazine blogger was even more blunt about the ankle-dwelling mob, explaining that we are "a nation of dodos" that is "too dumb to thrive."

Obama joined the parade in the State of the Union address when, with supercilious modesty, he chided himself "for not

explaining it (health care) more clearly to the American people." The subject, he noted, was "complex." The subject, it also might be noted, was one to which the master of complexity had devoted 29 speeches. Perhaps he did not speak slowly enough.

Then there are the emotional deficiencies of the masses. Nearly every Democratic apologist lamented the people's anger and anxiety, a free-floating agitation that prevented them from appreciating the beneficence of the social agenda the Democrats are so determined to foist upon them.

That brings us to Part 2 of the liberal conceit: Liberals act in the public interest, while conservatives think only of power and self-interest.

It is an old liberal theme that conservative ideas cannot possibly emerge from any notion of the public good. The belief in the moral hollowness of conservatism animates the current liberal mantra that Republican opposition to Obama's social democratic agenda — which couldn't get through even a Democratic Congress and powered major Democratic losses in New Jersey, Virginia and Massachusetts — is nothing but blind and cynical obstructionism.

By contrast, Democratic opposition to George W. Bush — from Iraq to Social

Security reform — constituted dissent. And dissent, we were told at the time, including by candidate Obama, is "one of the truest expressions of patriotism."

No more. Today, dissent from the governing orthodoxy is nihilistic malice. "They made a decision," explained David Axelrod, "they were going to sit it out and hope that we failed, that the country failed" — a perfect expression of liberals' conviction that their aspirations are necessarily the country's, that their failure is therefore the nation's.

Then comes Massachusetts, an election Obama himself helped nationalize, to shatter this most self-congratulatory of illusions.

For liberals, the observation that "the peasants are revolting" is a pun. For conservatives, it is cause for uncharacteristic optimism. No matter how far the ideological pendulum swings in the short term, in the end the bedrock common sense of the American people will prevail.

The ankle-dwelling populace pushes back. It re-centers. It renormalizes. Even in Massachusetts.

Charles Krauthammer is a Washington Post columnist. Readers may write to him at letters@charleskrauthammer.com or Washington Post Writers Group, 1150 15th St. NW, Washington, D.C. 20071.

The paradox of black war heroes

Leonard Pitts

I t is the enduring paradox of our centuries here.

It is the paradox that stood its ground at Bunker Hill, paradox that made a doomed charge on Fort Wagner, paradox that stormed San Juan Hill, advanced through the Meuse-Argonne, landed on Iwo Jima, liberated Seoul and was taken prisoner in Hanoi.

It is the paradox: black men, will you defend America? Leave skin and blood in foreign lands fighting for ideals that do not include you?

Ideals like, We hold these truths to be self-evident that all men are created equal.

And, One man, one vote. And, Liberty and justice for all.

That paradox suffuses "For Love of Liberty," a moving new documentary airing this month — Black History Month — on some PBS stations. The program is a valuable compendium of black military history. Through narration and dramatic readings, a host of

their country called.

We get the runaway slave Crispus Attucks becoming the first person to die for American independence, and 5-foot-4 130-pound Pvt. Henry Johnson single-handedly driving off two dozen German attackers. We get Staff Sgt. Ruben Rivers, broken bone poking through his skin, refusing to be evacuated, refusing morphine, and leading his men against the Nazis in a battle that took his life. We get Pvt. Milton Olive throwing himself on a grenade in Vietnam. We get tombstones, reminding us that freedom bears a price.

But over, amid and above all that, we get the paradox.

One story paints the picture: It seems that

traveling by train through Louisiana. They were denied service in the dining area of a local cafe, given sandwiches and sent to eat them in a room off the kitchen. As they ate, the men watched through the window as German prisoners of war and the white soldiers guarding them entered the same dining area to be seated and served.

As one of the black men asked in a letter to a military magazine: "What is the Negro soldier fighting for? On whose team are we playing? I stood outside looking in, but could not help to ask myself these questions. Are these men sworn enemies of this country? Are we not American soldiers sworn to fight and die, if need be, for this, our country? Then why are the Germans treated better than we are?"

From time to time in this country, one hears people — sometimes implicitly, sometimes explicitly — question the patriotism, the "American-ness" of African-American

Barack Obama and, by extension, those of us who look like them, were insufficient in their love of country, lacking in fealty to its highest ideals.

It is always ... enlightening to be lectured on love of country by those whose heritage includes no paradox. One hopes a few of them will chance upon this program or its DVD.

One hopes they will see the stories of valor, watch American Marines denied seating at a table to which even Nazis are welcome, and marvel at the sheer love of country this bespeaks. Not love for the country as it is, but love for what it could someday be.

One hopes they will understand how much such love it takes to defy the paradox. Black men, it asks, will you defend America? Leave skin and blood in foreign lands fighting for ideals that do not include you? And always, the answer has been the same. Yes.

Leonard Pitts Jr. is a syndicated columnist. Readers

Instruction in Hydromatic Full Feathering Propeller, Chanute Field, Rantoul, Ill.

CHANUTE
AFB, ILL
PROPELLER
SCHOOL
ME
1953
USAF

SHAW UNIVERSITY BASKETBALL

BRIAN
#22
SENIOR
90-91
SEASON

MILDRED+MOM 1987 W.VA

Our dark history of coal

24 April 2010 Fayetteville Observer

By Scott Martelle

Watching the events unfold around Massey Energy Co.'s Upper Big Branch coal mine the last few weeks created an uneasy sense of deja vu. And it had less to do with 29 miners' bodies below ground than with power plays and corporate hubris above it.

The deadly West Virginia mine explosion came four days after the 100th anniversary of the start of a lengthy Colorado coal strike that eventually led to open guerrilla warfare between miners and the Colorado National Guard. The nadir of that showdown was what came to be called the Ludlow Massacre when, at the end of a daylong gun battle on April 20, 1914, National Guardsmen torched a strikers' tent colony where 11 children and four mothers were hiding in a large pit beneath the wooden floor of one of the tents. All but two of the mothers perished.

Few people these days have heard of the Ludlow Massacre. Fewer still know about the circumstances in which it occurred. In the face of abject regulatory failure, at least 75 people were killed over a seven-month period during the strike, as several thousand coal miners openly rebelled against a corrupt local political and economic system.

West Virginia has its own history of violent mining confrontations, including the 1921 march on Blair Mountain when 13,000 armed miners faced off against mine guards, local militia and government troops. Sixteen men, most of them miners, were killed before the U.S. government sent in one of its newest weapons — planes — to intimidate the miners into retreating. It worked.

But there had been no

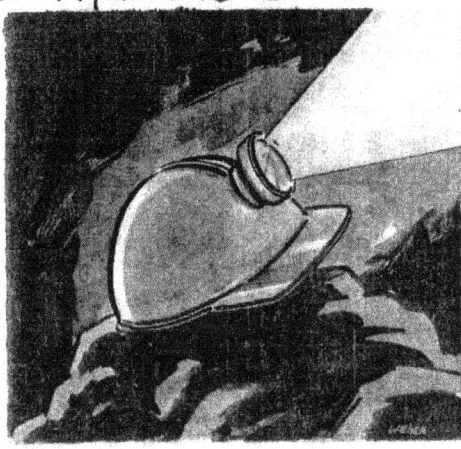

defusing the conflict in Colorado, where the mine owners — led by the Rockefellers' Colorado Fuel & Iron Co. — were so powerful that they effectively created their own laws, stole elections at will and installed mine superintendents to rule small fiefdoms enforced by hired thugs.

Upstaging the law

As if short-circuiting democracy wasn't bad enough, the coal operators ignored government safety regulations, considering them an intrusion on their right to make a profit. In the eyes of the Rockefellers' man in Colorado, Lamont Montgomery Bowers, the miners had a simple choice: Work under the operators' terms or find another job, safety be damned.

Don Blankenship, who runs Massey Energy, would have fit right in among those Colorado coal barons. Media reports have detailed Blankenship's efforts to dominate state politics, including trying to stack the state Supreme Court as it was considering cases involving Massey.

Other media reports

have detailed widespread safety violations at Massey mines. In one internal memo, Blankenship warned mine managers that they were to ignore any directive "to do anything other than run coal. ... This memo is necessary only because we seem not to understand that the coal pays the bills."

Bowers would have been proud.

The Colorado strike began in the northern mines on April 1, 1910. After it faltered, the United Mine Workers expanded the strike in September 1913 to southern Colorado, covering the eastern foothills of the Rockies. Most of the miners' demands were already required under Colorado law, including that they be paid for "dead work" they had been doing for free — namely, shoring up mine roofs with timbers so they wouldn't collapse and kill them.

"The companies created a condition which they considered satisfactory to themselves, and ought to be to the workmen, and jammed the workmen into it, and thought they were philanthropists," Ethelbert B. Stewart, a top

investigator for the new Department of Labor, wrote at the time. "That men have rebelled grows out of the fact that they are men."

The expanded strike was a nasty, brutal affair, and after a series of attacks and murders on both sides, Gov. Elias M. Ammons sent in the National Guard as peacekeepers. At the same time, state budget problems began delaying paychecks, which led many of the Guardsmen to walk away. The hated private mine guards took their places, and the peacekeepers morphed into the miners' enemy.

Then came the deaths at Ludlow on April 20, 1914. Over the next 10 days, amid a national union "call to arms," thousands of marauding miners and their supporters went on a rampage of retribution. At least 30 people were killed as the makeshift guerrilla army seized control of 275 miles of the Colorado Front Range.

Unable to stem the insurrection, Ammons sought help from President Woodrow Wilson, who sent in the Army to supplant the National Guard. The miners, with their immediate enemy gone, laid down their arms May 1, and the fighting was over, with the miners winning the war but losing. It would take an additional 13 years and the Wobblies to gain union recognition there.

Yet, much of the political and economic oppression in the region ended. To paraphrase Thomas Jefferson, a little revolution wasn't a bad thing for the miners of Colorado. Let's hope it doesn't take the same kind of action to redress the very deep grievances in West Virginia.

Scott Martelle is the author of "Blood Passion: The Ludlow Massacre and Class War in the American West." He wrote this for the Los Angeles Times.

8A WEDNESDAY, APRIL 28,

FAY OBS   SENATE INVESTIGATION 28 APR 10

AFGHANISTAN

Militants continue bombing attacks

The Associated Press

KANDAHAR, Afghanistan — The powerful half brother of President Hamid Karzai urged the international aid community not to pull out of the troubled southern city of Kandahar, where insurgents attacked Tuesday night, killing at least three and injuring dozens.

Kandahar Police Chief Sher Mohammed Zazai said militants detonated explosives near the city in an attack targeting a compound providing logistical support to NATO forces. He said at least three people were killed about a mile from Kandahar Air Field. Hospital workers said at least 35 others were injured.

Casualty reports were conflicting. Taliban spokesman Qari Yousaf said one suicide bomber and two armed insurgents killed 15 people and wounded 60 others and burned eight oil tankers on the site. Zulmai Ayubi, a spokesman for the Kandahar provincial governor, put the death toll at four and said 30 were injured.

Kandahar is the site of a planned offensive by Afghan and NATO forces that is intended to clear the city of Taliban fighters. President Obama has ordered 30,000 more troops into Afghanistan, in part to back up the Kandahar offensive, but the Taliban have launched increasingly deadly attacks ahead of the offensive.

On Monday, the United Nations announced that it had relocated several foreign employees from Kandahar to Kabul and told more than 200 Afghan workers to stay home.

Current and former Goldman Sachs employees are sworn in before a Senate subcommittee Tuesday. From left are Daniel Sparks, Joshua Birnbaum, Michael Swenson and Fabrice Tourre,

AP photo

Goldman executives deny any wrongdoing

■ Lawmakers criticize the company for its financial tactics.

By Marcy Gordon and Tom Raum
The Associated Press

WASHINGTON — Defending his company under blistering criticism, the CEO of Goldman Sachs testily told skeptical senators Tuesday that customers who bought securities from the Wall Street giant in the run-up to a national financial crisis came looking for risk "and that's what they got."

Lloyd Blankfein and other Goldman executives were lambasted by lawmakers for "unbridled greed" in an often-electric daylong showdown between Wall Street and Congress — with expletives frequently undeleted. Unrepentant, five present and two past Goldman officials unflinchingly stood by their conduct before a Senate investigatory panel and denied helping to cause the financial MELT DOWN +

See **BANK**, Page 4A

Greece, Portugal slide into junk credit ratings

WEDNESDAY, APRIL 28, 2010 **9A**

The Associated Press

ATHENS — Greece was pushed to the brink of a financial abyss and started dragging another eurozone country — Portugal — down with it, fueling fears of a continent-wide debt meltdown.

Stocks around the world tanked after ratings agency Standard & Poor's on Tuesday downgraded Greek bonds to junk status and downgraded Portugese bonds two notches, showing investors that Greece's financial contagion is spreading.

Greece is struggling with massive debt, and with prospects for economic growth weak it could end up in default. Its 15 eurozone partners and the International Monetary Fund have tried to calm the markets with a euro45 billion rescue package, but it hasn't worked.

Standard & Poor's warned that holders of Greek debt could take large losses in any restructuring, but a greater worry is that Greece's debt crisis is mushrooming to other debt-laden members of the eurozone.

WITNESSES AT COAL MINE HEARING 28.APR.10

Safety falls through loopholes

**By David Zucchino
and Kim Geiger**
Los Angeles Times

WASHINGTON — The company that operated the West Virginia coal mine where an explosion killed 29 miners this month was able to "game the system" by using a lengthy appeals process to avoid safety shutdowns, witnesses told a Senate committee Tuesday.

Massey Energy Co., which was cited 515 times for safety violations at the Upper Big Branch mine last year and 124 times this year before the April 5 explosion, was able to continue mining coal. Many of the violations were for improper ventilation of methane and coal dust, the suspected causes of the worst U.S. mine disaster in 40 years.

Because of loopholes in safety laws and a backlog of 16,000 safety violation appeals, federal inspectors are unable to shut down unsafe mine sections for more than short periods. The average appeal process drags on for 600 days, allowing coal companies to continue mining despite repeated safety citations.

And even when inspectors are able to shut down mine sections where inspectors find dangerous conditions, the mines are re-opened as soon as operators correct the violations.

"You just about have to have an explosion occur" to force a closure for imminent safety violations, Joe Main, head of the federal Mine Safety and Health Administration, told the Senate Committee on Health, Education, Labor and Pensions.

The hearing, the first since the disaster, was attended by family members of miners killed in other mine disasters, who held up photographs of their loved ones. They heard a mine workers' union leader angrily accuse Massey of knowingly operating unsafe mines and intimidating miners who complain about dangerous working conditions.

"The miners who work for Massey are scared to death," said Cecil Roberts, president of the United Mine Workers, his face reddening in anger. "They're intimidated. This company is run like it's 1921, not like it's the present day."

No Massey officials attended the hearing. A representative of the National Mining Association, an industry group, told the committee that current federal regulations are adequate to ensure mine safety.

"The tools are sufficient when properly used," said Bruce Watzman, the association's senior vice president.

Watzman pledged to work with Congress to eliminate the appeals process backlog, which he said "does not serve the interest of miners or mine operators."

Massey, which operated the Upper Big Branch Mine under a subsidiary, was hit with $1.24 million in penalties for safety violations there between January 2009 and the April 5 disaster, but paid only $180,000 because fines are not due until appeals are exhausted. Some fines imposed in 2006 still have not been paid by Massey, which contested 78 percent of its assessed penalties in its mines in 2009.

And even those fines that are paid are a pittance for a multibillion-dollar company like Massey.

"Unfortunately, the penalties for breaking the law are often so minimal that employers can dismiss them as simply the cost of doing business," said Sen. Tom Harkin, D-Iowa, who chairs the committee.

Sen. John D. Rockefeller IV, D-W.Va., holding aloft a 26-page sheaf of citations found at the Upper Big Branch mine since January 2009, called for "an end to the loopholes in the law that allow some mines to put profits over safety."

But when Main was asked why his agency had never used existing authority to shut down an unsafe mine, his response left senators baffled.

"That's a good question," Main replied.

Main repeated his earlier descriptions of regulations he said are too weak to hand out meaningful penalties and shutdowns.

Last year, federal inspectors issued 48 withdrawal orders requiring miners to evacuate dangerous sections at Upper Big Branch, but Massey was able to stall a shutdown of the mine.

"It's very easy to game the system," Main said, describing a "catch me if you can mentality" among mine operators.

President Obama, who demanded a detailed report of violations at Upper Big Branch that was delivered earlier this month, has described a system "so riddled with loopholes that they allow unsafe conditions to continue."

Labor Secretary Hilda Solis, who oversees the mine safety agency, has said of current regulations, "You could drive a truck through the loopholes that exist."

25.APR.10 ALASKA
Soldier suspected of killing wife, baby

ANCHORAGE — A 21-year-old military police officer who returned from Afghanistan two months ago likely shot his wife and 8-month-old baby to death, police said Tuesday.

The bodies of Racquell Lynch, 19, and Kyirsta Lynch were found Monday by an apartment manager who opened up their Anchorage unit at the request of military police.

Authorities had been looking for Spc. Kip Lynch, who had not shown up for duties at Fort Richardson Army Post. He was found severely wounded in another room and rushed to a hospital, where he underwent surgery.

The Associated Press

Somali soldiers defect to al-Qaida

By Katharine Houreld
The Associated Press

MOGADISHU, Somalia — Hundreds of Somali soldiers trained with U.S. tax dollars have deserted because they are not being paid their $100 monthly wage, and some have even joined the al-Qaida-linked militants they are supposed to be fighting, The Associated Press has learned.

The desertions raise fears that a new U.S.-backed effort beginning next month to build up Somalia's army may only increase the ranks of the insurgency.

Somalia's besieged U.N.-backed government holds only a few blocks of the Somali capital, Mogadishu, while Islamic insurgents control the rest of the city and most of the country. That turmoil — and the lawless East African nation's proximity to Yemen, where al-Qaida in the Arabian Peninsula is based — has fed fears that Somalia could be used to launch attacks on the West.

In an effort to rebuild the tattered Somali military, the United States helped fund a training program for nearly 1,000 soldiers in neighboring Djibouti last year, Western diplomats said. The French-trained troops were supposed to earn $100 a month, but about half of them deserted because they were not paid, Somali army Col. Ahmed Aden Dhayow said.

"Some gave up the army and returned to their ordinary life, and others joined the rebels," he said.

Somalia's state minister for defense, Yusuf Mohamed Siyad, confirmed some trainees had joined the al-Shabab militants, but he declined to specify the number of deserters.

The development highlights a key problem facing efforts to rebuild the bankrupt nation's army — guaranteeing funding for soldiers' salaries, not just their training.

Failure to resolve the pay issue could threaten the suc-

AP photo
Government soldiers cross a street in March during heavy fighting against Islamist insurgents in Mogadishu, Somalia.

cess of a U.S. and European Union training program beginning in Uganda next month that has been touted as the biggest effort to rebuild the army in 20 years.

Funding for the Somali army is a complex affair involving contributions from donor nations, the U.N. and the Somali government. Individual countries sometimes pledge to cover salaries for a limited number of soldiers for a few months, and when the money runs out, salaries don't get paid.

The U.S. has provided $2 million to pay Somali soldiers and purchase supplies and equipment in Mogadishu since 2007, according to the State Department. Another $12 million went toward transport, uniforms and equipment, but the U.S. has declined to say how much of that paid for training.

During a recent AP visit, dejected-looking soldiers said they had not been paid, some for months, and that their wages were intercepted by senior officials.

When pressed for details, mid-level officers glanced at colleagues clutching plastic bags of spaghetti, the day's lunch ration, and said they couldn't discuss the problem.

"There is not enough money to pay everyone," Col. Ali Hassan said as a group of officers listened.

Earlier this year, guns were taken from trainee soldiers and they were given sticks after a riot broke out between those who had been paid and those who had not. The African Union, which has peacekeepers at Camp Jazira, temporarily suspended payments over fears that men who had been paid would be killed by those who had not, an official involved with the training said.

Ariz. wants proof from Obama

The Associated Press

PHOENIX — Arizona lawmakers expressing doubt over whether President Obama was born in the United States are pushing a bill through the legislature that would require the president to show his birth certificate to get on the state's 2012 ballot.

The House passed the measure Wednesday on a 31-29 vote, ignoring protests from opponents who said it's casting Arizona in an ugly light and could give the elected secretary of state broad powers to kick a presidential candidate off the ballot.

"We're becoming a national joke," Rep. Chad Campbell, a Phoenix Democrat who opposes the measure, said Thursday.

The measure's sponsor, Republican Rep. Judy Burges of Skull Valley, said she isn't sure Obama could prove his eligibility for the ballot in Arizona and wants to erase all doubts.

So-called "birthers" have contended since the 2008 presidential campaign that Obama is ineligible to be president because, they argue, he was actually born in Kenya, his father's homeland. The Constitution says that a person must be a "natural-born citizen" to be eligible for the presidency.

Hawaii officials have repeatedly confirmed Obama's citizenship, and his birth certificate has been made public, along with birth notices from two Honolulu newspapers published within days of his birth in August 1961.

...

THE FAYETTEVILLE OBSERVER

25 APRI 2010 FAYETTEVILLE OBSERVER NC (handwritten)

IMMIGRATION

AP photo

Arizona Gov. Jan Brewer signs an immigration bill into law Friday in Phoenix. The sweeping measure would make it a crime under state law to be in the country illegally.

Inspector: SEC staffers viewed pornography

MarketWatch

WASHINGTON — During the past five years, top Securities and Exchange Commission staff members and contractors used government computers on official time to view pornography, according to an agency inspector general.

The SEC's inspector general found that 33 SEC employees or contractors violated commission rules and policies by viewing porn, according to a memo obtained

by MarketWatch. The investigation was requested by Sen. Charles Grassley, R-Iowa.

Rep. Darrell Issa, R-Calif., the Ranking Member of the House Committee on Oversight and Government Reform, said he was disturbed by the findings.

"This stunning report should make everyone question the wisdom of moving forward with plans to give

The legislation, sent to the Republican governor by the GOP-led legislature, makes it a crime under state law to be in the country illegally. It also requires local police officers to question people about their immigration status if there is reason to suspect they are illegal immigrants; allows lawsuits against government agencies that hinder enforcement of immigration laws; and makes it illegal to hire illegal immigrants for day labor or knowingly transport them.

Governor signs bill despite criticism

The Associated Press

PHOENIX — Gov. Jan Brewer ignored criticism from President Obama on Friday and signed into law a bill supporters said would take handcuffs off police in dealing with illegal immigration in Arizona, the nation's busiest gateway for human and drug smuggling from Mexico.

With hundreds of protesters outside the state Capitol shouting that the bill would lead to civil rights abuses, Brewer said critics were "overreacting" and that she wouldn't tolerate racial profiling.

Earlier Friday, Obama called the Arizona bill "misguided" and instructed the Justice Department to examine it to see if it's legal. He also said the federal government must enact immigration reform at the national level — or leave the door open to "irresponsibility by others."

POLICE: MAN WAS DRUNK WHILE DRIVING STUDENTS

■ A breath test is given to the driver after a vehicle rearends the school bus.

By Nick Needham
Staff writer

Police say a Cumberland County school bus driver was drunk while driving 18 middle school students Friday afternoon.

Charles Wynn, 49, of the 1800 block of Windlock Drive, was driving a bus from Lewis Chapel

Middle School when it was rear-ended by a Ford Expedition on Pritchett Road at 2:49 p.m., authorities say.

Police did a breath test on Wynn at the scene and found his blood alcohol level to be 0.2, more than two times the legal limit of 0.08. The test was given

A wrong can make a right

P resident Obama is right that Arizona's tough immigration law is "misguided." And Arizona Gov. Jan Brewer is right that her state has been "more than patient waiting for Washington to act." The two are not unrelated.

Enforcing our immigration laws is a federal responsibility which Washington has failed to meet. It's too bad that the Arizona law comes just as the Obama administration had started doing what must be done — and a plan for effective immigration reform has some Senate support.

After eight years of passivity under the Bush administration, Immigration and Customs Enforcement is actively going after companies found to be employing illegal workers. That and a weak economy are credited with having slowed the surge of illegal

Froma Harrop

immigrants into this country.

But as Brewer said, patience is gone. The result is a policy that is disturbingly unfair to Latino populations. The law makes it a crime to move around without immigration documents and lets police demand such papers from anyone suspected of being in the United States illegally.

You know who that means: people from Mexico or who look like they could be from Mexico. And, although the governor has promised to train officers against racial profiling, how could there not be? What would make an Arizona law

enforcer suspect that someone is here illegally other than that person's ethnic appearance?

Stopping brown people in the street is not the way to address the problem. Most illegal immigrants come for work so they can support their families.

Harassing countless innocents alongside illegal immigrants is a callous and futile way to stop massive flows of undocumented workers. The more successful approach is to remove the job magnet by fining and possibly jailing their employers.

It is already against the law to hire illegal aliens, but the lack of counterfeit-proof identification is a giant loophole. If the job-seeker presents a reasonably good-looking document, a company can't be held liable if that person is found to be working illegally.

An immigration reform

proposal put together by Sens. Charles Schumer, D-N.Y., and Lindsay Graham, R-S.C., would end that dodge by creating a Social Security card that contains fingerprints, eye scans or other biometric markers unique to every individual. Employers would check the information against a national database for all new hires, be they immigrant or native born.

No, Arizona is not going about this the right way. But its radical law may spur overdue action. Now is the best time for it, when a slow economy has deflated the cheap-labor argument that only illegal immigrants will wash dishes or mop floors.

Froma Harrop is a syndicated columnist. Readers may write to her at info@creators.com (with her name in the subject line) or Creators Syndicate, 5777 W. Century Blvd., Suite 700, Los Angeles, CA 90045.

650 ready for Afghanistan

Fort Bragg paratroopers will be gone for up to 120 days

By John Ramsey
Staff writer

Fresh off a 49-day deployment to Haiti, about 650 Fort Bragg paratroopers are ready to leave for Afghanistan as early as today.

Soldiers from the 1st Battalion, 325th Airborne Infantry Regiment, 2nd Brigade Combat Team, 82nd Airborne Division have orders for a 90- to 120-day training mission scattered across Afghanistan, said Lt. Col. Charles J. Masaracchia.

The goal is to help put Afghan security forces through a sort of basic train-

ing, teaching them skills such as marksmanship, patrolling and the military decision-making process, Masaracchia said.

"The hope is that they can then conduct their own training internally to a suitable standard," he said. "The goal right now is for us not to train private through sergeant first class. It is to train the sergeant first class and have him instruct his own people, which gives him credibility within his own force."

Training Afghans to be able to protect their own country is a key to eventually withdrawing U.S. troops.

Masaracchia found out 12 days ago that he would lead this mission. He took command of the battalion Friday.

On Tuesday, Masaracchia and his command sergeant major, Richard Clark, met with The Fayetteville Observer in the commander's office, which was littered with Masaracchia's packed bags.

This battalion was tapped for duty in Afghanistan because another unit wasn't going to be able to be there quickly enough, Masaracchia said. He said his men will be working alongside soldiers in the 10th Mountain Division — which needs more soldiers for the job — to train the Afghans to a standard level of proficiency. The mission is strictly training, joining

forces with Afghan soldiers on patrols or other operations. Afghans who complete the training will be passed along to other units that will team up with them on battlefield missions.

As part of the global response force, Clark said, the soldiers in 1st Battalion are prepared to go anywhere in the world in 18 hours or less.

Soldiers found out about the upcoming deployment late last week.

"We're ready to go," Clark said.

The leaders said they aren't worried about switching to combat mode so quickly after helping Haitians recover from an earthquake.

"It's much easier to train an organization and deploy an organization into a com-

Missing data hurting oil spill investigation

By Allen G. Breed and Curt Anderson
The Associated Press

A "black box" can reveal why an airplane crashed or how fast a car was going in the instant before an accident. Yet there are no records of a critical safety test supposedly performed during the fateful hours before the Deepwater Horizon oil rig exploded in the Gulf of Mexico.

They went down with the rig.

While some data were being transmitted to shore for safekeeping right up until the April 20 blast, officials from Transocean, the rig owner, told Congress that the last seven hours of its data are missing and that all written logs were lost in the explosion.

INSIDE

■ Rig owner enjoys low taxes in Switzerland, Page 5A

The gap poses a mystery for investigators: What decisions were made — and what warnings might have been ignored? Earlier tests, which suggested that explosive gas was leaking from the mile-deep well, were preserved.

"There is some delay in the replication of our data, so our operational data, our sequence of events ends at 3 o'clock in the afternoon on the 20th," Steven Newman, president and CEO of

An image from video shows oil spewing from a yellowish, broken pipe 5,000 feet below the ocean's surface.
AP photo

Transocean Ltd, told a Senate panel. The rig blew up at 10 p.m., killing 11 workers and unleashing a gusher that has spewed millions of gallons of oil into the Gulf.

Houston lawyer Tony Buzbee, who represents several rig workers involved in the accident, questioned whether what he called "the phantom test" was even performed.

"I can just tell you that the Halliburton hands were scratching their heads," said Buzbee, whose clients include one of the Halliburton crew members responsible for cementing the well to prepare for moving the drilling rig to another site.

Buzbee said that when Halliburton showed BP PLC and Transocean officials the results of the pressure tests that suggested gas was leaking, the rig workers were put on "standby." BP is the rig operator and leaseholder.

Buzbee said one of his clients told him the "Transocean and BP compa-

ny people got their heads together," and 40 minutes later gave the green light.

Meanwhile, out in the Gulf, BP settled on its next attempt to cut down on the spill: Undersea robots will try to thread a small tube into the jagged pipe that's leaking on the sea floor. The tube, which will suck crude to a ship on the surface, will be surrounded by a stopper to keep oil from leaking into the water.

BP said it wasn't sure how much of the roughly 210,000 gallons leaking daily would be captured by the improvised device.

If that doesn't work, engineers can still attempt to use a "top hat" box now on the sea floor to cover the leak and siphon the oil to the surface.

Details of a likely blowout scenario emerged this week for the first time from congressional and administrative hearings. They suggest there were both crew mistakes and equipment breakdowns at key points the day of the explosion.

Do people have 'a duty to die'?

Thomas Sowell

One of the many fashionable notions that have caught on among some of the intelligentsia is that old people have "a duty to die," rather than become a burden to others.

This is more than just an idea discussed around a seminar table. Already the government-run medical system in Britain is restricting what medications or treatments it will authorize for the elderly. Moreover, it seems almost certain that similar attempts to contain runaway costs will lead to similar policies when American medical care is taken over by the government.

Make no mistake about it, letting old people die is a lot cheaper than spending the kind of money required to keep them alive and well. If a government-run medical system is going to save any serious amount of money, it is almost certain to do so by sacrificing the elderly.

There was a time — fortunately, now long past — when some desperately poor societies had to abandon old people to their fate, because

there was just not enough margin for everyone to survive. Sometimes the elderly themselves would simply go off from family and community to face their fate alone.

But is that where we are today?

Talk about "a duty to die" made me think back to my early childhood in the South, during the Great Depression of the 1930s. One day, I was told that an older lady — a relative of ours — was going to come and stay with us for a while, and I was told how to be polite and considerate towards her.

She was called "Aunt Nance Ann," but I don't know what her official name was or what her actual biological relationship to us was. Aunt Nance Ann had no home of her own. But she moved from relative to

relative, not spending enough time in any one home to be a real burden.

Poor as we were, I never heard anybody say, or even intimate, that Aunt Nance Ann had "a duty to die."

I began to hear that kind of talk decades later, from highly educated people in an affluent age, when even most families living below the official poverty level owned a car or truck and had air-conditioning.

It is today, in an age when homes have flat-panelled TVs, and most families eat in restaurants regularly or have pizzas and other meals delivered to their homes, that the elites — rather than the masses — have begun talking about "a duty to die."

Many years later, while going through a divorce, I told a friend that I was considering contesting child custody. She immediately urged me not to do it. Why? Because raising a child would interfere with my career.

But my son didn't have a career. He was just a child who needed someone who understood him. I ended up with custody of my son and,

although he was not a demanding child, raising him could not help impeding my career a little. But do you just abandon a child when it is inconvenient to raise him?

Much of what is taught in our schools and colleges today seeks to break down traditional values, and replace them with more fancy and fashionable notions, of which "a duty to die" is just one.

These efforts at changing values used to be called "values clarification," though the name has had to be changed repeatedly over the years, as more and more parents caught on to what was going on and objected. The values that supposedly needed "clarification" had been clear enough to last for generations and nobody asked the schools and colleges for this "clarification."

Thomas Sowell is a syndicated columnist. Readers may write to him at www.tsowell.com, at info@creators.com (with his name in the subject line) or Creators Syndicate, 5777 West Century Blvd., Suite 700, Los Angeles, CA 90045.

Latest losers to America's anger

WASHINGTON — As we approached the Tuesday night with the most significant senatorial primaries of the year so far, I turned for guidance to a man who had already been through the fires that define the incendiary politics of 2010.

Ten days after he was barred from the ballot in the Utah Republican primary because the 3,500 delegates to the GOP state convention preferred to give more votes to his two challengers, three-term incumbent Sen. Bob Bennett was, as I expected, more analytical than angry, more thoughtful than embittered.

Bennett, 76, who followed his father to Washington and Capitol Hill, is the kind of legislator reporters value because he can speak thoughtfully and dispassionately about his colleagues' collective mood without subjecting you to gobs of self-serving rhetoric.

Now, I found him equally reflective of what had caused his fellow Republicans, who had elected him for almost 20 years and frequently told pollsters he was their most popular incumbent, to turn against him.

"I'll tell you what is new," he said. "There is this thing called the federal government. It's big and intimidating and it's out of control. And whoever you

David Broder

are, and whatever your title, or your history, or your individual voting record, if you are part of it, you find yourself having to defend it. And sometimes, it just looks indefensible to them."

Two days before activist Republican voters in Utah gathered for the county caucuses that chose the delegates to the state convention, they watched on television as Democratic Speaker Nancy Pelosi forced an unusual Sunday session of the House of Representatives to push through an amended version of the Obama administration's health care bill. "It was a Sunday, which is a very special day for me and my fellow Mormons," Bennett said. "And it was really a display of partisan political muscle.

"We prepared for the county conventions like we never had before. We had every precinct covered, and we set our turnout quotas at twice the level we had ever seen before. We hit or exceeded our quotas almost everywhere, and we were swamped. People came out of

the woodwork to vote against anyone they associated with the federal government."

In Bennett's view, his fate was sealed by the county conventions, and nothing that happened thereafter could change it. The efforts against him by out-of-state tea party people and other right-wing organizations simply let them claim credit for something they were late in joining, he said. And the efforts by wildly popular Mitt Romney and other establishment Republicans to save his candidacy were equally futile.

At the fringe, the movement to purge him took on aspects of ideological extremism, Bennett said. "I was asked several times about my position on the 17th Amendment, providing for the direct election of senators," Bennett said. "They viewed that as the opening effort by Washington to usurp the power that the Constitution had placed in the hand of state legislatures."

But mainly it was a mainstream reaction against the centralization of power in the capital, a combination of bank bailouts, health care guarantees and all the other ways in which Washington has found reasons — or excuses — to intervene and to spend money it does not have.

That reaction is not confined to Utah. And it may not even be representative of the state. If Bennett had

made the primary ballot, he claims, he would have won renomination easily.

But we saw the anti-Washington sentiment Tuesday in Kentucky, where the physician son of libertarian Rep. Ron Paul easily defeated Senate Minority Leader Mitch McConnell's handpicked candidate for the Republican nomination for a vacant Senate seat — and credited his win to the tea partiers.

The same sentiment carried to Arkansas, where incumbent Democratic Sen. Blanche Lincoln was forced into a runoff by her labor-backed challenger.

And it claimed its largest victim of the year so far in Pennsylvania's Sen. Arlen Specter. Run out of the Republican Party last year by a GOP challenger, he fell embarrassingly to a less-known younger congressman in a bid for the Democratic nomination. His failure showed the Obama White House once again to be a toothless tiger — with its endorsements now having failed in Virginia, New Jersey, Massachusetts and Pennsylvania. No good news for the president there.

David Broder is a Washington Post columnist. Readers may write to him at davidbroder@washpost.com or Washington Post Writers Group, 1150 15th St. NW, Washington, D.C. 20071.

GAYS IN THE MILITARY 25 MAY 10

Proposal to lift ban in doubt

By Anne Flaherty
The Associated Press

WASHINGTON — A lukewarm endorsement from Defense Secretary Robert Gates and opposition among some lawmakers cast doubt Tuesday on whether Congress this week would lift a 17-year-old ban on gays serving openly in the military.

Gay rights' groups predicted that the bill might pass the House but face a tough road in the Senate.

"The door isn't closed, but it's barely cracked," said Aubrey Sarvis, executive director of Servicemembers Legal Defense.

A compromise was struck Monday by the White House and a small group of Democrats who fear that repeal efforts will be doomed if Republicans regain control of one or both houses of Congress after fall elections.

The plan would overturn the "don't ask, don't tell" law but still allow the military to decide when and how to implement any changes to accommodate the new policy.

Gates has said that he supports repeal but would prefer that Congress wait to vote until he can talk to the troops and chart a path forward. A study ordered by

Gates is due on Dec. 1.

Some lawmakers took a similar stand. "I see no reason for the political process to pre-empt it," Sen. Jim Webb, a conservative Democrat from Virginia, said of the military study.

On Tuesday, Gates said he would support the White House compromise but wished it didn't have to happen now.

Gates and Adm. Mike Mullen, chairman of the Joint Chiefs of Staff, say they agree that the ban should be lifted but want time to complete a wide-ranging study on how to do so without causing turmoil.

WEDNESDAY, MAY 26, 2010   **10A**

AP photo

Douglas Inkley, with the National Wildlife Federation, works near an island affected by oil from the Deepwater Horizon oil spill in Louisiana's Barataria Bay on Tuesday.

BP readies 'top kill' to plug gushing pipe

By Matthew Daly
The Associated Press

WASHINGTON — Marking five disastrous weeks, BP readied yet another attempt to slow the oil gushing into the Gulf on Tuesday as a federal report alleged drilling regulators have been so close to oil and gas companies they've been accepting gifts and even negotiating to go work for them.

President Obama prepared to head to the Gulf on Friday to review efforts to halt the millions of gallons of contaminating crude, while scientists said underwater video of the leak showed the plume growing significantly darker, suggesting heavier, more-polluting oil is spewing out.

BP's next effort to stop the damaged oil well, perhaps today, will be to force-feed heavy drilling mud and cement into the well to plug it up. The tactic, called a "top kill," has never been tried a mile beneath the sea, and company executives estimate its chances of success at 60 to 70 percent.

On Capitol Hill, lawmakers continued feuding over a law that caps oil spill liability at $75 million for economic damages beyond direct cleanup costs. Democrats have tried to pass a bill raising the limit to $10 billion but have been blocked by Republicans.

A new report from the Interior Department's acting inspector general found that an inspector for the Minerals Management Service, which oversees drilling, admitted using crystal methamphetamine and said he might have been under the influence of the drug at work.

The report cited a variety of violations of federal regulations and ethics rules at the agency's Louisiana office. Previous inspector general investigations have focused on inappropriate behavior by the royalty-collection staff in the agency's Denver office.

The report adds to the climate of frustration and criticism facing the Obama administration, although it covers actions before the spill.

In a letter to Sen. Barbara

"Unfortunately, given the events of April 20 of this year, this report had become anything but routine, and I feel compelled to release it now," she said.

Her biggest concern is the ease with which minerals agency employees move between industry and government, Kendall said. While no specifics were included in the report, "we discovered that the individuals involved in the fraternizing and gift exchange — both government and industry — have often known one another since childhood," Kendall said.

Relationships took precedence over their jobs, Kendall said.

The report follows a 2008 report by then-Inspector General Earl Devaney that decried a "culture of ethical failure" and conflicts of interest at the minerals agency, which is part of the Interior Department.

Salazar called the latest report "deeply disturbing" and said it highlights the need for changes he has proposed, including a ???

365

KOREAN PENINSULA TENSIONS

THE FAYETTEVILLE OBSERVER

PROBATION VIOLATION

Ex-Detroit mayor gets prison time

By Corey Williams
The Associated Press

Kilpatrick

DETROIT — Time and again, Kwame Kilpatrick's exceptional oratory skills rallied Detroit voters to his side despite his frequent troubles as mayor.

But all his swagger and professions of love for family, God and the city failed to sway a judge Tuesday, who sent Kilpatrick to prison for up to five years for violating this probation stemming from his conviction for lying under oath about an affair with his chief of staff.

The former mayor's rehabilitation "clearly ... has failed," Wayne County Circuit Court Judge David Groner said before announcing his sentence.

The criticism was some of the harshest leveled at the one-time mayor and darling of Michigan's Democratic Party, who early in his political career displayed the bravado and eloquence to talk his way out of thorny situations.

Brash and arrogant, Kilpatrick was criticized during his first term for improperly using city credit cards to pay restaurant tabs. It was later revealed that his wife used a city-leased vehicle for her personal use. Each time, he asked for his constituents' forgiveness, and he came from behind to win re-election in 2005.

But his political fortunes soured when Kilpatrick testified in a whistle-blower lawsuit trial that he was not romantically involved with his chief of staff. Text messages between the two later showed he was lying.

At issue during Tuesday's hearing was $1 million Kilpatrick was ordered to pay the city after pleading guilty in 2008 to obstruction of justice. Groner ruled last month that Kilpatrick failed to report all of his assets and meet other conditions of his probation.

Pyongyang severs t

By Hyung-jin Kim
The Associated Press

SEOUL, South Korea — Relations on the divided Korean peninsula plunged to their lowest point in a decade Tuesday when the North declared it was cutting all ties to Seoul as punishment for blaming the communists for the sinking of a South Korean warship.

The announcement came a day after South Korea took steps that were seen as among the strongest it could take short of military action. Seoul said it would slash trade with the North and deny permission to its cargo ships to pass through South Korean waters. It also resumed a propaganda offensive — including blaring Western music into the North and dropping leaflets by balloon.

North Korea said it was cutting all ties with the South until President Lee Myung-bak leaves office in early 2013, the official Korean Central News Agency said in a dispatch monitored in Seoul late Tuesday.

The North's Committee for the Peaceful Reunification said it would expel all South Korean government officials working at a joint industrial park in the northern border town of Kaesong, and South Korean ships and airlin-

ers would be banned from passing through its territory.

The North's committee said it would start "all-out counterattacks" against the South's psychological warfare, and called its moves "the first phase" of punitive measures against Seoul, suggesting more action could follow.

Earlier Tuesday, one Seoul-based monitoring agency reported that North Korea's leader ordered its 1.2 million-member military to get ready for combat.

North Korea Intellectuals Solidarity said Kim Jong Il's order was broadcast last Thursday on speakers installed in each house and at major public sites throughout the country.

South Korean officials could not immediately confirm the report, and its military said it had no indication of unusual activity by North Korea's military.

Clinton visit

South Korea wants to bring North Korea before the U.N. Security Council over the sinking, and has U.S. support. U.S. Secretary of State Hillary Rodham Clinton was to visit South Korea today.

Clinton was in Beijing on Tuesday, wrapping up two days of intense strategic and economic talks with China,

Prot[...] a N[...] flag[...] Kore[...] defe[...] slog[...] the[...] Ass[...] Seo[...] Kor[...] Tues[...] AP p[...]

which respond[...] U.S. appeals t[...] international a[...] North Korea o[...] ship sinking.

The North a[...] technically rem[...] since the 195[...] War ended with[...] rather than a p[...]

Tensions ha[...] last week, when[...] ternational[...] concluded tha[...] from a North K[...] rine tore apart[...] warship on Mar[...] 46 South Korea[...]

The North flatly denies involvement in the sinking of the Cheonan and has warned that retaliation would mean war.

As part of its propaganda offensive, South Korea's military resumed radio broadcasts airing Western music, news and comparisons between the South and North Korean political and economic situation late Monday, according to the Joint Chiefs of Staff.

South Korea also will install dozens of loudspeakers and towering electronic billboards along the heavily armed land border to urge communist soldiers to defect.

FAYOBS NC

TUESDAY, MAY 25, 2010   **8A**

South Korea cuts trade with North

2 5 MAY 10

The Associated Press

SEOUL, South Korea — South Korea's president slashed trade to impoverished North Korea and pledged to haul Pyongyang before the U.N. Security Council, vowing Monday to make Pyongyang "pay a price" for a torpedo attack that killed 46 sailors.

President Obama offered his full support for South Korea's moves, and U.S. Secretary of State Hillary Rodham Clinton conferred with China — a veto-wielding permanent seat holder on the Security Council — on the next step in what she called a "highly precarious" security situation.

The March 26 sinking of the Cheonan in the Yellow Sea off the west coast was one of South Korea's worst

 Sign up for @lerts

■ Get breaking news delivered to your e-mail. Sign up for @lerts at **fayobserver.com**.

military disasters since the 1950-53 Korean War. A torpedo fired from a North Korean submarine tore the ship in two, an international team of investigators concluded last week.

President Lee Myung-bak called the attack the latest in a series of provocations from the North, and aimed to strike Pyongyang financially by cutting trade with the country in desperate need for hard currency.

South Korea has been North Korea's No. 2 trading partner, behind China, and

the measure will cost Pyongyang about $200 million a year, analysts say.

Pyongyang disputes the maritime border unilaterally drawn by U.N. forces at the close of the war, and the Koreas have fought three bloody skirmishes there, most recently in November. The Cheonan went down not far from the Koreas' sea border.

Defense Minister Kim Tae-young said the U.S. and South Korea would hold anti-submarine military exercises in the waters. The U.S. has 28,500 troops in South Korea.

Seoul carried out $1.68 billion in trade with North Korea in 2009, about 33 percent of Pyongyang's total trade, according to the Korea Trade-Investment Promotion Agency.

30 MAY 10 FAY OBS

President destroying his own country

The man in our White House is plunging our country into a civil war, dividing the citizens in this great United States. He is determined to destroy us, from within and from without, one way or another.

On the inside, he says states cannot take it upon themselves to enforce federal law to protect their state from drugs, drug lords, weapons sales, murder, kidnapping and destruction of property caused by illegal immigrants coming into the U.S.

On the outside, he is disarming our country, thinking he is encouraging peace and favor with our enemies when the enemy does nothing except lie. He apologizes for us being a free and patriotic people.

He has spent and is spending money like a man gone wild from day one, always in a helicopter or Air Force One going somewhere to politic or have a photo op.

He is going to cause our country to collapse under a mountain of debt with programs he proposed and a stupid Congress voted into law. We fear for our children and grandchildren.

What have some of the American people voted into the White House? A man gone greedy for power and control of the greatest nation on Earth. He is unpatriotic and pretends to be a Christian. How can we take three more years of this?

Another thought; why do we waste money venturing into outer space when it is needed so desperately on Earth? Hello, American leaders, are you in space or spaced out?

Betty Lowrance
Clinton

SHAW UNIVERSITY

Alumni association seeks board ouster

The Associated Press

RALEIGH — The national alumni association of Shaw University, one of the oldest historically black colleges in the South, has called for the board of trustees to step down or be dismissed because of continuing financial problems.

The News & Observer of Raleigh reported that the alumni association of Shaw University in Raleigh addressed its letter to the school board chairman Willie Gary, an alumnus and multimillionaire lawyer whose office is based in Stuart, Fla.

Shaw's board consists of educators, business people and Baptist officials in North Carolina, Florida and New York, as well as boxer Evander Holyfield and boxing promoter Don King, Shaw's website says. The school is searching for a new president and must renew its accreditation in 2012.

"We can no longer stand by and allow Shaw to appear to deteriorate due to poor judgment. ... We have serious concerns regarding conflict of interest, fiduciary responsibilities, adverse interest and commitment," says the May 14 letter from association president Emily Perry.

The letter isn't the first criticism from alumni about

Shaw, a school of about 2,700 students that has debt of more than $20 million. In March, the school's Florida alumni group sent a letter to Shaw administrators saying it was "amazed" that giving among board members totaled only $41,089 since July, despite Gary's pledge that each of the roughly 40 board members would chip in $50,000.

Gary said Thursday that he doesn't plan to step down or request that anyone else do so. He said he hasn't kept up with his 1991 pledge to donate $10 million, at the rate of $250,000 a year, because of the recession.

"Whether I've given any money to Shaw in the last year or so? No, because of the economic times," Gary said. "We don't have it."

He promised to resume his donations once the economy improves.

Perry's letter, which was sent to board of trustee and alumni association members, suggests the board eliminate ineffective members to make way for the future.

"Now is the time for a new board of trustees that can effectively attend to the fiduciary responsibilities of Shaw," the letter reads.

Earlier this year, Shaw University secured a $31 million federal loan with help from U.S. Rep. Bob Etheridge.

Oil: Third relief well could be drilled if the first two fail

From Page 1A

"The probability of them hitting it on the very first shot is virtually nil," said David Rensink, incoming president of the American Association of Petroleum Geologists, who spent most of his 39 years in the oil industry in offshore exploration. "If they get it on the first three or four shots, they'd be very lucky."

The relief well drilling and temporary fixes were being watched closely by President Obama, who planned to meet for the first time today with the co-chairmen of an independent commission investigating the spill. A senior administration official said the meeting will take place at the White House. The official spoke on condition of anonymity because the meeting had not been formally announced.

Relief wells

For the relief well to succeed, the bore hole must precisely intersect the damaged well. If it misses, BP will have to back up its drill, plug the hole it just created, and try again.

The trial-and-error process could take weeks, but it will eventually work, scientists and BP said. Then engineers will then pump mud and cement through pipes to ultimately seal the well.

As the drilling reaches deeper into the earth, the process is slowed by building pressure and the increasing distance that well casings must travel before they can be set in place.

Still, the three months it could take to finish the relief wells — the first of which started May 2 — is quicker than a typical deep well, which can take four months or longer, said Tad Patzek,

chair of the Petroleum and Geosystems Engineering Department at the University of Texas-Austin. BP already has a good picture of the different layers of sand and rock its drill bits will meet because of the work it did on the blown-out well.

On the slim chance the relief well doesn't work, scientists weren't sure exactly how much — or how long — the oil would flow. The gusher would continue until the well bore hole collapsed or pressure in the reservoir dropped to a point where oil was no longer pushed to the surface, Patzek said.

"I don't admit the possibility of it not working," he said.

A third well could be drilled if the first two fail.

"We don't know how much oil is down there, and hopefully, we'll never know when the relief wells work," BP spokesman John Curry said.

The company was starting to collect and analyze data on how much oil might be in the reservoir when the rig exploded April 20, he said.

BP's uncertainty statement is reasonable, given they only had drilled one well, according to Doug Rader, an ocean scientist with the Environmental Defense Fund.

Two relief wells stopped the world's worst peacetime spill, from a Mexican rig called Ixtoc 1 that dumped 140 million gallons off the Yucatan Peninsula. That plug took nearly 10 months beginning in the summer of 1979. Drilling technology has vastly improved since then, however.

So far, the Gulf oil spill has leaked between 19.7 million and 43 million gallons, according to government estimates.

GULF OIL SPILL

Relief wells likely to take 2 months

■ In the meantime, BP will try a cut-and-cap process to cover the leaking wellhead.

By Matthew Brown
The Associated Press

NEW ORLEANS — The best hope for stopping the flow of oil from the blown-out well at the bottom of the Gulf of Mexico has been compared to hitting a target the size of a dinner plate with a drill more than two miles into the earth and is anything but a sure bet on the first attempt.

Bid after bid has failed to staunch what already has become the nation's worst-ever spill, and BP PLC is readying another patchwork attempt as early as Wednesday, this one a cut-and-cap process to put a lid on the leaking wellhead so oil can be siphoned to the surface.

But the best-case scenario of sealing the leak is two relief wells being drilled diagonally into the gushing well — tricky business that won't be ready until August.

See OIL, Page 4A

SHOULD THE U.S. CANCEL OFFSHORE DRILLING PLANS IN THE WAKE OF THE BP OIL SPILL?

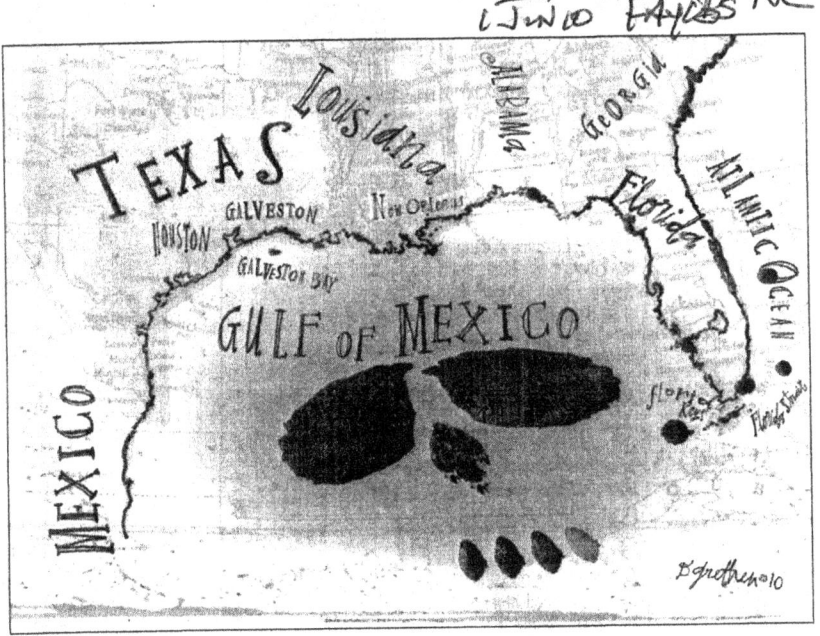

YES

Use subsidies for alternate energy

By Hal T. Nelson and Nicholas I. Cain
McClatchy News Service

The April 20 explosion that caused the calamity, and killed 11 workers, has spilled at least 6 million gallons of oil — and perhaps five times that amount — into the waters of the Gulf Coast.

Some estimates have put the cost of this disaster to fishing, tourism and the environment at more than $12 billion — but it will be years before the true cost is known. Given the deaths and the damage to the environment, one would think that advocates of offshore oil drilling would take a breath. But, amazingly, some are still preaching "drill, baby, drill."

appetite for oil, the United States has only a tiny fraction of the world's crude oil reserves.

Domestic U.S. oil production peaked in 1972, at almost 3.5 billion barrels per year. In the last 10 years, despite advances in extraction technology, annual domestic production has dropped to around 2 billion barrels.

The simple fact is that if we open all offshore waters to drilling, we would supply only one year of oil for the United States.

A better approach is to use our existing supplies more efficiently by investing in clean, green technology.

Instead of subsidizing oil production, the United States should expand support for efficient transportation technologies, such as hybrid

NO

U.S. can't afford to pass up gulf

By Mark J. Perry
McClatchy New Service

Those who disparage offshore drilling — and seem eager to ban it — ignore that the Gulf of Mexico accounts for one-third of U.S. oil production. Without domestic production, we would be spending even more on imported oil — which is already running $1.5 billion a day.

Any sensible response to the explosion on the Deepwater Horizon oil rig — and the huge oil spill that's fouling gulf waters — needs to recognize two facts. First, the demand for oil is expected to increase. Second, America cannot suddenly stop offshore drilling.

The best place in the United States to find new oil is in the gulf's untapped

50 miles from Florida.

The Gulf of Mexico is among the best areas to which U.S. companies still have access. Drilling for oil in the gulf is an opportunity we cannot afford to squander. Our energy security and economic growth depend on it.

Producing oil safely is essential. The offshore rig explosion that cost the lives of 11 men and threatens the gulf shores was such a shock that it has restarted a national debate on safety.

Imposing a ban on offshore oil development would be a mistake of historic proportions.

The fact is, before the Deepwater Horizon capsized, there had not been a large oil spill from an offshore drilling rig in

IF

-RUDYARD KIPLING

IF YOU CAN KEEP YOUR HEAD WHEN ALL ABOUT YOU
ARE LOSING THEIRS AND BLAMING IT ON YOU;
IF YOU CAN TRUST YOURSELF WHEN ALL MEN DOUBT YOU;
BUT MAKE ALLOWANCE FOR THEIR DOUBTING TOO,
IF YOU CAN WAIT AND NOT BE TIRED BY WAITING,
OR, BEING LIED ABOUT DON'T DEAL IN LIES,
OR, BEING HATED, DON'T GIVE WAY TO HATING,
AND YET DON'T LOOK TOO GOOD, NOR TALK TOO WISE;
IF YOU CAN DREAM-AND NOT MAKE DREAMS YOUR MASTER
IF YOU CAN THINK-AND NOT MAKE THOUGHTS YOUR AIM;
IF YOU CAN MEET WITH TRIUMPH AND DISASTER
AND TREAT THOSE TWO IMPOSTORS JUST THE SAME,
IF YOU CAN BEAR TO HEAR THE TRUTH YOU'VE SPOKEN
TWISTED BY KNAVES TO MAKE A TRAP FOR FOOLS,
OR WATCH THE THINGS YOU GAVE YOUR LIFE TO BROKEN,
AND STOOP AND BUILD 'EM UP WITH WORN OUT TOOLS;
IF YOU CAN MAKE ONE HEAP OF ALL YOUR WINNINGS
AND RISK IT ON ONE TURN OF PITCH-AND -TOSS,
AND LOSE, AND START AGAIN AT YOUR BEGINNINGS
AND NEVER BREATHE A WORD ABOUT YOUR LOSS;
IF YOU CAN FORCE YOUR HEART ND NERVE AND SINEW
TO SERVE YOUR TURN LONG AFTER THEY ARE GONE,
AND SO BOLD ON WHEN THERE IS NOTHING IN YOU
EXCEPT THE WILL WHICH SAYS TO THEM:"HOLD ON";
IF YOU CAN TALK WITH CROWDS AND KEEP YOUR VIRTUE,
OR WALK WITH KINGS-NOR LOSE THE COMMON TOUCH;
IF NEITHER FOES NOR LOVING FRIENDS CAN HURT YOU;
IF ALL MEN COUNT WITH YOU, BUT NONE TOO MUCH;
IF YOU CAN FILL THE UNFORGIVING MINUTE
WITH SIXTY SECONDS' WORTH OF DISTANCE RUN
YOURS IS THE EARTH AND EVERYTHING THAT'S IN IT,
AND-WHICH IS MORE YOU'LL BE A MAN, MY SON!

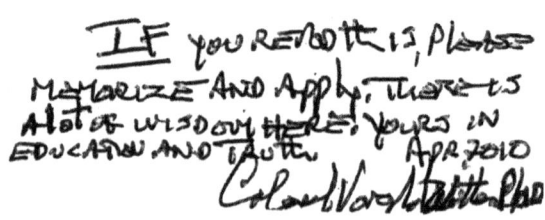

IF you read it is please memorize and apply, there is a lot of wisdom here; yours in education and truth, Apr 2010
Colonel Vaughan Witten PhD

18 JUNE 2010 FAYOBS, NC

Politics of self-preservation

The big oil spill in the Gulf of Mexico is bad enough in itself. But politics can make anything worse.

Let's stop and think. Either the government knows how to stop the oil spill or they don't. If they know how to stop it, then why have they let thousands of barrels of oil per day keep gushing out, for weeks on end? All they have to do is tell BP to step aside, while the government comes in to do it right.

If they don't know, then what is all this political grandstanding about keeping their boot on the neck of BP, the attorney general of the United States going down to the Gulf to threaten lawsuits — on what charges was unspecified — and President Obama showing up in his shirt sleeves?

This government is not about governing. It is about creating an impression. That worked on the campaign trail in 2008, but it is a disaster in the White House, where rhetoric is no substitute for reality.

If the Obama administration was for real, and trying to help get the oil spill contained as soon as possible, the last thing its attorney general would be doing is threatening a lawsuit. A lawsuit is not going

Thomas Sowell

to stop the oil, and creating a distraction can only make people at BP start directing their attention toward covering themselves, instead of covering the oil well.

If and when the attorney general finds that BP did something illegal, that will be time enough to start a lawsuit. But making a public announcement at this time accomplishes absolutely nothing substantive. It is just more political grandstanding. This is not about oil. This is about snake oil.

Nothing will keep a man or an institution determined to continue on a failing policy course like past success with that policy. Obama's political success in the 2008 election campaign was a spectacular triumph of creating images and impressions.

But creating political impressions and images is not the same thing as governing. Yet, Obama in the White House keeps on saying and doing things to impress people, instead of governing.

Once the elections were

over and the time for governing began, there was now a new audience to consider — the leaders of other countries around the world. However impressed the media and the Obama cult might be with the president's image, rhetoric and style, leaders of other countries — allies and enemies alike — are interested in results.

Even our domestic policies can affect foreign leaders, as Ronald Reagan's breaking of the air traffic controllers' strike impressed the Russians with what kind of man they were going to have to deal with.

Domestic bungling by Barack Obama sends a dangerous signal to countries hostile to us, in addition to the signal sent by his displays of amateurism on the world stage.

President Obama had barely settled into the White House before he began demonstrating his willingness to sell out this country's friends to appease our enemies. His trip to Moscow to try to make a deal with the Russians, based on reneging on the pre-existing American commitment to put a missile shield in Eastern Europe, was the kind of short-sighted betrayal whose consequences can come back to haunt a nation for years.

Obama spoke grandly about "pressing the reset button" on international relations, as if all the international commitments of the past were his to disregard. But if no American commitment can be depended upon beyond a current administration, then any nation that allies itself with us is jeopardizing its own national security, because dangers in the international jungle last longer than four or even eight years.

We are already seeing the consequences. Even Turkey is cozying up to Iran, now that it is painfully clear that Obama is not going to do anything that has any realistic chance of stopping Iran from going nuclear.

If leaders of other nations can't depend on the United States, then they need to make the best deal they can with our enemies. They understand that preserving their nations' security is a leader's top priority, even if Barack Obama doesn't.

Thomas Sowell is a syndicated columnist. Readers may write to him at www.tsowell.com, at info@creators.com (with his name in the subject line) or Creators Syndicate, 5777 W. Century Blvd., Suite 700, Los Angeles, CA 90045.

CONGRATS..

'NAM 64-73

AFGHAN WAR 01—

LONGEST WAR

MAY OBS - NC

The tragedy of black families

Forty-five years ago this summer, a report on serious declines in traditional black American family life leaked out of President Lyndon Johnson's labor department and exploded into controversy. We've been grappling with the issue ever since.

The report by Assistant Labor Secretary Daniel Patrick Moynihan is largely forgotten, but the sociopolitical arguments that it ignited continue to burn, often with more heat than light, in that rough terrain between raw emotions and rational thought.

"It proved enormously controversial and established its author's reputation as an iconoclast, yet today the Moynihan Report is largely forgotten," says James T. Patterson, history professor emeritus at Brown. "Sadly, its predictions about the decline of the black family have proven largely correct."

Tragically so. In 1963, a fourth of nonwhite births in this country were out of wedlock, eight times the proportion among whites. Today, black non-marital

Clarence Page

births have soared to more than 72 percent among non-Hispanic blacks, compared with about 28 percent for whites.

At the time of its publication, the report was denounced mostly by angry black leaders and social critics as wrong, insensitive and even racist. In his new and richly detailed book, "Freedom Is Not Enough: The Moynihan Report and America's Struggle Over Black Family Life From LBJ to Obama," Patterson concludes that controversy resulted from the report's timing, it's candid language and the race of its author.

When a major race riot broke out in the Watts section of Los Angeles later that summer and the Vietnam War escalated, the Moynihan Report and its "case for national action"

was shelved. With it went a missed opportunity, in Moynihan's and Patterson's view, for government to take such actions as, say, a focused effort to employ black fathers and make them more "marriageable," as Harvard sociologist William Julius Wilson has written.

Yet, what can government do about marriage? There's little dispute that kids who grow up with married parents at home tend to do better by all measures than those who don't. But the pro-marriage streak in mainstream American values rubs up against our love for personal freedom.

We now have a black president who has repeatedly expressed the same alarm over black family disintegration that touched off a culture war when Moynihan expressed it. Yet, we as a nation still seem to prefer to ignore the decline in marriage or argue about its causes than to take action to reverse it — or help the children whose upbringing is damaged by it.

Patterson finds hope in programs such as the nationally acclaimed Harlem Children's Zone, which "wraps

children in a community of love," as its founder Geoffrey Canada likes to say, often while they're still in the womb.

Serving 8,000 children in a 100-block area, the $58 million program includes a "baby college" for parents, all-day kindergarten classes, charter schools, after-school tutoring and a health clinic. The Zone offers young couples counseling and other help for their children from prenatal and preschool all the way to college. The program reaches out to parents before birth, if possible, a time when the young fathers often want to be involved but haven't a clue as to what to do.

President Obama promised in his 2008 campaign to help replicate the Zone in 20 cities. It's not the long-sought "magic bullet" to beat the problems of child poverty, but if there's any chance for us to fill the gap that vanishing marriage has left, all-inclusive community-based approaches such as this one are a good place to start.

Clarence Page is a syndicated columnist with the Chicago Tribune. E-mail him at cpage@tribune.com.

Gulf oil Spill
Louisiana, Miss, Alabama

21 JUN

Gulf oil '11

Fugitive gang leader in custody

The Associated Press

KINGSTON, Jamaica — Reputed gang leader Christopher "Dudus" Coke, who eluded a bloody police offensive in his slum stronghold last month, was arrested Tuesday by authorities outside Jamaica's capital, the island's top cop said.

Coke has been called one of the world's most dangerous drug lords by U.S. authorities and faces trial in New York on drug and arms trafficking charges. His arrest came nearly a month after 76 people were killed during a

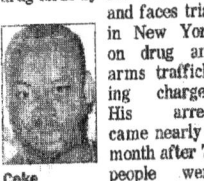

Coke

four-day assault by police and soldiers on the West Kingston slum of Tivoli Gardens, Coke's base that was defended by his armed followers.

At a news conference, Police Commissioner Owen Ellington said Coke was in good condition in police custody. He said Coke was captured by police manning a vehicle checkpoint along a highway, but said other "circumstances of (Coke's) arrest are being investigated."

The Rev. Al Miller, an influential evangelical preacher who facilitated the surrender of Coke's brother earlier this month, said that Coke was prepared to surrender to authorities at the U.S. Embassy in Kingston when police stopped his convoy on a highway outside the capital.

Miller said police captured Coke on the way to the embassy and then took him to the nearby Spanish Town police headquarters. He was then flown to Kingston, the preacher said.

'Useful idiots' have placed nation at risk

Thomas Sowell

When Adolf Hitler was building up the Nazi movement in the 1920s, leading up to his taking power in the 1930s, he deliberately sought to activate people who did not normally pay much attention to politics. Such people were a valuable addition to his political base, since they were particularly susceptible to Hitler's rhetoric and had far less basis for questioning his assumptions or his conclusions.

"Useful idiots" was the term supposedly coined by V.I. Lenin to describe similarly unthinking supporters of his dictatorship in the Soviet Union.

Put differently, a democracy needs informed citizens if it is to thrive, or even survive. In our times, American democracy is being dismantled, piece by piece, before our very eyes by the current administration in Washington, and few people seem to be concerned about it.

available at the discretion of politicians and bureaucrats, private individuals and organizations can be forced into accepting the imposition of powers that were never granted to the government by the Constitution.

If you believe that the end justifies the means, then you don't believe in Constitutional government. And, without Constitutional government, freedom cannot endure. There will always be a "crisis" — which, as the president's chief of staff has said, cannot be allowed to "go to waste" as an opportunity to expand the government's power.

When Franklin D. Roosevelt arbitrarily took the United States off the

Damaging policies

The president's poll numbers are going down because increasing numbers of people disagree with particular policies of his, but the damage being done to the fundamental structure of this nation goes far beyond particular counterproductive policies.

Just where in the Constitution of the United States does it say that a president has the authority to extract vast sums of money from a private enterprise and distribute it as he sees fit to whomever he deems worthy of compensation? Nowhere.

The man appointed by President Obama to dispense BP's money as the administration sees fit is only the latest in a long line of presidentially appointed "czars" controlling different parts of the economy, without even having to be confirmed by the Senate, as Cabinet members are.

Those who cannot see beyond the immediate events to the issues of arbitrary power are the "useful idiots" of our time. But useful to whom?

Thomas Sowell is a syndicated columnist. Readers may write to him at www.tsowell.com, at

Other states want to copy Arizona

■ North Carolina is among those with campaigns to enact tougher immigration laws.

By John Miller
The Associated Press

BOISE, Idaho — Arizona's sweeping new immigration law doesn't even take effect until next month, but lawmakers in nearly 20 other states are already clamoring to follow in its footsteps.

Gubernatorial candidates in Florida and Minnesota are singing the law's praises, as are some lawmakers in other states far from the Mexico border such as Idaho and Nebraska. But states also are watching legal challenges to the law, and whether boycotts over it will harm Arizona's economy.

The law, set to take effect July 29, requires police to check the immigration status of anyone they think is in the country illegally. Violators face up to six months in jail and $2,500 in fines, in addition to federal deportation.

Lawmakers or candidates in as many as 18 states say they want to push similar measures when their legislative sessions start up again in 2011. Arizona-style legislation may have the best chance of passing in Oklahoma, which in 2007 gave police more power to check the immigration status of people they arrest.

Bills similar to the law Arizona's legislature approved in April have already been introduced in Pennsylvania, Rhode Island, Minnesota, South Carolina and Michigan, but none will advance this year.

ARIZONA-STYLE IMMIGRATION LEGISLATION

Other states that have shown interest or have introduced bills similar to Arizona's controversial illegal immigrant enforcement bill.

States with interest in illegal immigration legislation
▨ Have introduced legislation   ▨ Suggested filing in 2011

Source: National Conference of State Legislatures   AP graphic

Business, agriculture and civil rights groups oppose such legislation, saying legal residents who are Hispanic would be unjustly harassed and that immigration is a federal rather than a state responsibility. Supporters say police will not stop people solely on the basis of skin color and argue that illegal immigrants are draining state coffers by taking jobs, using public services, fueling gang violence and filling prisons.

Arizona Gov. Jan Brewer said Friday that most illegal immigrants entering Arizona are being used to transport drugs across the border, an assertion that critics slammed as exaggerated and racist. Brewer said the motiva-

tion of "a lot" of the illegal immigrants is to enter the United States to look for work, but that drug rings press them into duty as drug "mules."

"I believe today, under the circumstances that we're facing, that the majority of the illegal trespassers that are

poll this month found that 85 percent of people rank immigration as an important issue, and about half disapprove of how Obama has handled it.

Even lawmakers in states far from the U.S.-Mexico border say illegal immigration is hurting their constituents.

N.C. effort

William Gheen, president of the North Carolina-based Americans for Legal Immigration Political Action Committee, said the more states that sign on, the more likely Congress will be to act. Gheen has led a grassroots campaign to get legislatures to take up Arizona's bill and believes the topic could become the litmus test in an election year when people are already slamming Washington.

"Any candidate that wants to survive the bloodbath that's approaching this November needs to come out in support" of Arizona's law, Gheen said. He sends regular e-mail messages

Panetta: U.S. is struggling with Taliban

■ The director of the CIA says insurgents have grown in violence and aggression.

By Anne Flaherty
The Associated Press

Panetta

WASHINGTON — The U.S. has driven al-Qaida into hiding and undermined its leadership, but is struggling to oust its primary sympathizer, the Taliban, from Afghanistan, the nation's spymaster said Sunday.

sacked this past week in a stunning shake-up in U.S. military leadership after his critical comments about the White House.

"We're seeing elements of progress, but this is going to be tough," Panetta told ABC's "This Week."

He said al-Qaida's evolving attack strategy increasingly relies on operatives

AFGHANISTAN

Obama's forgetting the details

FAJOBS, NC

22 JUNE 2010

Roger Simon

We are going to "mobilize." We are going to have a "battle plan." We are going to set up a "fund." And we are going to get the tourists "to come back."

We are going to have a "long-term Gulf Coast Restoration Plan." We have established "a National Commission." And we are going to build "a new organization."

We are in a crisis because of "a lack of political courage and candor." But "the time to embrace a clean energy future is now."

"There are costs associated with this transition," but the one thing the president "will not accept is inaction."

But do not worry.

"Even if we don't yet know precisely how to get there," said the president, "we know we'll get there."

How? Why? Because we won World War II. And we landed "a man safely on the surface of the moon."

All we need now is "courage." And a "hand" to guide us "towards a brighter day."

And that was pretty much President Obama's entire speech to the nation.

The president is trying to pull off a tough trick: He is trying to do what Lyndon Johnson did when Johnson used a stunning tragedy — the assassination of John F. Kennedy — to bludgeon Congress into passing Johnson's Great Society. And Johnson succeeded. He got the Civil Rights Act, the War on Poverty, Medicare and Medicaid.

But that was then. And this is now, and the nation is not stunned the way it was when Kennedy was killed. Today, the nation is nervous, twitchy, angry.

Why is that evil black cloud of oil still gushing? Who is going to stop it? When? How? And why haven't they done it already?

"What sees us through — what has always seen us through — is our strength, our resilience and our unyielding faith that something better awaits us if we summon the courage to reach for it," the president said.

Uh, yeah. Nobody is more impressed than I am in the president's ability to inspire. But I am not sure his speech was all that inspirational.

Maybe the location was wrong. Maybe using the Oval Office — and it was the first time the president has used it for a speech — upped the ante too much. Maybe we expected too much.

Like details.

I interviewed Obama, and he told me that what the American people "hope and expect is for the president to do everything that's within his power. They don't expect us to be magicians."

But I am not so sure that is true. Don't we expect our presidents to be just a little magical, to be able to do things that ordinary mortals cannot? Isn't that why we elect them?

"If something isn't working, we want to hear about it," the president said Tuesday. "If there are problems in the operation, we will fix them."

Well, something isn't working, Mr. President. And there are problems in the operation.

So maybe now is the time to dig real deep in your hat and see if you can find a rabbit. Or two.

Roger Simon is the chief political columnist of politico.com, an award-winning journalist and a New York Times best-selling author.

![World's Highest Standard of Living cartoon]

McChrystal wasn't the problem

I feel sorry for Stan McChrystal. He got sacked because his aides were too honest with a Rolling Stone reporter. They rashly exposed a problem that is undercutting the war effort: the infighting among civilian and military officials in Kabul and Washington.

The general's aides shouldn't have mocked top civilian officials, and he deserved to be chastised. However, President Obama, in explaining the general's firing, said the war requires "unity of effort." If so, he'll need to do more than send the general home.

McChrystal's staff made snide remarks to Rolling Stone about Vice President Biden, Ambassador Richard Holbrooke and National Security Adviser James Jones. The general complained about being "betrayed" by Karl Eikenberry, the U.S. ambassador to Kabul. Obama argued that the Rolling Stone piece "erodes the trust necessary for the team to work together."

What trust? The article reflects serious tensions between Obama's civilian and military advisers in Kabul, fed by the conflicting positions of White House and Cabinet officials on Afghan strategy. These tensions make it impossible to fashion a coherent policy that Americans — and Afghans —

Trudy Rubin

can understand.

McChrystal and Eikenberry differed over how to wage the war and how to deal with Afghan President Hamid Karzai. The relationship between embassy and military commanders in Kabul remains distant and mistrustful.

To complicate matters further, the president's special envoy to the region, the brilliant but brusque Richard Holbrooke, is resented by embassy staff as well as many in the military. His infrequent presence causes confusion among Afghan officials about who speaks for the president.

Obama's D.C. team adds to the confusion, with Biden making statements about Obama's 2011 pullout deadline that conflict with those of the secretaries of defense and state, Robert Gates and Hillary Clinton. The president has yet to clarify whose interpretation he endorses.

"This is a highly dysfunctional team," said former U.S. Ambassador to Iraq Ryan Crocker, referring to those who work on the war in Afghanistan. "You can't

win the big war if we're fighting the small ones with each other. And unity has to start at the top."

Indeed, the only good that might emerge from McChrystal's exit is if Obama — and Gen. David Petraeus, his choice to succeed McChrystal — can finally weld these players into a team that works together. Otherwise, the sacking will only aid those who are cheering American disarray.

It was very risky for Obama to fire McChrystal, who never challenged the president's Afghan strategy. McChrystal leaves at a key juncture, with efforts to stabilize southern Afghanistan, the Taliban heartland, faltering.

That said, we are fortunate Petraeus is willing to step down from a broader command of Mideast operations (including Afghanistan and Pakistan) to take the job of NATO and U.S. commander in Kabul. He is wholly familiar with the strategy and the players, and has a history, in Iraq, of making counterinsurgency work.

Of critical import, he made military-civilian cooperation a virtual religion when he worked with Crocker in Baghdad. If he wants to counteract the downside of McChrystal's exit, Obama should give Petraeus all the

backing he needs.

And the president should use McChrystal's departure to send the message that his entire Afghan team needs to start cooperating with each other.

Obama needs to lead by example. If Gates, Petraeus and Clinton believe (wisely, in my book) that the 2011 deadline depends on conditions on the ground, and Biden says otherwise, the president should clarify his position and keep everyone on message.

Indeed, if the president really seeks "unity of effort" on the war, it's time to summon Biden, Jones, Gates and Clinton, along with Eikenberry and Petraeus, for separate and collective consultations, to see whether they are ready to cooperate. If not, more changes of personnel are needed.

It's tragic enough that a talented general has been disgraced. But at least this episode should serve some purpose. Otherwise, the civilian-military divisions that brought down McChrystal will continue to haunt Petraeus and undercut our efforts in Afghanistan.

Trudy Rubin is a columnist and editorial-board member for the Philadelphia Inquirer. Write her at: Philadelphia Inquirer, P.O. Box 8263, Philadelphia, Pa. 19101, or e-mail trubin@phillynews.com.

BP: Relief well on target

to worries.

By Michael Kunzelman
The Associated Press

NEW ORLEANS — BP's effort to drill a relief well through 2½ miles of rock to stop the Gulf spill is on target for completion by mid-August, the oil giant said Friday. But BP's stock tumbled anyway over the mounting costs of the disaster and the company's inability to

The loss of an American institution

By Marilyn Johnson

The United States is beginning an interesting experiment in democracy: We're cutting public library funds, shrinking our public and school libraries, and in some places, shutting them altogether.

These actions have nothing to do with whether the libraries are any good or whether the staff provides useful service to the community. This country's largest circulating library, in Queens, N.Y., was named the best system in the United States last year by Library Journal. Its budget is due to shrink by a third.

If you visit public libraries, you will see an essential service in action, as librarians help people who don't have other ways to get online, can't get the answers they urgently need, or simply need a safe place to bring their children.

The people who welcome us to the library are idealists, who believe that accurate information leads to good decisions and that exposure to the intellectual riches of civilization leads to a better world. While they help us get online, employed and informed, librarians don't try to sell us anything. Nor do they turn around and broadcast our problems, send us spam or keep a record of our interests and needs, because no matter how savvy this profession is at navigating the online world, it clings to that old-fashioned value, privacy. They represent the best civic value out there, an army of resourceful workers that can help us compete in the world.

Instead of putting such conscientious, economical and service-oriented professionals to work helping us, we're handing them pink slips. The school libraries and public libraries in which we've invested decades and even centuries of resources will disappear unless we fight for them.

Those in cities that haven't preserved their libraries, those less fortunate and baffled by technology, and our children will be the first to suffer. But sooner or later, we'll all feel the loss as one of the most effective levelers of privilege and avenues of reinvention begins to disappear.

Marilyn Johnson is the author of "This Book Is Overdue!" She wrote this for the Los Angeles Times.

Another kind of depression

The economic effects of the Great Recession have been easy to see: a stock market crash, a sickening drop in home values and household wealth, and the throbbing pain of persistent unemployment.

But a deep recession does more than economic damage. When short-term unemployment turns into long-term unemployment, as it has in this recession to a level unseen since the 1930s, rates of depression (the psychiatric kind) increase, anxiety rises and behavior changes in ways both expected and unexpected.

Take birthrates, for example. They have fallen during the last two years, most sharply in states with high unemployment and mortgage foreclosure rates.

Here's something more surprising: As the recession deepens, participation in civic activities — community organizations, volunteer groups, even church attendance and social clubs — is likely to drop. Sociologists once assumed that during hard times people would naturally band together, if only to protest their plight or to give each other solace. It turns out that the opposite is true: Economic distress causes people to withdraw.

Jennie E. Brand of UCLA

Doyle McManus

studied the ripple effect of unemployment among families in Wisconsin, and she says there are several reasons: People who lose their jobs feel depressed; they sometimes feel ashamed of their financial troubles; they lose some of their trust in society; and some of them move to new communities where they have no ties.

Brand's most important finding is that the social and psychological effects of unemployment can be lifelong, even if the economic distress is only transient.

"People who lost their job even once, were roughly 30 percent less likely to participate in community activities, and that lasted through their lives," she said her Wisconsin study. "Twent[y] years later, they were still l[ess] likely to participate."

A study just released by the Pew Research Center suggests that if this recessi[on] has a similar effect, the impact on American societ[y] could be deep and long.

IRAQ
Suicide bombers kill scores in attacks

■ Sunni fighters who turned against al-Qaida are targeted.

By Barbara Surk
The Associated Press

BAGHDAD — A suicide bomber ripped through a line of anti-al-Qaida Sunni fighters waiting to collect their paychecks near an Iraqi military base as nearly 50 people were killed in violence west of Baghdad.

The attack is the deadliest this year against the groups that turned against the terror network amid an apparent campaign by insurgents to undermine confidence in the government security forces and their allies.

The attacks on the Awakening Council members highlighted the daunting security challenges the country faces as the U.S. works to withdraw all combat troops in Iraq.

The first attack Sunday morning by a single bomber with an explosive vest killed at least 45 people and wounded more than 40 at a checkpoint near a military base in the mostly Sunni district of Radwaniya southwest of Baghdad.

About 150 Sunni fighters had lined up to collect their paychecks when the bomber

See IRAQ, Page 4A

July 18 FEDERAL BENEFITS *FA-1085* *NC*

Obama: Post-traumatic stress help 'long overdue'

By Julie Pace
The Associated Press

WASHINGTON — The government is taking what President Obama calls "a long overdue step" to aid veterans with post-traumatic stress disorder, making it easier for them to receive federal benefits.

The changes that Veteran Affairs Secretary Eric Shinseki will announce Monday fulfill "a solemn responsibility to provide our veterans and wounded warriors with the care and benefits they've earned when they come home," Obama said in his week-ly radio and online address Saturday.

The new rules will apply not only to veterans of the Iraq and Afghanistan wars, but also those who served in previous conflicts.

No longer will veterans have to prove what caused their illness. Instead, they would have to show that the conditions surrounding the time and place of their service could have contributed to their illness.

"I don't think our troops on the battlefield should have to take

See **PTSD**, Page 5A

PTSD

From Page 1A

notes to keep for a claims application," the president said. "And I've met enough veterans to know that you don't have to engage in a firefight to endure the trauma of war."

Veterans advocates and some lawmakers have argued that it sometimes could be impossible for veterans to find records of a firefight or bomb blast.

They also have contended that the old rules ignored other causes of PTSD, such as fearing a traumatic event even if it doesn't occur. That could discriminate against female troops prohibited from serving on front lines and against other service members who don't experience combat directly.

"This is a long overdue step," Obama said. "It's a step that proves America will always be here for our veterans, just as they've been there for us. We won't let them down. We take care of our own."

A study last year by the RAND Corp. think tank estimated that nearly 20 percent of returning veterans, or 300,000, have symptoms of PTSD or major depression.

A senior official at the Department of Veterans Affairs said the agency doesn't expect the number of veterans receiving benefits for PTSD to rise dramatically, as most veterans with legitimate applications for benefits do eventually get claims. The goal is simply to make the claims process less cumbersome and time-consuming, said the official, who would speak only on condition of anonymity ahead of the VA's announcement.

5-star rank generally only given to a few

Q: I was getting a haircut the other day and my barber asked me how many five star generals there have been in the history of the U.S. military. I knew there were five, but I could only think of two, Gen Eisenhower and Gen Bradley. — D.I., Fayetteville

A: You're right, there were five. Four of them were appointed within five days in December 1944: George Marshall, Douglas MacArthur, Dwight D. Eisenhower and Henry H. Arnold. Omar Bradley followed six years later.

The five-star insignia was created in 1944 to accompany the rank of General of the Army. The rank was introduced to give American commanders the same rank as their field marshal equivalents in the British army during World War II.

The rank still exists and can be bestowed in times of war, but hasn't been since Bradley.

An earlier version of the General of the Army title was created in 1866 and given to Ulysses Grant, but came with only four stars. At that time, the title could only be held by one general at a time. Upon his installation as president in 1869, Grant was succeeded by William T. Sherman as General of the Army. Philip Sheridan followed in 1888, but died the same year and the rank was not passed on.

There is one higher rank in the U.S. Army: General of the Armies. Note the plural. It's only been used twice. John J. Pershing received it in 1919 for his service during World War I, and it was bestowed posthumously upon George Washington as part of the bicentennial celebrations in 1976. — G.P.

FAY OBS   TUESDAY, JULY 20, 2010   3A

WAKE COUNTY SCHOOL BOARD

19 arrested as racial tensions rise

AP photo

Andrea Charity, left, and Monique Davis march down Fayetteville Street in Raleigh on Tuesday.

■ Protesters angry over a busing system disrupt a meeting and take to the streets.

By Mike Baker
The Associated Press

RALEIGH — Protesters and police scuffled Tuesday at a school board meeting in North Carolina over claims that a new busing system would resegregate schools, roiling racial tensions remi-

niscent of the 1960s.

Nineteen people were arrested, including the head of state NAACP chapter who was banned from the meeting after a trespassing arrest at a June school board gathering.

"We know that our cause is right," the Rev. William Barber said shortly before police put plastic handcuffs on his wrists before the meeting started.

Inside, more than a dozen

See **PROTEST**, Page 4A

The Rev. William Barber, head of the state NAACP chapter, was arrested outside the Wake County School Board's offices in Raleigh on Tuesday.

YEARLONG DEPLOYMENT   20 July 10

Guard to patrol border

By Suzanne Gamboa
The Associated Press

WASHINGTON — National Guard troops will head to the U.S.-Mexico border Aug. 1 for a yearlong deployment to keep a lookout for illegal border crossers and smugglers and help in criminal investigations, federal officials said Monday.

The troops will be armed but can use their weapons only to protect themselves, Gen. Craig McKinley, chief of the National Guard Bureau, told a Pentagon news conference. The troops will undergo initial training and be fully deployed along the nearly 2,000-mile southern border by September.

The announcement provides details on how the government will implement President Obama's May decision to bolster border security and comes as drug-related violence has escalated in Mexico, where several people died over the weekend in a car bombing and in a separate massacre at a private party. It also comes as the U.S. debate over illegal immigration has intensified in an election year.

"The border is more secure and more resourced than it has ever been, but there is more to be done," said Alan Bersin, commissioner of Customs and Border Protection, part of the Homeland Security Department.

The 1,200 troops will be distributed among four border states, with Arizona getting 524; Texas, 250; California, 224 and New Mexico, 72. Another 130 would be assigned to a national liaison office.

Bersin said the Homeland Security Department will provide six more aircraft, including helicopters, to the border. He said at least 300 Customs and Border Protection agents and inspection officers will be sent to the Tucson area, along with mobile surveillance vans and addi-

been somewhat deficient, and they're bolstering that."

Arizona Gov. Jan Brewer, a Republican, said the deployment isn't enough "nor tied to a strategy to comprehensively defeat the increasingly violent drug- and alien-smuggling cartels that operate in Arizona on a daily basis."

U.S. Reps. Ann Kirkpatrick and Gabrielle Giffords, both D-Ariz., separately called the announced actions welcome but insufficient.

"This is the kind of action we want from the administration — not suing the state," Kirkpatrick said, referring to the Department of Justice's challenge to the new Arizona immigration enforcement law.

Deployed by Bush

President George W. Bush

grants. The troops' deployment ended in July 2008.

McKinley said even though the four border states are contributing 54,000 troops to the wars in Iraq and Afghanistan, they still have a sizable number available for other deployments or disaster response. More can be deployed at state cost if governors wish, but the 1,200 are being paid for by the federal government, he said.

"Right now I cannot see a case where we would be overextending the National Guard for this effort," he said.

Immigration and Customs Enforcement also is beefing up its presence in Arizona, said John Morton, the Homeland Security Department assistant secretary overseeing the agency.

USDA employee pressed to resign over remark

20 July 10

By Ben Evans and Mary Clare Jalonick
The Associated Press

WASHINGTON — The Obama administration is standing by its quick decision to oust a black Agriculture Department employee over racially tinged remarks at an NAACP banquet in Georgia, despite evidence that her remarks were misconstrued and growing calls for USDA to reconsider.

Shirley Sherrod, who until Tuesday was the Agriculture Department's director of rural development in Georgia, says the administration caved to political pressure by pushing her to resign for saying that she didn't give a white farmer as much help as she could have 24 years ago when she worked for a non-

profit group.

Sherrod says her remarks, delivered in March at a local NAACP banquet in Georgia, were part of a story about racial reconciliation, not racism. The white farming family that was the subject of the story stood by Sherrod and said she should keep her job.

"We probably wouldn't have (our farm) today if it hadn't been for her leading us in the right direction," said Eloise Spooner, the wife of farmer Roger Spooner of Iron City, Ga. "I wish she could get her job back because she was good to us, I tell you."

The NAACP, which initially condemned Sherrod's remarks and supported Sherrod's ouster, joined the calls

for her to keep her job. The civil rights group said it and millions of others were duped by the conservative website that posted partial video of her speech on Monday.

"We have come to the conclusion we were snookered ... into believing she had harmed white farmers because of racial bias," said the NAACP statement.

The website, biggovernment.com, gained fame last year after airing video of workers at the community group ACORN counseling actors posing as a prostitute and her boyfriend. It posted the Sherrod video as evidence that the NAACP, which recently passed a resolution condemning what it calls racist elements of the Tea Party, condones racism of its own.

Rangel faces ethics charg

**By Lisa Mascaro
and Michael A. Memoli**
Tribune Washington Bureau

WASHINGTON — Democratic Rep. Charles B. Rangel, once among the most powerful members of Congress, will face a hearing next week on charges that he violated House ethics rules after a panel of his peers formally accused him of wrongdoing Thursday following a two-year investigation.

The veteran New York congressman was accused by House ethics investigators who have been poring over records of his travel and record keeping in response to complaints over his corporate-paid trips, his use of sev-

eral rent-controlled apartments and other allegations.

Rangel, 80, could face reprimand, censure or expulsion if the House Ethics Committee determines he has violated rules. Any such sanction would be subject to a vote of the full House.

Not since 2002, when Congress was investigating then-Rep. James Traficant of Ohio, has the secretive Ethics Committee convened such a proceeding. Rangel, who has been in Congress for 40 years, is expected to mount a vigorous defense.

"For over two years I've been asking them to look at this and to throw out what I believe has no substance."

Rep. Charlie Rangel, D-N.Y., speaks to reporters Thursday on Capitol Hill.
AP photo

Rangel told reporters at the Capitol on Thursday. "I don't have any fear at all, politically or personally, what they come up with."

The committee announced that a public hearing would begin next Thursday. It could take several days for

lawmakers on the panel to decide whether ethics investigators have proven their case. No formal charges have yet been made public.

Rangel requested the Ethics Committee investigation in July 2008 following published reports concerning

corporate-pa
Caribbean, h
rent-stabiliz
New York
fundraising a
volved the u
tionary.

A spokes
Speaker Na
Calif., said t
tee's action
the independ
ethics comm
moving forw

But the pi
ceeding is l
amid a Dem
retain contro
this fall's mi
and Thursd
ment carried
overtones.

So much for racial tolerance

Weren't we supposed to enter a new age of tolerance with the election of President Barack Obama?

His half-black, half-white ancestry and broad support across racial lines suggested that at last Americans judged each other on the content of our characters — not the color of our skin or our tribal affiliations.

Instead, in just 18 months of the Obama administration, racial discord is growing and relations seem to have been set back a generation.

Black voters are galvanizing behind Obama at a time of rapidly falling support. White independents, in contrast, are leaving Obama in droves.

The National Association for the Advancement of Colored People has claimed that the loosely organized Tea Party includes "racist elements." The National Council of La Raza has ripped the state of Arizona for its new anti-illegal alien legislation. Jesse Jackson characterized aspects of the multimillion-dollar bidding war to acquire basketball superstar LeBron James in terms of masters and

Victor Davis Hanson

slaves. Pundits are arguing whether the fringe racist New Black Panther Party is analogous to the Klan.

Indeed, race seems to be the subtext of almost every contemporary issue. In times of growing deficits, white people are stereotyped as being angry over supposedly paying higher taxes to subsidize minorities, while minorities are stereotyped as being mostly on the receiving end of entitlements.

Why the escalation of racial tension in the supposed postracial age of Obama?

First, Obama's reputation as a racial healer was largely the creation of the media. In fact, Obama had a number of racially polarizing incidents that probably would have disqualified any other presidential candidate of the past 30 years.

His two-decade

apprenticeship at Trinity Church under the racist and anti-Semitic Rev. Jeremiah Wright has never been adequately explained. Obama indulged in racial stereotyping when he wrote off the white lower-middle class of Pennsylvania as clueless zealots clinging to their guns, religion and xenophobia. Obama also characterized his grandmother as a "typical white person" when he implied that her supposed fear of young black males symbolizes the prejudices of the entire white community.

The president himself criticized Cambridge, Mass., police for acting "stupidly" when they arrested his friend, Harvard professor Henry Louis Gates.

Attorney General Eric Holder blasted America as "a nation of cowards" for not talking more about race on his terms. Supreme Court Justice Sonia Sotomayor was almost obsessive in self-referencing herself as a "Latina." She also suggested that her racial background and experiences made her "wise" in a way white male colleagues could never be.

Recently, Obama

appealed to voters along exclusionary race and gender lines when he called upon "the young people, African-Americans, Latinos and women, who powered our victory in 2008."

We are a racially diverse society of Asians, blacks, Hispanics, whites, and mixtures of all that and more. Race is no longer necessarily a guide to politics.

The more the president appeals to his base in racial terms, the more his appointees identify themselves as members of a particular tribe, and the more political issues are framed by racial divisions, so all the more such racial obsession creates a backlash among the racially diverse American people.

America has largely moved beyond race. Tragically, our president and a host of his supportive special interests have not.

Victor Davis Hanson is a classicist and historian at the Hoover Institution, Stanford University, and the author of "The Father of Us All: War and History, Ancient and Modern." E-mail him at author@victorhanson.com.

Clearing the air on more Social Security myths

In last week's column, I took on some allegations from a diatribe called a "Social Security History Lesson" that's floating around on the Internet.

This week, I am looking at more misleading allegations.

Allegation: The Internet document asks, "Which political party started taxing Social Security annuities?" And it answers the question this way: "The Democratic Party, with Al Gore casting the tie-breaking vote."

Fact: President Reagan first started taxing Social Security benefits when he signed the Social Security Reform Act of 1983.

At the time, there were

Your Social Security
Tom Margenau

only enough reserves left in the Social Security trust funds to keep the system running for another five years or so. Reagan created the National Commission on Social Security Reform and named Alan Greenspan to head the panel. They produced a series of proposals that Reagan signed into law — some of which cut benefits and some of which raised revenues. Their actions are in large part responsible for keeping the Social Security system solvent to this day.

It was the Clinton administration that modified the tax rules in 1993 by raising the portion of benefits subject to taxation for wealthier people from 50 percent to 85 percent.

The majority of Americans don't pay taxes on their benefits. In order to have your benefits taxed, your overall income has to exceed certain thresholds that depend on whether or not you are married and on your tax filing status.

Allegation: The Internet history lesson asks this question, "Which political party decided to start giving Social Security payments to immigrants?" And it answers, "That's right! Jimmy Carter and the Democratic Party. Immigrants move into this country, and at age 65, they begin to receive Social Security payments. The Democratic Party gave these payments to them, even though they never paid a dime into it!"

Facts: No one can get Social Security retirement benefits unless he or she has worked and paid enough Social Security taxes to become insured.

Also, from the time the original Social Security Act was passed in 1935, the law has never set a citizenship test for benefit eligibility. As long as you had worked long enough to be insured, you could receive retirement benefits at age 62. And a small fraction of those benefits are paid to immigrants who are living in this country legally.

While Jimmy Carter was president, the first international Social Security treaty agreements were signed. Often, citizens of one country were working in another country. But this led to all kinds of issues with respect to Social Security taxes and eventual Social Security benefits: Should you pay Social Security taxes to your native country or to the country in which you are working? Should you get Social Security benefits from your native country or from the country where you were working? These are the kinds of issues the Social Security treaty agreements are designed to deal with.

President Carter signed the first of these treaties in the late 1970s with Italy and Germany. Today, we have such agreements with about 25 countries.

Send questions to Tom Margenau at yoursocialsecurity@comcast.net, or write to Social Security Office, P.O. Box 120190, San Diego, CA 92112-0190.

Creators Syndicate

No, we couldn't

Syndicated columnist Cal Thomas:

America — or at least the part of it that voted for Barack Obama for president — has made a big mistake. Some of those teary-eyed people in Chicago's Hyde Park neighborhood on Election Night 2008 would probably admit it if they were interviewed. Many bumper stickers still display fading "Obama '08" stickers, but you'd find fewer that read, "Yes We Can!"

There is no shame in making a mistake. Everybody makes plenty in a lifetime, even in elections.

The mistake made by those who voted for Obama, thinking it would be different with him, is their belief that it would be different with him. A politician is a politician. That is not necessarily an evil thing. We must have politicians, I suppose, but like the metaphorical crazy aunt who is kept in the attic, a politician should be kept in his or her place, lest the house become chaotic.

Fayetteville Observer, NC

MILITARY   SUNDAY, AUGUST 1, 2010   3D

Agent Orange countdown nears

The Department of Veterans Affairs likely will begin in October to pay thousands of disability claims to Vietnam veterans with ischemic heart disease, Parkinson's disease and B-cell leukemia – illnesses newly associated with exposure to defoliants, including Agent Orange, used in that war.

A 60-day countdown to the day that VA can start compensating up to 86,000 veterans retroactively for these diseases will begin when VA publishes its final implementing regulation, which could be this week.

Congress sent a strong signal of support to these veterans in July when first the Senate and, on Tuesday, the House passed the Supplemental Appropriations Act of 2010 (HR 4899) which included $13.4 billion for VA to pay the first wave of compensation claims for

Military Update
Tom Philpott

these diseases.

VA estimates this expansion of Agent Orange-related claims, which VA Secretary Eric Shinseki announced last October, will benefit over time more than 153,000 and cost more than $42 billion in its first decade of payments.

The White House's Office of Management and Budget is near to clearing the VA regulation through its last review hurdle. Once the final regulation is published in the Federal Register, Congress will have 60 days to review and possibly block

the regulation.

Sen. Jim Webb, D-Va., showed his intent to lead that review by adding language to the war supplemental stating that, as the Congressional Review Act requires, none of the $13.4 billion can be spent for 60 days. This gives Congress time to weigh the cost and review the science behind the decision.

Sen. Daniel Akaka, D-Hawaii, chairman of the Senate Veterans Affairs Committee on which Webb serves, has scheduled a Sept. 23 hearing where presumably VA officials and independent medical researchers will explain why these diseases should be compensable for any veteran who suffers from them and served even a day in Vietnam.

Webb has argued the VA is interpreting the Agent Orange Law of 1991 too liberally, linking ailments

generally associated with aging to wartime exposures, and committing VA to billions of dollars in added compensation payment, because Congress chose to forfeit its own oversight responsibilities.

Webb notes that the 2001 decision linking Type II diabetes to Agent Orange has resulted in more than 220,000 veterans – nearly one in 10 who served in Vietnam – drawing disability compensation for an illness often associated with unhealthy diets, aging or family history.

That Congress kept $13.4 billion in the war supplemental to pay for expansion of Agent Orange presumptive diseases dampens prospects that Webb can block the regulation at this late hour.

E-mail milupdate@aol.com or write to Military Update, P.O. Box 231111, Centreville, VA, 20120-1111.

THE FAYETTEVILLE OBSERVER

Joint Chiefs chair says strike plan for Iran in place

By Anne Gearan
The Associated Press

WASHINGTON — The U.S. military has a plan to attack Iran, the chairman of the Joint Chiefs of Staff said Sunday, although he thinks a military strike is probably a bad idea.

Not long after Adm. Mike Mullen's comments aired on a Sunday talk show, the deputy chief of Iran's Revolutionary Guard was quoted as saying there would be a strong Iranian response should the U.S. take military action against his country.

Mullen, the highest-ranking U.S. military officer, often has warned that a strike on Iran would have serious and unpredictable ripple effects around the Middle East. At the same time, Mullen said the risk of Iran's developing a nuclear weapon is unacceptable.

"I think the military options have been on the table and remain on the table," Mullen said on "Meet the Press" on NBC. "It's one of the options that the president has. Again, I hope we don't get to that, but it's an important option and it's one that's

well understood."

The official Iranian news agency IRNA quoted Revolutionary Guard deputy chief Yadollah Javani as saying Sunday that security in the Persian Gulf would be jeopardized "if Americans commit the slightest mistake."

"The Persian Gulf is a strategic region. If the security of this region is endangered, they will suffer losses, too, and our response will be firm," Javani said.

Iran repeatedly has threatened to target the heart of Tel Aviv, the second-largest city in Israel, should the U.S. or Israel take military action against it.

The U.S. and Iran are at odds over the goals of Iran's nuclear program. Iran contends that it's aimed at peaceful uses while the U.S. claims Iran is gearing up to create a nuclear weapon.

Waters to face ethics trial

By Larry Margasak
The Associated Press

WASHINGTON — California Democrat Maxine Waters faces a House trial this fall on three charges of ethical wrongdoing, setting the stage for a second election-season public airing of ethics problems for a longtime Democratic lawmaker.

The charges focus on whether Waters broke the rules in requesting federal help for a bank where her husband owned stock and had served on the board of directors. She denied the charges Monday.

Persons familiar with the case said Waters is accused of violating:

■ A rule that House members may not exert improper influence that results in a personal benefit.

■ The government employees' ethics code, which prohibits granting or accepting special favors, for the employee or family members, that could be viewed as influencing official actions.

■ A rule that members' conduct must reflect creditably on the House.

The persons were not authorized to be quoted by name on allegations not yet made public.

The House ethics committee's announcement comes just days after it outlined 13 charges against Rep. Charles Rangel, D-N.Y., including

Rangel, the former House Ways and Means Committee chairman who has served for 40 years, faces a trial in the fall.

Waters is a senior member of the House Financial Services Committee, which handled the recent rewrite of legislation that regulates financial institutions and has strong protections for consumers.

In a statement, Waters said, "I have not violated any House rules. Therefore, I simply will not be forced to admit to something I did not do and instead have chosen to respond to charges made by the House Committee on Standards of Official Conduct in a public hearing."

AP photo

Rep. Maxine Waters, D-Calif., has been charged by a House investigative panel with violating ethics rules.

failing to disclose assets and income, delayed payment of federal taxes and improper

use of a subsidized New York apartment for his campaign office.

Identity thieves target children

3Ave6

■ Authorities say the sale of Social Security numbers in a new type of fraud could pose a threat to the nation's credit system.

By Bill Draper
The Associated Press

KANSAS CITY, Mo. — The latest form of identity theft doesn't depend on stealing your Social Security number. Now thieves are targeting your kid's number long before the little one even has a bank account.

Hundreds of online businesses are using computers to find dormant Social Security numbers — usually those assigned to children who don't use them — then selling those numbers under another name to help people establish phony credit and run up huge debts they will never pay off.

Authorities say the scheme could pose a new threat to the nation's credit system. Because the numbers exist in a legal gray area, federal investigators have not figured out a way to prosecute the people involved.

"If people are obtaining enough credit by fraud, we're back to another financial collapse," said Linda Marshall, an assistant U.S. attorney in Kansas City. "We tend to talk about it as the next wave."

The sellers get around the law by not referring to Social Security numbers. Instead, just as someone might pay for an escort service instead of a prostitute, they refer to CPNs — for credit profile, credit protection or credit privacy numbers.

Fty OBSERVER

",SO, ANYONE LUCKY ENOUGH TO HAVE A JOB BETTER HANG ON TO IT AND HELP US TO MAKE ENDS MEET— MORNING, GRAN'MA— UNTIL THIS SLUMP IS OVER."

CALIFORNIA CHALLENGE

Gay marriage issue may end up before high court

**By Lisa Leff
and Paul Elias**
The Associated Press

SAN FRANCISCO — A federal judge overturned California's gay-marriage ban Wednesday in a landmark case that could eventually force the U.S. Supreme Court to confront the question of whether same-sex couples have a constitutional right to wed.

The ruling by Chief U.S. District Judge Vaughn Walker touched off a celebration outside the courthouse. Gay couples waved rainbow and American flags and erupted with cheers in the city that has long been a haven for gays.

Shelly Bailes held a sign reading "Life Feels Different When You're Married" as she embraced her wife, Ellen Pontac. People in the Castro neighborhood toasted with champagne as word of the ruling spread.

In New York City, about 150 people gathered outside a lower Manhattan courthouse.

See **MARRIAGE**, Page 4A

4 AUG10

Marriage: Judge rejects every argument posed by ban sponsors

From **Page 1A**

They carried signs saying "Our Love Wins" as organizers read portions of the ruling.

Walker methodically rejected every argument posed by sponsors of the ban in response to a lawsuit filed by two gay couples who claimed Proposition 8, the voter-approved ban, violated their civil rights.

"Proposition 8 singles out gays and lesbians and legitimates their unequal treatment," the judge wrote in his 136-page opinion. "Proposition 8 perpetuates the stereotype that gays and lesbians are incapable of forming long-term loving relationships and that gays and lesbians are not good parents."

Standing in front of eight American flags at a news conference, the two couples behind the case beamed and choked up as they related their feelings of validation.

"Our courts are supposed to protect our constitutional rights," lead plaintiff Kris Perry said as Sandy Stier, her partner of 10 years, stood at her side. "Today, they did."

Protect Marriage, the coalition of religious and conservative groups that sponsored the ban, said it would immediately appeal the ruling to the 9th U.S. Circuit Court of Appeals.

"In America, we should uphold and respect the right of people to make policy changes through the democratic process, especially changes that do nothing more than uphold the definition of marriage that has existed since the founding of this country and beyond," said Jim Campbell, a lawyer on the defense team.

Despite the favorable ruling for same-sex couples, gay marriage will not be allowed to resume immediately.

ION   THE FAYETTEVILLE OBSERVER

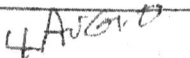

TEA PARTY RACISM

Blacks dispute claims

By Philip Elliott
The Associated Press

WASHINGTON — Black members of the tea party movement on Wednesday rejected charges that the group's activists are racist, saying they oppose President Obama because of his policies, not his skin color.

The members gathered at a Washington news conference in the wake of allegations about its rank and file, heightened by the recent split with a Tea Party Express leader who had posted a letter on his blog written from "Colored People" to Abraham Lincoln. The post suggested that black people would choose slavery over having to do real work.

The black members said the racism that has been attributed to the tea party movement came from outsiders who infiltrated the groups to discredit their work and it should be rejected.

"These people do not oppose Barack Obama because of his skin color. They oppose him because of his policies,"

said Lloyd Marcus, a spokesman for the group.

The NAACP last month approved a resolution condemning racism within the tea party movement and called on activists to "repudiate the racist element and activities" within the political movement.

Criticism of Obama

At the news conference, several members assailed Obama and the Democrats, often in harsh terms.

"Democrats have re-enslaved America," said Kevin Jackson, president of the Black Conservative Coalition.

He said tea party activists, if successful, would reduce the size of government and set in motion another Emancipation Proclamation, the document that President Abraham Lincoln signed that effectively ended slavery.

"This time, even the white folks get freed," said Jackson, who accused Obama of viewing fellow blacks as "mongrels."

Democratic National Committee spokesman Hari Sevugan declined to respond to the tea party leaders' criticism. The White House also declined to comment.

Other tea party speakers called Democrats white supremacists and elitists. Conservative Moms for America leader Mary Baker said Democrats were pushing "anti-God politics."

"Destroy America. That's what the D in Democrat Party means," she said.

Alan Keyes, who unsuccessfully ran for the U.S. Senate against Obama in 2004, said the president "got elected on a virulent form of racism" by exploiting his race during the 2008 campaign.

The Tea Party Express, one of dozens of libertarian-leaning and anti-tax groups, organized the meeting with reporters to denounce racism and then accused its opponents of using allegations of racism to censor dissent.

Walker said he wants to decide whether his order should be suspended while the proponents of the ban pursue their appeal. He ordered both sides to submit written arguments by Friday on the issue.

The appeal would go first to the 9th Circuit then to the U.S. Supreme Court if the high court justices agree to review it.

Proposition 8

California's electorate passed Proposition 8 with 52 percent of the vote in November 2008 after the most expensive political campaign on a social issue in U.S. history.

Supporters argued the ban was necessary to safeguard the traditional understanding of marriage and to encourage responsible childbearing.

Walker, however, found it violated the Constitution's due process and equal protection clauses while failing "to advance any rational basis in singling out gay men and lesbians for denial of a marriage license."

"Indeed, the evidence shows Proposition 8 does nothing more than enshrine in the California Constitution the notion that opposite-sex couples are superior to same-sex couples," the judge wrote.

He also said proponents offered little evidence that they were motivated by anything other than animus toward gays — beginning with their campaign to pass the ban, which included claims of wanting to protect children from learning about same-sex marriage in school.

"Proposition 8 played on the fear that exposure to homosexuality would turn children into homosexuals and that parents should dread having children who are not heterosexual," Walker wrote.

Walker heard 13 days of testimony and arguments since January during the first trial in federal court to examine if states can prohibit gays from getting married.

Currently, same-sex couples can only legally wed in Massachusetts, Iowa, Connecticut, Vermont, New Hampshire and Washington, D.C.

In war on cheating, it's tech vs. tech

But Big Brother methods may not be the best way to stop plagiarism

By Trip Gabriel
THE NEW YORK TIMES

ORLANDO, Fla. — The frontier in the battle to defeat student cheating may be here at the testing center of the University of Central Florida.

No gum is allowed during an exam: Chewing could disguise a student speaking into a hands-free cell phone to an accomplice outside.

The 228 computers that students use are recessed in-to desk tops so that anyone trying to photograph the screen — using, say, a pen with a hidden camera, in order to help a friend who will take the test later – is easy to spot.

Scratch paper is allowed — but it is stamped with the date and must be turned in later.

When a proctor sees something suspicious, he records the student's real-time work at the computer and di-rects an overhead camera to zoom in, and both sets of images are burned onto a CD for evidence.

Dr. Taylor Ellis, the associate dean who runs the testing center within the business school at Central Florida, the nation's third-largest campus by enrollment, said that cheating had dropped significantly, to 14 suspected incidents out of 64,000 exams administered during the spring semester.

"I will never stop it completely, but I'll find out about it," he said.

As the eternal temptation of students to cheat has gone high-tech – not just on exams, but by cutting and pasting from the Internet and sharing of homework online like music files — educators have responded with their own efforts to crack down.

This summer, as incoming

SEE **CHEATING**, PAGE 7A

7/5/10

389

Bureaucrats' new rule of law

FAJOBS— NC   9 AUG 10

WASHINGTON — Recently, a draft memo surfaced from the Homeland Security Department suggesting ways to administratively circumvent existing law to allow several categories of illegal immigrants to avoid deportation and, indeed, for some to be granted permanent residency. Most disturbing was the stated rationale. This was being proposed "in the absence of Comprehensive Immigration Reform." In other words, because Congress refuses to do what these bureaucrats would like to see done, they will legislate it themselves.

Regardless of your feelings on the substance of the immigration issue, this is not how a constitutional democracy should operate. Administrators administer the law, they don't change it. That's the legislators' job.

When questioned, the White House downplayed the toxic memo, leaving the impression that it was nothing more than ruminations emanating from the bowels of Homeland Security. But the administration is engaged in an even more significant power play elsewhere.

A 2007 Supreme Court ruling gave the Environmental Protection Agency the authority to regulate carbon emissions if it could demonstrate that they threaten human health and the environment. The Obama EPA made precisely that finding, thereby granting

Charles Krauthammer

itself a huge expansion of power and, noted The Washington Post, sending "a message to Congress."

It was not a terribly subtle message: Enact cap-and-trade legislation — taxing and heavily regulating carbon-based energy — or the EPA will do so unilaterally. As Frank O'Donnell of Clean Air Watch noted, such a finding "is likely to help light a fire under Congress to get moving."

Well, Congress didn't. Despite the "regulatory cudgel" (to again quote the Post) the administration has been waving, the Senate has repeatedly refused to acquiesce.

Good for the Senate. But what to do when the executive is passively aggressive rather than actively so? Take border security. Sen. Jon Kyl, R-Ariz., reports that President Obama told him about pressure from his political left and its concern that if the border is secured, Republicans will have no incentive to support comprehensive reform (i.e., amnesty). Indeed, Homeland Security's abandonment of the "virtual fence" on the southern border, combined with its lack of interest in

completing the real fence that today covers only one-third of the border, gives the distinct impression that serious border enforcement is not a high administration priority absent some Republican quid pro quo on comprehensive reform.

But border enforcement is not something to be manipulated in return for legislative favors. It is, as the administration vociferously argued in court in the Arizona case, the federal executive's constitutional responsibility. Its job is to faithfully execute the laws. Non-execution is a dereliction of duty.

This contagion of executive willfulness is not confined to the federal government or to Democrats. In Virginia, the Republican attorney general has just issued a ruling allowing police to ask about one's immigration status when stopped for some other reason (e.g., a traffic violation). Heretofore, police could inquire only upon arrest and imprisonment.

Whatever your views about the result, the process is suspect. If police latitude regarding the interrogation of possible illegal immigrants is to be expanded, that's an issue for the legislature, not the executive.

How did we get here? I blame Henry Paulson. The gold standard of executive overreach was achieved the day he summoned the heads of the country's nine largest banks and informed them that henceforth the federal government was their business

partner. The banks were under no legal obligation to obey. But they know the capacity of the federal government, when crossed, to cause you trouble. They complied.

So did BP when the president summoned its top executives to the White House to demand a $20 billion federally administered escrow fund for damages. Existing law capped damages at $75 million. BP, like the banks, understood the power of the U.S. government. Twenty billion it was.

Again, you can be pleased with the result (I was), and still be troubled by how we got there. Everyone wants energy in the executive (as Alexander Hamilton called it). But not lawlessness. In the modern welfare state, government has the power to regulate your life. That's bad enough. But at least there is one restraint on this bloated power: the separation of powers. Such constraints on your life must first be approved by both houses of Congress.

That's called the consent of the governed. The constitutional order is meant to subject you to the will of the people's representatives, not to the whim of a chief executive or the imagination of a loophole-seeking bureaucrat.

Charles Krauthammer is a Washington Post columnist. Readers may write to him at letters@charleskrauthammer.com or Washington Post Writers Group, 1150 15th St. NW, Washington, D.C. 20071.

HE OBSERVER 10 Aug 10

Preference goes to current
; will be edited and cannot
our name, street address and
and hometown will be
anonymous letters. Six weeks
n the same writer. Letters must
gns the letter, and exclusive to
l Page Editor, The Fayetteville
lle, NC 28302, or fax to (910)
yobserver.com.

Tea Party vs. taxers and spenders

If the Democratic party is so happy to raise taxes, why not let all of the registered Democrats pay for them?

When the rest of the civilized world has decided to cut back on taxes and expenditures, why does the Obama government want to keep on spending and taxing everything in sight?

Does anyone have a better idea? I would sure like to hear it above the loud din of an overwhelming liberal news media.

The United Kingdom is moving away from National Healthcare while the United States moves toward it.

Why would all of the doctors needed now and in the future be foolish enough to opt for socialized medicine?

Americans who are proud to live in the best and most free country in the world are not taking this lying down. The Tea Party folks are showing their mettle. They are strong patriots unafraid to show their love and respect for our great country and "for which it stands."

Doesn't that loyalty to our country give you a warm, proud feeling — to know they represent the huge silent majority of Americans who are busy trying to keep the nuts and bolts together for a better future?

Nobody ever said it would be easy, but don't you feel thankful that we can still "Take Back America" from those who have been bamboozled with a lot of meaningless but harmful words and endless speeches?

Long live our Republic!
Dorothy Bursey
Sanford

Having big waist linked to risk of death

Los Angeles Times 10 Aug 10

LOS ANGELES — Having a large waist is associated with a host of potentially serious health issues, such as heart disease, high cholesterol, Type 2 diabetes and inflammation. According to a new study, it may also be linked to death.

Researchers from the Epidemiology Research Program of the American Cancer Society in Atlanta looked at data among 48,500 men and 56,343 women ages 50 and older who took part in the Cancer Prevention Study II Nutrition Cohort. Most of the participants were white. In 1997 they supplied their weight and waist circumference. At the beginning of the study, the average age was 69 for men and 67 for women.

The study participants were followed until 2006, at which point 9,315 men and 5,332 women had died. Having a very large waist — at least 47 inches for men and 43 inches for women — was associated with about twice the risk of death compared with men with waists measuring 35 inches or less and women with waists measuring 30 inches or less. Having intra-abdominal fat is considered to be a bigger health risk than fat underneath the skin, or subcutaneous fat, since visceral fat surrounds the internal organs.

The study was released Monday in the journal Archives of Internal Medicine.

AP photo/Greensboro News & Record, Joseph Rodriguez

Back to school
10 Aug 10

A sign is misspelled Monday on a newly paved road leading to Southern Guilford High School in Greensboro.

Our politics anything but post-racial

By Jonathan Bean

The Obama presidency increasingly reminds me of the 1961 best-seller, "Black Like Me."

The author of that classic in civil rights literature was Texas journalist John Howard Griffin, a white man who darkened his skin to pass as a black in the segregated South. By pretending to be something he was not, Griffin awakened the world to the plight of American blacks living under the racist policies of the Jim Crow South.

Sadly, President Obama's racial fixation has become disturbing in recent months. By pandering to racial pride and grievance, he is betraying the liberal tradition that enabled him to become president — a tradition represented by Frederick Douglass, Branch Rickey, Zora Neale Hurston, Stanley Crouch and others who spoke out against racial injustice and defining individuals by their color.

By obsessing with racial issues, Obama makes a mockery of a tradition that sought to "get beyond" race.

Seeing beyond color

The cornerstone of that tradition was the notion of a colorblind society. Indeed, as recently as 1967, the NAACP — which stirs the racial flames today — agitated for no racial identification whatsoever on any form, such as birth certificates, marriage licenses, or loan applications.

Zora Neale Hurston, one of the 20th century's preeminent black writers, spoke for the colorblind ethic when she said, "Why should I be proud to be black? Why should anyone be proud of their skin color? Races have never done anything. All that is good and excellent is the work of individuals." And she meant it.

By way of contrast, President Obama in April pandered to black voters by making a public display of his "black-only" Census identification. The president who once said he "could not disown his white mother and grandmother" did just that.

A second foundation of the liberal tradition of racial harmony was the notion of equal justice for all.

The NAACP's founder, a white man — Moorfield Storey — would cringe at the president and NAACP today.

The NAACP's McCarthyist name-calling and "guilt by association," directed at members of the so-called Tea Party movement, together with President Obama's selective outrage at injustices both at home and abroad, would strike Storey as disturbingly similar to the white supremacist principles he fought against with the NAACP.

The president and the NAACP need to remember that the civil rights movement also attracted a fringe element. Even people that many now glorify, such as Malcolm X, spewed the worst anti-Semitism and anti-white racism. The Rev. Martin Luther King Jr. was accused of accepting the help of communists and socialists — and individuals with such ties were indeed part of the civil rights "movement," because, in a free country, everyone has the right to petition the government for redress of grievance.

More disturbing than the NAACP's political posturing is the president's one-sided view of justice. What kind of signal does it send to the country when the Department of Justice refuses to prosecute members of the New Black Panther Party for intimidating whites at a polling place? Justice is supposed to be colorblind, not wear blinders.

President Obama, originally grabbed the imagination of the American people after a speech, now reprinted in countless books, speaking of biracialism and a desire to transcend race. A small cottage industry of books emerged describing the shift to "post-racial politics." That was then, this is now. His popularity plummeting, President Obama now turns inward into his "blackness" and turns the other way as his supporters project all opposition to his party and policies as racist. This is wrong.

The president needs to remember his own biracial roots and remind his administration and supporters that criticism is not the same as hate. He also needs to re-read the classics of civil rights literature. Frederick Douglass could teach him a thing or two, as could the earlier figures of the NAACP.

A race-obsessed Mr. Hyde appears to be living within President Obama's Dr. Jekyll at 1600 Pennsylvania Ave. The president needs to be rid of him.

Jonathan Bean is a research fellow at the Independent Institute and a professor of history at Southern Illinois University and editor of "Race and Liberty in America: An Essential Reader."

AID WORKERS KILLED

Afghanistan ambush described as swift, ruthless

By Deb Riechmann
and Amir Shah
The Associated Press

KABUL, Afghanistan — The first sign of danger was the crackle of gunfire over their heads. Ten gunmen, their faces covered, rushed toward terrified humanitarian workers and began shouting, "Satellite! Satel-

lite!" — a demand to surrender their phones.

Moments later, 10 of them lay dead, including two women hiding in the back seat of a car that the attackers hit with a grenade, according to an Afghan official familiar with the account the sole survivor gave police.

It is the first detailed narra-

tive of the slayings of six Americans, two Afghans, one German and a Briton on Aug. 5 in remote northern Afghanistan.

They were ambushed and shot after journeying about 100 miles — much of it on foot and horseback — through the Hindu Kush mountains, giving eye care and other medical care to

impoverished villagers.

Afghan and U.S. investigators spent at least four hours this week questioning the survivor, a 24-year-old father of three named Safiullah. He was employed as a driver for International Assistance Mission, a nonprofit Christian organization that has worked

See **AFGHANISTAN**, Page 4A

The Fayetteville Observer

Sacrilege at Ground Zero

WASHINGTON — A place is made sacred by a widespread belief that it was visited by the miraculous or the transcendent (Lourdes, the Temple Mount), by the presence there once of great nobility and sacrifice (Gettysburg), or by the blood of martyrs and the indescribable suffering of the innocent (Auschwitz).

When we speak of Ground Zero as hallowed ground, what we mean is that it belongs to those who suffered and died there — and that such ownership obliges the living to preserve the dignity and memory of the place, never allowing it to be forgotten, trivialized or misappropriated.

That's why Disney's early '90s proposal to build an American history theme park near Manassas Battlefield was defeated by a broad coalition fearing vulgarization of the Civil War. It's why the commercial viewing tower built right on the border of Gettysburg was taken down. It's why, while no one objects to Japanese cultural centers, the idea of putting one up at Pearl Harbor would be offensive. And why Pope John Paul II ordered the Carmelite nuns to leave the convent they had established at Auschwitz. He was teaching them a lesson in respect: This is not your place, it belongs to others.

Charles Krauthammer

is clear: If the proposed mosque were controlled by "insensitive" Islamist radicals either excusing or celebrating 9/11, he would not support its construction

But then, why not? By the mayor's view of religious freedom, by what right do we dictate the message of any mosque?

Location matters. Ground Zero is the site of the greatest mass murder in American history — perpetrated by Muslims of a particular Islamist orthodox in whose cause they died and in whose name they killed.

Which makes you wonder about the good will behind Imam Feisal Abdul Rauf's proposal. This is a man who has called U.S. policy "an accessory to the crime" of 9/11 and, when recently asked whether Hamas is a terrorist organization, replied, "I'm not a politician. ... The issue of terrorism is a very complex question."

America is a free country where you can build whatever you want — but not anywhere. That's why

Even New York Mayor Michael Bloomberg, who denounced opponents of the proposed 15-story mosque and Islamic center near Ground Zero as tramplers on religious freedom, asked the mosque organizers "to show some special sensitivity to the situation." Yet, the government has no business telling churches how to conduct their business, shape their message or show "special sensitivity" to anyone about anything. Bloomberg was inadvertently conceding the claim of those he excoriates for opposing the mosque, namely, that Ground Zero is indeed unlike any other place and therefore unique criteria govern what can be done there.

Bloomberg's implication

we have zoning laws. These restrictions are for reasons of aesthetics. Others are for reasons of common decency and respect for the sacred. No commercial tower over Gettysburg, no convent at Auschwitz — and no mosque at Ground Zero. Build it anywhere but there.

The governor of New York offered to help find land to build the mosque elsewhere. A mosque really seeking to build bridges, Rauf's ostensible hope for the structure, would accept the offer.

Charles Krauthammer is a Washington Post columnist. Readers may write to him at letters@charleskrauthammer.com or Washington Post Writers Group, 1150 15th St. NW, Washington, D.C. 20071.

The kids are not all right

The Ottawa (Ontario) Sun, on children and teenagers headed in the wrong direction:

For years now, it's been plain to anyone with eyes that children and teenagers are gradually getting lazier, fatter, less respectful of authority and narcissistic.

The evidence is everywhere: In schools, playgrounds, on the ice and in the courts.

Academics have had a field-day with this. They churn out study after study linking excessive screen time — TV, web networking and video games — with a slew of emotional, behavioral and physical ailments, led by obesity.

It's a worldwide problem. Researchers in the southern Chinese city of Guangzhou recently found 13- to 18-year-olds who spent more than five hours a day on the Web were one-and-a-half times more likely to suffer depression than moderate users.

No wonder they're depressed. Who wouldn't be, staring at a screen all day, lost in a world that isn't real?

Col. Dave Grossman, former U.S. Army psychiatrist and world-leading author on the effects and causes of violence, argues video games are teaching U.S. teens to kill — without pity and without remorse — while at the same time turning them into couch whales.

Coupled with this we have a school system that drills children with the mantra they can do no wrong. So when a parent or teacher comes along and says get off your behind, go kick a ball, they're met

with blank stares — at best.

Let's pressure the school boards to reintroduce deportment and basic discipline as core objectives of education. And let's talk about a year of compulsory military or community service at age 18.

Most of all, let's stop pointing the finger and get off our own lazy, lard-layered butts.

Trading exports for sustainability

The China Daily, Beijing, on China's booming export growth:

China's swelling trade surplus has presented yet again remarkable proof of the resilience of Chinese exporters and, at the same time, the increased difficulty of cutting down the country's reliance on exports for growth.

Latest statistics show that China's monthly trade surplus trumped almost all forecasts to hit an 18-month high, up 170 percent from a year earlier to $28.7 billion. In view of the fragile global recovery, most observers believed China could hardly run an even larger monthly trade surplus than what it posted in June, a whopping $20 billion.

With a trade surplus close to the largest China has ever seen and record overseas sales in July, Chinese exporters have shown impressive capacity to survive what is arguably the worst global recession in more than half a century.

It seems likely that the export sector will remain a powerful growth engine of the Chinese economy for many more years.

That may disappoint people who anticipated a steady decline in China's trade surplus to reduce global

Obama supports ground zero mosque

By Margaret Talev
McClatchy Newspapers

WASHINGTON — Weighing in for the first time on the emotionally charged issue, President Obama gave his blessing Friday to a Muslim group's plans to build a mosque near ground zero in New York, saying, "This is America, and our commitment to religious freedom must be unshakeable."

In making his case for supporting the Cordoba House project, Obama, who once taught constitutional law, referred to the Constitution and the words of Thomas Jefferson.

However, the audience to whom he addressed his remarks looked strikingly different from the Founding Fathers: dozens of Muslim-American men and women in politics, government, business, academia, faith and activism, all his guests at a White House "iftar," the evening meal that breaks the daily fast during the holy month of Ramadan.

"As a citizen, and as president, I believe that Muslims have the same right to practice their religion as anyone else in this country," Obama said. "That includes the right to build a place of worship and a community center on private property in lower Manhattan, in accordance with local laws and ordinances."

He said the Sept. 11, 2001, attacks had been "a deeply traumatic event" for the nation, that emotions of opponents of the mosque project are understandable and that "we must all recognize and respect the sensitivities surrounding the development of lower Manhattan. Ground zero is, indeed, hallowed ground."

He also said that the United States has flourished because of religious freedom.

"The principle that people of all faiths are welcome in this country, and will not be treated differently by their government, is essential to who we are."

MOSQUE NEAR GROUND ZERO

Reactions are mixed to Obama's defense

■ The president says he believes in the right but won't comment on the 'wisdom' of the project.

By Pauline Jelinek and Julie Pace
The Associated Press

PANAMA CITY BEACH, Fla. — Weighing his words carefully on a fiery political issue, President Obama said Saturday that Muslims have the right to build a mosque near New York's ground zero, but he did not say whether he believes it is a good idea to do so.

Obama commented during a trip to Florida, where

Obama

he expanded on a Friday night White House speech asserting that Muslims have the same right to freedom of religion as everyone else in America.

The president's statements thrust him squarely into a debate that he had skirted for weeks and could put Democrats on the spot three months before midterm elections where they already were nervous about holding control of the House and maybe even the Senate. Until

See **MOSQUE**, Page 5A

Waters disputes charges

By Larry Margasak
The Associated Press

AP photo
Rep. Maxine Waters speaks Friday on Capitol Hill.

WASHINGTON — A defiant Maxine Waters disputed charges that she violated House ethics rules and released documents Friday that could undercut the complaint that the 10-term California Democrat sought federal money to bail out a bank where her husband owns stock.

With midterm elections three months away and no trial date scheduled by the House Ethics Committee, Waters — like her House colleague Charles Rangel of New York — made her case in the court of public opinion.

"I have not violated any House rules," the senior member of the House Financial Services Committee told a news conference that included a power-point presentation of the documents.

Waters is charged with three counts: violating a rule requiring lawmakers' conduct to reflect creditably on the House; violating the spirit and letter of a rule prohibiting receipt of benefits by exerting improper influence; and violating a government code of conduct that prohibits dispensing or receiving special favors.

Waters' primary defense is that she contacted former Secretary Henry Paulson Jr., in September 2008 about a meeting for the National Bankers Association — a trade group of minority-owned banks. She said she turned the matter over to Rep. Barney Frank, D-Mass., the Financial Services Committee chairman, after learning OneUnited Bank was the association member actually needing the aid.

The case appears to hinge on whether Waters was trying to help the association or OneUnited, a bank where the congresswoman's husband, Sidney Williams, owns stock. The bank is headquartered in Frank's Massachusetts district.

The investment of Waters' husband was worth more than $352,000 at the end of 2007. But by late September 2008 — the month when Waters says she was helping the trade association — the investment had declined to $175,000.

Several documents released by Waters show that the association, not OneUnited, wrote to Paulson for federal help. In one internal Treasury Department document, the head of the federal bailout program for financial institutions said he had no knowledge of congressional intervention when the decision was made to give OneUnited $12 million in December 2008.

The dismantling of America

17 AUG 10 FAYOBS

"We the people" are the familiar opening words of the Constitution of the United States — the framework for a self-governing people, free from the arbitrary edicts of rulers. It was the blueprint for America, and the success of America made that blueprint something that other nations sought to follow.

At the time when it was written, however, the Constitution was a radical departure from the autocratic governments of the 18th century. Since it was something so new and different, the reasons for the Constitution's provisions were spelled out in "The Federalist," a book written by three of the writers of the Constitution, as a sort of instruction guide to a new product.

The Constitution was not only a challenge to the despotic governments of its time, it has been a continuing challenge to all those who think that ordinary people should be ruled by their betters.

While the kings of old have faded into the mists of history, the principle of the divine rights of kings to impose whatever they wish on the masses lives on today

Thomas Sowell

in the rampaging presumptions of those who consider themselves anointed to impose their notions on others.

The Constitution of the United States is the biggest single obstacle to the carrying out of such rampaging presumptions, so it is not surprising that those with such presumptions have led the way in denigrating, undermining and evading the Constitution.

While various political leaders have done things that violated either the spirit or the letter of the Constitution, few dared to openly say that the Constitution was wrong and that what they wanted was right.

It was the Progressives of 100 years ago who began saying that the Constitution needed to be subordinated to whatever they chose to call "the needs of the times." Nor were they content to say that the Constitution needed more amendments,

for that would have meant that the much disdained masses would have something to say about whether, or what kind, of amendments were needed.

The agenda then, as now, has been for our betters to decide among themselves which constitutional safeguards against arbitrary government power should be disregarded.

Attack on Constitution

The first open attack on the Constitution by a president of the United States was made by our only president with a Ph.D., Woodrow Wilson. Virtually all the arguments as to why judges should not take the Constitution as meaning what its words plainly say, but "interpret" it to mean whatever it ought to mean, in order to meet "the needs of the times," were made by Wilson.

To get their way, the elites must erode or dismantle the Constitution, bit by bit, in one way or another. What that means is that they must dismantle America. This has been going on piecemeal over the years, but now we have an administration in Washington that circumvents the Constitution wholesale,

with its laws passed so fast that the public cannot know what is in them, its appointment of "czars" wielding greater power than Cabinet members, without having to be exposed to pubic scrutiny by going through the confirmation process prescribed by the Constitution for Cabinet members.

Now there is leaked news of plans to change the immigration laws by administrative fiat, rather than congressional legislation, presumably because Congress might be unduly influenced by those pesky voters — with their constitutional rights — who have shown clearly that they do not want amnesty and open borders, despite however much our betters do. If the Obama administration gets away with this, and can add a few million illegals to the voting rolls in time for the 2012 elections, that can mean re-election, and with it a continuing and accelerating dismantling of America.

Thomas Sowell is a syndicated columnist. Readers may write to him at www.tsowell.com, at info@creators.com (with his name in the subject line) or Creators Syndicate, 5777 W. Century Blvd., Suite 700, Los Angeles, CA 90045.

By Aaron David Miller

Woody Allen got it wrong. Ninety percent of success in life isn't just showing up; it's showing up at the right time and knowing what to do once you get there.

Barack Obama has gotten it half right then. Like most of our consequential presidents, he arrived at the right time; unlike them, he may have badly misread his moment, and America's.

This intuitive capacity (or lack of it) to read the nation's mood and circumstances accurately is a crucial component of effective leadership. In Obama's case, it may well be that who he is and what he has wanted have prevented him from seeing clearly what most Americans want and need.

Matter of circumstance

Because we focus on the character and personal qualities (for good or ill) of our presidents, we often ignore the importance of circumstances and just plain dumb luck in elevating or constraining presidential performance.

Let's consider three undeniably great presidents, one a century. George Washington, Abraham Lincoln and Franklin Roosevelt can lay claim to greatness because they had a chance to be great, and that chance derived from circumstances over which they had little control. To oversimplify, Washington was there when a nation needed to be created, Lincoln was there to save it and FDR to shepherd it safely through the Depression and the world's greatest war.

Other consequential presidents had the good fortune to follow weak predecessors (Andrew Jackson, after John Quincy Adams), to arrive at moments when the country was ripe for real change (Lyndon Johnson after a martyred John Kennedy) or to show up at a favorable moment when one coalition or party is weakening and another is gaining strength (Ronald Reagan, after Jimmy Carter).

The point is that the hour, the circumstance and the season set up the great man. But this kind of luck only creates the possibility of change, not its certainty. For this, you need the marriage of a skillful president and his moment. And near the top of that president's must-have qualities is the acute capacity to grasp where the nation is and where it can go.

Washington found just the right balance between the fear of too much national government and the threats that would have undermined the new nation without enough government.

Lincoln's willful and principled commitment to the Union without slavery was married to tactics that contained enough zigs and zags so that he could maintain confidence and trust and ask great sacrifice of the half of the nation he represented.

FDR's mix of ironclad confidence and reassurance, together with practical experimentation and use of government-as-remedy in response to 30 percent unemployment, captured the mood of a nation, calmed its fears and sustained its hopes.

Moreover, all great transformers wrap their actions in values and ideals that, while bold, also are familiar and consistent with those of the nation's story. Lincoln and FDR sold revolutionary change by claiming that it was anchored in what the nation's founders had intended.

Man on a mission

Like other consequential presidents, Obama was a man

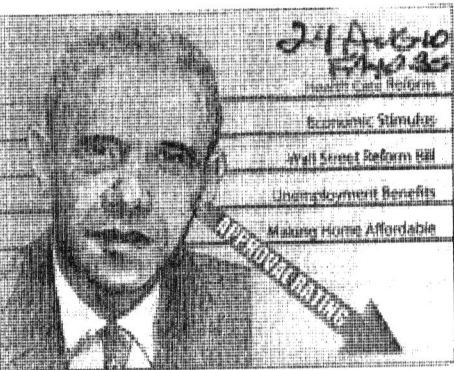

on a mission in 2008. But he has allowed his agenda to obscure his capacity to see where most Americans were and what they wanted.

First, he was convinced that the country was so badly served by his Republican predecessor that most Americans understood the need for sweeping change and were prepared to support it. Second, he misread his crisis: the recession. That crisis, though severe to be sure, was not so nation-encumbering that it forced the political system out of fear or desperation to become more pliable. When combined with a Republican Party determined to say no to just about anything, transformative change has proved difficult indeed.

Besides, Obama isn't FDR. He wasn't as skilled, as grounded in the American experience or, frankly, as likable as Roosevelt, and so he hasn't come to serve as a repository of the nation's trust and confidence. FDR, like Obama, was hated by many, but he also was beloved by millions.

Finally, unlike some of his predecessors, Obama hasn't found a unifying message situated in an American experience that is universally shared. Part of Obama's problem is his uniqueness: His professorial, detached and cool-to-cold nature, the racial prejudice against him and his outlier background make him a different kind of president than most Americans have known.

Obama may have had no choice but to introduce a large stimulus bill to stop the economic bleeding, but health care reform represented an overreach and stressed a political system that already was dysfunctional. It also convinced many, however unfairly, that he was a man of the left.

It isn't for nothing that Gallup ranked him as the most polarizing first-year president since its polling began. Liberals are unhappy, independents are running away, Republicans are rejoicing in his travail, and movements such as the "tea party" are gaining ground — all of which makes the case for Obama as polarizer in chief. Only 13 percent of Americans believe they have benefited from his economic policies, the most depressing statistic of all.

The president probably isn't all that worried. And as the second-term victories of Bill Clinton and George W. Bush suggest, we are hardly re-electing great presidents these days; average ones will do quite nicely, as long as the economy stays strong.

In fact, if Obama is re-elected in 2012, for only the second time in our history we will have had three different two-term presidents in a row. The last time this happened was in the early 19th century (Thomas Jefferson, James Madison and James Monroe). And what does this tell you? Americans aren't so much looking for great presidents, big ideas or historic transformations. They want satisfaction on mundane matters such as prosperity, keeping Americans safe from terrorist attacks and an end to the roller-coaster ride of partisanship, name-calling and celebrity politics that is Washington today.

The president may not have gotten that message the first time around; if he's lucky, maybe he'll get it the next time.

Aaron David Miller is a public policy scholar at the Woodrow Wilson International Center for Scholars. His book "Can America Have Another Great President?" will be published in 2012. He wrote this for the Los Angeles Times.

Missing the moment

Little bang for big tuition bucks

By Andrew Hacker and Claudia Dreifus

At Pomona College, a top-flight liberal arts school, this year's sticker price for tuition and fees is a hefty $38,394 (not including room and board). Even after adjusting for inflation, that comes to 2.9 times what Pomona was charging a generation ago, in 1980.

This kind of massive tuition increase is the norm. In New England, Williams College charges $41,434, or an inflation-adjusted 3.2 times what it did 30 years ago. Southern Cal's current tab of $41,022 is a 3.6 multiple of its 1980 bill.

Tuition at public universities, in a time of ailing state budgets, has risen at an even faster rate. The University of Illinois' current $13,658 is six times its 1980 rate after adjusting for inflation. San Jose State's $8,250 is a whopping 11 times more.

If you look at how that added revenue is being spent, it's hard to argue that students are getting a lot of extra value for all that extra money. Why? Colleges aren't spending their extra revenues, which we calculate to be about $40 billion a year nationally over 1980 revenues, in ways that most benefit students.

Athletics

One thing colleges are spending more on is athletic teams, which have become a more pronounced — and

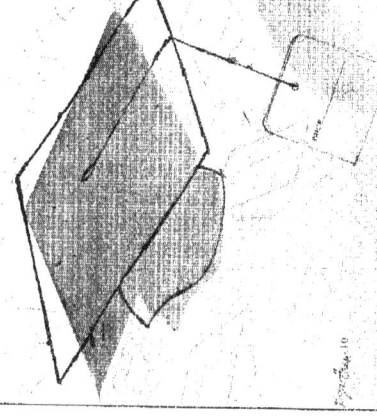

costly — presence on campuses everywhere. Currently, 629 schools have football teams — 132 more than in 1980. And all but 14 of them lose money, including some with national names.

Meanwhile, the cost of sports continues to rise. The average football squad has gone from 82 to 102 players, because of sub-specialties required by esoteric coaching strategies. The number of women's sports teams has also risen sharply. And teams cost money — often lots of it. Varsity golf at Duke, open to both genders, costs an estimated $20,405 per player per year. Because there are no revenues for most sports, the deficits often have to be covered by tuition bills.

directors; having more of them means higher bills for students.

Added tuition revenue has also gone to raise faculty salaries. Yale's full-time faculty members now average $129,400, up 64 percent in inflation-adjusted dollars from what they made in 1980. (Pay in other sectors of the U.S. economy rose only about 5 percent in this period.) Stanford's tenured and tenure-track professors are doing even better, averaging $153,900, an 83 percent increase over 1980.

We're told such stipends are needed to get top talent, but we're not so sure. Faculty stars may raise prestige, but they are often away from the classroom, having negotiated frequent paid leaves and smaller teaching loads —

underwritten, of course, by tuition. At Williams College this year, for example, three of seven religion professors are taking off all or part of the academic year.

Complete data on college presidents' pay is easily accessible only back to 1991. Yet even in that relatively short span, many college leaders have seen their salaries double in inflation-adjusted dollars. Carleton's president today gets 2.4 times more than the president did 19 years ago, at NYU, pay has risen by 2.7 times. Measured another way, it takes the tuitions of 31 Vanderbilt students to

Administrative costs

Another source of increased expense is administration. Since 1980, the number of administrators per student at colleges has about doubled; on most campuses their numbers now match the number of faculty. Here are some of their titles: senior specialist of assessment; director for learning communities; assistant dean of students for substance education; director of knowledge access services.

Needless to say, these officials claim that they offer needed services. Who can be opposed to ensuring access and assessment? Yet let's not forget that tuition pays for all these deans and

cover their president's $1.2 million annual stipend. We have yet to see evidence that lofting more money to the top enhances the quality of instruction.

In theory, all this extra tuition money should permit the hiring of more junior faculty, which might mean smaller introductory courses. But on many campuses, huge classes remain the norm. One reason is that most teaching budgets are consumed by senior professors. Amherst's full-time faculty absorb 77 percent of the cash available for full-time faculty. At Berkeley, they sop up 73 percent. At Northern Arizona, it's 75 percent. The little that's left is parceled out among junior professors and underpaid adjuncts, who despite rising tuition, are doing an increasing portion of the teaching.

Room and board

The cost of room and board has gone up sharply too, with charges often double or more in inflation-adjusted dollars. At Bowdoin and UCLA, they have gone up three times. Most college tours will show that student living standards have risen, too. Rooms once had only iron cots, military mattresses and battered desks. Now suites are wired for electronic gear, with fully equipped kitchens down the hall. Penn State enables students to legally download music — at last

count about 2 million songs a week.

As to dining, food costs may be lower than ever, but not on college campuses, where the quality of campus dining has become a marketing tool. If your memories of dorm food include mystery meat and overcooked vegetables, you'd be in for a shock on today's campuses. Here were some recent choices in the Middlebury College dining rooms: sun-dried tomato pizzas, African couscous, tandoori chicken, orange-ginger tofu steak, red beans and basmati rice. Whether these more elaborate menus make students more studious is not known.

The travesty of high tuition is that most of the extra charges aren't going for education. Administrators, athletics and amenities get funded, while history departments are denied new assistant professors. A whole generation of young Americans is being shortchanged, largely by adults who have carved out good careers in places we call colleges.

Andrew Hacker is on the faculty of Queens College and Claudia Dreifus teaches at Columbia University. Their book, "Higher Education? How Colleges Are Wasting Our Money and Failing Our Kids and What We Can Do About It," came out last month. They wrote this for the Los Angeles Times.

399

FAy OBS

STUDY OF CENSUS DATA

Illegal immigration numbers declining

By Michael Matza
The Philadelphia Inquirer

PHILADELPHIA — The number of illegal immigrants in America stopped growing for the first time since 1990 — dropping from a peak of 12 million to 11.1 million last year, according to a Pew Hispanic Center study released Wednesday.

The average annual influx of illegal immigrants dropped as well, from 850,000 in the first five years of the current decade, to 300,000 in 2009.

The findings, based on extrapolations of U.S. Census data, may be attributable to fewer jobs in the troubled U.S. economy and harsher enforcement on the Southern border, Pew demographer Jeffrey Passel said.

About 7 million illegal immigrants were employed in the United States in 2009, down from 8 million in 2007, according to the report.

Florida, Nevada, and Virginia saw the largest declines in illegal immigrants, according to Pew, a nonpartisan research organization.

Overall, illegal immigrants make up about 4 percent of the U.S. population.

The study is the latest talking point for all sides in the national debate about illegal immigration.

Christine Thurlow Brenner, a professor of public policy at Rutgers University-Camden believes the decline is mostly jobs-related.

"Some people will spin this to say the heightened security is working," Brenner said. "To me, the decline demonstrates that jobs really are the key attractor."

America: Land of contradiction

Can the city of New York tell the Greek Orthodox they have to relocate and there are height requirements for their new church, but can't tell an imam where to build a mosque?

Under freedom of religion, a mosque can be built near Ground Zero, but have a child take a Bible to school and watch what happens.

We can force Catholic charities to give employees reproductive health care, but can't tell an imam where to build a mosque.

Christians clamor for a candidate with their views; when they get one, they vote for the other candidate.

We can kick Americans out of college for their beliefs, but with open arms welcome illegal immigrants.

We can say we have compassion by helping illegal immigrants, but where is this same compassion when Americans are being raped, kidnapped, murdered and have their land seized by illegal immigrants?

Can U.S. citizens be charged with giving support to Somali insurgent groups, while our government is giving millions to terrorist organizations Hezbollah and Hamas?

Can denying same-sex marriage be called discrimination, while denying other sexual behavior such as polygamy or pedophilia those same rights?

Why must a U.S. military dependant show a certified birth certificate and military orders to enroll in school, but we're still awaiting President Obama's certified birth certificate?

Why must we show our job qualifications to be hired, but for the Supreme Court we hire the most unqualified?

Why do we reward bad behavior, CEO compensation packages and illegal immigration?

Joe Bierkortte
Hope Mills

Record rise in poverty may hurt Democrats

Census figures being released this week are expected to show an increase to 15 percent.

By Hope Yen and Liz Sidoti
The Associated Press

WASHINGTON — The number of people in the U.S. who are in poverty is on track for a record increase on President Obama's watch, with the ranks of working-age poor approaching 1960s levels that led to the national war on poverty.

Census figures for 2009 — the recession-ravaged first year of the Democrat's presidency — are to be released this week, and demographers expect grim findings.

It's unfortunate timing for Obama and his party just seven weeks before important elections when control of Congress is at stake. The anticipated poverty rate in-

Sign up for @lerts

Get breaking news delivered to your e-mail. Sign up for @lerts at fayobserver.com.

crease — from 13.2 percent to about 15 percent — would be another blow to Democrats struggling to persuade voters to keep them in power.

"The most important anti-poverty effort is growing the economy and making sure there are enough jobs out there," Obama said Friday at a White House news conference. He stressed his commitment to helping the poor achieve middle-class status and said, "If we can grow the economy faster and create more jobs, then everybody is swept up into that virtuous cycle."

Should the estimates hold true, some 45 million people in this country, or more than 1 in 7, were poor last year. It would be the highest single-year increase since the government began calculating

poverty figures in 1959. The previous high was in 1980, when the rate jumped 1.3 percentage points to 13 percent during the energy crisis.

Among the 18-64 working-age population, the demographers expect a rise beyond 12.4 percent, up from 11.7 percent. That would make it the highest since at least 1965, when another Democratic president, Lyndon B. Johnson, launched the war on poverty that expanded the federal government's role in social welfare programs from education to health care.

Demographers also expect the report to show:
- Child poverty increased from 19 percent to more than 20 percent.
- Blacks and Latinos were disproportionately hit, based on their higher rates of unemployment.
- Metropolitan areas that posted the largest gains in poverty included Modesto, Calif.; Detroit; Cape Coral-Fort Myers, Fla.; Los Angeles; and Las Vegas.

TEA PARTY

Rallies resonate across country

By Robin Hindery and Kevin Freking
The Associated Press

SACRAMENTO, Calif. — Originally billed as a chance to reflect on the Sept. 11 terrorist attacks, a series of raucous tea party rallies around the country on Sunday ended up focusing almost entirely on an event still to come — the Nov. 2 election.

INSIDE
Palin, Beck recall 9/11 attacks at Alaska event. Page 5A

"We are your everyday, average, churchgoing families, we represent the majority of people in this nation, and we're ready to take back our government," said Pam Pinkston of Fair Oaks, Calif., one of about 4,000 people to attend Sacramento's "United to the Finish" gathering.

Thousands of tea party activists also turned up at

Rallies: Events an opportunity to build momentum before election

From Page 1A

rallies in Washington, D.C., and St. Louis to spread their message of smaller government and focus their political movement on the pivotal congressional elections in November.

Several thousand people marched along Pennsylvania Avenue from the Washington Monument to the Capitol, many carrying signs reading "Congress You're Fired" and "Let Failures Fail" and "Impeach Obama."

"It wouldn't bother me to make a clean sweep," said Michael Power of Decatur, Ala., endorsing term limits for members of Congress. "There are some good ones, but we can lose those."

Leslie and Gary Morrison

Kurt Amschoer of Sacramento, Calif., waits for the start of the 'United to the Finish' gathering held at the former McClellan Air Force Base in Sacramento on Sunday.

ous rallies wore red, white and blue clothing and carried yellow flags with the picture of a snake coiled above the inscription, "Don't Tread On Me,"

what they describe as big government run amok and to recall the sense of national unity Americans felt the day after the attacks of Sept. 11,

ington rally. "People are scared. If we do not succeed in November, all that once was good and great about this country could someday be gone."

Most of the rally-goers were already faithful tea party activists, and it will take a lot more than just them to make real waves at the polls, acknowledged Tea Party Patriots co-founder Mark Meckler.

"We want to fire people up today, so that then they'll go out and get the new people," Meckler, of Nevada City, Calif., said backstage at the Sacramento event.

Tea Party Patriots claims to be the nation's largest tea party group, with 2,700 chapters, including at least 175 in California.

FAY OBS 12 SEPT 10

SUSPICIONS RUFFLE FAITH'S FOLLOWERS

By Rachel Zoll
The Associated Press

NEW YORK — Nine years of denouncing terrorism, of praying side-by-side with Jews and Christians, of insisting "I'm American, too." None of it could stop a season of hate against Muslims that made for an especially fraught Sept. 11.

Now, Muslims are asking why their efforts to be accepted in the United States have been so easily thwarted.

"We have nothing to apologize for, we have nothing to fear, we have nothing to be ashamed of, we have nothing that we're guilty of — but we need to be out there and we need to express this," said Imam Mohammed Ibn Faqih in a sermon at the Islamic Institute of Orange County

See MUSLIMS, Page A4

Suspicion remains

Sultan Ahmed, left, and Mohammed Sadik take part in a demonstration Saturday in support of the proposed site for an Islamic cultural center near ground zero in New York.

THE FAYETTEVILLE OBSERVER

Muslims: Poll participants say they know little about Islam

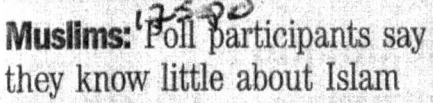

From **Page 1A**

in Anaheim, Calif., the day before the 9/11 anniversary.

There is no simple way for American Muslims to move forward.

Images of violence overseas in the name of Islam have come to define the faith for many non-Muslims at home. The U.S. remains at war in Afghanistan, and although America has formally declared an end to its combat operations in Iraq, U.S. troops there continue to fight alongside Iraqi forces.

Within the U.S., domestic terror has become a greater threat, while ignorance about what Islam teaches is widespread. More than half of respondents in a recent poll by the Pew Forum for Religion & Public Life said they knew little or nothing about the Muslim faith.

Center of controversy

The summer frenzy about Islam in America has revolved around Park51, a community center and mosque planned two blocks from New York's ground zero.

to America starting in the 19th century. The hierarchical Catholic church was denounced as a threat to the separation of church and state. Synagogues were banned in many states, and Jews were viewed as undermining the nation's Christian character.

Mark Silk, director of the Greenberg Center for the Study of Religion in Public Life at Trinity College in Connecticut, said the experience of Japanese Americans in World War II more closely parallels the current plight of Muslims. After the Pearl Harbor bombing, Silk said Americans asked, "Are our Japanese different from those Japanese?"

"I don't think we're about to round up all the Muslims and put them in concentration camps," Silk said. "But I don't think we've ever seen the degree of legitimacy given by people in positions of authority to straight-up, anti-Islamic expression."

In recent months, mosques in Tennessee, California, New York and elsewhere have been shot at and vandalized. Threatening messages were left at one mosque. A Florida pastor caused a global uproar with his ultimately unfulfilled threat to make a bonfire of Qurans on Sept. 11.

Many Jewish, Roman Catholic, mainline Protestant, evangelical, atheist and other groups have responded with an outpouring of support for Muslims, but suspicion remains high among many Americans.

Islamic centers have become a focus of non-Muslim fears. Federal authorities have placed informants in mosques, saying doing so is a critical counterterrorism tool. Muslim groups have separately created national campaigns encouraging congregations to monitor for any sign of radicalization, but they also have complained bitterly about the use of informants, worried the innocent will be caught up in the net police have set for criminals.

Historians, and several Muslim leaders, see similarities to the prejudice Roman Catholics and Jews experienced as newcomers

U.S. Muslim condemnations of terrorism have failed to persuade other Americans.

This year, in response to recent cases of young Americans lured into jihadist movements by Internet preaching, nine prominent U.S. Muslim scholars made a YouTube video denouncing radicalism. Other American Islamic scholars have written edicts, or fatwas, saying violence is contrary to Islamic teaching.

However, suspicion persists among other Americans that Muslims say one thing in public and something different among themselves. U.S. Muslim groups that still accept foreign funding are the most vulnerable to this charge.

It doesn't help that many of the statements against violence are delivered in heavily accented English at a time of heightened anti-immigrant feeling in the United States.

"I think that part of the reason the general American public is not listening is the common human impulse to fear and mistrust what we don't know or understand," said Abdullahi An-Na'im, an expert in Islam and human rights at Emory University School of Law.

SEXUAL ABUSE ALLEGATIONS

Embattled pastor vows to fight claims

By Errin Haines
The Associated Press

LITHONIA, Ga. — Casting himself as the Bible's ultimate underdog, Bishop Eddie Long went before thousands of faithful supporters at his megachurch Sunday and promised to fight accusations that he lured four young men into sexual relationships.

"I feel like David against Goliath. But I got five rocks, and I haven't thrown one yet," Long said in his first public re-

marks since his accusers filed lawsuits last week claiming he abused his "spiritual authority." He stopped short of denying the allegations but implied he was wronged by them.

"I have never in my life portrayed myself as a perfect man," he said. "But I am not the man that's being portrayed on the television. That's not me. That is not me."

Long's brief addresses to the congregation at New Birth

See **PASTOR** Page 6A

AP photo

'I have never in my life portrayed myself as a perfect man,' Bishop Eddie Long told his congregation at New Birth Missionary Baptist Church in Lithonia, Ga., on Sunday. 'But I am not the man that's being portrayed on the television.'

Pastor: Many churchgoers say they support leader

From **Page 1A**

Missionary Baptist Church were met with thunderous applause and an outpouring of support during services that were equal parts rock concert and pep rally.

The sanctuary was nearly filled to its 10,000-seat capacity for the 8 a.m. and 11 a.m. services. Many lined up two hours before the doors of the church opened.

Long became one of the country's most powerful independent church leaders in the past 20 years, turning a suburban Atlanta congregation of 150 to a 25,000-member powerhouse with a $50 million cathedral and a roster of parishioners that includes athletes, entertainers and politicians. And there was almost no sign Sunday that his flock wanted to turn him away.

Followers prayed, sang and embraced one another as they rallied around their senior pastor. Wearing a cream-colored suit as he strode into the church sanctuary hand-in-hand with his wife, Vanessa, Long paused to soak in the adoration.

During the second service, however, one young man in a blue shirt stood up and shouted: "We want to know the truth, man!" He was quickly escorted out and did not return.

New Birth. "We love our place of worship. My son goes to school here. We do everything here."

It is unclear whether Long faces any risk of being removed by his church's board, but the allegations at the very least guarantee months of scrutiny as the lawsuits move forward.

Gay marriage opponent

Long is a father of four who has been an outspoken opponent of gay marriage and whose church has counseled gay members to become straight. Two young men say he groomed them for sexual relationships when they were enrolled in the church's LongFellows Youth Academy, a program that taught teens about sexual and financial discipline.

Two other young men — one of whom attended a satellite church in Charlotte — have made similar claims.

The men say they were 17 or 18 when the relationships began. Federal and state authorities have declined to investigate because Georgia's age of consent is 16.

"I've been accused. I'm under attack. I want you to know, as I said earlier, I am not a perfect man," Long said. "But this thing, I'm going to fight."

came up seven times.

'Simple, direct'

Cheryl Barnett, who has attended New Birth since Long became senior pastor more than 20 years ago, said she was "very much fulfilled with what he had to say."

"It was simple. It was direct. He's standing in the scriptures. That's what we would expect from our minister," she said.

Long addressed the media briefly during a news conference between services, but media access to the services was tightly controlled. Reporters were required to check in with church officials and were led to a separate part of the church to view the service. The media also were told not to interview church members inside the sanctuary or on church property.

After Long's remarks during the 8 a.m. service, an Associated Press reporter was escorted out of the sanctuary by church officials who said the press was not allowed in the sanctuary during worship.

Members clapped and swayed in their seats as the first service began, with several people with microphones singing on stage. Later in the service, hundreds began dancing and chanting, "Jesus, Jesus."

Census: 1 in 7 in poverty

16 Sept 10 FA JOBS

Figures show last year's rate climbed to 14.3 percent.

By Don Lee
Tribune Washington Bureau

WASHINGTON — The recession and longer-term economic troubles have pushed the nation's poverty rate to levels not seen in over a decade and close to what it was when President Lyndon Johnson launched the "War on Poverty," bringing more straited lives to millions of Americans and adding to the financial challenge facing the whole country.

And the face of the poor has changed ominously, Census Bureau data released Thursday showed. No longer the old stereotype of the inner-city single mother collecting welfare checks, those falling below the poverty line today are likely to be full-time workers who cannot earn enough to meet their needs or middle-class workers driven into the ranks of the poor by lost jobs.

The higher poverty levels meant higher costs for government programs such as Food Stamps and unemployment compensation, potentially heavier tax burdens for the country as a whole, and more straited lives and financial pressures for millions of Americans.

For the United States as a whole, the rise in the poverty level that began a decade ago and accelerated during the recession has wiped out all the gains made during the long run of economic growth and prosperity in the 1990s.

The Census Bureau said 43.6 million people, or 14.3 percent of American residents, lived below the poverty line last year, compared with 13.2 percent in 2008 and 11.3 percent in 2000. The number of people counted as living below the poverty line in 2009 was the largest number since records began being kept in the 1950s, though the total population is larger.

The increase would have been greater without growth in Social Security payments and unemployment insurance benefits, which kept several million more Americans from falling below the line. With the economy faltering, more elderly people also began collecting the federal retirement benefit, adding to the financial pressures on the program.

The poverty threshold in 2009 was $10,956 for one person and $21,954 for a family of four.

The rate for Latinos grew last year to 25.3 percent from 23.2 percent in 2008, higher than other groups. The poverty figures for whites went up to 12.3 percent from 11.2 percent in 2008, and for blacks rose to 25.8 percent from 24.7 percent.

Economists said the latest poverty figures and data on overall median household income — which declined 0.7 percent last year to $49,300 — were better than they had expected given the severity of the recession.

A key difference, they said, appeared to be the government's much-derided stimulus bill — the Recovery Act — which expanded unemployment benefits and Social Security payments, among other things.

---

20 Sept 10 **4 DAYS IN BRITAIN**

Vatican says pope's visit was a success

The Associated Press

BIRMINGHAM, England — The Vatican declared Pope Benedict XVI's four-day visit to Britain a "great success" Sunday, saying the pontiff was able to reach out to a nation wary of his message and angry at his church's sex abuse scandal.

On his final day, Benedict praised British heroics against the Nazis to mark the 70th anniversary of the Battle of Britain and moved an Englishman a step closer to possible sainthood.

Vatican spokesman the Rev. Federico Lombardi said the important thing wasn't so much the turnout — crowds were much smaller than when Pope John Paul II visited in 1982 — but that Benedict's warning about the dangers of an increasingly secularized society had been received "with profound interest" from Britons as a whole.

"Everyone is agreed about the great success, not so much from the point of view of the numbers, but ... by the fact that the message of the pope was received with respect and joy by the faithful," Lombardi told reporters.

Prime Minister David Cameron, in his farewell speech before Benedict's departure ceremony, said the pope had "challenged the whole country to sit up and think, and that can only be a good thing."

Amputee's channel swim successful

PARIS — A Frenchman whose arms and legs were amputated swam across the English Channel this weekend using leg prostheses that have flippers attached.

Philippe Croizon, 42, had expected the tough crossing to take up to 24 hours — and instead, he finished in only 13½.

"I did it, I'm happy, I'm so happy, I can't believe it, it's crazy," he told France-Info radio, sounding giddy on arrival late Saturday.

The Associated Press

404

Black Leaders sacrifice own people

Road paved with good intentions

Few things have captured in microcosm what has gone so painfully wrong, where racial issues are concerned, like the recent election for mayor of Washington.

Mayor Adrian Fenty, under whom the murder rate has gone down and the school children's test scores have gone up, was resoundingly defeated for re-election.

Nor was Mayor Fenty simply a passive beneficiary of the rising test scores and falling murder rates. He appointed Michelle Rhee as head of the school system and backed her as she fought the teachers' union and fired large numbers of ineffective teachers.

Mayor Fenty also appointed the city's chief of police, Cathy Lanier, who has cracked down on hoodlumism, as well as crime.

Either one of these achievements would make mayors local heroes in most other cities. Why then was he clobbered in the election?

One key fact tells much of the story: Mayor Fenty received more than 70 percent of the white vote in Washington. His opponent received more than 80 percent of the black vote.

Both men are black. But the head of the school system that he appointed is Asian and

Thomas Sowell

the chief of police is a white woman. More than that, most of the teachers who were fired were black. There were also bitter complaints that black contractors did not get as many of the contracts for doing business with the city as they expected.

In short, the mayor appointed the best people he could find, instead of running a racial patronage system, as a black mayor of a city with a black majority is apparently expected to. He also didn't spend as much time schmoozing with the folks as was expected.

A political blunder

So what if he gave their children a better education and gave everybody a lower likelihood of being murdered?

The mayor's faults were political faults. He did his job, produced results and thought that this should be enough to get him re-elected. He refused to do polls and focus groups, and he ignored what his political advisers

were warning him about.

No doubt Mayor Fenty is now a sadder and wiser man politically. While that may help him if he wants to pursue a political career, Adrian Fenty's career is not nearly as important as what his story tells us about the racial atmosphere in this country.

How did we reach the point where a city is so polarized that an overwhelming majority of the white vote goes to one candidate and the overwhelming majority of the black vote goes to the opposing candidate?

How did we reach the point where black voters put racial patronage and racial symbolism above the education of their children and the safety of everyone?

There are many reasons but the trend is ominous. One key factor was the creation, back in the 1960s, of a whole government-supported industry of race hustling.

President Lyndon Johnson's "war on poverty" — a war that we have lost, by the way — bankrolled all kinds of local "leaders" and organizations with the taxpayers' money, in the name of community "participation" in shaping the policies of government.

These "leaders" and

community activists have had every reason to hype racial resentments and to make issues "us" against "them."

One of the largely untold stories of our time has been the story of how ACORN, Jesse Jackson and other community activists have been able to transfer billions of dollars from banks to their own organizations' causes, with the aid of the federal government, exemplified by the Community Reinvestment Act and its sequels.

Racial anger and racial resentments are the fuel that keeps this lucrative racket going. How surprised should anyone be that community activist groups have used mau-mau disruptions in banks and harassed both business and government officials in their homes?

Lyndon Johnson once said that it is not hard to do the right thing. What is hard is knowing what is right. We can give him credit for good intentions, so long as we remember what road is paved with good intentions.

Thomas Sowell is a syndicated columnist. Readers may write to him at www.tsowell.com, at info@creators.com (with his name in the subject line) or Creators Syndicate, 5777 W. Century Blvd., Suite 700, Los Angeles, CA 90045.

405

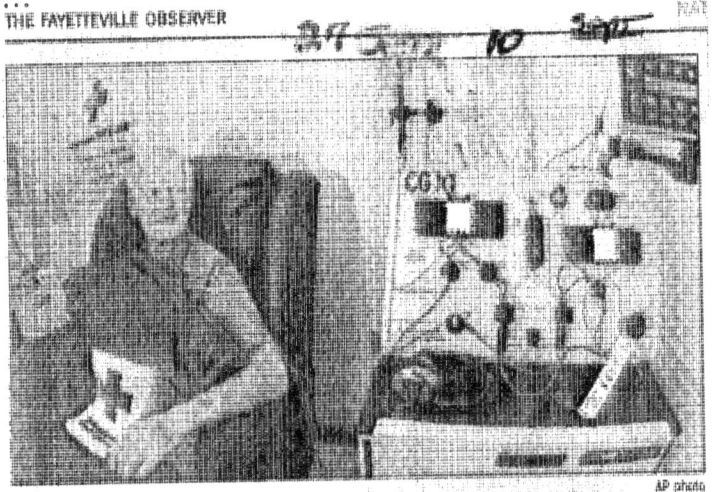

THE FAYETTEVILLE OBSERVER

AP photo

Bob Svensson is hooked up to a blood infusion machine Aug. 16 at the American Red Cross in Dedham, Mass., as he undergoes prostate cancer treatment.

New cancer drugs may cost $100,000

■ Medicare and insurance companies are debating whether it's worth spending that much to add an average of four months to people's lives.

By Marilynn Marchione
The Associated Press

BOSTON — Cancer patients, brace yourselves. Many new drug treatments cost nearly $100,000 a year, sparking fresh debate about how much a few months more of life is worth.

The latest is Provenge, a first-of-a-kind therapy approved in April. It costs $93,000 a year and adds four months' survival, on average, for men with incurable prostate tumors. Bob Svensson is honest about why he got it: insurance paid.

■ Check your e-mail in the morning for top stories.

Sign up for Alerts at *layobserver.com*.

layoffs in the recession. The nation's new health care law eliminates these lifetime limits for plans that were issued or renewed Sept. 23 or later.

Celgene Corp.'s Revlimid pill for multiple myeloma, a type of blood cancer, can run as much as $10,000 a month; so can Genentech's Avastin for certain cancers.

A gamble

Unlike drugs that people can try for a month or two and keep using only if they keep responding, Provenge is an all-or-nothing $93,000 gamble. It's a one-time treatment to train the immune system to fight prostate tumors, the first so-called cancer vaccine. Part of why it costs so much is that it's not a pill cranked out in a lab, but a treatment that is individually prepared, using each patient's cells and a protein found on

stomach cancers in remission. Three such cases were recently described in the New England Journal of Medicine, and all those patients suffered relapses.

■ Retirements are being delayed to preserve insurance coverage of cancer drugs. Holly Reid, 58, an accountant in Novato, Calif., hoped to retire early until

■ Lifetime caps on insurance benefits are hitting many patients, and laws are being pushed in dozens of states to get wider coverage of cancer drugs.

■ Tens of thousands of people are seeking help from drug companies and charities that provide free medicines or cover copays for low-income patients.

■ Doctors and insurers increasingly are doing the cruel math that many cancer patients want to avoid, and questioning how much small im-

406

Red herring politics

Thomas Sowell

Some of the longest-serving members of Congress, whose party has overwhelming majorities in both houses, are having far closer election races than they are used to. These include Senate Majority Leader Harry Reid and Speaker of the House Nancy Pelosi, not to mention 18-year veteran Sen. Barbara Boxer.

Despite their long records, they seem to want to talk about everything except their records. They could tell us why they voted for ObamaCare and huge stimulus bills, without time enough to read them. Instead, they have come up with enough red herrings to stock an aquarium.

One of the big distracting talking points is that the Republicans in Congress have been "the party of No." Given the overwhelming majorities of the Democrats in both houses, in addition to their control of the White House, whether the Republicans said "yes," "no" or "maybe" could not stop the Democrats from doing anything they wanted to do.

It also should be noted that the Democrats were in power

in Congress before President Obama got to the White House. So "the mess" that he constantly reminds us he "inherited" includes runaway spending by Congressional Democrats, of whom Sen. Barack Obama was one of the more prominent big spenders.

Sen. Harry Reid is playing the race card, saying that he can't see how any Hispanic can vote for Republicans. But this is the same Harry Reid who in 1993 rejected "those who ask us to wink at illegal immigration" and warned against having "the social and cultural makeup" of the country "radically altered" by these immigrants.

In 1993, Sen. Reid introduced a bill — the Immigration Stabilization Act — to cut back on all immigration, both legal and illegal.

Sen. Reid said: "Our federal wallet is stretched to

the limit by illegal aliens getting welfare, food stamps, medical care and other benefits, often without paying taxes." He said, "Safeguards like welfare and free medical care are in place to boost Americans in need of short-term assistance," and added: "These programs were not meant to entice freeloaders and scam artists from around the world."

Today, of course, Sen. Reid is singing an entirely different tune.

Instead of talking about the track records of people who have been wielding power in Washington for years, much of the mainstream follows the scent of the red herrings that have been dragged across their trail and focuses on the personal lives of the candidates who are challenging the incumbents.

Whether it is Meg Whitman's housekeeper or remarks that Christine O'Donnell made when she was a teenager, or how much money Carly Fiorina made when she was a corporate CEO, the media are right on it — and right off the serious issues about what the incumbents have been doing

to this country.

If everyone who made silly remarks when they were teenagers were prevented from being elected, at least half the elective offices in the country would be vacant. And since when is earning a high income in private industry a disqualification for holding public office?

The Obama administration has fewer people with real-world experience in the private sector than any other administration in years. Maybe if they had more people with practical experience in the economy, we wouldn't be in the mess that politicians created.

The big question for the election next month is whether the voters keep their eye on the ball and judge candidates by what policies they advocate or whether they can be thrown off the track by red herrings

Thomas Sowell is a syndicated columnist. Readers may write to him at www.tsowell.com, at info@creators.com (with his name in the subject line) or Creators Syndicate, 5777 W. Century Blvd., Suite 700, Los Angeles, CA 90045.

FAYOBS

Study: Hispanics should outlive blacks, whites

By Mike Stobbe
The Associated Press

ATLANTA — U.S. Hispanics can expect to outlive whites by more than two years and blacks by more than seven, government researchers say in a startling report that is the first to calculate Hispanic life expectancy in this country.

The report released Wednesday is the strongest evidence yet of what some experts call the "Hispanic paradox" — longevity for a population with a large share of poor, undereducated members. A leading theory is that Hispanics who manage to immigrate to the U.S. are among the healthiest from their countries.

A Hispanic born in 2006 could expect to live about 80 years and seven months, the government estimates. Life expectancy for a white is about 78, and for a black, just shy of 73 years.

Researchers have seen

LATINO LONGEVITY

Hispanics born in 2006 can expect to live longer than their black and white counterparts in the U.S.

U.S. LIFE EXPECTANCIES, 2006

Female   Male

	Female	Male
Hispanic	83.1	77.9
White	80.4	75.6
Black	76.2	69.2

Source: Centers for Disease Control and Prevention   AP

signs of Hispanic longevity for years. But until recently, the government didn't calculate life expectancy for Hispanics as a separate group; they were included among the black and white populations. The new report projecting future life spans is based on death certificates from 2006.

An estimated 40 percent of Hispanics are immigrants, who in some cases arrived after arduous journeys to do taxing manual labor. It takes a fit person to accomplish that, suggesting that the United States is gaining some of the healthiest people born in Mexico and other countries, said Dr. Peter Muennig of Columbia University.

Compared with the estimate for all U.S. Hispanics, life expectancy is nearly two years lower in Puerto Rico, more than two years lower in Cuba, and more than four years lower in Mexico, according to World Health Organization figures.

However, experts say that immigrant hardiness diminishes within a couple of generations of living here. Many believe it's because the children of immigrants take up smoking, fast-food diets and other habits blamed for wrecking the health of other ethnic populations.

Instigators fan the flames of hatred

This is in response to Jesse Washington's Sept. 26 article, "Bigotry alive and well in online comments."

As long as we have the human race, we will have bigotry, just as we will have crime, poverty and ignorance. Almost everyone is a bigot in one way or another. I once heard a New Yorker say, "Southerners are rednecks and bigots." He didn't see the irony in his statement.

The article mentions proposals to require real names in online comments, or to prohibit racist remarks altogether. But would that stop people from having bigoted thoughts or attitudes? Only a Pollyanna would believe that bigotry can be eliminated, but I think it can be toned down.

Racism among many — not all — whites would end if this push to punish whites for the sins of their ancestors were halted. Many whites see it as "two wrongs do not make a right." But some black leaders have a vested interest in keeping the flames of racism burning, and continue to brainwash blacks into believing that all whites are evil and owe them restitution.

Most blacks and whites whom I know are content to live and let live, to work at making a living, love their families, enjoy their friends and just go about their daily lives. Rodney King asked, "Why can't we all just get along?" The answer is that there are those who make it their business to see that we don't.

Donald H. Sullivan
Fayetteville

Working-class whites favor GOP choices

By Alan Fram
The Associated Press

WASHINGTON — Working-class whites are favoring Republicans in numbers that parallel the GOP tide of 1994 when the party grabbed control of the House after four decades.

The increased GOP tilt by these voters, a major hurdle for Democrats struggling to keep control of Congress in next month's elections, reflects a mix of two factors, an Associated Press-GfK poll suggests: unhappiness with the Democrats' stewardship of an ailing economy that has hit this group particularly hard, and a persistent discomfort with President Obama.

"They're pushing the country toward a larger government, toward too many social programs," said Wayne Hollis, 38, of Villa Rica, Ga., who works at a home supply store.

The AP-GfK poll shows whites without four-year college degrees preferring GOP House contenders 58 percent to 36 percent. That 22-point bulge is double the edge these voters gave Republican congressional candidates

in 2006 and 2008, when Democrats won House control and then padded their majority.

Ominously for Democrats, it resembles the Republicans' 21-point advantage with working-class whites in 1994, when the GOP captured the House and Senate in a major rebuke to the Democrats and President Bill Clinton. The advantage is about the same as the 18-point margin this group gave Republicans in 2004, when President George W. Bush won re-election and helped give the GOP a modest number of additional House and Senate seats.

"Obama ran as a centrist, and clearly he's not been that," said GOP pollster David Winston. "People who have been part of our majority coalition are looking to come back to us."

Working-class whites have long tilted Republican. Many were dubbed Reagan Democrats in the 1980s, when some in the North and Midwest who had previously preferred Democrats began supporting conservative Republicans.

The Democrats can hardly afford further erosion from a group that comprises about four in 10 voters nationally.

To lure them, Obama has used televised chats in people's backyards to emphasize his efforts to lift the economy for average Americans. The Democratic-led Congress passed legislation with tax cuts and loans for small businesses before breaking for the election. On the campaign trail, Democrats pounced on Connecticut GOP Senate candidate Linda McMahon's refusal last week to rule out reducing the minimum wage to help ailing companies.

"Democrats have to make it a choice between two individual candidates, not a referendum on do you like where things are or not, because no one likes where things are," said Democratic pollster Dave Beattie.

Working-class whites' views contrast with whites who have college degrees, who the AP-GfK Poll shows are split evenly between the two parties' candidates. Minorities decisively back Democrats.

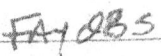

Trouble by the numbers

David Broder

WASHINGTON —
Sometimes the most
important clues are
hiding in plain view. That was
the case in late June, when the
Gallup Organization reported
that the share of voters who
describe themselves as
conservative had increased
from 37 percent to 42 percent
in the past two years.

That does not sound like a
big change. But given the
long-term stability of these
basic philosophical alignments,
the reaction it measured to the
economic troubles and the
performance of the new
Democratic administration is
very significant.

The most recent number,
a cumulative figure based on
surveys during the first half
of 2010, drew some attention
because it was the highest
percentage for conservatives
in any such poll since Gallup
started asking this question
in 1992. The five-point gain
came equally from the ranks
of moderates and liberals,
who fell to 35 percent and
20 percent, respectively.

What was less noticed at
the time were the

state-by-state Gallup figures,
but thanks to the busy
calculators at Third Way, the
moderate Democratic
advocacy and political action
group, the implications of
those numbers for the
midterm election have
become clear in a memo now
circulating around
Washington.

They explain why so many
Democratic candidates are
struggling in states such as
Wisconsin and Washington,
which have been kind to their
party in the recent past. And
they argue that President
Obama may have been
focused on the wrong target
when he kicked off his fall
campaigning at the
University of Wisconsin in the
liberal stronghold of Madison.

The message emerges
from some pretty basic math

calculations — work done by
Lydia Saad of Gallup and
then overlaid by Anne Kim
and Jon Cowan of Third Way.

Saad ran the Gallup
numbers for individual
states, with few surprises.
Wyoming, Mississippi, Utah
and South Dakota checked in
with 50 percent or more
conservatives. At the other
end, Rhode Island,
Connecticut, Vermont,
Massachusetts and Colorado
were the most liberal states
— but only in Rhode Island
did the percentage top 30.

Then Kim and Cowan
added their own assumptions:
Suppose Democratic
candidates run as well as
Obama did nationally in 2008,
taking 20 percent of the
conservatives, 60 percent of
the moderates and 89 percent
of the liberals. And suppose,
too, that turnout rates are the
same for all three groups.

With the updated Gallup
figures, a 2010 Democratic
candidate who matched
Obama's national percentages
would still win Colorado,
Connecticut, Delaware,
Oregon and Washington. But,

with more conservatives and
fewer liberals in the mix, the
Democrat would come up
short in 13 other competitive
states and barely break even
in California, Illinois and New
Hampshire.

As anyone who is following
the election campaign knows,
this kind of analysis makes no
allowance for the possible
impact of Lisa Murkowski's
write-in effort in Alaska or
the crash-and-burn
Republican gubernatorial
campaign in Colorado.

If Gallup is right, and I
believe its methodology is
solid, there simply are fewer
liberal votes to be won this
time. And, as the Third Way
memo says, "While the
middle has always played a
pivotal role in American
electoral politics, where they
swing this fall will certainly
decide the fate of the
Democratic majority."

*David Broder is a Washington
Post columnist. Readers may
write to him at
davidbroder@washpost.com or
Washington Post Writers Group,
1150 15th St. NW, Washington
D.C. 20071.*

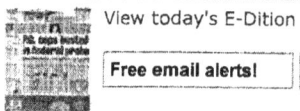

View today's E-Dition

Free email alerts! [Go]

washingtonexaminer.com

The Examiner

COLUMNS AND OPEDS

[Print] [Email]   SHARE 🔲 🔲 🔲   1 retweet

David Limbaugh: President Obama is stuck playing the same note

By: DAVID LIMBAUGH
Examiner Columnist
September 10, 2010

I never expected President Obama to be promoting my new book, "Crimes Against Liberty," but that's virtually what's happened with his recent speeches on the economy. It's as if he's determined to validate every premise I assert in "Crimes Against Liberty."

All the elements are there: his thin-skinned narcissism, his deceit, his militant partisanship, his bullying and his dogged adherence to his disastrous policy agenda against all evidence of its failure and against the express will of the American people.

His full-throated class warfare was on clear display. With him, it's always us against them. He praised "Wisconsin's working men and women," that is union members, as if no one else works or contributes to the economy or society.

Expanding on this theme, he paid homage to the middle class -- the people whose taxes "in any form" he promised he would never raise -- before signing the excise tax on tobacco, trying to pass the cap-and-trade bill, shoving through Obamacare and its 14 to 19 new taxes, which will total some half a trillion dollars over the next decade and fall hardest on middle-income groups. A value-added tax is even on the table.

He claims to be the middle class's greatest champion but fails to explain why his economic policies -- not George W. Bush's, not John Boehner's -- are devastating that very group and bankrupting our children's futures.

No, the acceptance of personal accountability is not in his makeup. It's still Bush's fault that our unemployment rate hovers between 9 and 10 percent despite Obama's promise that it would not exceed 8 percent if he passed his stimulus bill. Now he says "there's no silver bullet" to fix these problems. But that's not what he said during the campaign. He was the silver bullet who would cause the oceans to subside and whose policies would "jump-start this economy again."

He ratcheted up his class warfare theme with this assertion that only those at the top of the economic ladder are doing well, while the middle class is being left behind. If that's true, does it mean he will finally acknowledge the failure of his policies? After all, the middle class (and all groups) fared far better under President Bush. But don't hold your breath.

Next, this self-professed "fierce advocate for the free market" proceeded to savage capitalism, saying it's always rewarding greed and recklessness.

What evidence does he have that America's free market system tilts toward criminals? He's the one, with his government hand-picking of winners and losers, who skews the natural workings of the market in favor of his friends and supporters.

He also engaged, as usual, in scapegoating, demonizing and bullying groups of people instead of discussing the merits of his policies. He went off again on "Wall Street," those he consistently and unpresidentially derides as "fat cat bankers," who are responsible for our economic problems because they took "reckless risks and cut corners to turn huge profits."

Wrong again. The Democratic-led Congress pressured banks to take ridiculously reckless risks not for profits, but to realize its Utopian scheme of "affordable housing," which involved making un-creditworthy loans to people who couldn't pay them back.

He then turned his sights on the unemployment problem, saying that having a job is about more than a paycheck; it's about people's having "a sense of purpose."

That's very true. But this is Obama's economy now. His economic agenda has largely been implemented, and the economy is utterly stagnating.

Yet he remains in campaign mode, as if he were still an outsider. It's surreal. If he truly wants to give people the sense of purpose that only their jobs can provide, then why does he extend unemployment benefits in perpetuity and create a disincentive for people to go back to work?

Amazingly, Obama's stated prescription to jump-start the economy now is to spend another $50 billion of money confiscated from the private sector for infrastructure improvements. This is becoming cartoonish.

If an almost $800 billion stimulus bill didn't get the economy moving, how does he expect us to believe a mere fraction of that amount would do it? And don't get me started about how he presented his stimulus bill as an infrastructure booster and then allocated only 7 percent of those funds toward infrastructure. Nor should I comment on his otherworldly claim that he is "committed to fiscal responsibility."

And he has the audacity to complain about being mistreated. "They treat me like a dog"? You mean they treat you like you and your party have been treating Bush for 10 years, including your slanders in your speeches this week?

This whole thing is disgraceful, and people across America now recognize it. Obama has about five notes, and he plays them over and over in cacophonous disharmony.

The more he talks the less people believe him. It's not as if we can't compare his rhetoric with the results.

Examiner Columnist David Limbaugh is nationally syndicated by Creators Syndicate.

More from David Limbaugh
- O'Donnell looks to the Constitution; Coons looks to the Supreme Court
- Just because GOP may win doesn't mean it'll be loved
- Americans are outraged about violations of their liberty
- Obama spurns Tea Parties for not being more like him
- Obama doesn't know how to stop digging that hole

Topics
David Limbaugh

The Fayetteville Observer

Here&There

Obama in a squeeze

Time columnist Mark Halperin:
Barack Obama is being politically crushed in a vise. From above, by elite opinion about his competence. From below, by mass anger and anxiety over unemployment. And it is too late for him to do anything about this predicament until after November's elections.

With the exception of core Obama administration loyalists, most politically engaged elites have reached the same conclusions: the White House is in over its head, isolated, insular, arrogant and clueless about how to get along with or persuade members of Congress, the media, the business community or working-class voters. This view is held by Fox News pundits, executives and anchors at the major old-media outlets, reporters who cover the White House, Democratic and Republican congressional leaders and governors, many Democratic business people and lawyers who raised big money for Obama in 2008, and even some members of the administration just beyond the inner circle.

The politically good news for Obama is that no matter what the outcome of the midterm elections, everything changes in January. Republicans will have a greater obligation, politically and morally, to help govern, rather than thwart and badger. The president will get a chance, in his State of the Union address and in his budget proposal, to show he is turning the page on the political horrors of 2010 for his party and the nation.

Michael Godwin
Fayetteville

Saggy pants positively indecent

On Oct. 1, I read a newspaper article about a man exposing himself at a car wash. It said "Indecent exposure is a misdemeanor offense." Based on that, I say arrest all of the men wearing pants that hang below their buttocks. They walk, no, I mean limp because they cannot walk normally, and the decent citizens are forced to see their undergarments.

Undergarments are supposed to be just that — under the pants.

Just because they have been programmed like robots to imitate Hollywood, that does not give them a right to do so in public. If they are that desperate for attention, they should seek counseling, not force innocent people to be exposed to their indecent behavior.

WOW! 2.6 MiLLiON KiLLED JOBS! CAN I HAVE YOUR AUTOGRAPH?!

Black preachers exhort their flocks to go to the polls

By Errin Haines
The Associated Press

ATLANTA — On the Sunday before Election Day, preachers told black churchgoers across the country to get out and vote — and defy predictions that they'll be complacent or uninterested in a year that President Obama isn't on the ballot.

Tying the vote to nostalgia and obligation, black pastors invoked the civil rights movement and Obama's historic 2008 victory. At Ebenezer Baptist Church in Atlanta — the spiritual home of the Rev. Martin Luther King Jr. — the Rev. Raphael G. Warnock warned attendees that not voting would be nothing short of a sin.

uing to sputter.

Polls indicate that minority voters may not turn out at the same level as they did two years ago, but analysts say a solid showing among blacks could still swing several House, Senate and gubernatorial races, especially in the South.

Mike Thurmond, currently Georgia's labor commissioner, currently lags behind popular GOP incumbent Sen. Johnny Isakson. Thurmond — hoping to become the first black senator elected in Georgia and the first elected in the South since Reconstruction— attended Greater St. Stephen Full Gospel Baptist Church in Atlanta as he made his campaign rounds Sunday. Thurmond said the

"Go to the polls Tuesday in the name of our ancestors," Warnock said to cheering listeners who rose to their feet. "Know that your ballot is a blood-stained ballot. This is a sacred obligation."

Among those in the pews in black churches across the country were Democratic candidates hoping congregations would heed the message. Indeed, many pastors and worshippers said this election was more important than 2008, with Democrats struggling to hold on to large majorities in the House and Senate and Obama still working to put his agenda in place. Several voters said in interviews with The Associated Press that they planned to get to the polls, believing Obama needs more time to implement his plans.

The black electorate, one of the Democratic Party's most loyal constituencies, voted in record numbers to help elect the country's first African-American president two years ago, and Democrats are hoping at least some of that enthusiasm hasn't faded. Obama has in recent weeks tied a midterm vote for Democrats to continued support for his agenda

polls are flat wrong.

"This whole notion about a lack of enthusiasm was an illusion, and a propaganda scheme at worst, designed to depress turnout," he said.

At the historic Dexter Avenue King Memorial Baptist Church in Montgomery, Ala., the Rev. Michael Thurman opened his sermon Sunday by asking parishioners to vote. He said he did not endorse any candidates, but he said this election would be even more important than 2008's historic vote.

"This one's going to decide the direction that the nation goes in from here," Thurman said.

Negative ads

The sea of negative political ads — many accusing Democratic candidates of being a rubber stamp for Obama's agenda — has quelled the enthusiasm of many black voters, said Calvin Johns, a retired medical doctor. African-Americans could be especially key to Blue Dog Democrat Bobby Bright, who narrowly won his first term two years ago with the help of black voters.

"T...

ANALYSIS

Voters united only in anger

By Liz Sidoti
The Associated Press

WASHINGTON — America is united in its frustration over the economy, over Washington, over where the country is heading.

But it's deeply split about how to fix some of the nation's biggest woes — a ballooning federal debt, near 10 percent joblessness and a sluggish recovery.

Now a divided government could be taking shape, with President Obama and ascendent Republicans facing only two options: compromise or stalemate.

Can this new power structure — one with different ideological philosophies to fix increasingly complex problems — actually lead a sharply polarized country that can't agree on where it wants to go? Will the politicians even try?

If voters don't know what they want beyond something different from the status quo, how can a government deliver, much less one that's divided?

These will be the central questions of the next two years as a weakened Obama, diminished Democrats and resurgent Republicans try to figure out how to meet the demands of a suffering electorate that now seems to perpetually crave change. And how to keep their jobs in 2012.

For now, this much is clear from Tuesday's elections: a country in economic crisis is — from the voters to the politicians — enormously conflicted over the way forward.

An Associated Press analysis of preliminary exit poll results and pre-election polls shows that 39 percent of voters say the budget deficit should be the next Congress' top priority; roughly the same slice say spending money to create jobs should be job No. 1; and 19 percent say cutting taxes should come first.

Disagreements are even in the details: 39 percent say broad tax cuts enacted under George W. Bush should be continued for all. About the same number say the tax cuts should be extended for all but the wealthiest wage earners, while 15 percent say they should expire for everyone.

On another huge issue, close to half of voters want to repeal the health care overhaul Obama enacted this year, while about the same number want to expand it even further or leave it in place.

For all the differences, most voters agreed that they were deeply dissatisfied with Obama and the Congress. And they didn't have a favorable view of either the Democratic or Republican parties. They also were intensely frustrated with the way the federal government is working. And most thought the country was seriously on the wrong track.

Nearly all voters were worried about the future direction of the economy, and about 4 in 10 said they are worse off financially than they were two years ago. Yet again, solutions differed dramatically: A third apiece thought the government's $814 billion stimulus program helped the economy, hurt the economy or made no difference.

With economic fears fueling an antiestablishment fervor, Americans were taking out their anger on the party in power.

Republicans were on track to post huge gains at all levels of government, perhaps large enough to rise to power in the House if not the Senate. It would be a stunning rebuke to a Democratic president and his Capitol Hill allies who — as the economy tanked — pumped in enormous amounts of money to try to stop the slide.

It was a deeply serious campaign

Charles Krauthammer

WASHINGTON — In a radio interview that aired Oct. 25 on Univision, President Obama chided Latinos who "sit out the election instead of saying, 'We're gonna punish our enemies and we're gonna reward our friends who stand with us on issues that are important to us.'" Quite a uniter, urging Hispanics to exact political revenge on their enemies — presumably, for example, the near-60 percent of Americans who support the new Arizona immigration law.

This from a president who won't even use "enemies" to describe an Iranian regime that is helping kill U.S. soldiers in Afghanistan. This from a man who rose to prominence thunderously declaring that we were not blue states or red states, not black America or white America or Latino America — but the United States of America.

This is how the great post-partisan, post-racial, New Politics presidency ends — not with a bang, not with a whimper, but with a desperate election-eve plea for ethnic retribution. Nice.

Yet press secretary Robert Gibbs' dismay is reserved for Senate Republican leader Mitch McConnell and the "disappointing" negativity of his admission that "the single most important thing we want to achieve is for President Obama to be a one-term president."

McConnell, you see, is supposed to say that he will try very hard to work with the president after the election. But it is blindingly clear that nothing of significance will be enacted. Over the next two years, Republicans will not be able to pass anything of importance to them — such as repealing Obamacare — because of the presidential veto. And the Democrats will be too politically weakened to advance, let alone complete, Obama's broad transformational agenda.

That would have to await victory in 2012. Every president gets two bites at the apple: the first 18 months when he is riding the good will honeymoon, and a second shot in the first 18 months of a second term before lame-duckness sets in.

Over the next two years, the real action will be not in Congress but in the bowels of the federal bureaucracy. Democrats will advance their agenda on Obamacare, financial reform and energy by means of administrative regulation, such as carbon emission limits imposed unilaterally by the Environmental Protection Agency.

But major congressional legislation to complete Obama's social-democratic agenda? Not a chance. That's why McConnell has it right. The direction of the country will be determined in November 2012 when either Obama gets a mandate to finish building his "New Foundation" or the Republicans elect one of their own to repeal it, or what (by then) remains repealable.

Gibbs' disapproving reaction to this obvious political truth is in keeping with the convention that all things partisan or ideological are to be frowned upon as "divisive." This is pious nonsense. What is the point of a two-party democracy if not to present clear, alternative views of the role of government and, more fundamentally, the balance between liberty and equality — the central issue for any democracy?

The beauty of this year's campaign, and the coming one in 2012, is that they actually have a point. Despite the noise, the nonsense, the distractions, the amusements, this is a deeply serious campaign about a profoundly serious political question.

Obama, to his credit, did not get elected to do midnight basketball or school uniforms. No Bill Clinton he. Obama thinks large. He wants to be a consequential president on the order of Ronald Reagan. His forthright attempt to undo the Reagan revolution with a new burst of expansive liberal governance is the theme animating this entire election.

Charles Krauthammer is a Washington Post columnist. Readers may write to him at letters@charleskrauthammer.com or Washington Post Writers Group, 1150 15th St. NW, Washington, D.C. 20071.

Voters approve ban on felons as sheriffs

The Associated Press

RALEIGH — North Carolina voters overwhelmingly agreed Tuesday to amend the state Constitution to permanently bar convicted felons from running for or serving as a county sheriff.

With about three-quarters of the precincts reporting, unofficial results show 85 percent of voters casting "yes" ballots in favor of the amendment, compared to 15 percent who voted "no."

The amendment, which will be added to the state Constitution later this year, will bar anyone convicted of a state or federal felony from being a sheriff.

The state sheriffs association pushed for the measure at the General Assembly last summer after six known felons ran for the office in the May primary. All lost.

Current law allows a convicted felon to be elected sheriff or to another elected office once the felon's rights of citizenship are restored.

■ Republicans take back seats from Democrats in the Senate, but likely won't have total control.

By Charles Babington
The Associated Press

WASHINGTON — Republicans grabbed Senate seats from Democrats in Wisconsin, Arkansas, North Dakota and Indiana on Tuesday, but a Democrat's win in West Virginia may preserve his party's Senate majority.

Veteran Democratic Sens. Russ Feingold of Wisconsin and Blanche Lincoln of Arkansas lost their reelection bids. But West Virginia Gov. Joe Manchin held off millionaire Republican John Raese to keep a Democrat in the seat held for half a century by the late Robert C. Byrd.

To gain the 10 seats they need for a Senate majority, Republicans would have to win all the remaining tight races, and pull off upsets in California and Washington.

Tea party champions won high-profile races in Florida and Kentucky, spearheading a likely cadre of libertarian-leaning Republicans who will press party leaders to be more adamant about lower taxes, less spending and smaller government.

Rand Paul of Kentucky and Marco Rubio of Florida rocked the GOP establishment last spring by routing leadership favorites in

party primaries. Then they beat back Democrats' efforts to paint them as too extreme, winning comfortably on Tuesday.

"Tonight there's a tea party tidal wave," said an exultant Paul.

Feingold, a three-term Democrat, lost to GOP newcomer Ron Johnson in Wisconsin. Best known for efforts to tighten campaign finance laws, Feingold was the only senator to vote against the so-called Patriot Act passed after the 2001 terrorist attacks, calling it a dangerous infringement on civil liberties.

Lincoln fell to GOP Rep. John Boozman in Arkansas, where President Obama lost by 20 percentage points two years ago.

Conservatives said Lincoln, who won her first two Senate elections comfortably, was too close to Obama, while liberals said she wasn't loyal enough.

Indiana voters sent Republican Dan Coats back to the chamber after a 12-year absence. Coats, who spent a decade in the Senate before stepping down in 1998, defeated Democratic Rep. Brad Ellsworth. The seat is being vacated by Democrat Evan Bayh.

In North Dakota, Republican Gov. John Hoeven easily won the Senate seat that retiring Democrat Byron Dorgan held for 18 years.

But Connecticut's attorney general, Richard Blumenthal, kept his state's Senate seat in Democratic hands, fending off pro wrestling entrepreneur Linda McMahon.

Senate breakdown

37 seats at stake
51 needed for a majority

51

Democrats 45

Republicans 4

Undecided

— Projected party breakdown
as of 12:40 a.m. today

Paul, who beat Democratic state Attorney General Jack Conway, is an ophthalmologist who had not sought office before. His father is Rep. Ron Paul of Texas, a hero to many libertarians. He won the seat vacated by GOP Sen. Jim Bunning.

Rubio, a former Florida House speaker, defied his party's estab-

lishment by refusing to stand aside for Gov. Charlie Crist in the Senate race. Crist ran as a third-party candidate, but Rubio defeated him and Democratic Rep. Kendrick Meek.

Tea partiers were hoping for up to three more Senate victories in western states. They included Nevada, where Sharron Angle hoped to beat Senate Majority Leader Harry Reid, and Colorado, where Ken Buck took on Democratic Sen. Michael Bennet.

A tempestuous three-way race in Alaska threatened to let Democrat Scott McAdams win a once-hopeless race for GOP Sen. Lisa Murkowski's seat. Murkowski was running a rare write-in campaign after losing the Republican primary to another tea partier, Joe Miller.

Rob Portman won the Ohio Senate race, keeping a Republican in the seat that Sen. George Voinovich is vacating. Portman spent 12 years in the U.S. House starting in 1993. He later was budget director and then U.S. trade representative under President George W. Bush. Portman defeated Democratic Lt. Gov. Lee Fisher.

A nine-seat Democratic loss would produce a 50-50 tie that Vice President Joe Biden, the Senate's official president, would break in the Democrats' favor.

Democrats technically hold 57 Senate seats, but two independent senators caucus with the party.

President, new speaker united on little

By Ben Feller and Julie Hirschfeld Davis
The Associated Press

WASHINGTON — United on almost nothing, Barack Obama and John Boehner are the two faces of America's divided government, the humbled president and the triumphant House leader. Both claim to speak for the people, yet they have had little to say to each other.

This is the relationship that will drive everything.

On first appearance, both men put on a public display Wednesday intended to emphasize what voters want: cooperation to create jobs. A reflective Obama acknowledged the drubbing his party took in Tuesday's elections; Boehner, the speaker-in-waiting, seemed intent not to gloat.

Yet the clearer reality is that these are men of vastly different agendas, styles and backgrounds. And it was telling that just about every mention of cooperation be-

AP photos

President Obama, right, will have to find common ground if he's to forge progress with Ohio's John Boehner, left, the new House speaker, and Kentucky's Mitch McConnell, the Senate minority leader.

tween them was accompanied by insistence on more give by the other — essentially the same formula for bitter gridlock that existed before voters tilted power toward Republicans.

These are men who simply see solutions to problems differently. Likewise, their ways of going about their business.

There's really no connection between them when they do talk. That's how Boehner bluntly put it before the election, and the White House does not dispute the feeling. Obama is known to poke fun at Boehner's perpetual tan, and they both enjoy a good round of golf, but Obama surely has it right when he says the finding of common

Obama is the Ivy League-educated law professor who is known for keeping his composure and publicly yielding few flashes of anger. When he was in the Senate, Obama stayed above much of the political back-and-forth. And with both houses of Congress controlled by Democrats in the first half of his term, Obama didn't need much help, if any, from Republicans to pass his signature policy initiatives.

Boehner was a prime Obama target during the lead-up to the midterm elections, with the president criticizing the Ohio congressman by name and setting him up as the embodiment of unwise Republican ideas, past and future.

The two men have been involved in some bitter face-to-face exchanges. Obama did call to congratulate Boehner on Tuesday night. However, the president made only a vague reference to looking forward to working together and to meeting in

ground will not be easy.

Boehner is an amiable political animal, a happy warrior who came of age on Capitol Hill during the messy years of the so-called Republican revolution under former Speaker Newt Gingrich. He is a backslapper with a sarcastic wit and a penchant for getting worked up.

the next few weeks. There is no expectation of a meeting between the men before Obama leaves on Friday for a 10-day trip to Asia.

Republicans regard Obama as haughty and unwilling to engage, Boehner himself accused the president earlier this year of offering "finger-wagging lectures" instead of leadership. And Obama and Boehner are not believed to have ever met one-on-one, with their dealings conducted in group meetings or through senior aides.

Obama also must deal with the Republican Senate leader, Mitch McConnell of Kentucky. McConnell doesn't enjoy the majority status that House Republicans will soon have, but he will be part of a larger, emboldened minority that will take glee in working to stop Obama. "We'll work with the administration when they agree with the people," McConnell said at Boehner's side or Wednesday, "and confront them when they don't."

419

4/10/10 FALORS

Tuesday's narrative a telling tale

NEW YORK — Two words: Narrative, schmarrative.

Democrats have talked endlessly about the importance of narrative — missing in President Obama's case. We've heard over and over about the lack of smart messaging and the president's failure to communicate. If only Obama could better express himself, all would be well.

Seriously? This is the same president whose soaring rhetoric once sent his ratings into the heavenly realm and who, after assuming office, never stopped expressing himself.

For months, he was everywhere. Talking, talking, talking. Admit it. How many times did you flip on the tube and say, "Omigod, he's talking again"? Several teleprompters had to take early retirement from sheer exhaustion.

Here's a narrative: You can't sell people what they don't want, no matter how mellifluous your pitch. This is the clear message of the midterm elections, and who didn't know?

Only Democrats, apparently.

They — the imperial "they" — say that the people weren't voting against the president. Check. Most Americans don't dislike the president, as in the person. Obama didn't create this dismal economy, and most

Kathleen Parker

acknowledge that fact. But voters were clearly casting a ballot against his policies.

And no, the tea partiers weren't voting against his pigmentation, as my colleague Eugene Robinson suggested in a recent column. "Take back the country," the popular tea party refrain, doesn't mean reclaim it from "the black man." It means reclaim it from a rogue government.

There were so many clues, even the clueless should have seen what was coming.

In February 2009, Obama had an approval rating of 76 percent. Few but God poll better. Obviously, one can only go downhill from there, but you can't pin the slide on racism. All those people didn't suddenly realize their president was African American and become racists.

Are there racists in America? Sure. And some of them show up at tea party rallies. Say what you will about the tea party, and there's plenty to say, but it is fundamentally unfair to say the tea partiers are racist. It is also just plain incorrect to say that opposition to Obama

is anti-black. The election was a referendum on policies that are widely viewed as too overreaching and, therefore, ultimately, threatening to individual freedom.

The essential question that voters were answering was whether government or the private sector is better suited to create jobs. This is a question on which historians and economists disagree, but it was the crux of Tuesday's election. At the risk of oversimplifying, the midterm bloodbath was a fight over capitalism.

Whether candidates could properly articulate market arguments was less important than whether they understood that expanded government means less individual freedom.

Obama's declining popularity since his planet-realigning ascendancy is easy enough to graph. The dipping points in his approval ratings correspond to specific agenda items, such as the stimulus bill and health care reform. Interspersed among those major initiatives were red flags the size of Chile.

In November 2009, New Jersey and Virginia both elected Republican governors — Chris Christie and Bob McDonnell, respectively. These two elections were referendums on Obama's agenda, specifically tied to health care. Then in January came Republican Scott Brown in Massachusetts,

another Democratic state, thundering into the Senate to fill the slot left vacant by Ted Kennedy's death.

That's narrative for you. Yet somehow Democrats couldn't see it. They turned a blind eye and did the very thing Americans loathe: telegraphed disdain for the misinformed masses and insisted that people would like what their government was doing for them once they understood it.

Instead of hearing the people's voices, Democrats and the White House doubled down and began to demonize the opposition. John Boehner, today the presumptive speaker of the House, became a target du jour. In an echo of some of the tea party's worst moments, the White House advanced the them-versus-us mantra.

They're the problem. Except, alas, "they" were The People. And their voices were being ignored. For better or worse, our system of governance doesn't include a monarchy.

Obama didn't need to be a better communicator. He needed to be a better listener. End of story.

Kathleen Parker is a syndicated columnist. Readers may write to her at kathleenparker@washpost.com or the Washington Post Writers Group, 1150 15th St. NW, Washington, D.C. 20071.

Time for Obama to govern 4 NORD FAY ORS his own way

WASHINGTON — The message to President Obama from Tuesday's election could not have been plainer: Don't abandon your goals. Change your way of operating.

There will be a temptation to interpret the Democrats' loss of their House majority and of at least six Senate seats as a rejection of Obama's first-term agenda, the one on which he was elected in 2008.

American voters are not that flighty or unsettled. What happened was that Obama ran into several crises that he and others had not anticipated, and the cumulative weight of those problems ended up frustrating him.

The biggest problem by far was the economy, the virtual collapse of the financial system starting in the autumn of 2008 while George W. Bush was still president. That eased Obama's path to the presidency but it saddled him with a huge and lingering burden once he was in office.

He also was burdened by the legacy of two wars and a backlog of unmet domestic needs, ranging from a dysfunctional health care system to undernourished infrastructure and energy sectors.

David Broder

Democratic politics of Capitol Hill, the less incentive there was for any Republican to contribute to his success.

Thus, a double setback to the hopes that had been aroused by his election. Instead of cooperation, the worst kind of partisanship returned. And instead of changing the way Washington operated, he seemed to ratify business as usual.

Continued partisanship

Facing all these challenges at once, Obama did what seemed natural. He turned to his outsize Democratic majorities in Congress and said essentially, "Folks, I need you to fix this."

The Democrats on Capitol Hill were eager to respond, but they did so in the way that they always will. Instead of acting promptly and with discipline, they dallied and used the delays to bargain for better benefits for their constituents and contributors.

What began as a sound economic stimulus, along with health care and energy bills, became a swollen, expensive and ineffective legislative monstrosity.

Somewhere along the way, Obama lost sight of his campaign pledge to enlist Republican ideas and votes. Maybe they were never there to be had, but he never truly tested it. And the deeper he became enmeshed in the

Lessons learned

What lessons should Obama draw? The worst mistake would be for him to abandon or reject his own agenda for government. If health care is to be repealed, let it be after the 2012 election.

Instead, he should return to his original design for governing, which emphasized outreach to Republicans and subordination of party-oriented strategies. The voters have in effect liberated him from his confining alliances with Nancy Pelosi and Harry Reid and put him in a position where he can and must negotiate with a much wider range of legislators, including Republicans.

The president's worst mistake may have been avoiding even a single one-on-one meeting with Senate Minority Leader Mitch McConnell until he had been in office for a year and a half. To make up, the outreach to McConnell and likely House Speaker John Boehner should begin at once.

Obama tried governing on the model preferred by congressional Democrats and the result was the loss of Democratic seats and his own reputation. Now he should try governing his own way. It cannot work worse, and it might yield much better results.

David Broder is a Washington Post columnist. Readers may write to him at davidbroder@washpost.com or Washington Post Writers Group, 1150 15th St. NW, Washington, D.C. 20071.

421

State-by-state results: The other races

ALABAMA
William Barnes, D............ 36%
*Richard Shelby, R (i) 64%

ALASKA
Scott McAdams, D
Joe Miller, R
Lisa Murkowski, write-in (i)

ARIZONA
Rodney Glassman, D 35%
*John McCain, R (i) 59%

ARKANSAS
Blanche Lincoln, D (i) 39%
*John Boozman, R............ 56%

COLORADO
Michael Bennett, D (i)........ 49%
Ken Buck, R.................... 45%

CONNECTICUT
*Richard Blumenthal, D 52%
Linda McMahon, R............ 46%

DELAWARE
*Christopher Coons, D........ 57%
Christine O'Donnell, R 40%

FLORIDA
Kendrick Meek, D............ 49%
*Marco Rubio, R.............. 20%
Charlie Crist, independent.... 29%

GEORGIA
Michael Thurmond, D........ 39%
*Johnny Isakson, R (i)........ 59%

HAWAII
*Daniel Inouye, D (i)
Cam Cavasso, R

IDAHO
Tom Sullivan, D 24%
*Mike Crapo, R (i)............ 73%

INDIANA
Brad Ellsworth, D 40%
*Dan Coats, R 55%

IOWA
Roxanne Conlin, D............ 34%
*Chuck Grassley, R (i)........ 64%

KANSAS
Lisa Johnston, D 27%
*Jerry Moran, R................ 69%

LOUISIANA
Charles Melancon, D 38%
*David Vitter, R (i)............ 57%

MARYLAND
*Barbara Mikulski, D (i)...... 61%
Eric Wargotz, R................ 37%

MISSOURI
Robin Carnahan, D 38%
Roy Blunt, R.................... 57%

NEW HAMPSHIRE
Paul Hodes, D 36%
*Kelly Ayotte, R................ 61%

NEW YORK
*Kirsten Gillibrand, D (i) 62%
Joseph DioGuardi, R 36%

NEW YORK
*Charles Schumer, D (i) 65%
Jay Townsend, R 33%

NORTH DAKOTA
Tracy Potter, D................ 22%
*John Hoeven, R.............. 77%

OHIO
Lee Fisher, D.................. 38%
*Rob Portman, R 58%

OKLAHOMA
Jim Rogers, D 26
*Tom Coburn, R (i) 71

OREGON
*Ron Wyden, D (i) 57
Jim Huffman, R 40

SOUTH CAROLINA
Alvin Greene, D 28
*Jim DeMint, R (i)............ 63

SOUTH DAKOTA
*John Thune, R (i)
uncontested

UTAH
Sam Granato, D 39
*Mike Lee, R.................. 56

VERMONT
*Patrick Leahy, D (i).......... 65
Len Britton, R 30

WASHINGTON
Patty Murray, D (i) 51
Dino Rossi 49

WISCONSIN
Russ Feingold, D (i) 48
*Ron Johnson, R............ 51

THURSDAY, NOVEMBER 4, 2010 **8A**

ACLU files suit over 'stop, frisk' searches

By Patrick Walters
The Associated Press

PHILADELPHIA — A civil liberties group filed a federal lawsuit Thursday challenging the use of "stop and frisk" searches by Philadelphia police, alleging that the policy is violating the rights of blacks and Latinos who have done nothing wrong.

The American Civil Liberties Union of Pennsylvania filed the lawsuit on behalf of eight men — including a state lawmaker — it says were subjected to illegal searches since the city started using "stop and frisk," a controversial element of first-term Mayor Michael Nutter's 2007 mayoral campaign.

In the lawsuit, the ACLU cites city data showing that 253,333 pedestrians were stopped last year, compared with 102,319 in 2005. More than 70 percent of the people stopped last year were black and only 8.4 percent of the total stops led to an arrest, the ACLU said.

The lawsuit, which seeks class-action status, seeks unspecified damages and a court injunction.

In Philadelphia, the lawsuit filed Wednesday tells the stories of state Rep. Jewell Williams, a 52-year-old Philadelphia Democrat, and seven others who said they were stopped without reason by Philadelphia police. In March 2009, Williams said he was handcuffed and pushed into a police vehicle after asking questions during a traffic stop involving two other men; police Commissioner Charles Ramsey later apologized to Williams.

Another plaintiff, Mahari Bailey, a 27-year-old lawyer, said he was stopped on four occasions over a year and a half.

Make way for the gridlock

4-Nov-10
Fri DBS

The Republican electoral wave that rolled across America on Tuesday was propelled by two powerful currents, overlapping in places and diverging in others.

It will take a day or more to sort out precisely where these results rank among the great congressional swings of the past century, but we do know that they were propelled by both the "tea party" movement and the disenchantment of independents, many of whom voted for Barack Obama two years ago but this time deserted the Democrats in droves. These tendencies were both driven, in part, by an angry disillusion felt by many voters. Polling has found that popular confidence in every big American institution — political parties, business, labor, organized religion, the media — is at an all-time low.

On Tuesday, CNN's national exit poll found that a solid majority of voters disapproved of both the Democratic and Republican parties. In many cases, the GOP may have benefited from the fact that the most visible symbol of the status quo was President Obama, a Democrat.

The voters who registered their discontent Tuesday did not all come from the same perspective. The tea party populists have an ideological antipathy to government and

Tim Rutten

a visceral hostility to the give-and-take of politics. They believe government and political compromise are the real sources of the country's problems. Independents, on the other hand, are by their nature non-ideological, instinctive believers in what Arthur Schlesinger called "the politics of remedy." They're angry and disenchanted because they believe government and politics have failed catastrophically. That's particularly true of voters older than 65, who cast almost one in four of Tuesday's ballots.

The Republicans' congressional leaders also are likely to resist compromise, though for reasons of their own. (If you're getting a sense of conflicting agendas as opposed to clear mandates, there's a reason.) Rep. John A. Boehner of Ohio, who barring something unforeseen will be the next speaker of the House, has said repeatedly on the stump that "there will be no compromise" in the next Congress. Another House Republican leader, Mike

Pence of Indiana — a likely presidential candidate — told a television interviewer that "there will be no compromise in ending this era of runaway spending, deficits and debt, no compromise on repealing Obamacare lock, stock and barrel."

Current Senate Minority Leader Mitch McConnell of Kentucky says the main objective of the next two years will be ensuring Obama's defeat in 2012. That's what's really on the Republican establishment's mind. They believe their party squandered a historic opportunity when they won 52 seats in 1994, but then pursued an overly ambitious agenda under then-Speaker Newt Gingrich. That mistake resulted in a disastrous government shutdown, which, in turn, forced a series of compromises with President Clinton, who won re-election two years later.

Neither Boehner nor McConnell wants to let that happen again. For the same reason, congressional Republicans won't be pursuing anything like the fundamental overhaul of government that tea party members would like to see. Boehner, who will be the first speaker since Democrat Tom Foley to have previously served as the chairman of a congressional committee, is a firm believer in traditional seniority and a

committee system with powerful chairmen, and he already has signaled that he doesn't intend to alter that.

One of the first tests of his ability to discipline populist revolutionaries fresh from the electoral barricades will come when the new Congress is asked to raise the federal debt limit from $12.4 trillion to $14.3 trillion. No Congress has ever refused to approve such an increase and, if such a refusal were to occur, the consequences for the global financial system would be apocalyptic. Many of the new senators and House members have pledged to vote against an increase in the debt.

Neither is there likely to be a vote, quick or otherwise, that the insurgents want on a repeal of health care reform. Instead, there probably will be a series of procedural, regulatory and funding votes — the grinding legislative equivalent of trench warfare.

There will be a heated struggle, but it will be between the White House and the congressional leadership, a purely rhetorical battle over who can offer the country the best explanation for governmental stalemate, one that fixes the blame on the other side.

Timothy Rutten is a columnist for the Los Angeles Times. E-mail him at timothy.rutten@latimes.com.

Cell phones set to detonate bombs

Tribune Washington Bureau

WASHINGTON — Two package bombs shipped from Yemen were likely designed to be triggered by an alarm set on a cell phone attached to a syringe filled with chemical material to detonate the explosives, two U.S. officials said Thursday.

Militants are believed to have tested the length of time it took a package to travel from Yemen to Chicago during a dry run shipment of books and compact discs in September, and likely set the cell phone alarms to go off while the cargo planes were in the air, authorities previously said.

John Brennan, President Obama's top counterterrorism adviser, had said on Sunday that the bombs were designed to be "self-contained" and "didn't require somebody to go in and sort of manually sort of press a syringe."

On Thursday, two U.S. officials confirmed that a syringe in the bomb was intend-

ed to act as a blasting cap initiated by a phone alarm.

When the alarm went off, electrical current from the phone battery would have run through a thin wire filament, similar to those in light bulbs, that would have ignited a small amount of combustible liquid and detonate the bomb.

Once the bomb had the parts, the bombs would not be difficult to assemble, Dave Williams, a retired bomb expert.

"If you could make brownies from a Hines box mix, you make this device," he said Thursday.

ELECTION 2010

Republicans ready to bend Democrats to their will

**By David Lightman
and William Douglas**
McClatchy Newspapers

WASHINGTON — Republicans on Thursday began plotting strategy for the next Congress by vowing to be unified and relentless in their insistence that this year's health care overhaul be repealed and that most domestic spending be frozen or cut drastically.

The GOP, which gained at least 60 seats in the House of Representatives and six in the Senate in Tuesday's election, showed no appetite for bipartisan cooperation.

debate shut down, and the new Senate will have at least 46 Republicans, the GOP moderates probably won't be needed for close votes they're not comfortable with.

In the House, where 218 votes are needed for a majority, current projections show the GOP winning 239 seats, so the GOP leadership could lose 20 or more Republicans and still win.

2012 strategy

One centerpiece of the Republican strategy is to build for 2012, when 21 Senate Democrats, two independents who caucus with the Democrats and 10 Republicans face re-election.

"We have a reasonable shot of getting a majority in the near future," McConnell said.

As part of that push, one of his party's major themes will be to build a case that Democrats are woefully out of touch.

That's particularly important to the tea party loyalists.

"The mandate for change is directed at the other guys," said Senate Republican leader Mitch McConnell of Kentucky. "We are right where we have been."

Where they've been for the past two years is marching mostly in lockstep on issues central to the Republican platform, such as health care, global warming and spending — and against the Democrats' agenda.

Don't look for much change, GOP leaders said.

They'll want Bush-era tax

See **ELECTION**, Page 4A

"Believe me, they're in a no-compromise stance," said McInturff. "They don't want engagement with the president, they don't want to work across party lines; they want now-former Speaker Pelosi's agenda totally and irrevocably stopped and reversed."

That's the theme that congressional leaders are stressing.

Democrats "set about dismantling the free market, handing out political favors at taxpayer expense, expanding government and creating a more precarious future for our children," McConnell charged.

"In other words, Democrat leaders used the crisis of the moment to advance an agenda Americans didn't ask for and couldn't afford. And then they ignored and dismissed anyone who dared to speak out against it."

From **Page 1A**

cuts extended permanently.

"The best thing we could do for families and job creation is to extend the current rates as soon as possible for as long as possible," said Rep. Dave Camp, R-Mich., who is expected to chair the House Ways and Means Committee.

They'll want votes on repealing the health care overhaul, even though they know that President Obama would veto any such effort.

McConnell conceded that his party won't be successful right away on health care. But, he said, "We can compel administration officials to attempt to defend this indefensible health spending bill and other costly, government-driven measures."

Democrats fired back.

"Republicans have always been the party of putting big business over the middle class," said Jim Manley, spokesman for Senate Majority Leader Harry Reid of Nevada, "and they are wasting no time in trying to jam through favors for big corporations at the expense of hardworking families who are struggling to make ends meet."

Dissent possible

Theoretically, two potential cracks in Republican unity could emerge — from the right and the middle — but given the solidarity in GOP ranks over the past two years, chances that their ranks will splinter now appear slim.

Still, here's how it could happen: The tea party movement backed an estimated 110 winning House Republicans, but at least three of its seven Senate candidates lost.

Rep. Michele Bachmann of Minnesota, a tea party favorite, will challenge Texas Rep. Jeb Hensarling for the

fourth-ranking House Republican leadership position. Hensarling has the backing of Rep. Eric Cantor, R-Va., the likely House majority leader. Their showdown could rupture GOP ranks.

Analysts warned that Republicans need to be careful with tea party backers.

"This is trouble for the party," said GOP pollster Bill McInturff. He found about one-third of Republican voters say they're not tea party people, while another third are Republican but "really think of myself as a tea party person."

The final third says, "I'm a Republican and tea party, but when you ask, I think myself more as a Republican."

The danger to the GOP is that a rift might emerge between tea party purists and more established Republican lawmakers schooled in compromise.

However, Sal Russo, the Sacramento, Calif.-based political guru behind the Tea Party Express, said the movement is unified over reining in the growth and expansion of the federal government. Tea party backers are politically practical, he said, to a point.

"I think most people recognize that you have to give to get sometimes," Russo said. "What we're saying is we expect 100 percent fidelity on our issue — you've got to rein in the scope and the range of the federal government."

The other potential dent in Republican unity could come from the few remaining GOP moderates. Up for re-election in 2012 are Sens. Scott Brown of Massachusetts, Richard Lugar of Indiana and Olympia Snowe of Maine.

Still, since only 41 votes are needed in the 100-member Senate to avoid having

425

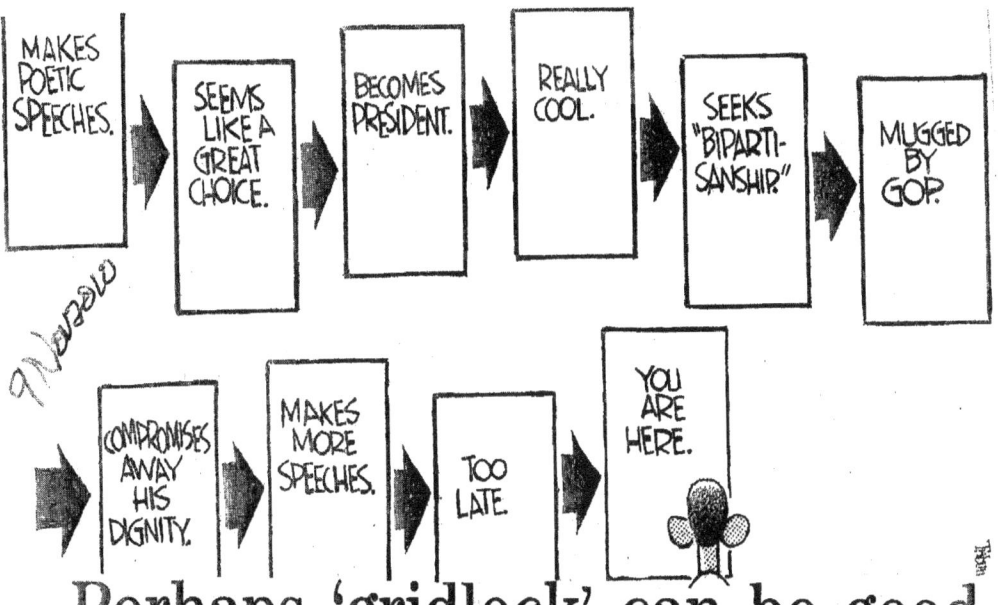

Perhaps 'gridlock' can be good

Thomas Sowell

Whenever the party that controls the White House does not also control Capitol Hill, political pundits worry that there will be "gridlock" in Washington, so that the government cannot solve the nation's problems.

Almost never is that fear based on what actually happens when there is divided government, compared to what happens when one party has a monopoly of both legislative and executive branches.

The last time the federal government had a budget surplus, instead of its usual deficits, there was divided government. That was when the Republicans controlled the House of Representatives, where all spending bills originate, and Bill Clinton was in the White House. The media called it "the Clinton surplus."

By the same token, some of the worst laws ever passed were passed when one party had overwhelming majorities in both houses of Congress, as well as being led by their own President of the United States. ObamaCare is a product of the kind of arrogance that so much power breeds.

It was the same story back in the famous "first hundred days" of the New Deal in 1933. The National Industrial Recovery Act of 1933 clamped down on the American economy the kind of pervasive government control seldom seen outside of totalitarian countries.

Fortunately, the Supreme Court eventually declared the National Industrial Recovery Act unconstitutional. But, before that happened, the N.I.R.A. probably did more to prevent the economy from recovering from the Great Depression than any other law or policy.

You cannot tell what effect a law or policy will have by what politicians call it, whether they label it a "recovery" program or a "stimulus" program.

Those who fear gridlock in Washington today implicitly assume that government actions are needed to "solve" the economy's "problems." That assumption has been so pervasive over the past 80 years that many people fail to realize that the republic existed for nearly twice that long before the federal government intervened to get the economy out of a recession or depression.

During all that time, no depression ever lasted even half as long as the Great Depression of the 1930s.

For most of the history of this country, there was no Federal Reserve System, which was established in 1914 to prevent bank failures and the bad effects of large expansions or contractions of the supply of money and credit. But bank failures in the 1930s exceeded anything ever seen before the Fed was established. So did the contraction of money and credit during the Great Depression.

The seductive notion that some Big Daddy in Washington can solve our problems for us — whether healing the sick, preventing poverty or "growing the economy" — is encouraged by politicians for obvious reasons, and the media echo the idea.

Both in Washington and in the media, there is virtually zero interest in comparing what actually happens when the federal government intervenes in the economy and when it does not.

More than a century and a half of ignoring downturns in the economy never produced a depression as deep or as long as the 1930s depression, with its many federal interventions.

The unemployment rate was 6.3 percent when the first big intervention took place, during the Hoover administration. It later peaked at 25 percent, but its fluctuations were always in double digits throughout the 1930s, as President Roosevelt tried one thing after another. As late as the spring of 1939, nearly a decade after the stock market crash of 1929, unemployment hit 20 percent again.

But there is no way that Barack Obama is going to stop intervening in the economy unless he gets stopped. Only gridlock can do that.

Thomas Sowell is a syndicated columnist. Readers may write to him at www.tsowell.com, or info@creators.com (with his name in the subject line) or Creators Syndicate, 5777 West Century Blvd., Suite 700, Los Angeles, CA 900-

THURSDAY, NOVEMBER 18, 2010   **3A**

Challenges loom large for black caucus

By David Goldstein
McClatchy Newspapers

WASHINGTON — As Democrats in the House of Representatives regroup after major losses in the midterm elections, the Congressional Black Caucus chose Missouri Rep. Emanuel Cleaver on Wednesday to lead them through the new political terrain.

He'll become chairman of a group next year whose 42 members all survived the midterm elections, even as many of their more moderate and conservative colleagues are now packing up their offices and preparing to head back home.

 Cleaver

'Walking together'

After his unanimous approval, Cleaver, a minister and former Kansas City mayor, told the group, "Because we now occupy the minority, the challenge we are faced with will be greater. ... If we walk together, we will accomplish our aim."

He was elected one day after a House ethics panel found Democratic Rep. Charles Rangel of New York, one of the caucus' most prominent and formerly powerful members, guilty of 11 ethics violations.

Another senior Democratic member of the black caucus, Rep. Maxine Waters of California, also faces ethics charges. The ethics committee is looking into whether she interceded with federal regulators on behalf of a bank with ties to family members.

But the direction of the House Democrats over the next two years will be where

Cleaver will put his energy. He now leads the largest caucus in the House, a liberal stronghold that will bolster what appears to be the direction that House Democrats will likely pursue.

Earlier in the day, they re-elected California's Nancy Pelosi, currently speaker of the House, as their minority leader in the next Congress.

The black caucus has been a strong supporter of Pelosi But in the days leading up to the vote, it balked on supporting her and others in the leadership unless she addressed its concerns about Rep. Jim Clyburn of South Carolina.

Currently the House majority whip, Clyburn is the highest-ranking African-American in Congress. Traditionally, the Democrats would lose one leadership slot when it becomes the minority party in January. But the black caucus insisted that Clyburn remain in a position with some power, and Pelosi offered him a new leadership post.

Voter turnout

The black caucus will be expected to play an important role in helping to increase the African-American turnout in 2012, when President Obama is expected to run for re-election, and Democrats will try to regain the House.

Compared with 2008, about 8 million fewer African-Americans went to the polls this year, according to David Bositis, a senior analyst at the Joint Center for Political and Economic Studies, which focuses on issues affecting African Americans and other minorities.

THURSDAY, NOVEMBER 18, 2010   **5A**

Iraq president is opposed to hanging Aziz

By Barbara Surk
The Associated Press

BAGHDAD — Iraq's president declared on Wednesday that he will not sign off on the hanging of Tariq Aziz, joining the Vatican and others in objecting to the death sentence for a man who for years was the international face of Saddam Hussein's regime.

President Jalal Talabani's statement sets up a showdown between those seeking maximum punishment for key figures of the ousted regime and groups calling for reconciliation.

"I feel compassion for Tariq Aziz because he is a Christian, an Iraqi Christian," Talabani, a Kurd, told France's 24 TV. "In addition, he is an elderly man — aged over 70 — and this is why I will never sign this order."

However, Talabani's opposition does not necessarily mean Aziz, 74, will escape the noose. Aziz was sentenced in October for his alleged role in a campaign of persecuting, killing and torturing members of Shiite opposition and religious parties that now dominate Iraq.

The Iraqi constitution says death sentences must be ratified by the president before they can be carried out. But there are mechanisms to bypass the president — such

as an act of parliament or the approval of one of Talabani's deputies.

Justice Ministry spokesman Abdul-Sattar Bayrkdar said death penalties can be carried out regardless of the president's refusal to sign the order.

"If the president refuses to sign an execution that is not a veto on a verdict," Bayrkdar said.

Although Talabani says the death penalty violates his socialist principles, many convicted criminals and members of the former regime — including Saddam himself — have been executed during his presidency.

Talabani has tried to block only one proposed execution — that of Saddam's defense minister, Sultan Hashim al-Taie, a popular figure among the country's Sunni minority. Al-Taie, who was sentenced to death three years ago, is still alive.

"I want to reassert that my father's execution sentence was a political decision. Therefore, it's null and void," said Aziz's son, Ziad, speaking from neighboring Jordan. "

The Vatican expressed "great satisfaction" at Talabani's comments, calling them a step forward for human rights.

427

Post: Narrative, Articles and Cartoons

When you are writing a book about your youth, life experience, world view and future outlook; the more you write and experience simultaneously with your writing over an eight year span, you realize that you always have something to add and it is difficult to bring it to an absolute close. There is just so much to say, and after you have said it, you realize that you have still left out much that you didn't say, but wish you had. It is impossible to capture on two hundred or so pages, a life time of 75 plus years. So in that context please allow me to continue for just a bit more. I want to now summarize the various elements of my life.

Family- Wonderful. My early life in West Virginia was a blessing of my adventure, love and education beyond anything I could conceive of at the time. I took everything for granted and had no fear of the present or future. For me, life was great and would get better for though I knew I was poor, my spirit and belief in success in the future was unassailable. I was blessed with wonderful parents, sibling, teachers and friends that supported me in my positive view of life and their cumulative effect was that I was cloaked with the power of belief in myself that has sustained me-with the over arching protection of God.

Marriage- Wonderful for 50 years, with of course some dry patches early when I was somewhat reckless with gambling, but I was always diligent, loving and protective of Mildred and our children, so she forgave me. It really wasn't all that bad. I only lost my pay check once, but it was enough that I almost lost Mildred. After I grew up over that episode, we struggled at times and prospered at times, but overall were steady and prosperous. In the last days preceding Mildred's death, she was very sick with many serious ailments, I loved her, but was worn down with her care and I guess she detected my frustration of not being able to provide a cure or amelioration of her pain and disability. She died of a heart attack at the kitchen table in my presence. 911 and the hospital couldn't save her, but she had been blessed by God for 77 years. Both of our names are on the grave stone with my date to be filled in later. As for my sons, I'm very proud of Brian, a college graduate at Shaw and U.S. Army Veteran. As for Scott, nothing, I am very disappointed in him and have disowned him, for good reason, not disclosed. We had dogs over 50 years who Mildred loved very much: Kippy, Huey,

Nancy, Murphy and Malcom who is now blind. I loved them very much also.

Career- Great. The Air Force was my ticket out of West Virginia and other than my basic upbringing was the best thing that happened to me, other than Mildred. We were made for each other, the military I mean. I was ahead of the Air Force in discipline and duty when I joined. So it was basically easy for me for 27 years, except the separation from Mildred in England, Greenland, Azores, Vietnam, Japan, Philippines, Greece and Thailand. I attained the highest possible enlisted ranks of E-9 Command Chief Master Sergeant and broke many color barriers with my performance and educational level.

After retirement, I served at Shaw University for 32 years as Psychology Associate Professor and 10 years as Vice President of Student Affairs under two administrations. I have discussed this earlier, yet hold the school in high regard, but not its administrators.

United States cultural decline: I observed a rapid plunge in the integrity, order, love, trust, honesty and work ethic of the general population, especially blacks. Many Whites also became weak, unpatriotic, corrupt and greedy leaving the country in bad shape that may not survive much longer. The anti Christian movement is striving for homosexual marriage, illegal immigration, and half hearted support for our military makes me sick with disgust. The Marxist, Socialist agenda of the President and the liberal movement port ends a dangerous future if the masses do not wake up and see their impending doom, that is disregarded by the media.

I am reluctant to reference Adolph Hitler in his analysis of the collapse of German society after the WWI wherein he observed the poisoning of the German soul and the failure of the educational system to teach character in his book Mein Kampf that he wrote in prison in 1923 before he came to power. To him the so called liberal press actually engaged in digging the grave of the German people just as the present American liberal press of CNN, MSCBS, ABC and NBC are digging our grave as they support the Democratic agenda of Socialism, homosexuality and hatred for America. While observing the decline of personal responsibility and power of the press, he divided the reader into three categories or groups. In this regard, the soul of America is being poisoned and many won't know it until it until it is too late.

For Hitler, "First, into those who believe everything they read, second into those who have ceased to believe anything; and third those who critically examine what they read and judge accordingly. Numerically, the first group is the largest. It consists of the great mass of people and consequently represents the simplest-minded part of the nation. It cannot be listed in terms of professions, but at most in general degrees of intelligence to it belongs all those who have neither been born nor trained to think independently, and partly from in capacity and partly from incompetence and believe everything that is set before them in Black and White. To them the influence of the press is enormous.

The second group is smaller in number. It is partly composed of elements which previously belonged to the first group, but after long and bitter disappointments shifted to the opposite side no longer believing anything that comes before their eyes in print. They hate every newspaper for they believe they only contain lies and falsehoods. He says these people are hard to handle since they are suspicious even in the face of the truth.

The third group which is by far the smallest, consists of the minds with real mental subtlety, whom natural gifts and education have taught them to think independently and form their own judgment of thing. They regard journalists as rascals on principles, who tells the truth only once in a blue moon."

This Hitlerian analogy is dangerously similar to what's happening in America, with the press ignoring the truth and propagating lies about incompetent, Islamic oriented, politically correct, man-children who hate America and purport to be something that they are not-and of course the first group swallows the bait hook, line and sinker.

It's ironic that we can learn some good even from a historical villain and the only one thing I mention of value-while damning his evil ways and achievement of killing millions of innocent people and seeking European and eventual world conquest for German expansion, is the concept of the Big Lie. The Big Lie strategy is now being used by Obama and his minions. I do not trust them. They have turned our world upside down.

It goes like this. For Hitler surmised that the traitorous elements of Germany that contributed to her defeat in 1917 was the magnitude of lies that took the weapon of moral right from the one dangerous accuser,

Ludendorff, who could have risen against the traitors. He says the underminers of freedom of the people proceed with the principle that the magnitude of a lie always contains a certain factor of credibility, since the great masses of the people in the very bottom of their hearts tend to be corrupted rather than consciously and purposely evil and due to the simplicity of their minds more easily fall victim to a Big Lie than a small one, since they themselves lie in little things and would be ashamed of lies that were too big. Such a falsehood will never enter their heads, and they will not be able to believe in the possibility of such monstrous misrepresentations, but even when enlightened, they will continue to accept a least some of the lie as true. "Therefore, something of even the most insolent lie will always remain and stick." He used this philosophy of the Big Lie in the propaganda of World War II and it worked.

Let us beware of the Big Lie-for if it is told often enough many will believe it. I will now pause until 2 November 2010 elections for my final push to finish this book. This date is important for it is when the American people who had been fooled by Obamania and drank the "Kool Aid" of his hope and change will have a chance to partially rectify their mistake in 2008 and vote the Democrats out and hopefully take back the House and Senate for the Republicans, perhaps then we can stop this madness and take back America that we love and are proud of. The rise of the Tea Party, disillusionment of the Independents, low poll ratings of Obama and loss of even some of his "True Believers indicates that his party is over and will effectively be a lame duck until 2012 and then voted out of office that November. Oh, by the way, the Big Lie is today referred to as "spin". The truth is spun to make Black-White or vice versa.

The problems of 12 million illegal aliens, Mexicans mostly and still coming, a $1 ½ trillion budget deficit. A$13 trillion national debt, bailouts to GM, AIG, labor unions and untold others, a despised Health Care Bill and the President calling Blacks a "mongrel race" and afraid to call radical Islamist terrorist after they killed 3,000 Americans on 911 and try to blow up our airplanes, I would think this should be enough to wake up even a dead liberal.

3 November 2010

My Son Brian

433

BRIAN

BRIAN #32 JUNIOR HI BASKETBALL
JR HIGH, Fayetteville, NC
DOUGLAS BYRD   1983

It's time to listen to the people

The GOP now controls both North Carolina's House and Senate for the first time in 112 years. Now there's no reason to keep a constitutional amendment recognizing marriage as only between one man and one woman from moving forward (blocked six years in a row by Democrats).

We are the only state in the South without this. Indeed, in a loop from Arizona to Virginia, every state except N.C. has this. The only reason the Democrats blocked it each year was to kowtow to their homosexual political allies.

If a state expects to receive God's blessings, then we must defend marriage at the highest levels, so that no activist judge can strike down what we presently have on the books: a mere state law. Latest polls show 70 percent of North Carolinians favor this.

Remember "One Nation Under God," and "God Bless America?" Listen to the people.

MEDAL OF HONOR

President Obama presents the Medal of Honor to Staff Sgt. Salvatore Giunta on Tuesday.

AP photo

Highest award salutes bravery in Afghan war

By Darlene Superville
The Associated Press

WASHINGTON — For Army Staff Sgt. Salvatore Giunta, the tribute to his heroism was bittersweet. It recalled a bloody day in Afghanistan's Korengal Valley, and the soldier he brought back later died.

"I would give this back in a second to have my friends with me right now," Giunta said Tuesday afternoon on the rain-soaked White House driveway after President Obama hung the nation's highest military honor around his neck.

Giunta is the first living winner of the Medal of Honor from

See MEDAL, Page 4A

Conclusion

3 November 2010
(Back to Sanity)

Judgment Day Yesterday

Tuesday November 2, 2010. I have been waiting for months to see how most Americans would respond and vote in response to the madness of the Obamaville Liberal, Socialist Anti Business, Anti American values, Pro Abortion Pro Homosexual agenda and administration. After yesterday's crushing defeat of Obama Democrats where the Tea Party and Republicans cleaned their clock with a winning of 63 new House seats – taking over the House of Representatives – getting rid of that stupid Nancy Pelosi, and picking up 6 new Senate seats giving the Republicans a healthy 45 seats to fight the Democrat majority of 55 seats. They will now have a hedge against the two Rino-Repulicans in name only Senators Collins and Snow from Maine who were essentially Democrats and couldn't be counted on in critical votes.

I am very happy with the results that America is coming to it's senses and realize they were duped and flim flamed in 08 by the hope and change rhetoric of Obama. I knew it was all a farce. But now with 9.6% unemployment, 4 million jobs lost, 13 trillion dollars in debt, failure to even try the Black Panthers for video taped voter intimidation, failure to even call people who killed 3000 Americans on 9-11-2001, terrorist and more. Even the most naïve rational Americans, real Americans or conservative Americans realize that they made a mistake if they voted Democrat in 2008.

For all those who didn't drink the "kool Aid" of 08, they woke up as I predicted and voted out the radical Liberal House of Representative, 6 radical Senators and the Obama madness. Yes, I am a Black Republican, even Tea Partier if you will. I'm an American that wants America to remain free and proud and good like it used to be. Not sold down the river by the Saul Alinsky's, Marxist, liberals of the world. So now that many are drinking tea or will be and not drinking Obama Kool Aid, I believe we have a chance to survive terrorism and all the social and political problems we now endure.

As for my job at Shaw University, we had a pretty good Interim President for one year in Dr. Yancy. She brought fiscal stability and reorganization of our debt but did nothing for the internal corruption of the upper administration or resolution of faculty and staff abuse and arbitrary treatment by the ones with power. Everyone is still afraid to stand up or even speak out about the repressive situation for fear of losing their job. Morale is as low as the Titanic and the mission continues to suffer. We did bring in a new young Black female president, but I think she is good at talking rhetoric but see no substance in her purported ability to change things, but I could be wrong. Fortunately for me, this is my last year here anyway. So I won't suffer anymore but I feel sad and sorry for my colleagues I leave behind.

So this is my farewell paragraph. I have done my best and leave this document as an illustration or articulation of my legacy and proof of my existence for my 3 score and 15 years so far. Good-bye and I hope you have enjoyed or gained something from this book if you happen to read it.

THE FAYETTEVILLE OBSERVER

First-class stamps will now be 'forever'

The Associated Press

WASHINGTON — Rummaging around for 1- and 2-cent postage stamps when postal rates go up is heading the way of the Pony Express. Beginning in January, all new stamps good for 1 ounce of first-class mail will be marked as "forever."

The move is designed to help customers cope with postage increases, a U.S. Postal Service official said Tuesday.

Postmaster General Patrick R. Donahoe plans to announce the new policy Jan. 14, the official said.

When the Postal Service unveiled its first-class commemorative stamps for 2011 on Tuesday, all were marked "forever" instead of the current rate of 44 cents.

The initial first-class stamp under the new policy will be the Lunar New Year: Year of the Rabbit stamp, to be issued Jan. 22. It will be followed by stamps commemorating Kansas statehood on Jan. 29 and, in February, the centennial of President Ronald Reagan's birth.

The Forever Stamp, first issued in April 2007 and featuring the Liberty Bell, was designed for use regardless of changes in postal rates. They are sold at the prevailing price of 1 ounce of domestic first-class postage.

The Postal Service says that 28 billion Forever Stamps have been sold since, generating $12.1 billion in total revenue. The stamps without denominations already account for 85 percent of its stamp program, the service says.

2011 OUTLOOK

Get used to higher prices for gas

■ Experts say costs at the pump likely will keep increasing.

By Drew Brooks
Staff writer

Don't expect to pay less than $3 for gasoline any time soon.

Industry experts are predicting that pump prices will continue to rise in 2011, perhaps surging as high as $4.

Average prices already have topped $3 in Fayetteville for the first time in two years, reaching $3.036 for regular gasoline Thursday, according to AAA's Fuel Gauge Report. That was slightly above the statewide average of $3.025, and below the national average of $3.071.

Tom Crosby, a spokesman for AAA Carolinas, said he believes prices will continue to inch upward and possibly still be rising by summer, the peak driving season.

"We're not going to have a good new year when it comes to gas prices," Crosby said.

Historically, gasoline has followed a seasonal pattern in which prices rise during the summer and drop after Labor Day, according to the U.S. Energy Information Administration, a subdivision of the Department of Energy.

But this year, the national average price has risen more than 30 cents per gallon since

See GAS PRICES, Page 4A

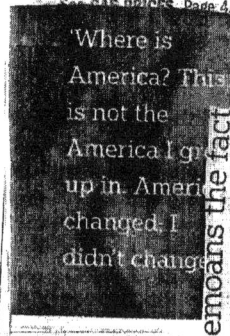

'Where is America? This is not the America I grew up in. America changed. I didn't change'

n Mitchell Shird bemoans the fact ... of plenty, there's no longer enough

Gas prices: Some analysts think return to $4 a gallon is possible

From Page 1A

Labor Day, the largest increase during that period since the government began tracking the data in 1990, according to the EIA.

In past years, gas prices have fallen an average of 22 cents during the same period, the agency said. The exception was 2008, when gas prices skyrocketed to more than $4 before crashing.

INCREASING GAS PRICES

The price of gasoline is on the rise again, with Fayetteville seeing its highest prices at the pump in recent history. Here's a look at how prices have changed in the past year, according to AAA's Fuel Gauge Report.

IN FAYETTEVILLE			
	CURRENT	WEEK AGO	MONTH AGO	YEAR A
Regular	$3.036	$2.949	$2.796	$2.60
Mid	$3.222	$3.129	$2.967	$2.76
Premium	$3.364	$3.267	$3.098	$2.88

Highest recorded average price for regular $4.027 on July 16, 2008

STATEWIDE

"At one time, America was about life," Shird said from a corner bedroom of the vacant house where he sleeps at night. "But now that America is about money, there's not enough for everyone. Being homeless doesn't mean I'm not happy. I'm content. God has given me enough, and this is not my home."

No one forgot she was white excelling in a black musical genre. It simply failed to matter.

Yet, race still matters. It remains the way we judge each other and our lives.

A Rasmussen poll last fall reported that fewer Americans than ever before believe race relations are improving. Nearly a third of respondents believe black-

white relations are deteriorating, a noticeable increase in the percentage who gave similar responses in a poll last summer. Questions about Hispanic-black/white relations showed similar tensions.

The results are surprising to those who just two years ago heralded the dawning of a post-racial society ushered in by the election of Barack Obama.

But the poll only underscored for me what I've already suspected: Whether the topic is music or politics, race remains the thing Americans stumble over most.

Even as the president carries out policies left over from the previous administration, tax cuts and two wars to name a few, the growing sense is that we need to "take our

country back." Teena Marie overcame fears that she was taking soul music from African-Americans. One can only hope Obama quells the fears of those who think he's taking America away from them.

Change comes slowly but it does come. White soul singers are not exactly a dime a dozen, but they no longer raise eyebrows. No one tries to hide the

stumble over race

How the giant lost its might
(USA)

Leonard Pitts

I tem: Only 28 percent of high school science teachers consistently follow National Research Council guidelines encouraging them to present students with evidence of evolution. Thirteen percent "explicitly advocate creationism or intelligent design ..."

These are among the findings of Penn State political scientists Michael Berkman and Eric Plutzer after examining data from a representative survey of 926 high school biology teachers. Writing in the Jan. 28 issue of Science magazine, they report that most science teachers — 60 percent — cheat controversy by such stratagems as telling students it does not matter if they "believe" in evolution, so long as they understand enough to pass a test. Or they teach evolution on a par with creationism and encourage students to make up their own minds.

■ ■ ■

Once upon a time, there lived a stupid giant.

The giant had not always been stupid. Or, perhaps it is more accurate to say the giant had once revered intelligence, reason and the byproducts thereof. Indeed, the giant was renowned for an ingenuity and standard of living that made it the envy of the world.

Much of the world did more than envy the giant. Much of the world admired and respected it. Its basic decency, along with its strength and intelligence, set it apart. There came a time, however, when, though the giant retained its strength and arguably even its decency, it lost its intelligence.

Stupidity crept over the giant with the stealth of twilight, a product less of one abrupt moment than of a thousand moments of complacency, of resting on laurels, of allowing curiosity to be teased and bullied out of bright children, of dumbing down textbooks so kids could get better grades with less work, of using "elite" like a curse word. And, of behaving as if knowing things, and being able to extrapolate from and otherwise make critical use of, the things one knows, was a betrayal of some fundamental human authenticity — some need to keep it real

Stupidity stole over the giant until it could no longer tell science from faith, or conventional wisdom from actual wisdom and in any event, valued ideological purity above them all. Stupidity snaked over the giant until science teachers shrank from teaching science, history books contained history that wasn't history, political leaders told outright lies with blithe smiles and no fear of being caught.

Some regarded the giant's stupidity as a danger. They reasoned that when one is so big that one's merest movement or slightest utterance affects the entire world, it's a good idea if those movements and utterances are animated by something more than autonomic function.

Others saw the giant's stupidity as an opportunity. They learned eagerly until they surpassed the giant's intellect. They grew until they rivaled the giant's size and strength. They did not attempt to match the giant's decency. They considered decency a hindrance.

And the giant? It sat on its haunches in the mud as the world changed about it and new giants rose and shook their fists. The giant did not notice. It was watching "Jersey Shore" on MTV. And it lived obliviously ever after.

Leonard Pitts Jr. Is a syndicated columnist. Readers may write to him at lpitts@herald.com or the Miami Herald, 1 Herald Plaza, Miami, FL 33132.

Double Oops

Taking this long to complete the final product and the three week Christmas 2010 holiday from work, I had a lot of time to think and reminisce about the past and some important things I forgot and failed to mention so far. These are unconnected odds and ends that relate to some of the episodes I mentioned in previous chapters.

I forgot to mention my Washington High school friends and classmates: Ian Pearis, Joe Cameron, Bobo Murray and Clyde Kelly in my listings. All great guys. Also about Billy Dabbs who was such a joyful person. He was our local milk man also. He drove a real small milk truck early in the morning and dropped off bottled quarts of milk and picked up empties. Most every one had ice boxes to keep milk cold. Ice was a penny a pound and we would get a ten pound block every day or so and I am not sure about how much milk. We also bought milk from the company store. Billy was only about 5 feet tall but he had the heart of a giant. Henry Wallace was a baseball player (pitcher), so good that the Pittsburg Pirates were looking at him. I don't know what happened.

About "Tackhead" Ely. He was also small as was I, but could kick a football like someone in the National Football League (NFL) when he was 15. I don't know how he did it but he had a natural gift to punt a football. Sometimes I would challenge him in kicking in a field near the little one cell Cedar Grove jail and I had no chance. By the way, Cedar Grove had one police officer at a time. Eventually, a white friend of ours only about 21, named Wetzel Bowe became the police. He was friendly and looked awesome in his black uniform, gun, and the shinny bullets around his waist. We grew up with him playing sand lot baseball. Remember that's how I learned to catch. He and his brother Chester were the best players, but much older than us, so it was reasonable that they were. You see the three years between 15 and 18 is huge regarding physical capabilities compared to 3 years difference of say 35 and 38. So in my case I was like a boy among men in the sports context and only achieved what I did out of sheer iron will power, desire and spunk as they called it in those days. My real power and advantage over my counterparts were my mental power coupled with will and spunk. I sound self serving but it is true. At this stage in life I am not ashamed to blow my own horn. Like Cassius Clay, aka (Mohammed Ali) used to say - if you brag but can back it up - it is not bragging. Jesse Woodson was the best Black player in about everything. He went on to play for Mr. Merrows in high school.

Also, about Tackhead, he would swim the river with Leroy, Bobby and I. There were two large piers in the Kanawha River in Cedar Grove for the Coal barges. We called them "cribs". They were about 30 feet high and we would dive off them into the muddy river. I must admit I was afraid to jump off that pier into the water that often had submerged logs floating by that you couldn't see. One boy did hit one and broke his back. But you know I, we, were young and stupid and thought we were immortal and did many things even when we were afraid. That's why the military wants young men in its ranks.

As for getting frequent beatings from my dad, my mom didn't tell him all the bad things I did, so she saved me from him sometimes. She knew he was ruthless once he started the beating. I loved her for that and many, many other things.

As for Shaw, I was right. This new President, McClaurin doesn't have it. She is too controlling and inexperienced to deal with the people of an HBCU. Though she is Black I think she thinks White. That's okay as long as you know how to manage the different Black-White ethos and world view. I wish her well, but most everybody dislikes her style including the Trustee Board. She may last a year, two tops. For my Psychology Department they have dredged up a viper from hell to be in charge and she appears to be a certifiable whacko, over compensating for childhood pain, abuse, lack of love and other factors that contribute to the development of tyrants and weirdoes. Lucky for me this is my planned last semester (Spring 2011) and I will soon be free of this dismal situation. I have reported her to the administration but nothing has been done. My colleagues are so afraid of losing their jobs that they remain mute and just take her demeaning, disrespectful treatment. Plus we have a few quislings in our midst that will betray us in a nano second. A quisling is a traitor-deceiver. The name quisling comes from the President Quisling of Norway in 1940 World War II, when he betrayed the Norwegian people to Hitler and the Nazis. We have a few quislings in the Knotty Heads Anonymous also. They don't know that I know. There is an old adage that evil men succeed only when good people stand silent. And I found this to be true. There is another one that says, if you don't stand on your feet to your enemy, you deserve to crawl on your knees. Well on this one you have to mitigate it because of the family factor. You see it is noble to suffer and sacrifice to sustain and protect your family. But even then there is a limit to how much you will allow yourself to be abused and controlled by others. But alas, this is above my pay grade and I can't save or fix the world. Besides with the ignorance and corruption permeating Shaw, I am not sure it is fixable or savable.

But, I love and respect my colleagues for their work and sacrifice for Shaw but feel sad for them to have to continue to be beat down.

I am not sure what I will do after I resign-retire in July. I will go to West Virginia for a week or two and just revisit my past - what is still there. The jungle, forest, nature has reclaimed most of the old coal towns and fields including Ward. But I will just see what I see. Charleston of course is still vibrant, growing, clean and beautiful. But go ten miles out and you see the real West Virginia. Relatively poor and primitive, but proud, good, hard working people. I will have about a $60,000 a year fixed income so that should sustain me if I don't have any big bills.

I am and intend to remain single since Mildred passed away four years ago. I admit I did have an eye on a certain lady, but she seemed to have kicked me to the curb. She just disappeared and can't be contacted. I am not sure what happened. So I surmise that was for the best. God has his hand in these things and saved me from her. Besides if Rene Descartes, the equivalent of Plato and Socrates as the smartest man in the world in the 18th Century who said among all his vast achievements as soldier, engineer, philosopher, inventor and statesman - the greatest thing he did was remain celibate all his life. So if he could do it, so can I from hence forward.

So I guess this finally, finally does it. I want to thank James Elledge the Printer-Publisher <u>A Place to Copy</u> for his patience with my adding pages, for he is such a nice, gentle prince of a man. Also, I again thank Mrs. Mildred Hooker, who is like an angel and Mrs. Kimberly Tidwell for their support and typing my manuscript. <u>Farewell!</u>

A List to Live By

The most destructive habit	WORRY
The greatest joy	GIVING
The greatest loss	SELF-RESPECT
The most endangered species	DEDICATED LEADERS
The most satisfying work	HELPING OTHERS
The ugliest personality trait	SELFISHNESS
Our greatest natural resource	OUR YOUTH
The greatest "shot in the arm"	ENCOURAGEMENT
The greatest problem to overcome	FEAR
The most effective sleeping pill	PEACE OF MIND
The most powerful force in life	LOVE
The most crippling failure disease	EXCUSES
The most dangerous pariah	A GOSSIPER
The world's most incredible computer	THE BRAIN
The worst thing to be without	HOPE
The deadliest weapon	THE TONGUE
The most power-filled words	"I CAN"
The greatest asset	FAITH
The most worthless emotion	SELF-PITY
The most beautiful attire	A SMILE
The most prized possession	INTEGRITY
The most powerful channel of Communication	PRAYER
The most contagious spirit	ENTHUSIAM

For a Long Healthy, Wealthy, Wise Life, My Advice

* Love God, parents, and family
* Love America and fight for her when necessary
* Don't smoke, do drugs, or drink excessively
* Don't covet or envy
* Don't run red lights
* Don't mess with another person's wife or husband
* Read good books and all newspapers
* Eat breakfast
* Work hard and work smart
* Save some money
* Don't loan money to friends or anyone - It only makes enemies
* Get education – write a book and plant a tree
* Don't gossip
* Obey the law

NEVER REVEAL TO A FRIEND what you would do as an enemy

Everyone needs this list to live by... then everyone can really be successful!

443

Supplemental

The Journey
Supplemental

Today 28 September 2011, I took the day off and explored Fayetteville, particularly the Botanical Gardens and the Southern end of the 4.5 mile Cape Fear River Trail. Even for a boy who grew up in the wild, wonderful woods of West Virginia, I was amazed and taken back with the outdoor wooded splendor here right under my nose for 40 years. I fondly wish Mildred was here to see it. She would be thrilled. I suspect 90% of Fayetteville have not visited this wonder. The trail meanders through the woods close to the river with all kinds of trees, flora, periodic picnic tables, wooded seats to rest, and you just walk and walk taking in the beauty and serenity. It was ultra quiet, almost magical. I am so glad I came. I thought I would have to walk back to the entrance complex and I was actually tired, but guess what, the trail was designed in a round about circuitous circle, and I came out back at the other end of the complex. I was glad I didn't have to walk all the way back even though I enjoyed it so much.

But now back to the book. It's been seven months since I completed it including printing. I can't or won't release it until April of 2012 for personal reasons and, in the meantime I have thought of many anecdotes or stories I forgot to put in it. If as some have told me, this journey may be a future movie, I want to have as much about me, my family, friends, and West Virginians in it as I can. So I only have a few things to add. They won't be on the CD yet I will just insert a few pages at the back and add these pages to the basic book CD. Here goes... ... ...

Anecdote One - Fighting Bullies

I was always small and short as a youth and was only 120 pounds when I joined the Air Force. I barely made the minimum weight. So anyway, I was subject to being bullied in junior and senior high school. So my dad told me to defend myself by walking up to the biggest bully and hit him in the nose and eyes before they could stop me. They then could not see, and I would then get low and pick them up and slam them on the ground. They would be shocked as would the others watching.

Now, I knew I would eventually lose that fight, for the big bully would eventually get up and beat me up. But though I lost – he would never bother me again. In fact, most would then be my friend and most others would respect me or thought I was crazy and leave me alone (smile).

Anecdote Two - Fight With The Boston-Navy Thug, Big John

When I was courting Mildred in Boston, I took her to a pretty nice but not too expensive night club. I was weighing about 140 lbs. and had only poverty level airman first class money. But drinks didn't cost much, beer about 25 cents and liquor for maybe a dollar. So we were sitting at this table and this big drunk sailor comes in and starts messing with me for no reason. I guess because I was small and he said "what are you doing with that pretty woman". Before I go on with this episode let me tell you that Boston was a Navy town and this big sucker was the meanest, baddest dude in Boston. Even the police were scared of him. But I didn't know it at the time and challenged him to leave me alone. I have often wondered if I had acted differently if I had known. Anyway, he was a big Black guy in civilian clothes, and after I told him not to touch Mildred's earrings, he said "you think you're a bad little nigger don't you". I said "no, but I can take care of myself". So this guy pulls out a big long knife and walked toward me. Well now I was scared and started backing away reaching out to the near tables for a weapon of some kind to deal with him. After backing all the way to the stage whey they played music, I found a beer bottle on a table and broke it, held one jagged piece in my hand and jumped up on the stage above him. As he continued to approach me I intended to jam the beer bottle into his face before he could cut me. As it turned out the Club Manager –Bouncer, named Buffalo, came up behind him and took the knife to my great relief. Mildred, I and her sister Ethel - who had tried to help me by hitting this guy with a chair which didn't faze him, left the club immediately. I went back to my base in New Hampshire and didn't return to Boston for several weeks. But as luck would have it, as I was leaving the train in Boston's North station, he was getting on the train. I don't think he saw me but I had to clear the air with him now that he was sober, and once he recognized me, he apologized for what he did. I was glad because I didn't want to be ducking and dodging such a powerful force in Boston in the future. As it turned out the episode

446

with him had brought me a certain fame and status because no one-even the Boston thugs - had stood up to this guy. He and I became friends and the tough guys knew it and none of them bothered me after that. I now had insurance because of him. He remained stationed in Boston-Charlestown Navy station for a long time, even after I transferred to New Jersey. I don't remember his name exactly. It was Big something - I think Big John. What finally happened to him I don't know but I am glad the Bouncer, Buffalo intervened when he did.

Anecdote Three - The Lesson of the Tie

At Washington High in the 12th grade a very popular and nice student named Leroy Brockman showed me how to tie a necktie – specifically a Half Windsor. I will never forget him for that. By the way, he was the younger brother of two basketball heroes - Kenneth and Hamp Brockman. They were tall and seemed like giants to me but I was so small at the time. They probably were only 6 feet 2 or so in reality. But they were good and very friendly - all from Montgomery.

Anecdote Four - Dad Rescued Coal Mine Operation

One summer when the mines were closed for production during the annual week-long 4th of July holiday, our family went to Martinsville as we often did. This time, however, during the maintenance performed in this period, the main belt that brought and carried the coal from the mine in Shrewsbury across the highway, to the river barges broke down and they couldn't get the coal out. Well, daddy was the best miner and belt fixer in the mine and they needed his expertise. So the coal company superintendent - the Big Man, Mr. McBain - had the West Virginia State Police drive down to Martinsville, Virginia to get daddy to come back and fix the belt. After finding us they took him back to West Virginia where he told them how to fix the problem and they then brought him back two days later. He was a hero for the company and would have been promoted to a boss rank except the company would not make any Blacks a boss no matter how much they knew. It's ironic that in the mine everyone was Black so to speak, with the coal dust all over them. When the men came out of the mine you couldn't tell the whites from the Blacks except the whites had red lips.

Anecdote Five - Shaw President Fired

I said in the main body of this book that the Shaw President McClaurin was weird and incompetent and probably would not last a year. Well, I was right, she was fired after eleven months. I am not privy to all the reasons but it was rumored that she intended to spend $350,000 on her Inauguration and the Trustee Board just could not accommodate or condone her reckless spending and incompetent management anymore. So they let her go and brought back the previous temporary President who was very good and should have remained all the time. Also, the weird person in the Psychology Department was fired.

Anecdote Six - Universal Studios "Jaws" Experience

During the time 1975-1979, that Mildred and I were stationed in Arizona, we visited several times my sister Sandra in Los Angeles, about a 6 hour drive. Sandra was and is very smart, industrious and kind. We enjoyed visiting her and she was always gracious, taking us to see the sights and activities in Los Angeles. She did this even though she had a very important job as a nurse and director of a Kidney Dialysis Unit at Cedars of Sinai Hospital. So on this one occasion in about 1977 Mildred, I and our boys and Mildred's sisters Ethel and Sille who were visiting us in Arizona went to Los Angeles and Sandra took us to see Universal Studios. It was very exciting and enjoyable. Two unique things were memorable. One was about the movie "Jaws". We were all on this little train or cars hooked together touring the complex when we went though a shallow body of water and the "shark" Jaws arose out of the water and appeared to try and come into the cars. It was so sudden and surprising that everyone screamed, hollered and laughed. Of course it wasn't a real shark but it sure looked like one. The other thing was when we went into a studio where acting was going on. When we arrived, the lady in charge looked out and picked me to play a short role. I said ok. So the female on stage said "help, help, I need help" and I was supposed to say "I'll save you baby" and I did. Everybody laughed – it was fun. Sandra took us down to San Diego – Tijuana, Mexico and we had fun there also – but we didn't drink the water (smile). Sandra could do so many things, seemingly with no effort. She reminded me a lot of Mom.

Anecdote Seven - Mom's Love and Good Cooking

I have already spoken somewhat about my mother Arlene – but not enough. She did so much for others, not complain, or feel sorry for herself if things were bad. She just persevered and made things happen. There is no more an angel in heaven than my mother. She was the meaning of LOVE. And cook – oh my goodness, Pinto Beans, cornbread, meatloaf, lemon pie, Carmel cakes – Daddy loved Carmel cake – and on and on. She put butter on our rice. Mildred put gravy on hers. I liked them both. I could go on but you get the point. She loved us all equally and made us all confident and proud, never asking anything in return. But we did love her back in every way we could. Remember I took the 100 customer paper route for 3 years just to be sure she would get a free paper everyday and not pay the 65 cents per month. All of my sisters and brother could say the same thing about mom and I am just speaking for all of us.

Anecdote Eight - Dad DuPont - Firing

Dad worked in Martinsville a year or so after marriage – remember that's when I had Diphtheria in about 1937 or 38. I don't know or remember all the dynamics of my parents being there, but dad worked for DuPont, building a new DuPont Plant that eventually closed 50 years later. So you see in this time the typical wage was anywhere from 10 cents to 50 cents an hour and a nickel was huge. You could buy a soda pop, coke or candy bar for 5 cents; popcorn at the movie 5 cents and the ticket 15 cents, a loaf of bread, pound of Bacon, 10 pounds of ice, dozen of eggs - 10 or 15 cents. My dad being from West Virginia was used to more money than the 10 cent Martinsville economy. So he boldly asked DuPont for a 5 cents raise for himself and I think for everybody. So they fired him. I don't know the details, but I am pretty sure that's why he, mom and I went back to West Virginia and the Coal Mines. Oh, and you could fill your car with gas for less than 2 dollars.

Anecdote Nine - Diddie Wah Diddie

In Upper Ward hollow near the artificial coal related water pond, it was clear and cold from a small stream. I never knew what it was for. Anyway, Mr. B.J. Edmond and his wife, Ms. Lena, lived in a small scary, always dark house. Mr. B. J. was kind but strange, looked like a Black Indian with a very large hawk nose and Ms.

Lena was very nice, fat, and Black. I never saw her come out of the house. Most people were scared of them and wouldn't go in the house, thinking they did Voodoo or something. I wasn't scared and went often to talk to them. They liked me for some reason. Mr. B.J. would often make me laugh when he said the bad people of Ward would go to Diddie Wah Diddie or in other words Hell. I don't know what ever happened to them once I left for the Air Force.

Observation - Opinions

The most beautiful states by topography - Arizona, New Mexico, Utah, West Virginia

Friendliest people state - West Virginia

Friendliest people country - England, Philippines, Thailand

Cleanest state - Alabama

Cleanest city(s) - Oklahoma City, Charleston, W. VA, Montgomery, Alabama

Most uniquely beautiful campus - Virginia Tech

Most beautiful regular campus - Cornell, Duke, Princeton, Stanford

Most beautiful women - Puerto Rico, Thailand, Philippines, Iceland

Smartest discipline - Physics, Law, Psychology, Medicine

Toughest, hardest work - Coal Miners, Construction, Ship Builders, Public School Elementary Teachers, Policemen

Most greedy industry - Banks, Insurance, Wall Street

Most devious liars - Lawyers, Media-Print, TV, and Congressmen

Biggest threat to future U.S. - Illegal immigration, Naïve-Brain washed Blacks, Incompetent Dysfunctional Congress, Greedy Banks, Duplicitous PC Media, Black Race Baiters, Welfare Moochers, and Same-Sex Marriage.

Biggest Individual threat to future U.S. - Barack Obama

Biggest asset to future U.S. - Tea Party, Conservative Black College Professors, Hard Working Middle Class, Farmers, Scientists, and Medical Practitioners

Greatest Black Americans - W.E.B. Dubois, Fredrick Douglas, Booker T. Washington, Martin Luther King, Jr., Herman Cain, Alphonso Witten, Nat Turner, Denmark Vesey, Bryd Prillerman, Thurgood Marshall, Joe Louis, Colin Powell, Jackie Robinson, Hank Aaron, Buffalo Soldiers and Black Slaves 1619 to 1865, Louise Henderson, Shirley Chisholm, Mary McCloud Bethune.

ANECDOTE TEN

A few things I forgot but now add with additional printing.

1. In the early days of coal mining, there were several gases in the mines including methane which could or would explode, but the miners couldn't smell or detect it to avoid the danger. So what did they do? They used canaries in a small hand held cage, and the canary would usually pass out or die when they inhaled the gas -- thus warning the miners.

2. About My Bicycle -- it was a Shelby with fat tires -- not the expensive Schwinn with skinny tires. Anyway, I had it fixed up with lights all over it including a small generator held against the front tire with a spring for use at night. Also, a large basket in front and saddle bags on the rear fender to carry my newspapers. I think I already said how I woke up many miners in the morning with my paper hitting the door at 5:30 or 6:00AM. They would often check the paper to see if they hit the number at $5.00 for a penny played. If they hit, they would often take the day off and wait for the numbers man to payoff and take new bets.

3. There was a litany of people coming around to the houses every day selling stuff including the number man. You saw the ice man selling ice for a penny a pound. My mom would often buy 10 pounds every day or so for our ice box to keep butter, milk and other things cold. We all had electricity but no running water and no one had a refrigerator except for the mine bosses and a few more prosperous miners and some business men and the one doctor for the whole reservation. There was also a milk man, a wood man, insurance man, but I don't remember them all.

4. My first car that I purchased in 1954 for $600 with help of dad when I was home on leave from the Air Force in New Hampshire, was a 1949 Ford Coupe -- maroon car. I loved that car and even had insurance to keep it on base at Grenier. I mention this because I was stupid enough to let an airman friend use it to go to Boston one night. My daddy warned me not to loan the car because someone would tear it up. Well he was right. The airman totaled it in a wreck. That was a hard lesson for me. But I have never loaned my car to anyone since, and I have probably owned a dozen cars over the past 60 years. Also, if you got caught speeding in Massachusetts, the police would put you in jail for a few hours until you paid some money or talked your way out. Most of us had a lead foot and tip toed through the small towns where the police waited to grab you.

5. Mom washed our clothes on a wash board and eventually we got a wringer-electric washing machine. It was a big step up for us. She would put the clothes through the wringer to squeeze the water out and hang them outside on a clothes line -- like some do today -- using clothes pins. Even though the miner's clothes were very dirty with coal dirt, they always wore clean overalls to work the next day. We and most people had such great pride in those days. We believed cleanliness was next to Godliness.

6. Oh yes -- about football practice -- Mr. Meadows would beat us on our butts with a big paddle to make us work harder and be tougher with our playing. I avoided it most of the time -- besides, I got beat enough by my dad and didn't want anymore.

7. And one more thing, as a small boy I loved to build balsawood airplanes and even placed an engine on one but couldn't get it to fly. ☺ I would worry mama when I went to the store with her, to buy the cereal that had tiny toys in the box, especially air planes. She would get it for me. She was such an angel. Daddy did good too. He bought me a snare drum for the High School band – but probably regretted it when I made so much noise practicing on it at home. ☺

8. About Football – Again, the day before our Friday Night Games, Mr. Meadows would let us take our football shoes home to polish them. I was so proud to take them home and let people know I had them and might actually play in the game. I would be so excited that I never could sleep the night before the game. One other thing, Charles Day and a few other players were somehow involved in the National Guard in their senior year and had to go to Camp Pickett, Virginia for training for the Korean War. They came back much bigger and stronger – I believe for the 1952 season – and I think they won some games that year, or at least we didn't lose to Stratton and Garnet by the usual 50-0 score. ☺ I think I have this right, but remember it's been 60 years now.

Psychological Properties Of Colours

There are four psychological primary colours - red, blue, yellow and green. They relate respectively to the body, the mind, the emotions and the essential balance between these t⌷ The psychological properties of the eleven basic colours are as follows⌷⌷⌷⌷⌷⌷⌷⌷⌷⌷⌷⌷⌷⌷⌷⌷⌷⌷⌷⌷⌷⌷⌷⌷⌷⌷⌷⌷⌷⌷⌷⌷⌷

RED. Physical
Positive: Physical courage, strength, warmth, energy, basic survival, 'fight or flight', stimulation, masculinity, excitement.
Negative: Defiance, aggression, visual impact, strain.

Being the longest wavelength, red is a powerful colour. Although not technically the most visible, it has the property of appearing to be nearer than it is and therefore it grabs our attention first. Hence its effectiveness in traffic lights the world over. Its effect is physical; it stimulates us and raises the pulse rate, giving the impression that time is passing faster than it is. It relates to the masculine principle and can activate the "fight or flight" instinct. Red is strong, and very basic. Pure red is the simplest colour, with no subtlety. It is stimulating and lively, very friendly. At the same time, it can be perceived as demanding and aggressive.

BLUE. Intellectual.
Positive: Intelligence, communication, trust, efficiency, serenity, duty, logic, coolness, reflection, calm.
Negative: Coldness, aloofness, lack of emotion, unfriendliness.

Blue is the colour of the mind and is essentially soothing; it affects us mentally, rather than the physical reaction we have to red. Strong blues will stimulate clear thought and lighter, soft blues will calm the mind and aid concentration. Consequently it is serene and mentally calming. It is the colour of clear communication. Blue objects do not appear to be as close to us as red ones. Time and again in research, blue is the world's favourite colour. However, it can be perceived as cold, unemotional and unfriendly.

YELLOW. Emotional
Positive: Optimism, confidence, self-esteem, extraversion, emotional strength, friendliness, creativity.
Negative: Irrationality, fear, emotional fragility, depression, anxiety, suicide.

The yellow wavelength is relatively long and essentially stimulating. In this case the stimulus is emotional, therefore yellow is the strongest colour, psychologically. The right yellow will lift our spirits and our self-esteem; it is the colour of confidence and optimism. Too much of it, or the wrong tone in relation to the other tones in a colour scheme, can cause self-esteem to plummet, giving rise to fear and anxiety. Our "yellow streak" can surface.

GREEN. Balance
Positive: Harmony, balance, refreshment, universal love, rest, restoration, reassurance, environmental awareness, equilibrium, peace.
Negative: Boredom, stagnation, blandness, enervation.

Green strikes the eye in such a way as to require no adjustment whatever and is, therefore, restful. Being in the centre of the spectrum, it is the colour of balance - a more important concept than many people realise. When the world about us contains plenty of green, this indicates the presence of water, and little danger of famine, so we are reassured by green, on a primitive level. Negatively, it can indicate stagnation and, incorrectly used, will be perceived as being too bland.

VIOLET. Spiritual
Positive: Spiritual awareness, containment, vision, luxury, authenticity, truth, quality.
Negative: Introversion, decadence, suppression, inferiority.

The shortest wavelength is violet, often described as purple. It takes awareness to a higher level of thought, even into the realms of spiritual values. It is highly introvertive and encourages deep contemplation, or meditation. It has associations with royalty and usually communicates the finest possible quality. Being the last visible wavelength before the ultra-violet ray, it has associations with time and space and the cosmos. Excessive use of purple can bring about too much introspection and the wrong tone of it communicates something cheap and nasty, faster than any other colour.

ORANGE.
Positive: Physical comfort, food, warmth, security, sensuality, passion, abundance, fun.
Negative: Deprivation, frustration, frivolity, immaturity.

Since it is a combination of red and yellow, orange is stimulating and reaction to it is a combination of the physical and the emotional. It focuses our minds on issues of physical comfort - food, warmth, shelter etc. - and sensuality. It is a 'fun' colour. Negatively, it might focus on the exact opposite - deprivation. This is particularly likely when warm orange is used with black. Equally, too much orange suggests frivolity and a lack of serious intellectual values.

PINK.
Positive: Physical tranquillity, nurture, warmth, femininity, love, sexuality, survival of the species.
Negative: Inhibition, emotional claustrophobia, emasculation, physical weakness.

Being a tint of red, pink also affects us physically, but it soothes, rather than stimulates. (Interestingly, red is the only colour that has an entirely separate name for its tints. Tints of blue, green, yellow, etc. are simply called light blue, light greenetc.) Pink is a powerful colour, psychologically. It represents the feminine principle, and survival of the species; it is nurturing and physically soothing. Too much pink is physically draining and can be somewhat emasculating.

GREY.
Positive: Psychological neutrality.
Negative: Lack of confidence, dampness, depression, hibernation, lack of energy.

Pure grey is the only colour that has no direct psychological properties. It is, however, quite suppressive. A virtual absence of colour is depressing and when the world turns grey we are instinctively conditioned to draw in and prepare for

Psychological Properties Of Colours - Colour Affects

hibernation. Unless the precise tone is right, grey has a dampening effect on other colours used with it. Heavy use of grey usually indicates a lack of confidence and fear of exposure.

BLACK.
Positive: Sophistication, glamour, security, emotional safety, efficiency, substance.
Negative: Oppression, coldness, menace, heaviness.

Black is all colours, totally absorbed. The psychological implications of that are considerable. It creates protective barriers, as it absorbs all the energy coming towards you, and it enshrouds the personality. Black is essentially an absence of light, since no wavelengths are reflected and it can, therefore be menacing; many people are afraid of the dark. Positively, it communicates absolute clarity, with no fine nuances. It communicates sophistication and uncompromising excellence and it works particularly well with white. Black creates a perception of weight and seriousness.
It is a myth that black clothes are slimming:

The truth behind the myth is that black is the most recessive colour a matter of not drawing attention to yourself, rather than actually making you look slimmer.

WHITE.
Positive: Hygiene, sterility, clarity, purity, cleanness, simplicity, sophistication, efficiency.
Negative: Sterility, coldness, barriers, unfriendliness, elitism.

Just as black is total absorption, so white is total reflection. In effect, it reflects the full force of the spectrum into our eyes. Thus it also creates barriers, but differently from black, and it is often a strain to look at. It communicates, "Touch me not!" White is purity and, like black, uncompromising; it is clean, hygienic, and sterile. The concept of sterility can also be negative. Visually, white gives a heightened perception of space. The negative effect of white on warm colours is to make them look and feel garish.

BROWN.
Positive: Seriousness, warmth, Nature, earthiness, reliability, support.
Negative: Lack of humour, heaviness, lack of sophistication.

The Journey – Vaughan Witten

<u>**A Funny Turtle Story**</u>

I know this page is out of place but I didn't think of this story until after the book was finished, printed and bound, so I had to find an open space –page to add it after the publication. It is so unbelievable, yet true, that I can't not report it. It goes like this: One Saturday, summer morning, outside Fayetteville in about 1981, Mildred, I, and the boys went to White Lake in Bladen County for a picnic along with many other friends and neighbors. I don't remember who they were now. Anyway, my son Brian about 14 or 15 at the time and I ended up together in our car and were a few minutes behind the others on the highway this hot morning in July, as I recall. I was going about 50 mph on the two lane road when I saw this turtle moving slowly across the road and directly in my path. Brian called out "look at the turtle, don't hit it." I said I would try not to but not sure if I could – but guess what – the turtle rose up and ran off the highway. We could see its legs. Brian and I looked at each other dumfounded. We couldn't believe it. We laughed and continued on. I almost can't believe it today 30 years later. But it is a true story. I didn't know turtles could run – but this one did (smile). I should have stopped to see what kind or what was special about him or if I could have found it, but I didn't.

One other thing I forgot is that Sandra and Emma, my sisters, both became nurses and were very successful in the medical field. James, my younger brother was an army paratrooper, served in Vietnam a year ahead of me and worked successfully in th electronic field, especially with Digital inc. Janita graduated from college with a degree in Sociology from a school in Hampton – Christopher Newport University, I believe, raised a beautiful family as did all the others, and her husband, Lee received an artificial heart for 6 months in a Norfolk, VA hospital until he received a real heart and he is still recovering and doing well. I did not know you could survive 6 months on a mechanical heart, he did. Finally, Audrey, bless her sweet wonderful heart raised a beautiful family in Saginaw, Michigan, but has Alzheimer's – for which I am sad. I wanted to get this in because I think I forgot to mention these details about my siblings.

Not feeling the love for Obama policies

Jonah Goldberg

"I f you love me, you've got to help me pass this bill."

That was part of Barack Obama's response to an exuberant fan who shouted "I love you!" at a campaign rally.

And so it has come to this. "The One" has gone from messiah to pleading like a teenage boy on a date. "Come on, baby. If you love me, you'll do it."

According to the standard calendar, autumn is fast approaching. According to the White House calendar, we're finishing up our second "Recovery Summer." But for the president, this is the darkest winter.

When Obama unveiled his first stimulus, he promised it would lift 2 million people out of poverty. Instead, the Census Bureau announced this week that

2.6 million more people fell below the poverty line last year, pushing the number of poor people to the highest level in a half-century.

That stimulus was also intended to jump-start a new economy, fueled by high-paying clean energy jobs. The crown jewel of that multibillion-dollar effort was a solar power company called Solyndra, which not only closed its doors and fired its workers but has exposed the White House as at best politically incompetent and ideologically blinkered.

Now, in fairness, the Department of Energy considers the bankrupt company a winner. "The project that we supported succeeded," Damien LaVera, a Department of Energy spokesman, told the New York Times. "The facility was producing the product it said it would produce, and consumers were buying the product. The company struggled because the market has changed dramatically."

That's true. If Obama had been able to pass cap-and-trade as the market once foolishly expected, things might have been different. He wanted to make electricity rates "skyrocket," which could have made Solyndra's expensive products profitable. As it is, Solyndra

was only marginally more legitimate an enterprise than Paul Newman's bookie parlor in "The Sting".

Then there's the politics. On Tuesday afternoon, even as polls remained open in congressional elections in New York and Nevada, high-level Democratic donors and strategists gathered on a conference call. A participant in the discussion told Politico that the mood was "awful." "People feel betrayed, disappointed, furious, disgusted, hopeless," he added.

That was before the election results came in. In Nevada, the Republican crushed a top-flight female Democratic candidate by 22 points. In New York, the seat that once belonged to Geraldine Ferraro, Chuck Schumer and Anthony Weiner went to

Republican Bob Turner — the first time the seat has gone Republican since 1923. A liberal strategist put a rosy spin on it: "The mine hasn't collapsed, but the loss in New York is definitely a dead canary."

In both races, the Democrats used their trump card: scaring seniors by telling them the GOP wants to take away their Medicare and Social Security. It didn't work.

This came against a backdrop of abysmal poll numbers showing Obama's approval falling with every constituency, including Democrats, independents, Hispanics and African-Americans. That might be why congressional Democrats are openly balking at his must-pass stimulus do-over.

But don't share this with

AttackWatch.com, the third and newest operation set up by this president inviting good and decent Americans to band over the names of critics who say mean things about the president.

It seems ominous, but the truth is, it's sad In 2008, the "politics of hope" campaign trained volunteers to testify about how they "came to Obama" the way one talks of "coming to Jesus." Now, they ask supporters to help build a digital enemies list. Which they'll do, of course. But not because they love him.

Jonah Goldberg is editor-at-large of National Review Online and a visiting fellow at the American Enterprise Institute. You can email him at JonahsColumn@aol.com, or via Twitter @JonahNRO.

THURSDAY, OCTOBER 6, 2011

■ The Fayetteville Observer

Schools can help black male studer

By Tawannah Allen

Cumberland County public school officials continue to face a stubbornly persistent problem that demands immediate attention.

The problem — the underperformance of African-American male students — is masked by a modest 2 to 3 percent increase in the overall African-American graduation rate since 2003 — an increase driven largely by improvements in the academic performance of black females.

Poor academic performance begins early in the schooling experiences of the black male. For Cumberland County black and white males in grades three through eight, for example, there was a 30 percent gap in the pass rate on end-of-grade tests in reading and math in 2010-11. Trend data on student performance on standardized tests reveal that this gap in the pass rate has existed for least a decade.

For black males who underperform in grades three through eight, research reveals that the dropout rate is exceptionally high, especially at the ninth grade, which roughly corresponds to the age at which they are old enough to quit school. Even those who manage to graduate from high school and enter college, studies reveal, are prone to dropping out in the freshman year, largely due to poor or inadequate academic preparation.

School failure imposes a significant fiscal burden on our communities. In contrast to the average high school graduate whose lifetime net fiscal contribution is an estimated $287,000, the average dropout will reportedly cost taxpayers over $292,200 in lower tax revenues, higher cash and imposed incarceration costs. Given the current economic and fiscal pressures we are facing, Cumberland County schools must develop effective strategies to address the African-American male achievement gap — and by extension, the dropout problem.

Here's what Cumberland County school administrators and teachers can do immediately to improve academic outcomes for their black male students.

Principals must create a culture of equity within their schools. That is, they must make decisions and allocate resources based upon the needs of struggling students and their most successful teachers. A culture of equity is not about treating everyone fairly. Principals also must strive to create a more inclusive school culture. That is, they must establish open and trusting relationships with black males and their parents, who often feel excluded from the education process. Research suggests that the development of a more positive-inclusive school culture will increase both parent involvement and the academic performance of their black male children.

Teachers also must strive to build strong and mutually helpful relationships with their black male students and their parents or caregivers. This will require patience, persistence and resilience.

To achieve success, teachers must first recognize that black boys' perception of the education process often is shaped by the limited educational experiences of their parents. Given this reality, teachers must strive to facilitate and nurture not only cognitive but also social and emotional growth of their black male students. This will require teachers to use multiple ways to facilitate learning, including kinesthetic (doing), auditory (hearing), visual (seeing) or tactile (touching), and to continuously search for ways to incorporate both the interests and real-life experiences of black males in classroom activities and to use multiple methods to facilitate learning.

Activities designed to build self-confidence, along with teachers offering positive criticism, can increase a student's desire to contribute in the classroom. Students often need assurance that their input will be valued.

Addressing the needs of the whole student, not just their academic needs, is key in promoting success within the clas Often, teachers as being the at friend or even Understanding unwritten roles build trust, con motivation, not the teacher, bu the class.

Teachers an administrators and communic expectations fo males. These e should be coup arrive opportu participate in a contribute mea class and activ

Through the strategies, impr male achieveme graduation rate Cumberland Co is a mission tha possible.

Tawannah Allen, associate profes director of the E Leadership Doct at Fayetteville St University.

Grads lack tools for a job

Fay JOBS - NC SALU

Jobs, jobs, jobs, we keep hearing. But for whom, whom, whom? Certainly not for the many young Americans being graduated from colleges that have prepared them inadequately for the competitive marketplace in which they find themselves. The failure of colleges and universities to teach basic skills, while coddling them with plush dorms and self-directed "study," is a dot-connecting exercise for Uncle Shoulda, who someday will say — in Chinese — "How could we have let this happen?"

We often hear lamentations about declining educational quality, but the focus is usually misplaced on SAT scores and graduation rates. Missing from the conversation is the quality of what's being taught. Meanwhile, we are mistakenly wed to the notion that more people going to college means more people will find jobs.

A learning curveball

Obviously, the weak economy is a factor in the highest unemployment rate for those ages 16-29 since World War II. But there's more to the story. Fundamentally, students aren't learning what they need to compete for the jobs that do exist.

These facts have been well documented by a variety of sources, not to mention the common experience of employers who can't find applicants who can express themselves grammatically.

A study published by the Association of American

Kathleen Parker

Colleges and Universities has found that 87 percent of employers believe that higher education institutions have to raise student achievement if the U.S. is to be competitive in the global market. Sixty-three percent say recent college grads don't have the skills they need to succeed. And, according to a separate survey, more than a quarter of employers say entry-level writing skills are deficient.

One of the most damning indictments of higher education came early this year with a book, "Academically Adrift: Limited Learning on College Campuses," by Richard Arum of New York University and Josipa Roksa of the University of Virginia. It's a dense tome that could put Ambien out of business, but the authors' findings are compelling. Just two examples:

■ Gains in critical thinking, complex reasoning and writing skills are either "exceedingly small or nonexistent for a larger proportion of students."

■ Thirty-six percent of students experience no significant improvement in learning (as measured by the Collegiate Learning Assessment) over four years of higher education. Undoubtedly, critics of

Arum and Roksa will find reason to diminish their findings. But Americans know something is wrong with higher education, and the consensus is growing that young adults aren't being taught the basic skills that lead to critical thinking.

Most universities don't require the courses considered core educational subjects — math, science, foreign languages at the intermediate level, U.S government or history, composition, literature and economics.

The nonprofit American Council of Trustees and Alumni has rated schools according to how many of the core subjects are required. A review of more than 1,000 colleges and universities found that 29 percent of schools require two or fewer subjects. Only 5 percent require economics. Less than 20 percent require U.S. government or history.

Outdated at the core

Critics of ACTA's findings insist that the core curriculum is outdated and accuse the organization of being "conservative." (Founders included Lynne Cheney, as well as Joe Lieberman.) Some also insist that such "old-fashioned" curricula merely encourage memorization and rote learning rather than critical thinking. Ridiculous, says ACTA President Anne Neal.

"How can one think critically about anything if one does not have a foundation of skills and knowledge? It's like suggesting that our future

leaders only nee Wikipedia to de direction of our

College stude undereducated, I not dumb and m short-changed. A Roper Organizat found that nearl recent graduate: think they got tl money's worth. problem with ed isn't money — v plenty — but qu instead of figuri to make educati future dividends, educational insti building better c flat-screen TVs, theaters and tan salons, according recent CNN rep parents aren't fu they're not payir attention.

In the lost sp loco parentis, Ne Arum have team take these findin upon whom ultir responsibility fal nation's 10,000 c university truste letter sent a few ago, Arum wrote institutions not d a rigorous curric actively contribu degradation of te and learning. The putting these stuc our country's futu risk."

That's a provo charge and a call Let's hope truste and heed.

Kathleen Parker is syndicated column Readers may write kparker@kparker.co. Washington Post W Group, 1150 15th Washington, D.C. 2

Physicists cheer signs of particle

5 July 12

By John Hellprin
The Associated Press

GENEVA — Scientists at the world's biggest atom smasher hailed the discovery of "the missing cornerstone of physics" Wednesday, cheering the apparent end of a decades-long quest for a new subatomic particle called the Higgs boson, or "God particle," which could help explain why all matter has mass and crack open a new realm of physics.

First proposed as a theory in the 1960s, the maddeningly elusive Higgs had been hunted by at least two generations of physicists who believed it would help shape our understanding of how the universe began and how its most elemental pieces fit together.

As the highly technical findings were announced by two independent teams involving more than 5,000 researchers, the usually sedate corridors of the European Center for Nuclear Research, or CERN, erupted in frequent applause and standing ovations. Physicists shed tears reflecting on the decades of work that brought them to this momentous occasion.

The new particle appears to share many of the same qualities as the one predicted by Scottish physicist Peter Higgs and others and is perhaps the biggest accomplishment at CERN since its founding in 1954 outside Geneva along the Swiss-French border.

Rolf Heuer, director of CERN, said the newly discovered subatomic particle is a boson, but he stopped just shy of claiming outright that it is the Higgs boson itself —

Sign up for @lerts

■ Get breaking news delivered to your e-mail. Sign up for @lerts at **fayobserver.com**.

an extremely fine distinction.

The Higgs, which until now had been purely theoretical, is regarded as key to understanding why matter has mass, which combines with gravity to give an object weight.

The idea is much like gravity and Isaac Newton's early theories: Gravity was there all the time before Newton explained it. The Higgs boson was believed to be there, too. And now that scientists have actually seen something much like it, they can put that knowledge to further use.

The center's atom smasher, the $10 billion Large Hadron Collider on the Swiss-French border, sends protons whizzing in a circle at nearly the speed of light to create high-energy collisions. The aftermath of those impacts can offer clues about dark matter, antimatter and the creation of the universe, which many theorize occurred in an explosion known as the Big Bang.

Most of the particles that result from the collisions exist for only the smallest fractions of a second. But finding a Higgs-like boson was one of the biggest challenges in physics: Out of some 500 trillion collisions, just several dozen produced "events" with significant data, said Joe Incandela, leader of the team known as CMS, with 2,100 scientists.

... THE FAYETTEVILLE OBSERVER

FULL-TERM BABIES

More time in womb matters in school

By Lindsey Tanner
The Associated Press

CHICAGO — Even for infants born full term, a little more time in the womb may matter.

The extra time results in more brain development, and a study suggests perhaps better scores on academic tests, too.

Full term is generally between 37 weeks and 41 weeks; newborns born before 37 weeks are called premature and are known to face increased chances for health and developmental problems.

The children in the study were all full term, and the majority did fine on third-grade math and reading tests. The differences were small, but the study found that more kids born at 37 or 38 weeks did more poorly than did kids born even a week or two later.

The researchers and other experts said the results suggest that the definition of prematurity should be reconsidered.

The findings also raise questions about hastening childbirth by scheduling cesarean deliveries for convenience — because women are tired of being pregnant or doctors are busy — rather than for medical reasons, the researchers say.

Women should "at least proceed with caution before electing to have an earlier term birth," said lead author Dr. Kimberly Noble, an assistant pediatrics professor at Columbia University Medical Center.

The study involved 128,000 New York City public school children and included a sizable number of kids from disadvantaged families. But the authors said similar results likely would be found in other children, too.

Of the children born at 37 weeks, 2.3 percent had severely poor reading skills and 1.1 percent had at least moderate problems in math. That compares with 1.8 percent and 0.9 percent for the children born at 41 weeks.

Children born at 38 weeks faced only slightly lower risks than those born at 37 weeks.

Compared with 41-weekers, children born at 37 weeks faced a 33 percent increased chance of having severe reading difficulty in third grade, and a 19 percent greater chance of having moderate problems in math.

Liberals, hostility and illogic

Thomas Sowell

Random thoughts on the passing scene:

■ For a long time, Democrats have gone to Washington to win at all costs, while too many Republicans went to Washington to compromise with Democrats. The rise of the Tea Party may change that.

■ Those who favor huge cuts in military spending seem not to understand that our military exists not simply to win wars, but to present such overwhelming superiority to potential enemies as to prevent having to fight a war.

■ Some people who are belatedly seeing what Obama is really like are saying that he has changed. This is probably easier to say than admitting that you were blind to the man's whole history before, and were taken in by his rhetoric and geniality.

■ Wishful thinking is not idealism. It is self-indulgence at best and self-exaltation at worst. In either case, it is usually at the expense of others — the opposite of idealism.

■ The hostility of liberals against Sarah Palin is something that liberals themselves ought to be concerned about. After all, she is just someone who has a different opinion about politics and a different social background. What I fear the liberals most resent is their perception that she is someone who is talking back to her betters.

■ When Harry Truman was president, he had a sign on his desk that said: "The buck stops here." If Barack Obama had a sign, it would say: "The buck stops with Bush."

■ Does anyone seriously believe that short dresses, exposing bony knees, make women look attractive?

■ In most discussions of the problems of American public schools, the low intellectual quality of people who come out of our schools of education is the 800-pound gorilla that keeps getting ignored. Such teachers cannot give their students abilities that they themselves don't have.

■ Did we have to wait for the Solyndra and other government "investment" disasters to learn what economic nonsense political "investments" are? Reckless spending to win votes, or campaign contributions, from the recipients of government largesse is still reckless spending, regardless of what other words are used to try to dignify it — whether these words are "stimulus," "jobs" or whatever.

■ In liberal logic, if life is unfair then the answer is to turn more tax money over to politicians, to spend in ways that will increase their chances of getting reelected.

Thomas Sowell is a syndicated columnist. Readers may write to him at www.tsowell.com, at info@creators.com (with his name in the subject line) or Creators Syndicate, 5777 West Century Blvd., Suite 700, Los Angeles, CA 90045.

If having it all, what's the 'it'?

Froma Harrop

Two cultural events have caught our attention this season. One is the stern graduation speech at Wellesley (Mass.) High School in which teacher David McCullough Jr. told pampered students, "Do not get the idea you're anything special." The other was an article in The Atlantic magazine by Anne-Marie Slaughter titled, "Why Women Still Can't Have It All."

Somehow the two belong together.

Slaughter's story: While deeply engaged as a high official in the Obama State Department (after serving as dean at Princeton's Woodrow Wilson School of Public and International Affairs), she decided that her two teenage sons needed more of her presence and so left the helm to spend more time at home.

The conclusion: Ambitious women can't have it all.

The implication: They ought to.

My confusion: What the heck do you mean by "it"?

The one thing that's clear: There's never enough of "it."

Worship. Barbecue ribs. Ride horses. Bet on horses. Get a good night's sleep. The worker-drone existence also swallows male executives, at the expense of their cultural growth and pleasure. Are they having it all?

Incredibly, Slaughter refers to a 10-month sabbatical she, her husband and their children took in Shanghai as a time of merely treading water, as "putting money in the family bank." How many Americans get paid sabbaticals? What Slaughter regarded as one of the "plateaus" in her career, others would consider the pinnacle.

Rather than quietly accepting the tradeoffs she's made, she demands recognition for taking care of her family.

Greatness and what it means

Can you say why America is the greatest country in the world?

The question proceeds, of course, from an assumption: that America is, indeed, the greatest nation on Earth. When it is posed by a chipper college student to Will McAvoy, the dyspeptic cable news anchor played by Jeff Daniels in the new HBO series "The Newsroom," he gores that assumption with acid glee.

By no standard — or at least, no standard he cares to acknowledge — does McAvoy believe America is still the world's greatest nation. Freedom? That's hardly unique, he says, noting that Canada, the United Kingdom, France, Germany and Japan are all free. And he ticks off a number of other measures — literacy, life expectancy, math, exports, infant mortality — by which, he says, America now lags much of the world.

Therefore, he says, America is, in fact, not the greatest nation on the planet. There is something telling and true in the crestfallen expressions with which the audience greets that declaration. It's as if someone has switched off the sun.

America believes in

Leonard Pitts

nothing quite so deeply as its own greatness.

There is something quintessentially us about that belief. The Japanese, we may presume, love Japan. Surely the Canadians feel a swelling pride at the sight of their flag and the Spanish stand a little straighter at the playing of their national anthem. But does any other nation feel the need to so routinely assure itself and remind others that it is the most excellent of them all?

"America," says Sean Hannity with numbing regularity, is "the best, greatest nation God has ever given man on the face of the Earth." It might be said that the seed of American greatness lies in the very need to be great, to raise the foam index finger and chant "USA! USA!" — to live up to our own self-image.

Unfortunately, the seed of American self-delusion lies in the same place. To read the test scores, to

watch the clown show that passes for TV news, to walk the boarded-up streets of downtown Wherever, USA., to talk to a father about his kids' future, is to take the fictional news anchor's point:

Namely, that there is something sad about yelling, "We're number one!" when you are, in fact, not.

But — and a character on the show reminds McAvoy of this — we can be, always. The potential of it lies in America's endless capacity for reinvention, the path to it in America's matchless sense of mission. The nation has always risen to the challenge of greatness when it had a goal, a purpose to unite behind, a thing to get done. That is the story of the Revolution, the Union victory, the Great Depression, the Second World War, the Marshall Plan, the Berlin airlift, the Civil Rights Movement, the moon landing.

So what is our mission now? What is the goal toward which we strive in 2012? And therein lies the problem: you don't know either, do you? Bill Clinton did mention something about a bridge to somewhere or other. George W. Bush was handed a mission — fighting

terrorism — on a golden tray and bungled it. President Obama, unlike candidate Obama, has yet to articulate a goal that excites and unites.

Like a knife's blade, greatness requires a whetstone to sharpen itself against. No whetstone presents itself in a nation where, as McAvoy notes, people define themselves by who they voted for in the last election, a nation whose depth of division and lack of unifying principle now poison the very air, a nation where, to speak of greatness is, increasingly, to speak of history.

But what of the future?

That will require mission and purpose, the realization that who we are is bound up in the things — audacious and spectacular things — we come together to get done. We ought to spend more time deciding what those things will be, and less reassuring ourselves of our own wonderfulness.

True greatness, after all, is not declared. It is achieved.

Leonard Pitts Jr. is a syndicated columnist. Readers may write to him at lpitts@miamiherald.com or the Miami Herald, 1 Herald Plaza, Miami, FL 33132.

Policing method predicts crime before it happens

By Greg Risling
The Associated Press

LOS ANGELES — Los Angeles police are aiming to beat suspects to the scene of a crime by using computers to predict where trouble might occur.

The Los Angeles Police Department is the largest agency to embrace an experiment known as "predictive policing," which crunches data to determine where to send officers to thwart would-be thieves and burglars. Time Magazine called it one of the best inventions of 2011.

Early successes could serve as a model for other cash-strapped law enforcement agencies, but some legal observers are concerned it could lead to unlawful stops and searches that violate Fourth Amendment protections.

In the San Fernando Valley, where the program was launched late last year, officers are seeing double-digit drops in burglaries and other property crimes. The program has turned enough in-house skeptics into believers that there are plans to roll it out citywide by next summer.

"We have prevented hun-

dreds and hundreds of people coming home and seeing their homes robbed," said police Capt. Sean Malinowski.

Crime mapping has long been a tool used to determine where the bad guys lurk. The idea has evolved from colored pins placed on a map to identifying "hot spots" via a computer database of past crimes and possible patterns.

Over the past decade, many large police departments, including Los Angeles and New York City, have used CompStat, a system that tracks crime figures and enables police to send extra

462

464

IF

-RUDYARD KIPLING

IF YOU CAN KEEP YOUR HEAD WHEN ALL ABOUT YOU
ARE LOSING THEIRS AND BLAMING IT ON YOU;
IF YOU CAN TRUST YOURSELF WHEN ALL MEN DOUBT YOU;
BUT MAKE ALLOWANCE FOR THEIR DOUBTING TOO,
IF YOU CAN WAIT AND NOT BE TIRED BY WAITING,
OR, BEING LIED ABOUT DON'T DEAL IN LIES,
OR, BEING HATED, DON'T GIVE WAY TO HATING,
AND YET DON'T LOOK TOO GOOD, NOR TALK TOO WISE;
IF YOU CAN DREAM-AND NOT MAKE DREAMS YOUR MASTER
IF YOU CAN THINK-AND NOT MAKE THOUGHTS YOUR AIM;
IF YOU CAN MEET WITH TRIUMPH AND DISASTER
AND TREAT THOSE TWO IMPOSTORS JUST THE SAME,
IF YOU CAN BEAR TO HEAR THE TRUTH YOU'VE SPOKEN
TWISTED BY KNAVES TO MAKE A TRAP FOR FOOLS,
OR WATCH THE THINGS YOU GAVE YOUR LIFE TO BROKEN,
AND STOOP AND BUILD 'EM UP WITH WORN OUT TOOLS;
IF YOU CAN MAKE ONE HEAP OF ALL YOUR WINNINGS
AND RISK IT ON ONE TURN OF PITCH-AND -TOSS,
AND LOSE, AND START AGAIN AT YOUR BEGINNINGS
AND NEVER BREATHE A WORD ABOUT YOUR LOSS;
IF YOU CAN FORCE YOUR HEART AND NERVE AND SINEW
TO SERVE YOUR TURN LONG AFTER THEY ARE GONE,
AND SO BOLD ON WHEN THERE IS NOTHING IN YOU
EXCEPT THE WILL WHICH SAYS TO THEM:"HOLD ON";
IF YOU CAN TALK WITH CROWDS AND KEEP YOUR VIRTUE,
OR WALK WITH KINGS-NOR LOSE THE COMMON TOUCH;
IF NEITHER FOES NOR LOVING FRIENDS CAN HURT YOU;
IF ALL MEN COUNT WITH YOU, BUT NONE TOO MUCH;
IF YOU CAN FILL THE UNFORGIVING MINUTE
WITH SIXTY SECONDS' WORTH OF DISTANCE RUN
'YOURS IS THE EARTH AND EVERYTHING THAT'S IN IT,
AND-WHICH IS MORE YOU'LL BE A MAN, MY SON!

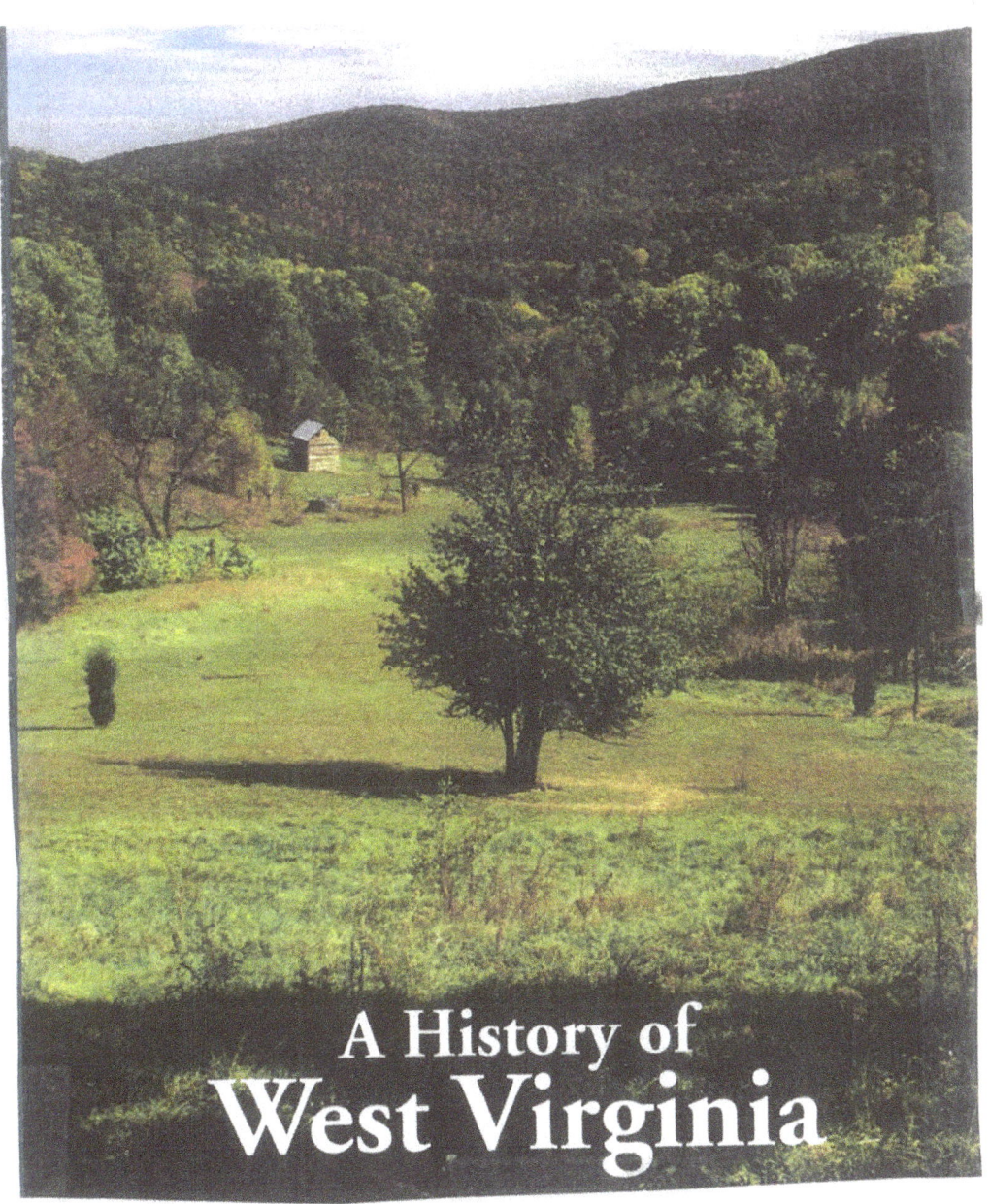

A History of
West Virginia

Introduction

In 1671, an English explorer stood at the top of a Virginia mountain. He looked out over the rugged land that would someday be part of West Virginia. The mountains seemed to go on forever. They looked like giant ocean waves. To this explorer, whose name was Robert Fallam, the mountains were beautiful. They were also, in many ways, frightening. How could anyone ever travel across them, he must have wondered.

The mountains *were* hard to cross. They cut western Virginia off from the eastern part of Virginia, and from the rest of the country. The mountains were one reason why, in the 1860s, western Virginia broke away from Virginia and became the state of West Virginia.

The history of West Virginia is a story of struggle—of white settlers against the Native Americans, of neighbor against neighbor in the Civil War, of coal miners fighting for fair pay and a safe workplace.

The history of West Virginia is also the story of a place whose hills and hollows are a part of its people, a place where family has always been important. It is the story of people proud to call this beautiful, rugged land home.

Claiming the Land

First White Explorers

Explorers were the first white people who came into the area that is now West Virginia. In 1671, the English explorers Thomas Batts and Robert Fallam reached the New River. They claimed it, and all the land drained by it, for England.

467

In 1716, Alexander Spotswood, a Royal Governor of Virginia, led a group of explorers across the Blue Ridge Mountains and into the Shenandoah Valley. When they started their trip, they must have looked like they were going on a picnic. They wore fancy clothes. They were loaded down with good things to eat and drink. Along the way, hornets stung the horses. One horse was bitten by a rattlesnake. Two men got the measles. Everyone's fine clothes were torn.

Finally, Spotswood and his men reached the Shenandoah Valley. They saw it was a land rich in timber and grass for grazing animals. They claimed it for the King of England. Spotswood gave each gentleman a little golden horseshoe. The group became known as the "Knights of the Golden Horseshoe." Their exploring opened the area to settlers.

First White Settlers

In 1722, a treaty was signed between the Iroquois and the Virginia government. This allowed Virginians to settle in the valleys between the Blue Ridge Mountains and the highest ridge of the Allegheny (Al-a-GAY-nee) Mountains.

Shepherdstown, Jefferson County

We cannot be sure who first settled the area. A man named Morgan Morgan is often called the first white settler in what is now West Virginia. As early as 1727, a group of Germans settled at New Mecklenburg. Today it is called Shepherdstown.

The Governor of the Royal Colony of Virginia encouraged people to settle in this land between the mountains. Many did. They came from the colonies of Pennsylvania and New Jersey. Many came from northern Ireland and Germany. Others came from Scotland and Wales. By 1750, much of the land between the mountains was settled. People began to look toward the land west of the Allegheny Mountains as a possible place to live.

The French and Indian War

France Claims Ohio Valley

France was not ready to give up its claim to the area that is now West Virginia. In 1749, the French buried lead plates at the mouths of all the major streams flowing into the Ohio River. The writing on these plates said that all the land drained by the Ohio River belonged to the King of France. This included most of western Virginia.

The French began to build forts to protect their claim. They built an important fort where the Ohio River begins. They called it Fort Duquesne (Du-KANE). This is where Pittsburgh now stands.

English Fight French and Indians

At that time, George Washington was a young man. He led a group of Virginia soldiers in two battles against the French. He won the first battle. He lost the second. He and his men were taken prisoner. They were sent back to Virginia with a message from the French. The message ordered the English to stay out of the Ohio Valley. Most of the Native Americans decided to fight on the side of the French. They thought the French would win the war.

In 1755, the English sent General Braddock and 1,400 British troops to aid the Virginians. General Braddock had spent 50 years in the British Army. He was used to fighting with soldiers lined up in rows. His soldiers wore red and white uniforms. They marched to the beat of battle drums. This style of fighting made them easy targets.

About 10 miles from Fort Duquesne, the French and Native Americans attacked Braddock's army. They shot at the British soldiers from behind trees and rocks. They defeated Braddock's army. Braddock was wounded. He died a few days later.

Settlers Live in Fear

This defeat struck fear in the settlers who had moved into the area between the Allegheny Mountains and the Ohio River. They had hoped the British Army would save them. Now they knew they were on their own. They would have to try to protect themselves.

This battle was part of a nine-year war between England and France that was fought in many parts of the world. In America, it was called the French and Indian War.

The defeat of General Braddock left the settlers open to attacks. Almost all of the settlements in the New River, Greenbrier (GREEN-bry-er), and Monongahela (Ma-non-ga-HE-la) areas were destroyed. Many settlers moved back across the mountains into the safer area of the Shenandoah Valley.

George Washington was now in charge of all of the Virginia soldiers. He almost gave up his command. He knew he would not be able to protect the settlers.

Rugged Land Makes Fighting Harder

In February of 1756, the Governor of Virginia sent soldiers to attack the Shawnee villages in Ohio. The Governor did not know how rugged the land was. It rained for days. The creeks and rivers were overflowing their banks. The men had to cross the flooded Big Sandy River 66 times in the span of 15 miles. Rain turned to snow. Starving packhorses were left behind. There was only a little bit of flour left for food, and hunters could find no wild animals. Many men deserted. Finally the officers voted to return home. This would not be the last time that the rugged land of western Virginia caused problems for soldiers.

The Native Americans continued their attacks. They attacked forts, but mostly they attacked the settlers who lived far apart from one another.

470

England Finally Wins

In 1757, British soldiers won major victories against the French. In 1758, General Forbes led 6,000 British soldiers against the French at Fort Duquesne. The French commander knew his soldiers were outnumbered. He ordered his men to blow up the fort and retreat north toward Canada. In the Ohio Valley, many Native Americans who had fought for the French now made peace with the British.

The Revolutionary War

Colonies Fight for Independence

By the late 1770s, many Americans were tired of being ruled by the British. The colonies began fighting to be free of England. Many men in western Virginia joined the army to fight the British. We call this struggle the "Revolutionary War" or the "War for Independence." Not many young men were left to guard the settlements.

Settlers Battle British and Indians

The British gave guns and bullets to the Native Americans. They wanted them to attack the settlers. In 1777, only two years after signing the peace treaty, the Shawnee, Mingo, and Wyandot (WHY-an-dot) tribes attacked the settlers who remained in western Virginia. The year 1777 became known as the "bloody year of the three sevens."

Chief Cornstalk had become a peacemaker between the tribes and the white settlers. He came to the fort at Point Pleasant to warn the settlers that he could no longer keep the Shawnee from attacking them. He and his son were taken prisoner and held in the fort. When Native Americans killed two white men near the fort, angry soldiers killed Cornstalk and his son. Five white men were

Fort Henry in 1777, located at what is now the city of Wheeling.

charged with the murders. They were set free when no one would testify against them.

Raids and battles continued. On August 31, 1777, Native Americans attacked Fort Henry on Wheeling Creek. The fort held out for three days but almost half its men were killed. Native Americans attacked settlements and smaller forts along the Greenbrier, Monongahela, and Ohio Rivers.

In September 1782, Fort Henry was attacked again. Ammunition inside the fort was almost gone. According to legend, a 16-year-old girl named Betty Zane saved the fort by running for gunpowder as bullets whizzed around her. This second battle of Fort Henry was the last big battle against the Native Americans in western Virginia.

Settlers Win, Become a Free Nation

East of the mountains, the British surrendered to the Americans led by George Washington in October 1782 at the Battle of Yorktown. The Revolutionary War was over. The settlers were no longer English colonists. They were Americans. A peace treaty was signed between England and the United States. England gave up claim to the land south of Canada and east of the Mississippi River.

After the war, thousands of settlers came over the mountains. In 1794, President George Washington sent 3,000 soldiers to make the land west of the mountains safe from attacks by Native Americans. Led by General Anthony Wayne, they defeated the Native Americans in Ohio at the Battle of Fallen Timbers. The Shawnee left their burned villages and moved farther west. The land which was to become West Virginia was now open to white settlers.

Owning Land

Who owned the land? Often, many people claimed the same plots of land in western Virginia. This was a problem for people who wanted to own the land they lived on. The same land could have been claimed by the first settlers, then given to soldiers as part of their pay for serving in the French and Indian War. Many soldiers sold their land to speculators. Speculators hoped to get rich by buying a lot of land for little money. They hoped to sell the land later and make a profit.

Most speculators lived outside the mountains of western Virginia. They hired surveyors to mark off their land. Many of these surveyors did not do a good job. Sometimes the stones or trees they used as markers were removed. During most of the 1800s, lawyers were kept busy trying to figure out who owned what land. Because of this confusion, many people moved farther west. There, they could be more sure that the land they bought would be their own.

Building Towns

Nevertheless, throughout the 1800s the population of western Virginia grew. Settlements became towns. New counties were formed. Roads were built. Ferry boats began business at important river crossings. Farms were started. Some were large but, because of the rugged land, most were small. Farmers grew the crops and raised the animals they needed to supply food for their families. Any extra was taken to market. It was sold to buy the things the farmer was not able to grow or make for himself.

The Whiskey Rebellion

Monongalia County

Many farmers in western Virginia found that it was easier to ship their extra corn to market if they made it into corn whiskey. The whiskey also sold for a much higher price than bushels of corn. When the government put a tax on whiskey, farmers became angry. In 1794, some farmers in Monongalia County forced a tax collector to leave. They joined Pennsylvania farmers in this struggle against the government which became known as the Whiskey Rebellion. Government troops were sent in to enforce the law and the rebellion ended.

The Split Begins

In many ways, western Virginia and eastern Virginia had been growing apart ever since the first settlements were founded west of the mountains. When western Virginia split from eastern Virginia, it was not a sudden event. It was the result of many differences that built up over the years.

Background Differences

Many of the settlers who came over the mountains after the Revolutionary War did not come from the eastern part of Virginia. They came from Pennsylvania, New Jersey, New England, and New York. Some came from England, Ireland, Scotland, and Wales. Many settlers in the northern part of eastern Virginia were German and Scotch-Irish. Many of these settlers had no attachment to eastern Virginia.

Land Differences

The land itself made western Virginia different from eastern Virginia. East of the mountains, much of the land was rich and flat. It was suitable for large farms. The main crop was tobacco. Large landowners used slaves to work this crop. Most of the tobacco was shipped down eastern Virginia's rivers and then across the ocean to markets in Europe.

Western Virginia was rich in natural resources: iron, coal, natural gas, oil, timber, and salt. As these industries grew, western Virginia became more different than ever from eastern Virginia which depended on its large tobacco farms and slave labor.

Political Differences

Other differences were political. People in the two areas had different ideas about who should be able to vote. According to the Virginia constitution, only white men who owned land were allowed to vote. Most people in western Virginia felt this gave too much power to the rich landowners. More landowners lived in eastern Virginia than in western Virginia.

Also, many government officials were chosen by other government officials. Most western Virginians thought government officials should be elected. Eastern Virginia had many more representatives in state government than did western Virginia. Western Virginians did not think this was fair.

Western Virginians Want Change

In 1829-1830, a convention was held in Richmond. The convention rejected the changes the western Virginians wanted. Wheeling newspapers began to call for western Virginia to separate from eastern Virginia.

Lewisburg,
Greenbrier County

In 1842, leaders of western Virginia met in Lewisburg to demand changes in the Virginia constitution. They also demanded improvements in transportation. The government in Richmond ignored their demands.

At a convention held in Richmond in 1850, western Virginians finally won more political power. All white men over the age of 21 could now vote. Many political officials who had been appointed now had to be elected. For the first time, the governor of Virginia was from western Virginia. He was Joseph Johnson from Harrison County.

Transportation improvements were made in western Virginia. The Baltimore and Ohio Railroad was built over the Allegheny Mountains. In 1852, the B&O, as the railroad was called, reached Wheeling. The railroad opened up western Virginia more than the roads ever had.

Harrison County

Leaders in both eastern and western Virginia seemed more willing to try to work things out. But, at the same time, the country itself was being pulled into two separate parts—the North and the South. Virginia was on the border. It was a mix of both North and South.

The Civil War

Slavery

On the eastern side of the mountains, thousands of slaves worked on the big Virginia farms that were called plantations. There were fewer slaves in western Virginia. These had been brought over the mountains by Virginia farmers.

Farms on the west side of the mountains were much smaller than the farms on the eastern side. On the small farms in western Virginia there were not many slaves. Often, farmers and slaves worked together in the fields. But a slave was still a slave and not a free person. Runaway slaves were often whipped in public. Families were split up as members were sold to different owners. In the saltworks of the Kanawha Valley, slaves were treated as if they were animals.

John Brown

More and more people opposed slavery as time passed. There were slave rebellions, one led by Nat Turner in eastern Virginia in 1831. Later, a man named John Brown began to work on a plan to wipe out slavery. He was willing to use violence to do it.

In 1856, Brown and four of his sons attacked and killed five pro-slavery settlers in Kansas. In 1857, Brown started gathering weapons for his battle to free the slaves.

John Brown

In 1859, he moved to a farm in Maryland that was near Harpers Ferry. On October 16, 1859, Brown and his followers took control of the government's guns at the arsenal in Harpers Ferry. Brown planned to give the guns he captured to slaves. He thought if slaves had guns they would rise up against their owners. During the raid, two of Brown's sons and many of his followers were killed. Brown was captured. On December 2, 1859, he was hanged.

After his death, Brown became a hero to many people who were against slavery. His actions and his death widened the split between those who approved of slavery and those who did not.

476

North and South
Disagree About Slavery

The North and the South were becoming more and more divided over the issues of slavery and the rights of states to decide matters for themselves. In November 1860, Abraham Lincoln was elected the 16th president of the United States. Leaders in the southern states were afraid that he would do away with slavery.

One month after Lincoln's election, South Carolina separated from the Union. Six other states followed. Virginia tried to decide which way to go.

War Begins;
Virginians on Both Sides

On April 12, 1861, near Charleston, South Carolina, Confederate guns fired on Fort Sumter. The Civil War had begun. Now Virginia had to decide whether to stay in the Union or join other Southern states in the new government that called itself the Confederate States of America.

John Carlile of Clarksburg led the fight to keep Virginia in the Union. Waitman Willey of Morgantown, who had freed his own slaves, warned that Virginia would break apart if it left the Union.

On April 17, 1861, Virginia delegates voted 88 to 55 to join the Confederacy. Most of the delegates from northwestern Virginia voted to stay with the Union. Fighting between Virginia's northern and southern troops began within a month.

"Stonewall" Jackson

Meanwhile, Confederate Colonel Thomas Jackson was in Harpers Ferry. He was busy capturing locomotives and railroad cars to send south for use by the Confederate soldiers. Jackson sent four locomotives down the rails to Winchester, Virginia, where the tracks ended. From there, teams of horses dragged the locomotives over 20 miles of road to Strasburg, Virginia. There they were put back on the railroad.

Around mid-June, the Union army was near Harpers Ferry. When Jackson was ordered to retreat, he blew up the railroad bridges. He set fire to what was left of the cars and locomotives. He didn't want them to be of any use to the Union Soldiers.

WV State Archives

Thomas "Stonewall" Jackson

The Civil War's first large battle was the Battle of Bull Run. It was fought near Manassas, Virginia. At first it looked as if the Union soldiers were going to win. They were stopped by a group of Southern soldiers under Jackson's command who stood "like a stone wall" in their way. The Confederates won the battle. Jackson was known from that day on as "Stonewall" Jackson.

Moving Toward Statehood

The fighting grew worse. Wheeling newspaper editor Archibald Campbell wrote that a new state should be formed in western Virginia. He said that the new state should be free of slaves. Many people agreed with him. About three times as many western Virginians were fighting for the Union as were fighting for the Confederacy.

In July of 1861, Union soldiers won an important victory at Rich Mountain in Randolph County. In September, Union troops defeated the Confederates at Gauley River. Union soldiers now controlled all of northwestern Virginia, most of the Kanawha Valley, and the B&O Railroad. Confederates still held the Greenbrier and other southeastern valleys.

By the end of 1861, Union soldiers were in control of most of western Virginia. The way was clear for the forming of a new state.

A New State

It was not easy to make a new state from part of an old state. It took many legal steps.

On May 11, 1861, western Virginians who wanted to stay in the Union met in Wheeling. They decided an election should be held so that voters of western Virginia could make their wishes known. On May 23, 1861, most voters voted in favor of the Union.

Wheeling, Ohio County

A New Government

On July 13, 1861, the Second Wheeling Convention was held. Delegates voted to form a new Virginia government. It was called the Reorganized Government of Virginia. It was loyal to the Union.

Francis H. Pierpont of Marion County was elected Governor of the Reorganized Government. John Carlile and Waitman Willey, the men who had led the fight to keep Virginia in the Union, were chosen to be the new government's senators in the U.S. Congress.

All of this allowed a new state to be formed within the borders of the old state of Virginia. In an election held in October 1861, voters approved the creation of this new state.

A New Name

In November 1861, another convention was held in Wheeling. Delegates wrote a constitution for the new state. Also, the new state needed a name. Many names were suggested. New Virginia, Allegheny, and Kanawha were some of them. Finally the name West Virginia was chosen. Most people wanted the entire B&O Railroad line to be in the new state. That is why the counties in the northeast part of Virginia were included, even though they were more sympathetic to the Confederacy than to the Union.

479

The Issue of Slavery

On May 29, 1862, Senator Willey presented West Virginia's application for statehood to the U.S. Senate. Congress said that slavery had to be outlawed in the state. Willey proposed an amendment that would, over time, do away with slavery in West Virginia. The Senate passed the bill with the amendment attached. Then the U.S. House of Representatives passed it. Now it was up to President Lincoln to sign the bill that would create the new state of West Virginia.

Lincoln Must Decide

Lincoln was worried. The Constitution of the United States clearly said that no state could be divided against its will. While Lincoln thought about what to do, Archibald Campbell, the editor of a newspaper called the *Wheeling Intelligencer*, wrote a letter to try to persuade the President. Governor Pierpont threatened to resign if Lincoln vetoed the bill.

Half of Lincoln's cabinet was in favor of the new state. Half was against it. This was a time of war. Lincoln felt that West Virginia could do more good in the Union than outside it. On December 31, 1862, he signed the bill.

West Virginia Becomes a State

Lincoln then issued a proclamation stating that West Virginia would become the 35th state on June 20, 1863. On that date, West Virginia became the 35th star in the American flag. Arthur H. Boreman of Parkersburg became the first governor of the new state of West Virginia.

Statue of Abraham Lincoln on State Capitol grounds in Charlest

Fighting Continues

The Civil War was still far from over. In West Virginia, Union soldiers had only shaky control. Confederates called "bushwhackers" struck fear in people who supported the Union. Bushwhackers were more horse thieves and criminals than they were soldiers. They beheaded a Union message carrier. People were often shot to settle past family or neighborhood fights that had nothing to do with the war.

Large armies were of no use against the bushwhackers. In West Virginia's rugged land, a few dozen sharpshooters at a steep place in the mountains could hold off hundreds of soldiers.

Union General Robert Milroy was so frustrated by the bushwhackers that he ordered people who supported the Confederates to pay for the property the bushwhackers stole or destroyed. If they refused, he said, their houses would be burned and they would be shot. Milroy later canceled the order. Union soldiers controlled most of the towns. Soldiers on both sides took what they needed wherever they could find it.

Women's War Roles

Women, children, and older men were left to take care of the farms. They lived in constant fear of raids by

bushwhackers. Anna Jarvis of Grafton started a work club to provide food and medicine to women who had lost everything because of the war.

Women worked as spies for both the Union and the Confederacy: Belle Boyd of Martinsburg charmed Union generals into telling important military secrets that she passed on to the Confederacy. She was arrested seven times. Nancy Hart Douglas, who lived in the Summersville area, became a member of the Moccasin (MOCK-a-sin) Rangers when her brother-in-law was killed by Union soldiers. She passed Union plans on to the Confederates. After escaping from prison in Summersville, she led the Confederates in burning the town.

Martinsburg,
Berkeley County

Summersville,
Nicholas County

Stonewall Jackson Dies

On May 2, 1863, Stonewall Jackson was shot by his own men. In the darkness, they had mistaken him for a Union soldier. He died eight days later. The Confederacy lost one of its greatest generals. Although Jackson remained loyal to Virginia, this Clarksburg native is honored as one of West Virginia's heroes. No general was better than Jackson at moving his troops quickly and surprising the enemy.

By the end of 1864, Union forces swept through the South. The Union controlled almost all of West Virginia. The bushwhackers were still raiding and killing, but the end of the war was near.

Civil War Ends

On April 9, 1865, Confederate General Robert E. Lee surrendered to the Union Army at Appomattox (Appa-MAT-ox) Court House in Virginia. The Civil War was over. Soldiers who had fought on both sides came home to a new state. In West Virginia, the Civil War had torn apart families and communities. It would take years for all the hurts to heal.

After the War

Freed Slaves Face New Problems

After the Civil War, thousands of former slaves came into the Shenandoah and Potomac Valleys of West Virginia. They were ready to start a new life. What they found was not what they had dreamed of. They lived in tent camps. Conditions were bad. Disease and sickness spread. Babies, young children, and old people were especially hard hit.

Martinsburg, Berkeley County

Charles Town, Jefferson County

On the plantations, slaves had not learned how to read. They were often punished if they were caught reading, or trying to learn.

Schools for African Americans were set up in the towns in the Eastern Panhandle by the Free Will Baptists. White people who did not want African Americans to have schools threatened the life of a teacher in Charles Town.

African Americans in Martinsburg raised $50 a

month to keep their school open. Whites broke the

windows and did what they could to stop the classes.

In the Kanawha Valley, African American preachers raised money from the people in their churches to set up their own schools.

Booker T. Washington

Booker T. Washington, who became a great educator, went to one of these schools.

After the Civil War, the state government passed laws to punish people who had been Confederates. Former Confederates could not vote, teach, hold office, or practice law.

Charleston Becomes State Capital

Charleston, Kanawha County

In 1870, people who had been Confederates were allowed to vote again. Democrats won power in West Virginia. They moved the capital from Wheeling to Charleston. At that time, Charleston was a small village. Within five years, lawmakers changed their minds and moved the capital back to Wheeling. When the people were given the chance to vote, Charleston won.

In 1885, state records were loaded onto a barge and moved back to Charleston for the last time.

State Seal Created

French-born Joseph Diss DeBar became the state's commissioner of immigration. He designed the state seal of West Virginia. On it is a farmer, a miner, and the state's motto, "Montani Semper Liberi." The words are Latin. They say, "Mountaineers are always free."

State Seal 6

483

Factories, Farms, and Revenuers

Diss DeBar tried to get industry and new people to come to West Virginia. He thought industry would be good for the state. West Virginia was rich in timber, coal, oil, and natural gas. These were needed by a country that was growing fast. In the rest of the nation, many people were leaving their farms to work in factories in the cities.

Before industry came to West Virginia, the land provided the people with most of the things they needed. Whole families worked together to make the best life they could for themselves.

The railroad expansion came at a price. We do not know how many men died while building the railroad. Many men were crushed by cave-ins in the tunnels. Others died in other kinds of accidents.

Workers dug a 6,000-foot tunnel through Big Bend Mountain in southern West Virginia. The hard red shale of this mountain caused many rock falls. The story is told that the bodies of men killed were buried in the pile of rocks and stones outside the tunnel opening. The people in charge of building the tunnel had the bodies buried at night because they were afraid the workers would quit if they knew how many men had been killed. Big Bend Tunnel was completed in July of 1872. At that time, it was the longest tunnel in the country.

Big Bend Tunnel, Summers County

The Legend of John Henry

A legend grew up around one African-American worker who helped dig that tunnel. His name was John Henry. He was a powerful man. With his hammer, he said he could beat a steam-powered drill at breaking through the rock in the tunnel. According to the legend, John Henry beat the steam drill, but the effort caused his heart to burst. Through stories and songs, people all over the world know about John Henry, the man who "died with a hammer in his hand."

Land and Mineral Rights
Are Bought Up

Industry spread into the mountains and valleys of West Virginia. With industry came people who saw land as something to buy and use in order to make money. They bought up all the land and mineral rights they could.

Mineral rights were the rights to own, and remove, the oil, coal, and gas in the earth. When landowners sold only the mineral rights, but kept title to their land, the sales contract they signed was called a "broadform deed."

Land sold cheaply. One land agent gave people sewing machines in return for their land. Other agents bought land for as little as one dollar an acre. The land was often bought by companies who did not care how they used it, how they left it, or what happened to the people who had lived on it.

Most people who had settled and lived on this land did not realize the value of what they sold so cheaply. They did not understand the broadform deeds that they

signed. They did not understand that the owners of the minerals under their land could destroy the top of their land to get the minerals out. They did not see ahead to the drilling platforms, the railroad sidings, the coal-mining buildings, and the strip mines that would tear up and destroy their land.

485

The Hatfields and McCoys

As the companies were moving in and taking over the land, the rest of the country was hearing about West Virginia. They were reading about the feud between the Hatfields and the McCoys.

Anderson Hatfield was a great bear hunter. When he killed his first bear, he described himself as "fit to face the devil." Maybe his nickname, "Devil Anse," comes from that. No one knows for sure. In addition to being a great bear hunter, Anse Hatfield was also a large landholder in Logan County. Both he and Randolph McCoy, who lived on the Kentucky side of the Tug Fork River, made money selling timber. The feud began when Randolph McCoy's son attacked Devil Anse's brother, Ellison. When Ellison died, the Hatfields captured the McCoys who were responsible for his death and shot them. The feud continued. More people were killed on both sides.

Logan County

Newspapers covered the story. They exaggerated

Devil Anse Hatfield middle row, second from left) and his family. This photograph was taken in 1897, several years after the feud that made him famous.

it to make it more interesting. Eleven people were killed, but the news stories said that hundreds died. They described the people as hillbillies who carried guns and jugs of whiskey. That was the picture of West Virginians that was given to the rest of the country.

Oil and New Products

Sistersville, Tyler County

Meanwhile, industry was changing West Virginia. Oil was discovered along the Ohio River. By 1893, Sistersville had the largest producing oilfield in the world. By 1900, Wheeling and the area around it had about one-third of West Virginia's factories. Over half of Wheeling's labor force worked at making steel, pottery, cloth, and tobacco products.

Timberland Laid Bare

Another one of West Virginia's valuable resources was timber. Forests that had never been cut covered two-thirds of the state. Then logging railroads were built up into the forests from the main railroad lines. Once again, it was often the immigrants, the people who had just moved here from other countries, who laid the tracks. Logging camps were built in the woods. A crew of six men could cut 200 trees in one day. All of the trees were cut until a mountain was bare.

When the lumberjacks—or wood hicks, as they were called in West Virginia—came to town on Saturday nights, many of them came to drink. Fights spilled out of saloons such as those in Brooklyn across the Greenbrier River from Cass.

Large companies from other states owned most of the timber industry in West Virginia. They bought the best timberland for just two to five dollars an acre. The lumber from a tree that cost them 50 cents often sold for as much as $200.

West Virginians had jobs but these jobs lasted for only a short time. They lasted only as long as the trees.

King Coal

The United States was growing. Coal was needed for factories, ships, and locomotives, as well as for home furnaces. Before 1900, most coal came from coalfields north of West Virginia.

After the railroads were built into the coal-rich areas of West Virginia, dozens of small companies opened up mines. Many of the operators of these mines were former miners from England, Wales, and Scotland. Some of them had mined coal in Pennsylvania, and then moved to West Virginia.

From Small Mines to Big Ones

Most of these early coal operators borrowed money to open up small mines not far from a railroad. The mines were usually far away from towns. The coal operators had to bring in everything they needed, or they had to build it on the spot. Often, one of the first things they built was a sawmill. This supplied them with lumber to build houses.

A lot of men who had worked on the railroad stayed to work as coal miners. Small coal companies also hired local farmers to work in the mines. These men mined only part of the year. They returned home in the spring to plant their crops and in the fall to harvest them. Many of them took off work to go hunting or fishing. Coal operators did not think these farmers were good mine workers.

As the coal operations grew larger, the operators hired immigrants. They came from many countries—Italy, Hungary, Russia, Germany, Greece, and Poland. Also, thousands of African Americans came from the southern states to work in the mines.

By 1900, there were 20,000 coal miners in West Virginia. About 6,000 of them were immigrants, and about 4,000 were African American. Many were native West Virginians who had left their farms.

Coal Camps and Coal Towns

In places where mines were located far away from towns, most of the miners and their families lived in coal camps. The camps were made up of small houses that the operators built near the mines. When mines were small, operators and workers lived together in these camps. When the operators grew richer, they moved their families out of the coal camps.

Coal mining gradually changed from small operations to big business. Due to competition, most small operations were forced to join together

Metal scrip.

or sell out to big corporations. Coal camps grew into company-owned towns. In southern West Virginia, 80 percent of the coal miners lived in company towns. Everything in a company town was controlled by the coal company. Doctors, preachers, and store clerks were on the company payroll. Company-sponsored baseball teams played each other on Sunday afternoons.

Paper scrip.

Miners often were paid in "scrip." Scrip was the word for metal tokens or paper coupons that stood for a certain amount of money. Scrip could be used only at the mine's company store. The store often charged high prices for food and clothes. Most miners had no choice; they had to buy everything they needed there. Many times, workers were in debt to the company store.

Harsh Living Conditions

In the coal camps that were far away from towns, the railroad was usually the only way in and out. Some coal towns were clean. Houses in towns such as Holden and Gary were well-built, but in many coal towns the houses were shacks that were put up in a hurry. African Americans and immigrants had to live in their own separate areas, often in the most run-down houses. The company owned the houses and set the rent. Coal dust made everything black. Raw sewage polluted the creeks.

Women spent hours every day trying to keep at least the inside of their houses clean. They tended gardens, often large ones. Many kept chickens and pigs in pens. Cows ran free.

The company controlled everything. On election day, workers were sometimes given a list of people they should vote for.

Harsh Working Conditions

Miners were paid by the weight of the coal they mined, not by the hours they worked. Operators would often underweigh the coal. Miners were supposed to be

Young boys worked in the mines.

at least 14 years old, but boys as young as nine worked in the mines. The boys worked long hours.

Coal mines were the most dangerous places to work in the United States. From 1877 to 1928, at least 10,000 men died in West Virginia coal mines. No records were kept on the number of boys who died. Safety regulations were weak and hardly ever enforced. Inspectors

490

were usually given their jobs because they were friends of office holders. In the 1890s, Governor MacCorkle vetoed a bill that would have made safety laws stronger. He said that nothing should burden the coal industry because the good of the state depended on it.

Miners who complained about their working or living conditions were fired. They and their families were thrown out of their company-owned houses. Sometimes, their names were put on a "blacklist." This marked them as troublemakers and no other mine would hire them.

Miners Unite and Strike

Miners knew they could not improve things individually. They learned that if workers joined together in a union they had more power. If the union called a strike, the mine could not operate.

Before 1900, there were small local strikes. In 1902, the United Mine Workers of America (UMWA) called for a big strike in the Fairmont, Kanawha, Pocahontas, and New River coalfields. The strike was for union recognition. About one-fourth of West Virginia's miners went on strike. The companies fought back with injunctions, state militia, strikebreakers, and scabs. Injunctions were legal orders against striking and picketing. The state militia were men called out by the governor to protect company property. They were supposed to keep order. Most often they were used to help the companies fight the unions. Strikebreakers were armed guards hired and paid by the company to keep out the union. A "scab" was the union term for a person who worked during a strike.

The UMWA brought in Mary Harris Jones. The miners called her "Mother Jones." Even though she was in her 70s, she helped organize and lead the miners. She was afraid of no one and the miners loved her.

Work Becomes More Dangerous

The 1902 strike ended with contracts in most of the Kanawha Coalfield but not in the southern coalfields. Many owners found ways around the contracts to increase their profits. If pay was based on filled coal cars, the company just increased the size of the cars. Living conditions were still bad. Working conditions were more dangerous than ever, with cave-ins, slate falls, and gas-filled mines.

On the afternoon of December 6, 1907, an explosion tore through the Fairmont Coal Company mine at Monongah, West Virginia. Flames and smoke shot out of the ground. The force of the blast blew buildings across the West Fork River.

Monongah, Marion County

A total of 361 miners lost their lives. No one knows how many boys working in the mine were killed. The disaster made widows of 250 women. The company gave each of them $150. "Quite a Christmas present," a company lawyer said.

Strikes Become More Deadly

In 1912, coal operators on Paint Creek in Kanawha County refused to renew the contracts they had with the union. The miners went on strike. In the next valley, Cabin Creek miners joined the struggle. The miners, who often worked 12 or more hours a day, wanted a nine-hour day

Striking miners and their families being evicted from company houses.

and better housing. They wanted to be paid in money instead of the scrip that had to be used at the company store.

The company fired the striking workers. The company wanted order, and said outside people brought in by the union were trying to stir up trouble. The company hired Baldwin-Felts detectives as mine guards. The guards were armed with rifles, shotguns, and machine guns. They threw striking miners out of their company houses and put their furniture out on the road.

The UMWA set up tent camps for the striking miners. Mother Jones, who was then in California helping other workers, returned to West Virginia to help the

miners. "There is no peace in West Virginia because there is no justice in West Virginia," she said. She dared the mine guards to shoot her. In August, she led 3,000 miners in a march on Charleston.

Miners shot at guards and at trains carrying strikebreakers. On the night of February 7, 1913, mine guards and a company official got on an armored train called the "Bull Moose Special." As it traveled through Holly Grove, the guards fired hundreds of shots into the tents of sleeping miners and their families. It was a miracle that only one miner was killed. A few days later, miners marched on Mucklow, now Gallagher, on Paint Creek. Twelve miners and four guards were killed.

Paint Creek & Cabin Creek, Kanawha County

Governor Glasscock sent the state militia–citizens armed with weapons–to try to keep order. At least 300 miners were arrested and sent to jail. Mother Jones, now more than 80 years old, was put under house arrest. A friendly guard smuggled out her messages encouraging the striking miners and telling the rest of the country what was happening.

In the tent camps, many people were sick with smallpox, measles, and diphtheria. There was hardly any food.

A Forced Compromise Ends Strike

On March 5, 1913, West Virginia's new governor, Henry D. Hatfield, paid a visit to the area. He was a doctor. He was also Devil Anse Hatfield's nephew. He ignored warnings that he might be shot. Hatfield spent two days in Holly Grove taking care of the sick. He came back to Charleston determined to settle the strike.

Under the terms of a compromise agreement, workers could trade at non-company stores and both the company operators and the workers could have their own people check the weight of the coal that was mined. There were already laws requiring this, but they were not enforced. Miners were given the right to organize, but the operators were not required to recognize the union. The miners rejected the agreement. Hatfield threatened more troops and prison terms if the miners did not accept the compromise. The miners felt they had hardly won anything, but they went back to work. Hatfield freed Mother Jones and the striking miners who had been put in jail.

At the end of 50 years as a state, West Virginia had seen more than its share of bloodshed: first the fighting of the Civil War and then the struggle for the union in the coalfields.

War in Europe, War in the Coalfields

World War I Needs State's Resources

World War I, which lasted from 1914 to 1918, changed West Virginia in many ways. More than 60,000 West Virginians served in the armed forces. At least 200 were army nurses. The war took West Virginians out of the hills and sent them into the world.

West Virginia's industries were needed to win the war. In Wheeling, steel mills worked night and day. Mustard gas and explosives were produced by the new chemical industries in the Kanawha Valley.

Coal was so important to winning the war that coal miners were not drafted. During the war there was peace between the coal operators and the union.

494

Post-War Union Efforts Begin

When the war ended, John L. Lewis, president of

Logan County

Mingo County

the UMWA, began to try to get the miners in southern West Virginia to join the mineworkers' union. He especially wanted to recruit miners in Mingo and Logan Counties. These two counties had about one-third of the non-union miners in the state.

After the war, the country did not need as much coal. The price of coal dropped. Coal operators wanted to keep coal miners' wages low so they could continue making a good profit. The coal operators were ready to do anything to keep the union from organizing the miners.

Matewan Is Center of Conflict

The union effort in Mingo County was based in the town of Matewan. Sid Hatfield was Matewan's 28-year-old chief of police. Many sheriffs and policemen were paid by the coal companies to work against the union. Hatfield was different. He promised to protect the miners who joined the union.

On May 19, 1920, Albert Felts and his brother Lee came to Matewan with a group of Baldwin-Felts detectives. They spent the day evicting striking miners and their families from homes owned by the Stone Mountain Coal Company. The Baldwin-Felts men piled the miners' furniture out on the roads.

When Albert and Lee Felts and their detectives returned to the train station, they were met by Sid Hatfield and a group of miners armed with guns. When Hatfield tried to arrest the Baldwin-Felts men, they tried to arrest him. Shots were fired. Seven detectives—including both Felts brothers—plus two miners, a bystander, and the Mayor of Matewan were killed. Because of conflicting evidence, Hatfield and the other defendants were found not guilty of causing the deaths.

Murder Leads to Armed Strike

The following year, Sid Hatfield and his friend Ed Chambers were murdered as they walked up the steps of the McDowell County Courthouse at Welch.

"They shot Sid down like a dog," one miner said. At the trial, no one was found guilty. Miners were enraged at the murder of Sid Hatfield. Now they felt they had nothing to lose by joining the union and going out on strike. Many of the miners felt it was time to take up guns to get what they wanted. They wanted the pay and benefits that union miners had won in the northern part of the state. Coal operators brought in strikebreakers to keep the mines working. During the 28 months of the strike, 3,000 striking miners and their families lived in tents along the roads.

Federal troops were called in three times to keep order. In August 1921, thousands of armed miners gathered at Marmet to begin a march to Logan. They were marching to support the striking miners in Logan and Mingo Counties. Union organizers were afraid that the marchers would begin shooting. They were afraid the march would do more harm than good. Union leaders talked the miners into stopping the march. But then, on August 28, state police tried to arrest some of the miners—not for marching but on some other charge. Two miners were killed and three were wounded. After that, the miners were determined to march to Logan.

The Battle of Blair Mountain

Don Chafin was the sheriff of Logan County. He vowed he would not let the miners go through his county. On August 31, more than 1,200 state police, armed guards, and others, many of them paid by the coal companies, tried to stop the miners at Blair Mountain. The battle lasted for four days and was fought over a 25-mile front. Over 2,000 U.S. troops were brought in, as well as a chemical warfare unit and airplanes with crude bombs. Faced with such a force, and unwilling to shoot U.S. soldiers, the miners stopped fighting.

The "Battle of Blair Mountain" got the nation's attention. People all over the country knew about the striking miners of Logan and Mingo Counties. But none of this attention brought with it the right to belong to a union. By the end of the 1920s, membership in the union had dropped from 50,000 to 600.

The Great Depression
And World War II

In the 1920s, West Virginia began to build better roads. This changed the way many people lived. They moved down out of the hills. Many farms were sold or abandoned. People built houses, schools, and businesses along the roads. Towns and cities grew. People wanted electricity, indoor plumbing, and telephones. Many women began to work outside the home. People began to hope for a better life. That hope ended with the Great Depression.

What Caused the Depression

The stock market crashed in October 1929. In 1930, there was little rain in the country's farmland. With few crops to sell, farms failed. Factories had been producing more goods than people could buy. As a result, many factories and businesses closed or cut back on production. They didn't need as much coal, lumber, or steel. So West Virginia's industries suffered. Many people lost their jobs. Some could not afford to pay back money they had borrowed. Many banks closed. Some people lost all their savings. Almost everyone suffered in the 1930s. Many people grew gardens for food. Some people warmed their homes with pieces of coal they picked up along the railroad tracks.

Hawks Nest, Fayette County

Tragedy at Hawks Nest

In 1930, the Union Carbide Corporation began digging a tunnel through Gauley Mountain at Hawks Nest. Part of the New River was to flow through the tunnel to make electricity at a power plant several miles downstream.

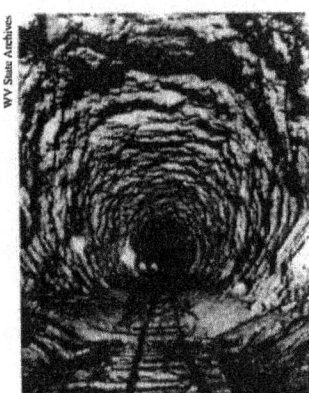

Hawks Nest Tunnel

Men who badly needed work signed up for the job of digging the tunnel.

Most of the 3,000 men hired were African Americans who had come from the South looking for work. The rock they drilled through was almost pure silica. The company wanted the tunnel dug fast. Safety rules were ignored. Wet drilling was not used because it would take longer to build the tunnel. Silica dust filled the air. The dust clogged the lungs of the workers who breathed it in. Over 700 men, DIED.

World War II Starts

On December 7, 1941, Japanese warplanes bombed Pearl Harbor in Hawaii. The United States was again at war. Just as in World War I, West Virginia's mines and factories were needed to win the war. Unemployed coal miners were called back to work. Thousands of men were drafted into the armed forces. Women were hired to keep the mills and factories running. Wheeling Steel made weapons. Chemical plants along the Kanawha River made explosives and man-made rubber.

Altogether, 218,665 West Virginians served in the armed forces; and 5,830 of them died in the war.

World War II ended in 1945. By 1946, union coal miners were again being called out on strikes by their leader John L. Lewis. These strikes made a lot of Americans mad. The strikes hurt other industries that needed coal in order to run.

Machines Replace Workers, Cause Black Lung Disease

By 1950, Lewis had won better health benefits and higher wages for coal miners, but new contracts allowed big machines to be used in the mines. The machine called the "continuous miner" made it possible to mine coal with far fewer miners. Many miners lost their jobs. African American miners were the first to lose their jobs because many companies refused to train them to work the new machines. The continuous miner filled the air in the mines with coal dust—much more dust than was raised by previous mining methods. Many miners became sick with "black lung."

Health and Safety Improved by Law

It was not until 1969 that the federal Coal Mine Health and Safety Act was passed. Ken Hechler was one of West Virginia's congressmen. He added words to the bill that gave benefits to miners suffering from black lung. The words he added also set a limit on the amount of coal dust allowed in mines.

For a while it looked as if the bill would not become a law. Too many coal companies were fighting against it. Members of the Black Lung Association (BLA), an organization made up of miners and former miners, went to Washington. Widows of some of the 78 miners killed in a mine explosion in 1968 in Farmington went to Washington. They told the congressmen about the bad conditions in the coal mines. It was their personal stories that got the bill passed. It was a great victory. The law made underground mines safer and healthier.

Farmington, Marion County

A Beautiful Place

West Virginia is one of the most beautiful states in the country. It is rich in natural resources. New roads have been built. Every year, more and more people come to West Virginia to ski and to go white water rafting. They come to camp and to enjoy the state parks. More highways are planned. West Virginians need to be careful that the natural beauty of the state is preserved. West Virginia's land and

West Virginia has other riches besides land and water. Since the time when industry came to the state, West Virginia has been home to many different peoples. Families from southern and eastern Europe and thousands of African Americans brought with them their own talents, ideas, and customs. West Virginia has benefited from this rich mix of peoples.

West Virginia has award-winning writers, musicians, and athletes. West Virginia has museums and art galleries. West Virginia has dozens of festivals that celebrate everything from apple butter and ramps to the old-time music, dance, stories, and crafts.

A Place of Pride

Throughout the history of the state, West Virginians have struggled to make a good life for themselves and their families in this hard but beautiful land. They have not given up. West Virginians have good reasons to be proud.

499

The Culture Center
1900 Kanawha Blvd., E.
Charleston, WV 25305-0300

Randall Reid-Smith, Commissioner

Phone 304.558.0220 • www.wvculture.org
Fax 304.558.2779 • TDD 304.558.3562
EEO/AA Employer

January 13, 2013

Dr. Colonel Vaughan Witten
539 Alleghany Road
Fayetteville, NC 28304-3290

Dear Dr. Colonel Witten:

This past week we received your publication *The Journey: Appalachia to Paradise to Purgatory*, which you have donated to the West Virginia State Archives. Congratulations on the completion of this extremely valuable work. Historians will undoubtedly utilize your book for research purposes, as you provide insight into growing up in southern West Virginia. I especially enjoyed the information on African-American high schools in West Virginia and the history of Washington High School, and the detailing of your extensive experiences in the military. We are truly grateful for your generosity and thoughtfulness in donating the copy of your book, which will be preserved in the State Archives for future generations of researchers. Thank you very much for your service to our country, and for this important publication.

Sincerely,

Joseph N. Geiger, Jr., Director
West Virginia Archives and History

West Virginia Division of Culture & History • An
Charleston, WV 25305-0300 • Phone: (
E-Mail: jos

500

This book has been viewed or downloaded in 136 countries over the past 8 years from 2014. It is monitored and reported by google analytics daily and has recorded over 40,000 hits so far up until 2022.

Colonel Vaughan Witten PhD
CMSGT U.S.A.F. RET.
Psychologist & Author

☎ (910) 583 8508

✉ colonel29witten@hotmail.com

🌐 www.colonelvaughanwitten2.com

📍 539 Alleghany Rd.
Fayetteville,NC 28304

THE JOURNEY
(APPALACHIA TO PARADISE TO PURGATORY)

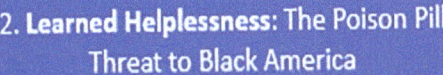

www.colonelvaughanwitten2.com

MY TWO OTHER BOOKS ARE ALSO AVAILABLE FOR PURCHASE IN AMAZON ,BARNES & NOBLE AND OTHER BOOK RETAILERS!

1. **Black Escape from Freedom**: The Fallacy of Victimism, and Resulting Self Defeating Behavior and Avoidance of Responsibility

2. **Learned Helplessness**: The Poison Pill Threat to Black America

www.ingramcontent.com/pod-product-compliance
Lightning Source LLC
Chambersburg PA
CBHW041532120626
46551CB00019B/2666